Krishna

Krishna

A Sourcebook

Edited by
EDWIN F. BRYANT

OXFORD
UNIVERSITY PRESS

2007

OXFORD
UNIVERSITY PRESS

Oxford University Press, Inc., publishes works that further
Oxford University's objective of excellence
in research, scholarship, and education.

Oxford   New York
Auckland   Cape Town   Dar es Salaam   Hong Kong   Karachi
Kuala Lumpur   Madrid   Melbourne   Mexico City   Nairobi
New Delhi   Shanghai   Taipei   Toronto

With offices in
Argentina   Austria   Brazil   Chile   Czech Republic   France   Greece
Guatemala   Hungary   Italy   Japan   Poland   Portugal   Singapore
South Korea   Switzerland   Thailand   Turkey   Ukraine   Vietnam

Copyright © 2007 by Oxford University Press, Inc.

Published by Oxford University Press, Inc.
198 Madison Avenue, New York, New York 10016

www.oup.com

Oxford is a registered trademark of Oxford University Press

Library of Congress Cataloging-in-Publication Data
Krishna : a sourcebook / edited by Edwin F. Bryant.
    p. cm.
Includes bibliographical references.
ISBN 978-0-19-514891-6; 978-0-19-514892-3 (pbk.)
1. Krishna (Hindu deity)—Literary collections.   2. Devotional literature, Indic.
I. Bryant, Edwin.
BL1220.K733 2007
294.5'2113—dc22   2006019101

9 8 7 6 5 4 3 2 1
Printed in the United States of America
on acid-free paper

Contents

PART IV   Hagiography and Praxis

Contributors

Vidyut Aklujkar is a research associate at the Centre for India and South Asia Research at the University of British Columbia. Her bachelor's and master's degrees were in Sanskrit from Poona University, Pune, India, and her Ph.D. in Philosophy is from the University of British Columbia. She has taught Hindi, Indian literature, and Indian mythology at the UBC, and Sanskrit at Harvard University. Her areas of research are epics in Sanskrit, particularly Ananda-ramayana, and literature in Sanskrit, Hindi, and Marathi. In addition to more than twenty-five research publications in international journals and anthologies, she has six books of fiction, essays, and translations published to date. She has edited a book on Goan Konkani proverbs and an anthology of Marathi short stories. In 2005, she was honored by the BMM award of excellence for her writing in Marathi by the Brihan Maharashtra Mandal of North America. She has been the co-editor, editor, and now serves as the consulting editor for *Ekata*, the quarterly journal of Marathi literature published from Toronto, Canada.

Paul Arney was educated at Columbia University and the Australian National University. He is an independent scholar based in Perth, Western Australia.

Richard Barz has a Ph.D. in Hindi from the University of Chicago. He is a member of the Faculty of Asian Studies at the Australian National University where he teaches Hindi and Urdu. He is the author of *The Bhakti Sect of Vallabhacarya* (1992), *An Introduction to Hindi and Urdu* (2000), and other books and articles on

Hindi in India and Mauritius and on *bhakti* literature and philosophy. He is currently preparing a Hindi documentary film on the pilgrimage to Gangotri and Gomukh in the Uttarakhand Himalaya.

Edwin F. Bryant is Associate Professor of Hinduism at Rutgers University. His publications include: *The Quest for the Origins of Vedic Culture: The Indo-Aryan Migration Debate* (2001); *Krishna: The Beautiful Legend of God* (2004); *The Hare Krishna Movement: The Post-charismatic Fate of a Religious Transplant* (2004); and *The Indo-Aryan Controversy Evidence, Politics, History* (2005). He has recently completed a translation of the Yoga Sutras and their traditional commentaries.

Francis X. Clooney, S.J., is the Parkman Professor of Divinity and Professor of Comparative Theology at the Harvard Divinity School, and Professor in Harvard University's Department of Sanskrit and Indian Studies. His areas of research interest include Vedanta, Tamil Vaishnavism, and the historical and comparative study of Hindu and Christian theologies. His most recent books are *Hindu God, Christian God* (2001), *Divine Mother, Blessed Mother* (2005), and *Fr. Bouchet's India: An 18th-Century Jesuit's Encounter with Hinduism* (2005). He is currently writing a study in comparative spirituality on the Shrimad Rahasyatrayasara of Vedanta Deshika, and the Treatise on the Love of God of Francis de Sales, and also a Christian commentary on the rahasya mantras of the Shrivaishnava tradition.

Satyanarayana Dasa received his Ph.D. from Agra University and is founder and director of the Jiva Institute for Vedic Studies in Vrindavan. His publications include the *Bhagavata Mahatmya* from the *Padma Purana*; the *Hitopadesha* of Narayana Pandita; *In Vaikuntha Not Even the Leaves Fall*; *The Yoga of Dejection*; and *Nama Tattva*. He has completed a translation of the six-volume philosophical treatise *Shat Sandarbhas* of Jiva Goswami, and he is presently working on a translation of the *Tarka Samgraha*, along with its *Nyaya Bodhini* and *Dipika* commentaries, as well as Jiva Goswami's Sanskrit grammar, the *Harinamamrita-vyakaranam*.

Neal Delmonico received his Ph.D. from the Department of South Asian Languages and Civilizations of the University of Chicago in 1990. He has taught in the Religious Studies Program at Iowa State University and in the Social Sciences Division, philosophy, and religion at Truman State University. He is the translator of numerous works from Sanskrit and Bengali. His publications include *First Steps in Vedanta* (2003) and *Nectar of the Holy Name* (2005) and he is a frequent contributor to the *Journal of Vaisnava Studies*. In addition to collaborating on an online text repository for Sanskrit and Bengali texts, available at www.granthamandira.org, he currently manages and edits for Blazing Sapphire Press.

David L. Haberman is Professor and Chair of the Department of Religious Studies at Indiana University at Bloomington. He received his Ph.D. in the history of religions from the University of Chicago Divinity School in 1984 and taught at the University of Arizona and Williams College before joining the faculty at Indiana University. Although he is a student of all religious traditions, he specializes in the religions of India, where he has lived for over six years studying the Hindu temple and pilgrimage cultures of that country. He has published many scholarly articles and several books, including the American Academy of Religion Prize–winning *Journey through the Twelve Forests: An Encounter with Krishna* (1994); *Acting as a Way of Salvation: A Study of Raganuga Bhakti Sadhana* (1988, 2001); an annotated translation, *The Bhaktirasamrtasindhu of Rupa Gosvamin* (2003), and *River of Love in an Age of Pollution: The Yamuna River of Northern India* (2006). He is currently working on a book about tree shrines in northern India.

John Stratton Hawley is Professor of Religion and Chair of the Department at Barnard College, Columbia University. His most recent books on India are *Three Bhakti Voices: Mirabai, Surdas, and Kabir in Their Time and Ours* (OUP, 2005) and *The Life of Hinduism* (2006), the latter co-edited with Vasudha Narayanan. Hawley's largest and longest-standing work, a verse translation and poem-by-poem analysis of lyrics attributed to Surdas in the sixteenth-century, is forthcoming from Oxford as *Sur's Ocean*. It draws on the critical edition prepared by Kenneth E. Bryant, with which it will appear conjointly.

Alf Hiltebeitel did his dissertation in the History of Religions at the University of Chicago on Krishna in the Mahabharata, and developed it into his first book (1976, 1990). He has worked widely on Indian religion and history, with work continuing to focus especially on the classical period and the Indian epics, and on the Tamil cult of the Mahabharata heroine Draupadi based on still ongoing fieldwork in Tamilnadu. He is currently working on a book titled *Dharma*, and on various essays on the epics following up his 2001 book, *Rethinking the Mahabharata*.

Steven P. Hopkins received his Ph.D. from Harvard University in the Comparative Study of Religion and is currently Associate Professor and Chair of the Department of Religion at Swarthmore College in Pennsylvania. He is a published author and poet, the recipient of the Eisner Prize in Literature at the University of California at Berkeley. His major field is South Indian Vaishnavism with special attention to the work of Vedantadeshika. In addition to *Singing the Body of God: The Hymns of Vedantadesika in Their South Indian Tradition* (OUP, 2002) and *An Ornament for Jewels: Love Poems for the Lord of Gods by Vedantadesika* (OUP, 2007), Hopkins has co-edited a book with John B. Carman entitled *Tracing Common Themes: Comparative Courses in the Study of Religion* (1990). He is currently at work on a long-term project on space, time, love, and memory in Sanskrit sandesha-kavyas or "messenger poems" in medieval South Asia, and a comparative book on religious transformations of the love lyric from Southern France to South India.

Ekkehard Lorenz received his M.A. in Indology with a focus on medieval and ancient Sanskrit at the Institute for Oriental Languages at the University of Stockholm. He is specialized in the medieval Bhagavata Purana commentarial tradition and is presently researching the authenticity of Madhva's unknown sources in the Bhagavatatatparyanirnaya.

Robert N. Minor is Professor of Religious Studies at the University of Kansas. He holds a Ph.D. from the University of Iowa in the history of religions. Besides his interest in history of religions methodology, his research concentrates on Indian religious thought and texts, and their interpretations in the modern period, religion and the secular state, and religion and gender. Among his publications are eight books, three of which were published simultaneously in the United States and India: *Sri Aurobindo: The Perfect and the Good*; *Bhagavad-gita: An Exegetical Commentary*; and *Modern Indian Interpreters of the Bhagavad-Gita*. Most of his interests coalesced in his *The Religious, The Spiritual, and The Secular: Auroville and Secular India*.

Nancy M. Martin, associate professor of Religious Studies at Chapman University and co-founder and associate director of the Global Ethics and Religion Forum, is an historian of religion with expertise in South Asian religions, gender issues, and comparative religious ethics. She is the author of *Mirabai* (forthcoming) and is currently completing a book examining low-caste traditions of Mirabai and Kabir in rural Rajasthan, entitled *The Renunciant Rani and the Weaver of Protest*. In addition she is the editor of a series of volumes on ethical issues and the world religions and producer of the documentary "Patterns for Peace: India as a Model for Peace in a Multi-Religious Society."

Bijoy M. Misra hails from Puri, India, and was raised in a family of scholars on Shri Jagannatha. He is a physicist and works as the Principal Scientist for General Dynamics at Massachusetts Institute of Technology Lincoln Laboratory. He is a writer in Oriya language and a scholar in Sanskrit. His edited *Sri Krishna Yoga*, a compilation of the lectures of the eminent monk Swami Sarvagatananda at MIT, was published by Advaita Ashrama in India in 2005. He is associated with the Department of Sanskrit and Indian Studies at Harvard University and acts as the Convener of the Outreach Program.

Vasudha Narayanan is Distinguished Professor in the Department of Religion and Director, Center for the study of Hindu Traditions (CHiTra) at the University of Florida. She is a past president of the American Academy of

Religion (2001–2002). She is the author and editor of six books, including, most recently, Hinduism (2004) and *A Hundred Autumns to Live: An Introduction to Hindu Traditions* (OUP forthcoming). She is currently working on Hindu temples and Vaishnava traditions in Cambodia. Her fields of interest include the Sri Vaishnava tradition; Hindu traditions in India, Cambodia, and America; and gender issues.

Lance E. Nelson is Professor of Theology and Religious Studies and chair of the department at the University of San Diego. His research focuses on medieval Hindu theology, particularly Advaita Vedanta, and his writings on aspects of South Asian religion have appeared in books, reference works, and scholarly journals published in North America, Europe, and India. He edited *Purifying the Earthly Body of God: Religion and Ecology in Hindu India* (1998) and is a past president of the Society for Hindu-Christian Studies.

Deepak Sarma is an assistant professor of Religion at Case Western Reserve University. He has a Ph.D. in the philosophy of religion from the University of Chicago. Madhva Vedanta has been the focus of his research since his undergraduate days at Reed College. He is the author of *An Introduction to Madhva Vedanta* (2003) and *Epistemologies and the Limitations of Philosophical Inquiry: Doctrine in Madhva Vedanta* (2005). He has published articles in the *Journal of Indian Philosophy*, the *Journal of the American Academy of Religion*, *Method and Theory in the Study of Religion*, and the *Journal of Vaishnava Studies*, as well as other journals. His areas of interest include Madhva Vedanta, comparative philosophy of religion, Hindu and Jain bioethics, and theory and method in the social sciences and in religious studies.

Graham M. Schweig did his graduate studies at Harvard University and the University of Chicago and received his doctorate in Comparative Religion from Harvard. He has taught at Duke University and the University of North Carolina and is currently Associate Professor of Philosophy and Religious Studies and director of the Indic Studies Program at Christopher Newport University, as well as Visiting Associate Professor of Sanskrit at the University of Virginia. His work focuses on the devotional theistic traditions of India, forms of love mysticism in world religion, especially Christian and Vaishnava traditions, and the psychology of religion. He is the author of *Dance of Divine Love: India's Classic Sacred Love Story: The Rasa Lila of Krishna from the Bhagavata Purana* (2005); *Bhagavad Gita: The Beloved Lord's Secret Love Song* (Harper San Francisco, forthcoming); *Bhagavad Gita Concordance: Comprehensive Word Reference* and *The Bhakti Sutra: Concise Teachings of Narada on Divine Love* (both forthcoming).

Paul H. Sherbow holds a B.A. in Middle Eastern Studies from Columbia University and is renowned as a Sanskritist. He served as Sanskrit editor at the

Bhaktivedanta Book Trust during the 1970s, and was cofounder as well as senior editor of the *Journal of Vaishnava Studies.* Active in interreligious initiatives, he has been assisting the director general of the International Shinto Foundation (ISF) in its United Nations and academic programs since 1997. He is presently senior researcher for the International Secretariat of the World Conference of Religions for Peace (WCRP) in New York City, with special assignments in India.

Neelima Shukla-Bhatt is a Visiting Professor in South Asia Studies at Wellesley College. She received her Ph.D. in Study of Religion from Harvard University (2003). Her doctoral dissertation was titled "Nectar of Devotion: Bhakti-Rasa in the Tradition of Gujarati Saint-Poet Narasinha Mehta." She has contributed articles on modern Hindu female religious leaders to the second edition of the *Encyclopedia of Religion* (2005). Several of her articles are forthcoming in books and journals. Her research focuses on *bhakti*, cultural/religious forms that open space for women and other marginalized groups as well as religion and globalization. She is presently examining garba, a dance form of Gujarat, as a ritual for Goddess worship and as a cultural form.

William L. Smith received his doctorate in Indology at the University of Stockholm, where he taught until 2004. His books include *The One-Eyed Goddess* (1980); *The Ramayana in Eastern India* (1988); *Bengali Reference Grammar* (1997); *W. L. Smith on Shankaradeva* (2000); and *Patterns in Indian Hagiography* (2004) and he has edited *Maithili Studies: Papers Presented at the Stockholm Conference on Maithili Language and Literature* (2003). He has published numerous articles on the medieval languages and literatures of Eastern India. He is at presently Professor of South Asian Languages at the University of Uppsala.

Krishna

Introduction

Edwin F. Bryant

Krishna is undoubtedly one of the most beloved deities of Hindu India. As a pan-Indian deity, his worship takes on distinctive forms and unique flavors that today dominate entire regions all over the subcontinent—Radha Krishna of Braj in North India, Jagannath in Orissa to the east, Shrinathji in Rajasthan and Ranchor in Gujarat to the west, Vitobha in Maharashtra in central India, Udupi Krishna in Karnataka and Guruvayor in Kerala in the South, to name but a few. Even in the West, one need only visit an art museum with a decent collection of Indian art and iconography to encounter representations of this deity in a variety of media, or attend a performance of classical Indian dance, where there is every chance that a scene from Krishna's life will be enacted, or browse the selections of devotional songs in any Indian grocery store to gain a sense of how embedded this deity is in the religious landscape of South Asia. His presence there can be attested for at least two and a half millennia.

Considered to be an incarnation of the Vedic deity Vishnu, who emerges in the later Vedic period as the supreme being, or, for some sects, as the supreme source being himself, Krishna is most readily encountered in the literary traditions of South Asia. The two great epics of India both feature incarnations of Vishnu—Rama in the *Ramayana*, and Krishna in the *Mahabharata*. While he is not the protagonist of the *Mahabharata*, the epic highlights a divine Krishna throughout its narrative at pivotal moments (see Hiltebeitel, chapter 1 here), and includes a sizeable appendix, the *Harivamsha*, dedicated exclusively to his life and incarnation (see Lorenz, chapter 3 here). Within the *Mahabharata* is embedded the famous *Bhagavad*

Gita, the best known and most often translated Hindu text, which is a theological discourse delivered by Krishna to his friend and disciple Arjuna (see Minor, chapter 2 here). While it has been argued that the text's prominence may have been somewhat enhanced in the colonial period,[1] anyone over the last twelve centuries or so interested in founding a new line of Vedanta—the school of philosophical thought that has emerged as the most influential and definitive of "Hinduism"[2]—was expected to write a commentary on the *Gita* as one of the three main textual sources of scriptural authority.[3] Indeed, all the principal commentators of the Vedanta who founded new schools of thought were Vaishnavas, devoted to Vishnu and his incarnations (or, at least, in the case of Shankara, accepted Krishna as *Ishvara*, God; see Nelson, Clooney, Sharma, Dasa and Barz, chapters 13–17 here). Krishna's influence, then, as will be evidenced in the pages of this book, has permeated every aspect of Hindu religious, aesthetic, cultural, literary and intellectual life.

The worship of Krishna as a divine figure can be traced back to well before the Common Era (the earliest evidence pertaining to the figure of Vishnu, of whom Krishna is generally held to be an incarnation, need not detain us here).[4] There is no obvious reference to Krishna in the *Rigveda*, the oldest Indic text, dated to circa 1500 B.C.E., although the name does appear a handful of times in the hymns[5] (a few scholars have unconvincingly tried to connect these instances with him, or with some proto-figure from whom he evolved).[6] Most instances of the word *krishna* in the *Rigveda*, however, are simply in its meaning as the adjective "black." It is in the late Vedic period, as represented by the *Chandogya Upanishad*, a philosophical text of around the sixth century B.C.E., that we find the first plausible—but still questionable—reference to the Puranic Krishna. This reference (3.17) has provoked considerable discussion as to whether or not it refers to an older portrayal of the Puranic Krishna, but this ultimately remains inconclusive.[7]

Less questionable references, however, emerge subsequent to this point in time. In Yaska's *Nirukta*, an etymological dictionary of around the fifth century B.C.E., there is a reference to the Shyamantaka jewel in the possession of Akrura, a motif from a well-known Krishna story.[8] There is a brief reference to Krishna under his patronymic of Vasudeva in the famous Sanskrit grammar, the *Ashtadhyayi* of Panini, dated around the fourth century B.C.E., which is important because, given similar references in other texts of this period, it may indicate that the author considered Krishna a divine being.[9] In the *Baudayana Dharma Sutra*,[10] also of around the fourth century B.C.E., there is an invocation to Vishnu using twelve names including Keshava, Govinda, and Damodara, which are names associated with Vishnu in the form of Krishna, thereby pointing to the latter's divine status in this very period. These names also reveal an awareness of several stories that are fully developed in later texts,[11] as do, in the same period, a number of references in the *Arthashastra*, a Machiavellian political treatise. Along the same lines, in the *Mahanarayana*

Upanishad of the *Taittiriya Aranyaka*, around the third century B.C.E., a *gayatri mantra* associates Vasudeva with Narayana and Vishnu.[12] Another significant source of references prior to the Common Era is Patanjali, the commentator on the famous grammar of Panini in the second century B.C.E. In his commentary (3.1.26), Patanjali mentions one of the most important episodes in Krishna's life, *Kamsavadha*, the killing of Kamsa, as represented in tales and theatrical performances, adding that the events were considered to have taken place long ago. Patanjali further makes a number of other clear references to Krishna and his associates as they are known in later texts.[13]

Krishna surfaces at key junctures of the *Mahabharata* narrative, and much has been written about his role as a divine figure in the epic (see Hiltebeitel, 1979, for a summary of views). There has long been a difference of opinion regarding the date of the core of the *Mahabharata*, with opinions ranging from the traditional one of 3100 B.C.E. to the fourth century C.E. (see Brockington, 1998, for a summary of views). A number of scholars date the core of the epic to the ninth century B.C.E, and almost all hold it to be at least as old as the fourth century B.C.E.[14] Enclosed within the *Mahabharata*, of course, is the well-known *Bhagavad Gita* spoken by Krishna to Arjuna on the battlefield of Kurukshetra, a text that is also assigned various dates by scholars. (Minor, chapter 2 here, opts for 150 B.C.E.; see his 1982 exegetical commentary for a discussion of differing views.) Here Krishna unambiguously declares himself to be the supreme being throughout the entire text.[15]

In terms of sources outside of the subcontinent prior to the Common Era, Megasthenes, a Seleucid ambassador to the court of the Indian emperor Chandragupta Maurya at the end of the fourth century B.C.E., provides interesting evidence from ancient Greek sources relevant to the early history of the divine Krishna. Megasthenes wrote a book called *Indika*, the original of which has not been preserved, but it was quoted extensively by other ancient classical writers whose works are extant.[16] According to Arrian, Diodorus, and Strabo, Megasthenes described an Indian tribe called the Sourasenoi, who especially worshiped Herakles in their land, and this land had two great cities, Methora and Kleisobora, and a navigable river, the Jobares. As was common in the ancient period, the Greeks sometimes described foreign gods in terms of their own divinities, and there is little doubt that the Sourasenoi refers to the Shurasenas, a branch of the Yadu dynasty to which Krishna belonged; Herakles to Krishna, or Hari-Krishna; Methora to Mathura, where Krishna was born; Kleisobora to Krishna *pura*, meaning "the city of Krishna"; and the Jobares to the Yamuna, the famous river in the Krishna story. Quintus Curtius also mentions that when Alexander the Great confronted Porus, Porus's soldiers were carrying an image of Herakles in their vanguard.

Early Buddhist sources also provide evidence of the worship of Krishna prior to the Common Era. The *Niddesa*, one of the books of the Pali canon of the fourth century B.C.E., speaks somewhat derogatorily of those devoted to

Vasudeva (Krishna) and Baladeva (Krishna's brother) (Bhandarkar, 1913, 3). The Buddhist *Ghata Jataka* text also mentions characters from the Krishna story, albeit in a somewhat garbled fashion, suggesting confused reminiscence of the legend (38).[17] That both early Buddhist and Jain sources saw fit to appropriate these legends in some form or *fashionpoints* to their presence and significance on the religious landscape of this period.[18]

The earliest archaeological evidence of Krishna as a divine being is the Besnagar, or Heliodorus column in Besnagar, northwest Madhya Pradesh, dated to around 100 B.C.E. The inscription is particularly noteworthy because it reveals that a foreigner had been converted to the Krishna religion by this period— Heliodorus was a Greek. The column, dedicated to Garuda, the eagle carrier of Vishnu and of Krishna, bears an inscription in which Heliodorus calls himself a *bhagavata* (devotee of Vasudeva Krishna).

That the Krishna tradition was prominent enough to attract a powerful foreign envoy in the first century B.C.E. might suggest that it had already developed deep roots by this time. In addition to this, there are a number of other inscriptions referring to Vasudeva Krishna prior to the Common Era by Indian sponsors of the tradition.[19]

Moving forward into the Common Era, while inscriptions during the Kushana period of around the first to third century C.E. point to the continuity of Krishna worship, it is during this period that we find the first iconographic representations of Krishna: one bas-relief in stone found near Mathura dated to the early first century C.E. shows Krishna being carried across the river Yamuna after his birth, and another found in nearby Jatipara and dated to the second century C.E. depicts him lifting Mount Govardhan, a theme that also surfaces on a representation in a fort in Rajasthan around this time (both these stories are narrated in chapter 4, here). Further archaeological and epigraphic evidence surfaces increasingly in the Gupta period, which lasted from the fourth century until the middle of the seventh century C.E.

By the Gupta period, the worship of Krishna was widespread across the subcontinent. Epigraphic and numismatic evidence indicates that most of the Gupta sovereigns, while patronizing a number of different Hindu sects, were devout Vaishnavas; and a number of the Guptas referred to themselves as *paramabhagavatas*, "topmost devotees of Bhagavan," another title used to refer to Krishna.[20] It is during this period that the Puranic literary genre attained the final stages of its compilation, and it is in these texts that the story of Krishna reaches its fullest expression.

The word *purana*, in Sanskrit, signifies "that which took place previously," that is, ancient lore. Several *Puranas* list the total number of *Puranas* as eighteen, and these texts, as we have them today, are essentially a vast repository of stories about kingship; the gods and their devotees; sectarian theologies; traditional cosmologies; popular religious beliefs concerning pilgrimages, holy places, and religious rites; and *yogic* practices—the popular Hinduism of India today essentially stems from the *Puranas* rather than the old Vedic corpus of texts. The three chief gods in the *Puranas* are Brahma, the secondary creator,[21] Shiva, the destroyer, and Vishnu, the maintainer, and a number of stories speak of the competition between these three for ultimate supremacy. Brahma is never, in actuality, a serious candidate, and the main rivalry in the *Puranas* is played out between the two transcendent lords Vishnu and Shiva.[22] Despite the usually playful rivalry between Vishnu and Shiva, much in the *Puranas* point to the fact that it is Vishnu who as a rule occupies a position of preeminence in the earlier texts (Rocher, 1986, 105; Gonda, 1954, 194).[23]

Although Vishnu is a purely transcendent deity, he is generally said to have ten principal earthly incarnations[24] which appear according to time and place, some of them in animal form;[25] one of them is Krishna, and the stories of these different incarnations are related in detail in the various *Puranas*. While it is the *Bhagavata Purana* that occupies itself most particularly with the incarnation of Krishna, the Krishna story also occurs in significant detail in other *Puranas*, particularly the *Vishnu Purana, Padma Purana*, and the later *Brahma Vaivarta Purana*, and it is in this genre of literature that the stories and legends that developed around his incarnation find their fullest expression. There is little doubt that the earliest material from the older sections of the *Puranas* goes back to the Vedic age,[26] but most scholars hold that the finalized form of the material in most of the eighteen major *Puranas* as we find them today reached its completion by the Gupta period.[27]

The Guptas were also patrons of the aesthetic art forms of India, in which themes from the Krishna story would come to feature so prominently in later periods—indeed, the Gupta epoch is often viewed as something of a golden era for literature, dramaturgy, sculpture, art, architecture, and other aesthetic expressions. While not much has survived in terms of Gupta architecture, the birth of Krishna is depicted on a panel featuring Vishnu's ten incarnations in the oldest surviving temple of this era, the Dashavatara temple at Deogarh, from the beginning of the sixth century c.e. (Dandekar, 1982, 159). The earliest extensive drama of the Krishna story that has survived, the *Balacharita*, by the playwright Bhasa, was also written in the Gupta period sometime around the fourth century c.e. (Kunbae, 1968, 2), while the earliest extant poetry bearing references to Krishna motifs goes back a century earlier still, penned by the poet Hala.

In the South, Krishna, under the name Mayon, is found in some of the earliest Tamil texts the *cankam* poetic corpus, which surfaces after the turn of the Common Era. By the third century, Krishnaism had gained access to the two royal courts of Kanchi and Maturai in the lands of Tamilnadu (Hardy, 1983), and by the middle of the first millennium of the common era had firmly embedded itself on the popular religious landscape of the South, albeit conforming to Southern sentiments and literary conventions. Subsequently, devotion to Krishna finds particular prominence in the devotional poetry of the Alvars between the sixth through tenth century c.e. The South, in fact, placed its own distinctive stamp on the Krishna tradition, both aesthetically and, particularly in later times, intellectually, much of which has yet to receive the scholarly attention it deserves.[28] In short, Krishna can first be identified as a divine being at the tail end of the Vedic period, in the early centuries B.C.E., and heralds the rise of a new theistic religion based on loving devotion to a personal God, which soon spread across the entire subcontinent to pervade every aspect of Hindu religious, cultural, intellectual, and aesthetic life. This volume has been put together in an attempt to capture some of these myriad ways the Krishna tradition has surfaced in the literature of the subcontinent from the earliest written sources up to the sixteenth century.

The various contributions herein have been divided—unavoidably somewhat arbitrarily—into four parts for the purpose of attempting to provide some kind of organizational coherence to the volume. Part I focuses on the classical primary texts in which Krishna is featured, by which I intend pan-Hindu Sanskrit (as opposed to regional, vernacular, or sectarian) texts, which serve as source material for derivative literature such as poetry or theological treatises. The volume opens with the *Mahabharata*, which is generally accepted as the oldest text that features Krishna on any scale. In the Mahabharata we find Krishna machinating to bring about the destruction of the hosts of armies that were wreaking havoc on the earth—God with a mission. We also find a controversial Krishna, prepared to break the codes of *dharma*, righteous conduct, in order to protect his *bhakta* (devotee), Arjuna. Although Krishna's role in the epic as statesman and friend of the five Pandavas is pivotal to the development of the narrative, he is not the protagonist of the story; but he appears at essential nodes, goading the chain of events to their inexorable conclusion. Alf Hiltebeitel's translation and extensive contextualization of an episode, featuring the tragic hero Karna (chapter 1 here), is one of the most poignant sections of the narrative, and gives a good sense of the shrewd diplomatic Krishna of the epic, lurking behind the scenes while the main characters play out their predetermined roles, only to emerge periodically to ensure that events unfold according to a grand and divine master plan.

Embedded within the *Mahabharata*, as noted, is the *Bhagavad Gita*, which has emerged in the modern period as Hinduism's best known text. Here, we find Krishna in the role of teacher enlightening his friend and devotee Arjuna as Arjuna is undergoing a moment of personal crisis. In the *Gita* we have a conscious effort to subsume a number of important theological expressions on the religious landscape of ancient India under the spiritual cachet of Krishna as the supreme personal Being. We see here outlined the early phases of the devotional but intellectualized path of *bhakti*, the path of *yoga* based on a loving relationship between the devotee and Krishna. Robert N. Minor's contribution (chapter 2 here) includes some of the most important verses of the text asserting the supremacy of Krishna as absolute godhead, and the path of devotion, *bhakti*, as the highest process of *yoga* and the pinnacle of human existence.

There are three primary sources for Krishna's early life, the *Harivamsha*, the *Vishnu Purana*, and the *Bhagavata Purana*. Of the three, it is the *Harivamsha*, an appendix to the *Mahabharata*, that some scholars consider to be the oldest account. Ekkehard Lorenz's extracts from this text (chapter 3 here) provide a vivid sense of the world of a cowherding community in early historic India: the cow-dung, the bullfights, the simple-hearted cowherding people, the precariousness of life—even the overexploited landscape. The rustic and earthy quality of the *Harivamsha* contrasts noticeably with the literary polish and theological sophistication of the *Bhagavata Purana*, which was to emerge as the unparalleled Krishna text in terms of popular appeal; to appreciate the distinct flavor of the two texts, Lorenz's translation of Krishna's interaction with the *gopis*, the women cowherds, can be read alongside the treatment of this topic in the selections from the *Bhagavata* in Graham Schweig's contribution (chapter 18 here).

The *Bhagavata* (as the *Bhagavata Purana* is sometimes called) has undoubtedly been by far the most important work in the Krishna tradition, at least over the last millennium or so, and is the scripture par excellence of the Krishnaite schools. Its importance can be amply seen by the immense influence it has exerted, along with the *Ramayana*, on the aesthetic culture of India—dance, drama, theatre, poetry, art, and so on—up to the present day (or even by simply considering the fact that the majority of the contributions to this volume are predicated on its narratives). In the Braj section of the tenth book of the *Bhagavata Purana*, we see God, not as statesman or teacher, as in the *Mahabharata* or *Gita*, but God as a child absorbed in play, *lila*—stealing butter, hiding from his mother, frolicking with the cowherd-girls. My selections (chapter 4 here) encompass the source narrative for some of the most beloved and popular *lilas*, pastimes, of Krishna as a mischievous but irresistible cowherd boy of Braj.

Part II consists of regional literary expressions—Assam, Orissa, Gujarat, Rajasthan, Maharashtra, and Tamil Nadu—all except one in non-Sanskritic vernaculars of India, with a view to representing the Krishna traditions in the various regions and languages of the subcontinent (selections from Bengali are presented in the section on praxis). We start with the two prose pieces, the first of which is the Oriyan *Mahabharata*. Although the Oriyan Krishna tradition, like much regional material, has yet to receive the academic attention it deserves, it contributes unique material to the Krishna worship of the subcontinent. Orissa is famed for its Jagannath temple, where a form of Krishna is revered passionately by almost all Hindus in the state; the temple also attracts millions of pilgrims from all over India, especially for the annual *Ratha-yatra* chariot procession. Local traditions link this deity with the Krishna of the *Puranas* and the epic in intriguing ways: specifically, the Oriyan *Mahabharata*, written by Sarala Dasa in vernacular in the fifteenth century, connects the origin of the Jagannath deity with the physical form cast off by Krishna in classical sources prior to his return to his divine abode. Bijoy M. Misra's contribution (chapter 5 here) presents the Oriyan version of the *mausala parva*, the sixteenth book of the *Mahabharata*, a fascinating regional rendition of the events that transpired after Krishna decided to relinquish his earthly incarnation.

In the next contribution (chapter 6 here), William L. Smith provides another East Indian sample of Krishna literature in the form of a play in the vernacular Assamese language. As is the case with most of the regional poets, Shankaradeva, a prolific and multilingual author, is enormously popular in a particular linguistic region, in this case the East Indian state of Assam, where almost every village is associated with one of the hundreds of monasteries and religious structures stemming from him and his specific form of Krishna devotion. Unlike other founders of Vaishnava lineages, however, Shankaradeva was not a Brahmin—indeed, he underwent persecution at the hands of the Brahmins, a very common motif in hagiographies of the devotional traditions— nor did he attempt to formulate a philosophical system. Perhaps his main contribution to his region was rendering some of the most important Sanskrit texts into Assamese, adding his own personal touch and innovative flavorings to the product. The play is a humorous and mildly irreverent rendition of two scenes from the *Bhagavata Purana*, where we find a henpecked Krishna berated and manipulated by his wife Satyabhama.

The remaining contributions in Part II are poems. These are headed by the Alvars, the earliest Vaishnava devotee saints who left extensive devotional poetry for posterity. As a group, they set the tone for the *bhakti* (devotional) traditions in general, by transcending gender and caste and by writing in the vernacular, in this case the Tamil language of the South. Their writings in the collective are given the highest veneration by the Shri Vaishnava lineage, a sect especially associated with the theologian Ramanuja, whose writings (presented in chapter 14) are indeed referred to as the fifth *Veda*.[30] Krishna, as can be seen in Vasudha Narayanan's selections (chapter 7 here), is viewed more as one facet of Vishnu in these poems than as a distinct incarnation; he is, furthermore, depicted with a specific southern aesthetic and within a South Indian regional landscape.

Scholars sometimes like to speak of three "families" of ecstatic devotee poets dedicated to Vishnu and his incarnations—the earlier southern one of the Alvars, featured in chapter 7, stemming from the sixth century c.e.; the northern one, represented later in Part II, which includes Sur, Mira, and other notables of around the sixteenth century from Uttar Pradesh and Rajasthan; and an intervening one from the central Indian state of Maharashtra. Vidyut Aklujkar's contribution (chapter 8 here) consists of samples from these latter Marathi *sants*, as they are called, a group spanning a period from the thirteenth to sixteenth century c.e. Devoted to the deity Krishna in the form of

Vitobha at Pandharpur, the poet-saints of Maharashtra absorbed themselves in the exploits of the Krishna of Braj and, like the other saints, wrote heartfelt poetry that has been savored by people in the region for centuries. In contradistinction to the later devotee poets who were to follow them in the North and highlighted the amorous Krishna of the *gopis*, the poetry of the Maharashtrian saints reveals a delightful devotion to God in the mood of *sakhya*, friendship. Here, we find an immediately engaging Krishna, complete with a runny nose, as he wrestles with his friends, or being humored by them when he sulks about not getting his way!

Moving up chronologically and geographically to the north of the subcontinent, perhaps the best known and beloved poet of Krishna in the homeland of the tradition, Braj—indeed in the Hindi-speaking belt in general—is Surdas, whose songs are today blasted over loudspeakers at religious events all over this area. John Stratton Hawley's contribution (chapter 9 here) provides an excellent glimpse into the magic of this poetry and its powerful ability to pull the reader or, in its more traditional context, listener into the world of divine *lila*, pastime, with its rich imagery and narrative strategies, such that one can almost experience the narrative as participant. These selections present us with some of the best-loved motifs of this genre—Krishna's birth, his appetite for butter, the tongue-in-cheek criticisms of his admirers, his seductive flute, and his amorous activities.

Nancy Martin (chapter 10 here) contributes a selection of poetry by a woman devotee of Krishna—a not isolated but nonetheless somewhat rare occurrence in Indic traditions. Mirabai is the best known and loved of the women saints devoted to Krishna, at least in the north of the subcontinent, due in large measure to the compelling nature of her story and her songs, which transcend gender, caste, and class. Considering Krishna to be her only spouse, Mira refused to consummate her marriage in the real world to her royal husband; her subsequent suffering and triumph over all adversities due to her unshakeable love for Krishna find expression in her own hagiography, as well as in the corpus of poetry that developed around her name. Mira's relationship with her worshipful Lord is *madhurya*, conjugal—that between a lover and the beloved—combining the flavors of union and separation, and the intensity of her voice sometimes blurs the boundaries of author and subject matter, the *gopis,* lovers of Krishna. She thus serves as a bridge between Krishna's idyllic and transcendent divine realm of Goloka and the immediate world of angry husbands, malicious and slandering family, and gossiping neighbors.

Narasimha Mehta's poetry, featured in the next contribution, focuses on an aspect of Krishna that generally receives much less attention outside of his home state of Gujarat. In traditional narrative, Krishna actually spent most of his adult life in Dvaraka, one of traditional Gujarat's coastal cities, which he established as his earthly capital. While it has generally been the youthful Krishna of Braj who has captivated the devotional imagination of his devotees, it is this Dvaraka Krishna who is reflected in Narasimha's poetry. Like Surdas and Mirabai, Narasimha is a solitary figure who remained independent from sectarian identification in life and (unlike Surdas) from posthumous sectarian appropriation as well. He, too, was persecuted by the Brahmins—as noted, this is a more or less standard motif in devotional hagiographies in general—and his immersion in the *lila* of Krishna has caused him, like his more famous counterparts elsewhere, to be beloved by almost every Gujarati, Hindu or non-Hindu. Neelima Shukla-Bhatt's contribution (chapter 11 here) thus provides a regional expression of Krishna devotion, which, like other sources in this volume, merits a greater audience than it has generally received.

Steven P. Hopkins's contribution (chapter 12 here) concludes Part II by providing a perspective of Krishna in the refined Sanskrit poetic tradition, specifically in the poetry of Vedanta Deshika in the medieval period in South Asia. Arguably second in importance only to Ramanuja himself in the Shri Vaishnava lineage, Vedanta Deshika, as philosopher, poet, multilingual literary connoisseur, and *acharya*, or spiritual head of a religious community, was one of the numerous prodigies of Indian intellectual culture peppering the landscape of premodern India that remain as awe-inspiring today as they must have been in their time. His poem, the *Gopalavimshati*, translated here, combines the local literary conventions and landscape of Tamil poetry with the aesthetic prestige and command of classical Sanskrit. Here we find the lines between Krishna and Vishnu blurred, as is not uncommon in Tamil poetry, affording us a vivid glimpse of how Krishna is worshiped in the Tamil genre of *stotra*, or "praise" poetry.

Part III is dedicated to philosophy and theology, and the first three chapters examine the role of Krishna in the work of the earlier three great Vedantic exegetes, Shankara, Ramanuja, and Madhva, all intellectual colossi from the south of India. Lance E. Nelson (chapter 13 here) discusses the ontological position of Krishna as *Ishvara*, the personal supreme Lord, in Shankara's system of nondual thought, *advaita*, which was propogated by him in the ninth century of the Common Era. While the notions of a personal God, the individual soul, and the world are all ultimately false appearances erroneously superimposed out of ignorance upon an undifferentiated absolute truth, *Brahman*, for Shankara, Krishna's lordship and transcendence, from the perspective of conventional reality, is as real as the existence of any other entity or object in conventional reality. Shankara's defense of the existence of *Ishvara*, and acceptance of his grace as essential for liberation, thus demonstrate serious theistic intent, albeit a theism that must eventually be discarded as one approaches the level of ultimate "transtheistic" reality. Nelson's contribution includes selections from a later adherent of this school, Madhusudana Sarasvati, who combines fervent devotion to Krishna with the *advaita* presuppositions of this sect.

Later Vedantins were to debate Shankara vigorously, since, as the most influential Vedantic commentators, he was to set the terms of the discussion to which all subsequent Vedantic exegetes had to respond in order to establish their own metaphysical specifics. For Ramanuja, who lived a couple of centuries after Shankara (eleventh to twelfth centuries c.e.), *Ishvara* was eternally real, not a false superimposition on *Brahman*; indeed, *Ishvara* is the highest aspect of *Brahman*, whom Ramanuja correlated with the personal deity Narayana/Vishnu. While acknowledging the nondual nature of the absolute, as evidenced in the label he assigned his own system, *vishistha-advaita*, "differentiated nonduality," Ramanuja nonetheless opposed Shankara's basic premises by holding that *Brahman* as Narayana contained eternally real and individual conscious souls as well as unconscious matter as parts of himself, thus rejecting the notion that these are all false appearances. Ramanuja to a great extent plays the role of apologist to the devotional tradition, incorporating it into mainstream philosophical discourse by writing commentaries on principle texts, and thus assuring it a level of status and prestige in intellectual circles. Francis X. Clooney's selections from the *Gita* (chapter 14 here) outline Ramanuja's and the subsequent commentarial tradition's theological defense of Narayana's incarnation into the world as Krishna, and convey the flavor of the exegetical, logical, and apologetic tenor of Ramanuja's philosophical writings, and that of his successors.

Madhva, a century later, is the third, chronologically, of the three great Vedantic exegetes. In his theology, the differences among the soul, Vishnu, and the world receive more emphasis than in the theology of Ramanuja. Both agree, however, that Krishna is an incarnation of Vishnu, even as Krishna is worshiped by lay Madhvas above all other incarnations and is the central deity in the Madhva stronghold in Udupi in South India. As Sharma's sample translations indicate, Madhva, like Ramanuja, opposed various aspects of Shankara's nondualistic thought, focusing particularly on the ontological status of ignorance, which Shankara posited as the underlying cause of the illusory superimpositions that appear to create the differentiated world of objects, as the Achilles heel of the *advaita* school. Deepak Sarma's contribution (chapter 15 here) gives a basic and brief introduction to Madhva's theology and his critique of the *advaita* viewpoint, examines the role of Krishna in this system, and then provides sample translations to illustrate both these areas.

Moving forward to the sixteenth century and the theologies of what are sometimes referred to as the Krishnaite schools, we find the emergence of organized Krishna lineages that reversed the commonly held relationship between Vishnu and Krishna, positing Krishna as the source of Vishnu rather than a derivative incarnation of Vishnu. In the six *Sandarbhas* of Jiva Gosvamin, featured in Satyanarayana Dasa's contribution (chapter 16 here), we see the Krishna tradition of the Chaitanya line branching out of the popular emotionalism that often characterized the sect, and harnessing Vedantic categories to systematize its understanding of the relationship of Krishna as supreme being with the world and the souls embedded within it in accordance with the standard philosophical terms and concepts of the day. As Ramanuja had done a few centuries earlier for the intellectualized *bhakti* of the Vishnu tradition, Jiva aspired to bring the emotionalized *bhakti* of the Krishna tradition into dialogue with the more established philosophical schools of his time, in conformity with the epistemological and metaphysical categories of the day, and thus confer status and authority on the budding Krishna lineage.

Rupa Gosvamin was the uncle of Jiva, and also had a significant influence on the Krishna devotionalism in the North. As a predominant figure among the theoreticians in the Chaitanya or Gaudiya lineage, and as a direct student of Chaitanya, Rupa's reconfiguring of the *rasa* theory of classical Indian literary aesthetics into a uniquely Krishnaite theology is still vitally influential in the Braj area today. Chaitanya and his followers theologically reconfigured *rasa* to denote various flavors of love of Krishna, subdividing it into five specific types or modes in which this love manifested—the highest, for Rupa, being *madhurya*, the conjugal. One can thus interact with God as one's lover in Gaudiya theology, and Rupa concerned himself with detailing the various stages and symptoms in the development of such love, as well as the means to attain it. David Haberman presents (chapter 17 here) in this regard one of the most important chapters of Rupa's seminal text, the *Bhaktirasamritasindu*, "Ocean of Nectar of the *Rasa* of Devotion."

In the final chapter of Part III, Graham Schweig examines the feminine dimension in Krishna theology. In the heartland of Krishna devotion, the Braj area of India, the worship of Krishna independent of the worship of his consort Radha is inconceivable—indeed, some Krishna communities direct more devotional attention to Radha than Krishna. By far the most popular motif in artistic and literary expressions of Krishna-*lila*, as several of the contributions to this volume exemplify, is Krishna's relationship with the *gopis*, the cowherd-women of Braj, and this mode of conjugal *bhakti* is upheld by several Krishna sects as the apex of love of God. Schweig first considers the androgynous qualities of Krishna himself, and then presents passages from the *Bhagavata Purana* featuring Krishna's interactions both with his royal queens in Dvaraka and with the *gopis* of Braj. A selection follows of poetic expressions of Radha-Krishna love poetry in various genres. Schweig concludes with a delightful selection on the topic of Yogamaya, Krishna's divine illusory potency, without whom there would be no *lila*.

Part IV is dedicated to praxis and hagiography. Richard Barz's contribution (chapter 19 here) bridges from part III by first outlining the basic contours of the *shuddhadvaita*, the "pure nonduality" devotionalized Vedantic philosophy as conceived by the sixteenth-century teacher Vallabha, and then highlighting some of the distinctive features of the devotional path of *bhakti* associated with this school, known as the *Pushtimarga*. Vallabha, a contemporary of Chaitanya, is one of the major formulators of *bhakti* thought, and his followers, with their distinctive red sectarian forehead markings, are today mostly clustered in parts of Gujarat, Rajasthan, and the Gokul area of Braj. The preeminent vernacular text for this lineage is the *Chaurasi Vaishnavan ki Varta*, which consists of noteworthy episodes in the lives of eighty-four exemplary practitioners of the *Pushtimarga*. Barz presents us with the account of Kumbhandas, whose down-to-earth, no-nonsense personality has made him an accessible role model to members of the sect, thus providing the volume with one sample of the multifaceted hagiographical traditions that have built up around well-known and less well-known saints devoted to Krishna across the centuries.

From the perspectives of the same *Pushtimarga* community stemming from Vallabha, as Paul Arney notes in the next chapter, the real purpose of devotional ideology is not to know the deity intellectually but to effect an inner transformation that will enable the devotee to experience, relate to, and interact with the ultimate truth in a highly personal and esoteric manner. This interaction is effected for Vaishnavas in general through a relationship between the devotee and Krishna in his *svarupa*, or deity form. Such praxis is an indispensable part of Vaishnava devotional life, both public and private, and the *pushtimarga* community has developed the practice of *seva*, or service to the *svarupa*, to a degree perhaps unsurpassed in both immediacy and lavishness even among other Vaishnava communities. Arney translates a sixteenth-century manual of precepts and practice that instructs followers of this lineage in the duties of *seva*, allowing a glimpse into this profoundly intimate and all-consuming relationship between God as deity and devotee as servant.

Another fundamental aspect of Krishna praxis is pilgrimage. Places where incarnations or epiphanies of Vishnu appeared in the physical realm are repositories of transformative divine forces, and act as magnets for devotees, as spiritual progress on the path of devotion may be exponentially increased by residence in such places, or by visiting them at particular times of the year. Paul Sherbow (chapter 21 here) provides selections from the *Puranas* and derivative literature glorifying the birthplace of Krishna in Mathura and other sites associated with his earthly incarnation, highlighting the times of year when pilgrimage to such sites is especially beneficial.

The final contribution to Part IV focuses on the power of Krishna's sacred names. Although the centrality and power of sacred sound has been perhaps the most enduring and ubiquitous aspect of the Indic traditions stemming from the Vedic age, perhaps none have placed more stress on the holy names than the Chaitanya Vaishnava tradition. Chaitanya took quite seriously the Puranic idea that chanting the divine names is the proper form of religious practice for the current age, and his followers developed an elaborate theology wherein Krishna's names are seen as a perpetually accessible sonic *avatara*, or sound incarnation, of Krishna. Neal Delmonico presents selections (chapter 22 here) primarily from Bengali sources (with some Puranic samplings in Sanskrit) on this sect's theological understanding of Krishna in vibratory form. Since the history of this tradition is filled with the stories of saints who have experienced ecstatic symptoms and trance states in the context of *kirtana* (congregational chanting), some hagiographical material is included in these selections to illustrate chanting as praxis.

Again, clearly there is much that is arbitrary in the categorization of these contributions into these four parts, and I offer it merely as a simplistic orga- nizational schema in an attempt to impose some sort of order on the volume. A number of the authors featured here wrote in a variety of genres—Vallabha could have been included in the philosophy section, as could Vedanta Deshika; Rupa wrote plays and poetry; and so on. And obviously there are countless expressions of the multifaceted Krishna tradition that perforce do not grace these pages at all—esoteric *pancharatra* ritual texts, Bengali poetry, Kerala puppet plays, women's folk songs from the villages of India, and a myriad more—due to the usual constraints of edited volumes in terms of size and the availability and willingness of specialists to contribute in such desirable areas. Nonetheless, if something of the range, complexity, richness, and charm of this captivating figure, and the myriad ways his presence has been preserved and handed down through the generations, has been portrayed in these pages, or if they inspire the reader to explore and uncover further facets and meanings of the multifarious Krishna tradition, then the book has attained its goals.

NOTES

1. See Sharpe, 1989, for discussion.

2. Vedanta emerged from the post-Vedic period as the most influential of the six classical Hindu schools of philosophical thought.

3. The other two sources in the *prasthana traya* were the Upanishads and the Vedanta.

4. For a history of early Vishnu worship, see Gonda (1954).

5. There is a *rishi*-sage, the father of one Vishvaka, by the name of Krishna, who composed hymn 8.85 and dedicated it to the Ashvins. In hymn 1.101, there is a reference to *krishnagarbha*, which is understood by the commentator Sayana as "fe- tuses in the pregnant women of the *asura* [demon] Krishna," and by the medieval commentator Skandasvamin, as "fortified places of the *asura* [demon] Krishna." In hymn 2.20.7, a synonymous compound, *krishnayoni*, is used.

6. For example, in hymn 8.96.13–15, there is a battle of Indra against an army of ten thousand led by Krishna Drapsa, which a number of earlier commentators saw as a reference to a pre-Aryan Krishna battling the Indra deity of the intruding Indo- Aryan tribes.

7. The reference is plausible because it describes Krishna as Devakiputra, the son of Devaki, who is indeed Krishna's mother in the later tradition, but the

correspondence nonetheless remains questionable, because this Upanishadic Krishna is the recipient of some esoteric teachings from the sage Ghora Angirasa, and there are no stories connecting the later Puranic and epic Krishna with Ghora Angirasa, or with such teachings. Krishna's boyhood teacher was Sandipani Muni, and his family guru was Garga Muni.

8. See, for example, *Bhagavata Purana* 10.56–57.

9. In *Ashtadhyayi* 4.3.98, the *sutra* (aphorism) "*vasudevarjunabhyah vun*" is presented, where '*vun*' is given as a special affix to denote *bhakti*. for Vasudeva (a name of Krishna) and Arjuna. The fact that this aphorism referred to *bhakti* (devotion) provoked a debate among scholars as to whether the term *bhakti* had the same connotations in this early period as it did later, and therefore whether it was evidence that Krishna was considered to be a divine being in the fourth century B.C.E. Certainly Patanjali, Panini's commentator in around the second century B.C.E., accepts the reference in this sense when he says that Vasudeva, as mentioned in this verse, is "worshipful." While some scholars felt that the matter was not incontrovertible, there are clearer references to Krishna's divinity in contemporaneous texts, which add some support the view of those who consider Panini to be intending a divine being. Panini also mentions the tribes associated with Krishna—the Andhakas and Vrishnis.

10. *Dharma-Sutras* are texts outlining the requirements of *dharma*, the variegated socioreligious duties of the different castes.

11. "Keshava" is a name of Krishna meaning "the killer of the Keshi demon," from a story described in Puranic texts; Govinda means "tender of the cows" and points to Krishna's entire childhood in Braj; and Damodara means "he whose belly is bound," from another story in the Puranic texts.

12. The same *mantra* appears in the much earlier *Yajur Veda* without mentioning Vasudeva. Narayana is another name for Vishnu in traditional Vaishnavism.

13. These include the fact that Krishna was an enemy of his maternal uncle Kamsa (2.3.36) and the fact that Vasudeva (a name of Krishna) killed Kamsa. There are also references to: Krishna and Sankarshana (2.2.24); Janardana (a name of Krishna, 6.3.6); a palace or temple of the lord of *dhana*, wealth (Kubera); Rama, and Keshava (a name of Krishna); followers of Akrura and of Vasudeva (a name of Krishna, 4.2.104); tribes associated with Krishna—the Andhakas, Vrishnis, and Kurus; as well as the names Ugrasena, Vasudeva, and Baladeva (1.1.114; references and further discussion in Preciado-Solis, 1984, 23).

14. Certainly the full one-hundred-thousand-verse epic predates the sixth century C.E., since it is mentioned in a land-grant at this time.

15. The *Shvetashvatara Upanishad* (3.1–4), which is slightly older than the *Gita*, identifies Rudra as the supreme Lord who creates and annihilates the worlds, and, earlier still, Vishnu is declared to be the Vedic sacrifice (e.g. *Shatapatha Brahmana* 5.2.3.6) thus suggesting his supremacy in this period. But these are relatively passing references, and the *Gita* represents the first time a deity makes such a claim about himself throughout a text encompassing over seven hundred verses.

16. These references have been culled by Dahlquist (1962).

17. The text presents Vasudeva and his brothers as the sons of Kamsa's sister Devagabbha (Devaki) who were handed over to a man called Andhakavenhu (which seems to be a compound of Andhaka and Vrishni, two kindred Yadava tribes) and his

wife Nandagopa (a compound of Nanda and Gopa, or Yashoda) who were attendants of
Devagabbha. The Jatakas are stories about the Buddha's previous lives. However,
although The Buddhist Pitaka texts of the fourth C.B.E. contain Jataka legends, and
bas-reliefs from the third century B.C.E. illustrate a number of Jataka stories, scholars
do not consider all the Jatakas to have been written at the same time.

18. See Jacobi (1988) for the Jain borrowings, and Lüders (1904) for the Buddhist ones.

19. Two inscriptions in the state of Rajasthan of the first century B.C.E. bear the
same text referring to a temple of Sankarshana and Vasudeva. Another Garuda column from Besnagar, dated c. 100 B.C.E., refers to a temple of Bhagavat and a king
called Bhagavata. From central India, also in the first century B.C.E., an inscription by
Queen Naganika in the Nanaghat cave is preserved that mentions Sankarshana and
Vasudeva, along with other deities, in its opening invocation. Eleven kilometers from
Mathura, Krishna's birthplace, a sculpture in a well in Mora records the installation of
the "five heroes of the Vrishnis" in a stone temple. Also from Mathura, another
inscription records the erection of a railing and doorway for a temple of Bhagavat
Vasudeva, both just at the turn of the Common Era (c. 10–25 C.E.).

20. Although *bhagavan* is not a title exclusive to Krishna, it is the term used to
refer to him in the quintessential Krishna-centered texts, the *Bhagavad Gita* and the
Bhagavata Purana, as can be seen from their titles.

21. Brahma is the creator of all the forms in the universe in the sense of being
their engineer, but he is not the creator of the primordial universal stuff itself. He is
born from the lotus stemming from Vishnu's navel.

22. A later Purana, the *Devi Bhagavata Purana*, marks the ascendancy into the
Puranic genre of Devi, the Goddess, as the supreme matrix.

23. Vishnu is generally associated with the *guna* of *sattva*, the influence of
goodness and enlightenment, and Shiva with that of *tamas*, the influence of ignorance
and bondage. Shiva claims fewer Puranas than Vishnu—the Linga, Skanda, and Shiva
are primarily Shaivite—and, according to Rocher (1986), each of these have encountered difficulties being accepted as a Mahapurana, or principle Purana. Moreover,
it is Vishnu who dominates in the Puranas that are considered to be earlier. Even
if the later texts dedicated to Shiva attribute to him the roles of creator and preserver,
in the broader Puranic scheme, he is the destroyer. It should be noted that followers of both traditions accept and extol the supreme, absolute, and transcendent nature
of the other deity but claim their deity to be the source of the other, a noteworthy
feature of Hindu monotheism.

24. The *Bhagavata Purana*, while mentioning twenty-two principal incarnations,
says that they are actually innumerable (1.3.26).

25. The commonly accepted list of these incarnations in the Puranas is as
follows: Matsya, the fish; Kurma, the tortoise; Varaha, the boar; Narasimha, the
man-lion; Vamana, the dwarf; Parasurama, the warrior; Rama, the prince; Krishna,
the cowherd-boy (the incarnation for the present day and age); Buddha, the founder of
Buddhism; and Kalki, the future warrior incarnation who will ride a white horse and
terminate the present world age of the Kali-yuga.

26. Many of the Vedic hymns assume common knowledge of bygone persons
and events to which they briefly allude and which would have been remembered

through tradition, and some of these are also mentioned in the Puranas. As early as the *Atharvaveda* of 1000 B.C.E., there is a reference to "the Purana" in addition to the *Vedas* (5.19.9). The *Chandogya Upanishad*, around the sixth century B.C.E., also explicitly refers to the Purana (3.4.1–2; 7.1.2 & 4) as one in a list of texts, as does the fourth century B.C.E. *Arthashastra* text of Kautilya and a number of Dharmashastra texts. The *Mahabharata*, which took its final form before the fifth century C.E. but, like the Puranas, contains material going well back into the first half of the first millennium B.C.E., is peppered with references to the Puranas and, indeed, even calls itself a Purana.

27. The Puranas are a fluid body of literature that went on transforming along the centuries through the process of transmission and adaptation. There is abundant evidence for this: there are differences in language between different sections of the text; while there are early references to archaic Vedic narratives, some of the stories in the texts are manifestly late, and deal with incidents occurring in later historical time, some of them cast as prophetic; different and sometimes inconsistent doctrines sometimes coexist in the same Purana; sometimes the same story is repeated in different places in the same text; and the very fact that many Puranas refer to eighteen Puranas indicates that such references must have been inserted after the eighteen Puranas had already been divided. One reason for concluding that the Puranas had attained their written form by the Gupta period is that neither the later dynasties nor later famous rulers, such as Harsha in the seventh century C.E., occur in the king lists contained in the texts.

28. The three most influential theologians of the Vedanta tradition over the centuries, all represented in part III of this volume, were from the South.

29. See Chakravarti (1876), Bhandarkar (1913), Bhattacharya (1928), Jaiswal (1967), Raychaudhuri (1920), and Preciado-Solis (1984) for overviews of the issue with further references.

30. The earliest Indic sacred texts are the four *Vedas*, which, nominally at least, are assigned the highest epistemological value by most Hindu sects.

REFERENCES

Bhandarkar, R. G. 1913. *Vaisnavism, Saivism and Minor Religious Systems.* Strassburg.
Bhattacharya, S. K. 1928. *Krsna-Cult.* Delhi: Associated Publishing House.
Brockington, John. 1998. *The Sanskrit Epics.* Leiden: Brill.
Chakravarti, Atul Chandra. 1876. *The Story of Krsna in Indian Literature.* Calcutta: Indian Associated Publishing.
Dahlquist, Allan. 1962. *Megasthenes and Indian Religion.* Delhi: Motilal Banarasidass.
Dandekar, R. N. 1982. *The Age of the Guptas and Other Essays.* Delhi: Ajanta.
Gonda, J. 1954. *Aspects of Early Visnuism.* Delhi: Motilal. Reprint, 1969.
Hardy, Friedhelm. 1983. *Viraha Bhakti.* Delhi: Oxford.
Jacobi, H. 1886. "Die Jaine Legende von dem Untergang Dvaravatis und dem Tode Krsnas." *Zeitschrift der Deutschen Morgenländischen Gesellschaft* 42, 493–529.
Jaiswal, Suvira. 1967. *The Origin and Development of Vaisnavism.* Delhi: Munshiram.
Hiltebeitel, Alf. 1979. "Krsna and the Mahabharata." *Annals of the Bhandarkar Oriental Institute, Poona,* 65–107.

Kunbae, B. 1968. *Avimaraka Balacarita*. Delhi: Lacchmandas.

Lüders, H. 1904. "Die Jatakas und die Epik—Die Krsna-Sage." *Zeitschrift der Deutschen Morgenländischen Gesellschaft* 58, 687–714.

Minor, Robert N. 1982 *Bhagavad Gita: An Exegetical Commentary*. New Delhi: Heritage

Preciado-Solis, Benjamin. 1984. *The Krsna Cycle in the Puranas*. Delhi: Motilal.

Raychaudhuri, Hemchandra. 1920. *Materials for the Study of the Early History of the Vaishnava Sect*. Delhi: Oriental Books Reprint Corporation. Reprint, 1975.

Rocher, L. 1986. *The Puranas*. Wiesbaden: Otto Harrassowitz.

Sharpe, Eric J. 1985. *The Universal Gita*. La Salle, Illinois: Open Court.

Tadpatrikar, S. N. 1930. "The Krsna Problem." *Annals of the Bhandarkar Oriental Research Institute* 10, 269–344.

Winternitz, M. 1927. *A History of Indian Literature*. New York: Russell.

PART I

Classical Source Material

I

Krishna in the *Mahabharata*: The Death of Karna

Alf Hiltebeitel

Whatever one makes of a few slight references to Krishna in texts that are probably older than the *Mahabharata*, and of the many efforts to imagine him prior to his literary debut *in* the epic, the *Mahabharata* is the first text to portray him as both divine and human, and to conceive of his humanity and divinity on a forceful and complex scale. From his almost casual introduction in the epic's first book as a knowing bystander at the wedding of Draupadi[1] to his death—along with the deaths of all his kinsmen—as the outcome of a drunken clan brawl in book 16, one can trace Krishna's epic involvement through an arc. Along this arc, his prominence reaches its peak from books 5 to 11: from the *Udyogaparvan*, or "Book of War Preparations," through the *Striparvan*, or "Book of the Women," that ends the war with the epic's mothers, wives, sisters, and daughters mourning over their slain menfolk. These central books give Krishna the role of ringmaster on the text's center stage.

To select a passage representative of Krishna along this curve, it seems best to catch him at its top. The one selected for translation here describes his involvements in the killing of the Kaurava hero Karna: a continuous narrative from the last five *adhyayas* ("chapters," "lessons," or "readings") at the end of the *Karnaparvan* (*Mahabharata* 8.65.16–69.43), the book in which Karna is—for two days, the sixteenth and seventeenth in the eighteen-day Kurukshetra war—the marshal and virtually the last hope of the Kaurava army.[2] The passage exemplifies the forcefulness and complexity of Krishna's wider epic portrayal; it reveals the depth and intricacy of his being God, and of the epic's delineation of *bhakti*; and it is a famous episode rich in its subsequent Sanskrit and vernacular unfoldings.[3]

The passage is also illustrative of the textual issues that bear upon strategies of reading and interpreting the *Mahabharata*. I present it on the assumption that *this* epic is a work of written literature, and not a product of oral composition. Although many hold the latter view in one form or another, for this passage it must suffice to mention the work of Mary Carol Smith, who argues on the basis of a preponderance of irregular metric features in this segment and throughout much of the *Karnaparvan* that it preserves signs of archaic oral composition.[4] While it is important to recognize metric variation and to appreciate that it would enhance recitation *from* the text, it is clear that by the time the *Mahabharata* was composed, its authors used varied meters for stylistic effects, including juxtaposition and archaization. What needs to be stressed—since it has been trivialized by so many modern interpreters inclined to see some kind of pristine oral core behind its literary "monstrosity"—is that the *Mahabharata* was written to move people, that it succeeded in doing so, and that what it has to say about Krishna is vital to both the authorial motivation and the text's success. Krishna's divinity is not a literary after-effect.[5]

Whatever may have preceded the *Mahabharata* orally, cultically, or in other unknown forms, the Poona critical edition of the *Mahabharata* shows that for about two millennia, the work that has moved people has been a book, and in that sense one can speak of all its audiences as *readers*.[6] Moreover, the manuscript evidence reveals the beginning of a literary history. The Poona critical edition makes this history sufficiently accessible through its apparatus for one to get a reasonable purchase on the flavor of what is stable and what has been "improved." In the passage given here, for instance, one can see that it is carefully constructed. It shows artistry: in framing devices; in its play of tropes, especially irony; in the juxtaposition of Vedic and Puranic allusions; in the swirl of affinities between heroes and deities;[7] and in the orchestration of epithets. It also requires of us a sense of pacing: an awareness of what has come before it and of what will follow it. One is alerted to the epic's wider representations of authorship, audience, and character.[8] Noteworthy is the positioning of characters at key moments in their unfolding: not only the principal opponent, Karna, but the deepening portrayals—indeed, the "character development"—of the side-characters Yudhishthira and Dhritarashtra. On the other hand, some of the main characters—Arjuna, Shalya, and Krishna, for example—do nothing surprising in this segment. Indeed, as Yudhishthira tells Krishna in bringing the scene to closure, all Krishna had to do to make things turn out right was to act *in* character. By this time in the war, Yudhishthira knows almost as much about Krishna's doings as the reader.

A. Immediate Setting and Wider Background

The preparations for the final fight between Arjuna and Karna begin with a passage (8.63.30–62) in which the two heroes' divine fathers, Indra (king of the gods and storm god) and Surya (the sun god), lead the gods and demons, other celestials, and various classes of beings, incarnate texts, and cosmic entities in declaring their preferences in the incipient duel. In the course of this side-taking, Indra reminds Brahma and Shiva that Arjuna's victory is certain (*dhruva;* 50): Arjuna and Krishna are the invincible "two Krishnas" and are the ancient rishis Nara and Narayana (53–54). Since Krishna, who joins Indra's son Arjuna on the chariot, is ultimately Vishnu incarnate, Indra hereby invokes the sanction of the epic's three most supreme deities, Vishnu, Shiva, and Brahma, in effect anticipating the classical doctrine of the *trimurti,* or "three forms," of the Hindu godhead.[9] Arjuna and Krishna as "the two Krishnas on one chariot" have behind them their further paired identities not only as Nara and Narayana but as the Vedic "friends" Indra and Vishnu. The passage evokes all these associations, and makes the last the most mysterious.

The pivotal character of this duel is thus underlined by the attention drawn to all the divine and cosmic agencies that converge not only to witness it but also to have some kind of substantial part in its unfolding. Its decisiveness can be measured by the fact that it is the only duel in the *Mahabharata* war in which divinities choose sides, as they do not only in the *Iliad,* repeatedly, but just before the climactic chariot duel between Cúchulainn and the "horn-skinned" Fer Diad in the *Táin Bó Cúalnge.*[10] Yet to appreciate that the result is already known on high is only to begin to register that the death of Karna is probably the most overdetermined event in the *Mahabharata* war—indeed, in the entire *Mahabharata.* Karna is beset by a skein of fatalities that unravels to bring upon him a gathering sense of doom. As we find him in his final scene, he is left to imagine—and readers, too, insofar as they sympathize and forget for a moment, like him, that his defeat is divinely certain—that had it not been for these fatalities, he *could* have defeated Arjuna; had it not been . . . for Krishna, whose divinity Karna himself does not fail to recognize.[11] Indeed, given what the same reader comes to know about not only Krishna but about Vyasa, the author, Karna really didn't stand a chance.[12] Yet it is typical of God, authors, and texts to leave openings, and, as we shall see, it is never quite that straightforward.

B. Opening the Book on a Hero's Life

Around Karna's life, one can discern two framing passages: one (at 1.104) that virtually introduces him by his birth;[13] the other (at 12.1–5) that ends all narration of his life with a stark and knowing postmortem. The debut birth passage is jewel-like in its glimpses into facets of Karna's destiny that problematize themselves as his story unfolds, particularly in the more fully developed birth narration in book 3, at the point when Indra robs him of his natural-born armor and earrings. Full of possibilities but also signs of danger, the debut birth passage contrasts with Narada's sad but knowing obituary at the beginning of book 12. Both passages, however, leave out what they wish among the many forces that stack up against Karna. I will concentrate on these fatalities as they close in upon him, filling out the picture between these frames, especially as it relates to Krishna. The skein of occurrence, as best I can reconstruct it from the critical edition,[14] includes the following thirteen episodes, all of which are significant for the death passage in one way or another. As we shall see, Narada's postmortem will also describe further episodes, showing that the list that follows is incomplete. In introducing the main passage here, however, I will concentrate primarily on episodes 7, 11, and 13 in this sequence, since they have the most to do directly with Krishna.

1. Karna is abandoned at birth by his mother Kunti (1.104; 3.297–98).

2 and 3. Karna is doubly cursed. First, after he has inattentively killed a brahmin's cow, the brahmin curses him: may the earth swallow his wheel at a time of greatest peril. Second, after he has pretended to be a brahmin in order to obtain a Brahma-weapon from the brahmin weapon-master Rama Jamadagnya, the latter curses him: may he forget the weapon at the time he will be killed (8.29; 12.3, especially verse 31).

4. Although Karna exhibits matchless valor at a tournament of arms, the appearance of his low-caste *suta* father brings ridicule upon him. Duryodhana, however, sees a formidable ally in Karna and appoints him king of Anga.

5. The snake Ashvasena escapes the Fire (Agni)-feeding slaughter, by Arjuna and Krishna, of almost all the creatures at Khandava Forest and enters Karna's quiver, becoming a snake arrow determined to kill Arjuna in revenge (1.218).

6. Arjuna swears he will kill Karna after the humiliation of Draupadi at the dice match (2.68.32–36).

7. Karna is possessed by Naraka Bhauma (3.240.19).

8. Indra, disguised as a brahmin, begs the gift of Karna's natural-born earrings and armor, which make Karna immortal; Karna, not fooled by the disguise but bound by his vow of gifting, flays his body, earning the name Vaikartana, "the flayed," and gives the earrings and armor in exchange for Indra's infallible spear that will kill whomever it strikes but can be used by Karna only once, whereupon it will return to Indra (3.284–94).

9. Shalya, king of Madra, promises Yudhishthira he will destroy Karna's energy, or *tejas* (5.8).

10. During a Kaurava war-meeting, Karna recalls (reveals?)[15] the fraud of pretending he was a brahmin to Rama Jamadagnya, but reassures Duryodhana, "That weapon is still completely with me." But Bhishma, knowing better, says Karna lost his *dharma* and *tapas* when he lied to "the blameless lord Rama" for that weapon. Karna now decides for the first time to lay down his weapons until Bhishma has fallen (5.61).

11. Karna rejects the temptations offered by Krishna and Kunti (5.138–144).

12. Asked by Duryodhana to rank his warriors before battle, Bhishma says, "Because of Rama's curse and the Brahmin's speech [*abhishapac ca ramasya brahmanasya ca bhashanat*]," he rates Karna only "half a warrior." Here Bhishma mentions the double curse, and Karna makes his second refusal to fight until Bhishma is slain (5.165). Karna's life is so disjointed at this point that van Buitenen was led to admit, mistakenly, in a note on this verse: "Rama's curse: this incident is unknown to me; at any rate it is probably Bala-Rama" (1978, 555)!

13. Karna uses up the never-failing spear against Ghatotkacha (7.154–158).

14. Arjuna kills Karna (8.65–68).

After the fatalities at 2 and 3, which occur together, it does not seem possible to determine their order in relation to the fatalities at 4, 5, and 7. Unlike Yudhishthira and Arjuna, who as winning heroes are the subject of consecutive narrative, Karna is the subject of a fragmented countertext—what David Quint calls a loser's epic of resistance[16]—that the poets leave readers to piece together from segments where he is part of the main story and patches where he is the subject of selective memories—not only others' memories but his own.[17] Indeed, because it is so fragmented, I had to abandon an original intention of arranging Karna's fatalities in the order of their mention in the text rather than in the reconstructed order of their occurrence in his life. Yet some order emerges when we recognize that most of Karna's troubles cluster around three connections: those with his mother, Kunti, those with brahmins (including Indra disguised as one), and those with Krishna. Karna's debut passage, which mentions events in his life up to his obtaining Indra's spear in exchange for his own armor and earrings, occurs before Krishna enters the *Mahabharata*, which he does at the wedding of Draupadi. But by the time Karna and Indra actually make this exchange, it is the last year of the Pandavas' exile, and Krishna has become involved. Nonetheless, even the opening passage anticipates that Krishna will be the son of Kunti's younger brother

Vasudeva, and thus her nephew (at least in terms of her family of birth). Accordingly, Karna is not only the unknown elder brother of the Pandavas; still more hiddenly, he is, as much as Arjuna, a crosscousin of Krishna—known from the start to Kunti, soon known to Krishna, and eventually known to Karna himself. As far as I can recall, this relationship goes unmentioned. But it points up one facet of a deep and largely unexpressed rapport between Karna and Krishna that we must explore.

C. Karna Is Possessed by Naraka Bhauma (Episode 7)

During the epic's seventh book, in which Drona marshals the Kaurava army, Krishna saves Arjuna by intercepting a weapon intended for him, receiving it on his chest. Arjuna protests that when Krishna agreed to drive Arjuna's chariot, he vowed to be a noncombatant. Krishna then explains his intervention by telling a "secret of old." This weapon just hurled by Bhagadatta, king of Pragjyotisha (Assam), was the Vaishnava weapon, and no one else could have neutralized it. Bhagadatta got it from the former Pragjyotisa king Naraka Bhauma, "Naraka the son of Earth," who got it from Krishna's fourth [chaturthi] form [murti].[18] Prithivi (Earth) had requested the Vaishnava weapon for her son Naraka to make him invincible by gods and demons. After Krishna had killed Naraka,[19] the weapon passed on to Bhagadatta, whom Arjuna, says Krishna, should now "divest of that supreme weapon as I formerly slew Naraka" (7.28.16–35).

Naraka Bhauma would thus seem to have gotten his weapon long, long ago; but when did Krishna kill him? If a sequence in the *Narayaniya* is to be taken as implying consecutiveness, Krishna killed Naraka after Krishna and his Yadava clan had moved to Dvaraka, and before the killing of Jarasandha, an event that occurs near the beginning of book 2.[20] Krishna's slaying of Naraka is first recalled at the beginning of book 3. When Krishna first visits the Pandavas in the forest and is enraged at their exile, Arjuna calms him by reciting his past deeds; among them are the following: "You slew Naraka Bhauma taking the two jeweled earrings [*nihatya narakam bhaumam ahritya manikundale*]. . . . The Mauravas and Pashas have been set down, Nisunda and Naraka slain; the road to Pragjyotisha city has again been made secure [*kritah kshemah punah pantha puram Pragjyotisha prati*]."[21] And this victory is soon recalled in other passages that laud Krishna's past deeds, three of them in book 5.[22]

In addition to getting the Vaishnava weapon from his mother Earth, Naraka Bhauma thus stole Aditi's earrings, which Krishna killed him to retrieve. The epic does not say what Krishna did with these earrings. But in what appears to be the first full account in the *Harivamsha* (91.5–92), once Krishna slew her son Naraka, Bhumi (Earth) picked up the earrings and gave them to Krishna, saying, "Even given by you, Govinda, so this one is made to fall by you; as you desire, so you are like a child at play with his toys. Protect these two earrings, O God, and his children."[23] Krishna then gave the earrings to Indra on Mount Meru, and he and Indra then returned them to Aditi (*HV* 92.46–56). But now one may recall that Karna's earrings were once Aditi's to give to Surya (3.291.16–23). If they are the same earrings that Surya then gave to Karna, Surya must have gotten them from Aditi after they were recovered from Naraka. But that would seem difficult to square with Karna's being born with them, which would seem to have been earlier than Krishna could have retrieved them. For if Krishna carries out this mission after having settled the Yadavas in Dvaraka, he must have slain Naraka and retrieved the earrings after his childhood, and thus apparently fairly recently. So, more likely, Surya would have gotten a different pair of Aditi's earrings directly from her, as her son, and imparted them to Karna. By the time Indra has gotten the latter earrings from Karna, Aditi has already gotten back Naraka's earrings, and we are in the dark as to what Indra then did with Karna's.

So if Aditi's jewelry were all that connected Karna and Naraka, the two pairs of earrings would be a dead end. But there is more that connects Naraka and Karna. Both are born virtually immortal: Karna with his earrings made of *amrita*; Naraka with a boon of immortality. Each rules with some question of illegitimacy: Karna, the low-caste *suta's* son, rules Anga as a gift of Duryodhana; Naraka is a demon named "Hell" who menaces the gods. Their countries are both to the east: Anga is to the east of Madhyadesha, the Kauravas and Pandavas' "middle land"; Pragjyotisha means "lighted from the east" or "eastern/eastward light." Along with retrieving the stolen earrings, Krishna comes from Dvaraka in the west to "make safe the road to Pragjyotisha, the Eastward Light."[24] Karna worships the morning sun at such lengths that his back gets burnt. Naraka's full name, Naraka Bhauma, can mean "Hell on Earth," as in the story of Yayati, who is bounced from heaven;[25] afterward, this "Hell on Earth" is his destination.[26] Karna's life becomes a kind of hell on earth. Indeed, this Earth defines both their mothers. Naraka's is Bhumi or Prithivi, Earth herself; Karna's is Pritha, "Broad (like the Earth)." This affinity is so tangible that Pandav Lila folklore makes Bhumi and Kunti sisters, with Kunti as Mother Earth's *elder* sister! Mother Earth's son Bhaumasura (Earthly Demon, a fitting shorthand for Naraka) is thus Karna's cousin, as is Krishna. He is also the father of Bhagadatta, who agrees to help Arjuna find the path to the underworld when Arjuna bribes him with golden earrings![27] It is as if there were an implicit micromyth linking two pairs of solar earrings with demonic realms to the east that capture them, and from which they must be retrieved for a way to be opened.[28] Karna and Naraka do not have parallel careers, but it is as if they were drawn from the same metonymic gene pool and the same stock of cosmological images.

Moreover, there is an actual fusion between Naraka and Karna. Shortly before Indra robs Karna's earrings, the despairing Duryodhana, determined to fast to death, is spirited to the underworld realm of demons[29] by a *kritya*—a female personification of black magic, or *abhichara*[30]—whom the demons have sent for him. There Duryodhana's demon hosts tell him that Naraka has possessed Karna: "the soul [*atman*] of the slain Naraka resides in the form of Karna [*karnamurtim upashritah*]" (3.240.19ab). Indeed, it is "knowing this" that Indra will now rob Karna of his earrings (20–21)! For as we learn further from the epic's main narrator, Vaishampayana, Karna's possession by Naraka has intensified Karna's cruelty in his determination to kill Arjuna: "Karna too, his mind and soul possessed by the inner soul of Naraka [*avishtacittatma narakasyantaratmana*], then set his cruel mind [*kruram akarot sa matim tada*] on Arjuna's death" (32). Indeed, not only has Naraka possessed Karna; Bhishma, Drona, and Kripa have also now been possessed by *danavas*, and the Samshaptakas have been possessed by *rakshasas* (33–34)—all, it would seem, within the same recent time frame that includes Karna's possession by Naraka. It would appear that Naraka's affinities with Karna have drawn Naraka to possess Karna as a means of revenge against Krishna, his slayer.

Yet if Karna is demonically possessed from at least this time to his death,[31] as would seem to be implied, this fusion will have its limits.[32] As the epic ends, Yudhishthira will find Duryodhana in Heaven, and, rather than reside there with his former enemy, he will demand to be with his loved ones, even if they are in Hell, Naraka. There Yudhishthira's presence redeems them all, and of Karna, in particular, Vaishampayana says: "Nor was the truth-speaking hero Karna, O King, long worthy of Naraka [*narakarhash chiram*]" (18.3.36cd). So Karna was no more worthy of hell than of the demon who possessed him.

D. Karna's Temptations by Krishna and Kunti (Episode 11)

As a series of failed negotiations gives way to full preparation for war, Krishna, the last negotiator to find peace beyond reach, saves for the end of his embassy a conversation with Karna. Once Krishna leaves, Karna is also approached by Kunti. These two conversations take Karna into the depths of his predicament, confront him with his own truths, and reveal that, no matter how many forces work against him and no matter how base he has at times been or how possessed he might become, he is a great hero and a good man. As Krishna will put it—with terrible irony—after Karna's death: "He who announced Krishnaa [with the long "a," or double "a," as seen here; this refers to Draupadi] won by dice, the vilest of good men [*satpurushadhamah*]—today the earth drinks that *suta's* son's blood" (8.69.17).

Krishna takes Karna on Krishna's chariot out from the Kaurava capital, and tells him he is legally a son of Pandu (5.138.1–9). That being so, he offers to consecrate him king and promises, rather shockingly, that even "Draupadi will come to you at the sixth time" (9, 15, 18). Karna says he doesn't doubt that Krishna speaks "out of friendship and affection, and so as a friend [you] have my best interests at heart" (139.1). Their surprising friendship on Krishna's chariot resonates with other epic pairings between charioteers and warriors: in particular, the contrast between the Krishna and Arjuna as friends on Arjuna's chariot and Shalya and Karna as antagonists on Karna's chariot.[33] Karna knows details about his birth beyond what Krishna tells him, suggesting he already knows he is Kunti's son. He will remain loyal to Duryodhana and continue to cast his lot with the *sutas*, who have loved, raised, and married him into their lineage (3–16). It is thus for the best, he tells Purushottama,[34] that they suppress their conversation, for if Yudhishthira were to know Karna as his elder brother, he would not accept the kingdom; and if Karna were to accept it he would give it to Duryodhana. Better, he says, that "Yudhishthira be king forever, he who has Hrishikesha for his guide [*neta*],[35] Dhanamjaya as his warrior" (20–23, 57). Karna foresees that Duryodhana will now perform a great "sacrifice of weapons" at which Krishna will be witness and the Adhvaryu (ringmaster) priest (29). He admits that he now "burns from the *karma*" of his harsh words (*katukani*) to the Pandavas, uttered to please Duryodhana (45), and we must grant that these would include his insults to Draupadi.[36] He asks the Lotus-Eyed one that the *kshatriyas*, "old in learning and old in days," may by death in battle ascend to heaven "on the Kuru field, holiest even in the triple world" (52–54)—a favor Krishna grants (140.16–20). Karna's worship of the Sun thus does not eclipse his deeper acknowledgment of Krishna *bhakti*. Krishna smiles, then laughs and asks, "Does this offer of a kingdom not even tempt you?"[37] With Karna's resolution, the Pandavas' victory is now certain beyond a doubt (140.1–3). Karna asks Krishna why "you wish to bewilder me [*mam . . . sammohayitum icchasi*]" when you already know my answer, and admits that he is among the Kauravas bringing destruction to the earth (141.1–2). After their final words, Karna, having "clasped Madhava tightly," descends from his chariot, and Krishna speeds back to the Pandavas (47–49).

The Kaurava elder Vidura now goes to Kunti and tells her he can't sleep (142.1–9). "Sick with woe herself," Kunti broods over Karna's obstinacy and the danger he poses to the Pandavas (17). Recalling her vulnerabilities at his conception, she asks herself "Why should this *kanina* [son of an unmarried girl], who has returned to me as a son, not do my word that is so salutary for his brothers?" (25). Kunti is right that Karna would be covered by the law's retrospective intent regarding unwed mothers. But she would get no support from *The Laws of Manu* (9.160) on the crucial point of Karna's status as inheritor of the kingdom: a *kanina* is one of six types of sons "who are *relatives but not heirs*"![38] Karna would not inherit the kingdom, but of course Yudhishthira would "give" it to him, as Karna has just said to Krishna. Yet Kunti is drawing on another resonant theme here: sons should listen to their mothers. Indeed, she is used to having her sons take her word as absolute command, for it was she who once told them "Share it all equally," when she thought they were coming back with alms and instead they were talking about a "girl" just like she once was herself, Draupadi, whom Arjuna had just won in marriage.[39] So Kunti goes to the Ganga to find Karna. There she hears him reciting and stands behind him, waiting for him to finish. While he faces east with his arms raised, she stands in the shade of his upper garment like a withered garland of lotuses, hurting from the sunburn. At last, "having prayed up to the burning of his back [a prishtatapaj japtva] he turned around, and seeing Kunti he saluted her with joined palms, as was proper, this proud man of great *tejas*, the best of *dharma*'s upholders" (30). It is a precise evocation both of the *tejas* Shalya has sworn to destroy, and of the conditions under which Karna, while praying, gives boons "to brahmins especially, and always to all who are good [*sarvesham sarvada satam*]" (3.286.6cd).[40] So we know that Kunti might have done best had she come to make her request with a brahmin. It would now be sometime in the early afternoon, and she has, moreover, waited until Karna has *finished* his prayers. So he need give her nothing. Perhaps she knows all this and waits to make it clear that she is not trying to trap him. By the end he will make her a great gift of his own devising.

Kunti tells Karna he was her first-born, a *kanina*; about Surya being his father, the earrings, armor, and so forth (143.2–5)—nothing new to him, but perhaps she doesn't know that. Then she gets to the point: "It is not proper, son, especially for you, that, without knowing your brothers, you serve the Dhartarashtras from delusion [*mohad*]. In decisions about men's *dharma*, *this* is the fruit of *dharma*, son—that his father, and one-eyed mother too,[41] are satisfied" (6–7). Is she saying that as the fruit of *her dharma* Karna should satisfy *her*? In any case, she tells how splendid it would be if Karna joined forces with Arjuna and the rest, and concludes: "Endowed with virtues, eldest and best among relations who are the best, you will no longer be called '*suta*'s son.' You are a heroic Partha" (12). An elitist, Kunti appeals to what can only be Karna's sorest spot. And just at this point Karna hears "a voice [that] issued from Surya, difficult to transgress, affectionate, and uttered like a father: 'Kunti has spoken the truth, Karna, do your mother's word'" (5.144.1–2b). Unlike the Pandavas, who have *only* their mother's word to obey when she orders them to share equally,[42] Karna hears his mother's command reinforced by his father's. This is a lot of pressure from these absentee parents, but "Karna's thought did not waver, for he was firm in truth" (3). He tells Kunti he does not doubt her word; it would be his gateway to *dharma* to carry out her command (*niyoga*).

> But by casting me away, the wrong you have done me, destructive of fame and glory, is irreversible.... When there was time to act, you did not show me this crying out [*anukrosha*]. And now you have

summoned me, whom you have denied the sacraments. You never
acted in my interest like a mother, and now, here you are, enlightening
me solely in your own interest! (4–8)

He will not do her bidding; he will fight her sons with all his strength. But her
effort will not be vain: he will spare her other four sons in battle and only seek
to kill Arjuna; whether it is he or Arjuna who dies, five will survive. Why does
Karna say this? It is, he says, "while trying to persevere in the conduct of
noncruelty that befits a good man [*anrishamsyam atho vrittam rakshan satpur-
ushocitam*]" (144.19ab). To Kunti's self-serving "crying out" (*anukrosha*), Karna
responds with "noncruelty" (*anrishamsya*)! It is these two virtues, especially
befitting of a king, that Yudhishthira spends a lifetime learning to put together.[43]
But in this impasse, the two cannot be one—unless they are implicitly one in
Karna. "Having heard Karna's answer, Kunti shuddered from sorrow." But her
closing words are remorseless. Embracing Karna, recognizing that his words
mean destruction for the Kauravas and that "fate is all-powerful," she says:

"promise your commitment to that pledge you have given
[*tvaya . . . dattam tat pratijanihi samgarapratimocanam*], enemy-
plougher, for the safety [*abhayam*] of your four brothers. Good
health and good luck." . . . Pleased, Karna saluted her [*tam karno
'bhyavadat pritas*]. Then they both went their separate ways. (24–26)

It is an iconic moment, this "pleased" salute, for he has made his sad amends
with God and his mother.

E. Karna Uses Up the Never-Failing Spear (Episode 13)

Indra gave Karna the never-failing spear in exchange for his golden armor and
earrings. In the terrible night battle after the fourteenth day of war, Bhima's
half-*rakshasa* son Ghatotkacha wreaks havoc. The Kauravas panic and, in a
surprisingly brief appeal, press Karna to use the spear against him (7.154.48–
50). Caught in the moment, Karna hurls it and kills Ghatotkacha, but the spear
is gone: "that resplendent spear soared aloft in the night entering the intervals
of the constellations [*nakshatranam*[44] *antarany avishanti*]" (51–57)—to disappear, one assumes, into the nighttime outer space where Indra awaits its return to his hand.[45] The Kauravas rejoice (62–63). But the poets are not interested in the weapon's fate or even the fall of Ghatotkacha, who as Dhritarashtra
soon realizes, "was as insignificant as straw [*trinabhutam*]" (158.10d); they are
interested in the import of Karna's wasting this weapon, and, with that, in
imagining what might have been otherwise.

The Pandavas weep over the death of Bhima's son (155.1)—until Krishna
shocks them: "But Vasudeva was filled with great delight. As if agitating, he

shouted leonine shouts, Bharata, and shouting great shouts he embraced Phalguna. Shouting great shouts and tying the reins, he danced wrapped with joy like a tree shaken by the wind" (155.2–3). Krishna's joy mounts until Arjuna, finding that it looks unseemly, asks, "If it is not a secret . . . Madhusudana, tell me what has removed your gravity today; I think the levity of your action, Janardana, is like the drying up of the ocean or the creeping along [*visarpanam*] of Mount Meru" (9c–10).[46] Krishna replies that Karna was invincible with his never-failing spear. From the time he got it for his armor and earrings, which also made him invincible, he

> always thought you were slain in battle, but even with it gone he can only be slain by you. . . . He has now become human [*so 'dya manu-shatam prapto*]. . . . There will be only one means [*eko hi yogo*] to his death, in an opening brought on by his own inattentiveness. In that difficult situation, you should kill him when his chariot-wheel is sunk. I will signal you beforehand. (23, 27e, 28)

So Krishna knows Karna's whole story in advance, from the two curses on. Having found the means (*yogais*; 29) to kill other wicked foes, Krishna implies that it was he who was behind the slaying of Ghatotkacha—a *rakshasa*, moreover, who hated brahmins and sacrifices and violated *dharma*; had Karna not killed him, Krishna would have had to do it himself "for the sake of the establishment of *dharma*,[47] my imperishable vow" (156.25–28). Krishna must conjure up generic *rakshasa* traits here to justify killing Ghatotkacha, whose epic profile and stories hardly support the charge that he hated brahmins and the rest.

Dhritarashtra soon recalls that Krishna did indeed dispatch Ghatotkacha to nullify Karna's spear. He has just heard Samjaya narrate those very events (7.148.21–52): with Karna blazing like the Sun at night, Yudhishthira had urged Arjuna to fight him, but Krishna had said that so long as Karna still held Indra's spear, it was not yet time for that (34). Krishna had convinced Arjuna that Ghototkacha should fight Karna, and then told Ghatotkacha to use the advantages *rakshasas* have at night (51–52). So now, recalling that Arjuna had vowed to meet any challenge, Dhritarashtra asks why didn't Karna challenge Arjuna while he *had* the spear? What was wrong with Duryodhana's intelligence (*buddhi*) and counselors? "Vasudeva has cheated Karna of that spear through Ghatotkacha. As a *bilva* fruit would be snatched from the hand of a withered arm by a stronger man, so the never failing spear has become a failure [*shaktir amogha sa moghi bhuta*] in Ghatotkacha" (157.3–5, 6c–7). Samjaya replies that Krishna has just saved Arjuna with another of his *yogas*: "Having known what Karna wished to do, king, the slayer of Madhu commanded the lord of *rakshasas* to duel with Karna. . . . That spear would have killed Kaunteya like a tree hit by a thunderbolt" (11, 16).[48] Hearing Samjaya tell him that Dhritarashtra's own "bad counsel" (12) is in part to blame,

Dhritarashtra tries to shift the blame to Samjaya: "Why was this great goal also neglected by you, Gavalgani; why weren't you wise to it, greatly wise one?" (18). Samjaya says he was always in the inner circle where it was resolved every night: Karna should use the spear against Arjuna; or if Arjuna falls, kill Krishna; or kill Krishna even before Arjuna, since he is the root of all the Pandavas' successes (19–26). Daily they would awake with this resolution (*buddhi*)

> regarding the immeasurable Hrishikesha, lord of the thirty gods, but at the time of battle it was confounded [*vyamuhyata*]; and Keshava also always protected Arjuna.... He never wished to place him facing the *suta's* son in battle.... That is how the never-failing spear was made a failure. (27–29)

Not only that, Samjaya heard Krishna tell his kinsman Satyaki that it was he himself who baffled Karna's plan for the spear:

> I confused [*mohayami*] Radheya.... I do not regard my father, mother, yourselves, my brothers, or my breaths [as] so worthy of protection as Bibhatsu[49] in battle.... So it was that the *rakshasa* was sent by me to fight Karna; surely there was no other to withstand Karna in a battle at night. (36, 40, 43)

Dhritarashtra is now all the more dissatisfied with the Kauravas, and tells Samjaya "and you especially, son [*tata tava visheshatah*]," did not see to it that Karna hurled the spear "at Phalguna or the son of Devaki" (158.1–3). Samjaya repeats that Karna went to battle every day with that advice,

> but when morning came, king, Karna's and the other warriors' intelligence was destroyed by divine destiny [*daivataih ... buddhir nashyate*]. I think fate [*daivam*] is supreme, since Karna, with that [spear] in hand, did not kill Partha or Krishna the son of Devaki in battle. That spear held in his hand was raised like the Night of Time! Karna was a lord who possessed an intelligence afflicted by fate [*daivopahata buddhitvan*]. Confused by the gods' illusion [*mohito devamayaya*],[50] he did not release that Vasavi [weapon of Vasava, Indra] for death's sake into Devaki's son Krishna or into Partha. (6–9)

Dhritarashtra is then given the last word, speaking in the second person, perhaps as if to all of us: "You are destroyed by fate, by your own intelligence, and by Keshava; the Vasavi is gone, having slain Ghatotkacha who was as insignificant as straw" (10); and with no more to say on the matter, he asks Samjaya, So what happened next...?

The passage takes us to new and uncharted depths. There have been hints elsewhere that although Karna offers his devotions to Surya by day, the power that links him to Surya is strongest at night.[51] After debating every night how to use the spear, it is now in the dead of night when Karna burns fiercest with his "spear raised like the Night of Time"—probably an image of the *pralaya*, in which, after seven suns desiccate and burn the triple world, they leave not much, if any, time for night—until they bring on the cosmic night known as the night of Brahma.[52] It is the power of *rakshasas* at night that provides Krishna with the pretext to order Ghatotkacha to his death as the means to extract the spear, which sails off into the night sky.

It is also, I believe, a revelation that Karna and the Kauravas consider the option of killing Krishna. Could Karna—and this never-failing spear—really have done that? We are left to ponder the death of God. And what did Karna think of this option? We do not have his words. Maybe he was a *Suryabhakta* only pro tem, and only by default.[53] We could imagine he only listened to such advice, determined as he was to fight only Arjuna, and lifted by Krishna's friendship and his promise of heaven for the *kshatriyas* who would die at Kurukshetra. And then, too, Karna would know that Krishna was his cousin, the son of his mother's younger brother. But he also knows more than that, as does the reader. This is one of those passages that confirms Madeleine Biardeau's insight into the importance of the poets' contextual use of epithets, and in particular the selective and intensified uses of the name *devakiputra*, "Son of Devaki"—closing with three usages in seven verses—to underscore that the *daiva* has been the play of Krishna from the day his mother Devaki bore him.[54]

The passage is thus artful in unfolding Krishna's relation to fate: that when all is said and done, he *is* fate, but never without ambiguity.[55] If Dhritarashtra says he thinks fate (*daiva*) is supreme and that Karna's *buddhi* was "afflicted by *daiva*," it is uncertain whether "his *buddhi* was destroyed by destiny," as seems smoothest in the translation just given, or "by divinities" (*daivataih*), which looks odd but is at least equally accurate. Similarly, when Dhritarashtra says Karna was *mohito devamayaya*, does he mean Karna was "confused by the gods' illusion," as translated earlier, or "confused by the illusion of the god?" We know that it is really the latter.

F. Toward Karna's Death

Taken in isolation and looked at sequentially, these three moments in the life of Karna appear to have little in common, other than that among the fatalities that drive things toward his death, they are the three that have the most to do with Krishna. Nonetheless, they do align the hero toward this end by tracing his affinities and connections in three different spheres: the first in the realm of the demonic; the second in the human domain of family and friends; and the third in relation to God. In that, we might say there is some movement.

As the final duel with Arjuna takes shape, Karna recognizes Krishna as "the creator of the universe [*srashto jagatas*]" (8.22.49) even as he tries to counteract him by demanding Shalya as his charioteer.[56] More than any other Kaurava or Kaurava partisan, Karna is not just the Pandavas' problem but Krishna's. All the other great Kaurava heroes either make their pact with death with Yudhishthira or pose just momentary challenges to Arjuna. Only Karna is possessed by a demon whom Krishna has slain. Only Karna meets with Krishna alone. Only in foreseeing Karna's death does Krishna do such a dance. Flawed and demonically possessed as Karna may be, more than any foe Krishna finds the means to kill, Karna inspires admiration, affection, and a wish for things to have gone otherwise, as is ultimately expressed by Kunti and Yudhishthira. That Karna does inspire such things thus deepens Krishna's problem with him, and the reader's problem with Krishna. Says Krishna, losing his spear made Karna human. Until then, like Krishna, was he divine? For readers he was always more human than divine. Or perhaps one could better say, more than being divine, or for that matter demonic, he was always human. Approaching this point from other astute angles, Aditya Adarkar sees Karna having the "psychological strength of a child who has been raised by loving parents" (2001, 187)—that is, of course, his foster parents; Madeleine Biardeau, savoring his boastfulness, or "rodomontade," says that it is Karna's possession by a demon that humanizes him (2002, II, 119–20); while for Patricia Greer, "he uniquely represents the audience" (2002, 58).

G. Postmortem

Once Karna is killed and his identity as the Pandavas' eldest brother is revealed to them, it is left to the great Krishna *bhakta* Narada to give some narrative form to Karna's life. He does this in response to a tortured question of Yudhishthira that opens Yudhishthira's lengthy postwar grieving in the *Shanti* and *Anushasana Parvans*: "Why did the Earth swallow his wheel in battle? Why was my brother cursed?" (12.1.43a–44a). After unveiling a number of hitherto untold tales,[57] Narada closes with words steeped in irony that are nonetheless an elegy.

> To secure your[58] welfare the chief of the gods begged of Karna the divine natural-born and supremely radiant earrings, and also the natural-born armor, and he was confused by the god's illusion [*mohito devamayaya*].[59] Deprived of those earrings and natural-born armor, he was killed in battle by Vijaya while Vasudeva watched. Because of the curse of the high-souled brahmin Rama, because he granted Kunti's wish, because of Shatakratu's[60] illusion, because of Bhishma's contempt while tallying the warriors that he was but half a chariot warrior,[61] because of Shalya's destruction of his *tejas*, and by the lead[62] of Vasudeva, Karna Vaikartana, of brilliance equal to the sun's, was slain in battle by the Gandiva bowman who had

received divine weapons from Rudra, the king of the gods, Yama, Varuna, Kubera, and Drona, and also the high-souled Kripa. So your brother was cursed and also deceived by many [*evam shaptas tava bhrata bahubhish chapi vanchitah*]. Do not grieve. That tiger among men surely gained death in battle (12.5.8–15).

H. The Death of Karna

Following some preliminary fighting and some last-minute thoughts of reconciliation, the duel between Karna and Arjuna begins. The two warriors range against each other like elephants or mountains, each urged on by his allies, until Bhima goads Arjuna into doing better, offering to kill Karna himself with his mace if Arjuna is not up to the task (65.1–15). We pick up from there, with Krishna prodding Arjuna further by offering to lend him his discus. (*Trishtubh* verses are rendered line by line and numbered sequentially; *shloka* portions are rendered in paragraph and numbered as units.)[63]

> 65.16. Then, having seen the chariot and arrows thwarted,
> Vasudeva[64] also spoke to Partha,[65]
> "What is this, Kiritin,[66] that Karna has now crushed
> your weapons with his weapons?
>
> Why are you stupefied? Are you not attentive?
> The joyful Kurus are dancing!
> Honoring Karna, surely they all saw
> your weapon downed by his weapons.
>
> With the resolution that has destroyed the weapon of darkness
> from *yuga* to *yuga*, and also, in wars, terrible *rakshasas*
> and *asuras* sprung from pride,[67]
> with that resolution of yours, slay the *suta*'s son.[68]
>
> Or with that razor-edged
> Sudarshana[69] entrusted[70] by me,
> cut off the head of this foe by force,
> just as Shakra[71] did with the thunderbolt to the foe Namuchi.[72]
>
> 20. And with the strength by which you completely satisfied
> the lord who took the form of a hunter,[73]
> regaining that firmness, hero,
> kill the *suta*'s son together with his followers.
>
> Then bestow the abundant earth with her
> belt of oceans, towns, and villages,
> and her host of foes destroyed, on the king.[74]
> Obtain unequalled fame, Partha."

Challenged by Bhima and Janardana,[75]
remembering himself, considering his mettle,[76]
and having understood about the coming of the great-souled one,[77]
he spoke purposefully to Keshava.[78]

"I will bring forth this great fierce weapon
for the good of the world, for the destruction of the *suta's* son.
May you—and also the gods, Brahma,
Bhava,[79] and all who know Brahman—permit me to use it."

Thus invoking the invincible Brahma weapon
that was manageable only by the mind, he brought it forth.
Then the many-splendored one shrouded all the regions
and the intermediate points with missiles.
The Bharata bull also released high-speed arrows
numerously by the hundreds.

25. In the midst of combat Vaikartana[80] also
released hosts of arrows by thousands.
Resounding, they approached the Pandava
like torrents of rain released by Parjanya.[81]

And having struck Bhimasena and Janardana
and Kiritin too with three arrows each,
of inhuman feats and terrible might,
he roared awfully with a great sound.

Having seen Bhima and Janardana
struck with Karna's arrows, Kiritin
could not bear it, and again Partha
drew out eighteen arrows.

Having pierced Sushena[82] with one arrow
and Shalya with four and Karna with three,
he then hit Sabhapati,[83] clad in golden armor,
with ten that were well released.

The headless, armless prince
then fell without horse, driver, or banner
from the front of his chariot, his luster demolished,
like a *shala* tree cut down with axes.

30. Having again struck Karna with three, eight,
twelve, and fourteen arrows,
having slain four hundred tuskers equipped with weapons,
he slew eight hundred chariot warriors,
a thousand horses and horsemen,
and eight thousand brave foot-soldiers.

Then the pounding became very great
between that Arjuna and Adhiratha, O King,
the two striking one another with arrows
like two elephants with the fierce blows of their tusks.[99]

5. Then Karna, wishing to remove Phalguna's[100] head in battle,
aimed the foe-slaying serpent-mouthed arrow
that was well-sharpened, burning, terrible, well-rubbed in battle,
so long kept secret with Partha as its object,

ever-worshiped, bedded in sandalwood powder
and lying in a golden quiver,
of great venom,[101] blazing, and born
in the lineage of Airavata.[102]

Having seen Vaikartana, his arrow aimed,
the high-souled Madra king[103] said to him,
"This arrow will not reach his neck, Karna.
Having marked distinctly, fix a head-destroying arrow!"

Thereupon, his eyes reddened with wrath,
Karna said to Shalya, holding the arrow in check,
"Karna does not fix an arrow twice, Shalya.
Those like me are not given to deceit."

Having so spoken, he shot that snaky arrow
that he had worshiped for many years.
"Phalguna, you are slain," he said.
So hastening, he sent it forth strengthened.

10–11. Having seen that snake aimed by Karna, Madhava,[104]
the best of the strong, stepped powerfully on the chariot with
    his two feet.
When the chariot was immersed in the earth, the horses went
    to their knees.
Then the arrow struck that insightful one's diadem.[105]

With rage and great pains at discharging
that powerful weapon, the *suta*'s son thus struck off
Arjuna's head-ornament—celebrated through
the earth, sky, heaven, and the waters—from his head.

Having the brilliance of the planets, fire, moon, and sun,
adorned with nets of jewels, pearls, and gold,
it was carefully made with austerity for the sake of Puramdara[106]
by the inciter of the world himself.[107]

Having beauty of great worth, bringing fear to foes,
and fragrant, it kindled exceeding joy.

The lord of the gods, favorably minded, gave it himself
to Kiritin when he had attacked the gods' enemies.[108]

15. What Vrisha[109] forcibly struck off with the snake was
    unassailable
by the protectors known as Hara, the Lord of Waters, and
    Akhandala;[110]
by the foremost darts, the thunderbolt, the noose, and the
    Pinaka bow;[111]
and even by the foremost gods.[112]

Torn off by that best of arrows, that supreme diadem of Partha's,
burning with the fire of venom,[113] radiant,
dear over the earth, fell
like the blazing sun from the Asta Mountain.[114]

The snake then[115] forcibly struck off
the diadem adorned with many jewels from Arjuna's head
like great Indra's thunderbolt striking a lofty tree-bearing
    summit,
with fine sprouts and flowers, from a mountain.

As the earth, sky, heaven, and waters
appear agitated by the wind,
just so was the sound among the worlds then.
Perturbed folk strove and stumbled.

Then Arjuna, standing unperturbed, having bound
up his hair with a white cloth,
shone with his head so arranged like Udaya Mountain[116]
with the sun at full radiance.

20. Then, sped from Karna's arms, the serpentine arrow,
the great snake who had made enmity with Arjuna,
of great radiance like sun or fire,
having struck down the diadem, arose.[117]

It said to him,[118] "Know him[119] to have committed an offense
    against me,
Krishna, an hostility now born of the death of my mother."
Then Krishna said to Partha in battle,
"Slay the great snake who has made enmity with you."

Thus addressed by Madhusudana,[120]
the wielder of the Gandiva bow,[121] whose bow was fierce
    to foes,
said, "Who now is my snake
who has come on his own into the mouth of Garuda?"[122]

Krishna said, "When you were holding the bow
invigorating the god of variegated luster at Khandava,[123]
this multiform snake went to the sky, his body cut by arrows.
His mother was slain."[124]

Then Jishnu,[125] eschewing leftovers,[126]
cut the snake moving in the sky,
as if flying upward, with six keen arrows.
His body cut, he fell on the earth.[127]

25. At that time, with ten
stone-whetted peacock-feathered shafts,
Karna struck that foremost hero among men,
Dhanamjaya, who was glancing obliquely.

Then Arjuna, delivering with twelve
keen arrows released from the ear,
quickly released an arrow stretched fully to his ear,
its speed equal to venom.

The foremost of arrows, well-released,
having riven Karna's armor, as if driving out his breath,
having drunk his blood,
entered the earth smeared with bloody feathers.

Then Vrisha, angry at the fall of that arrow,
like a great snake beaten with a rod,
as one acting quickly, released the finest arrows
like a snake of great venom spewing the ultimate venom.

He pierced Janardana with twelve arrows,
and Arjuna too with ninety-nine;
and again, having pierced the Pandava with a terrible arrow,
Karna roared aloud and laughed.

30. The Pandava paid no heed to his joy.
Knowing about the vital points, he then cut his vital points.
Having the prowess of Indra he struck the foe with feathered arrows
even as Indra struck Bala[128] with energy.

Then Arjuna released on Karna ninety-nine arrows
that were like death's rod.[129]
His body, severely pained by those arrows, trembled
like a mountain riven by a thunderbolt.

That one's head-ornament, adorned with gold,
precious jewels, and the finest diamonds,
was pierced by Dhanamjaya with feathered arrows and fell down
on the earth, as did his fine earrings.

His fine and shining very costly armor,
carefully made by the best of craftsmen
working for a very long time, the Pandava
cut in a moment into many pieces with his arrows.[130]

Thereupon, angered, he[131] pierced the armorless one
with fine arrows, four of them.
Struck forcibly by his foe, Karna trembled exceedingly,
like a sick person with bile, phlegm, wind, and wounds.

35. With whetted arrows released from the circle of his great bow
discharged with care and action, and with strength,
Arjuna chopped at Karna with many of the best arrows,
and so too speedily cut his vital points.

Hard-struck by Partha's feathered arrows
of fierce speed and varied sharp points,
Karna shone like a mountain reddened with ores of red chalk
flowing with cascades of red water.[132]

Kiritin then covered Karna and his horses and chariot
with calf-toothed arrows, Bharata,
and, with every care, he shrouded the regions
with arrows feathered with purified gold.

Covered by those calf-toothed arrows, the broad
and thick-chested Adhiratha shone
like a well-flowered *ashoka, palasha,* or *shalmali* tree,
or a mountain furnished with *spandana* and sandalwood trees.

With those arrows manifoldly sticking to his body,
Karna shone in battle, O King,
like a great mountain[133] possessing auspicious *Karnikara* flowers
amid ridges and glens filled with trees.

40. He dispatched hosts of arrows with his bow;
Karna shone radiating masses of arrows
like the sun facing the Asta Mountain,
its blood-red disc beaming crimson.

Having assailed the regions, keen-pointed arrows
released from Arjuna's arms scattered
the blazing arrows like mighty snakes
released from the bend of Adhiratha's son's arms.[134]

Then his wheel fell into the earth.
When his chariot was reeling from the brahmin's curse
and the weapon obtained from Rama no longer shone,
the *suta*'s son was agitated in battle.

Not tolerating those misfortunes, he shook
his hands reviling,[135] saying, "*Dharma* protects
those eminent in *dharma*, so those who know *dharma* always say.
But now it is sunk[136] for me.
It does not protect its devotees.
I think *dharma* does not always protect."[137]

So saying, shaken from the injury to his vital points
by the fall of Arjuna's weapons, unsteady in his actions,
his charioteer and horses staggering,
he again and again censured *dharma*.

45–50. Then Karna pierced Partha in battle with three fiercely sped
arrows, and wounded him with seven. Then Arjuna released seventeen sharp-edged unswerving ones that were like fire and terrible
as Indra's thunderbolt. Having pierced him with terrible speed, they
fell on the earth's surface. Shaken to the core, Karna displayed motion with power. Thereupon, steadying with strength, he invoked a
Brahma weapon. Seeing it, Arjuna summoned an Indra weapon.
Having blessed the Gandiva bow and arrows, Dhanamjaya released showers of arrows like Indra releasing rains. Then those
energized high-potency arrows released from Partha's chariot appeared in the vicinity of Karna's chariot.

51–56. The great chariot warrior Karna then baffled those shot in
front of him. When the weapon was destroyed, the Vrishni hero[138]
then said, "Release the foremost weapon, Partha. Karna swallows
arrows." And Arjuna, having intoned the Brahma weapon, thereupon
fixed it. When Arjuna had then shrouded Karna and roamed about,
Karna, angered, cut his bowstring with well-sharpened arrows. Putting on and polishing another bowstring, the Pandava filled Karna
with blazing arrows by the thousands. Between the cutting of his bow
and his attention to restringing it in battle, it was so quick that
Karna did not perceive it. That was like a wonder. Radheya[139]
counteracted Savyasacin's weapons with weapons. Displaying his
own prowess, he did better than Partha.

57–65. Then Krishna, having seen Arjuna tormented by Karna's
weapon, considering, said to Partha, "Use a superior weapon." Then
Dhanamjaya, having blessed another iron-made divine arrow that
looked like fire and was equal to a serpent's venom, taking hold of a
Raudra weapon,[140] desired to shoot. Then the earth swallowed Radheya 's wheel in the great fight.[141] Then Radheya, his wheel swallowed, wept tears out of wrath, and said to Arjuna, "O Pandava,

forebear a bit. Having seen this wheel of mine swallowed by fate, Partha, abandon the intention practiced by cowards. As kings do not attack a king, Arjuna, so heroes do not attack in combat one with disheveled hair, one facing away, a *Brahman*, one with joined palms, one who has come for refuge, one whose weapon is lowered, one also who has gone to ruin, one without arrows, one whose armor has fallen, or whose weapon has fallen or broken. You are a hero, Kaunteya.[142] Therefore, forebear a bit, Dhanamjaya, while I draw this wheel out of the earth. Standing on your chariot, you cannot slay me standing ill-equipped on the earth. I fear neither from Vasudeva nor from you, Pandaveya.[143] Surely you are a *kshatriya*, one who shows compassion, an increaser of a great lineage. Recalling instruction about *dharma*, forebear a bit, Pandava."

67.1. Then Vasudeva, standing on the chariot, said,
"Luckily you remember *dharma* here, Radheya!
Sunk in disasters, when it comes to renouncing life those who are base
blame fate, not their misdeeds, whatever they are.

"Having led Draupadi singly clad into the hall—
you, along with Suyodhana,[144]
Duhshasana, and Shakuni, the son of Subala—[145]
your *dharma* did not become evident there, Karna.

3–5. "When the dice-knowing Shakuni vanquished the dice-ignorant Kaunteya Yudhishthira in the hall, where did your *dharma* go then?[146] When Krishnaa[147] was having her period, standing under Duhshasana's power, you laughed in the hall, Karna. Where did your *dharma* go then?[148] Again, Karna, covetous of kingship, you summoned the Pandava, relying on the Gandhara king.[149] Where did your *dharma* go then?"[150]

6–11. When Radheya was addressed this way by Vasudeva, his sharp anger fixed on the Pandava, remembering things about Dhanamjaya. At his anger, rays of luminous energy[151] appeared from every pore, O Maharaja. That was like a wonder. Having perceived him then, Karna again showered a Brahma weapon on Dhanamjaya, and made an attempt to abandon his chariot.[152] Covering that weapon with his own weapon, the Pandava attacked. Kaunteya then, having aimed at Karna, released another arrow that was dear to Jatavedas.[153] It blazed forth harshly. Karna then appeased the fire with a Varuna weapon,[154] and with clouds he made all the regions shrouded with darkness. But the unfazed energetic Pandaveya,

within Radheya's sight, then dispelled the clouds with a Vayu
weapon,[155]

and with arrows, the best of elephant girth-cords[156]
adorned with gold, pearls, gems, and diamonds, very beautiful,
highly exempt from the quality of darkness,
made with care by the best craftsmen with time and effort,

always bringing strength to your army,
which terrorized enemies, of adorable form,
as celebrated in the world as the sun,
its light equal to the sun, moon, and fire.

Then the high-souled Kiritin, engrossed with the
keen, gold-feathered, razor-sharp arrow of Adhiratha,
cut off the great chariot warrior Adhiratha's flagstaff
that was radiant with prosperity.[157]

15. O worthy friend,[158] the Kurus' fame, *dharma*, victory,
hearts, and all things dear
then fell with that banner;
and there was a great sigh, "Alas."[158]

Thereupon the Pandava, to kill Karna quickly,
took out from his quiver an Anjalika[160] that was
like a rod of fire and the thunderbolt of the great Indra,
its fine ray like the thousand-rayed sun's,

able to pierce the vital points, smeared with flesh and blood,
resembling Vaishvanara,[161] very precious, a destroyer
of the lives of men, horses, and elephants, measuring three
    cubits
and six feet, of straight course and fierce speed,

its radiance equal to the thousand-eyed god's[162] thunderbolt,
exceedingly unbearable like the one who eats whole corpses,[163]
resembling the Pinaka bow and Narayana's discus,
frightful, destructive of those bearing life.[164]

Having joined Gandiva with this supreme great weapon,
knowing *mantras*, having drawn, he said aloud,
"If I have performed austerities, satisfied my gurus,
and heard what is desired from friends,

20. "by that truth[165] may this great weapon,
an arrow of incomparable firmness, destroying bodies,
taking away lives, and hard-hearted, may this
well-bitten arrow be invincible upon my foe Karna."

So uttering, Dhanamjaya released
that terrible arrow for the death of Karna,
as fierce as a sorceress of the Atharva-Angirasas,[166]
blazing, irresistible in battle even by death.

Highly thrilled, Kiritin said,
"May this arrow of mine be the bearer of victory.
Vengeful,[167] splendid as the sun and moon,
reaching Karna, may it lead him to Yama."

With that choicest of victory-bearing arrows
whose radiance was equal to the sun and moon,
the diadem-crowned one, of thrilled aspect, vengeful,[168]
his bow drawn, halted his foe.[169]

Of radiance like the risen sun,
like the sun moving midway in the autumn sky,
that marshal's[170] head fell on the earth
like the red-disked sun from Asta Mountain.[171]

25. The embodied soul of that one of lofty deeds
abandoned the handsome body, ever raised in happiness,
with exceedingly great difficulty,
like a lord of great wealth the house to which he was attached.

Cut with arrows, the tall lifeless body
of Karna, who was deprived of armor, fell
with its wound streaming like a lightning-struck mountain peak
flowing with red chalky water.

Then from Karna's overthrown body
a blazing luminosity[172] soon entered the sky.
All the men and warriors saw this wonder,
O king, after Karna was slain.

The delighted Somakas, seeing him slain and lying down,
bellowed with the troops.
Exceedingly thrilled, they beat their musical instruments
and waved their arms and garments.
Others, endowed with strength, danced.
Embracing one another, they shouted, roaring,

having seen Karna cut down from the chariot,
slain by darts, like a fire scattered by a great wind
when it is at rest in the morning
at the termination of a sacrifice.[173]

30–34. Karna's body shone like the sun with its rays, its every limb
filled with arrows and bathed in streams of blood. Having scorched the

hostile army with burning rays of arrows, Karna was a sun led to the Asta Mountain by Arjuna as powerful time. When going to Asta Mountain, the sun thereupon departs, having taken away its luster; just so did the arrow go,[174] taking away Karna's life. In the late afternoon, O worthy friend, the *suta*'s son's head, cut off in battle by the Anjalika, fell with the body. Higher and higher, rising straightly, that arrow quickly snatched away the head and body of Karna, that enemy of warriors.

35. Having seen the fallen hero Karna
lying on the earth filled with arrows,
his limbs smeared with blood, the Madra king
went away with the chariot, its flagstaff cut.

When Karna was slain, the Kurus fled,
overcome with fear and gravely wounded in battle,
repeatedly glancing at Arjuna's great flagstaff
shining with beauty.

That one whose acts equaled those of the god of
    a thousand eyes,[175]
whose face was beautiful like a thousand-petaled lotus,
like the thousand-rayed sun at the close of day,
so his head fell to the earth.

68.1. Seeing the troops crushed with arrows
in the struggle between Karna and Arjuna, Shalya,
glancing at the approaching Duryodhana,
beheld the Bharata battlefield.

Duryodhana, having seen his army
with its elephants, horses, and chariots beaten down
and the *suta*'s son slain, his eyes full of tears,
repeatedly sighed, a picture of woe.

Then they stood surrounding Karna, desirous of seeing
the hero fallen on the earth
filled with arrows, his limbs smeared with blood,
as if Surya had happened to drop.

Among the enemy and among your own were
those who became thrilled, terrified, despondent, or forgetful;
so also others gave way to grief,
each according to their respective natures.

5. Seeing Karna slain by Dhanamjaya,
his energy[176] destroyed, his armor, ornaments, garments,

and weapons in disarray, the Kurus fled
like a confused herd of cows whose bull is slain.

Having seen Karna lying on the earth
harshly slain by Arjuna like an elephant by a lion,
the Madra king, terrified,
slid away quickly with the chariot.

And the Madra lord, his mind stupefied,
having gone quickly to Duryodhana's side with the chariot
whose banner was removed,
addressing that one beset with woe, said this word,

"The foremost chariot warriors, horses, and elephants are
    shattered.
Slain, your army is like the realm of Yama,
with its men, horses, and elephants like mountain peaks
after having attacked one another.

There has never been such a battle, Bharata,
as was the one now between Karna and Arjuna.
The two Krishnas[177] together were surely swallowed by Karna,
and all the others who are your enemies.

10. But what is the fate brought forth from its own sway
that protects the Pandavas and kills us?
Surely all the heroes who promoted your success and purpose
are forcibly slain by the enemy.

Heroes mighty as the Lord of Waters,
Kubera, Vaivasvata, and Vasava[178]
with their manliness, heroism, and strength,
and endowed with all manner of abundant great merits,

fit to be unslayable, Indras among men
desirous of your purpose, were slain by the Pandaveyas.
Don't grieve over it, Bharata. It is settled.
Success takes its course. There is not always success."

Hearing this word of the Madra lord
and reflecting on his own misconduct,
Duryodhana, wretched at heart, at wit's end,
sighed again and again, a picture of woe.[179]

To him who was silent in thought, miserable, and severely afflicted,
Artayani[180] said this wretched sad word:
"Hero, behold this terrible battlefield arrayed with
slain elephants, horses, and men;

15–16. "with fallen elephants, huge as mountains,
suddenly wounded, their vital spots
pierced with arrows, agitated and lifeless,
garlanded with gold, bathed with their armor,
weapons, and reins in streams of blood,
their standards, lances, hooks, and bells in disarray,
like lordly mountains whose herbs, trees, deer, and rocks
are scattered, riven with thunderbolts;

"and arrayed with fallen horses pierced with arrows,
others breathing hard and vomiting blood,
with wretched moans, their eyes rolling,
biting the earth and neighing pitifully;

"arrayed also with pierced horse- and elephant-warriors—
some with little life left, some with their life departed—
and with crushed chariot warriors, elephants, horses, and men;
the earth is hard to look at like the great Vaitarani;[181]

"with elephants whose limbs, trunks, and hind feet are cut,
trembling, fallen on the earth;
with famous elephant-, chariot-, and horse-warriors;
and with foot-soldiers slain fighting their enemies face to face,
their weapons, garments, ornaments, and armor shattered,
as if the earth was covered with tranquil fires;

20. "with the great armies seen fallen by thousands,
afflicted by the attacks of arrows,
their wits lost, panting again,
it is as if the earth came to have its fires extinguished;
with its waters fallen from the sky, the stainless earth
is like the night sky with its planets ablaze.

"The arrows released from the arms of Karna and Arjuna,
having riven the bodies of men, horses, and elephants,
quickly taking away their breaths, entered the earth
everywhere like great snakes with weapons[182] toward their dwelling.

"With the elephants, horses, and men slain in battle,
with chariot warriors killed by
Dhanamjaya and Adhiratha's arrows on the way,
the earth became very hard to traverse.

"With chariots shattered by weapons, bent and separated,
their traces, yokes, axles, and wheels cut,
their warriors and flagstaffs, choice weapons, horses,
and inseparably connected charioteers crushed by choice shafts,

"with iron-made devices that were released and knocked down,
their joins struck, bent, and disconnected,
their broken seats adorned with gold and jewels,
the earth was strewn like a sky with autumn clouds.

25. "With speedy, ornate, and well-equipped battle chariots
drawn by fleet steeds, their lords slain, fleeing quickly
with masses of men, elephants, chariots, and horses
your forces are smashed on every side.

"Golden tiaras fell, as did bludgeons, axes,
sharp pikes,[183] clubs, sharp-edged spears,
spotless unsheathed swords,
maces bound with golden cloth,

"bows ornamented with golden rings
and arrows with beautiful golden feathers,
and spotless unsheathed tempered lances,
darts, and swords with golden luster,

"umbrellas, fans, and conches
and garlands beautiful with flowers and the finest gold,
variegated elephant cloths, emblems, and cloth turbans,
diadem-crowns and beautiful tiaras,

"and cloths scattered and dispersed,
and necklaces chiefly of rubies and pearls,
tight upper-armbands, the finest bracelets,
collars for the neck with strings of gold,

30. "the best of gems, pearls, gold, and diamonds
and auspicious jewels high and low,
and bodies accustomed to unending happiness,
their heads and faces like the moon—

"having abandoned their bodies, enjoyments, and retinues
and even the happinesses known to the mind,
and acquiring great steadiness in their own *dharma*,
they together went with glory to the celebrated worlds."

Having thus spoken, Shalya stopped.
Duryodhana, his mind seized with grief,
saying "Oh Karna! Oh Karna!" was distressed,
senseless, his eyes filled with tears.

Then the lords of men, the son of Drona[184] first among them,
having all comforted him, went on,
glancing back repeatedly at the great banner of
Arjuna ablaze with glory.

The earth sprinkled with red blood born from
the bodies of men, horses, and elephants,
from union with the gold, garlands, and red cloths,
was like a radiant woman accessible to all.[185]

35. Perceiving her highly illustrious form covered with blood
at that terrible hour, O King,
the Kurus did not even stand.
All pledged to the world of the gods,

they were very miserable about Karna's death,
saying, "Oh Karna! Oh Karna!"
Beholding the sun reddened, O King,
they set forth quickly to their camps.

But Karna, his horses smeared with blood from the
sharp gold-feathered arrows sped from Gandiva,
his body covered with arrows, shone on earth even though he
    was slain
like Surya himself with his wreath of rays.

Having touched with his hands[186] the blood-besprinkled
body of Karna, the lord Vivasvat,[187]
his form blood-red, compassionate toward his devotee,
went to the other ocean desiring to bathe.

As if so reflecting, the universally celebrated
hosts of gods and rishis went each to his home.
And the folk,[188] having reflected, flowed away
as they wished to heaven and the surface of the earth.

40. Having seen that wonder causing fear to all
bearers of breath, that battle between the two
foremost Kuru heroes Dhanamjaya and Adhiratha,
those amazed folk then left applauding.

41–46. Though his armor was cut through with arrows, though the
hero was slain in battle, Fortune[189] did not leave Radheya even though
his life was gone. Adorned with various ornaments, O King, his
bracelets made of polished gold, the slain Vaikartana lay like a tree
possessing sprouts. Resembling the finest gold, aflame like the Purifier,[190] having burnt the Pandavas and Panchalas, O King, with
the energy of his weapons, that tiger among men together with his
sons was quieted by Partha's energy. The one who also said "I
give," and not "It is not so," when sought by seekers, a good man
always with the good,[191] that Vrisha was slain in the chariot duel. The
high-souled one whose entire wealth of self belonged to brahmins;

he for whom there was nothing, even his own life, he would not give
to brahmins; always dear to men,[192] a giver whose gift was dear—
he has gone to heaven having taken away from your sons their armor, protection, and hope for victory.

47. When Karna was slain, the streams did not flow,
and the sun went soiled to the Asta mountain;
and a slantwise planet, Yama's son,[193] had the color
of burning fire for its rising, O King.

Thereupon the sky split, the earth roared,
and violent high-velocity winds blew;
the regions blazed forth violently with smoke
and the great noisy oceans trembled.

Multitudes of mountains shook with their forests,
and hosts of beings shuddered, O worthy friend.
The planet *Brihaspati*,[194] oppressing the constellation *Rohini*,
took on the same color as the sun or moon.

50. When Karna was slain, the regions did not disclose
    themselves;
the sky was covered in darkness, the earth roamed about,
meteors of blazing light fell, and
night-stalkers[195] too were thrilled.

When Arjuna with his razor-sharp arrow toppled
Karna's head, its face radiant as the moon,
folk in the atmosphere, heaven, and here
repeatedly cried, "Alas!"

Having slain the foe Karna in battle,
who was honored by gods, men, and *gandharvas*,
Arjuna Partha shone with utmost energy
like the thousand-eyed one after slaying Vritra.[196]

Then with the chariot that roared like a bank of clouds,
that glittered like the sun at midday in the autumn sky,
whose emblemed banner had a terrible roar,[197]
that shone like snow, the moon, a conch, or crystal,
that was adorned with coral, diamond, pearls, and gold
and was fast beyond measure,

the two best of men,[198] the Pandava and the crusher
    of Keshi,[199]
lofty like the sun or fire,
fearless and quick in battle, shone
like Vishnu and Vasava mounted on the same vehicle.

55. With the sounds of their wheels, palms, and bowstring,
having forcibly destroyed their enemies' lusters,
having extinguished the Kurus with showers of arrows,
the one with the monkey on his banner and the one with the
    best of birds[200] on his banner
then took up with their hands their fine-sounding conches
that were covered with webs of gold

and dazzling as snow, and, forcibly blowing them loudly,
sank the hearts of their foes.
The two best of men[201] with the two best of faces
kissed the two best of conches and blew them jointly,

57. and from both, from Devadatta and the blare of
    Panchajanya,[202] it filled the earth, atmosphere, and heaven,
    and even the waters.
Those two heroes, making the forests, mountains,
streams, and regions resound with the sound
of their conches, terrified your son's army
and gladdened Yudhishthira.

Then, having heard the conches' agitating blare,
the Kurus departed with speed,
having deserted the Madra lord and also
the lord of the Bharatas, Duryodhana, O Bharata.

60. Hosts of beings together applauded Dhanamjaya
of many splendors in the great battle,
and Janardana too,
as if the two were risen suns.

Covered with Karna's arrows, the two foe-tamers
Achyuta[203] and Arjuna both shone forth in battle
like the sun or the rabbit-marked moon with its wreath of rays,
risen spotless, having destroyed the darkness.

Removing those bunches of arrows, the two lords[204]
of unrivaled prowess, flushed with happiness,
came surrounded by friends to their camp
like Vasava and Achyuta invoked by the attendees of a sacrifice.

Then they were honored by *charanas*,[205] men, and *gandharvas*
with the gods, and even the great snakes, *yakshas*,[206]
and the great *rishis* for their supreme strengthening of victory,
having slain Karna in that peerless battle.[207]

69.1–6.[208] Samjaya said, After Karna had thus fallen and your
army had fled, joyfully embracing Partha, Dasharha[209] said this word,

"Vritra was slain by the destroyer of Bala;[210] Karna by you, Dhanamjaya. People will tell the death of Vritra and Karna as a dou-
blet.[211] Vritra was slain in battle by the many-splendored possessor of
the thunderbolt. Karna was slain by you with the bow and sharp
arrows. Let the two of us, Kaunteya, report this prowess spread in
the world and bearing your fame to the intelligent Dharmaraja. Having reported to Dharmaraja the death of Karna in battle that was
so long intended, you will discharge your debt."[212]

6–11. When Partha said "Yes," the bull of the Yadus, deliberate[213]
Keshava, turned around the chariot of that best of chariot warriors.
And Govinda[214] said this word to Dhrishtadyumna, Yudhamanyu,
the two sons of Madri, Wolfbelly, and Yuyudhana,[215] "Bless you! May
you stand watchful facing the foe until the king is informed that
Karna is slain by Arjuna." Given leave by those heroes, he went to the
king's encampment. And having taken Partha, Govinda saw Yudhishthira, that tiger among kings, lying down on the finest of gold
beds. The delighted pair then touched the king's feet. Beholding their
joy and their superhuman blows, thinking that Radheya was slain,
Yudhishthira rose up.[216]

12–18. Then the sweet-speeched Vasudeva, delighter of the Yadus,
narrated the death of Karna to him just as it happened. Slightly smiling then, Krishna Acyuta, palms folded, addressed King Yudhishthira whose foe was slain. "Luckily the wielder of the Gandiva bow
and the Pandava Wolfbelly and you too and the two Pandava sons of
Madri are well, O King, freed from this hair-raising battle that has
been destructive of heroes. Quickly do the things that are yet to
be done, king. Harsh Vaikartana, the *suta*'s son of great might, is slain.
Luckily you triumph, Indra among kings. Luckily you increase, Pandava. He who announced Krishnaa won by dice, the vilest of good
men[217]—today the earth drinks that *suta*'s son's blood. Kuru bull, that
enemy of yours lies on the earth with his limbs torn by arrows. Look at
him, tiger among men, broken by many arrows."

19–25. Then the thrilled Yudhishthira paid homage to Dasharha; he
said, "Luckily luckily," Indra among kings,[218] and he gladly said
this: "It is not strange in you, great-armed son of Devaki,[219] that, with
you as his charioteer, Partha would now do what is manly." And
the law-supporting Partha, best of Kurus, having grasped his braceleted right arm, spoke to both Keshava and Arjuna, "Narada has
told that you are the two gods Nara and Narayana, the two ancient best of men[220] joined in the establishment of *dharma*.[221] The
wise great-armed lord Krishna Dvaipayana[222] has also told me this

divine story repeatedly. By your power,[223] Krishna, Dhanamjaya with Gandiva conquered the foes who faced him and never faced away. Our victory was firm. Defeat was not to be ours when you undertook Partha's charioteering in battle."

26–34. Having thus spoken, Maharaja, that great chariot-warrior, a tiger among men, having mounted that gold-decked chariot yoked with ivory-white black-tailed horses, surrounded by troops, pleasantly assenting to the heroic Krishna and Arjuna, then came to see the battlefield of many tidings. Conversing with the two heroes Madhava and Phalguna, he saw the bull among men Karna lying on the battlefield broken in pieces everywhere by arrows sped from Gandiva. Having seen Karna and his sons slain,[224] King Yudhishthira praised both Madhava and the Pandava, those tigers among men, saying, "Today, Govinda, with my brothers I am king of the earth, protected on every side by you, our lord, hero, and sage. Having seen the death of the proud tiger among men Radheya,[225] that wicked-souled son of Dhritarashtra[226] will be hopeless about life and kingdom now that the great chariot-warrior Karna is slain. By your grace, bull among men, our goals are met. Delighter of the Yadus, you and the wielder of the Gandiva bow are victorious. Luckily you triumph, Govinda. Luckily Karna is fallen." So, O Indra among kings, the much-delighted Dharmaraja Yudhishthira praised Janardana and Arjuna.[227]

35–40. Then the great chariot-warriors filled with joy magnified the king surrounded by all his brothers, beginning with Bhima. And the Pandavas Nakula, Sahadeva, and Wolfbelly, and Satyaki the foremost chariot-warrior of the Vrishnis, O Maharaja, and Dhrishtadyumna and Shikhandin, and the Pandus, Panchalas, and Srinjayas[228] honored Kaunteya at the *suta*'s son's fall. Behaving like conquerors, devoted to war, those tested champions, having magnified King Yudhishthira, lauded the two foe-taming Krishnas with words joined with songs of praise. Thus filled with joy, the great chariot-warriors went to their own camp. Thus this destruction, a very great hair-raising occurrence, came about on account of your evil policy, O King. Why do you grieve excessively now?

41–43. Vaishampayana said, Having heard this unpleasantness, the much-pained Kauravya lord of earth Dhritarashtra fell helpless on the earth, as did Gandhari, the true-vowed lady who saw *dharma*. Then Vidura and also Samjaya took hold of the lord of men, and the two also undertook to comfort the lord of the earth. So too the royal ladies raised Gandhari. The king, taking heart for the two of them, became silent, discerning.[229]

NOTES

1. See Hiltebeitel ([1976] 1990), 81–85.

2. Much has been written recently on Karna in the *Mahabharata*, mostly involving comparison with other myths and epics in fascinatingly different ways—most remarkably, three doctoral dissertations: McGrath (2001), seeking an "archaic" Karna to exemplify pre-*Mahabharata* features of Indo-European heroism; Adarkar (2001), examining the question of literary character around Karna; and Greer (2002), exploring how Karna is knotted into the *Mahabharata's* literary "net"—an image similarly used by Adarkar (189). Adarkar and Greer are to me the most persuasive and stimulating. See also Biardeau (2002, 1:743–754, 993–1119; 2:116–119, 219–229, 271–387, 523–532); Jarow (1999); Woods (2001, 43–46); Jarow (1999). For earlier treatments, see Dumézil (1968, 124–144); Biardeau (1975–76, 173–174; 1976–77, 143–146; 1978, 129–130, 170–175; 1978–79, 147–151; 1979–80, 171–174; 1980–81, 223–227); Biardeau and Péterfalvi (1985, 1986); Hiltebeitel (1980, 1982); Shulman (1985, 380–387); and Adarkar (2001, 48–56) (a review).

3. Especially the Sanskrit play *Karnabhara*, ascribed to Bhasa, on which see Miller (1991), and the *Terukkuttu*-style Tamil play *Karnamotcam*, attributed to Pukalentippuluvar, on which see de Bruin (1998, 1999); Hiltebeitel (1988, 395–413). On other South Indian treatments of Karna, see Shulman (1985, 380, 387–400). On *Mahabharata* folk epic traditions on Karna in North India, see Sax (2000, 2002, 157–185); Hiltebeitel (1999, 102–103 [in the Rajasthani *Pabuji*] and 121–262 [in the Hindi *Alha*]). See further Adarkar, 2001, 43–45.

4. See Smith (1972, 1992). Most of the epic (about 90 percent) is in *shloka* verses of two sixteen-syllable lines, while most of the rest is in *trishtubh* verses, regularly of four eleven-syllable lines. Smith has argued that *trishtubhs* form the epic's "core" and irregular *trishtubhs* its "nucleus" (1972, 65).

5. See Hiltebeitel (2005a, 98–107) for further discussion of "the book on Karna"; on the notion of "literary monstrosity," see Hiltebeitel (2001b, 1).

6. As A. K. Ramanujan has so nicely put it, "no Hindu ever reads the *Mahabharata* for the first time" (1991a, 419), and "in India . . . no one ever reads the *Ramayana* or the *Mahabharata* for the first time" (1991b, 46). See Hiltebeitel (2000). See also Hiltebeitel (2006).

7. Karna is like Rudra (65.36), but so is Arjuna, who must be reminded of the ways he is like Rudra, Krishna, and Indra (65.18–20). Arjuna is like Indra (65.37), but then so is Karna, fallen and beheaded, "one whose acts equaled those of the god of a thousand eyes" (i.e., Indra; 67.37).

8. On authorship, see Hiltebeitel (2001b, 32–91, 278–322); on character, see Adarkar (2001); on reader response, see Greer (2002).

9. See Biardeau (2002, 1:432; 2:318).

10. See Hiltebeitel (1982, 106). The extensive parallels between these episodes in the Irish and Indian epics remain to me an intriguing puzzle.

11. Karna recognizes Krishna as "the creator of the universe [*srashto jagatas*]" (8.22.49) even as he tries to counteract him by demanding Shalya as his charioteer; see Hiltebeitel (1982, 89; 1984, 9).

12. See Hiltebeitel (2001b, 59): Vyasa drops in on the battlefield to prevent Yudhishthira from fighting Karna (7.158.51–62), thus keeping Yudhishthira "in

character" and appearing to save his life and kingship but, more important, steering matters, like Krishna, to assure that the decisive duel will be between Arjuna and Karna.

13. Prior to this, he is described only in a partly formulaic verse (1.63.82), the last line of which occurs two other times (1.104.11ab, 1.126.2ab): "The great chariot-warrior Karna was begotten by Surya on the virgin Kunti; his face alight with earrings, he wore natural-born armor [*sahajam kavacam vibhrat kundaloddyotitananah*]."

14. Thus leaving out Draupadi's rejecting Karna as a suitor.

15. It is possible to infer, as Biardeau does (2002, 1:745), that the Kauravas would not know about Rama Jamadagnya's curse when Karna says in book 3 that, after befriending Duryodhana and studying archery with Drona at Hastinapura, he obtained "the fourfold canon of weapons [*astragamam caturvidham*]" from Drona, Kripa, and Rama (3.293.15–17). Indeed, Karna does not even seem to tell Surya of the curse when he tells him he obtained weapons from Rama Jamadagnya (3.286.8). So this could be where Bhishma learns about it. However, by the time Karna and Bhishma reconcile, after Bhishma's fall, Bhishma reveals that he has learned about Karna's birth from Narada, Vyasa, and Krishna (6.116.9), so he also could have heard about the curses from one or more of these as well—and, of course, done so earlier.

16. See Quint (1993, 11): "episodic dismemberment of narrative" in stories with no place to go; "deliberately disconnected and aimless" stories, over and against the "master narratives" (15) of "epic triumphalism" (41).

17. As early as 3.42.20, Arjuna (whose memory is often conveniently weak) gets a strong hint as to Karna's siring by Surya when, just after he has obtained the Pashupata weapon from Shiva, Yama gives him his staff-weapon and says, "Karna, who is a particle of my father, the god who sends heat to all the worlds, the mighty Karna will be slain by you, Dhanamjaya." As to Karna, see especially 8.29.31–32b, where he suddenly remembers the brahmin's curse concerning the wheel after first recalling the curse of Rama Jamadagnya.

18. Indeed, Krishna's secret story is deeper still. He continues: "Eternally engaged in protecting [*trana*] the worlds, I have four forms. Dividing my own self here, I bestow the worlds' welfare. One form, stationed on earth, does the practice of *tapas*. Another beholds the right and wrong done in the universe. Another, having resorted to the human world, performs action. The fourth, however, lies in sleep for a thousand years. My form that awakens at the end of a thousand years gives at that time the best of boons to those worthy of boons. Prithivi [Earth], having known that time to have arrived, then asked me for a boon for the sake of Naraka. Listen to it" (7.28.23–27). A similar terminology is used in a devotional section of *Shantiparvan* called the *Narayaniya*, where Nara, Narayana, Hari, and Krishna are said to be the four forms [*caturmurti*] of Narayana, "born into the house of Dharma" (12.322.2ab; see 326.13; 332.19; 335.1). It is not certain, however, how one might correlate the "four forms" in the two texts, and I leave the topic in the hope of discussing it elsewhere.

19. It is not clear how Krishna overcomes Naraka's alleged invincibility. Perhaps as a man Krishna is neither *deva* nor *asura*.

20. See 12.326.82–89; Dvaraka is mentioned at 12.326.84–85. See *Harivamsha* 91.4–92: Krishna comes from Dvaraka against Naraka riding with his wife,

Satyabhama, on his divine "mount," the great bird Garuda! On the *Narayaniya*, see note 18 here.

21. 3.13.16ab and 26. Between these verses Arjuna also recalls that Krishna, as Vishnu, is the son of Aditi and younger brother of Indra (23), perhaps suggesting that the earrings link these stories.

22. The gods had been unable to wrest the earrings from the robber [*dasyu*] Naraka in "Pragjyotisha, the terrible invincible fort city of the *asuras* [*durgam puram ghoram asuanam asahyam*]"; when Krishna succeeded, they gave him the boons of no fatigue in battle, the ability to step on water and air, and impenetrability to weapons (5.47.74–81). Further, Krishna slew Naraka, and other foes such as Kamsa and Shishupala, "as if in play [*kridann iva*]" (5.66.4); "having cut the nooses of Muru," slain Naraka Bhauma, taken the jeweled earrings, various other gems, *and* sixteen thousand women [to become his wives, according to the *Harivamsha*], he obtained his Sharnga bow (5.155.8–9; *Harivamsha* 92.18–35). The speakers in these passages are Arjuna as reported by Samjaya, Samjaya, and Vaishampayana, respectively. Dhritarashtra also knows of the killing of Naraka and Muru among Krishna's feats (7.10.5) and the *Narayaniya*, in an ancient prophetic voice, foretells as a future act of Narayana-Krishna (12.326.83–85).

23. *Harivamsha* 91.59 and 1083* (the middle line about the toys being an interpolation).

24. Perhaps it is significant that he comes with Satyabhama, whose name means "light of truth" (Biardeau, 2002, 1:910).

25. *Mahabharata* 1.85.3–9, 187.6–7; see Dumézil (1973, 30–37). See the story of Somaka, who sacrificed his only son to get all his wives pregnant with sons. It worked, but when he died and found that his priest had gone to Naraka for officiating, he decided not to leave hell without him (3.128)—Somaka negotiates this with Yama Dharmaraja in a story told to Yudhishthira, who faces a similar quandary at the end of the *Mahabharata*.

26. Biardeau (2002, 1:683), sees Naraka as "the asura who gives his name to the hell reserved for men."

27. See Sax (2002, 71–74). Bhagadatta seems to have become a brahmin in this story. Kunti's great old age is a recurrent theme in Pandav Lila folklore; see 144, 154.

28. I use the term *micromyth* in the sense defined by Doniger (1998, 88): "an imaginary text, a scholarly construct that contains the basic elements from which all possible variants could be created."

29. They are terrible (*raudrah*) *daityas* and *danavas* who dwell in Patala or Rasatala (3.239.18 and 25), not in Naraka (hell); see note 25 and 26 here.

30. See Hiltebeitel (2001b, 190–91), noting that Draupadi has *kritya* traits; and so does Kunti, with her *abhichara mantra* from Durvasas. On *abhichara*, see further Türstig (1985).

31. Karna has a modified demonic nature in the Draupadi cult Terukkuttu (a point missed in Hiltebeitel, 1988, 400); see de Bruin (1999, 294–296, 315). It comes to him at birth from the demon Tanacuran, the "gift-demon" or "liberal *asura*" (295), no doubt a fabulous transformation (a thousand heads, two thousand earrings) of Naraka. Karna's being demonic from birth could be pertinent, as de Bruin suggests,

to his "black, 'demonic' side" at Draupadi's disrobing (294). And of course even in the Sanskrit *Mahabharata*, Naraka *could* have possessed Karna by then.

32. If the case of Nala is a *Mahabharata* parallel, such possession is an off-and-on matter; see Hiltebeitel (2001b, 220–236); Biardeau (2002, 2:516): Karna, "possédé par *l'asura* Naraka, ne lui a pas plus cédé que Nala n'a cédé au Kali."

33. See Adarkar (2001, 96 n. 36). We learn at the end of this exchange that Samjaya has come too (5.141.48), which explains how he can narrate the dialogue to Dhritarashtra and not need the "divine eye," which he gets only later from Vyasa (6.2.9–13), to narrate the war. But when does Samjaya tell this to Dhritarashtra? Clearly, he and Dhritarashtra know things about Karna that they will keep from Duryodhana.

34. 5.139.20b. Uses of this name for Krishna play between its ordinary resonance as "best of men" and its theological import as Krishna's highest divine name, equivalent to God or Supreme Being (see Krishna's explanation of his *uttamah purushah*, or "supreme spirit," in *Bhagavad Gita* 15.17).

35. Arjuna follows Krishna's "lead." Krishna is "guide" as Hrishikesha, "master of the senses"; the name also can mean "he whose hair bristles with joy" (Biardeau, 2002, 1:595).

36. See Hiltebeitel (1981, 101–103). On the night before he takes command of the Kaurava army, Karna even shares regrets with Duryodhana, "recalling the pain they had caused Krishnaa [Draupadi] at the dicing" (8.1.7).

37. Literally, "burn you" (*tapet*). Krishna would be able to explain his silence on this exchange as a promise to Karna, but no one ever asks.

38. Olivelle (2005, 199): See *The Laws of Manu* 9.172.

39. See Hiltebeitel (1988, 200).

40. See 1.104.14–17: While growing up, "he worshiped Aditya (the Sun) up to the burning of his back [*a prishthatapad adityam upatasthe*], at which time while muttering prayer [*yasmin kale japan aste*] there was nothing the great-souled hero, true to his word, would not give at that time to brahmins [*nadeyam bramaneshvasit tasmin kale*]."

41. Van Buitenen has a note (1975, 553): "Nilakantha: 'having eyes only for her son,' but I suspect an idiom here: a mother without her husband, the son's father."

42. "Mother Kunti's orders" are nicely thematized in the Pandav Lilas of Garhwal; see Sax (2002, 71), and especially (153–155) where Arjuna follows them to find out who Draupadi and Kunti really are: the two chief "hags" (*panchali*, "bird"— Hindi *pakshi*, and evoking Draupadi's name Panchali) among the sixty-four *yoginis* who have determined the outcome of the *Mahabharata* war! Indeed, as this episode reflects, the Pandavas end up marrying a woman rather like their mother, pushed to do so by Kunti's unintended word that she utters absent the higher word of the Pandavas' deceased father. See Ramanujan (1991a, 437), on "autonomous action complexes" that can move from one character to others (I would add, "especially within a family"), so that "once set into motion, the act chooses its personae, constitutes its agents"; characters are "not quite 'fixed,' or 'finite' as they are open to past lives as well as other lives around them" (440).

43. See Hiltebeitel (2001b, 202–214, 230–231, 268–277; Lath 1990).

44. According to Monier-Williams ([1899] 1964, 524), "sometimes collectively 'the stars,' and more specifically "an asterism or constellation through which the moon passes."

45. See 3.294.24–25.

46. In effect, the simile suggests that Krishna looks like the pivot of the universe turning into a snake.

47. Echoing *Bhagavad Gita* 4.7–8 with the phrase *dharmasamsthapanartham* (156.28c).

48. Note that Krishna will then dance "wrapped with joy like a tree shaken by the wind," as just cited.

49. Implying recognition of Arjuna's reluctance to kill Karna as requiring this protection?

50. The same phrase—*mohito devamayaya*—will refer to Indra's deception of Karna in Narada's postmortem, the passage next cited.

51. E.g., "the radiant one [Surya] showed himself [to Karna] at night, at the end of a dream" (3.284.8ab) to warn him about Indra. As we shall see, Surya will take his son Karna back to himself as he descends into night. It seems Karna seeks to draw strength from Surya with his prayers up to the early afternoon, and is weakest—as Krishna knows—when the sun sets; see Biardeau (2002, 2:345).

52. From a different angle, see Biardeau (1976–77, 143–145; 1978, 173–174 [Karna as the errant Sun of the *pralaya*]; 2002, 2:531–532 [the apocalyptic face of Surya]).

53. See Biardeau (2002, 1:752): "Peut-être sa piété pour Surya—sa longue louange d'adoration quotidienne au dieu—lui cache-t-elle Vishnu?"

54. Biardeau argues that the poets use Krishna's name Devakiputra to evoke his double association with divine fate and divine play as a linguistic play on the two roots *div-*: one (alternately *dyu-*) behind associations with the gods (*deva*), the day sky (Dyaus), and fate (*daiva*), the other behind the play of dicing (*dyuta, devana*). The name's occurrence in *Chandogya Upanishad* 3.17.6 also provides Krishna's sole anchor in the Vedic revelation. See Biardeau (2002, 1:405, 574 and n. 4; 2:319, 358 n. 37)— she does not highlight the usages in this particular passage (see her summary of it: 2:226–228).

55. Matilal (1991) on Krishna's nonomnipotence (notably 414–415): "as the inner manipulator of every being, [Krishna] would bring about the intended destruction"; but "courses of certain events cannot be stopped. All that Krishna was able to do was to salvage justice at the end of the battle." See Woods (2001, 39–58, 146), and notably (54): although he is the "master magician [*mayavin*]," Krishna is "in the final analysis . . . himself . . . a product of this *maya*." Indeed, the author, the Island-Born Krishna Vyasa, works hand in hand with Krishna Vasudeva to shape the illusions and fates of epic characters (see Hiltebeitel, 2001b, 90–91, and note 12 here), often tipping his hand of *authorial* omnipotence, as when he tells Dhritarashtra: "Still, the character [*shila*] that is born in a man at his birth, that, they say, great king, does not leave him before he dies" (3.9.10; van Buitenen, 1975, 236; see Woods, 2001, 57)—to which Dhritarashtra replies that he blames fate (*vidhi*; 3.10.1) rather than himself for all that has happened up to this point, and all that will inevitably follow. Vyasa can only agree while complicating matters further. See Biardeau (2002, 1:405): "le *daiva* reste imprévisible et Krishna lui-même doit s'y conformer"—as with his absence from the dice match.

56. See Hiltebeitel (1982, 89; 1984, 9); see note 11 here.

57. Before Karna went to Rama Jamadagnya, he sought instructions in weapons from Drona, but was denied them because he was a *suta* (12.2.9–13). Then, some time after the double curse by the two brahmins (the second being Rama Jamadagnya), while serving as a charioteer (*rathin*) for Duryodhana at the *svayamvara* ("self-choice" marriage ceremony) of the princess of Kalinga, Karna helped Duryodhana abduct the bride after she snubbed Duryodhana; Karna fought off all the other kings, including Shishupala, Jarasandha, Shrigala, and Ashoka (12.4.2–21; 6–7 on these defeated kings). Third, Jarasandha wanted to test the might Karna had shown at Kalinga, and challenged him to a wrestling match; Karna ruptured the seam that held Jarasandha's body together (later to be split fully by Bhima). Gratified with Karna's prowess, Jarasandha gave him the city of Malini, and, after this, Karna "became king of the Angas" (55.1–7)—presumably the tournament at which Duryodhana appointed Karna to the Anga throne would have come after the bout with Jarasandha, but Narada does not mention that episode. It is then, once he has told these stories, that Narada now strings together other later episodes in the postmortem elegy now quoted. On the possible Buddhist allusions in these stories linking Karna, Jarasandha, and Duryodhana with Ashoka and Kalinga, see Biardeau (2002, 2:54, 527–532, 757). See also Hiltebeitel (2005b, 118).

58. He is speaking to Yudhishthira.

59. See the discussion of *mohito devamayaya* at the end of the section before the previous one. Following Tokunaga ([1991] 1994), these are the only two usages of this phrase in the *Mahabharata*.

60. Shatakratu is Indra, the god of a hundred sacrifices.

61. 5.165.6: When asked by Duryodhana to rank his warriors before battle, Bhishma had belittled Karna in this fashion, leading Karna to reply in kind and refuse to fight until Bhishma was slain (11, 27)—this being the second time a provocation from Bhishma leads Karna to vow not to fight until Bhishma's fall; see 5.61.12–13. When Bhishma has fallen and accepted Karna's gestures of reconciliation, he tells Karna that he used harsh words as "occasion for the destruction [of your] *tejas* [*tejo-vadhanimittam*]" (6.117.10)—that is, to the same end as Shalya (as mentioned by Narada here next); see Hiltebeitel (2001a, 267): Karna learns here (6.117.9) that Bhishma knows him to be Kunti's son from Vyasa, Narada, and Keshava. See Adarkar (2001, 213). See episodes 10 and 12 in the list of fatalities in section B.

62. *Nayena*; see Krishna as *netri*, "guide" or "leader" (at note 35 here), from the same root *ni-*, "to lead." See further Biardeau (1978–79, 150; 2002, 1:872).

63. On these meters see note 4 here.

64. Krishna, "son of Vasudeva"; also one of the most theologically charged of Krishna's names: for Hudson (1996, 68), "God who dwells in all things and in whom all things dwell," citing *Bhagavad Gita* 7.1–19, the last verse of which uses this name (one of four such usages in the *Gita*). Names and titles will be glossed here for their first appearance only.

65. Son of Pritha: here and throughout this passage, Arjuna; though it could also refer to Yudhishthira or Bhima. It would also be an implicit name for Karna as Pritha's hidden firstborn son.

66. Arjuna: the one who wears the diadem, a tiara, on his head.

67. *Dambhodbhavash chasuras*; Dambodbhava is a "prideful" *asura* slain by Nara and Narayana (*Mahabharata* 5.94). Krishna is rekindling Arjuna's awareness that he is Nara.

68. Karna.

69. "Of beautiful aspect," Krishna's *cakra*, or discus.

70. It could be that *nisrishta* means "hurled [by me]," but the imperative is directed at Arjuna.

71. Indra.

72. On this and further allusions to Indra's conquests of the demons Namuchi and Vritra, see note 211 here.

73. Shiva, who took the guise of a mountain hunter (*kirata*) when Arjuna sought the Pashupata weapon from him (*Mahabharata* 3.40–41).

74. Yudhishthira.

75. Krishna, "tormentor of people," a name often used when Krishna is awesome, overwhelming, and frightening.

76. His *sattva*: goodness, higher nature.

77. Ganguli, *Karna Parva* ([1884–96] 1970, 7:361), takes this as Arjuna "calling to mind the object for which he had come into the world." But *mahatmanas* seems to refer to Krishna rather than Arjuna.

78. Krishna, as having attractive hair.

79. Shiva.

80. Karna; on this name see episode 8 in section B.

81. Usually a name for Indra, *parjanya* could also mean a rain cloud.

82. One of Karna's sons.

83. A little-known warrior on the Kaurava side.

84. *Jana*, "folk" or "people" of heaven and earth, translated throughout, rather for lack of anything better, as "folk."

85. Pandava allies, a branch of the Panchalas, Draupadi's people.

86. Karna, as adoptive son of the *suta* Adhiratha.

87. Numerous northern texts add "at play in the middle of the crematorium during the terrible hour, his limbs wet with blood (*prakridamano 'yam shma-shanamadhye / raudre muhurte rudhirardragatrah*)" (8.1072*).

88. Arjuna, "Winner of wealth."

89. Krishna, "the unfallen."

90. Krishna as "best of men" or "supreme male," God; see note 34 here.

91. Ganguli, *Karna Parva* [1884–96] 1970, 7:268): "(in the waters of the Bhogavati in the nether region)."

92. Takshaka is a prominent *naga*, or snake, and the arrows are thus snake arrows.

93. Arjuna.

94. *Marmani*. These are an important topic in Indian medicine and martial arts.

95. Arjuna, "left-handed archer," "one who draws with the left hand."

96. Samjaya is addressing Dhritarashtra.

97. Probably released with a *mantra* from the *Atharva Veda*.

98. Rama Jamadagnya; see episodes 2–3 in section B.

99. Here, the critical edition notes two mainly northern insertions: the first (app. 1, no. 39, of four *trishtubhs*) tells of such fighting that heavenly beings applaud; the second (app. 1, no. 40, of five *trishtubhs*, five *shloka* lines, and one more *trishtubh*) tells how the snake Ashvasena, who, unlike his mother, survived the burning of Khandava Forest, flies out of the underworld into the sky to see the battle, and, to avenge Arjuna's killing his mother, enters Karna's quiver in the form of an arrow (l. 12: *shararupadhari*)—this in seeming contradiction to what is noted elsewhere (see episode 5 in section B) and, that Karna has long worshiped this snake arrow kept in his quiver. The net of arrows from the two combatants spreads darkness. *Apsaras* (nymphs) come to fan the heroes in their fatigue, and Indra and Surya brush their sons' faces. Then, as Karna realizes he cannot defeat Arjuna, he recalls the arrow in his quiver.

100. Arjuna's: Phalguna is a Vedic name for Indra and a spring month.

101. Here and throughout this segment, "poison" is always that of a serpent, and thus "venom."

102. Airavata is another prominent *naga*. Star passages 8.1083* and 1084* are inserted here. (A so-called star passage is deemed an interpolation in the critical edition's apparatus.) In the first, a *trishtubh*, the world regents and Shakra wail at the filling of the sky with meteors, when the arrow in snake form is fixed to Karna's bow; in the second, a half-*trishtubh*, Karna did not know that Ashvasena had entered his quiver with the aid of *yogabala*, "yoga power."

103. Shalya; this would seem to be one of the points where he seeks to undermine Karna's *tejas*; see epidsode 9 in section B.

104. Krishna, as named after another month in spring.

105. Vaidya (1954, 695–696), as editor of the *Karnaparvan* for the critical edition, includes these stanzas (10–11) "most reluctantly," arguing that doing so "is not fully justifiable. All the same, they are included, on the sole consideration that their contents are supported by all the MSS." His main argument is that the manuscripts agree in "substance" but not in form: Sharada/Kashmiri manuscripts in *shlokas*, which provide his reconstituted text, "have parallel versions," some of them "shorter" and in *trishtubhs*, in central and southern groups of texts—notably 8.1089*, which he regards as the southern *trishtubh* stanza that "first introduced" the theme, which northern versions then took up, modifying the meter. Vaidya can thus argue that the *shlokas* are metrical "misfits," that without them there would be no break and that the "ballad-form" of the duel "would improve" with their absence. Opening on to what he recognizes as "higher criticism" and speaking "from the rationalistic point of view" (of which his "I do not think that Shalya played treacherous with Karna" is further instance), his "explanation is that the subject-matter of these stanzas was introduced . . . at a considerably late stage, to glorify the divine power of Krishna, when the Krishna-cult influenced the redactors of the Epic." But there is no reason to think that the Krishna cult was late in influencing the epic. Vaidya's "first introduced" *trishtubh* could thus indeed be "original":

Having seen that blazing [arrow] rushing forward
moving in the air, the chief hero of the Vrishni lineage,
having forcefully pressed down on the chariot's wheel,
caused it to sink five finger-breadths, a hero indeed. (8.1089*)

Indeed, this *trishtubh* stanza eliminates the second *shloka's* doubling in advance of the arrow's hitting Arjuna's diadem. The critical edition's standing preference for the northern Sharada/Kashmiri manuscripts may account for Vaidya's choice of the poorer text and his overlooking the better explanation, in support of which it may be noted that this southern verse appears quite prominently among southern recension manuscripts in the Malayalam group (otherwise it appears only in Grantha manuscripts and two Telugu manuscripts), which should probably have provided the editors with testimony of equal value to that of the Sharada/Kashmiri manuscripts (see Hiltebeitel, 2006, 252–53).

106. Indra.

107. *Bhuvanasya sununa*; the reference is not clear to me. If the translation is right, it would suggest the sun god, which seems incongruous here, given Surya's favoritism for Karna. *Sunu* could also mean "son," giving us "son of the world" or "son of the earth"—which do not readily explain themselves either. The vulgate and numerous texts have *vibhuna svayambhuva*, "by the self-born lord," probably Brahma, who could be meant here in either case.

108. While residing in Indra's heaven, Arjuna received the diadem from Indra (3.171.5) after he had defeated some foes of the gods.

109. Karna.

110. Shiva, Varuna, and Indra, respectively.

111. Shiva's bow.

112. Vaidya (1954, 696), says the verse is "one of the so-called Kutashlokas [purposefully enigmatic verses] commented on by Vimalabodha." A northern insert adds: "That wicked-natured [*dushtabhava*] snake...swept away the diadem from Arjuna's head, and it fell to the earth" (8.1093*–1094*).

113. From the snake.

114. The western Sunset Mountain.

115. The verse reads repetitively. Perhaps "then" (*tatas*) suggests ongoing description rather than "next."

116. The Sunrise Mountain.

117. Here a patch of inserts: 1098*: the snake urges Karna to shoot him again, and Karna asks who this fierce-formed snake is; 1102*: the snake reveals his enmity for Arjuna; 1103*: even if Indra protects him, he will go to the land of the fathers; 1104*: Karna will not, he says, rely on another's might to win victory, or shoot the same weapon twice; 1105*: he will continue using his own weapons; 1106*: the snake, unable to bear these words, resumes the form of an arrow determined to kill Arjuna on his own.

118. Presumably, though it would seem unexpectedly, the snake addresses Krishna.

119. Arjuna.

120. Krishna as "destroyer of Madhu," one of two demons Vishnu slays upon awakening from his cosmic sleep. The epic poets frequently use the name where Krishna is linked with killing.

121. Gandiva is the name of Arjuna's bow.

122. Vishnu's heavenly bird-mount and a proverbial devourer of snakes.

123. Feeding Agni (Fire) at the Khandava Forest. Here and in what follows, see episode 5 in section B.

124. At 8.1114* Krishna adds that Arjuna should now remember him and shoot him from the sky.

125. Arjuna, "the victorious," and a name connecting him, at least to the ear, with Vishnu.

126. Leftovers (sheshan) may evoke the great world-snake, Shesha.

127. At 8.1115* is added: "When that snake had been slain by Kiritin, the lord Purushottama, himself of mighty arms, O king, quickly lifted up [samujjahara] the chariot from the surface of the earth with his two arms."

128. A demon.

129. Antakadandasamnibhah. Antaka is death as the Finisher, and a name for Shiva and Yama. The danda is the rod of punishment.

130. These earrings and armor have replaced Karna's originals, which he gave to Indra.

131. Arjuna.

132. App. 1, no. 41, of six trishtubhs, comes here: Arjuna hits Karna with another deadly arrow; Karna reels. Arjuna prefers not to kill him while he is in distress. Krishna then rebukes him: no warrior of mettle lets a foe regain his strength; kill him as Indra slew the (largely Vedic) demon Namuchi. Arjuna says "So be it," honors Janardana, and strikes Karna with arrows as Indra did Samvara, another of his Vedic foes.

133. I follow those manuscripts (the vulgate and others) that have mahagiri rather than the critical edition's mahendra (Indra) here, since it better fits the simile.

134. Here comes a series of inserts: 1120*: Recovering his dhairyam, firmness, Karna hits Arjuna and Krishna with ten and twelve snakelike arrows; 1121*: Dhanamjaya shoots an iron weapon that is like venom, fire, and Indra's thunderbolt; then (more widely attested than the previous or following):

> Invisible Kala (Time), O king, because of the curse of the brahmin,
> indicating the death of Karna, speaking,
> said, "The earth is swallowing your wheel,"
> when the time for Karna's death had arrived.
> The great Brahma weapon was destroyed in his mind
> which the great-souled Bhargava had given him.
> The earth swallowed the left wheel.
> O hero among men, when that time for death had arrived,
> the chariot then whirled about, O lord of men,
> from the curse of that best of brahmins. (8.1122* and 1123*)

Alternately, the southern recension's trishtubhs make Kala the presence of death that comes with the earth's swallowing the left wheel, and causes the chariot to reel because of the curse (1124* and 1125*).

135. Yudhishthira censures dharma at the end of the Mahabharata with the same verb (vi-garh-; 18.2.50c); see Hiltebeitel (2001b, 274).

136. The verb seems to combine dharma with the sunken wheel, implying a dharmachakra, or "wheel of dharma."

137. See Halbfass (1988, 318; see 325, 329–330) on dharma as that which "protects its protectors." See Hiltebeitel (2001b, 203–205).

138. Krishna, who comes from the Vrishni clan of the Yadavas.

139. Karna as the son of the *suta* Adhiratha's wife Radha. Here begins a series of pointed and increasingly ironic uses of epithets, beginning with only the narrator Samjaya juxtaposing Karna as son of Radha with Arjuna as Partha, son of Pritha or Kunti, when, of course, both are sons of Kunti. Soon the two combatants are calling each other by these pregnant names, *as is Krishna, who knows what the names conceal.*

140. A weapon of Rudra-Shiva, possibly his Pashupata weapon; see Hiltebeitel (1982, 107).

141. 8.1130*: Karna descends (*avatirya*) to try to lift the wheel, but instead raises the earth four fingers.

142. Son of Kunti (see note 139 here). Although Arjuna doesn't know it, Karna is appealing to him—with what looks like intended irony—as his couterine brother.

143. Arjuna, a metrically longer way of saying Pandava.

144. Duryodhana as "easy to combat"; see Biardeau (2002, 1:886 n. 4, 900).

145. Duhshasana, the second oldest Kaurava, who tried to disrobe Draupadi after she was gambled away, and Shakuni, the dicing master whose trickery won her, have been, along with Karna, who ordered her disrobing, Duryodhana's inner circle; see note 36 here.

146. In inserts, Krishna adds: Where was your *dharma* when Duryodhana ordered the poisoning of Bhima (8.1142*); or at the lacquer house (1143*)? when the time in the forest was over and the Pandavas were not given back their kingdom (1144*)?

147. Draupadi, the Dark Woman.

148. At 8.1145* Krishna adds: And when you insulted Draupadi, saying, "Your husbands are in Hell; choose another"?

149. Shakuni, to do the dicing.

150. Other additions: or when Abhimanyu was encircled? (8.1146*); Why go on with false words? You now speak for virtue, but it won't save your life. The Pandavas will regain their kingdom like Nala, and the Kurus will meet destruction (1147*); Karna hangs his head in shame, his lips quiver with rage, but he continues to fight. Krishna tells Arjuna to dispatch him (1148*).

151. *Tejas.*

152. At 8.1150*, Arjuna also uses a showery Brahma weapon on Karna.

153. Agni.

154. A watery weapon, Varuna being god of waters.

155. A windy weapon of the wind god. App. 1, no. 42, now adds, beginning with four *shlokas*, the rest in *trishtubhs*: Karna aims a fiery arrow making the gods weep and the Pandavas despair. It hits Arjuna's chest like a mighty snake penetrating an anthill. He reels. His grip loosens on Gandiva.

> Obtaining that interval, the great chariot warrior Vrisha,
> wishing to extricate his chariot's wheel
> that had been swallowed by the earth,
> leapt from his chariot and seized it with his two hands.
> But by fate he did not succeed, even with his great strength.

Then Kiritin, the high-souled radiant Arjuna, recovering his senses,
took up the Pranjalika, an arrow like the rod of Yama.
Then Vasudeva said to Partha,
"Sever the head of this enemy under refuge
before Vrisha climbs back onto his chariot."
Just so, having honored that lord's word,
he took up that blazing razor-pointed arrow and struck
the elephant girth-cord bright as the spotless sun (on Karna's flagstaff)
while the great chariot warrior's chariot-wheel was still sunk. (ll. 17–30)

156. The emblem on Karna's chariot flag, as in the passage in the previous note.

157. Or royal splendor, *shri*.

158. *Marisha.* Samjaya addresses Dhritarashtra with a certain intimacy from time to time.

159. At 8.1152* it adds, "The Kurus lost hope of victory at the sight of the flagstaff's fall."

160. An unusual weapon for the *coup de grâce,* named after "the *anjali,* the gesture of salutation with semi-closed hands raised to the bowed forehead . . . that denotes reverence, benediction, and friendship, as when . . . Arjuna joins his hands in the *anjali* at Krishna's bedside (5.7.7) in the scene where he secures Krishna's friendship (*sakhyam;* 10) and his service as charioteer" (Hiltebeitel, 1982, 108). Its use is mentioned four other times in the *Mahabharata*: the Pandavas shoot *anjalikas* against the Magadha elephant forces (6.58.31); Bhishma likewise against the Pandavas (104.30); and Ghatotkacha uses one twice, first against Ashvatthaman (7.31.93) and then against Karna (50.78). According to Ganguli, *Bhishma Parva* (1970, 5:173), they are "arrows with crescent-shaped heads." See further note 165 here, and, in the background, Karna's welcoming and farewell "salutes" to Kunti, discussed in section D.

161. Agni, as "belonging to all men."

162. Indra's.

163. Agni.

164. Southern and a few northern texts continue with ten *trishtubh* lines (8.1154*): Seeing this weapon able to defeat the gods and *asuras,* the *rishis* cried out: "May it be for the well-being of the universe [*svasti jagat syad*]" (l. 7).

165. As Arjuna's "act of truth," or *satyakriya,* ends on the note that he has "heard what is desired from friends (*maya yadishtam suhridam tatha shrutam*)" (67.20ab), it "brings its final focus onto the theme of friendship . . . [and] especially his friendship with Krishna." But with the choice of the *anjalika* weapon (see note 160 here), it is also "as if the implicit theme of fratricide is resolved symbolically into a death which affirms that the final salutation is that of brothers who are inherently friends" (Hiltebeitel, 1982, 108). See further Hiltebeitel (1988, 411 and n. 23); Biardeau and Péterfalvi (1986, 214): "la geste des deux mains jointes du suppliant . . . sans doute en manifestant son respect intérieur pour Karna"; and Biardeau (2002, 2:384): "un ultime salut respecteux et suppliant à la victime! Sans doute Arjuna a-t-il l'obscur pressentiment qu'il a tué un ennemi qui ne devrait pas être un."

166. The sorceress is a *kritya,* a type of female personification of black magic that the epic invokes and evokes at various points; see note 30 here. In the same vein,

Atharva-Angirasas probably suggests practitioners of Atharva Vedic black magic *ab-hichara* rites. See Türstig (1985).

167. See Monier-Williams ([1899] 1964, 420), on *jighamsur*: desirous of destroying or killing; revengeful.

168. He is like his arrow (see previous note).

169. At 8.1159* it adds that Arjuna struck off Karna's head, like Indra removing Vritra's, with the *mantra*-inspired Anjalika weapon, making Karna's trunk fall on the earth.

170. Karna has for two days, days 16 and 17 of the eighteen-day war, been marshal (*senapati*) of the Kaurava army.

171. Karna's sun-like head falls in three phases, collapsing a year into a day by the mention of autumn.

172. *Tejo diptam*; numerous texts say "his blazing *tejas* entered Surya [*suryam . . . vivesha*]."

173. A complex image, if Karna is like a fire dispersed after a *night* sacrifice. Shulman (1985, 386), argues for "a coherent semantics of sacrificial fate" in Karna's portrayal. Note the shift now to *shlokas*.

174. Suggesting an "arrow of time."

175. Indra.

176. *Ojas*, not *tejas*, here.

177. Arjuna and Krishna.

178. Varuna, Kubera, Yama, and Indra, the gods of the four directions.

179. Here app. 1, no. 43, follows—a long *adhyaya* in the vulgate: How did the armies fare, crushed and scorched during, after, and while fleeing the fight between Karna and Arjuna? Twice Duryodhana rallies his troops like the *asura* Bali against the gods, the second time saying that as there is no place to flee, they should fight like warriors.

180. Shalya, he whose course is orderly, truthful!

181. The foul, corpse-strewn underworld river of the dead.

182. What *astraih*, "with weapons," is doing here is not clear.

183. I revert to the vulgate's *shitash ca shula* here; the critical edition reads *ka-dangarayo*, for which there does not seem to be a sound explanation.

184. Ashvatthaman.

185. On the battlefield-earth as a seductive, beautiful, and ultimately triumphant woman and redeemed goddess, see Hiltebeitel (1980, 106–109).

186. Surya's hands are his rays.

187. Surya.

188. See note 84.

189. Lakshmi.

190. Pavaka, Agni.

191. *Sadbhih sada satpurushah*. See section D, at note 43: Karna "persevere[d] in the conduct of noncruelty that befits a good man."

192. The vulgate and some other texts have instead *strinam*, "always dear to women."

193. This planetary "son of Yama" eludes me. The vulgate has instead *somasya putra*, "son of Soma," which Ganguli, *Karna Parva* ([1884–96] 1970, 7:290), names as

Mercury. Monier-Williams ([1899] 1964, 846), gives Saturn as a name for Yama himself in the *Harivamsha*.

194. Jupiter.

195. *Nishacharas*, most typical of whom are *rakshasas*. The term is not used for Ghatotkacha, but he is one, and it would be fitting for his kind to take vengeful delight in Karna's death.

196. The critical edition regards this line about Vritra as uncertain, but all texts cited refer here in some way to Indra's slaying of Vritra. On this and further allusions to Indra's conquest of the demons Vritra and Namuchi, see note 211 here.

197. The monkey Hanuman roars from Arjuna's banner.

198. *Narottamau*. Nara being a name for Arjuna's ancient Rishi-identity that links him with Krishna's form Narayana, and *nara* being equivalent to *purusha* as "man," the title "two best of men" evokes Krishna's identity as Purushottama (see note 90 here) as well as Arjuna's identity with Krishna that makes them "the two Krishnas on one chariot."

199. The name recalls Krishna's killing of the horse-demon Keshi when he was a child in Vrindavan.

200. Garuda appears on Krishna's banner, Hanuman on Arjuna's (see note 197 here).

201. *Nrinam varau* now! The poets are clearly having fun in this verse. See note 198 here.

202. The conches of Arjuna and Krishna, respectively.

203. The "Unfallen," a name of both Krishna (see note 89 here) and Vishnu (as implied in what follows by the connection with Indra). Note the building allusions to the Vedic sacrifice that begin here.

204. *Ishvarau*.

205. Celestial singers.

206. Unpredictable cousins of *rakshasas*, given alternately to menacing, protective, and fructifying behaviors.

207. At 8.1197*, one *trishtubh* is added in closing: they were lauded like Indra and Vishnu after the overthrow of Bali. Then follows app. 1, no. 44: the Kauravas broke, fled, in despair. Duryodhana took Shalya's advice and withdrew the army. Various heroes and forces are described returning to the Kaurava camp. No Kaurava warrior wished to continue the fight. Duryodhana lets them rest for the night.

208. This *adhyaya* has a variant text in its entirety (8.1224*), mostly in the southern recension, and is thus wavy-lined as the preferred text of the editor. The variant has nothing of Krishna's mysterious words to Arjuna, is much thicker in Yudhishthira's "*bhakti*" paean to Krishna—"Govinda's" grace, and lacks the ironies of the northern passage (ll. 23–33).

209. Krishna, "worthy of respect" (see Biardeau, 2002, 1:105 n. 23).

210. Indra. See note 128 here.

211. Krishna's mysterious evocation of an identity between these combats, and thus between Karna and not only Vritra but Namuchi (see nn. 72, 132, 169), provides

a Vedic "deepening" of Karna's demonic rapport with the *asura* Naraka by possession
(see section C). The Vedic Indra conquers Vritra and Namuchi thanks to his "friend"
Vishnu and, in Namuchi's case, by a violation of friendship. The epic seems to reemplot
this thematic set into the web of true and false friendships surrounding Karna (see
Hiltebeitel [1976] 1990, 255–266; 1982, 93–107). With the exceptions of the initial
reference to Namuchi and 68.52d on Vritra, these Vedic allusions are found only in
the northern recension. For further discussion, see Hiltebeitel (2005a, 101).

212. At 8.1198* two *shlokas* are added on how Yudhishthira was turned back in
battle by Karna.

213. *Avyagra*: unconcerned, unconfused, steady, deliberate.

214. Govinda is probably the epic's most affectionate and salvific name for
Krishna (Hiltebeitel, 2001b, 67, 251–253, 256, 259 n. 54, 276; Biardeau, 2002, 2:273 n.
4, 317: probably from *gopa-indra*, "king of cowboys"), as it is in the cult of Draupadi
(Hiltebeitel, 1988, 236, 275–81).

215. Two of Draupadi's brothers, the Pandava twins, Bhima, and Krishna's
kinsman Satyaki, respectively.

216. *Samuttasthau*. One could say he "altogether rises."

217. Cited at the beginning of section D. See also note 191 here.

218. Samjaya to Dhritarashtra.

219. On the resonances of this epithet, see note 54 here.

220. *Purushauttamah*; see notes 34 and 90 here.

221. Echoing *Bhagavad Gita* 4.8.

222. Vyasa as "the island-born Krishna"; the author.

223. *Prabhava*, probably implying mysterious divine power. Yudhishthira is
consistent in praising Krishna rather than Arjuna.

224. Effectively eliminating Karna's sons as heirs whom Yudhishthira might see
himself obliged to enthrone in his own stead.

225. Again, the irony of the naming of Karna Radheya, Yudhishthira having yet
to know that he is a son of Kunti.

226. Duryodhana.

227. Various northern texts, including the vulgate, have Samjaya add: "Having seen Karna slain together with his sons by the arrows of Partha, the son of the
Kuru clan thought himself born as it were again [*punar jatamiva atmanam mene*]!"
(8.1212*). There is a Fisher King quality to Yudhishthira's recovery. See the translation at note 216 here.

228. Like the Somakas, a branch of the Panchalas.

229. The vulgate and other manuscripts have for this last line, "The king considered fate and necessity to be paramount" (8.1217*). A *phalashruti* (a passage on
"the fruits of hearing" the *Karnaparvan*) follows in many northern texts, and includes these rewards: "Whoever recites this great sacrifice of battle of Dhanamjaya
and Karna obtains the fruit from hearing a desired sacrifice rightly performed" (1219*
ll. 1–4)—adding that "Vishnu is the sacrifice [*makho hi vishnur*]" (l. 6); "And since
it is God, the eternal lord Vishnu, who is glorified everywhere [in this *parvan*],
the happy man [who recites it] acquires his desires, as the word of the great Muni
[Vyasa] is respected" (1222*).

REFERENCES

Adarkar, Aditya. 2001. "Karna in the *Mahabharata*." Ph.D. diss., University of Chicago.

Biardeau, Madeleine. 1975–81. "*Comptes rendus* of seminars on the *Mahabharata*." *Annuaire de l'École Pratique des Hautes Études*, pt. 5, 84, 165–185, 85, 135–167, 87, 145–171, 88, 167–182, 89, 221–250.

———. 1978. "Études de mythologie hindoue: 5. Bhakti et avatara." *Bulletin de l'École Française d'Extrême Orient* 65, 111–263.

———. 2002. *Le Mahabharata: Un récit fondateur du brahmanisme et son interprétation.* 2 vols. Paris: Éditions du Seuil.

Biardeau, Madeleine, and Jean-Michel Péterfalvi, trans. 1985–86. *Le Mahabharata.* Vol. 1, bks. 1–5. Vol. 2, bks. 6–18. Paris: Flammarion.

de Bruin, Hanne M. 1998. *Karna's Death: A Play by Pukalentippulavar.* Publications of the Department of Indology, 87. Pondicherry: Institut Français de Pondichéry.

———. 1999. *Kattaikkuttu: The Flexibility of a South Indian Theatre Tradition.* Groningen: Egbert Forsten.

Doniger, Wendy. 1998. *The Implied Spider: Politics and Theology in Myth.* New York: Columbia University Press.

Dumézil, Georges. 1968. *Mythe et épopée.* Vol. 1. *L'Idéologie des trois fonctions dans les épopées des peuples indo-européens.* Paris: Gallimard.

———. 1973. *The Destiny of a King.* Translated by Alf Hiltebeitel. Chicago: University of Chicago Press.

Greer, Patricia Meredith. 2002. "Karna within the Net of the Mahabharata: Reading the *Itihasa* as Literature." Ph.D. diss., University of Virginia.

Halbfass, Wilhelm. 1988. *India and Europe: An Essay in Understanding.* Albany: SUNY Press.

Hiltebeitel, Alf. 1976. "The Burning of the Forest Myth." In *Hinduism: New Essays in the History of Religions*, edited by Bardwell L. Smith. Leiden: Brill, 208–224.

———. [1976] 1990. *The Ritual of Battle: Krishna in the Mahabharata.* Albany: SUNY Press.

———. 1980. "Draupadi's Garments." *Indo-Iranian Journal* 22, 97–112.

———. 1982. "Brothers, Friends, and Charioteers: Parallel Episodes in the Irish and Indian Epics." In *Homage to Georges Dumézil*, edited by Edgar Polomé. Journal of Indo-European Studies monograph no. 3. special edition, 85–112.

———. 1984. "The Two Krishnas on One Chariot: Upanishadic Imagery and Epic Mythology." *History of Religions* 24, no. 3, 1–26.

———. 1988. *The Cult of Draupadi.* Vol. 1. *Mythologies: From Gingee to Kurukshetra.* Chicago: University of Chicago Press.

———. 1999. *Rethinking India's Oral and Classical Epics: Draupadi among Rajputs, Muslims, and Dalits.* Chicago: University of Chicago Press.

———. 2000. "The Primary Process of the Indian Epics." *International Journal of Hindu Studies*, Indian literature issue, edited by Bruce Sullivan.

———. 2001a. "Bhishma's Sources." In *Vidyaravavandanam: Essays in Honour of Asko Parpola*, edited by Klaus Karttunen and Petteri Koskikallio. Studia Orientalia 94. Helsinki: Finnish Oriental Society, 261–78.

————. 2001b. *Rethinking the Mahabharata: A Reader's Guide to the Education of the Dharma King*. Chicago: University of Chicago Press.

————. 2003. The Primary Process of the Hindu Epics. *International Journal of Hindu Studies* 4 (3): 269–88.

————. 2005a. Weighting Orality and Writing in the Sanskrit Epics. In Petteri Koskikallio, ed. Epics, Khilas, and Puranas: Continuities and Ruptures. Pp. 81–111. Proceedings of the Third Dubrovnik Conference on the Sanskrit Epics and Puranas. September 2002. Zagreb: Croatian Academy of Sciences and Arts.

————. 2005b. Buddhism and the Mahabharata: Boundary Dynamics and Textual Practice. In *Federico Squarcini, ed. Boundary Dynamics and Construction of Traditions in South Asia*. Pp. 107–31. Florence: university of Florence Press.

————. 2006. The *Narayaniya* and the Early Reading Communities of the Mahabharata. In Patrick Olivelle, ed. *Between the Empires: Society in India 300 BCE to 400 CE*. Pp. 227–55. New York: Oxford University Press.

Hudson, Dennis. 1996. "Arjuna's Sin: Thoughts on the *Bhagavad Gita* in Its Epic Context." *Journal of Vaishnava Studies* 43, 65–84.

Jarow, E. H. Rick. 1999. "The Letter of the Law and the Discourse of Power: Karna and the Controversy of the *Mahabharata*." *Journal of Vaishnava Studies* 8, no. 1, 59–76.

The Karnaparvan. 1954. Edited by Parashuram Lakshman Vaidya. In *The Mahabharata for the First Time Critically Edited*, edited by Vishnu S. Sukthankar and S. K. Belvalkar, vol. 10. Poona: Bhandarkar Oriental Research Institute.

Lath, Mukund. 1990. "The Concept of *Anrishamsya* in the Mahabharata." In *The Mahabharata Revisited*, edited by R. N. Dandekar. New Delhi: Sahitya Akademi, 113–119.

The Mahabharata. [1884–96] 1970. Translated by Kisari Mohan Ganguli. New Delhi: Munshiram Manoharlal.

Matilal, Bimal Krishna. 1991. "Krishna: In Defense of a Devious Divinity." In *Essays on the Mahabharata*, edited by Arvind Sharma. Leiden: Brill, 401–418.

McGrath, Kevin. 2001. "The Sanskrit Hero: Karna in Epic Mahabharata." Ph.D. diss., Harvard University.

Miller, Barbara Stoller. 1991. "*Karnabhara*: The Trial of Karna." In *Essays on the Mahabharata*, edited by Arvind Sharma. Leiden: Brill, 57–68.

Monier-Williams, Monier. [1899] 1964. *A Sanskrit-English Dictionary*. Oxford: Clarendon Press.

Olivelle, Patrick, ed. and trans. 2005. *Manu's Code of Law: A Critical Edition and Translation of the Manava-Dharmashastra*. New York: Oxford University Press.

Quint, David. 1993. *Epic and Empire: Politics and Generic Form from Virgil to Milton*. Princeton: Princeton University Press.

Ramanujan, A. K. 1991a. "Repetition in the *Mahabharata*." In *Essays on the Mahabharata*, edited by Arvind Sharma. Leiden: Brill, 419–443.

————. 1991b. "Three Hundred *Ramayanas*: Five Examples and Three Thoughts on Translation." In *Many Ramayanas: The Diversity of a Narrative Tradition in South Asia*, edited by Paula Richman. Berkeley: University of California Press, 22–49.

Sax, William S. 2000. "In Karna's Realm: An Ontology of Action." *Journal of Indian Philosophy* 28, 295–324.

————. 2002. *Dancing the Self: Personhood and Performance in the Pandav Lila of Garhwal*. New York: Oxford University Press.

Shulman, David Dean. 1985. *The King and the Clown in South Indian Myth and Poetry*. Princeton: Princeton University Press.

Smith, Mary Carol. 1972. "The Core of India's Great Epic." Ph.D. diss., Harvard University.

————. 1992. *The Warrior Code of India's Sacred Song*. New York: Garland.

Tokunaga, Muneo. [1991] 1994. *Machine-Readable Text of the Mahaabhaarata Based on the Poona Critical Edition*. First rev. version. Kyoto.

Türstig, Hans-Georg. 1985. "The Indian Sorcery Called *Abhicara*." *Wiener Zeitschrift für die Kunde Sudasiens* 29, 69–117.

van Buitenen, J. A. B. 1973. *The Mahabharata*, vols. I: 1. *The Book of Beginnings*. Chicago: University of Chicago Press.

————. 1975. *The Mahabharata*, vol. II: 2, *The Book of the Assembly Hall; 3, The Book of the Forest*. Chicago: University of Chicago Press.

————. 1978. *The Mahabharata*, vol. III: 4, *The Book of Virata; 5. The Book of the Effort*. Chicago: University of Chicago Press.

Woods, Julian F. 2001. *Destiny and Human Initiative in the Mahabharata*. Albany: SUNY Press.

2

Krishna in the *Bhagavad Gita*

Robert N. Minor

In approximately 150 B.C.E., a devotee of the god Krishna composed a seven-hundred-verse poem that came to be known as the
Bhagavad Gita, the "Song of the Beloved One." His intention was to
expand on a scene from a tale already in its earliest form in a larger
epic poem that has come to be known as the *Mahabharata*.

It is clear that his addition was meant for a particular dramatic
moment in the epic.[1] It was added at the very beginning of the
account of a great world war that would decide the final fate of
both sides in what had begun as an intrafamily feud. Just as this
"great Bharata" war is about to begin, and when the "arrows have
begun to fly," Krishna, the charioteer of the epic hero/warrior Arjuna,
begins a dialogue/sermon to convince Arjuna that he must fight in
the war, even though the other side includes members of his family and revered gurus.

In the first chapter of the *Bhagavad Gita*, Arjuna surveys the
participants of the battle on both sides and throws down his bow,
refusing to fight. By creating this new-found reluctance for the
hero, the author of the *Bhagavad Gita* provided himself with an opportunity to teach his hearers about *dharma*, the crucial epic concept
of the truth and duty that is built into the universe. Existentially
relevant is the fact that *dharma* includes Arjuna's duty, as well as
that of all his listeners.

The author of the *Gita* (as the text is often abbreviated) was also a
devotee of earlier compositions that we know today as the *Upanishads*. He both refers to and quotes these books, which became part
of the larger body of scriptures called the *Vedas*. Composed between

800 and 200 B.C.E., the *Upanishads* were the product of the teachers or gurus of a variety of schools of thought. Their common goal was to attain *moksha*, liberation from what they understood to be the continual rounds of rebirth and redeath (*samsara*) all creatures must endure. The author of the *Gita* so revered this Upanishadic tradition that he took pains to show that what he believed and taught was also affirmed in the *Upanishads*, even if he had to reinterpret those texts to suit his particular religious purposes.

The Upanishadic tradition eschews desire and attachment to the everyday elements of this life. The *Gita's* connection to that tradition of nonattachment seems to have blunted the emotional elements usually associated with devotion to Krishna. In the *Gita*, *bhakti*, or devotion, lacks its later passionate expression. Here in the *Gita*, the sense of "attachment" to Krishna has little to do with human emotions. It occurs instead on the deepest level of the self within and not the emotions, intellect, or body that surround the self. The true self is free from desire and loathing of anything other than Krishna's essential nature.

Numerous alternative "paths," or *yogas*, were available in the religious milieu of the second century B.C.E. Some of these paths the text rejects, and others it reinterprets to suit the comprehensive path to *moksha*, liberation, that it recommends. The *Gita* rejects actionless behavior by reinterpreting the idea of "nonaction." It relegates the sacrificial system of the early Vedic literature to a path that goes nowhere because it is based on desires. And it is clear that, though it recognizes other deities, they are subordinated to the god Krishna. Worship of Krishna is the highest worship.[2]

As a part of the epic, the basic themes found in the text are referenced by later devotees. Later religious thinkers composed commentaries on the *Gita* as if it were an important scripture separate from the *Mahabharata*. But the *Gita* as a distinct popular text really came into its own in the modern period. For modern Indian nationalists, its compact size was manageable and its call to battle provided a vision of an active, even militant lifestyle that could respond to British oppression and counter the Western criticism that "Hinduism" was a passive religion that discouraged outward action. Since more recent commentators view "Hinduism" as an inclusivistic religion, many modern Hindus have interpreted the *Gita* as a text that teaches that "all paths" lead to the highest goal. But the text itself—and traditional commentators—was much more exclusivistic.

The *Gita* begins with Arjuna's reluctance to fight the battle before him. Arjuna drops his bow due to what Krishna labels unmanliness, weakness, pity, and emotional attachment. Krishna convinces Arjuna to do his manly duty (*dharma*) as a member of the warrior class (*varna*). Threats to the system of class must have been part of the author's society, for crucial to the text's worldview is the teaching that Krishna created the four *varnas* and that maintenance of its structure is essential to maintenance of the universe itself. Twice (3.35; 18.47) the *Gita* says that it is better to do poorly the duty assigned to one's own class than to do that assigned to another class well. And how best to maintain the system of classes is at the foundation of the disagreement that begins the dialogue. Just as in chapter I Arjuna refuses to fight, asserting that this class structure would be preserved best if there were no battle, so Krishna argues in the remainder of the text that it will be best preserved if the battle is fought. To maintain the social structure, which is foundational to the universe (*loka-samgraha*, 3.20; 25), Arjuna must fight. "Nothing better exists for a warrior than a battle required by *dharma*," Krishna says in 2.31.

The sermon, however, does not stop there. Krishna also explains to Arjuna *how* to perform his actions so as not to have them affect or hinder him. Action (*karma*) is good, required by *dharma*, and inevitable, Krishna says. It is impossible not to act. To be freed from the results of one's actions, from their *karmic* consequences, however, one is to do the actions required by one's class duty without concern for the "fruit" or results they produce. This nonattached action has been called *nishkama-karma*, "action without desire," though that phrase is not used in the text. It has also been interpreted as action done without concern for personal consequences, though the text says there should also be no concern for their results on others.

In a progressive style of revelation that unfolds as the *Gita* continues, Krishna adds to this nonattached action a nonattached mental-consciousness stance one is to take as one acts. One is to practice through mental reflection and meditation a concentration upon the unchanging self (*atman*) within, which is eternally unaffected by all that goes on in what Krishna calls Nature (*prakriti*). With a dualistic ontology quite similar to that of classical Sankhya-Yoga thought, Krishna provides a metaphysic for nonattached action. In addition to the Sankhya-Yoga assertion that the true self or soul is unchanging and not attached to the ever-active Nature, Krishna adds that the self within is actually eternally affected by its devoted relationship to Krishna, who is Lord of the Universe. The self is always and only attached to the Lord Krishna and affected by that attachment. Thus, in the great vision in *Gita* II, Arjuna's inner self (*antar-atman*) is shaken by the vision, a very un-Samkhya-Yoga assertion.

The author of the *Gita* took the approach of progressively adding devotion to the text, beginning with the more immediate issues of the battlefield and appropriate action and slowly adding teachings of Krishna's place beyond and over the universe and his relationship to the individual. The fact that Krishna is no mere human charioteer and companion is progressively revealed in the text beginning in chapter 4, both in word and in the frightening vision in chapter II. Arjuna learns that Krishna descends into the world to adjust its *karma* and restore the *dharma* when evil (*a-dharma*) has become dominant. In the *Gita*, we may have the earliest reference to a god descending as an *avatara* to protect the *dharma* when things seem to have gotten out of hand.

Arjuna also learns that Krishna is "Lord of Yoga," that Krishna runs the universe in the same nonattached fashion he calls human beings to run their lives and Arjuna to fight the battle before him—doing his duty without concern for the results. In chapter 7, Krishna reveals that the unquenchably active Nature is actually Krishna's own lower nature (*prakriti*). What Nature does, therefore, completely conforms to Krishna's will, even to the point that the *Gita* seems ultimately to teach that all one can do is be Krishna's instrument for Krishna's activities. At times it appears that Arjuna himself has little say in his actions and will be compelled to do Krishna's will no matter what Arjuna decides.

Krishna also reveals that there is an eternal, unchanging loving relationship between the individual soul and Krishna encompassed by the term *bhakti*, devotion. Though later texts will see this in highly emotional terms, there is little emotion to *bhakti* in the *Gita*. The teachings of the text thus appealed traditionally more to religious thinkers than common devotees. In the *Gita*, devotion to Krishna is a mental-consciousness stance that is unconcerned with its effects on Nature, a stance that is not attached to the world that is not the true self. It is exclusively identified with the self within each one, a self that is solely attached to its Lord, Krishna, the Lord of the Universe.

In the *Bhagavad Gita*, devotion to Krishna develops slowly out of the surrounding battle scene. Though that development never quite reaches the depths of attachment of later Krishna *bhakti*, the text provides an image of Krishna who is both the Lord of the Universe and one who incarnates in this world again and again to set things right and protect the *dharma*. As the nonattached Lord, he is unapproachable except as we are in touch with our deepest and unmoved selves, who are eternally attached to him. As the incarnate one, there is a possibility that he can be approached by his devotees. Arjuna, he says, is somehow dear to him, as are all those who practice his unique *yoga*. That relationship, however, would be more fully developed only by later devotees. And the vision of chapter 11 is less comforting than frightening. Though Arjuna asks to "see" Krishna as *yogic* Lord of the Universe, he is happier for the vision to come to a close. To the *Gita*'s author, it seems better to recognize the distance between the Lord and the devotee, at least on the cosmic level.

The text is actually spoken by Samjaya, the charioteer of the blind king Dhritarashtra, who describes the scene to the king. Krishna's words are preceded by the phrase "The Beloved One (Shri Bhagavan) said."

The following excerpts were chosen because they have most to do with the concept of *bhakti*, or devotion to Krishna, in the *Bhagavad Gita*. We begin in chapter 4.

> The Beloved One said:
> I have had many births as have you, Arjuna.
> I know them all; you do not, Oh Scorcher of the Enemy.
> Though I am not really born, My own Soul is eternal, and
>   I am Lord of all Beings,

Still, on the basis of My Nature and My mysterious power, I
come into being in this world.

Because whenever there appears to be a diminishing of *dharma*,
Arjuna,

Or a growth in *a-dharma*, I choose to descend.

To protect the good people, to destroy those who do evil,

I descend in age after age, to establish *dharma* again.

Whoever therefore really knows My miraculous birth and all
that I do,

When that one dies, he is no longer reborn, but comes to abide
with Me, Arjuna.

Many, freed of attraction, fear, and anger, their life absorbed
in Me, depending on Me,

Purified by the austerity of knowledge, have attained My state
of being.

In whatever way any approach Me, in just that way I return
their love;

People follow My path in every way, Son of Pritha.

Desiring the success of actions in this world, they sacrifice to
the Vedic gods.

The success that comes from these acts comes quickly in this
human world.

I created the system of four classes with each class having
distinguishing characteristics and actions.

Yet, though I do such actions, You should know Me as one who
effectively is eternally inactive.

The actions I do actually do not count as actions because I have
no interest in the results of My actions.

The one who understands Me in this way is also not bound by
the actions that he does.

The ancient seekers of liberation knew this secret and acted.

So, you should do your actions this way too, just the way the
ancients did them. (4.5–15)

The Beloved One said:

O Son of Pritha, neither here on earth nor there above, is
there any destruction for that one,

For no one who does what is right comes to an unfortunate
result, My friend.

Attaining the worlds of those who do good, abiding there for
endless years,

One who has fallen from *yoga* is reborn in the home of the
happy and prosperous.

Or else he comes to be in a family of learned *yogins*.
Such a birth as that is more difficult to attain in this world.
There that one continues on with the depth of intellect from
    his former embodiment,
And strives once more from that point toward perfection,
    O Son of Kunti.
That one is carried forward by that former practice even against
    his will.
Even the one who merely wishes to know *yoga*, transcends the
    Brahman of words.
However, the *yogin* who perseveres, controlled, completely
    cleansed of evil,
Perfected through many births, then comes to the supreme goal.
The *yogin* is superior to ascetics; he is even superior to those
    with knowledge,
And the *yogin* is superior to those who are just active. Therefore,
    be a *yogin*, Arjuna.
Moreover, of all the *yogins*, the one whose inner self has
    gone to Me,
Who is devoted to Me, filled with faith, that one I consider the
    best *yogin*. (6.40–47)

All true seekers are worthy, but I say that the one who embraces
    the knowledge I teach is Mine,
Because that one through his own *yoga* relies only on Me as his
    highest goal.
When his many rebirths end, the one who truly knows relies
    on Me;
That rare, great soul is the one who thinks: "Krishna is all."
People do rely on other gods when they are robbed of knowledge
    by various desires,
Following various teachings, and limited by their own
    karmic Nature.
Yet whatever divine form any devotee seeks to worship,
It is I who grants unswerving faith to them.
When that devotee, practicing *yoga*, faithfully seeks help from
    those gods,
And receives what he desires, it is because I am the one who
    distributes it.
But what they receive is not permanent due to their lack of
    understanding;
Those devoted to the gods go to those gods, while My devotees
    go to Me.

The foolish think that I just come into being from nothing, like
    any mortal or god.
They do not understand that I am essentially eternal and
    supreme.
Not every one sees Me, because I am concealed by the
    mysterious power of My *yoga*.
These people are deluded and unaware that I am unborn and
    imperishable. (7.18–25)

The Beloved One said:
But this most esoteric thing I shall explain to you, since you are
    not a critic.
When you have learned this combination of theoretical and
    practical knowledge, you shall be freed from evil.
This royal knowledge, this royal secret, is a supreme purifier,
Easily comprehensible, in touch with *dharma*, easy to practice,
    eternal.
People who put no faith in this *dharma*, O Scorcher of the Foe,
Are reborn in the path of death and *samsara*, and fail to attain
    Me.
I pervade all of this universe in the form of the Unmanifest;
Every being lives in Me, but I am not dependent on them.
Notice that this is My divine mystery, for paradoxically beings
    do not live in Me.
My essential being supports beings and causes them to be but
    does not reside in or depend on them.
Just as the great wind that is everywhere constantly resides in
    space,
It is certain that in the same way all beings live in Me.
All beings, Arjuna, return into My Nature
At the end of each age; and with a new age I send them forth
    again.
I continue to send them forth using My own Nature.
I do so for these powerless beings through My active Nature.
Yet I am not bound by these actions I do, Arjuna;
Unattached to My actions, I sit as one on the sidelines.
I oversee the actions of Nature that bring forth the moving and
    unmoving beings,
And so through this force the world goes on.
They who despise Me in this human form I have assumed
    are foolish
For they do not know My transcendent nature as the Great
    Lord of Beings.

Their desires, actions, and knowledge are in vain; they lack insight.
They live out of a delusive, evil, and demonic nature.
But the great-souled ones who live out of a divine nature
Are devoted to Me and, without wavering, know Me as the origin
  of all beings, the Imperishable.
They always glorify Me and set their hearts on Me.
They worship Me with devotion, constantly practice My *yoga*
  and serve Me.
Still other people worship and wait upon Me through knowledge
Of My unique, various, and innumerable, omnipresent forms.
Such as: I am the act of ritual and the action of worship, the
  offering to the dead and the medicinal herb.
I am the *mantra*, the only butter for sacrifice, the sacrificial fire,
  and the offering itself.
I am the father, mother, founder, and grandfather of this world.
I am the object of true knowledge, the purifier, the syllable *om*,
  and the Vedic verses, chants, and rituals.
I am the goal, supporter, lord, witness, resting place, refuge,
  friend of all.
I am the origin, maintenance, and dissolution of all as well as
  its treasure and imperishable essence.
I give the heat, and send and hold back the rain.
I am both immortality and death as well as what is existent and
  nonexistent, Arjuna.
Those who follow the three *Vedas*, who drink the sacrificial
  beverage, who are purified of evil through their ritual
  worship, desire heaven.
They do attain the well-deserved heaven of Indra himself and
  experience what the gods enjoy.
Yet when their *karma* is exhausted and they have enjoyed this
  higher world, they return to the realm of mortals.
They desire what results from following the practices of the
  three *Vedas*, and they get them, impermanent though they be.
Those who think of Me without any other thoughts, who serve Me,
When they persist faithfully, I see to it that they receive and
  permanently possess their goals.
For those who are devotees of other gods and always worship
  them with faith,
It is really I, Arjuna, that they are worshiping, though not
  appropriately.
For I am actually both the one who receives and the Lord over
  all acts of worship.

They just don't recognize this as they should and therefore, they
    return to birth.
Those who worship the gods go to them, those who worship the
    departed spirits go to them.
Those who worship inferior spirits go to them. Just so,
    worshipers of Me come to be with Me.
Whoever offers even a leaf, a flower, fruit, or water to Me
    in devotion,
That is a meaningful offering I accept from those whose souls
    are truly devoted.
Whatever you do, whatever you eat, whatever you offer as an
    offering or gift,
Whatever self-sacrifice you make, Arjuna, do it as an offering
    to Me.
In this way you shall be freed from good and evil results that are
    the bonds of karma.
Thus freed, with your soul attached to this *yoga* of renunciation
    of results, you shall go to Me.
I am no more attached to one being or another, none is hateful
    or dear to Me,
But those who worship Me with devotion are united in Me and I
    in them.
If even one who has done great evil worships Me with single-
    minded devotion,
In spite of the evil done, that one is considered a holy one
    because of his zeal.
Quickly the evildoer's soul becomes righteous and attains eternal
    peace.
Son of Kunti, you can count on this: no devotee of Mine is
    ever lost.
Because if anyone chooses Me, Arjuna, even if they are from
    evil births
Like women, and those of the lowest classes, even then they go
    to the highest end.
So how much more likely are the righteous of the sage class or
    the royal seers?
This world is impermanent and unfulfilling, so while here,
    devote yourself to Me.
Concentrated on Me, devoted to Me, sacrificing to Me, and
    calling upon Me,
Thus following this *yoga*, totally intent on Me, you shall come to
    Me alone. (9.1–34)

The Beloved One said:
Once again, O Great Warrior, listen to My supreme message,
Which I shall speak to you who revels in it out of a desire for the
    best for you.
The many gods and the great seers do not know My beginning
Because I am the beginning of both the gods and the great seers.
Whoever does know Me as the unborn, the one without
    beginning, and the Great Lord of the World,
That one is no longer deluded and among all mortals is freed
    from all the evil of rebirth. (10.1–3)

I am the origin of all that exists, and everything emanates
    from Me.
The enlightened who are endowed with My state of being know
    this and are devoted to Me.
Their thoughts are on Me, their life given to Me, they enlighten
    one another,
To these, constantly nonattached to all else and devoted to Me,
I give a path of mental *yoga* that leads them to Me.
In order to show compassion to these devotees, I take the
    darkness born of their ignorance
And dispel it with the light of true knowledge, all the time
    remaining nonattached.

Arjuna said:
You are [the one called] the Highest *Brahman*, the Highest
    Abode, the Supreme Purifier,
the Eternal Divine Person, the Primordial God, and the Unborn
    Lord.
So [You are] called by the ancient seers, the divine seer Narada,
Asita Deva, and Vyasa, as well as in what You yourself have
    told me.
I believe that all that You say is true, Krishna,
For, O Beloved, neither the gods nor their enemies know that
    You are this.
You alone know your true Self by Your true Self, O Highest Person,
Sustainer of Beings, Lord of Beings, God of Gods, Lord of the
    Universe. (10.8–15)

Arjuna said:
As a favor to me, You have spoken about the highest mystery
    that pertains to the true self.
Because of this my misunderstanding has vanished.
For I have heard You tell me of the origin and dissolution of
    beings in detail,

And of Your own great and imperishable Self, O Lotus-Petal-Eyed
   One.
It is as You yourself say it is, O Supreme Lord. Now,
I long to actually see your form as the Lord, O Supreme Person.
If You think it is possible for me to see it, O God,
O Lord of *Yoga*, then show Your imperishable Self to me.

The Beloved One said:
Behold My innumerable forms, Son of Pritha,
Forms that are divine, variously colored, of various types, and
   of various shapes.
Behold also the divine beings: Adityas, Vasus, Rudras, the two
   Ashvins, and the Maruts.
Behold the many marvels never seen before, Son of Bharata.
Behold this day the unity of the whole universe with its moving
   and unmoving beings
Here in My Nature, Gudakesha, and behold whatever else you
   desire to see.
But you can't see Me as I am with your everyday eyes,
So I give you the eye of the gods. Now, behold, the *Yoga* of the Lord.

Samjaya narrates:
Upon saying this, Oh king, Hari, the Great Lord of *Yoga*,
Revealed to the Son of Pritha his Supreme Form as the Lord:
A form of many mouths and eyes, of many marvelous sights,
Of many dazzling ornaments, and awe-inspiring, exalted weapons.
Wearing priceless garlands and vestments, perfumes and lotions,
The infinite God is made of all breath-taking marvels, and faces
   everywhere.
If the light of a thousand suns should suddenly fill the sky
It would be like the brilliance of that Exalted One.
The whole world in its unity and diversity there
In the Body of the God of Gods the Son of Pandu then beheld.
Filled with wonder, with his hair standing on end, Arjuna
Lowered his gaze before the God, put his hands together in
   reverence and said:

Arjuna said:
Oh God, I see all the gods and the variety of other beings in
   Your body,
Lord Brahma sitting on a lotus, the Vedic seers, and divine serpents.
I see you of infinite form, with many arms, bellies, mouths,
   and eyes,
Without beginning, middle, or end of You, O Lord of All, O Form
   of All.

As a great brilliance, glowing from everywhere, with crown,
 mace, and discus,
Though it is hard to look at, I see you with the immeasurable
 glory of the flaming fire and the sun.
I know You are what is "the Imperishable," "the Supreme Object
 of Knowledge," "the Supreme Foundation on which the
 Universe rests,"
You are "the Imperishable Guardian of the Everlasting *Dharma*";
 "the Eternal Person."
I see you without beginning, middle, or end, with infinite power
 in your innumerable arms, the sun and the moon as eyes,
Your mouth a flaming fire that burns this entire universe with
 its brilliance.
For the expanse between heaven and earth and all directions is
 filled with you alone.
Seeing this, your wondrous, terrible form, the three worlds
 tremble, O Great Self. (11.1–20)

Your great form, O Mighty Warrior, with many mouths and eyes,
 many arms, thighs, and feet,
With many bellies, and showing many fangs, having seen (this),
 the worlds quake and so do I.
Touching the sky, blazing with many colors, with mouth gaping
 and enormous flaming eyes,
Seeing you thus, my deepest self trembles, and I find no stability
 or tranquility, O Vishnu.
And having seen Your mouths with their many fangs, glowing
 like the fires of the dissolution of the universe,
I have lost my sense of direction and find no safe place. Have
 mercy, O Lord of Gods, You in whom the universe dwells!
And, indeed, into You all the sons of Dhritarashtra along with
 the throngs of kings,
Generals Bhishma, Drona, and Karna, the son of the charioteer
 there also, together with our leading warriors,
Rush into Your frightening mouths that gape with many fangs,
Some appear stuck between Your teeth with their heads
 crushed.
Just as the many torrents of waters rush toward the sea,
So those who are heroes in the world of humans enter Your
 mouths with their consuming flames.
As moths rush blindly to their destruction in the blazing flame,
Just so the worlds of humans speed into Your mouths to their
 destruction.

Lapping up all the worlds on every side, and swallowing them
with flaming mouths,
Your terrifying brilliance fills all the universe and your terrible
radiance consumes it, O Vishnu.
Tell me who You of such terrifying form are. Homage to You,
O Best of Gods. Have mercy!
I want to understand You, the Primordial One, for I do not
comprehend your intentions now.

The Beloved One said:
I am Time, ripe, cause of the world's destruction, come forth
here to destroy the worlds.
Even without any action of yours, all the warriors drawn up before
you will cease to exist.
Therefore, arise and seize the glory. Enjoy a prosperous kingship
by conquering your enemies.
These have already been slain by Me. Be the mere instrument,
O Left-Handed Archer. (11.23–33)

The Beloved One said:
This highest form has been revealed by My own *yogic* action
because I grant you grace.
My form, splendorous, filling the whole cosmos, infinite, primeval,
has never been seen by anyone except you.
Not through Vedic sacrifices or recitation, or through gifts, rituals,
or gruesome austerities,
Can I be seen in this form in this human realm by anyone but
you, Hero of the Kurus.
Don't tremble or be confused because you have seen My
frightening form;
Do not be afraid, but rejoice in your heart. Behold now My
previous form.

Samjaya narrates:
Having spoken this to Arjuna, the Son of Vasudeva manifested
again his own form,
And the Great One comforted his fear by assuming his gentle
appearance.

Arjuna said:
Now that I see this gentle human form of yours, O Agitator
of Men,
I have become composed with my heart restored to normal.

The Beloved One said:
This form of Mine that you have seen and that is difficult to see,

Even the gods unceasingly wish to see this form.
Not through the Veda, austerity, gifts, or rituals
Can I be seen in the way that you have just seen Me.
But, Arjuna, by unswerving devotion can I in such a way
Be known, truly seen, and entered into, Scorcher of the Foe.
He who does My work, depending on Me, devoted to Me, free
    from attachment,
Free from hostility to all beings, comes to Me, Son of Pandu.
    (11.47–55)

Arjuna said:
Those who unceasingly practice the *yoga* of nonattachment and
    are devoted to You in their worship,
And those who revere the Imperishable, Unmanifest—which of
    these understands *yoga* the best?

The Beloved One said:
Those who, fixing their mind on Me, worship Me with the *yoga*
    of nonattachment,
Endowed with supreme faith, those I consider to be the best
    yogins.
But those who worship the Imperishable, Ineffable, Unmanifest,
The All-Pervading and Inconceivable, Unchanging, Immovable,
    Eternal,
By subduing the many senses, with equal nonattachment toward
    everything,
Rejoicing in the welfare of all beings, they also reach none but Me.
Those who have their minds fixed on the Unmanifest have greater
    anguish,
Because the Unmanifest goal is attained with difficulty by
    embodied souls.
But those who, casting all actions on Me, hold Me as highest,
With undistracted nonattached *yoga*, meditating on Me,
    worshiping Me,
For them I become the Rescuer from the sea of death and *samsara*
Immediately, for those whose thoughts have entered into Me,
    Son of Pritha.
Fix your mind only on Me, make your intellect enter Me,
From then on you will dwell in Me. There is no doubt about this.
But if you are not able to fix your thought constantly on Me,
Then seek to reach Me by the practice of nonattached *yoga*,
    O Conqueror of Wealth.
If you are unable to even practice, be completely devoted to
    My work;

Performing actions just for My sake, you will achieve perfection.
But, if you are even unable to do this, then, by depending on
My *Yoga*
At least act with abandonment of all the fruit of action, controlling
yourself.
For knowledge is more valuable than practice, meditation is
preferred to knowledge,
And abandonment of the fruit of actions is even more valuable
than meditation. With abandonment peace is immediate. (12.1–12)

The Beloved One said:
Still further I shall teach you the highest knowledge, the best of
all knowledge,
By knowing which all the seers have left this world to reach
supreme perfection.
Depending on this knowledge and arriving at a state of likeness
with Me,
Even at the creation of the next age, they are not reborn, nor do
they tremble at its dissolution.
For Me Great *Brahman* is a womb in which I plant the seed;
And from that comes the origin of all beings, Son of Bharata.
Whatever forms come to be in all wombs, Son of Kunti,
Great *Brahman* is the womb. I am the seed-sowing Father. (14.1–4)

Arjuna said:
O Lord, what are the characteristics that describe one who has
transcended the threads of Nature?
What actions? And how does that one pass beyond these threads?

Krishna said:
Brightness and activity and delusion, Son of Pandu,
Those one does not despise when they are present, nor desire
when absent.
As one sitting separately on the sidelines who is unmoved by the
threads of Nature,
Thinking that it is merely those threads at work, and standing
firm and undisturbed,
Unmoved by pain and pleasure, by a lump of earth, a stone,
or gold; centered in the self,
Unmoved by the lovable and the hated, by criticism and praise;
steadfast,
Indifferent to honor and dishonor, to friend and enemy,
Abandoning all activities that would attach – that one, it is said,
transcends the threads of Nature.
And the one who serves Me with an unwavering *yoga* of devotion,

Transcending these threads of Nature, is qualified to become
  Brahman
Because I am the foundation of the Immortal and Imperishable
  Brahman,
And of everlasting *dharma,* and of the only true bliss. (14.21–27)

The brightness that radiates from the sun, that illuminates the
  entire universe,
That is in the moon and the fire, know that it is My brightness.
And I maintain all beings by entering the earth though My power;
And I cause all plants to thrive, by becoming the juicy soma.
Entering the body of all living beings, becoming the digestive fire
  of humans,
And joining with the upper and lower breaths within, I digest the
  four kinds of food.
And I have entered into the heart of all; from Me come memory,
  knowledge, and reasoning.
I alone am the One who is known by all the *Vedas.* And I am the
  author of *Upanishadic* thought and knower of the *Vedas.*
In this world here there are two "persons": the perishable and
  the imperishable.
The "perishable" is all phenomenal beings; the "person" unmoved
  by this is called the "imperishable."
But there is another highest "Person" called the Supreme Self,
Which, by entering into the three worlds as the Eternal Lord,
  supports them all.
Since I transcend the "perishable" and am even higher than the
  "imperishable,"
Therefore I am proclaimed "the Highest Person" in the world
  and in the *Veda.*
The one who, not deluded, knows Me to be the Supreme
  Person,
That one knows all and devotes himself to Me with his entire
  being, Son of Bharata.
Thus I have proclaimed the most secret teaching, Blameless One,
The one awakened to this truth would be truly enlightened and
  with nothing left to be done, O Son of Bharata. (15.12–20)

With intellect unattached to anything, with the self conquered,
  free from desire,
One attains to the supreme perfection of nonaction through
  renunciation.
Hear from Me briefly how that one, having attained such
  perfection, also attains *Brahman,*

Son of Kunti, which is the highest state of knowledge.
Yoked with a pure intellect and controlling himself with firmness,
Abandoning sounds and the rest of the objects of sense, and
    putting away desire and hatred,
Cultivating solitude, eating lightly, controlling speech, body,
    and mind,
Continually engaged in the *yoga* of meditation, taking refuge in
    passionlessness,
Abandoning egotism, strength, pride, desire, anger, and clinging,
Unselfish, and calm, that one conforms to *Brahman*.
Having become *Brahman*, with a serene soul, that person neither
    mourns nor desires,
Is the same toward all beings, and attains to supreme devotion
    to Me.
Through devotion he comes to know Me, how great and who
    I really am.
Then, thus really knowing Me, he thereupon enters into
    My presence.
That one who relies always on Me, even though he continues to
    perform actions,
Attains, by My grace, the eternal, unchanging, abode.
Casting all actions on Me with your thoughts, devoted to Me,
Depending on the *yoga* of the intellect, constantly think of Me.
Through My grace, if your mind is on Me, you shall pass over any
    difficulties.
But if you will not listen due to egotism, you shall perish.
If, taking refuge in egotism, you think "I will not fight,"
This decision would be useless. Nature will coerce you.
O Son of Kunti, since you are bound by your own nature
    and *karma*,
Even what, out of delusion, you desire not to do, you will do
    against your will.
The Lord dwells in the heart of all beings, Arjuna,
Causing all beings by His mysterious power to move as if
    mounted on a mechanism.
Seek refuge in Him alone with your whole being, Son of Bharata;
From that grace, you shall attain to supreme peace and an eternal
    abode.
Thus, I have taught you the knowledge that is more secret than
    any secrets.
After considering this fully, act as you choose.
Once again, listen to My supreme message, the deepest secret
    of all.

You are truly loved by Me. Therefore I shall speak for your benefit.

Fix your mind on Me, devoted to Me, sacrificing to Me, paying homage to Me,

And I promise you, as one who is dear to Me, that you shall certainly come to Me.

Abandoning all *dharma*, take refuge only in Me.

I shall rescue you from any evil; so do not despair.

You must not speak of this to one who neglects austerity, nor to one without devotion,

Nor to one who has no desire to hear what is said, nor to one who speaks evil against Me.

Whoever does set forth this supreme secret to My devotees,

Having practiced the highest devotion to Me, shall come to Me, without a doubt.

And no human being shall do more pleasing things for Me,

Nor shall there be anyone more pleasing to Me on the earth than this one.

And whoever shall retell this dialogue on *dharma*,

I shall consider that one a lover of Me through the sacrifice of knowledge.

Even the one who hears it with faith, without scoffing,

That one also will be liberated and will attain the joyful worlds of those whose actions are pure. (18.49–71)

NOTES

1. For the most complete discussion of the evidence for dating the *Bhagavad-gita*, determining its relationship to the *Mahabharata*, and other introductory matters, see Robert N. Minor, *Bhagavadgita: An Exegetical Commentary* (Columbia, MO: South Asia Books, 1982), xxi–lx.

2. Robert N. Minor, "The *Gita's* Way as the Only Way," *Philosophy East and West* 30, no. 3 (July 1980), 339–354.

3

The *Harivamsa*: The Dynasty of Krishna

Ekkehard Lorenz

According to Hindu tradition, the Sanskrit text known as the *Harivamsa* (*HV*) was compiled by the sage Vyasa, along with the *Mahabharata* and the *Puranas*; no historical or human author is credited with the work.[1] *Harivamsa* means "the dynasty of Hari," and "Hari" is a name of Vishnu. The text describes itself as *mahakavya* (great long ornate religious poem), *Purana, charita* (account of heroic deeds), and *akhyana* (legend),[2] while the *Mahabharata* says that the *Harivamsa* is one of its appendices (*khila*) and calls it a *purana*.[3] Two versions of the *Harivamsa* currently exist in print: the vulgate[4] and a critical edition (CE).[5]

The vulgate, a text of 16,137 marked stanzas, is divided into three sections, or *parvans*. They are called *Harivamsaparvan, Vishnuparvan,* and *Bhavishyatparvan,* and have 55, 128, and 135 chapters, respectively. While the CE formally retained these three divisions, their length was reduced to 45, 68, and 5 chapters, respectively.[6] The chapters of the CE are numbered 1 through 118, across the three sections of the work. The following discussion of the *HV* refers to the CE.

The adventures of Krishna and Sankarshana are narrated in the *Vishnuparvan*. The two brothers are described as incarnations of Vishnu. They are said to be one entity with one mind and one single purpose, but two bodies. The *Vishnuparvan* begins by narrating the events leading up to the birth of Krishna, and ends with Krishna's return to Dvaraka, after his fights with Bana and Varuna. The text remains silent about Krishna's demise.

Scholars have variously called the *HV* a *mahakavya,* a *Purana,* or even the "Ur-*Purana*." Daniel H. H. Ingalls argues that the *HV* is a specimen of *mahakavya.*[7] He refers to Dandin's list of features that *kavya* texts are required to have, and points out that nearly all these requirements are met by the *HV.* Sivaprasad Bhattacharyya, on the other hand, holds that "the *Harivamsa* is *shastra* and occasionally but rarely appears remodeled, as it were, in the form of a *shastrakavya;* but nowhere, as in other *Puranas,* has it trespassed into the domain of *kavya* proper, in its formal manifestation."[8]

Ludo Rocher did not include the *HV* in his discussion of *Puranas,*[9] and Bhattacharya does not grant it *purana* status either: "It is, however, extravagant, to include it in the class of much-tampered *Puranas.* From the viewpoints of plan, execution and manner of expression it is more homogeneous than any other work of this type."[10] Numerous scholars, however, tend to regard the *HV* as a genuine *Purana.* In his abridged edition of the *HV,* Keshavram K. Shastree holds that "according to the mention of contents of the MBH, the HV is, no doubt, a Purana as said above (*MBH.* 1-2-69)."[11] He proceeds to name the five topics that a genuine *Purana* should deal with, and lists the chapters of the *HV* in which these topics have been covered. A. M. T. Jackson considered the *HV* to be not merely a *Purana* but the original *Purana* after which all subsequent *Puranas* were modeled:

> In the earliest enumerations of Sanskrit literary works we find the *itihasa-puranam* mentioned in such a way as to imply that there was but one Purana, and that it was regarded as a supplement to the Itihasa. As the latter name belongs *par excellence* to the Mahabharata, it is hard to avoid the conclusion that the Purana in question was what has now become the Harivamsa. It must, however, have originally had all the five characteristics of a Purana, including a cosmological section, which was omitted most probably when the legends relating to Krishna and the other incarnations of Vishnu were amplified at the expense of the other constituents of the original work. The latter still survives in parts of the modern Puranas, all of which are derived from one common original, but now subsist as independent works, no longer connected with the Mahabharata.[12]

Walter Ruben, while not attempting to show that the *HV* was the original *Purana,* believed that the text of the present vulgate was based on a much shorter and older version, possibly the *Brahmapurana.*[13] At present, however, most scholars seem to agree with Ludo Rocher that "The Brahmapurana has numerous passages in common with other puranas: Vishnupurana, Markandeyapurana, Sambapurana, and Vayupurana, as well as with the Harivamsa, and the Anushasana and Shanti *parvans* of the Mahabharata. In all these cases the Brahma is reputed to be the borrower."[14]

In order to determine whether the *HV's* account of the Krishna legend is earlier than that of the *Puranas*, one would have to decide which portions of the text constitute the original *HV*. P. L. Vaidya proposed that the first 98 chapters of the CE might have been current around 300 C.E., and suggested that the last twenty chapters could have been added in the period from 300 C.E. to 1050 C.E.[15]

Sivaprasad Bhattacharyya, who holds that already Ashvaghosha (first century C.E.) referred to the *HV*, finds internal and external evidence that "the *H.V.* was certainly an authoritative text by the first century A.C. and its later redaction took place about the end of the second or beginning of the third century A.C."[16] Ingalls, who, like Bhattacharyya, observes that the *HV* has much in common with the *Ramayana*, considers the *HV* to be the later work.[17] Since the CE of the *HV* became available in print, however, attempts have been made to assign far greater antiquity to the text.[18] K. K. Shastree, for example, in his abridged version of the *HV*, argues that the text could be possibly as early as the sixth century B.C.E.[19]

Not only the content of the *HV* but also its form, especially its metrical apparatus, have been analyzed to find clues that could help determine its date. Bhattacharyya, who studied the meters in the vulgate, concluded that the metrical patterns he found betrayed the antiquity of the work.[20] The CE, however, shows much less metrical variety. It contains no prose and has none of Bhattacharyya's archaic irregular meters.[21]

Absence of a large variety of artfully arranged classical meters does of course not establish the antiquity of a work. A more detailed analysis of the prosodical patterns in the *HV* will possibly add further insights that might be helpful in determining its date.[22]

It will be appropriate, at this point in the discussion, to compare the *HV* with that text that contains the most popular account of the Krishna legend: the *Bhagavatapurana* (*BhP*).[23] While the *HV* shows less metrical variety than the *Mahabharata* or even the *Ramayana*, the *BhP* stands on the opposite end of the scale of prosodic diversity. Apart from prose passages, *arya*, and uneven *anushtubh*, it features twenty-five different types of even meters, plus the semi-even meters *upajati*, *sundari*, and *pushpitagra*. Some of its hymns are composed entirely in almost flawlessly executed classical meters. The *HV* tends to repeat certain patterns of expression, and has long passages with strings of nouns that all have the same case endings, while the *BhP* has a broader vocabulary and is richer in grammatical forms. Blessings to the reader or reciter, at the end of a chapter or larger section, are far less common in the *HV* than in the *BhP*. The *HV* has only a few hymns to Vishnu or Krishna, for example, Indra's prayer in CE 62 and Narada's in CE 67. The *BhP* has many more hymns. In the tenth *skandha* there are fifteen hymns with more than ten stanzas each, plus a large number of shorter prayers.[24]

The text samples shown here are near literal translations of four chapters of the critical text of the *HV*. "Breaking Two Arjuna Trees," "The Wolves Appear," and "Arriving at Vrindavan" are a series of three consecutive chapters. "Krishna Plays with the Cowherd Women" follows ten chapters later in the narration.

Chapter 51, "Breaking Two Arjuna Trees," is narrated in thirty-seven *anushtubh* stanzas. It contains the adventure that gave Krishna his name "Damodara." In the *BhP* this story is spread over three chapters.[25] Some passages in this chapter are similar or identical to corresponding passages in the *BhP*.[26] In the *BhP* the two trees that Krishna uproots are the sons of Kuvera, who, in their previous life, had been cursed by Narada for parading naked in front of his eyes. They offer ten stanzas of praise to Krishna, their liberator—a pattern often repeated in the *BhP* but practically absent in the *HV*. In the *HV* the trees are not described as persons. They are said to be the oldest or tallest, and that people used to pray to them for blessings.[27] Both in the *HV* and in the *BhP*, the herdsmen, after seeing the uprooted trees, talk about moving their camp to another place. In both accounts they list other inauspicious events that have happened earlier. While the *BhP* then factually narrates how the cowherds move to Vrindavan, the *HV* proceeds to chapter 52, which describes a rather unexpected turn of events.

Chapter 52 of the *HV* describes how Krishna creates wolves from the hairs of his body. The wolves terrorize the herdsfolk. They devour people, cows, and calves, and they abduct small children at night. This incident is not found in any other account of Krishna's activities. Krishna tells his brother that he needs to create an impetus that will convince the herdspeople that it is time to move the camp to another location. The wolves he created are described as bearing the mark of *shrivatsa* (an emblem on the chest of Vishnu) and having the same dark complexion as Krishna. The incident appears to violate the narrator's dictum at the end of the next chapter: "Neither calves, nor cows, nor any other creatures suffer where Madhusudana [Krishna] stays for the well-being of the worlds."[28] The wolf story will perhaps appear less striking if one considers that the *HV* also describes cattle slaughter and meat eating. In chapter 60, for example, the herdsmen promise Krishna to slaughter buffaloes and other animals to prepare an offering for Mount Govardhan, a feast that is then eaten by the assembled herdsfolk.[29]

Chapter 53 of the *HV* describes how the camp is moved to Vrindavan in order to save the cows from the onslaught of the wolves. Both *HV* and *BhP* describe how the new camp is laid out by arranging wagons in the shape of a half moon. This chapter is an instance where the *HV* presents more detail than the *BhP*. Both the moving away from the old camp and the buzzing activity at the new campsite are narrated more elaborately than in the *BhP*.

The first sixteen stanzas of chapter 63 of the *HV* describe a dialogue between Krishna and the cowherds, and the remaining nineteen stanzas tell about Krishna's erotic adventures with the *gopis,* or cowherd girls. Some see in this chapter a description of the famous *rasa* dance of the *BhP,* but there is not much in the *HV* to support this view. The short account in the *HV* does not present any explicit theology or moral instructions, as in the *BhP,* where the whole affair takes up five chapters. Krishna does not attract the *gopis* by his nocturnal flute-playing. In fact, Krishna of the *HV* is not a flute-player at all. In the *HV,* it is the girls who take the initiative in the autumnal lovemaking. The *HV* does not explicitly mention that Krishna made love to married wo-men, while the *BhP* is clear about this.[30] Both accounts compare the love-making of Krishna and the *gopis* to the mating of an elephant bull with a troop of females. The *gopis'* imitating Krishna's deeds and praising him in song, which in the *HV* happens in Krishna's presence—a sort of foreplay, as it were—is described in an elaborate separate chapter in the *BhP.* But there, the *gopis* act in the absence of Krishna, who has left them in order to teach that one should not be proud in the presence of god. In the *HV* the term "*rasa* dance" is not used, nor is there mention of a *rasa-mandala,* the celebrated circular arena of the dance.

Yamalarjuna-bhangah (Breaking Two Arjuna Trees)
Harivamsa, Chapter 51 (CE)

Vaishampayana said: The two cheerful boys received the names Krishna and Sankarshana. As time went by, they began to crawl. Krishna and Sankarshana were an inseparable pair. From their early childhood they were like-minded and acted in identical ways. Together they looked as beautiful as the young moon combined with the rising sun. Krishna and Sankarshana looked very similar and acted in the exact same childlike ways. They shared the same beds, sat on equal seats, ate the same meals, and dressed alike. These two powerful forms of the one performed the deeds of the one with the will of the one. They were the one in the shape of two chil-dren. These two humans engaged in the works of the gods were the Lords of the whole world. As protectors of the entire universe they had assumed the shapes of two cowherds. Mutually intertwined in their games, they looked like the sun and the moon that had taken hold of each other's rays in the sky.

Krishna and Sankarshana had arms like serpent hoods, and as they moved about, their bodies covered by dust, they resembled a pair of proud young elephants. Sometimes smeared with ashes, some-times sprinkled with cow dung, the two would roam about like the youthful sons of fire. Bodies and hair powdered with dirt, they crawled around on their knees while playing in the cowsheds. At other times the two beautiful children amused their father, laughingly playing tricks on the cowherd people. Hair falling over their eyes, those two charming boys, tender little children with moon-like faces, shone brilliantly.

Seeing them so determined to roam all over the camp, the cowherd Nanda could not restrain the two wild ones. Thereupon the enraged Yashoda took the lotus-eyed Krishna to her wagon, rebuked him many times, and even bound him to a grinding mortar with a rope tied around his waist. "Now move if you can!"—she said, and went to her work. Then, while Yashoda was busy, Krishna left the courtyard.

Krishna, who was playing like a small child, amazed the herdscamp folk when he came forth from the courtyard, dragging the mortar behind. With the mortar in tow, Krishna proceeded away from the other children toward a pair of mighty *arjuna* trees in the forest. The mortar to which Krishna was bound toppled and got stuck between the two *arjuna* trees. And as he continued to drag, he pulled them both down, right from their roots. Then he just sat there, laughing, amid their forcefully shattered roots and branches.

Krishna had done all this to demonstrate his supernatural powers to the cowherds. It was through the powers of this boy, for example, that the rope had been made strong.

The cowherd women on the path along the banks of the Yamuna saw little Krishna and rushed to mother Yashoda with cries of astonishment. Visibly bewildered, the women told her: "Come Yashoda, come on! Hurry, what do you delay! Those two *arjuna* trees that people in our camp worship for benedictions, those two trees have fallen, with your son on top! Your little son is sitting right there laughing, bound like a calf with a strong rope around his waist. Get up, come on! Thinking yourself so learned, you silly, dull-witted woman believed your son to be alive, while he has just escaped from the mouth of death!"

Frightened, Yashoda at once got up and exclaiming "Ah, Alas!" she went to the place where the two great trees had fallen. She saw her child right between the two trees, a rope tied around his waist, pulling a mortar.

Soon the whole camp—women, men, elders, and youths—surrounded the spot to see the great miracle. Those forest-roaming cowherds pondered and pondered: "Why did these two most excellent trees in our camp fall? "Without wind, without rain, without a lightning stroke, without being harmed by a human hand? How did these trees crash down?" "Alas, alas! These uprooted *arjuna* trees no longer shine. They look like a pair of waterless clouds fallen to the ground! O Nanda, although they came to be uprooted like this, these trees were merciful to you, for your little boy escaped unharmed. This is already the third calamity that happens in this camp. Putana was destroyed, the cart was destroyed, and now these trees. Our herds camp should not remain in this place, for the disasters we have seen here forebode nothing good."

Nanda hastened to untie Krishna from the mortar and for a long time kept him on his lap, as if Krishna had returned from death. Then, rebuking Yashoda, Nanda went home, and all the other cowherd people returned to the camp too.

From then on the herdswomen in the camp celebrated Krishna by the name Damodara ["whose belly is tied with a rope"], because he had been bound by a rope.

This, then, O foremost of the Bharatas, was the marvelous feat of the little boy Krishna, who lived among the cowherds.

Thus ends the fifty-first chapter of the *Harivamsa.*

Vrika-darshanam (The Wolves Appear)
Harivamsa, Chapter 52 (CE)

Vaishampayana said: Thus Krishna and Sankarshana spent the first seven years of their childhood in that one particular camp. Soon the two black-haired boys began to herd the calves. Dressed in blue and yellow garments and smeared with white and yellow pigments, the handsome boys played melodious tunes by blowing into folded leaves. They looked charming, like three-hooded serpents, as they roamed in the woods. With garlands of forest flowers on their chests, peacock feather ornaments on their arms, and flower-blossom chaplets on their heads, they appeared like a pair of young trees. Wearing lotus-flower crowns and carrying their ropes like sacred threads, the two, with their water gourds dangling, played on their cowherd flutes. Sometimes they laughed at each other, sometimes they played with each other, and at other times they would grope for each other when fast asleep on beds of leaves. Thus, herding the calves and beautifying the great forest, they happily roamed about like restless young horses.

One day, beautiful Damodara said to Sankarshana: "O noble one, it is impossible to play with the cowherd boys in this forest. It is disgusting that we are still trying to enjoy all this, after it has already been used up by us. Grass and wood are destroyed, and the cows have wasted the trees.

"The groves and forests, once so dense, look sorry now, like a gaping void. And these trees of imperishable luster, which had been turned into fences and wooden bolts, have all met destruction in our campfires. There used to be wood and grass near at hand, but now it has to be sought at distant places. With little water, few hideouts, and no shelter, with resting places hard to find and trees being scarce, this dreadful forest stands amid useless vegetation, abandoned by birds.

"Joyless, tasteless, and devoid of suitable breezes, this birdless, desolate forest is just like unseasoned food. As our locally grown wood and vegetables are being sold, and our wealth of grass is being depleted, our camp is turning into a city! As a herdscamp is the ornament of the hills, so the forest is the ornament of the herdscamp. Let us therefore go to another forest with green grass and fresh fuel. And since the cows wish to enjoy new pastures, let those wealthy cowherds move to a forest that has young grass.

"Herdspeople use no doors, no locks, no borders, they own no houses and no fields. They are in fact world famous for being free like migratory birds. The cows do not enjoy the grass that really just grows in their own stool and urine. It has a pungent flavor, and is not good for their milk. Let us move with our cows to a lovely, nearly flat region with charming virgin forests. The camp has to be brought together immediately!

"For I have heard of a delightful forest with an extensive grass cover. It is known by the name of Vrindavan and has delicious plants, fruits, and water. Free from crickets and thorns, Vrindavan is endowed with all the virtues of a forest. It is sheltered at the banks of the Yamuna and consists almost entirely of *kadamba* trees. With its gentle, cooling breezes, that forest is a beautiful abode of all seasons. Its charming, wonderful inner recesses will lend themselves to the pleasures of the herdswomen. Not very far from Vrindavan, the great Mount Govardhan shines with its lofty peak, like the Mandara mountain near the Nandana gardens. At the center of Mount Govardhan stands a banyan tree called Bhandira. With its huge branches extending over miles, it is beautiful like a dark blue cloud in the sky. And through the middle of that dark cloud, the River Kalindi draws a dividing line—parting the hair as it were—just as the Nalini, the best of rivers, passes through the Nandana gardens.

"Happily roaming there, the two of us shall always behold Mount Govardhan, the lovely river Kalindi and Bhandira, the king of trees. There we should have our herdscamp! We must abandon this useless forest! Let us do something that will cause the camp to come together, if you don't mind."

After the intelligent Vasudeva had spoken in this way, and as he kept reflecting, hundreds of blood-, flesh-, and fat-eating creatures appeared. They rushed forth from the hairs of his body: everywhere, hundreds of dreadful, dangerous wolves. Great panic spread among the cowherds when they saw the wolves rushing at cows, calves, men and women alike. To their terror, some wolves formed packs of five or ten, some came in troops of twenty or thirty, while yet others counted up to a hundred. Because they had issued forth from Krishna's own body, all the wolves had his blackish complexion and bore the mark of *shrivatsa*.

Panic broke out in the cowsheds as the wolves were devouring calves and stealing away small children at night. The entire herds-camp was devastated. It was impossible to protect the cows. No one could cross the river or go out to get anything from the forest. In this way the wolves, fierce like tigers in their attacks, forced the community to suspend its activities and stay in one spot.

Thus ends the fifty-second chapter of the *Harivamsa*.

Vrindavan-praveshah (Arrival at Vrindavan)
Harivamsa, Chapter 53 (CE)

Vaishampayana said: It became increasingly difficult to face the onslaught of the wolves. Seeing this, the men and women of the herds-camp resolved: "We cannot remain here. Let us move to another great forest that is auspicious and delightful, and will give only pleasure to our cows."

"What are we waiting for? Let us leave right away with our valuable cows, so that the entire camp will not be put to a gruesome death by these wolves!"

"We spend our nights in fear of these howling wolves, who have protruding teeth, ripping jaws, and blackish faces, and whose limbs are of a smokey, dark red color!"

In every house people were crying: "My son has been killed by the wolves!" "My brother has been killed by the wolves!" "My calf and my cow have been killed by the wolves!"

As the women were crying and the cows mooing, the assembly of elders decided to move the camp. When Nanda came to know that the elders, for the well-being of the cows, had decided to move the camp to Vrindavan, and when he understood that they were determined to leave, he spoke like Brihaspati as he gave his mighty commands:

"If you have firmly concluded that we should leave right away, then the camp has to be informed at once and you have to get ready without delay!"

The common people then loudly spread the order in the camp: "Quick! Gather the cows and yoke the wagons! Collect the calves and pack your equipment! The camp has to be moved from here to Vrindavan!"

Hearing Nanda's well-spoken message, the entire camp rose up, eager to leave at once. Shouts of: "Come on! Get up! We're going! Don't sleep! Move! Yoke up!"—sprang up in the camp. It was a big commotion. When the camp got on its way, crowded with wagons and roaring like the ocean, a thunderous, tiger-like sound arose.

A file of herdswomen hastened away from the old camp, their heads crested with jugs and jars, like a line of stars appearing above the horizon. Another line of women proceeding down the road, their breasts tied up in blue, yellow, and red cloths, resembled a rainbow. Walking along the road with their burden of ropes and cords dangling from their shoulders, some cowherd men looked like banyan trees. With its brilliant stream of rolling wagons, the camp glittered like the ocean with its rushing, storm-tossed waves. Within a moment's notice the campsite turned into a desert, bereft of people and utensils, yet filled with bands of crows.

At last the herdspeople arrived at the forest of Vrindavan and set up a large camp to accommodate their cows. The camp was laid out in the shape of a half moon. Its circumference was formed by wagons and stretched over two *yojanas*, while the straight line of its diameter extended over one *yojana*. Densely grown brambles and thorny trees, as well as strong stakes pointed at the top and dug into the ground, protected the camp well on all sides.

Churns were being put up throughout the camp, and churning rods set into motion by cords spilled water from the churns. The camp was fortified by overturned wagons and strong, upraised wooden posts, tied together with ropes and strings. Pulling cords were being wrapped around the tops of churning rods, and straw for the construction of grass huts was being spread. Cowsheds had been swept clean with brooms made from twigs, and mortars had been put in place. Fires glowed in the east of each house, and cots had been furnished with calf-hide covers. Herdswomen cleansed the entire forest by pouring water and collecting branches. Energetic herdsmen, young and old alike, quickly felled the trees and cut up the timber with axes.

That campsite, a truly charming forest residence abounding with groves, shone brilliantly, as if thoroughly showered with heavenly nectar. And the cows, who could give as much milk as one desired, had now reached Vrindavan, the forest that could supply grass at all times, and that resembled the Nandana gardens.

Krishna, the forest ranger and friendly benefactor of cows, had of course already seen this forest earlier. Grass thrived there even throughout the last part of the hot season, when Indra showered his nectar-like rains.

Neither calves, nor cows, nor any other creatures suffer where Madhusudana stays for the well-being of the worlds.

In this way the cows and the cowherd people, as well as the youthful Sankarshana, happily lived in the place Krishna had chosen.

Thus ends the fifty-third chapter of the *Harivamsa.*

Krishna-gopi-krida (Krishna Plays with the Cowherd Women)
Harivamsa, Chapter 63 (CE)

Vaishampayana said: After Indra left, Krishna, the glorious lifter of Mount Govardhan, entered the camp while the herdsfolk worshiped him. Krishna's relatives, elders, and companions welcomed him saying: "We are fortunate, we are obliged to you for holding up the mountain. Through your kindness the cows have escaped the dreadful rains and we were able to endure this great calamity, O Govinda of god-like glory! O Krishna, lord of the cows, after seeing your superhuman deed of lifting the mountain, we think you must be an immortal being. Who are you, O mighty one? Are you a Rudra, a Marut, or perhaps one of the Vasus? For what purpose did you become Vasudeva's son? Your childish play in the forest, your humble birth among us and your supernatural deeds make us suspicious, O Krishna. For what purpose do you enjoy yourself among us in the lowly dress of a cowherd? And why do you herd cows, while you are in fact just like one of the world-protecting gods? Whether you are a god born as one of us, a *danava,* a *yaksha,* or just a *gandharva*— whoever you are—we bow unto you. For whichever purpose you may have chosen to live here: we have sought refuge in you and are all at your service."

Having heard the words of the cowherds, lotus-eyed Krishna smilingly addressed his assembled kinsmen: "Let it be understood that I am not what all you formidable heroes have thought me to be. I am your friend and kinsman. But if you absolutely need to know it, you must wait for the proper occasion. Then your good selves shall hear and see the truth about me. If I am your praiseworthy friend, illustrious like a god, and if I am acting for your benefit, then why ask what is my business?"

So addressed by the son of Vasudeva, the cowherds fell silent and dispersed in all directions, hiding their faces.

At night, however, when Krishna saw the blooming youth of the moon and the freshness of the autumnal nights, he began to think of lovemaking. Courageous Krishna arranged fights between rutting bulls in the dung-adorned streets of the herdscamp. Valiant Krishna also set up contests between fiercely powerful cowherds, and in the forest, the hero caught cows just like an alligator.

Valuing youth and knowing the right moment to act, Krishna brought together the young women and girls of the camp and enjoyed himself with them at night. With their eyes, those lovely cowherd women drank at night the beauty of Krishna's face that resembled the moon descended on earth. Gracefully dressed in soft silken garments of yellowish glow, Krishna appeared all the more lovable. Adorned with a crown and bracelets, decorated with an excellent garland of forest flowers, Govinda beautified the herdscamp.

"Obeisance unto Damodara," the cowherd girls in the camp would say since they had witnessed radiant Krishna's wonderful adventures. Their faces casting restless glances, those beautiful women pressed their upraised breasts against Krishna. When checked by their fathers, brothers, and mothers, those young cowherd women, eager to make love, sought out Krishna at night. Then, combining into pairs, all of them joyfully praised Krishna's enchanting adventures in song. These beautiful young women, their eyes fixed upon Krishna, were playing out Krishna's exploits, behaving just like him. Some of the cowherd girls were clapping hands, while others enacted Krishna's forest adventures. The happy girls playfully imitated Krishna's dancing, his singing, and his lusty smiling glances. The lovely women, totally engrossed in Damodara, happily went on singing, out there in Braja that had become so sweet because of their love.

Their bodies covered with powdered cow dung, they surrounded Krishna, satisfying him like female elephants excited by an elephant bull. Other women, not satiated, drank Krishna with their cheerful eyes wide open out of love, eyes like those of the black antelope. Fixing their gaze on Krishna's mouth, other cowherd girls, thirsting and eager for the pleasure of love, entered the nocturnal lovemaking and drank. Thrilled with joy by his sighing "Ah" and "Oh," these beautiful women delighted in the gentle sounds Damodara made.

Their orderly tied and parted hair, now disarrayed from lovemaking, beautifully fell over the tips of their breasts. Thus adorned by circles of herdswomen, happy Krishna enjoyed himself during the moonlit nights of the autumn season.

Thus ends the sixty-third chapter of the *Harivamsa.*

NOTES

1. A number of Jaina works, like those of Jinasena (784 C.E.) and Pushpadanta (965 C.E.), deal with the life of Krishna and are also called *Harivamsapurana.* See *Harivamsapurana: Ein Abschnitt aus der Apabhramsha-Welthistorie "Mahapurana Tisatthimahapurisagunalankara" von Pushpadanta,* Herausgegeben von Ludwig Alsdorf, Alt- und Neu-Indische Studien 5 (Hamburg, 1936). *Harivamsa* is also the name of a Bengali poem by one Bhavananda (sixteenth–seventeenth century): *Harivamsa* (Dhaka: University of Dhaka 1932).

2. *The Harivamsa: The Khila or Supplement to the Mahabharata, Text as constituted in Its Critical Edition,* in *The Mahabharata, Text as constituted in Its Critical Edition,* vol. 5 (Poona: The Bhandarkar Oriental Research Institute, 1976); *mahakavya, purana, charita,* and *akhyana* are mentioned in 118.43, 49, and 50.

3. *Mahabharata* (CE) 1.2.69ab: *harivamsas tatah parva puranam khilasamjñitam.*

4. *The Harivamsapuranam* 2 vols. (Delhi: Nag Publishers, 1985). This is a reprint of an undated Venkateshvara Steam Press Mumbai edition of the Sanskrit text with Hindi translation. It has 318 chapters with a total of 16,137 marked stanzas. The *Harivamsaparvan* has 3,111 marked stanzas, the *Vishnuparvan* 7,817, and the *Bhavishyatparvan* 5,205.

5. See note 2 here; vol. 5 of the *Mahabharata* CE, text without apparatus. The critical text with apparatus is *The Harivamsa: For the First Time Critically Edited by P. L. Vaidya,* 2 vols. (Poona: The Bhandarkar Oriental Research Institute, 1969).

6. The *Harivamsa-parvan* of the CE has 2,442 marked stanzas, the *Vishnuparvan* 3,426, and the *Bhavishyatparvan* 205. The entire text consists of 118 chapters with a total of 6,073 marked stanzas.

7. D. H. H. Ingalls, "The *Harivamsa* as a Mahakavya," in *Melanges d'Indianisme à la mémoire de Louis Renou* (Paris: Editions E. de Boccard, 1968), 381–394. Ingalls points out that classical *kavya* is required to employ descriptions of seasons, of sunrise and sunset, of amorous scenes, of an army on the march, etc. He refers to Dandin (eighth century), who lists these requirements in his *Kavyadarsa* (1. 15-17). See *Kavyadarsa of Dandin* ed. S.K. Belvalkar (Poona: Bhandarkar Oriental Research Institute, 1924).

8. Sivaprasad Bhattacharyya, "Kalidasa and the *Harivamsa,*" *Journal of the Oriental Institute Baroda* 7, no. 3 (March 1958), 188.

9. Ludo Rocher, *The Puranas* (Wiesbaden: Harrassowitz, 1986).

10. Sivaprasad Bhattacharyya, "The Approximate Date of the *Harivamsa,*" *Journal of the Asiatic Society (Letters)* 22, no. 2 (1956), 156.

11. Keshavram K. Shastree, *The Hari-Vamsa,* abridged ed. (Poona: Bhandarkar Oriental Research Institute, 1978), vi.

12. A. M. T. Jackson, "Some Miscellaneous Notes: The Date of the *Harivamsa*," *Journal of the Royal Asiatic Society* (1908), 530.

13. Walter Ruben, "The *Krishnacharita* in the *Harivamsa* and Certain *Puranas*," *Journal of the American Asiatic Society* 61 (1941), 115–127.

14. Rocher, *Puranas*, 155.

15. P. L. Vaidya, ed., *The Harivamsa*, vol. 1, introduction, critical text, and notes (Poona: Bhandarkar Oriental Research Institute, 1969), xxxix.

16. Bhattacharyya, "Approximate Date of the *Harivamsa*," 161.

17. "If anything, one would say that the Harivamsa's style with its parataxis, its lack of sophistication, its occasional brutality of language, is somewhat more archaic than the *Ramayana*. And yet, from the evidence at our disposal we must judge the *Harivamsa* to be the later work." Ingalls, "The *Harivamsa* as a Mahakavya," 393.

18. That the poet Valmiki, author of the *Ramayana*, is mentioned in the vulgate 2.3.18 indicated that the *HV* could not have been composed before the *Ramayana*. Similarly, the mention of a Roman coin, the denarius, in the vulgate 2.55.50, suggested that the *HV* could not have been composed before the introduction of this currency. Neither of these passages is included in the critical text of the *Harivamsa*.

19. Shastree, *The Hari-Vamsa*, viii. In Shastree's abridged text, the 6,073 stanzas of the CE have been further reduced to a mere 1,808 marked stanzas. Shastree excludes all passages (like, for example, CE 65.43) that could point to a later date of the work.

20. Sivaprasad Bhattacharyya, "The Approximate Date of the *Harivamsa*," *Journal of the Asiatic Society (Letters)* 22, no. 2 (1956), 157–158.

21. There are only eight non-*anushtubh* meters in the critical text of the *Harivamsa*. All in all, there are only twenty-six stanzas composed in non-*anushtubh* meters in the CE. The entire rest of the work, 6,047 marked stanzas, is composed in the *anushtubh* meter. This metrical apparatus, then, would probably further point toward an early date of the work. The *Ramayana* has thirteen different meters; the *Mahabharata* has eighteen.

22. The *HV* possesses a prosodical feature that sets it apart from many *Puranas*: compound words that extend beyond the boundaries of verse feet are extremely rare in the CE, but they are a common phenomenon in the *Bhagavatapurana*, the *Vishnupurana*, and the *Brahmapurana*. In the entire text of the CE, I found only four cases in which a compound word extends beyond the boundaries of a *pada*. In the 1,323 stanzas of the *Brahmapurana* that deal with the Krishna story, there are 93 such occurrences, and in the 3,973 stanzas of the tenth *skandha* of the *Bhagavatapurana*, there are 303.

23. *Maharshivedavyasapranitam Shrimadbhagavatamahapuranam (mulamatram)* (Gorakhpur: Gita Press, 1996).

24. For a more detailed comparison of the Krishna story in the *HV* with that in the *BhP* and the *Vishnupurana*, see: Noel Sheth, *The Divinity of Krishna* (Delhi: Munshiram Manoharlal, 1984); Benjamin Preciado-Solis, *The Krishna Cycle in the Puranas* (Delhi: Motilal Barnasidass, 1984); M. M. Pathak, "Krishnacharitra in Vishnupurana Harivamsa and Bhagavata—A Comparative Study," *Journal of the Oriental Institute Baroda* 41, nos. 3–4 (March–June 1992), 327–337.

25. *Bhagavatapurana,* tenth *skandha,* chaps. 9, 10, and 11 (only the first six stanzas in chap. 11).

26. *HV* 51.14: *vyagrayam tu yashodayam;* and *BhP* 10.9.22: *vyagrayam matari prabhuh; HV* 51.17: *tiryaggatam udukhalam;* and *BhP* 10.10.26: *tiryag-gatam ulukhalam.*

27. *HV* 51.22: *vraje satyopayachitau;* see also *Ramayana* 2.68.16: *nikulavriksham asadya divyam satyopayachanam.*

28. *HV* 53.34: *na tatra vatsah sidanti na gavo netare janah / yatra tishthati lokanam bhavaya madhusudanah //.*

29. *HV* 60.13: *vishasyantam cha pashavo bhojya ye mahishadayah;* in the corresponding passage in the *BhP,* Krishna instructs the cowherds in what exactly they should cook and fry, and gives them a thoroughly vegetarian menu.

30. *HV* 63.24ab: *savaryamanah pitrbhir bhratrbhir matrbhis tatha. BhP* 10.29.8ab: *ta varyamanah patibhih pitrbhir bhratrbandhubhih.*

4

Krishna in the Tenth Book of the *Bhagavata Purana*

Edwin F. Bryant

Although Krishna is perhaps best known in the West as the speaker of the *Bhagavad Gita*, it is *the Shrimad Bhagavata Purana*, "The Beautiful History of God," popularly referred to as the *Bhagavata Purana*, or just the *Bhagavata*, that is the principal textual source dedicated to the actual narrative of Krishna's incarnation and activities.[1] It has not been Krishna's influential teachings in the *Bhagavad Gita* or his statesmanship in the *Mahabharata* that have produced the most popular and beloved stories about this deity. Rather, it has been his childhood *lilas*—play, pastimes, or frolics—during his infancy, childhood, and adolescence in the forests of Vrindavan, popularly known as Braj, among the cowherd men and women that have been most especially relished all over the Indian subcontinent over the centuries. This very personal depiction of God is the primary subject matter of the tenth book of the *Bhagavata Purana*.

The *Bhagavata* forms part of a corpus of texts known as the *Puranas*. The word *purana*, in Sanskrit, signifies "that which took place previously," that is to say, "ancient lore." These texts are vast repositories of social, cultural and religious information and devotional stories about the gods and their devotees such that almost everything that has come to be associated with "modern Hinduism" has its roots in the *Puranas* (see introduction). Several *Puranas* list the total number of *Puranas* as eighteen, one of which is the *Bhagavata*. The *Bhagavata Purana* occupies itself almost exclusively with Vishnu and his incarnations, and most particularly, in its tenth book, with the incarnation of Krishna. The work consists of twelve *skandhas*—cantos, subdivisions, or books—out of which the tenth book disproportionately makes up about one-quarter of the entire text.

It is this tenth book that has caused the *Purana* to be indisputably recognized as the most famous work of *Purana* literature, and this can be evidenced by the overwhelming preponderance of traditional commentaries on the text. Whereas most of the other *Puranas* have produced no traditional commentaries at all, and others only one or two, the *Bhagavata* has inspired eighty-one commentaries in Sanskrit alone that are presently available, and there were others that are no longer extant.[2] It has been translated into almost all the languages of India, with forty or so translations on record in Bengal alone. It was the first *Purana* to be translated into a European language: three different French translation were completed between 1840[3] and 1857, and these were followed, in turn, by a translation of the *Panchadhyaya*, the five chapters of the tenth book dedicated to Krishna's amorous pastimes with the *gopis*, in 1867, again in French.

The *Bhagavata* is unambiguously a Vaishnavite text (that is to say, it views Vishnu as the supreme deity), and its first nine books discuss in greater or lesser detail all the major incarnations prior to Krishna. The entire tenth book (which takes up about four thousand out of a total of a claimed eighteen thousand verses)[4] is dedicated to Krishna, and, indeed, as in the *Bhagavad Gita*, it is Krishna under his title of Bhagavan who gives his name to the entire *Purana*. While the *Bhagavata Purana*, then, is a Vaishnavite text in general, it is a Krishna-centered text in specific. Indeed, the Krishnaite theologies that emerged in the sixteenth century, initiated by influential teachers such as Vallabha and Chaitanya, find grounds to hold that it is not Krishna who is an incarnation of Vishnu but Vishnu who is a partial manifestation of Krishna. These sects extol Krishna as the supreme Absolute Truth from whom all other deities, including Vishnu, evolve, and the *Bhagavata Purana* is presented as the epistemological authority in this regard.

It is a thoroughly inconclusive task to assign specific dates to the *Puranas*, as exemplified by the considerable variation in the dates assigned by scholars to the *Bhagavata* itself. Not the least of the problems is that the *Puranas* are a fluid body of literature that went on transforming along the centuries through the process of transmission and adaptation. Unlike the genre of texts known as *shruti*,[5] which could never be tampered with, the *Puranas*, which are *smriti*,[6] had much more flexible expectations associated with them. While nonetheless sacred and authoritative, the *Puranas* transmit information for the general populace, and thus adjustments according to the day and age are not viewed askance—indeed, such fluidity is inherent in the claim made by most *Puranas* of presenting the "essence" of the *Veda* according to time and place, of explaining, expanding on, and even superseding the contents of previous scriptures, of revealing secret truths not contained elsewhere. They are thus ongoing revelation.

As the story goes, Vyasadeva, in the *Bhagavata* (1.5.1 and following), remained unfulfilled after compiling all the *Vedas*, the great Mahabharata Epic, and other *Puranas*, until the sage Narada informed him that the cause of his despondency was that he had not described the highest goal of knowledge. The result was the *Bhagavata*, the *galitam phalam*, the ripened fruit of the Vedic tree (1.1.3). Indeed, the Bhagavata describes itself as the essence of all the *Vedas* and *Itihasa* Epic (1.2.3; 1.3.42).

While the present *Puranas* contain recent material that can be traced well into historical times, they also contain ancient narratives and anecdotes from the earliest period of protohistory in South Asia.[7] It is thus futile to speak of absolute dates for any *Purana* as a whole, since one would have to speak of the age of individual sections within individual *Puranas*. I will simply note here that most scholars hold that the bulk of the material in most of the eighteen *Puranas*, as we find them today, was compiled by the Gupta period in around the fourth–sixth century c.e.[8] Understandably, then, there is no consensus regarding the date of the *Bhagavata Purana*, that is to say, the version of the text that has been handed down in its present form, although a number of scholars have considered it to be the latest of the eighteen primary *Puranas* composed in the South. There are a number of reasons to question this view,[9] and I am inclined to leave open the possibility that the *Bhagavata*, too, could have reached its final compilation in the Gupta period along with the other *Puranas*.

In terms of theology, in the *Mahabharata*, the *Harivamsha*, and the *Vishnu Purana*, there is no doubt that Krishna is an incarnation of Vishnu the transcendent Supreme Being. The roles, for the most part, have been somewhat reversed in the *Bhagavata*, as already mentioned: while there are abundant passages in the text that relate to Vishnu without explicitly subordinating him to Krishna, particularly in the books prior to the tenth, the general thrust of the tenth book prioritizes Krishna. In many ways, the very structure of the *Purana* culminates in the story of Krishna's incarnation, with the first nine books forming a prologue to the full glory of *Bhagavan* in the tenth book.

The books prior to the tenth teach various aspects of *bhakti-yoga*, the path of devotion, and are actually mostly associated with Vishnu as the goal of devotion. The reader of the text encounters the most famous Vaishnava role models in the first nine books—Prahlad, Dhruva, Gajendra, Ajamila, Bali, and so on—and these and other well-known stories familiarize the devotee with the requirements and expectations for the path, as well as providing illustrations of successful exemplars. The tenth book reveals the goal: Lord Krishna himself. Thus the prior books prepare the reader for the *Bhagavata's* full revelation of God's personal nature that is disclosed in the tenth book, a fact suggested by the *Purana* itself (2.10.1–2). In this, the *Bhagavata*, along with the *Gita*, which also promotes Krishna as the Supreme Being, is one of the two primary sources of scriptural authority that the Krishna sects rely on in their prioritization of Krishna as the highest Absolute Truth and personal godhead.

The crucial verse in the *Bhagavata* the Krishna theologians utilize to justify the preeminence of Krishna over all other manifestations of godhead is 1.3.28. Situated after a number of verses listing previous incarnations, this verse says: "These [other incarnations] are *amsha*, or *kala*,[10] partial incarnations, but *krishnas tu bhagavan svayam*, 'Krishna is *Bhagavan*, God, himself.'" This verse becomes something of a *mahavakya*, a "pivotal," "most important," or "representational statement" for the theology of the Krishna sects.

In terms of its philosophy, traditional sources enumerate six schools of thought that emerged from the Upanishadic period of the late Vedic age. The philosophy of the *Bhagavata* is a mixture of Vedanta[11] terminology, Samkhyan metaphysics,[12] and devotionalized *yoga* praxis.[13] Correlating the *Ishvara*, personal God, of the Yoga and Nyaya schools and *Brahman*, the absolute truth underpinning all reality, from the Upanishads and the Vedanta tradition, with Krishna, the tenth book promotes Krishna as the highest absolute personal aspect of godhead—the personality behind the term *Ishvara* and the ultimate aspect of *Brahman*. It is especially of great importance to the compiler of the tenth book of the *Bhagavata*, given the authoritative nature of the *Vedanta Sutras*, to stress that Krishna is *Brahman*, the absolute truth beyond matter (10.14.32; 10.10.33; 10.13.61; 10.40.29; 10.49.13; 10.73.23; 10.85.39). The text repeatedly stresses that Krishna's body is not made of *prakriti*, matter, like the forms of this world (10.2.42; 10.14.2) but is pure *Brahman* (10.3.24; 10.80.17), made up of pure bliss and knowledge (3.13; 10.13.54; 14.22; 48.7), and pure being (10.3.24; 10.3.13). Krishna is beyond the flow of the *gunas*, which are the activating forces and essential ingredients inherent in the production of the *prakritic* bodies of earth, water, fire, air, and ether (10.3.19; 10.3.24; 27.4; 37.22; 27.4; 29.14, etc.).[14]

It is also important to note that the tenth book of the *Bhagavata* does not subsume Krishna's form, or personal characteristics, as a secondary derivation from some higher impersonal absolute, as the various monistic sects of Vedanta propose. It is never said that Krishna's form and personality ultimately and eventually merge or dissolve into some supreme formless and impersonal Truth. While *Brahman* is described in the usual impersonal Upanishadic phraseology in many sections of the text, particularly in the earlier books, the indications from the tenth book are that *Brahman* also contains an eternal personal element, a realm where Krishna and his form are eternal.[15]

In terms of Krishna's descent into the world, the tenth book can be divided into two distinct sections equal in size: the childhood pastimes of Krishna in Vrindavan, called Braj *lila*, and the post-Vrindavan adult activities. The moods of the two sections are quite distinct. Many of the chapters in the second section contain stories of Krishna's battles with numerous demoniac kings, narrations of his heroic martial exploits, descriptions of his winning the hands of his various wives, and accounts of his statesmanship and lavish royal household life. The second section is regal and resonates far more closely with the tone of the *Mahabharata* than does the first section. The stories of the first section, in contrast, paint a delightfully different and far more intimate picture of the Supreme Being, and it is in this section that the term *lila*, a term essential to the understanding of the theology of the text and of the devotional traditions predicated upon it, as is shown by numerous contributions to this volume, occurs most frequently. The term *lila* suggests pure play, or spontaneous pastime, and it is in this first section that we find God stealing butter from his mother, feeding it to the monkeys, and hiding from her in fear as she chases him with a stick; it is also here that we find the supreme *Brahman* making love to the married cowherd damsels in the forests of Braj—in other words, here we find God at play.

Although, in a sense, all of God's activities, including creation, are play, the proper noun *lila* is especially used in the tenth book of the *Bhagavata* when God is enjoying himself in the beautiful and idyllic landscape of Braj, interacting with his friends and loved ones, devoid of any sense of mission or purpose. It is rarely used once Krishna leaves Braj and sets out to accomplish his mission and fulfill his promise to Brahma to kill demons (although sometimes it is used in the instrumental form when he dispatches demoniac adversaries in the sense of "effortlessly" or "playfully"), and it is never used in the *Bhagavad Gita*. The *Gita* presents us with Krishna as God in the mood of teacher imparting spiritual knowledge, and the *Mahabharata* presents us with Krishna as God in the mood of diplomat machinating to bring about the destruction of the hosts of armies so as to remove the burden of the earth; both depict God with a mission. The Braj section of the tenth book presents us with a description of God with no agenda other than to engage in *lila* with his most intimate devotees.

According to the *Bhagavata* (10.47.58), to be an intimate associate of God able to play with him by participating in this *lila* is the highest possible perfection of human existence. The ecstatic states of love experienced by the dwellers of Braj are not paralleled anywhere else in the text; the adult post-Braj relationships of Krishna with his other devotees seem quite formal in contrast. As such, the residents of Braj are the ultimate role models for the devotional path of *bhakti-yoga*: upon seeing the intense devotion of Krishna's devotees in Braj, Uddhava hankers to be a shrub or plant in their midst, so that he might come in contact with the dust of their feet (10.47.61). Entrance into the *lila*, then, is the supreme goal of life for the *Bhagavata* school, a goal considered to be unobtainable to all except God's highest and most intimate devotees. The text repeatedly tells us that he who is beyond the reach of the greatest of *yogis* is bound by the love of the residents of Braj (10.9.9), even to the point of being "controlled by them like a wooden puppet" (10.11.7).

A further term essential to a discussion of *lila* is *yogamaya*, the power of "divine illusion." The unqualified term *maya*, in the *Bhagavata*, is generally used in the same negative way that it is used in the *Gita* (7.14–15), and in Hindu thought in general, that is, to refer to the illusory power that keeps the *jiva* souls bewildered by the sense-objects of this world and ensnared in the *karmic* cycle of birth and death in *samsara* (10.23.52–53; 10.40.23). *Maya* has another face in the *Bhagavata*, however. This role of *maya* is especially discernible under the name Yogamaya, which occurs in the context of Krishna's *lila*. Yogamaya covers the pure liberated souls in the *lila* with her power of illusion, such that they are unaware of Krishna's real nature and thus relate to him not as God but rather as their friend, lover, or child, and so on. Were Yogamaya not to extend her influence in this way, the souls would realize Krishna's true nature and be incapable of interacting with him in *lila* in these intimate ways (10.7.32; 10.11.2 and following; 10.16.14; 10.19.14; 10.20.1; 10.42.22; 10.61.2). To put it differently, how could God truly play spontaneously and unceremoniously with anyone in the role of a son or friend, if everyone knew he was really God?

Unlike that of her *samsaric* counterpart, Yogamaya's power of illusion, then, is a highly desirable and positive one obtained only by the highest yogis. Indeed, the text suggests that Krishna's incarnation has, in reality, two motives: one is the "official" motive articulated in the *Gita,* and opening verses of the tenth book of the *Bhagavata*, to unburden the earth from the intolerable buildup of demoniac military power and to thus protect the righteous (e.g., *Gita* 4.7–8; *Bhagavata* 10.1.17 and following). The other is to attract the souls lost in *samsara* to the beauty of *lila* with God, and thus entice them to relinquish their attachment for the self-centered indulgences in the world of *samsara*, which simply perpetuate the cycle of *karma*, and thus of repeated birth and death (11.16–17).

The *Bhagavata* vividly illustrates the essential role of *yogamaya* in the world of *lila* in the eighth chapter (of the tenth book), which is included in the following selections, when Krishna's mother, Yashoda, looks into her son's mouth to see if he has eaten dirt (10.8.36). Gazing at her child, she sees the entire universe in his mouth. Becoming enlightened as to the real nature of both herself and Krishna, she immediately loses her ability to interact with him as his mother and begins to bow down at his feet, spout Vedantic-type philosophy, and eulogize him. Krishna immediately re-covers her with his *yogamaya*, causing her to lose her memory of the event so that she can again place him on her lap and continue with her maternal duties. Krishna, in other words, doesn't want to be God all the time; he wants to enjoy *lila* with his friends as an equal, or with his parents as a subordinate. As the text puts it: "For those who could understand, Bhagavan Krishna manifested the condition of [submitting] Himself to the control of his dependents in this world" (10.11.9).

Being subject to the influence of *yogamaya* and hence able to play such intimate roles in God's *lila*, then, is the highest and rarest boon of human existence. The text repeatedly says that not even the gods, or the most elevated personalities, or even Vishnu's eternal consort, the goddess of fortune herself, enjoy the grace bestowed on the residents of Braj (e.g., 10.9.20). Krishna's mother Yashoda was able to chase Krishna in anger, to spank him whom the greatest *yogis* of all cannot reach even in their minds (10.9.9). So elevated are the residents of Braj.

Krishna's *lila* extends beyond the actual acts performed by Krishna. Meditating upon his *lila* is a process of *yoga*, "union with the divine." Five of the seventeen verses where the term is used in book 10 as a proper noun (10.11.33; 10.35.1; 10.35.26; 10.47.54; 10.69.39) occur in the context of the residents of Braj singing about Krishna's *lila*. Hearing, singing about, and meditating upon Krishna's *lila* are the primary *yogic* activities in the *Bhagavata* school and, indeed, head up the list of the nine processes of *bhakti-yoga* outlined in book 7: hearing about Vishnu/Krishna, singing about him, remembering him, serving him, worshiping him, offering obeisances to him, dedicating all one's actions to him, confiding in him as a friend, and offering one's body and belongings to his service (7.5.23–24). The entire *Purana* is recited because king Parikshit, who had seven days to live, asked sage Shuka what a person at the point of death should hear, chant, and remember (1.19.38); the answer is the chanting of Krishna's names (2.1.11) and meditation upon his personal form (2.1.19). *Bhakti-yoga* involves saturating the senses with objects connected to Krishna's *lila*, and constantly filling the mind with thoughts of him. It is a process that transforms the focus of the mind and senses, rather than attempting to shut them down, as outlined in the classical *yoga* of Patanjali, and a saint is one whose mind and senses are used in this fashion (10.13.2). Singing and hearing about Krishna's *lila* with the senses of tongue and ear are two prime activities in this regard, and the residents of Braj are constantly and spontaneously engaged in this type of *bhakti-yoga*. According to the *Bhagavata*, although the present age of Kali-yuga is a "storehouse of faults," it has one major redeeming quality: simply by chanting about Krishna, one is freed from self-centered attachments and attains the highest destination (12.3.51). The same applies to hearing the stories about Krishna (11.6.48–49; 10.90.46; 10.6.44). Echoing the *Gita* (8.6–7), the *Bhagavata* says that anyone whose mind is absorbed in Krishna's feet is liberated from the material world at the time of death (10.2.37; 10.90.50), does not experience suffering while still within it (10.11.58; 10.39.37; 10.87.40; 10.90.49), and ultimately attains Krishna's abode (10.90.50).

This leads to another striking feature of the *yoga* of the *Bhagavata*: not only are Krishna's devotees awarded liberation, but so, too, are even his enemies—Putana, a devourer of children (10.6.35); the demon Agha (10.12.33) and various others (10.74.45; 10.78.9–10l; 10.66.24; 10.87.23)—merely by dint of being absorbed in thoughts of Krishna, albeit in an inimical mood. Not surprisingly, if even those inimical to Krishna are involuntarily liberated simply by coming into contact with him, irrespective of their motives, then anyone and everyone is eligible to voluntarily engage in the process of *bhakti-yoga* and attain the goal of selfless devotion, irrespective of caste, social status, race, or gender. Indeed, in accepting the lowly *gopis* as the highest of all *yogis*, including even all other *bhakti-yogis*, the *Bhagavata* significantly surpasses the *Gita's* mere acceptance of women devotees as qualified for liberation (9.32), a statement that itself was radical for the times. (As an aside, it was these very *gopi* passages that incurred Victorian disapproval from certain quarters, and caused the *Bhagavata* to be disparaged by most Western scholars in the colonial period).

Before concluding, it is worthy of mention, if only in passing, that the final redactor of the *Bhagavata* is not only a philosopher or theologian but an epic poet; there are entire sections of the text, particularly the *panchadhyaya*, the five chapters of the tenth book dedicated to Krishna's amorous pastimes with the *gopis*, that exhibit all the characteristics of exquisite *kavya* poetry (e.g., as outlined in the literary text the *Sahityadarpana* 7.559). Overall, the tenth book of the *Bhagavata* ranks as an outstanding product of Sanskrit literature, a fact that has yet to receive the scholarly attention it merits. Perhaps more significantly, as this volume itself exemplifies, the *Bhagavata* has inspired more derivative literature, poetry, drama, dance, theater, and art than any other text in the history of Sanskrit literature, with the possible exception of the *Ramayana*.

Finally, as a text, the *Bhagavata* presents itself not just as a record of sacred history but as a literary substitute for Krishna after his departure from the world—the *vangamayavatara*, or literary incarnation of God. The concluding verse of the entire tenth book says that, by reading, hearing, and reciting the text itself, one is interacting directly with God (10.90.49–50). Likewise, the eleventh book, which concludes the narration of the Krishna story, ends with the same message in its final verse (11.31.28). The point is stressed still further by having the concluding verses of the entire *Purana* claim that those born after the departure of Krishna to his abode who are fortunate enough to encounter the *Bhagavata Purana*, listen to it, read it, and contemplate it constantly with a devoted heart will attain liberation, just as those who were fortunate enough to personally encounter Krishna when he was on earth were awarded liberation (12.13.18). The text thus presents itself as a fully empowered incarnation of Krishna for all future generations.

Be that as it may, the stories of the tenth book of the *Bhagavata* are well known and beloved to every Hindu household across the length and breadth of the Indian subcontinent. They have inspired numerous spiritual seekers to renounce the world in quest of Krishna's lotus feet, countless more to engage in the process of *bhakti-yoga*, and generations of artists, dramatists, poets, singers, writers, dancers, architects, and temple-patrons across the centuries to represent their narratives. One need only consider the number of contributions in this volume that are predicated on its narratives to get a sense of the significance of the tenth book on the religious landscape of Hinduism. The following selections attempt to capture the appeal of these stories by presenting some of the best known *lilas* from the text. (See Schweig, chapter 18 here, for a sample of the *gopi* passages.)

Chapter 3
Krishna's Birth

1. "In due course of time, an extremely auspicious moment endowed with all favorable qualities arrived. At the time of [Krishna's] birth, all the constellations and stars were benevolent. The constellation was Rohini, which is presided over by Brahma.

2. "The quarters were clear and the sky covered with clusters of visible stars. On the earth, there was an auspicious abundance of mines, pastures, villages, and towns.

3. "The rivers contained crystal-clear water and the ponds were beautiful with lotuses. Rows of trees offered eulogies with loud sounds of bees and birds.

4. "A fresh breeze blew in that region, pleasing the senses and carrying pleasant fragrances, and the sacred fires of the brahmins[16] blazed forth, undisturbed.

5. "The minds of the ascetics and the gods were peaceful, and kettle drums resounded in unison at the time when the unborn One was born.

6. "The *kinnaras* and *gandharvas* burst into song, the *siddhas* and *charanas* offered prayers, and the *vidyadharas* joyfully danced along with the *apsaras*.[17]

7. "The sages and demigods, overflowing with happiness, showered flowers, and the clouds rumbled very mildly in resonance with the ocean.

8. "At midnight, when deep darkness had arisen, Janardan[18] Krishna, was born. Vishnu who dwells in the heart of everyone appeared in Devaki, who resembled a goddess, just as the full moon appears in the eastern quarter.

9–10. "Vasudeva saw that amazing, lotus-eyed child, with his four arms wielding the weapons of the conch and the mace, and so on.[19] He bore the mark of *shrivatsa*, and the *kaustubha* jewel was radiant on his neck.[20] Clad in a yellow garment, he appeared as beautiful as a dark rain cloud. He was resplendent with a magnificent belt, and arm and wrist bracelets, and his profuse locks were encircled with the luster of a helmet and earrings made of valuable *vaidurya* gems.

11. "Upon seeing his son, Hari, Vasudeva was overwhelmed by the auspicious occasion of Krishna's incarnation. His eyes were wide

winged creatures, and thorns, or even perform their household duties, they experienced considerable agitation of mind.

26. After a short time, O kingly sage, Balarama and Krishna were walking easily in Gokula on their feet without bruised knees.

27. Thereafter, Bhagavan Krishna, along with Balarama, played with the boys of Braj of his same age, awakening the bliss of the women of Braj.

28. Observing the delightful childish restlessness of Krishna, the *gopis* assembled together and spoke tongue-in-cheek as follows [in the presence] of his mother, who was listening:

29. "Sometimes, he releases the calves untimely, and laughs when cries [of protest] are raised. Moreover, he eats the tasty milk and whey stolen by means of his thieving strategies. He divides [the curds and whey] and feeds the monkeys. If he does not eat, he breaks the pot. When goods are not available and he leaves angry with the household, he blames the children.

30. "When it is out of reach of his hands, he devises a system [to obtain it] by arranging benches and grinding mortars. Knowing what has been placed inside the pots hanging on rope slings, that cunning boy [makes] a hole [in them] during that time of day when the *gopis* are very absorbed in household chores. His own body, which bears clusters of precious jewels, functions as a light in the dark house.

31. "While he is perpetuating such audacities, he passes urine and other things in our houses. Although his deeds are accomplished by means of thieving strategies, he outwardly appears as if virtuous." In this manner, these affairs were related by the women as they gazed at Krishna's beautiful face with its fearful eyes. With a smiling countenance, Yashoda did not want to scold Krishna.

32. Once, when Balarama and the other cowherd boys were playing, they complained to Mother Yashoda: "Krishna has eaten mud."

33. Yashoda was concerned for his welfare, and so scolded Krishna, whose eyes appeared to be struck by fear. Grasping him in her hand, she said to him:

34 "Why have you eaten mud secretly, you unrestrained boy? These young friends of yours are making this allegation, and so is your elder brother."

35. "Mother, I didn't eat any mud. They are all spreading false accusations. If you think they are speaking the truth, then look into my mouth yourself."

36. "If that is the case, then open wide," she said. Lord Hari, Krishna, whose supremacy cannot be constrained, but who is God assuming the form of a human boy for play, opened wide.

37–38. Yashoda saw there the universe of moving and nonmoving things; space; the cardinal directions; the sphere of the earth with its oceans, islands, and mountains; air and fire; the moon and the stars. She saw the circle of the constellations, water, light, the wind, the sky, the evolved senses, the mind, the elements, and the three *guna* qualities.[26]

39. She saw this universe, with all of its variety, differentiated into bodies, which are the repositories of souls. She saw time, Nature, and *karma.* Seeing Braj as well as herself in the gaping mouth in the body of her son, she was struck with bewilderment:

40. "Is this actually a dream? Is it a supernatural illusion, or is it just the bewilderment of my own intelligence? Or is it, in fact, some inherent divine power of this child of mine?

41. "Therefore, I offer homage to his feet, which are the support of this world. From them, and through their agency, this world manifests. Their true nature cannot be known by the senses nor by reason. They are very difficult to perceive by thought, words, deeds, or intellect.

42. "He is my refuge. Through his illusory power arise ignorant notions such as: 'I am I; he over there is my husband; this is my son, I am the virtuous wife, protectress of all the wealth of the ruler of Braj; all the *gopis* and *gopas,* along with the wealth derived from the cattle, are mine.'"

43. Then the omnipotent supreme Lord cast his *yogamaya* power of illusion in the form of maternal affection over the *gopi* who had realized the truth.

44. Immediately, the *gopi's* memory was erased. She sat her son up on her lap and returned to her previous state of mind, with her heart full of intense love.

45. She considered Hari, Krishna, whose glories are sung by the three *Vedas,* the *Upanishads,* Samkhya *yoga* and the *satvata* sages,[27] to be her very own son.

Chapter Nine
Krishna's Favor Falls on the *Gopi Yashoda*

1. Once upon a time, when the house servants were engaged in other chores, Yashoda, the wife of Nanda, churned the milk herself.

2. Remembering the songs about the activities of her child, she sang them while she was churning yogurt.

3. Yashoda churned, revolving back and forth. Her bracelets were moving on her arms, which were tired from pulling the rope, and her earrings were swaying. *Malati* jasmine flowers dropped from her hair, and her face, with its beautiful eyebrows, was sweating. She

wore a linen cloth bound by a girdle on her broad sloping hips, and her two quivering breasts lactated due to affection for her son.

4. Hari, Krishna, approached his mother as she was churning, desiring to drink her breast milk. Grasping the stirring stick, he obstructed her, invoking her love.

5. He climbed on her lap. Looking at his smiling face, she allowed him to drink from her breast, which was lactating from affection. But she hastily put him down, while he was still unsatisfied, and rushed off when the milk that had been on the fire, boiled over.

6. Enraged and biting his quivering red lower lip with his teeth, Krishna broke the butter churning pot with a stone. With phony tears in his eyes he went inside to a hiding place, and ate the freshly churned butter.

7. Yashoda removed the boiling milk and reentered again. Noticing the broken vessel, she inspected that deed of her son. Not seeing him present, she laughed.

8. She spied him standing on top of the base of a mortar. He was wantonly distributing fresh butter to a monkey from a hanging pot, his eyes anxious on account of his thievery. She stealthily approached her son from behind.

9. Seeing her with stick in hand, Krishna hastily climbed down from there and fled, as if in fear. The *gopi* ran after him, whom the minds of *yogis*, directed by the power of austerity, are not able to reach.

10. The slender-waisted mother pursued Krishna, her progress impeded by the burden of her broad moving hips. Followed by a retinue of flowers fallen from her braid that had become loosened from haste, she seized him.

11. Grasping his arm she chastised him, making him fearful. Looking up with eyes agitated with fright, the guilty boy was crying and rubbing his two eyes, smearing the mascara with his hands.

12. Yashoda was affectionate to her child, and so threw away the stick upon realizing that her son was frightened. Unaware of the power of her son, she wanted to bind him with a rope.

13. Krishna has no beginning and end, no inside and no outside. He is the beginning and end and inside and outside of the universe. He is the universe.

14. The *gopi* bound him with a rope to the mortar as if he were a common being. She considered Krishna, who is the unmanifest Truth beyond sense perception in the form of a human, to be her own son.

15. That rope for binding her guilty child was short by two fingers. So the *gopi* joined another one together with the first.

16. When even that also was too short, she joined another one with that, but however many ropes she brought forth, they were also two fingers lacking.

17. In this way, while all the *gopis* chuckled with amusement, Yashoda joined together all the ropes in her household. Smiling, she was struck with wonder.

18. Seeing the exertion of his mother whose limbs were sweating, and whose wreath of flowers had fallen from her hair, Krishna became compliant in his own binding.

19. Indeed, by this act, dear Parikshit, the quality of subservience to a devotee was demonstrated by Hari, Krishna, despite the fact that his only constraint is self-induced. By him this universe, along with those who control it, is controlled.

20. Neither Brahma, nor Shiva, nor even Shri, the goddess of fortune, despite being united with his body, obtained the benediction that the *gopi* obtained from Krishna, the giver of liberation.

21. God, this son of the *gopi*, is not attained as easily in this world by embodied beings, nor by the wise, nor by the knowers of the self, as he is by those who have devotion.

Chapter 12
Playing in Braj (The Killing of the Demon Agha)

1. One day, Hari, Krishna, made up his mind to have breakfast in the forest. After arising at dawn and waking up his *gopa* friends with the pleasant sound of his horn, he set forth, herding the calves in front.

2. Thousands of adorable boys, equipped with flutes, bugle horns, staffs, and slings, joined him. Placing ahead their respective calves, which accompanied them in the thousands, they merrily set out.

3. Combining their own calves with the unlimited calves of Krishna, the cowherd boys diverted themselves in *lila* while they grazed their cows here and there.

4. Although they were decorated with gold, jewels, *gunja* berries, and crystals, they adorned themselves with minerals, peacock feathers, bunches of flowers, young shoots, and fruits.

5. They stole each others slings and other things and, when detected, they threw them to some distant spot. Those who were in that spot then threw them further still. Eventually they returned them, laughing.

6. If Krishna went off in the distance to view the beauty of the forest, they would enjoy themselves by touching him, saying "I was first, I was first!"

7. Some played their flutes, some blew their horns. Others hummed with the bees and still others cooed with the cuckoos.

8. They chased the shadowless birds, moved gracefully with the swans, seated themselves with the cranes, and danced with the peacocks.

9. Tugging at the young monkeys, they climbed the trees with them. Then, imitating them, they joined them in swinging through the trees.

10. Jumping about with the frogs, they got soaked by the splashes from the river. They laughed at their own shadows and hurled abuse at their echoes.

11. In this way, those boys who had accumulated heaps of merit roamed about in pleasure with Krishna.[28] He is the experience of the bliss of *Brahman* for the wise, the supreme Deity for those who are dedicated to his service, and the child of a human being for those who are absorbed in ignorance.

12. Although the dust of His feet is not obtained even after many births of austerities by *yogis* with controlled minds, He has personally become an object of vision for the residents of Braj. How, then, can their fortune be described?

Chapter 16
The Banishment of Kaliya

17. Searching for their beloved Krishna along the path by means of his footprints, which were marked with the signs of God,[29] the cowherd folk went to the banks of the Yamuna.

18. Seeing the footsteps of the Lord of their community interspersed here and there among the other footprints of the cows on the path, O King, they rushed along in haste. These footprints bore the marks of the flag, thunderbolt, goad, barley, and lotus.

19. Seeing Krishna motionless within that reservoir of water in the distance and enveloped in the coils of the serpent within the lake, and seeing the cows and cowherd men traumatized everywhere, the cowherd folk were struck with utter despair and cried out in distress.

20. The *gopis'* minds were attached to the unlimited Lord. Remembering his affectionate smiles, glances, and words, they were overcome with the utmost grief as their beloved was being seized by the serpent. They perceived the three worlds as void without their dearest.[30]

21. They prevented Krishna's mother from following her child [into the lake], although they were as distressed as she. Pouring forth their sorrow, and narrating stories about the darling of Braj, each one remained corpse-like, with their gaze fixed on the face of Krishna.

22. Lord Balarama was aware of the potency of Krishna. Seeing Nanda and the others, whose very life was Krishna, entering that lake, he restrained them.

23. Krishna remained for some time imitating the behavior of a human being in this manner. Then, seeing that His own Gokula community, including women and children, that had no shelter other than him, was completely distressed, he understood that this was on account of him and arose up from the bonds of the serpent.

24. The serpent, his coils tormented by the extended body of Krishna, released him. Enraged, the serpent raised up his hoods and drew himself erect as he looked at the Lord. His face had motionless eyes like burning charcoal, and his nostrils were breathing like frying pans of poison.

25. Krishna circled around him, toying with him. Just like Garuda, the king of birds,[31] Krishna likewise maneuvered around looking for His opportunity. The serpent had eyes fiery with dreadful poison and was repeatedly licking the two corners of his mouth with his forked tongue.

26. Bending the raised neck of the serpent, whose strength had been depleted by this circling around, Krishna, the Original Being, climbed onto its massive hoods. Then, that original teacher of all art forms danced, his lotus feet reddened by contact with the piles of jewels on the serpent's head.[32]

27. Then, his followers—the celestial *gandharvas*, *siddhas*, sages, *charanas*, and young wives of the gods—seeing that Krishna had begun to dance, immediately approached in delight with eulogies, offerings, flowers, songs, musical instruments, and various types of drums such as *mridangas*, *panavas*, and *anakas*.

28. Krishna, who chastises the wicked, crushed whichever head of that hundred-and-one-headed snake would not bend, with blows of his feet, O King. The snake's life span became depleted and he was whirling around. He vomited blood profusely from his nose and mouth and was overcome by utter desperation.

29. The serpent was breathing intensely out of anger and was discharging poison from his eyes. Whichever head he raised up, Krishna forced him to bow low, striking it with his feet as he danced. As he was being worshiped with flowers, that most ancient Being brought the snake under submission in the lake.

30. The serpent, his limbs broken, and his one thousand hoods battered by that wondrous dancing, was spewing out blood from his mouths, O King. He remembered that most ancient being, Narayana,[33] the teacher of all moving and nonmoving entities, and surrendered to him in his mind.

Chapter 25
Krishna Lifts Govardhan Hill

1. Shri Shuka said: "At this, O King, Indra understood that his own worship had been abandoned, and became enraged with the *gopas*, headed by Nanda, who had accepted Krishna as their Lord.

2. "Thinking himself to be Lord, Indra summoned the host of clouds called Samvartaka, which bring about the annihilation of the universe.[34] Furious, he spoke the following words:

3. " 'Just see the extent of the intoxication of the forest-dwelling *gopas* produced because of their wealth. They have taken refuge in Krishna, a mortal, and now they neglect the gods.

4. " 'Abandoning meditative knowledge, they desire to cross over the ocean of material existence through ritualistic so-called sacrifices that are like unstable boats.

5. " 'By taking shelter of Krishna, a boastful, childish, stubborn, ignorant mortal who thinks himself to be a great scholar, the *gopas* have made an enemy out of me.

6. " 'Destroy the arrogance of these people caused by the intoxication of riches. They are steeped in wealth and their egos have been inflated by Krishna. Bring destruction to their livestock.

7. " 'As for me, I will mount my elephant Airavata,[35] and follow you to Braj accompanied by the immensely powerful host of Maruts,[36] with the intention of destroying the cattle station of Nanda.' "

8. Shri Shuka said: "Ordered in this way by Indra, the clouds, unleashed from their moorings, vigorously released torrents of rain on Nanda's Gokula.

9. "Flashing forth with lightening bolts and roaring with claps of thunder, they showered down hail as they were urged on by the fierce hosts of Maruts.

10. "When the clouds had released incessant torrents of rain as thick as pillars, the earth became inundated with floods of water. Low ground could not be distinguished from high ground.

11. "The livestock, shivering because of the excessive wind and rain, and the *gopas* and *gopis*, afflicted by cold, approached Krishna for protection.

12. "Covering their heads and shielding their children with their bodies, shivering and tormented by the rain, they approached the soles of the feet of the Lord:

13. " 'Krishna, most virtuous Krishna, Master—you are compassionate to your devotees. Please protect Gokula, which accepts you as Lord, from the wrath of this divinity.'

14. "Seeing them being pounded unconscious by the excessive wind and hail, Lord Hari deliberated on what the incensed Indra had done:

15. "'Indra unleashes rain full of hail and unseasonal and excessive fierce wind in order to destroy us because we neglected his offering.

16. "'Under these circumstances, I will adopt the appropriate counter-measures through my mystic power. I will destroy the ignorance and pride born of opulence of those who, out of stupidity, think of themselves as lords of the world.

17. "'The bewilderment caused by thinking of oneself as lord is inappropriate for the demigods who are endowed with a godly nature. My breaking the pride of the impure for their peace of mind is a suitable thing to do.

18. "'Therefore, I make this pledge: I shall bring about the protection of the cowherd community by my own mystic power. They accept me as their Lord, their shelter is in me, and they are my family.'

19. "Saying this, Vishnu lifted up the mountain of Govardhan with one hand and held it effortlessly just like a child holds a mushroom.

20. "Then the Lord spoke to the cowherds: 'Mother, father, and residents of Braj, enter the cavity under the mountain along with your herds of cows at your leisure.

21. "'Please do not entertain any fear that the mountain might fall from my hand during this time. Enough of your fear of the rain and wind! I have arranged shelter from them for you.'

22. "At this, their minds were pacified by Krishna, and they entered the cavity with their wealth, herds, and dependents in accordance with the available space.

23. "Giving up concern for hunger and thirst, and any expectation of comfort, Krishna held up the mountain for seven days. Watched by those residents of Braj, he did not move from that spot.

24. "Subdued and helpless, and with his plan thwarted, Indra reigned in his clouds. He was completely astonished by Krishna's mystic power.

25. "When he saw that the sky was cloudless, the fierce rain and wind had desisted, and the sun had arisen, Krishna, the lifter of Govardhan hill, spoke to the *gopas*:

26. "'Give up your fear, O *gopas*, and come out with your wives, possessions, and children. The wind and rain have desisted, and the rivers are for the most part without [flood] water.'

27. "At this, those *gopas*, women, children, and elders took their respective cows and their paraphernalia, which had been loaded onto carts, and gradually came out.

28. "While all beings watched, Bhagavan, the Lord, effortlessly placed that hill back in its place where it had been previously.
29. "The residents of Braj were filled with the force of love, and approached him with embraces, or with whatever was appropriate. And the *gopis* happily offered auspicious benedictions, and lovingly worshiped him with yogurt, unhusked barley, and so on.
30. "Overwhelmed with love, Yashoda, Rohini, Nanda, and Balarama, best of the strong, embraced Krishna and offered benedictions.
31. "The hosts of gods, the *siddhas, sadhyas, gandharvas,* and *charanas* in the heavens praised Krishna with satisfaction, and released showers of flowers, O Parikshit, descendent of Prithu.
32. "Directed by the gods, they played conches and kettledrums in the celestial realms, while the leaders of the *gandharvas,* headed by Tumbaru, sang.
33. "Then, O King, Hari, along with Balarama, proceeded to his own cow-pen surrounded by the affectionate cow herders. The *gopis* happily went on their way singing about his deeds of this kind. Their hearts were touched."

The following narrative represents the adult Krishna after he has left the forests of Braj and set about his mission of reestablishing *dharma.*

Chapter 69
The Vision of Krishna's Householder Life

1. Shri Shuka said: "After hearing that Naraka had been killed, and that there had been a marriage of many women by one person, Krishna, Narada desired to see this:
2. "'It is really amazing that one person with one body has married sixteen thousand women, and lives simultaneously in many houses.'
3. "Saying this, the eager sage of the gods came to see Dvaraka. It resounded with swarms of bees and flocks of birds, and had flowery parks and pleasure groves.
4. "It was filled with the loud sounds of swans and cranes in lakes filled with blooming *kumuda* white lotuses, *kahlara* white lotuses, *ambhoja* lotuses, *indivara* blue lotuses, and water lilies.
5. "It was endowed with nine hundred thousand mansions made of silver and crystal with external appendages of gold and jewels, and was distinctive with great emeralds.
6. "It was charming with residences of gods, assembly halls and buildings, and laid-out markets, crossroads, paths, and throughways. Its terraces, streets, courtyards, and roads were sprinkled with water, and the heat was blocked by flying flags and banners.

7. "Hari's private inner chambers were in that city; they were beautiful, venerated by the celestial guardians of the quarters of the world, and exhibited the personal skill of Tvashta, the architect of the gods.

8. "Those chambers were beautifully decorated with sixteen thousand residences. Narada entered one of these magnificent houses of [Krishna's] wives.

9–11. "It was supported with coral pillars with choicest overlays of *vaidurya* gems, and decorated with walls made of sapphire, and floors whose luster never faded. There were canopies constructed by Tvashta, with hanging strings of pearls, and ivory seats and couches embellished with the best quality jewels. There were women dressed in beautiful garments with golden ornaments on their necks, and men wearing jeweled earrings, turbans, fine clothes, and armor.

12. "The darkness was dispelled by the light of clusters of jeweled lamps, O dear king. Peacocks danced there on the variegated pinnacles of the houses. Seeing the incense and *aguru* billowing forth from the holes [in the latticed windows], dear Parikshit, they thought them to be clouds and cried out.[37]

13. "The sage saw the Lord of the Satvatas with His wife in that house. She was always accompanied by a thousand maidservants who were equal in dress, age, beauty, and qualities, and she was fanning Krishna with an ox-tail fan with a golden handle.

14. "Bhagavan Krishna, the most eminent of those who uphold *dharma*, saw Narada and immediately rose up from the bed of Shri, the goddess of fortune. He offered homage to both Narada's feet with his head, which was bedecked with a helmet. Then, with his hands folded in respect, he insisted that [Narada] sit on his own personal seat.

15. "Although he is the ultimate *guru* of the world, and the water that washes his feet [the Ganga] is the ultimate holy place, Krishna, the Lord of the righteous, washed Narada's feet and actually carried the water from that on His own head. Brahmanyadeva, 'the Lord of Brahmins,' is the name applied to him for this quality.

16. "After worshiping the most eminent of the celestial sages according to scriptural injunctions, Krishna, the ancient sage Narayana, friend of mankind, spoke measured words as sweet as nectar: 'Pray tell, master, what can we do for your good self?'

17. "Shri Narada said: 'O almighty one, it is certainly not surprising that you, the master of all the worlds, are the friend of all creatures, and the chastiser of the wicked. You are widely praised, and we know well that your incarnation is due to your own free will. It is for the protection and maintenance of the world, and for [bestowing] liberation.

18. "'I have seen your two lotus feet that give liberation to people. Brahma and the other [gods] of profound intelligence meditate upon them in the heart. They are the grounds of deliverance for those fallen into the well of *samsara*, the cycle of birth and death. Bless me that my remembrance [of them] will remain, so that I can travel about meditating [on them].'

19. "Thereafter, Narada entered another residence of Krishna's wives, O dear king, desiring to witness the *yogamaya* of the Lord of the lords of *yoga*.

20. "There, he [saw] Krishna again, this time playing with dice with his beloved and with Uddhava. Narada was worshiped with the highest devotion, by [Krishna's] rising up to greet him and [offering] him a seat, etc.

21. "Narada was asked by Krishna, who appeared as if unaware: 'When did you arrive, sir? What can we, who are imperfect, do for those who are perfect?'

22. "'Therefore please tell us, O Brahmin, make this birth auspicious for us.' Narada was amazed. He rose silently and went to another residence.

23. "There, too, he also saw Govinda, Krishna, who was pampering his children and infants. Then, in another residence, Narada saw that preparations had been made for taking a bath.

24. "Elsewhere, Krishna was offering oblations into the three sacred fires,[38] worshiping with the five sacrifices,[39] feeding the twice-born, and eating their remnants.[40]

25. "In another place, Krishna was sitting down at dusk and silently chanting *japa mantras*.[41] In one place he was maneuvering around in the fencing area with sword and shield.

26. "Elsewhere, Krishna, the elder brother of Gada, was riding horses, elephants, and chariots, and somewhere else again, he was lying on a couch, being praised by bards.

27. "In one place, Krishna was consulting with his ministers such as Uddhava, while elsewhere he was enjoying water sports surrounded by women and courtesans.

28. "In another place he was giving nicely decorated cows to distinguished members of the twice-born castes, and listening to auspicious stories from the *Puranas* and epic histories.

29. "At some point, in some other house of a beloved, Krishna was laughing by telling jokes, while elsewhere he was pursuing *dharma*, *artha*, 'economic prosperity,' or *kama*, 'sensual enjoyment.'[42]

30. "In one place he was meditating on the supreme Being who is beyond *prakriti*, and serving his *gurus* with pleasures, desirable objects, and worship.

31. "And somewhere else, Keshava Krishna was preparing for war against some people, and elsewhere again, alliances with others. Still elsewhere, Krishna was contemplating the welfare of the righteous, along with Balarama.

32. "[Narada saw] him making arrangements with due pomp for traditional marriages for his sons and daughters, with suitable brides and grooms at the appropriate time.

33. "He saw great celebrations by the Lord of the lords of *yoga* for his children when they were sent off, and when they returned. The people were amazed at these.

34. "In some places, [Narada saw] Krishna offering sacrifices to all the gods with elaborate rituals, or fulfilling his *dharma* by [constructing] monasteries, groves, and wells.

35. "In other places, he was roaming about in the hunt, mounted on a horse from the Sindh province, and killing sacrificial animals, surrounded by the Yadu heroes.

36. "Elsewhere, the Lord of *yogis* was wondering about in disguise among his ministers in the inner section of the city, desiring to know the attitudes of each of them.

37. "After seeing this exhibition of *yogamaya* by Krishna, who was following human ways, Narada said to Hrishikesh Krishna smilingly:

38. " 'We know that your *yogamaya* is hard to perceive, even for magicians. But it will manifest, O Soul of the lords of *yoga*, by service to your lotus feet.

39. " 'Give me your leave, O God—I will wonder about the worlds, which are overflowing with your glories, singing about your *lilas*, which purify the earth.' "

NOTES

1. The material for this section is drawn from my translation of the tenth book, *Krishna: the Beautiful Legend of God: Srimad Bhagavata Purana Book 10* (London: Penguin, 2004).

2. Madhva, in the thirteenth century, refers to commentaries that are not presently available, as does Jiva Gosvamin in the sixteenth century.

3. Wilson's translation of the *Vishnu Purana* (Delhi: Nag, reprint 1980), also appeared in 1840.

4. The actual number is 16,256.

5. "That which is heard," or transhuman revelation not composed by humans, namely, the early Vedic corpus.

6. "That which is remembered," or indirect revelation, divine in origin, but composed via human agency, namely, most other pan-Indic classical texts later than the Vedic corpus.

39. According to the *Laws of Manu* (3.69–71), the *mahayajna*, "great sacrifice," consists of five offerings, to Brahma, the gods, the forefathers, humans, and ghosts.

40. As noted earlier, eating the remnants of food offered to the deity or to saintly persons is called *prasada*, and is considered purifying.

41. *Japa* is meditation upon the repetition of the name of a deity.

42. The fulfillment of *dharma*, *artha*, and *kama*, along with *moksha*, liberation, are the four *purusharthas*, or goals of human life.

PART II

Regional Literary Expressions

5

Orissa: Shri Krishna Jagannatha: The *Mushali-parva* from Sarala's *Mahabharata*

Bijoy M. Misra

On the eastern coast of India, on the shores of the Bay of Bengal, in the town of Puri in the state of Orissa, stands the magnificent temple of Shri Jagannatha, whom the local people worship as the "Lord of the Universe."[1] The massive structure (two hundred and fourteen feet high) and many smaller structures in the complex occupy a space of about forty-two thousand square feet, surrounded by a twenty-foot wall. The *nagara*[2]-style temple, called the Badadeula (Big Temple) in the local Oriya language, is about a thousand years old, constructed between the eighth and twelfth centuries. Together with the large temple complex at Bhubaneshwar and the "Black Pagoda"[3] of Konarka, the temple at Puri is among the finest specimens of Orissan art and architecture in post-Guptan India. The temple along with the other pilgrim sites in the town have made Puri a major destination for Hindu pilgrims since 800 c.e. The Ratha Jatra (Car Festival)[4] at Puri is world-famous for its pageantry, and for the faith and devotional ecstasy of the attendees.

The Deities

The mystery of the deities in the temple at Puri has been a topic of diverse speculation. There are four wooden deities about four feet high on the main pedestal. The simple lines and curves of the sculptures attest to the antiquity of their shape and construction. Vibrant colors made from vegetable dyes accent the facial curves and the eyes of the images and add to their beauty and majesty. The four images, from left to right, are: (1) white-colored Balabhadra, (2) yellow-colored Subhadra, (3) black-colored Jagannatha, and (4) red-colored Sudarshana. The Sudarshana image, hidden from direct public view, is nondescript and is installed behind the image of Jagannatha. The four colors have at times been interpreted as representing the colors of humanity on the planet. Every twelve to forty years (varying with astronomical calculations), the images are "buried" and new images are made out of a specially recognized *margosa* tree. During this rebirth, called *nabakalebara* (new body), a wrapped package of *brahma* (life) is removed from the old Jagannatha image and placed in the new one.[5] Besides the four images, metal images of Madhava,[6] Shridevi, and Bhudevi[7] are installed at the front of the pedestal. During all rituals and daily routines, the Jagannatha deity is treated as the King of Orissa, whom the rest of the people, including the past kings of the region and the present royal family, attend as servants.

Unlike most Hindu deities, who are worshiped using images made of stone or metals, Jagannatha, Balabhadra, Subhadra, and Sudarshana are unique in that they are the only deities who are worshiped using images made of wood. Among the four images, the image of Jagannatha is considered the most primitive, and the sanctity and faith associated with its worship is most peculiar. The rituals for all four deities follow tantric, Vedic, and Pauranic prescriptions. From the tantric point of view, Jagannatha is Bhairava;[8] from the Vedic point of view, he is Purushottama;[9] and from the *Pauranic* point of view, he is Narayana.[10] That these main currents of Indian tradition accept his importance enhances his mystique and lends complexity to his metaphysics.

The tantric rites of Jagannatha—especially the preparation of food offerings and the construction and painting of new images—are connected to the tribal culture of Orissa. It is claimed that the tribal *sabaras*[11] first discovered ("saw") the deity of Jagannath (before he was installed in the temple) and "owned" him. They continue to have the right of "seeing" the new image first. Jagannatha liked to "accept" their food offerings while in the forest and "continues to like" them in his new abode in the temple. A particular group of devotees called *daitas*, who are the descendants of the earlier *sabaras*, have the exclusive privilege of carrying the principal meals to the deities and caring for them during their "sickness" following the "bathing" festival in midsummer.

Interpretation

The Vedic invocation *Ado yaddaru plavate sindhoh pare apurusham tada rabhasva durhano tena gachha parastaram*[12] is interpreted by Sayana as: "There exists on the sea-shore in a far-off place the image of a deity of the name Purushottama [*apurusham*] which is made of wood floating as it were, on the sea. By worshipping that indestructible wood, attain the supreme place [of the Vaishnavite]."[13]

Natives of Puri recognize Jagannatha as Purushottama, and it is likely that the wooden image of Jagannatha predates the entry of Vedic religion into Orissa. Because all solid objects originated from "water," the legend may point to mysterious driftwood in the ocean as the precursor of the images.

The *Bhagavata Purana* teaches a modified Samkhya theistic hierarchy, whereby Vishnu enters the manifested creation as Narayana in the form of *kala* (time), the twenty-fifth element. The Supreme Being, by virtue of his divine power, pervades everything, internally as an indwelling spirit and externally as time. *Kala* is abstract and dark, and Jagannatha has been interpreted as *kala* in Narayana. Other aspects of Vishnu are manifest in the three other deities Balabhadra, Subhadra, and Sudarshana, who represent *jnana* (knowledge), *shakti* (energy), and *chaitanya* (consciousness).[14]

The triad of Jagannatha, Balabhadra, and Subhadra has been connected to the Buddhist troika, and the belief persists among some historians that the shrine at Puri contains mortal remains, possibly a tooth, of Gautama Buddha. This line of thinking emphasizes the legend of the *brahma* that Hindus believe is encased in the deity. The Car Festival most likely is rooted in Mahayana Buddhism. It is worth noting that the *Bhagavata Purana* incorporates Gautama Buddha into Hindu theology as an incarnation of Vishnu. Jagannatha is viewed as a symbol of the Buddha by many Oriya mystics.

Sarala Dasa's *Mahabharata*

The connection between Jagannatha of Puri and Krishna of Dvaraka is thought to have originated in the fifteenth century with the version of *Mahabharata* written by the Oriya poet Sarala Dasa.[15] His exact dates are not established; it is only known that he was a contemporary of King Kapilendra Deva, who reigned 1435–67 C.E. in Orissa. Sarala Dasa was born as Siddheshwara Parida in a farming family, in a village about forty miles from Puri. His Oriya version of the monumental epic is the first retelling of the original in any of the regional languages of India. While Sarala Dasa followed the themes and plot of the original story, he also added local stories, colloquialisms, and depictions of everyday Oriya life. The poet set the poem in the rustic *dandi*[16] meter of bardic poetry, and the characters speak in the voices of ordinary people. The composition highlights the poet's exceptional narrative and creative abilities.

Sarala Dasa created the story of Jagannatha in his retelling of the *Mausala* (*Mushali* in Oriya) *parva* (book 16) of the *Mahabharata*. It begins with this statement: "With the advent of the *Kali*[17] age, Shri Krishna decided to relinquish his earthly incarnation. All his kinsmen, the Yadavas, perished through mutual destruction, and Shri Krishna was slain by an arrow from the hunter Jara, who mistook his feet for the ears of a deer." From this point on, the story departs from the original.

Arjuna came and tried but failed to cremate Shri Krishna's body. He was advised by a voice from the sky to float Shri Krishna's *pinda*[18] in the ocean. Meanwhile, with the advent of *Kali*, Naryana hid in the forest and incarnated himself as Madhava[19] among the *sabaras*. The *sabaras* worshiped his image as Sabarinarayana. The Vaishnavite King Galamadhaba sent messengers to discover this image. When his messenger, the brahmin Vasu, succeeded in discovering its location, it disappeared from view, and the kings received celestial instructions to install a stone deity in Yamanika [Puri]. Thus, Puri became a place of pilgrimage for all the faithful.

Many centuries later, an expedition of another king, Indradyumna, reached Puri and learned of the local legend of the installation of Jagannatha and Shri Krishna's *pinda*. Indradyumna built a big temple at Puri [Nilagiri] and searched for the deity to install. The king was advised in a dream to meet the *sabara* Bishwabasu. The latter received the celestial message that Shri Krishna's *pinda* would appear as a wooden log in a well, the Rohini Kunda at Puri. The brahmin Vasu and the *sabara* Bishwabasu retrieved the log. The Lord commanded Bishwabasu to construct the deities. Bishwabasu was helped by the timely arrival of an old brahmin, who disappeared, leaving the deities not fully completed. The brahmin Vasu identified Jagannatha as Vishnu, Balabhadra as Shiva, and Subhadra as Brahma. The curse on Brahma to be invisible in Kali-yuga was confirmed.[20] By the order of the king, the families of the brahmin Vasu and the *sabara* Bishwabasu remained as custodians of the deities.

Sarala Dasa's tale has become a folk tradition in Orissa and has made Puri a prime center of the Vaishnava faith. Chaitanya's residence in Puri in the early sixteenth century added a final touch to the story of Krishna as Jagannatha. The three words "Hare," "Rama," and "Krishna" in the Vaishnava *mahamantra* (great chant)[21] represent the three deities in the temple. While the Gaudiya Vaishnavas emphasize Krishna as a spiritual entity, the *sabaras* in Puri go through a period of mourning, penance, and purification when Jagannatha leaves his body and new deities are constructed. This complex synthesis of pre-Aryan Indian culture and Aryan theology has still not been fully explored.

No other temple rivals Puri in offering a paradigmatic celebration of the family of Krishna. Service is first offered to Krishna's older brother Balabhadra, then to his sister Subhadra. Shri Krishna Jagannatha is only served at the end. The Car Festival of the deities may well have a Buddhist origin,[22] but it could also be connected to the *Shrimad Bhagavatam* story of Balarama and Krishna leaving Braja.[23] The nonbrahmin aspects of services at Puri are much akin to nonbrahmin practices in services in the Krishna temple at Dvaraka. Finally, the personal services offered at Puri resemble those in Dvaraka and have made Jagannatha a household deity in the state of Orissa.

No complete, critically edited version of Sarala's *Mahabharata* is yet available. For this translation, I have used Raja Kishore Das's popularly available compilation, and revised it with the edition of Artaballabha Mohanty. The *Mushaliparva* in the Das compilation has nineteen chapters, sixteen of which are linked with the Shri Krishna Jagannatha story. These sixteen chapters are included in the translation here. Sarala's story of Yadava women in Dvaraka and his description of the holy places of interest in Puri and their mythological significance are omitted. Local stories in these chapters are retained to the extent that they are directly related.

Oriya, a language derived from Prakrit and ultimately Sanskrit, has a lyrical tone.[24] Sarala's Oriya metaphors are often hard to render into English. Extending the style of the original *Mahabharata* stories, Sarala goes into an intricate web of fables, legends, and storytelling, one embedded in the other. I hope that the flavor and the contents of this rich story will be of interest for further research.[25]

Shri Krishna's Thoughts and Advice to Akrura

The king of Bilanka paid his respects to the sage Agasti and requested him to continue to tell him the story of the *Mahabharata*. "I am particularly interested," the king said, "in hearing what Hari [Krishna] did after his visit to Vishnu in heaven." The sage continued the story.

"On his return from heaven, Hari remained unhappy, remembering Vishnu's order that he must return to heaven. He kept thinking of ways to eliminate the Yadavas and what arrangements he might make for the women after the Yadavas perished. 'This land was under the control of a thousand kings,' he reflected, 'and now it's all mine.'

"Ten years passed: it was the day of *Kumarotsava*[26] in Dvaraka. Shri Krishna was playful and was in the mood to give away all his wealth. There were noisy celebrations. All the people in Dvaraka had gathered and were making merry. There were thirty two thousand women, one hundred sixty thousand and eighty children, and their wives. And there were thousands of grandchildren and great-grandchildren. There were innumerable members of the families descended from Yadu, Bhoja, Andhaka, Vrishni, and Chuhana.[27]

"Seeing the families and his own kinsmen, Shri Krishna was suddenly gloomy. Tears filled his eyes. 'How am I to destroy what I

have created?' he thought ruefully. Akrura noticed Shri Krishna's
tear-filled eyes. 'You are the Lord of all!' Akrura said. 'Whom do
you fear? You are on earth to remove distress. Thanks to you, there is
no death or old age in Dvaraka. You see everyone as a part of your
own soul. Why are you unhappy?' Shri Krishna informed him about
the message from Vishnu and ruminated on the attachment to his
own kinsmen. 'Keep the message secret,' he said. Akrura pleaded:
'How can you go away leaving me alone?'

" 'If you keep everything secret', Shri Krishna replied, 'I will take
you along when I leave.' Shri Krishna continued: 'In the early times
of the atrocities on earth, the demigods prayed to Vishnu. Vishnu
pulled two hairs from his thigh and ordered them to take birth
in black and white form. On his orders, I was incarnated as a fish,
recovered the *Vedas*[28] from Sankhasura, and gave them back to
Brahma. Then I was born as a tortoise and supported Mount Mandara
on my back. Taking the incarnation of a boar, I killed Hiranyaksha.
Coming as Narasimha to rescue Prahlada, I killed Hiranyakashipu.
I took the incarnation of Vamana to push Vali down to a subter-
ranean dungeon. I was born as Parshurama in the house of Jama-
dagni and slew Sahasrabahu at my father's order. I eliminated all the
kshatriyas from the earth twenty-one times. Then I was born as Rama
in the house of Dasharatha and killed demons like Ravana and
Kumbhakarna. Now we are born as Kanhu and Sankarshana in the
house of Vasudeva. In this incarnation, we killed such demons
as Kamsa. I have taken birth many times out of my own curiosity!'[29]

" 'At last I am thinking of eliminating my worldly attachments
here! Intoxicated by my own pride, I took many wives and have
made a large family. I am attached to my family. It's difficult for me
to leave now. So, I am unhappy! How, Akrura, am I to leave now and
who would take care of my wives and children? My parents would
lament for me, and thirty-two thousand women would miss me.
Where shall I leave my son Pradyumna? I love him so dearly! I
have been extremely anxious.'

"Akrura prostrated himself at Shri Krishna's feet. He reminded
Shri Krishna of all the services that he had performed. 'Please,' he
begged, 'take me along when you leave for Vaikuntha.'[30]

" 'It's impossible for you to go to Vaikuntha,' Shri Krishna said.
'I can only guide you. You can't go there if you have sins. No one
goes there in a mortal body even if one has lived a virtuous life on this
earth. Only a yogi well versed in the knowledge of *Brahman*[31] is
capable of going to Vaikuntha along with his body. Since you have
expressed an interest, let me help you with the knowledge of
Brahman.'

"Shri Krishna explained, 'First, master the eight stages of *yoga* and keep your mind steady. Sit in *yogasana* and practice the sixty-four *mudras*,[32] relinquishing all mental attachments. Stop the flow of air in all ten openings of the body and concentrate on Brahman. Block sensation in three nerves—*ida, pingala,* and *sushumna*[33]—and allow air to leave the body only through your head. Then turn your tongue and perform the *khechari mudra.*[34] So doing, you will never go hungry and you will not die! If you can prevent food and sleep, you will definitely protect your body.' Shri Krishna continued: 'I have told you this sacred knowledge because you are very dear to me. You must never reveal this to anyone. Now you should move to the Ekamra *tirtha*[35] near the Vindhyas and reach the site of Hatakeshwar *linga*[36] in the forest. Start these *yoga* austerities immediately.'

"Akrura asked, 'Where shall I see you again?' Shri Krishna said: 'Yama[37] will put my *pinda* under the *kalpabata*[38] tree at the Nilaparvata hills on the northern side of the ocean. I will be known as Purushottama. A king named Galamadhava will make arrangements for my stay. O Akrura, don't go home now. You should leave for the mountains directly.' Akrura left Dvaraka at midnight."

Unnatural Events in Dvaraka, the Destruction of the Yadus, and the Demise of Balarama

Agasti said to the king: "Shri Krishna was extremely anxious. He was at a loss how he could destroy all the people that he had created." He said, "Let me narrate the playful prank that Shri Krishna played to eliminate the Yadu clan."

"Dvaraka saw many unusual omens. There were violent earthquakes and meteor showers. Comets were seen during the day. Houses burned without fire. The temples fell down on their foundations. Animals roared loudly. Both sun and moon were seen together in the sky. There were eclipses. Family members were in conflict everywhere. Everyone was frightened. After a few days, an uncouth, ugly *kalapurusha*[39] showed up. He was of a reddish black color. His veins and bones were visible through his emaciated body. He moved menacingly through the streets, but people could hardly see him. Shri Krishna considered this to be an opportunity!

"Shri Krishna ordered his messengers to alert the town to the appearance of the *kalapurusha* in Dvaraka. Beating drums, they announced through the city: 'Listen, everyone! Be careful! A strange animal has entered the land. He can eat anyone alive! Shri Krishna has seen this strange animal, called Kokua.[40] It could swallow anyone who is seen on the road. Everyone, be careful!'

support all of them? All of my Yadavas are dead!' Utterly tired, he fell deep asleep. Morning dawned. The age of Kali had occupied the land. Shri Krishna was in *kalanidra*.[45]

"Next to the Kalindi hill was a *sabara* village. Jara lived in that village. He came from an established *sabara* family, headed by the patriarch Aja. Aja's son was Ajapati, the father of Gajaraja. Gajaraja's son was Biraja, and his son was Kalakunta. Jara was Kalakunta's son. That morning, Jara left home as usual in search of game. Jara carried his large wooden bow. He happened to carry the iron arrow that he had specially made.

"Jara hid in many of his usual haunts and waited for his prey. He did not succeed. This was unusual. He got tired and thirsty. Suddenly, at a distance, he noticed two fleshy protrusions with reddish tinge in the center. They looked like two ears of a deer to him. He targeted them with his bow and discharged an arrow. Lo, it pierced the left foot of sleeping Shri Krishna, who started up, saw blood oozing out from his foot, and felt a sharp pain. 'Who,' he wondered, 'could inflict such pain on me?'

"Jara came close and recognized Shri Krishna. Alarmed, he deeply apologized. 'What have I done! I have hit the One who is worshiped by Brahma and Rudra. O my Lord! I never learned my duties of worship and service. I didn't know what the future had in store for me.' Then, steadying himself, he cried, 'Why didn't you protect yourself, since you know the future!' Seeing the pain on Shri Krishna's face, he said, 'My Lord, let me get the arrow out. Let me apply medicine. You will be all right!' Shri Krishna replied: 'If you removed the arrow, I would immediately die. Get some water from the Yamuna and sprinkle it on my face.' Jara sprinkled the water and fanned Shri Krishna to comfort him.

"Shri Krishna inquired, 'How did you get the arrow that pierced me?' Jara replied, 'I have a friend, who is a fisherman. He gave me a fish. When my wife cut the fish, she found an iron spike inside the fish's stomach. She brought it to me. I had it sharpened by the blacksmith and kept it for use on rare occasions. Because I didn't find any quarry in my long day's search, I used the arrow so that I would not lose a deer!" Shri Krishna knew the story of the infamous iron spike and recalled the curse of the sage Ashtavakra.[46]

"Shri Krishna requested Jara to go to Indraprastha and fetch Arjuna. 'But don't tell anyone what has happened,' he said. Jara's wife was standing nearby, and Jara asked her to continue to fan Shri Krishna. He gave her the bow. 'Protect yourself. Do not let the wild animals come near you.' Jara left for Indraprastha.

Jara Informs Arjuna and Escorts Him to Kalindi

"Jara met Arjuna at Indraprastha in private and told him of Shri Krishna's request. Arjuna went to Yudhishthira to seek permission to leave immediately. Yudhishthira was confused and asked Sahadeva to explain to him what was happening. Sahadeva recounted the events at Kalindi.[47] Hearing Sahadeva's narration, Yudhishthira was very sad and prepared to go himself. Sahadeva dissuaded him: 'It is not possible for you to bear the pain of seeing Shri Krishna at this time. Let Arjuna go and we shall know the details on his return.' Sahadeva warned Arjuna— 'Never touch Shri Krishna's body!'

"Arjuna and Jara left Indraprastha and, on the way to meet Shri Krishna, entered a forest. The road looked unfamiliar. Puzzled, Arjuna asked Jara where they were going. Jara said, 'Shri Krishna is in Kalindi forest, not in Dvaraka. I have told you exactly what he asked me to convey! Shri Krishna ordered me to bring you to him as quickly as possible.'

"After a long journey, Jara and Arjuna met Shri Krishna. Arjuna saw him sleeping on the branch of the *salmali*[48] tree. Shri Krishna's face was dark. Unable to get up, he started crying. Seeing him helpless, Arjuna was perplexed. Approaching Shri Krishna, he asked, 'Have you given up all your worldly possessions?' Shri Krishna said, 'Well, this is all I have! I have to suffer the pain because of the curse of the sage Ashtavakra.' Arjuna retorted: 'You are the All-Knowing! How can someone curse you? You came to know of Kali's arrival and have decided to leave the earth. I know this since I have been with you all along!'

"Shri Krishna said: 'You have a task to perform. You have to go to Dvaraka and break the news of my departure there. Take the women across the river Balunka and shelter them on the other shore.' Then he begged: 'O Partha, the pain is making me restless. Come close. Embrace me!' Arjuna remembered Sahadeva's advice and declined. 'I just have a human body,' he said. 'How can I touch you, Narayana himself?' Shri Krishna cajoled, 'Remember, how many times I have helped you!' He again implored: 'O Kiriti, just stretch out your arm and touch me with your finger. I will feel much better.' Arjuna insisted, 'I don't have my brother's permission to do so.' 'If you can't touch me with your body, can you touch me with your bow?' Shri Krishna begged.

"Arjuna thought to himself: 'What do I do now? It is he who has been always a friend to the Pandavas. Thanks to him, we have subdued the world. And he is in utter pain!' Arjuna could not tolerate the pain in Shri Krishna's face and stretched his *gandiva*[49] toward him. At that moment, Jara removed the arrow from Shri Krishna's foot. Shri Krishna clasped the *gandiva* with his right hand and looked at Arjuna. His spirit left his body. It merged with Arjuna. He rode the *pushpaka*[50] and went to heaven. He had a big homecoming welcome and many words of felicitations. He had gone back where he had come from."

The Battle between Jara and Arjuna; Arjuna's Defeat

Agasti continued:

"Arjuna could not control himself and wept bitterly. He got very angry and trembled in anger. 'You, Jara Sabara!' he shouted, 'How could you kill the Lord of the universe? I will not let you go alive. I will tear you into pieces.' 'Please don't be angry with me,' the *sabara* begged: 'It never occurred to me that Shri Krishna would be sleeping there. I mistook him for a deer. Please don't say it's my fault.' Jara went on, calmly: 'I am an ignorant man and have committed such a deadly sin. I am a forest-dweller. I don't have much to receive from this earth. I would die happily any time! But think, if you get killed by me, you would be missed by the entire universe!'

"Arjuna would not listen. 'There is no point to my life when Shri Krishna has left his body!' he said to himself. Then he shot five arrows at Jara. Jara blocked each of them with counterarrows. Jara roared loudly, calling all the gods to witness: 'Hear! Arjuna, a King, wants to fight with me, a mere *sabara*!' Jara shot arrows at Arjuna. Arjuna defended himself with counterarrows. The battle continued. Arjuna was weak against Jara. Shri Krishna wasn't there to help him! It was remarkable to see two of Drona's disciples fighting with vigor. Arjuna dispatched the Agni, Bhairavi, and Satadhara[51] weapons. Jara countered with the Varsa, Trimbaka, and Sahasradhara[52] weapons.

"Arjuna desperately dispatched the Manabhedi[53] weapon and ordered it to kill Jara. In reply, Jara shot back the Manaharana[54] weapon with the order to kill Arjuna. Since both the weapons were accurately aimed, everyone was scared. The gods gathered in the sky and commanded both Jara and Arjuna to recall their weapons. The gods said: 'You both have only one soul. Arjuna, you and Jara have always been together. During Rama's time in the age of Treta, you were Sugriva and he was Angada, the son of Vali. Vali was not an enemy of Rama, but Rama killed him to protect Sugriva.[55] This was unfair. Vali's son was destined to kill Shri Krishna in the age of Dvapara. Now it is done. Arjuna, go and cremate Shri Krishna

on the Nilasundara hill.' Arjuna was subdued. He was happy to
know about Jara. He asked Jara's help to cremate Shri Krishna. He
was immersed in grief and reminisced about life and his experience with Shri Krishna. He wept again.

The Cremation of Shri Krishna; Worship of Narayana

"Arjuna asked Jara to look for aloe wood for the funeral pyre. Jara
searched all around, but to his utter amazement could not find a
single aloewood tree. He returned to Arjuna 'This is most unbeliev-
able!' he said. 'A tree I used to see right here has disappeared.' Then
he said, 'Let me tell you the story about the tree.'

"Jara said: 'The story of Nilamadhava[56] happened during the
time of my grandfather Vasu. One night, while he was moving in the
forest, he rested under the aloewood tree. He noticed a blue stone that
had the signs of conch, discus, club, and lotus; it also had markings of red lips. He prostrated himself and offered his respects to the
image. The stone turned into the image of Madhava in front of him.
Madhava told him: "I am the all-pervading Lord of the Universe.
Because Kali has entered the earth, I have hidden myself, taking the
form of this stone. You should worship me with leaves and water.
You should never tell this to anyone. If it is revealed, you and all your
family members will cease to live." After saying this, Madhava disappeared and became a stone again.'

"Jara continued: 'Madhava stayed at the aloewood tree, and Vasu
went on offering worship for many days. Vasu apologized for any
errors he might be making in worship. He would say: "I am not
trained in ritual worship. Please forgive me." Madhava would assure him that he was quite content with the service. After worship,
Vasu would offer cooked rice every day, and the Lord would eat
portions of it. Vasu would eat whatever remained. So it continued.
Nobody else knew anything about it. After some time, Vasu fell
sick and became feeble. He was unable to walk to the shrine. He was
greatly concerned how to offer food to the Lord. After much torment,
he thought he could teach the whereabouts of Madhava to his son
Gajaraja in secret. 'Inform the Lord that Vasu is suffering in high
fever,' Vasu said. Gajaraja reached the shrine of Madhava and offered the worship and food. The Lord would not receive food from
Gajaraja! Grieved at this, Vasu himself returned to offer food to
the Lord. The Lord would not receive worship, nor would he receive food!

" 'Vasu recounted these events to Ishwara,[57] who had been installed as a *linga*[58] in his village of Rudrapur. Ishwara pondered: "It is

not right that Narayana has assumed an incarnation in stone. It would be easy for everyone to get *moksha*[59] just by seeing him!" He ordered Yama to collect Shri Purushottama[60] back to the heavens and seclude him from the people on earth. Yama did so and installed Shri Purushottama in his own abode. Such has been the story behind this tree. I saw it only yesterday!' Jara said.

"Arjuna cried aloud, 'O Lord, how do I cremate your body when I am unable to obtain any aloewood?' Suddenly, to his utter bewilderment, the tree appeared again in its place. Arjuna pointed this out to Jara, who cut the tree and assembled the faggots. Arjuna arranged them in a pyre and then offered flower garlands on Shri Krishna's body. He was wailing and lamenting. He laid Shri Krishna's body on the pyre and lit the aloewood. 'Your body is like that of a black bee,' Arjuna sobbed, 'I, sinful as I am, am cremating it!' The funeral pyre burned for a day and night, but the fire did not touch Shri Krishna's *pinda*. Arjuna wondered at this. It is said that the *pinda* of someone who has sinned in life do not burn. Arjuna pondered what sins Shri Krishna might have committed. Then, recalling that he had touched the body with his mortal hands, he wondered whether his own action had tainted the *pinda*.

"Suddenly, a voice came from the sky: 'Fire can't destroy this *pinda*. The *pinda* will remain in the Nilasundara hills, to be worshiped there for a long time! Please extinguish the fire and float the *pinda* in the sea!' Arjuna put out the fire and collected the *pinda*. He floated it out into the sea and completed the last rites. Arjuna alerted Jara to look out for the *pinda* on the coast. 'Wherever it might come to shore would be a world-famous place!' he said.

"After bidding goodbye to Jara and his wife, Arjuna walked along the sea-coast to Dvaraka. He sat down on the Raivata hill and meditated on the sage Vyasa, who suddenly appeared and asked him all about Shri Krishna. 'While cremating the Lord, I heard a voice from the sky asking me to float the *pinda* in the sea. I have done that. I don't have the heart to tell this to the people in Dvaraka.' Vyasa declared, 'Shri Krishna's *pinda* will be worshiped for four hundred thirty two thousand years of the age of Kali.' Then Arjuna told Vyasa of Shri Krishna's instruction that the ladies in Dvaraka be sheltered on the other shore of Balunka river.

"Both Arjuna and Vyasa reached the palace. Rukmini and Satyabhama, two principal wives of Shri Krishna, welcomed them. Then followed the greetings from the other wives and all the ladies. Arjuna narrated what had happened during the previous night. Arjuna told Rukmini and Satyabhama: 'The Lord will come to you every day, and you should take care of all the other ladies.' All the women were sad and wept profusely. Vyasa said, 'No, none of you is a widow. Once you cross the Balunka River, you will meet Shri Krishna.' Everyone crossed the river at night. They built houses and lived there for some time. The ladies asked, 'Where is Shri Krishna? We don't see him.' Vyasa invoked Shri Krishna through *mantras*. Shri Krishna appeared there in divine incarnation. Everyone was happy. They had divine bliss."

Vasu Brahmin Locates Sabarinarayana[61]

Agasti continued:

"Some years went by. There came a king called Ritupurna in the clan of Hari. His son was Janughanta, whose son was Ashwamali. His son was Namagopala, whose son was Pashupatra. His son was Jayanata, whose son was Sadashiva. Sadashiva's son was Galavya, who had been childless. After serving the Lord for a long time, he was blessed with a son. He named the son Galamadhava. Galamadhava was extremely brave. He also devoted much time to the worship of Vishnu. When Shri Krishna's incarnation came to an end, Galamadhava refused to eat food. From his minister Madanavitta he came to know that Madhava had appeared near the Rudra River and that Shri Krishna's *pinda* was floating in the sea.

"The king sent messengers in four directions—Vishnu Dasa to the east, Hari Dasa to the north, Sudeva Dasa to the west, and Vasudeva Dasa to the south. Vasudeva reached the Kalindi lake and searched through the nearby forest. There he entered the village of the *sabaras* and met his namesake Vasu Sabara. Recognizing him as a brahmin, Vasu Sabara venerated him and offered him many tokens of respect. Brahmin Vasudeva appreciated these gestures. He decided to stay in the village for a few days. He became a good friend to Vasu Sabara and his family.

"The brahmin noticed that Vasu's father Jara left every day with water and leaves as though he were going for worship. One day he observed *puja*[62] marks on Jara's forehead. He ventured to ask Vasu's wife about Jara's excursions. She said she did not know but would find out. She asked her husband that night and found out that he did not know either. Both Vasu Sabara and the Vasu brahmin then went to Jara. After properly greeting him, the brahmin asked if he might accompany Jara on his trip. Jara replied, 'I do worship a deity, but it's too difficult to reach there. It's deep in the forest, where many wild animals lurk.' When Jara discouraged him, Vasu's wife made another plea. Jara gave his consent: 'I will take you along when I go tomorrow.'

"Next day, the brahmin rose early to be ready. 'Before we start,' Jara said, 'I have to blindfold your eyes.' The brahmin thought of a clever trick. He filled his *puja* vase with rice and sesame seeds and held the vase in one hand. Blindfolded, Vasu walked with his other hand holding the hand of his guide, Jara. Unknown to Jara, Vasu went on scattering the seeds as they walked.

"They reached the banks of the Rudra River, which was about four miles from the village. They walked to the place where the deity was worshiped. Jara removed the blindfold from the eyes of the brahmin. Vasu saw the image of Madhava and offered his prayers. He said to himself: 'I will report this to King Galamadhava, and the king will make appropriate arrangements for the service of the Lord! O Lord, your days of neglect in this remote forest should come to an end. You should bless the King and receive his offerings!'

"Vasu Brahmin inquired from Jara about the origin of the deity. 'The Lord appeared under the tree on his own accord,' Jara said. He explained how Shri Krishna was always generous to the *sabara* family. The brahmin said, 'It's scary here. We should leave!' Jara blindfolded him and led him out of the place. Vasu Brahmin again took rice and sesame seeds from his *puja* vessel and went on strewing on the path as they trekked back. After a month or so, Vasu Brahmin bade farewell to the *sabara* family and left for home.

Vasu Brahmin's Report to Galamadhava and the King's Fight with the *Sabaras*

"At Kanchi, the messengers had come back from east, north, and west. 'We looked everywhere and never found any image of Vishnu,' they said. King Galamadhava anxiously waited for Vasu's return from the south. Once Vasu arrived, the king was very happy. 'Perhaps Vasu has good news,' he wondered. After the brahmin had been welcomed and made comfortable, the king said, 'I have been eagerly waiting for you. If we cannot find Vishnu, I will relinquish my throne and go to the forest!'

"The brahmin told the story of his journey. 'Yama took away the image from the Kalindi forest and kept it in the heavens. Sinners would congregate and were liberated just by seeing the image. The heavens became filled with people! Yama did not like this and he eventually brought the image back to earth. He placed it on the northern side of the Rushikulya river. I located it there.'

"King Galamadhava immediately set forth toward the *sabara* village with his minister and the armed forces. They followed the

shoots of rice and sesame, and were led to the location of the shrine
by Vasu Brahmin. But to their surprise, when they reached the tree,
they did not see the deity! There were only flowers and some food.
Vasu Brahmin looked all around amazed. Everything was there
except the deity!

"The king asked the *sabaras* there if they could help locate the
deity. Nobody knew where it was. The king was upset. In his rage,
the king killed them all. Hearing of the carnage, Jara showed up. Jara
had a big fight with Galamadhava's forces. He killed most of the
king's soldiers. The king was frightened. He retreated.

"In the night, the king reflected on his adventure and prayed to
the Lord to save his soldiers from Jara's wrath. The Lord Madhava
appeared to him in his dream and said: 'Generations of *sabara*
families have been worshiping me. Yama took me away and placed
me back as *Sabarinarayana* among these *sabaras*. The *sabari*[63]
cooked for me the most delicious food, and I was most happy. What
you have done is unfair. Since you killed the kinsmen of my devotee, all the members of your own family will die and your clan
will become extinct! Please be friendly with the *sabara*. There must
be no enmity between you two!' Then the Lord said to Jara: 'I will
appear as a stone image. You should install me at the holy place of
Yamanika.[64] A member of your family must always stay near me!'
The Lord said to the king: 'You will carry my stone image by a boat
and install it on the top of Nilagiri.'

"The Lord disappeared, turning into a stone image. King Galamadhava transported and installed the image next to the great Ya-
meswara *linga* at the holy place of Yamanika."

Description of Nilasundara and Construction of the Big Temple

The king of Bilanka asked the sage Agasti to continue the story of Shri
Krishna's *pinda* in the sea. "What happened after Arjuna floated it
and how was it found?" the king asked. Agasti told the story of King
Indradyumna and the construction of the temple at Yamanika.

Agasti said:

"There was a king called Shri Madhukeshara in the clan of Birata.
His son's name was Indradyumna. In the course of an expedition, Indradyumna chanced to reach the holy place of Yamanika.
There the sage Shuka told him the stories of Galamadhava and the
prediction that the Lord would grace the place as a deity. Having
heard this, the king resolved to build a temple on the hill. The king's
minister then described to him the sanctity of the hill and told him

the story of Shri Krishna's *pinda*. 'I will build the temple,' the king said, 'and install Shri Krishna's *pinda* in it.'

"The King thought deep and hard how to construct the temple. After a few days a strange artisan showed up. 'Don't worry,' he told the king, 'I will help you construct it!' At an auspicious moment in the early morning on a Thursday, the fourth day after the full moon in Rohini *nakshatra*[65] in the month of Tula,[66] a brahmin boy named Vishwavasu made the invocation for the temple. A large and beautiful stone temple was built. Then the king thought deeply how to locate Shri Krishna's *pinda*. He went to Yameshwara *linga* to observe penance and austerities so that he would get clues. He meditated there for fourteen days without food. Ishvara was pleased with the king's determination and advised him to go to Markanda Brahma[67] and solicit his help.

King Indradyumna meets Jara; Appearance of Shri Krishna's *Pinda* in Nilagiri

"King Indradyumna went to Markanda Brahma and meditated for sixty-five days in austerities. Markandeshwara appeared before him in his dream. The king said: 'I have built a temple at the Yamanika kshetra, and I have come to ask your advice as to which deity to install there!' Markanda said: 'You need to get Shri Krishna, who has been hiding in the Nilagiri hills. You have to know more about him from Jara Sabara.'

"The king and his people went to look for Jara and met him in the holy place of Gosagara. The minister told the king about Jara's life and about Shri Krishna's cremation. He said that Jara had always been the protector of Shri Krishna's body. The king rewarded Jara with a hundred thousand gold coins and asked him if he would join him in worshipping Shri Krishna's *pinda*.

"The king asked: 'Have you seen the *pinda* that Arjuna floated in the sea? If you can find it, we should install it at Nilagiri.' Jara replied: 'I have been waiting from the day the *pinda* floated away. I wish to ask the Lord whether he wants to be worshiped on earth. I have no luck! You go to Chandrabhaga[68] and stay there overnight. I will meditate on Shri Krishna. I will come by and tell you if I find an answer.'

"The king left for Chandrabhaga and spent the night there. At the beach, Jara meditated on the Lord. Just then, Lord Shri Krishna came out of the sea and appeared before him. Jara paid his respects and requested 'My Lord, may you appear at Nilagiri!' Shri Krishna said: 'It is the wish of Lord Brahma that we should spend some time

on the earth during the Kali-yuga. We will appear in the incarnation of the Buddha. We will destroy the evil and protect the noble.
This is absolutely true!' Hearing the Lord, Jara begged: 'King Indradyumna desires to install you in the temple that he has constructed.' Shri Krishna replied: 'Escort him to Rohini Kunda. Our
bodies will be transformed there and you will see us as the Buddha.
My *pinda* will appear as a log of wood. Tell the king he should take
good care of me!' Lord Shri Krishna disappeared.

"Jara left for Chandrabhaga. The king saw him from a distance
and received him. Jara broke the good news to him and urged
everyone to proceed toward Nilagiri. Jara, the king, and his minister
Nakula came to Nilagiri. King Indradyumna showed Jara the beautiful temple he had built. Jara went around the temple and observed
all the splendid architecture and designs. He praised the king very
much. The King described to him how he had been advised by
Markandeshwara to install Lord Jagannatha in the temple and how
he had been directed to meet him. 'Dear friend Jara, I came to you
because you are a devotee of Shri Vishnu. If you can, please help
me to install the Lord Jagannatha in this temple.' Jara told him about
Shri Krishna's message that he would appear in Rohini Kunda.[69]

"The king, the *sabara*, and the minister went to Rohini Kunda
and waited to witness the appearance of the Lord. Meanwhile, Shri
Krishna in the heavens announced his desire to install himself at
Nilagiri as Shri Jagannatha. Other gods reflected that sinners
would get liberation merely by a *darshan!*[70] But they were helpless.
Ishwara said, 'I will join with you in Nilagiri as Balabhadra.' Brahma
said, 'I can't stay behind. I will go with you also.' Shri Krishna gave
assurance—'Yes, you will be always with us.'

"Next morning, Indradyumna saw a beautiful red aloe log inside
the Rohini Kunda. It had the shape of the glistening body of the
Lord. The king showed it to Jara, and the *sabara* confirmed that it was
the *pinda* of Shri Krishna. 'You have already gained liberation by
viewing it!' Jara said. The king called for the soldiers from the palace
and asked them to lift the log from the well. The heavy log could
not be lifted. It was evening, and the king was anxious. At night, Shri
Krishna spoke to the king in a dream: 'This log is not just a piece
of *agouru*.[71] It's my *pinda*. The entire *mahameru*[72] is contained in
it. Ordinary people cannot lift it. Only the *sabara* Jara and the brahmin Vasu can handle it!'

"The king called Jara and Vasu. He told them about the dream.
Then, Jara and Vasu helped to lift the log. They carried it to the
entrance of the temple. The king found that it was impossible to carry
the log inside the sanctum. Indradyumna once again received orders

from the Lord in a dream: 'Ask Jara to create images out of the log.' The king met Jara in the morning. 'It's true that I have built this temple, but the Lord said that it is you who know him well.' the King told Jara. 'The Lord has ordered that you create the images. He said that you would know what they should be.' The king hugged Jara, complimented him for the blessing of being close to the Lord, and gave him gifts. 'Do not worry. I will create the images!' Jara said and went inside the temple, closing the doors. Mysteriously, a brahmin arrived inside the temple. Both of them cut the log into three pieces—large, medium, and small. They made three images. The king waited outside.

"Days passed. It was a Thursday, the thirteenth day of Mithuna[73] in the star of Rohini. The king was anxious to check on the work inside the temple. He walked around the temple and tried to listen through the doors on all the four sides. He didn't hear any noise. He was worried. 'Could it be that Jara has disappeared?' he thought. The king was tense. He decided to break open the door. He entered the temple in the evening. On the Jagamohana[74] pedestal, he saw three magnificent images: one was white, one yellow, and the other black. The king was awe-struck. He prostrated himself in front of the deities."

The Mystery of the Deities

Vaivaswata Manu asked the sage Agasti how the mysterious brahmin had shown up in the temple and how he had disappeared. "Let me unravel the mystery," Agasti said.

"Jara went inside the temple and prayed hard. 'I don't know designs, nor do I know artistry. How am I to create these images, that all would worship?' Just then, Vishwakarma, the eternal architect, arrived there in the guise of a brahmin. He helped Jara to construct the three images. Vishwakarma disappeared after the construction. Lord Shri Krishna then commanded Jara: 'You must hide my *pinda* in a secret place. People must not see the color of my body since everyone will eventually merge in me. Get resin from a *sala*[75] tree and cover my *pinda* with it.' Jara went out in the night, collected the resin, and smeared it on the *pinda*. Shri Krishna's body then merged in the *pinda* in the log.

"Indradyumna asked Vasu to help him identify the three images. The brahmin said: 'The white image is that of Balarama. He is on the left and has the *saunaka* mace and the plough in his hands. He is Shri Krishna's elder brother. The yellow image in the middle is Brahma. Since Brahma has been cursed to be invisible in Kali-yuga, he appears as Subhadra, Shri Krishna's younger sister. And the image on the left, black and very beautiful to behold, holding the conch and discus, is the image of Lord Jagannatha.'"

Agasti continued:

"Rama, Krishna, and Subhadra—these three images represent Hara, Hari, and Brahma in the holy abode of Shri Purushottama. Since people in the Kali-yuga are bereft of devotion, they don't see the feet of the Lord. But they have the privilege of worshiping both Hari and Hara at the same shrine. Both Hari and Hara have the same soul but two bodies! Thus the Lord will stay for the four hundred thirty two thousand years of Kali-yuga."

"The king was very happy to hear the mystery of the images. He joined the brahmin Vasu in offering services to the deities. The king prayed to the Lord—'Let Vasu's family be eternally in your service'! Jara's family remained as constant protectors of the Lord's body. They became known as *daita*. They made medicines when the Lord fell sick."

Agasti concluded:

"All the divine beings then congregated and took their respective positions in the holy place of Nilagiri. They had their images constructed there, and each was able to get the *darshan* of the Lord every day!"

NOTES

1. I offer my sincere thanks to Mr. Thomas E. Burke, formerly staff at Harvard University, for having helped to edit the draft manuscript. I am grateful for the assistance of late Professor K. C. Mishra of the Institute of Orissan Culture in Bhubaneswar, India, and late Sri Yogesh Panda, poet and scholar at Harvard University, for bringing the legends of Sarala Dasa to my attention and to assist me in collecting the resource materials. I thank Swami Sarvagatananda of the Ramakrishna Vedanta Center in Boston, Dr. V. S. Rao of the High-Tech Yoga Institute of Lowell, Massachusetts, and the members of my family for encouragement in the work. This article is dedicated to the endearing memory of my late grandfather, Sri Nilakantha Misra of Birapratapapur village, Puri, India.

2. The architecture presenting a progressive elevation from the entrance to the main shrine.

3. Only the entrance to the temple at Konarka remains, and it looks like a pagoda. The main temple has been destroyed.

4. The deities are carried outside the Temple and travel in massive wooden chariots in the month of July.

5. A mysterious packet and its tradition of offering "life" to the deity continue to be transferred to the new image.

6. The image of Shri Vishnu.

7. Two wives of Shri Vishnu.

8. The male counterpart to the tantric *yogini*.

9. The manifestation of the cosmic consciousness. *Bhagavad Gita*, 15. 8.

10. The life-force of all existence in the creation. *Srimad Bhagavatam*, canto 3, chap. 26.

11. The primitive hunting tribe living in the hills of India.

12. *Rig Veda*, 10.155.3

13. K. C. Mishra, *The Cult of Jagannatha* (1984), Firma KLM Pvt Ltd, Calcutta.

14. Mishra, *The Cult of Jagannatha*.

15. Considered the father of the modern Oriya language.

16. A meter used in Orissa for folk singing. The two lines of the stanza can be of uneven length but rhyme together.

17. The last of the four Hindu eras: *Satya, Treta, Dvapara, Kali*.

18. The body residue, symbolizing the conscious spirit of life.

19. Hindus believe that the cosmic forces become deities in the age of *Kali*.

20. There is scriptural folklore saying that Brahma was cursed by Vishnu not to get worship on the earth because he had played pranks on Vishnu.

21. *Hare Rama Hare Rama Rama Rama Hare Hare, Hare Krishna Hare Krishna Krishna Krishna Hare Hare*.

22. There is historical evidence that Puri was a Buddhist center and Buddha's relics were carried in a procession on the festival days.

23. *Srimad Bhagavatam*, canto 10, chap. 39.

24. Oriya belongs to the Indo-European family of languages, along with Bengali and Assamese.

25. Sarala also wrote a version of the *Ramayana* and the *Chandi Purana* in Oriya. I will try to offer translations of other Sarala literature in the future.

26. A festival on the full-moon day of in the solar month *Ashvina*, which normally falls in October.

27. Various tribes in Dvaraka.

28. Hindus believe that the *Vedas* were kept hidden in the sea and were rescued.

29. Popularly ten incarnations of Vishnu have been accepted as a part of evolution.

30. The heavens, abode of Vishnu.

31. The nondescript consciousness, the Upanishadic concept of all-pervading spirit.

32. The divine symbols (seals) made by using hands, legs, fingers, and tongue to help seal air flow in and out of the body.

33. Three principal nerve channels in the body.

34. A special seal in which the tongue blocks the flow of air.

35. Holy place.

36. I.e., the *linga* (phallic monument) of Hatakeshwar (a name of Shiva). Shiva transforms himself into phallic symbols, and it is believed that success in yogic austerities is achieved with dedicated worship of Shiva.

37. The Hindu god Death.

38. The age-old banyan tree, considered to be wish-fulfilling for Hindus.

39. The mythological satanic figure that is believed to appear at the end of an era.
40. The name of a mythical animal in Oriya.
41. Night of the new moon.
42. Flowering tree made popular by Krishna through his plays.
43. Krishna's discus.
44. The yogic posture of meditation.
45. The timeless sleep before death.
46. The sage Ashtavakra had cursed Krishna to die violently.
47. Sahadeva, the youngest of the Pandavas, had the special skill of knowing the past and future.
48. A silk cotton tree.
49. Arjuna's bow.
50. The celestial vehicle.
51. "Fire," "destruction," "hundred streams."
52. "Rains," "pacifier," "thousand streams."
53. "That pierces the mind."
54. "That kills the mind."
55. The story is from the *Ramayana*. Sugriva offered to help Rama in rescuing Sita, who had been abducted. In order to gain the friendship of Sugriva, Rama killed Vali and enthroned Sugriva as the king.
56. "The blue-complexioned Madhava."
57. Shiva, the third of the Hindu trinity.
58. Shiva is worshiped as a phallic symbol.
59. The Hindu concept of liberation.
60. Another name for Narayana.
61. Another name for Nilamadhava.
62. Hindu ritual of offering worship to a deity.
63. The *sabara*'s wife.
64. Another name for the holy town of Puri.
65. The Rohini cluster of stars, the fourth asterism.
66. Libra.
67. The Brahma shrine in Puri. Devotees congregate there for meditation.
68. The wish-fulfilling river on the sea, known to bring good luck to the devotees.
69. The sacred well in Puri.
70. The Hindu ritual of "seeing" the deity.
71. Aloewood.
72. The mountain that supports the earth.
73. Gemini.
74. The platform on which the deities are installed.
75. Large tropical tree, widespread in Orissa, with broad leaves and resinous sap.

6

Assam: Shankaradeva's *Parijata Harana Nata*

William L. Smith

When the devotional movement came to Assam in the latter half of the sixteenth century, the region had long been associated with tantricism, witchcraft, and magic. It was there that the *Kalika Purana* and the *Yogini Tantra* were written, and it was the reputed site of *yogini* kingdoms where unwary travelers were transformed into beasts. It was also the home of the famous temple of the goddess Kamakhya and that of the dread Tamreshvari, or Kechai Khati, "eater of raw flesh," to whom human victims were annually offered. Assam was fragmented into different states, kingdoms, and chieftaindoms ruled by a great variety of peoples. In central Assam, the once powerful Hindu kingdom of Kamata was in decline; to the north of it were the warlike Bhutiyas, to the east the Kacharis, Chutiyas, and other tribes, as well as the more powerful Ahom, who would eventually dominate the country and give it their name; and, finally, to the west were the Koch, another tribal people who were about to found a powerful kingdom of their own. Much of the power of the Kamata had passed to a group of Hindu chieftains known as the Bara Bhuyan, the Twelve Lords of the Land. It was to one of their leaders, Kusumbar, that the leader of the Vaishnava reformation, Shankaradeva, was born.

Since the art of history was cultivated in Assam, we know a great deal about Shankaradeva's career, thanks to the numerous reliable biographies, or *charitas,* about him and his followers. The young Shankaradeva enjoyed a sound Sanskrit education and had assumed the duties of a Bhuyan leader, or *shiromani,* when his wife suddenly died and his life underwent a radical change of course.

Shankaradeva went off on a long pilgrimage and returned home to found the Eka Nama Sharana Dharma, the Refuge of the One Name, as his movement came to be known. Shankaradeva started his proselytizing career by constructing a prayer hall, or *nam ghar*, and by staging the *Chihna yatra*, a seven-day dance drama depicting the glory of Krishna. The play made a great impression on the audience, several of whom became the first converts to the Eka Nama Sharana Dharma. This launched Shankaradeva on a long career of preaching, writing, and organizing. Because of political unrest and religious persecution, his life was a peripatetic one: attacks on Bara Bhuyan territories by neighboring tribes caused him to flee to the Ahom kingdom, and thereafter one move followed another until he eventually ended his days at the court of the powerful king of the Koch, Naranarayana, where he passed away in 1568. During his career he was aided by many talented disciples, the most important of whom was his successor, Madhavadeva, who was almost as gifted a writer and organizer as he.

In many respects, the Eka Nama Sharana Dharma is much like Vaishnava groups elsewhere in northern India. It emphasizes the primacy of *bhakti*, which is considered more desirable than *mukti*, or liberation, and it is attained by listening to and repeating the names of God, as in the communal singing of *kirtans*. The texts held in the highest regard have been the *Bhagavad Gita* and the *Bhagavata Purana*, the latter especially in the form of Shankaradeva's Assamese rendering of its tenth book, or *Dasam*, as it is called. Shankaradeva emphasized the *dasya rasa*, approaching God in the attitude of a servant, and in his writings he usually refers to himself as *krishnar kinkara*, the servant of Krishna. In this he differs markedly from the Vaishnavas of nearby Bengal, who stress the *madhurya-rasa*, the erotic sentiment. In line with this, almost no attention is given to the figure of Radha in Assamese Vaishnava literature.

The Eka Nama Sharana Dharma is also indifferent toward image-worship. It is said that Shankaradeva's followers once had a statue of him carved, but when the saint saw it, he ordered it to be thrown into the Brahmaputra lest it be worshiped instead of Hari. In worship the deity is represented by a copy of the *Bhagavata Purana* or other sacred text placed on the altar in a pedestaled tray or *simhasana*. Shankaradeva staunchly opposed the worship of any deity other than Vishnu and was an especially vociferous opponent of animal sacrifice, which was very common among the Shaktas in his day. One of his close followers, Vyasakalai, whose duty it was to read the *Gita*, once offered worship to Shiva, feeling that this was his last chance after three of his sons had died of a disease and a fourth had come down with it. When Shankaradeva learned what he had done, he was immediately expelled from the movement. Toward the end of Shankaradeva's life, the Koch king Naranarayana asked for initiation, or *sharana*, as it is called, but Shankaradeva refused, since as a ruler Naranarayana had to preside in ceremonies in which other gods were honored.

Shankaradeva did not attempt to construct a philosophical system, nor did any of his successors. He knew well that the people he intended to reach with his teachings, Hindu peasants and tribal peoples, would have little interest in the subtleties of philosophy. Attitudes toward dietary practices, marriage regulations, and the caste system are comparatively relaxed, most likely in consideration of the heterogeneous character of the Assamese population. Shankaradeva, who was married twice, did not recommend celibacy and praised the role of householder, as well as supporting his family and relatives—and society, by aiding the needy. Even Madhavadeva, who was exceptional in that he was celibate himself, urged his followers not to follow his example. Like most other devotional sects, Shankaradeva's movement proclaimed that devotion was more important than caste and that all devotees were equal. It was unusual in that, to some extent, this ideal was actually realized in practice. Most striking is the fact that Shankaradeva himself was not a brahmin, as were the founders of all the other major Vaishnava sects, but a *kayastha*, a caste ranked in Assam as *shudras*. Madhavadeva was also a *kayastha*. This was resented by brahmins who claimed that a member of an inferior caste could not serve as guru to a brahmin. Brahmins also objected to Shankaradeva's having translated the *Bhagavata Purana* into Assamese, a complaint common elsewhere in India, and were angry because he forbade his followers to participate in Hindu ceremonies that involved the worship of deities other than Krishna. Brahmin harassment was a constant problem for Shankaradeva's movement. Brahmins urged both the Ahom and Koch king to persecute the sect, and once Shankaradeva was forced to go into hiding, and Madhavadeva spent nine months in house arrest. Some of their followers were tortured and sold into slavery, and the biographers describe how brahmins pelted them with rocks, tore off their garlands, and tied them to the tails of dogs.

Two institutions unique to Assamese Vaishnavism played a major role in the success of the movement: the *nam ghar* and the *satra*. The *nam ghar*, literally "house of the name," is an open rectangular hall used for prayer sessions and village meetings. It also serves as a theater and a center for cultural activities in general. Inside it is a smaller structure known as a *manikuta*, where sacred images, texts, and other valuable items are kept. At least one *nam ghar* is found in every Assamese village. The *satra* is a type of monastery that resembles the Buddhist *vihara* in some respects.[1] It usually consists of a *nam ghar* and living quarters for the monks, which are surrounded by a wall. A *satra* is headed by an *adhikara* and is populated by celibate monks called *kevaliya bhakats*. Lay devotees called *shishyas* live outside the monastery. Nonbrahmins serve as *adhikaras*, and there have been even a few isolated instances of women serving in the same capacity. Every Assamese village is affiliated with one of the region's five-hundred-odd *satras*. Assamese boys were expected to take initiation, and the *satra* also helped spread literacy, notions of hygiene, and other values. Still today, when one comments on the neatness of

Assamese villages, one is told that Shankaradeva deserves the credit. The *satra* institution not only played a major role in converting Hindus to Vaishnavas but in converting a large portion of the Assamese population to Hinduism.

The *Parijata Harana Nata*

Shankaradeva was a prolific author who wrote in several different languages. Most of his works are renderings of Sanskrit texts: he translated much of the *Bhagavata Purana* and the *Uttara-kanda* of the *Ramayana* into Assamese and wrote narrative poems such *as Rukmini Harana Kavya* and the *Harishcandra Upakhyana* based on puranic themes. These are not translations in the modern sense of the word, since Shankaradeva condenses, adds color and new detail, and combines elements from different texts, thus in many cases transforming his translation into a new work. His language is colloquial rather than Sanskritized; his work is free-flowing and idiomatic, and he is not averse to humor. Shankaradeva also wrote devotional lyrics, the best known of which are the *Bargit*, or Great Songs, and the *Kirtana-ghosha*, a collection of lyrics based on the *Bhagavata* and intended for congregational chanting. It is said that no Hindu home is without a copy of the *Kirtana-ghosha*. A doctrinal work, the *Bhakti-ratnakara*, another of his treatises, consists of Sanskrit verses dealing with Vaishnava ideas.

Shankaradeva is also the author of six plays belonging to a genre of dramatic literature known as *ankiya nat*, a term first employed by the *charita* writers. Shankaradeva himself preferred the terms *nata* or *nataka* and *yatra*. The Sanskrit term *anka* denotes a one-act play, and though efforts have been made to establish the origins of *ankiya nat* in Sanskrit models, this has proven difficult, since Assamese dramas violate many of the rules of Sanskrit dramaturgy and differ in structure, subject, treatment, and language. Shankaradeva must have been influenced by Maithili drama, which was flourishing at the time *ankiya nat* first appeared, but his plays do not follow Maithili models either. Shankaradeva was an innovator rather than an imitator.

One of the most distinctive features of Shankaradeva's plays is their language. Sanskrit plays were written in a mixture of Sanskrit and various Prakrits, and in contemporary Maithili dramas, while dialogue is in Sanskrit and Prakrit, songs are in Maithili. In Shankaradeva's dramas, aside from a sprinkling of Sanskrit couplets, the prose dialogue and the songs are written in a language scholars call Vrajavali, or Assamese Brajabuli. It is also the language in which the *Bar git* are written. It is usually described as a mixture of Maithili, Assamese, Braj Bhasha, and sometimes other languages. A Bengali counterpart, Brajabuli, was used for Vaishnava lyrics in Bengal. Recent research, however, suggests that both these Vaishnava literary idioms are little more than varieties of Early Maithili.[2] In the sixteenth century, Maithili was the oldest and the most highly developed vernacular in eastern India and was used in highly regarded lyrical and dramatic literature. As it was closely related to Assamese, it could be understood without much difficulty, so it is not difficult to understand why Shankaradeva decided to use it. An Assamese verse commenting on the mixture of languages in the *ankiya nat* says: "Sanskrit verses are composed as there will be scholars to grasp their meaning. The brahmins in the assembly will comprehend the meaning of the songs. The village folk will understand the Brajabuli words. The ignorant people will witness the masks and effigies."[3]

Ankiya nat are usually performed at night, during the winter when agricultural laborers have less work to do, religious occasions such as Janmashtami, or on full-moon nights and the like. The performance is usually held in a village *nam ghar,* and the villagers serve as the actors. Female roles are played by young men. All actors are amateurs and are not looked down on. The audience sits on mats or on the bare floor. Costumes, masks, and other props are used.

Shankaradeva's dramas begin and end with a benediction (*bhatima*). They are not divided into acts, and they have no *vidushaka,* or jester, unlike Sanskrit drama. On the other hand, they do have a *sutradhara,* or director; but in the Assamese plays, the *sutradhara* not only introduces the play and the characters as in classical drama but also continues in this role throughout its course, introducing each scene and explaining the action. The *sutradhara* also sings, dances, and delivers brief discourses. Sanskrit verses (*shlokas*) follow each change of scene, reiterating what the *sutradhara* has already said in Maithili (Vrajavali). Most of these verses were composed by Shankaradeva. The prose dialogue alternates with songs (*gitas*) sung in appropriate melodies (*ragas*), along with interludes of dancing; this gives the *ankiya nat* a certain similarity with modern Western musicals. They have also been called "lyrico-dramatic spectacles."

The *Parijata Harana* was written toward the end of Shankaradeva's life. The eminent Assamese scholar Maheshvar Neog describes it as "Shankaradeva's masterpiece with its well-developed dialogue, bold and almost realistic characterization, finely developed plot and humour."[4] The *Parijata Harana* retells two stories from the *Bhagavata* (10.59.1–45) and the *Vishnu Puranas* (5.29–31), especially the version in the latter. There we are told how Indra, ejected from heaven by the terrible demon Naraka or Narakasura, appealed to Krishna for aid. In response, Krishna, accompanied by his wife Satyabhama, flew on Garuda's back to Pragyotishapura and slew the demon and his generals after a fierce battle. On the way back to Dvaraka, Krishna stole the divine *parijata* tree from Indra, whose enemy he had defeated in battle, and planted the tree by Satyabhama's door. The story perhaps was especially attractive because of its connection with Assamese history. The demon Naraka, the son of the demon Hiranyaksha and the earth goddess, was the first ruler of Pragjyotishapura, ancient Assam. His son Bhagadatta, whom the *Mahabharata* refers to as a king of the Mlecchas, was killed by Arjuna. In Assam and Bengal there is a tradition that Duryodhana married Bhagadatta's daughter, Bhanumati.

In the following translation, the prose dialogue has been included in its entirety, as are the remarks of the *sutradhara* (abbreviated as *sutra*). Most of the songs have been condensed to save space. The translation is based on the editions of Birinchi Kumar Barua and Kaliram Medhi.[5]

The *Parijata Harana Yatra* of Shankaradeva

Hail Krishna, Vishnu Achyuta, the Supreme Lord.
Mounted on the shoulders of Garuda, he struck down his
    enemy.
In his joyful *lila* the son of Devaki
carried off the *parijata* flower for the sake of his beloved.
Victory to Krishna.

SUTRA   Render obeisance to Krishna, summon the audience and say:

Victory to Krishna, destroyer of Kamsa and his family.
His delightful form pervades the minds of his devotees,
like a hundred thousand wishing trees, he fulfills all their
    desires.
Concentrate your thoughts on his feet.
As death draws ever closer with a growl,
abandon all else and take refuge with Hari.
He is the subject of this play, its name is the *Parijata Harana*.
Listen, everyone, with devotion,
you have no other friend except Hari.
So says Shankara, the servant of Krishna.
Let everyone repeat the name of Rama!

SUTRA   Good people! He who is the Supreme Guru of the world, the Supreme Person, is entering the assembly along with his wives Rukmini and Satyabhama. He will perform the *Parijata Harana Yatra*. Watch, and listen carefully. Never stop repeating the name of Hari.

COMPANION   What is that music being played?

COMPANION   It is the instruments of the gods you hear.

SUTRA   Good people! As I said, the Supreme Lord Krishna is coming here with his wives for the sake of the *yatra*. Listen with great care.

He enters, mounted on the mighty bird Garuda.
A mere shard of his beauty eclipses that of the Love God.
His dark body glistens, his yellow robe shines,

he wears a gem-studded crown above his jewel-like face.
Bracelets dangle on his arms
and anklets jingle on his feet.
His splendid figure puts a hundred million Cupids to shame.
The radiance of his body fills all the directions.
With him are Rukmini and Satyabhama, the best of women.
So says Shankara, the slave of the slave of Hari.

SUTRA   After he dances with all his wives, Krishna is staying in a palace with Rukmini. Stayabhama is staying in her own palace. At that time god Indra arrived in the company of the celestial sage Narada. He bowed to Krishna and informed him about the depredations of the demon Narakasura. Then Narada gave obeisance to Krishna. Watch and listen with the greatest attention!

The god Indra comes astride his elephant Airavata,
a royal parasol above his head, thunderbolt in hand.
Before him is Narada, singing of the virtues of Hari.
Indra's lovely wife Shachi at one side,
walking with a graceful gait, arching her eyes.
So sings Shankaradeva: the Lord of the Gopinis is the way.

SUTRA   When Krishna saw Narada, he and his wives stood up and greeted him.

NARADA   (*Raising his hand*) May you live long!

SUTRA   After pronouncing his blessing, Narada places the *parijata* flower in the hand of Krishna and tells him about its wondrous qualities.

NARADA   Krishna, the perfume of the *parijata* can be sensed six kilometers away. Wealth, family, and glory never leave the home of a person who possesses a *parijata* flower. Because of the power of this blossom, the woman who wears it is exceptionally fortunate. Her husband will never leave her. What else can I say about this marvelous flower? (*He then sits in silence.*)

SUTRA   When Rukmini hears what the sage said about the qualities of the *parijata*, she gasps Krishna's feet with delight and says:

RUKMINI   (*her hands clasped*) My dear husband! Since I am your senior wife, O Lord of Life, please present me with that rare blossom!

SUTRA   Now listen to what happens when Rukmini asks for the flower.

Filled with delight, Rukmini bowed down to her husband's
     feet,
her hands joined together in supplication.
"Please Lord, let this *parijata* flower be given to me.

I learned of its qualities from the lips of the sage,
appease my pride.
You who are merciful to your devotees, I am begging you,
make me a present of the flower.
I am your foremost wife.
Please let my hopes be realized."
The lover Krishna smiled at his wife's words,
says Shankara, the slave of Krishna.

SUTRA   When he hears Rukmini's request, Krishna, laughing, lifts
her up and proudly sits her on his lap. The Lord of the World then
fixes the *parijata* flower in her hair. Her wish has been granted. Then,
sitting together with his wife, Krishna affectionately asks Narada for
news.

KRISHNA   Sage, are you faring well? Our city of Dvaraka has been
sanctified by your coming. I am thankful for having been graced with the
sight of you.

NARADA   Lord Krishna, your human deeds have enchanted the entire
world. It does not know you as the Lord. I know all about devotion. You
wish to enchant me? Listen Lord:

Parameshvara, Lord of the World,
I, Narada, am a slave at your feet.
I wander through all ten directions singing of your virtues.
You are the Guru of the World, the God of the gods.
May I serve your feet forever!
May my lips sing your praises forever!
I ask this boon of you.

NARADA   Krishna, you are the Supreme Person, you are Narayana.
You have descended to earth to remove its burden of evil. The demon
Naraka is causing the gods much grief at the moment. This is the reason why Indra and his wife Shachi have come to take refuge at your
feet. Look, Krishna, look!

SUTRA   With those words, Narada is silent. Indra falls at Krishna's feet,
and he and his wife praise him.

Victory to the Yadava Lord
in whose name are the four *rasas*.
Slayer of Agha, Baka, Dhenuka, and Kamsa,
you eased the earth of its burden of evil
and became an *avatara* for the sake of your devotees.
Now the sinful Naraka is committing great outrages.

He attacked heaven and carried off its riches.
I am pleading at your feet.

INDRA   Lord Krishna, is there any evil deed the demon Naraka hasn't
done? He has stolen the umbrella of Varuna and carried off all the
jewel mountain. O Krishna, what can I say, even the earrings of
Mother Aditi are not safe from him. What other recourse have I? O
Krishna, there is nowhere else for me to go save the refuge of your
feet. Please save me, Lord Jagannath, save me!

SUTRA   Once he has said this, Indra falls down before Krishna and
bursts into tears.

SHRI KRISHNA   Indra, cease your lamenting! Your enemy's final
hour has come! I will kill Narakasura right away for the sake of
the gods. You can be absolutely certain of this. Now go on ahead
to Amaravati. I will slay Narakasura today and follow you there.

NARADA   Indra, when Krishna makes a promise like this, your enemy
has as good as forfeited his head. Don't be afraid, go on ahead. Shri
Krishna has felt pity for you, so you don't need to worry. We will come
along later.

SUTRA   When he hears this promise of relief, Indra circumambu-
lates Narada and Krishna and then bows down to them. Taking leave, he
mounts his elephant Airavata and goes his way.

NARADA   Krishna, get ready to depart at once, as soon as I've seen the
fun in Dvaraka, I'll follow you.

SUTRA   When he says this, Narada departs. See what happened then!

> Narada left, singing the praises of Hari,
> and wandered to Dvaraka and gazed on its magnificence
>   with awe.
> All of Hari's houses were encrusted with jewels
> making them resemble celestial mansions.
> Then the sage spied a fabulous dwelling
> within which Satyabhama sat,
> her face gleaming like the moon waxed full.
> Narada greeted her with a smile
> and when the lady saw the sage,
> she bowed down before him
> and said, "Narada, may you live a long life!"

SUTRA   As she fans him with a cowry, the sage takes a seat.

NARADA   Queen Satyabhama, I have witnessed the dire deeds of your Krishna. Mother, you are indeed unfortunate. I have just found that out today.

SATYABHAMA   Muniraj, what are you talking about? I don't understand you at all.

NARADA   O dear, fate certainly has not been kind to you! Mother, what can I say, it pains me to have to tell you this.

SUTRA   Once he says this, the sage turns his head away and is silent. Satyabhama becomes nervous and asks:

SATYABHAMA   Muni, I know that there is no other woman as fortunate as I am. Krishna will never go off and leave me. What did you hear or see? Promise to tell me the truth right away. Muni, I'm very upset. Don't sit there and say nothing!

SUTRA   Seeing how determined the queen was, the sage says:

NARADA   Mother, O Mother! What can I tell you? It's wrong to speak about all these things. I brought down a precious *parijata* flower from heaven and put it in Krishna's hand. The wonderful qualities of the *parijata* flower make the woman who wears it very fortunate. I knew this when I told him that Satyabhama is worthy of the *parijata* flower. But then what did Krishna go and do? As he watched you out of the corner of his eye, he fastened the divine *parijata* in Rukmini's hair with his own hand with great affection. Oh, yours is an unlucky life! How can you endure witnessing the favor your co-wife enjoys? Mother, you're numbered among the dead though living. Oh, what more can I say?

SUTRA   When Satyabhama has heard about the great good fortune of her co-wife from Narada's lips, she becomes both enraged and overwhelmed with a feeling of humiliation and faints dead away. With her hair spread out, she looks like a clove tree uprooted by the wind. No breath stirs in her nostrils.

When Satyabhama's friend Indumati sees what happened, she shouts, "She's dead!" and holds her in her arms and sprinkles her head with water. Then she wipes her face with the hem of her sari and tries to comfort her as she weeps herself.

INDUMATI   My dearest friend, are you going to die of humiliation because of your co-wife? Is this any way to react? Won't your husband Krishna try to make it up to you? Mother, stop thinking these gloomy thoughts!

SUTRA   When Satyabhama has recovered to some extent, she sighs deeply as if she were in agony.

Tears poured from the lotus-like eyes of the lovely lady
as her body grew exhausted from sobbing.
All seemed to be darkness to her.
Her heart burned because of the success of her rival
and the pain welled up in her heart.
"Hari, my dear Hari, you have become like an enemy
since you slighted me so."
She rolled round on the floor groaning.

SUTRA   Satyabhama complains about her humiliation in this piteous way. Then the trouble-loving Narada returns to Krishna. Listen to what he told him!

NARADA   Shri Krishna, how can you be happy here? Satyabhama has stopped eating and drinking because of the insult of the *parijata* flower. She's dying of grief. Go to her quickly and see for yourself.

SUTRA   When he hears from the sage about his wife's grief, Shri Krishna is upset because of his deep affection for her. He asks the sage what has happened and then goes to see her.

Tell me sage, straight out, with no tricks,
is the love of my life alive?
That proud lady cannot bear the most trivial slight,
how can she survive my crime?
The suffering of my beloved sears me with pain.
By not giving her the flower, I caused her death.

SUTRA   Overwhelmed by affection, Krishna goes to his beloved. Her face is pale from weeping. She is heaving deep sighs and lying on the floor. Holding her in his arms, Krishna asks her what has happened. As tears stream from his eyes, he consoles her.

SHRI KRISHNA   Darling, I only gave a single flower to Rukmini; if this is the reason you feel slighted, then get up off the floor! I'll give you a hundred *parijata* flowers. My love, Rukmini and Jambuvati are not as favored as you are. You are as precious to me as my very life. Now you know this, so stop grieving. It breaks my heart to see you suffering in this way. Beloved, I swear it to you, get up, get up!

SUTRA   When she hears her husband's words, Satyabhama turns her back to him, sinks her head, and begins to sob in a heart-rending manner.

SATYABHAMA   My husband, why are you trying to bamboozle a miserable woman like me with your clever talk? Go to your beloved Rukmini instead! What's the point of your staying here?

SUTRA   Once she says this to Krishna, she laments. Listen and see!

"Keshava, now I have understood you.
Now I see how you behave.
Forget your tricks and go back to your dear wife.
Krishna, I didn't understand your wiles,
There's no woman as miserable as I.
I'm now aware of your lover's tricks,
now I know your mind.
Oh, I'll not outlive this insult,
I've left all hope of life."
The lady fell at her lover's feet moaning,
says Shankara the servant of Hari.

SATYABHAMA   Oh miserable me! I take second place to my co-wife!
You have humiliated me so terribly, how can I stay alive? My life is ruined!

SUTRA   Having said this, the queen faints and falls to the floor, tears
gushing from her eyes. When he sees that, Krishna cries out and takes
her in his arms, and his heart fills with tenderness. Tears run from her
doe-like eyes. He holds his beloved tight in his arms and comforts her
with the following words:

Dear, I see that your frail frame cannot bear your grief.
Tears are flowing from your lotus eyes.
My love, listen to what I have to say,
I did not give you a *parijata* flower
and I cannot get over that.
There is no one else as fortunate as you,
I gave Rukmini just one flower,
does that upset you so?
I'll pull up the *parijata* tree by the roots
and plant it by your door.
Listen my dear, I've told you the truth,
you must believe my words.
So stop crying princess,
my heart cannot bear to see your sorrow.
I swear I will do it,
get up, get up!

SUTRA   When he said this, Krishna held Satyabhama's hand.

INDUMATI   My dearest friend! Your husband is the Supreme God. He's
very upset and begging you to forgive him. What else can he to do to
satisfy you? Forget your grief, get up, get up!

SUTRA   When Satyabhama hears her husband's pleas, her heart is
somewhat calmed. Seeing that, Krishna lifts her up, sits her on

his thigh, and wipes away the dust with his yellow robe and binds up her hair. He puts betel and camphor into her mouth with his own hand.

Having gotten her way with her husband, Satyabhama bows to Krishna with a satisfied smile on her face and says:

SATYABHAMA   My dear husband, you promised to get a *parijata* tree for me. So fetch it right away and don't dawdle. I will not set foot into my home unless I see a *parijata* tree before it. I swear it!

SHRI KRISHNA   My dear, the evil demon Naraka has defeated the gods and carried everything they owned. So I first I have to kill him and help them. Then I can get you your *parijata* tree.

SATYABHAMA   You're right. First do the work of the gods, then fetch the *parijata* tree on the way. I'll go with you.

SHRI KRISHNA   My dear, you're a woman. It's not proper for you to go where fighting will be taking place.

SATYABHAMA   My husband, you have many other wives. It's not certain which one you will give the *parijata* flower to. There's no way I'll let you out of my sight.

SHRI KRISHNA   Dearest, if you're going with me, then get ready quickly.

NARADA   (*with irritation*) Krishna, I see that you're abandoning the work of the gods because of a woman. You've spent the whole day making up to her.

SHRI KRISHNA   Sage, what does a woman understand about fighting? I cannot get away from her. I'm on my way right now. Don't be angry.

SUTRA   With these words, Shri Krishna quickly sets off with his wife. He twanges his bowstring and the sound reverberates in all ten directions. Narada then comes up and says:

> The Lord of the Yadus has departed,
> *saranga* bow in hand, his wife at his side.
> He wears a yellow robe on his dark blue body
> which glistens like a new rain cloud.
> Jeweled anklets resound on his feet.
> Shankara says, "Immerse your mind in this!"

NARADA   I have not seen many men so far under their wife's thumbs as you. You can't even leave your wife when you go into battle. You are the Guru of the World. I wander through the three worlds singing of your glory. Oh, I feel ashamed!

SHRI KRISHNA   Listen, *muni*, what am I supposed to do? Satyabhama was on the brink of death because of the *parijata*. How much more of that could I take?

NARADA   Krishna, This is the way a man gets when he's lovesick. He has to do whatever his wife orders. So what! The demon Naraka is in Kamrup and this is Dvaraka, a four-month journey away. If you take a woman along, the journey will take two or three years. Is this doing the work of the gods? Do one thing. Summon Garuda, the king of the birds, your vehicle. Climb up on his shoulders and go kill Naraka.

SUTRA   When he had hears Narada's words, Krishna says to his wife:

SHRI KRISHNA   Dear, Narada is right.

SATYABHAMA   Husband, I can't go all the way by foot.

SHRI KRISHNA (*summoning Garuda*)   King of Birds: come quickly, come quickly!

GARUDA   My Lord, while I am here, there's no need to walk. Climb on my back and slay the evil Naraka.

SUTRA   Then Shri Krishna mounts on Garuda and flies off to perform his *lila*. Shri Krishna flies to Kamrup on Garuda with the speed of the wind. He sounds his conch Panchajanya, and when Naraka hears it, he comes running. Watch and hear how Krishna slew him.

> Govinda flew on the back of Garuda,
> eager to slay Naraka.
> The King of Birds went with the speed of the wind
> and reached Kamrup in the blink of an eye.
> Hari sounded his conch time and again,
> and the demons' hearts shook to hear it.
> They knew that Madhava was on his way
> and went off roaring to fight.
> Kettledrums announced the battle
> and cries of "kill, kill!" and "Hold, hold!" filled the air.
> Enraged, Naraka charged,
> intending to cleave Krishna with his sword.
> Hari twanged the string of his bow
> and plagued the demons with a flurry of missiles,
> slaughtering the demon warriors,
> slicing off arms, shoulders, and heads.
> Seeing this, the other demons fled
> as arrows struck and felled them.
> The angry Jagannath hurled his discus
> and cut off the evil Naraka's head.

The delighted gods
    beat the victory drums and tossed down flowers,
shouting "Jaya, jaya Yadava."
Let everyone repeat the name of Hari!

SUTRA Once Shri Krishna has killed Naraka, the gods celebrate the glorious deed, beating kettledrums and shouting "Jaya Krishna, jaya Krishna" and showering down flowers upon his head. Shri Krishna and Satyabhama are filled with joy. When Vasumati learns that her son Naraka has been slain, filled with grief, she takes her grandchild Bhagadatta to an audience with Shri Krishna. See what happened!

> Come to the beloved mother, come for *darshan* of Hari.
> Holding the child, Vasumati approaches with a graceful gait,
> her body pale from suffering at the sufferings of her son.
> Sighing, she wipes the tears from her eyes
> and bows to the feet of the Lord.
> Says Shankaradeva, "Rama is my heart and my goal."

SUTRA Holding her child, Vasumati prostrates herself before Shri Krishna. She then joins her hands together and says:

VASUMATI Lord Krishna, you are the Guru of the World, the Supreme Person in endless eons. My son Naraka was destroyed for the sin of opposing you. I place my grandson, Naraka's child Bhagadatta, at your feet. Please watch over him. I plead for peace at your lotus feet.

SUTRA Hearing her sad words, Shri Krishna consoles her, saying:

SHRI KRISHNA Vasumati, weep no more. Your son Naraka became a burden to the earth, and for that reason I slew him and removed it. I will do as you ask and install Bhagadatta as ruler of Kamrupa. You need worry no more.

SUTRA Shri Krishna then embraces Vasumati, and, after speaking some comforting words, he enters the demon's harem. He sends the sixteen thousand captive women he finds there to Dvaraka. After he takes the earrings of Aditi, the umbrella of Varuna, and the mountain of jewels, he and Satyabhama mount Garuda and fly off to heaven.

    Having slain the demon Naraka, Shri Krishna goes to heaven and joyfully sounds his conch. When all the gods hears the sound, they recognize it.

THE GODS Shri Krishna has come to heaven!

SUTRA The gods applaud Shri Krishna and beat the celestial kettledrums and shower him with flowers. When Satyabhama sees this, she asks her beloved:

SATYABHAMA   My dear husband, what place have we come to where kettledrums are sounding and flowers raining down? Introduce me to all of these people.

SHRI KRISHNA   Devi, don't you know that this is Amaravati and that these are the gods who have come to see me? Look, there's the god Indra sitting on the back of his elephant Aitavata. There's his queen Shachi, over there are the guardians of the directions, and there are the *siddhas* and the *vidyadharas.*

SATYABHAMA   My husband, what is that tree there shining on top of a celestial mansion?

SHRI KRISHNA   Don't you know, dear? That's the reason you were angry with me, that is the *parijata* tree.

SATYABHAMA   Why, I have obtained my heart's desire. I'll dress in *parijata* blossoms and put on a show in front of my cowives. Dear husband, do it right away!

SUTRA   Then Indra appears and receives them with pride. Shachi embraces Satyabhama and welcomes her.

INDRA   Krishna, we are grateful to you for killing the evil Narasura. You have saved us once again. There's no way for us to repay that debt.

SUTRA   When Indra spoke these words, tears of affection welled up in his eyes. He then stood in silence. Shri Krishna and Indra bowed to Mother Aditi. Satyabhama fell on her knees before her mother-in-law.

SUTRA   Aditi begins to praise Shri Krishna as supreme among the gods.

> "*Jaya, jaya* to the abode of the world.
> *Jaya, jaya* to the bane of demons.
> *Jaya, jaya* to the savior of his servants.
> *Jaya, jaya* to Lord Murari.
> King of the Yadus, show mercy to me.
> I have sought the refuge of your feet.
> Supreme Person, save me!
> There is no recourse save you.
> I have abandoned the things of the world
> and am praising you with palms joined."
> She then made a deep bow.
> Everyone, repeat the name of Rama!

SUTRA   Then, Krishna shows Aditi his knowledge and fills her heart with the spirit of Vaisnavism. He bows to her and says:

SHRI KRISHNA   Mother, you are the supremely merciful deity. Always give me your blessings.

SUTRA   Aditi hears this, embraces Shri Krishna, and says:

ADITI   My son, may you live long. Because of my boon, neither god nor demon can overcome you.

SUTRA   Then Shri Krishna takes leave of the goddess. He puts Varuna's umbrella and the jewel mountain in Indra's hand. Then, together with Satyabhama and Narada, he bids farewell to the gods and returns home.

> The handsome Murari, enchanter of the world,
>   continues his *lila*,
> walking gracefully with the best of women.
> There is a gentle smile on his lips,
> his body glistens like a new rain cloud,
> cloaked in a yellow robe.
> Anklets jingle on his delicate feet
> resembling the fresh shoots.
> He has descended to earth, bestowing devotion
>   and salvation,
> says the servant of Krishna.

SUTRA   The charming figure of Shri Krishna enchants them with his supreme *lila*. Now watch and see what happens next. Satyabhama becomes angry, grips Shri Krishna's yellow robe, and says:

SATYABHAMA   My dear husband, you've really kept your promise well, haven't you! You haven't brought me a *parijata* flower. I don't understand your heart at all.

SHRI KRISHNA   I forgot, dear. It's not my fault. (*Speaking to Narada*) Rishi, go quickly. Go find Indra's parijata tree and bring it here right away.

SUTRA   When he hears Shri Krishna's command, Narada goes to Indra and says:

NARADA   Oh Devaraja, Shri Krishna wants the *parijata* for his wife Satyabhama. Have it sent to him immediately!

SUTRA   When she hears Narada's command, Shachi, full of rage, retorts,

SHACHI   What bad luck! Does that petty mortal Satyabhama hope to wear the *parijata* flower of Indra's consort Shachi? Divine *rishi*, tell her that only a woman who has accumulated innumerable merits, one who is a resident of the Amaravati, the city of the gods, can wear that flower. Indra cannot give my *parijata* to her!

INDRA   Rishi, how can I give away a *parijata*? It is the possession of goddesses. Doesn't Krishna know anything about women? Go tell him, Narada!

SUTRA   Narada goes back and tells Krishna and Satyabhama what Shachi has said.

NARADA   Krishna, you sent me for the *parijata* flower. I am very ashamed. All that happened was that she heaped insults on Satyabhama. When Shachi heard me mention the *parijata*, she threw a fit and asked how a woman like Satyabhama could want to wear a *parijata* flower. She was in a rage; she said she had meditated and prayed in birth after birth for endless ages in order to become the mistress of Amaravati and earn the right to wear the *parijata* flower. Why, Krishna, when I heard the goddess's curses, my heart burned. How miserable I felt!

SUTRA   When Satyabhama hears that, shaking with rage, she says:

SATYABHAMA   My husband, why did you bring me here? Shall Shachi, that daughter of a *danava*, speak harsh words to me and keep the *parijata*? Oh Lord, what are you afraid of? Go and get the *parijata* right away!

NARADA   Well spoken, your majesty! Krishna should fetch the *parijata* right away.

SUTRA   Then, when Shri Krishna hears his wife's words, he goes up to the *parijata* tree and pulls it up by the roots. When the guards see that, they begin shouting,

GUARDS   Krishna, what are you doing taking Shachi's parijata tree?

SATYABHAMA   Guards, listen to me: Go and tell Shachi that I, Satyabhama, am taking her *parijata* tree. Now do your best to try and stop us!

GUARDS   [When the guards heard that, they went to Indra and Shachi, prostrated themselves before her, and said:] Mother Shachi, Satyabhama had her husband Krishna carry off your *parijata* tree. Do what is proper!

SUTRA   When she hears about the theft of the celestial tree, Shachi bursts into a rage and says to Indra:

SHACHI   Husband, is a mortal being taking away the *parijata* tree in your very presence? What are you good for? What's the use of your thunderbolt?

SUTRA   Once she has said this, she begins to weep before him.

INDRA   Darling, don't be upset! What is Krishna compared to me? I'll defeat him and bring back the *parijata* at once. Don't worry!

SUTRA   Indra then begins to make preparations for battle. He picks up his bow and arrows and rides off mounted on the back of his elephant Airavata. Shachi and the gods accompany him.

SHACHI Daughter of Satrajit, are you, a mortal, stealing my *parijata* flower? Now your luck has run out. If you don't want me to wipe you out along with the rest of your family with a thunderbolt, give it back at once!

SUTRA She roars out these words. Listen!

> "You're brave for a mere mortal.
> You stole our *parijata*.
> My husband Indra, who wields a thunderbolt,
> the annihilator of demons, is on his way.
> Give me back my *parijata* tree
> and save your life, princess.
> Your husband, the mortal Madhava
> was quite presumptuous to take it
> in the very presence of Indra. What is he?"
> Such was the blustering of Shachi.

SHACHI Satyabhama, I know all about your husband Madhava, the cowherd who ran after *gopis*. No woman in Gokula was safe from him. Why even Kamsa's humpbacked servant girl Kubji couldn't escape his clutches. What else can I say about him? Is this profligate puffed-up Krishna going to steal my *parijata*? He and his family are doomed!

SATYABHAMA Listen, Indrani, my husband is the Supreme Guru of the World. Merely by repeating his name, the world is saved from all sin. And you're insulting him! Why don't you drop dead, you shameless hussy! I feel disgust just saying the name of your husband Indra. You can't count all the dancing girls your Indra keeps here in Amaravati. What sort of things does he do? He seduced Ahalya, the wife of the sage Gautama, and made her lose caste. That's why his whole body was covered with vaginas. You wretch, is this the Indra you're boasting to me about?

> "You wretched woman, are you insulting him
> the dust of whose lotus feet you have taken?
> The Guru of the World before whom
> Brahma and Shiva fall.
> How can a slave like Shachi
> look him in the face and scold him?
> If you sing his name, you are cleansed from sin
> and gain both devotion and heaven.
> Are you insulting Govinda, you hussy?"
> Says Shankara at the feet of Hari.

SATYABHAMA Shachi, you daughter of a *danava*, what have you to brag about? We showed the greatest heroism by carrying off the *parijata*. Look at your husband Indra, let's see how he capable he is of fighting and retrieving the *parijata* from Krishna's hands. Then we'll see what your boasts are worth.

SUTRA　When Shachi hears these harsh words from Satyabhama, stung by the insult, she angrily says to her husband:

SHACHI　My husband, King of the Gods, what good are you? You just stand there listening to the insults of a mortal woman! You're not a hero at all! It's a mockery to call you Indra, the god Indra.

SUTRA　Then, wounded by the arrow-like insults of his wife Shachi, Indra flies into a rage, picks up his bow, and goes up to offer Krishna battle. Seeing him, Krishna twangs the string of his bow, climbs on Garuda's back, and goes to face Indra. Indra looks at him and says arrogantly:

INDRA　O Yadava, why did you steal Shachi's *parijata*? I will put an end to your life with my razor-sharp arrows. How can you withstand me?

SUTRA　Indra says much in this vein. Now hear and see how the two fired their divine missiles and clashed in battle.

> With a shout Indra fired his arrows.
> "Today I'll take your life," he cried.
> Holding his *saranga* bow, Hari looked at him
> and fired off arrows,
> shattering all Indra's shafts,
> and piercing his breast pierced with bolts.

SUTRA　Struck by Krishna's arrow, Indra falls unconscious. He recovers, gets up and says:

INDRA　O Shri Krishna, if you are going to give back the *parijata*, give it back. Otherwise, I'll finish you off with my thunderbolt.

KRISHNA　You evil king of the gods! Are you trying to frighten me? Let me see just how mighty you are.

> His strength restored,
> the Smasher of Cities held his thunderbolt aloft
> and aimed it.
> "I'll take your life," he cried.
> "Stay! stay!" retorted the Yadu king.

SUTRA　Not being able to overcome Krishna with his arrows, Indra, swollen with pride and rage, hurls his thunderbolt. Hari laughs, leaps into the air, and grabs it.

SHRI KRISHNA   You scoundrel king of the gods, you can see how I can withstand your blows. Now withstand mine!

SUTRA   With these words, Krishna raises up his discus. When Indra sees it, his heart shakes. Unable to keep his arms and legs from shaking, he flees on the back of his elephant, terrified. When he sees that, Krishna runs after him, laughing.

> In fear of his life Indra fled,
> right behind him ran Madhava grinning.
> "Hey Purandara!," shouted Murari,
> "Stop, where are you running to, thunderbolt-wielder?"
> Indra fled, not looking back,
> so sings Shankara, servant of Krishna.

SUTRA   Shouting at Indra to stop, Krishna pursues him. Finally Indra is unable to flee further. When Satyabhama sees that, she laughs and ridicules him.

SATYABHAMA   Purandara, why are you running? Why, it's not proper for you, the king of the gods, to flee in fear after being bested by the mortal Krishna. Shachi struts about before you decked out in her finery with a garland of *parijata* flowers in her hair. You're the hero who bears the thunderbolt. Why are you fleeing? Are you turning your back to shame? Oh poor Shachi! Look how brave your Indra is! Why don't you turn your husband around to face the other way? I, a mortal, am taking your *parijata* flowers. How can you stand that?

SUTRA   Then, when he hears his wife being insulted in that way, Indra turns around and says:

INDRA   Satyabhama, I am well aware that you are the fiercest and most headstrong of all Krishna's wives. Why are you making fun of me in this way? Look, I have been defeated by the Supreme Guru of the World, Krishna Narayana, whose lotus feet have been worshiped for endless eons by Brahma and Shiva. It that anything for me to be ashamed of? Women can't understand anything! There's no reason for you to mock me.

SUTRA   Once he said this, Indra begins to lament, sobbing, "Oh, I am a sinner who was so blinded by *maya* that I did battle with the Supreme Lord. Miserable me! His body trembling with terror, Indra joins his hands together, prostrates himself on the ground before Krishna, and says, "Save me! Save me"!

> *Jaya, jaya* Murari, crusher of Keshi and Kamsa,
> *Jaya, jaya* to the bearer of Govardhan,

> to him who eases the fears of the faithful,
> *Jaya, jaya* to the crusher of the poisonous Kali,
> to the dwarf who bettered Bali.
> Made blind by your *maya*, I did a great wrong in
>   fighting you.
> Forgive this crime of mine, I fall at your feet.
> Purge me of my evil-mindedness,
> I will follow the path of devotion to you.

SUTRA   After praising Krishna in this way, he lies with the greatest humility before Krishna and begins to wail. Seeing that he is overcome with terror, Krishna smiles, takes him by the hand, raises him up, and comforts him, saying:

SHRI KRISHNA   Purandara, you are my elder brother. I do not hold you at fault. You have nothing to be afraid of. Here, take your thunderbolt. I find no joy in the *parijata*, take it back.

SUTRA   When Satyabhama hears him say this, she scowls at her husband and says, chewing her lips in irritation:

SATYABHAMA   My dear husband, what in the world has come over you! You heard those wheedling words from Indra. Once again, he begged us to do battle with the demon Naraka and accomplish the work of the gods. You can have confidence in what he says. What right do you have to give away my *parijata*?

INDRA   Lord Krishna, take the *parijata*. I will send it to Dvaraka along with the divine assembly and all my wealth. As long as you remain on the earth, you can have use of it.

SUTRA   Accepting his offer, Krishna bids a respectful farewell to Indra, takes the *parijata* flower with his permission, and happily leaves with his wife.

> Taking the *parijata*, they graciously left.
> That gem of a woman smiled with pleasure
> and walked with the stately gait of the elephant.
> The dark-hued Krishna walked in delight with his wife
> who was like a elephant cow
> and he like a mighty elephant bull at play.
> The servant of Krishna sings,
> I bow at the feet of Hari.

SUTRA   Then Krishna and Satyabhama enter Dvaraka delighted by their adventure. When everyone learns of Krishna's arrival, a great celebration is held. Everywhere victory drums are sounded. When Rukmini learns that her husband has triumphed in battle, she goes to him with her ladies-in-waiting and bows down before him. Krishna embraces her and comforts her. Then Rukmini stands to one side with her ladies-in-waiting. Puffed up with pride, Satyabhama says to her:

SATYABHAMA   Oh princess of Vidarbha; your lord gave you a single *parijata* flower. Look, look here, he uprooted the entire *parijata* tree and brought it for me! Look at the great honor he rendered me!

SUTRA   When she hears Satyabhama's boastful words, Rukmini smiles and replies:

RUKMINI   My dear sister Satyabhama, what are you talking about? My husband Krishna is the Supreme Guru of the World. When one worships his lotus feet, can anything else in the universe seem precious in comparison? Then *dharma, artha, kama,* and *moksha* can be obtained with the greatest of ease. What is a *parijata* compared to that?

SUTRA   As she spoke of the greatness of devotion, love touches Rukmini. Hear how she describes service to the feet of Hari:

> What are you saying to me?
> With Hari as a husband, what do I lack?
> Meditating on his vermilion feet,
> I obtain the four *rasas*.
> Singing the virtues of his name,
> I am saved from sin.
> So says Shankara, there is no way but that of Hari.

SATYABHAMA   My lord Krishna, why are you neglecting me? Plant the *parijata* tree at once before my door.

SUTRA   When Krishna hears the words of his beloved, he plants the tree by his door with his own hands. The queen then says:

SATYABHAMA   My dear husband, what have you done? I have many co-wives. Think of all the problems there will be with people stealing *parijata* flowers! Don't put it there, plant it at my door!

SUTRA   Krishna, filled with thoughts of his wife, uproots the *parijata* again and plants by the door of her dwelling. Her wish fulfilled, Satyabhama bows to her husband, and she and her ladies-in-waiting praise him.

Krishna slew Narakasura, accomplishing the work of the gods, he defeated Indra, brought the *parijata* tree, and planted it at the door of his beloved. In this way Krishna performed his *lila* together with his wife.

Acting out his *lila* in this way, Krishna fulfilled the desires of his devout wives and remained in the city of Dvaraka. The devotion of those who listen to and repeat the story of Hari's theft of the parijata flower with faith will greatly increase. Knowing this, repeat the name of Hari!

> Victory to Murari, the Life of the World.
> Slayer of Kamsa, Keshi, Baka, and Agha.
> He is the ruler of the vast cosmos,
> ever granting salvation and devotion.
> Victory to Yadava, the slayer of Danuja,
> who punishes evildoers and rescues the faithful.
> Victory to the Supreme Person, the God of the gods
> whose feet are worshiped by Brahma and Shiva.
> This play has been composed with great care
> in various meters in order to spread devotion to Hari.
> *Parijata Harana* is its name.
> Listen, good folk, to the unparalleled virtues of Hari.
> This is the essence of religion in the Kali age,
> there is not, is not, any other path.
> See how Kali has leveled everything,
> making no distinction between virtue and vice.
> Foul-minded folk never understand
> that there is no other way but that of the Bearer of the
>   Saranga Bow.
> Concentrate your mind on Hari, leave all other hopes.
> Put firm faith in the name of Hari.
> It is the name of the King of Dharma.
> So says Shankaradeva, the servant of Krishna:
> repeat the name of Rama!

NOTES

1. For details see S. N. Sarma, *The Neo-Vaisnavite Movement and the Satra Institution in Assam* (1966; reprint, Guwahati: Lawyer's Book Stall, 1999).

2. See W. L. Smith, *Dr. W. L. Smith on Sankaradeva*, compiled by Prabhat Ch. Das (Guwahati: Oriental Institute for Sankaradeva Studies, 2001), and W. L. Smith, "Inventing Brajabuli," *Archiv Orientalni* (Prague) 68, no. 3 (2000).

3. Mahesvar Neog, *Early History of the Vaisnava Faith and Movement in Assam: Sankaradeva and His Times* (1965; reprint, Delhi: Motilal Banarsidass, 1983), 267.

4. *Ankiya Nat*, edited by Birinci Kumar Baruva (1940), 3rd ed. (Guwahati: Department of Historical and Antiquarian Studies in Assam, 1983).

5. *Ankavali*, ed. Kaliram Medhi (Guvahati: Jayanti Art Press, 1950).

7

Tamil Nadu: Weaving Garlands in Tamil: The Poetry of the *Alvars*

Vasudha Narayanan

Some of the earliest poems of Krishna and Vishnu in South India are found in the Tamil language and specifically in the poetry held sacred by the Sri Vaishnava tradition of South India. To understand these poems is not just to know the words; it is to know one Hindu tradition's notion of aural revelation, it is to explore the social and ritual context of a sacred text, it is to be sensitive to the traditions of recitation, music, and verbal and performative commentaries that have been associated with its transmission. While the earliest compositions to Vishnu are found in anthologies between the second and fifth centuries C.E., the body of literature that just focuses on devotion to Vishnu is called the *Divya Prabandham* (Sacred Collect), which includes the *Tiruvaymoli*, a poem of 1,102 verses.

The Sri Vaishnava tradition of South India became organized around the time of its fifth and most important teacher (*acharya*), Ramanuja (c. 1017–1137 C.E.). The phrase "Sri Vaishnava" occurs in the *Tiru Venkatam* (Tirupati) temple inscriptions as early as 966 C.E., and it is probable that a community bearing that name existed even from the ninth century. The Sri Vaishnava community emphasizes exclusive devotion to the lord Vishnu and his consort Sri. Like many of the other Hindu traditions, it accepts the Sanskrit *Vedas*, the epics *Ramayana* and *Mahabharata*, and the *Puranas* as scripture but, in addition to these, also claims that the poems of the *alvars* are "revealed." The word *alvar* is traditionally derived from the Tamil root *al* ("deep"), and the title *alvar* was given to eleven men and one woman who are said to have been immersed deep in the love of Vishnu. The twelve *alvars*, namely, Poykay,

Bhuttat, Pey, Tirumalisai, Kulasekara, Tondaradipoti, Tiruppan, Periyalvar, Andal, Tirumankai Nammalvar, and Madhurakavialvar, probably lived between the sixth and the tenth centuries C.E. Many of them traveled from temple to temple singing in praise of Vishnu. The twenty-four works of the *alvars*, combined, are about four thousand verses long, and they came to be known as the *Nalayira Divya Prabandham*, or the Sacred Collect of Four Thousand Verses. The Sri Vaishnavas refer to the poems simply as the *Divya Prabandham*. The poems of the *alvars*, as we have them today, are not arranged in the chronological order of their composition but are divided into four sections each containing about one thousand verses.

The poetry and the poems are socially significant. First, they were composed in the Tamil language, rather than Sanskrit; second, the poets were of many castes; and finally, there is one woman, Andal, in the group of *alvars*. The poets celebrate the Tamil language in which the poems are composed. For the first time within the Hindu complex of religions, in these poems devotion was expressed in a mother tongue, a "language . . . continuous with the language of one's earliest childhood and family, one's local folk and folklore."[1] Unlike Sanskrit, it was a spoken language, associated with powerful emotions. Some of the *alvars* were brahmins; others came from the other castes. Tiruppanalvar was said to be a *panchama*, or outcaste. Andal, a woman, is considered to be one of the most important of the poets. She was disdainful of the idea of marrying a human being, vowing to marry only Vishnu/Krishna himself. What we have here, therefore, is a scenario where devotees consider faith to be more important than caste or gender and the Tamil language to be a delightful medium in which they can express their emotions.

After the eleventh century C.E., the Sri Vaishnava community came to see one of the *alvars*, Sathakopan (ninth century), known affectionately as Nammalvar, or "our *alvar*," as a paradigmatic devotee, and his *Tiruvaymoli* as the equivalent of the *Sama Veda*. Andal, the woman poet, is also venerated with great enthusiasm. Her icon is consecrated and worshiped in Sri Vaishnava temples in India and around the world; in North America, we find her in several temples, including those in Toronto; Aurora and Lemont, Illinois (near Chicago); Malibu, California; Atlanta; Pittsburgh; Rochester, New York; and elsewhere. Her poems are recited daily in these temples.

The Sri Vaishnava community thinks of the entire Sacred Collect, but particularly Nammalvar's works, as equivalent to the Sanskrit *Vedas*. Canonized as scripture, the *Tiruvaymoli*, in particular, has been of seminal importance in the piety and liturgy of the Sri Vaishnava community of South India, and is extraordinarily significant in the history of Hindu literature. It was the first "vernacular" work within the Hindu consciousness to be considered "revealed"; it was also the first work in a mother tongue to be introduced as part of domestic and temple liturgy. Unlike the Sanskrit *Vedas*, which could only be recited by male members of the upper castes, the *Tiruvaymoli* has been recited by men and women of all castes of Sri Vaishnava society. It is historically significant as a key part of the Tamil devotional literature that influenced the religious patterns in medieval northern India. The devotion voiced in the *Tiruvaymoli* was transmitted through the Sanskrit text known as the *Bhagavata Purana* and possibly through the teacher Ramananda (c. 1360–1470), as well as through Sanskrit hymns and oral tradition, and appeared in different forms in the teachings of Chaitanya, Vallabha, Surdas, Kabir, and Guru Nanak.

According to Sri Vaishnava tradition, Nammalvar is said to belong to the landowning Vellalla Hindu community, which South Indian brahmins traditionally hold to be a low caste but in reality wields considerable economic power. Nammalvar claims in the *Tiruvaymoli* that the Lord speaks through him (7.9), and Sri Vaishnavas quote these verses to proclaim the "revealed" nature of the work. Very little historical information is available about the poet, but it is assumed that he lived about the ninth century c.e. Around the tenth century, the brahmin scholar known as Nathamuni (who was later hailed as the first teacher of the Sri Vaishnava community) was entranced by a set of eleven verses that he heard from wandering musicians, and he inferred from the eleventh "signature" verse that this set was part of a poem with a thousand stanzas. The verses that so moved Nathamuni were from the *Tiruvaymoli*. According to Sri Vaishnava tradition, in the course of his search to retrieve the other verses of the *Tiruvaymoli*, he was also blessed with the revelation of three other, shorter works of Nammalvar, and about twenty other poems composed by other Tamil poet-saints. The idea of the primary and, in fact, the "parent" status of the *Tiruvaymoli* and its author to all other poems and poets remains strong in Sri Vaishnava consciousness.

Andal, the woman poet, also has a special status in the Sri Vaishnava community. She composed two poems in which she particularly voices her love for Krishna. In the *Tiruppavai,* she imagines herself to be a *gopi* waking up her friends and then going on to wake up Krishna, whom she calls Rama, Mal, and the various names of Vishnu. In later centuries, the Sri Vaishnavas think of Andal as either the incarnation of the earth goddess (Bhu Devi) or as Nila Devi, a third consort of Vishnu.

Perhaps the first thing we notice about the *alvar* poems is that the devotion is addressed to Vishnu and not just to Krishna or to Rama. Unlike some North Indian poets who focused on either Rama or Krishna, in the South, the *alvars* composed primarily to Vishnu, especially in his enshrined form in the local temple. This form, called *archavatara* in Sri Vaishnava theology, is considered to be an actual incarnation of Vishnu, equivalent to Rama or Krishna. The local icon is considered to be absolutely, completely Vishnu— the same Vishnu who incarnated himself as the fish, the tortoise, and Rama and Krishna. The *alvars* moved seamlessly between Vishnu and his descents, identifying one with the other. Thus, we do not find a poet like Surdas or Tulsi, who focus primarily on Krishna or Rama—the *alvars* wrote to Vishnu, who is indistinguishable from his incarnations and from the form in the temple.

Periyalvar writes about the temple at Shrirangam:

> This is the temple of him who became
> the divine fish, tortoise, boar, lion, and dwarf.
> He became Rama in three forms, he became Kanna,
> and as Kalki he will end [these worlds].
> This is Srirangam, where the swan and its mate
> swing on the lotus blossoms, embrace on flowery beds,
> and revel in the red pollen strewn around the river.
> (*Periyalvar Tirumoli* 4.9.9)

It is the same Vishnu who is in the ocean of milk, who came as Krishna—who, so as to marry his cousin Nappinnai, killed seven bulls in a show of valor. The same god is Rama, who shot a single arrow through seven trees to defeat Vali and befriend Sugriva.

We find a uniquely Tamil milieu in the songs of the *alvars*. Vishnu is called Mal, the wondrous one; this name, in fact, is used often. Many characters and stories are also uniquely Tamil—Krishna's consort is not Radha, as in the North, but Nappinnai, who is his cousin. In South India, cross-cousin marriages are common, and Nappinnai is portrayed as the daughter of Krishna's maternal uncle, a relationship that is considered to be traditionally right for marriages in the Tamil country. In order to wed Nappinnai, Krishna tames seven bulls in a public tournament. The taming of the bulls is again unique to these parts and is still practiced in Tamil Nadu during the month of January.

Krishna is Kannan ("the darling"), and he sports in the Tamil landscape as much as on the banks of the Yamuna. The *alvar* poetry assumes the earlier Tamil views on landscape aesthetics and literature as a given—specific scenes signify specific emotions for the poet. The early Tamil Sangam poetry (the first few centuries C.E.) spoke of five landscapes and correlated them to five moods or situations one could encounter in matters of love. Thus, a poem set on the seashore indicated that there a lover was pining for her beloved; mountainous terrain suggested a rapturous union; and so on. The passionate poems of the *alvars* are set not just in the lush Tamil countryside, with its banana trees, coconut groves, and mango plantations, but also in this stylized, aesthetic, interior landscape with its crashing waves, stormy clouds, and mountain winds.

The *alvars* sang about temples in several cities, towns, forests, and mountains. After the poems were collected and redacted by Nathamuni, the Sri Vaishnava community began to celebrate the 108 places that the *alvars* glorified in their hymns. These included 106 places in India—most of them in the South—and two locations of afterlife. These two were Vaikuntha, or the heavenly permanent abode of Vishnu, and the ocean of milk, upon which Vishnu reclines.

Finally, a word about the reception of these songs. The hymns have been recited, sung, and danced at temples and at homes in front of the deities. During the annual festival of recitation (*adhyayanotsava*), held between December and January in the Sri Vaishnava temples, the Sanskrit *Vedas* are recited. After the time of the early *acharyas*—indeed, the late *alvars* themselves, according to some biographical traditions—the Sacred Collect, which the Sri Vaishnavas understand as equivalent to the *Vedas*, has been recited. In Shrirangam, Shrivilliputtur, and Alvar Tirunagari, these are danced by male brahmins who hail from a particular *araiyar* (cantor) family.

The imagery of vision and sound also dominates the ritual patterns of the annual Festival of Recitation at the Srirangam temple in South India. In Srirangam, as the camphor is lit in the Hall of a Thousand Pillars, and the flame lights up the visible form of Vishnu, the brahmin cantors at the other end of the hall begin the recitation of the *Tiruvaymoli,* or Sacred Utterance. Through light and sound, vision and recited words, with eyes and ears, the community is put in touch with the heavenly realm, which they believe descends to earth for the ten days that it takes to recite and act the poem. For the duration of these ten days, the "gates of heaven," large doors at the northern side of this temple, are flung open, and the pilgrims stream through to see the divine form of the deity and to hear the recitation of the holy words of the *Tiruvaymoli.*

The Sri Vaishnava's experience and understanding of the hymns of the *alvars*, therefore, involves a study of the hymns' revealed status, recitation schedules, musical renderings, oral and written commentarial traditions, and dramatic performances in temples. It involves an understanding of the learning process by which the verses are committed to memory, the details of the almanac that dictate the selection of verses to be recited every day, the process by which the commentaries were recorded, and the ritual context of the temples where the songs are performed. Hearing and seeing these verses performed is to participate in the centrality of sacred sound and vision in the Hindu tradition.

Alvar Poetry to Vishnu: A Sampling

The first words of the first alvar:

> With the earth as the lamp
> the sweeping oceans as the ghee,
> and the sun with its fiery rays
> as the flame,
> I have woven a garland of words
> for the feet of the Lord,

who bears the red flaming wheel,
so I can cross the ocean of grief.

Poykai Alvar, Mudal Tiruvantati 1

Yashoda's lullaby:

A colorful little cradle of hammered gold,
studded with gems, intertwined with diamonds,
Brahma brought with love for you.

My little dwarf, *talelo*,
O Lord who paced the worlds, *talelo.*[2]

Periyalvar, Tirumoli 1.3.1

Nammalvar urges us to sing about Krishna and states his reason for the avatara (incarnation):

To punish Kamsa who tormented the good,
the Lord left his primal form of light
up there and took birth here:
   What are people who cannot sing of him,
   the Lord placed first in the *Vedas,*
who cannot jump about
in the streets—
Why do the learned and the wise
chant and roll the beads?
Are they even human?

Tiruvaymoli 3.5.5

Two young girls play a game marveling at Krishna's accessibility and supremacy:

He became a cowherd for the ignorant,
   He delighted
in eating the fragrant butter from shining pots
   in Ayppati, look my friend!

For the golden stomach that delighted in eating
the fragrant butter from shining pots,
the water, the seas, and the worlds were not enough,
   O *calale!*[3]

Periya Tirumoli 11.5.2

Vishnu/Krishna's supremacy and accessibility:

My Lord,
As Nara and Narayana, revealed

without restriction the books of ethics.
   Let that be;
Look here, the other day
[at the time of dissolution]
he opened wide his mouth and throat
[to swallow] the flaring suns, the earth,
the foaming oceans, the mountains and fires.

And now
he has eaten the butter churned by the *gopis*
and stands bound by the rope.
   Is there a greater marvel than this?
         Periya Tirumoli 10.6.1

Nammalvar speaks of the salvific nature of thinking about Krishna's mischief:

Take note: leaving aside many kinds
of knowledge that hit the mark,
and penances performed over many ages,
in this very birth, in a few days,
I've attained their results,
my heart follows my Lord
who hid and ate in stealth
the butter and milk in the hanging pot,
ending the sorrows of being born.
         Tiruvaymoli 2.3.8

Periyalvar speaks about Govardhana:

Like the king of the serpents opening his many hoods
   and supporting the vast worlds on it,
The five fingers of Damodara's hand opened
   like the petals of a flower
   and held aloft Govardhana.
This is the hill where the monkeys carry their babies
   and sing in praise of Hanuman
   who caused such havoc in Lanka,
and lull their little ones to sleep.
         Periyalvar Tirumoli 3.5.7

Nammalvar identifies the Vishnu who sleeps on the serpent bed as Krishna, who won the hand of Nappinnai, and Rama, who killed Vali:

He lay on the serpent bed
in the ocean of milk;

have you seen him,
   this lord?
With a flowing robe of gold,
He, like a calf
dark as a thunderous cloud
comes
filling the streets—

we have seen him
   here, in Vrindavanam.
        Nacciyar Tirumoli 14.5

A prankster
who knows no *dharma*,
He whose eyebrows arch
like the bow Saranga
   in his hand,
handsome one
   without equal,
have you seen him?

He whose form is dark,
whose face glows bright
like the sun that fans
on the peaks
   of the rising hills,
   we have seen him
   here, in Vrindavanam.
        Nacciyar Tirumoli 14.6

The passion of the separation and union: the heroine seems "possessed" by Vishnu:

The words of the mother:

"I'm the earth, you see," she says.
"I'm all the visible skies," she says.
"I'm the fires,
   the winds,
   and the seas," she says.
Is it because our Lord dark as the sea
   has entered her and taken over?

How can I explain, my girl,
   to you who see nothing
   but this world?
        Tiruvaymoli 5.6.3

Nammalvar savors a quiet moment of union with Krishna:

> As ambrosia that never sates,
> he has mingled with my self
> that is nothing,
> my Lord Kannan,
> dark raincloud at its darkest:
> red coral does not equal
> his mouth, nor the lotus
> his eyes, feet,
> or his hands.
>> Great necklaces, long hair, waist-string
>> and much else: his ornaments are many.
>>> *Tiruvaymoli* 2.5.5

> Who is my companion? Frightened,
> I search, sinking like a ship,
> In a stormy sea of life and death.

> Radiant and glorious,
> bearing aloft his discus and conch,
> He comes and becomes one
> even with me, his servant.
>> *Triuvaymoli* 5.1.9

Krishna drives the chariot in the Bharata war:

> Dark as the blue seas, Kannan,
> the black diamond of the heavenly hosts,

> He is my dear life,
> the Light that sleeps on the many-hooded serpent—

> to destroy the army of the Hundred who came to kill,
> once upon a time he sided with the Five,

> and in that terrible war that day
> he drove a chariot—

> when will these eyes glimpse
> the sounding anklets on his feet, Oh when?
>> *Triuvaymoli* 3.6.10

> It's incredible—
> *You* were born! You grew up!
> You showed your strength
> At the great battle of Bharata!
> You showed your valor
> to the five brothers!

The wonder of all this!
  You enter my soul,
melt it, and eat it.
O radiant flame of the sky!
When can I reach you?
                    Triuvaymoli 5.10.1

O wondrous one who was born!
O wondrous one who fought the Bharata war!
Great one, who became all things,
    starting with primal elements:
    wind, fire, water, sky, and earth.
Great one, wondrous one,
    you are in all things
    as butter lies hidden in fresh milk,
you stand in all things
    and yet transcend them.
    Where can I see you?
                    Triuvaymoli 8.5.10

Rama is the Lord in Tillai-Chitrakutam (Chidambaram):

In the beautiful city of Ayodhya, encircled by towers,
A flame that lit up all the worlds appeared in the Solar race,
and gave life to all the heavens.
This warrior, with dazzling eyes,
Rama, dark as a cloud, the First one, my only lord
is in Chitrakuta, the City of Tillai.
    When is the day
    when my eyes behold him
    and rejoice?
                    Kulasekhara Alvar's *Perumal Tirumoli* 10.1

Another kind of separation—Dasharatha and Rama:

The words of Dasharatha:

Without hearing him call me "Father" with pride and with love,
Without clasping his chest adorned with gems to mine,
Without embracing him, without smoothing his forehead,
Without seeing his graceful gait, majestic like the elephant,
Without seeing his face [glowing] like the lotus,
    I, wretched one,
    having lost my son, my lord,
    Still live.
                    Kulasekara Alvar's *Perumal Tirumoli* 9.6

Hanuman presents his credentials to Sita in Ashokavana by telling her of an incident known only to her and Rama:

> *The testimony of Hanuman:*
>
> O lady, beautiful as a garland
> bursting with blossoming flowers,
> grant me leave to bow at your feet.
> Graciously listen to my words.
> O lady, gentle as a fawn,
> with eyes like twin flowers,
> a perfect match for each other,
> Recognize my story:
> Once, during the night,
> when it was time for sweet experiences,
> taking a huge garland of jasmine flowers,
> you bound [him], in your house.
> This is my proof.
>
> *Periyalvar Tirumoli* 3.10.2

Seeking surrender—the words of the demons defeated by Rama in Lanka:

> *The dance of the rakshasas (demons):*
>
> The other day, our king
> entered the forest of Dandaka,
> He abducted the perfect beauty,
> the chaste woman, and was ruined.
> We are not to blame,
> Do not kill, O king of your clan!
> Our tribe has been ruined by a woman,
> You have given life to the gods.
> And now we fear;
> O Son of Dasharatha,
> We beat our drums, we dance our surrender.
>
> Our Ravana,
> king with long red-gold hair,
> carried away a goddess called Sita;
> look, he held her captive
> in that fragrant grove.
> This was his undoing.
> Kumbha, and now Nikumbha
> have fallen in war.
> Death comes in the form of a man.
> Do not slay us with your bow,

> We fear,
> We beat our drums, we dance our surrender.
> > *Periya Tirumoli* 10.2.3 and 5

The first incarnation as a Fish:

> There was no higher ground;
> Leaving not a spot uncovered,
> > the mighty flood swept high,
> > covering the prosperous lands
> > of the immortal ones.
>
> The gods said:
> > we have no other refuge.
> To be their fortress,
> > He, by his grace,
> came as a fish.
> The bowels [of the fish] shook in its haste,
> > the waves and waters of the ocean
> > crashed and rocked,
> > as he bore on his back
> > the mountains
> > that scraped the skies.
> My heart, do not forget
> > to worship this Lord.
> > > Tirumankai Alvar's *Periya
> > > Tirumoli* 11.4.1

Theology—the paradox of Vishnu's form:

> If you say he exists, he does,
> his forms are these forms,
> If you say he does not,
> his formlessness
> is of these nonforms.
>
> If he has the qualities
> of existence and nonexistence,
> he is in two states,
> he who pervades without end.
> > *Tiruvaymoli* 1.1.9
>
> Being virtue and sin,
> Lovers' union and separation,
> being memory and forgetfulness,
> being what is and what is not,

being none of these,
the Lord dwells in sacred Vinnakar
surrounded by lofty mansions.
                    Tiruvaymoli 6.3.4

Being the ultimate body of light;
being a body crusted with filth;

being hidden and manifest,
standing straight and doing crooked things,

the Lord lives in sacred Vinnakar
where the gods bow their heads

at his feet that fulfill all desires:
there is no other refuge for anyone.
                    Tiruvaymoli 6.3.7

On the impermanence of life:

Less than a lightning flash
are bodies inhabited by lives.
Just think on this
for a moment.

Cut your bonds,
your life-breath
will reach heaven.

Destroy your bonds,
wish for lasting things,
let go, and hold fast
to the Lord.
                    Tiruvaymoli 1.2.1 and 5

Sacred Places

Tirumaliruncholai, near Madurai:

My heart! There is nothing to gain
    by performing wasteful deeds.

    Reach yonder hill:
    near Maliruncolai
    surrounded by thick enchanted forests.

    This is the temple,
    where he who has the hue of stormy cloud
        delights to dwell.[4]
                    Tiruvaymoli 2.10.3

Tiruvenkatam or Tirupati:

> Grace is your hue,
>   O Lord whose color is that of a beautiful cloud;
> My Lord of wonder!
>   Nectar that seeps into my mind and tastes so sweet!
> Lord of the immortal ones!
>
> Lord of the Sacred Venkata, where
>   the crystal waterfalls crash,
>   carrying the gems, gold, and pearls!
>
> My Lord! Only say the words for me,
>   your servant, to reach your feet.

Kutantai—Kumbakonam:

> Whether you end my sorrow or not,
> I've no other support,
>
> O lord of the wheel with the curving mouth,
> miraculous one who sleeps in Kutantai,
>
> when my body goes limp and soul falters,
> you then must will that I do not weaken
> my grip on your feet.
>   *Tiruvaymoli* 5.8.8

The golden age has dawned:

> Rejoice! Rejoice! Rejoice!
> The persisting curse of life is gone
> the agony of hell is destroyed,
> death has no place here.
> The force of the Kali age is destroyed.
> Look for yourself!
> The followers of the sea-colored Lord
> swell over this earth
> singing with melody,
> dancing and whirling with joy.
>   We see them.
>
> The dizzying age of Kali ends;
>   the divine ones also enter.
> The golden age dawns
> and waves of great joy
> flood the land.
> The followers of my Lord,
>   dark as a cloud,

colored like the sea,
fill this earth, singing with melody.
They have settled all over the land.

Tiruvaymoli 5.2.1 and 5.2.3

Serving the servants of Vishnu:

Age after age, and in every age
may it come to pass,
that I have as my rulers,
the servants of the servants,
of the servants,
   of the inseparable servants of the Lord—
my Lord, whose body has the hue
   of an exquisite *kayam* blossom;
my Lord who has four shoulders,
   and whose hand holds the golden wheel.
May I, a lonely person,
have the good fortune
of being in the clan of those
who serve these servants.

Tiruvaymoli 8.8.10

Containing the Lord and being contained by him:

The Lord who dwelt in the City of Names
said, "I shall not move from you!"
He entered and so filled my heart!
I have caught
the Lord whose stomach was not quite filled,
even when he ate the seven clouds, the seven seas,
   the seven mountains and worlds,
and I contain him!

Transfixed, he stands within my eyes.
He,
   greater than comprehension,
   subtle focus of all thought,
   sweetness of the seven notes,
He,
   Lord of the Sacred City of Names,
   surrounded by pavilions,
   studded with colorful gems,
entered my heart.

Tirvaymoli 10.8.2 and 8

Just whom can I turn to
if you let me stray outside your hold?
What is mine? Who am I?
Like red-hot iron drinking water
You drank my life to exhaustion[5] and
then became nectar, never-ending for me.

Becoming nectar that never can end for me,
My love, you dwelt in my soul, within my life,
and ate them as if you could not have your fill.
    What more can you eat?
You, dark as a *kaya* flower,
    eyes like lotus,
    lips red as fruit,
are the beloved of the lady of the flower,
    so fit for you.

                              Tiruvaymoli 10.10.5 and 6

Afterword:

With love as the lamp,
ardor as the fuel,
thoughts that drip passion
    as the wick,
With melting heart,
I lit the blazing flame of wisdom
for Narana.
who desire the wisdom of Tamil.

                    Bhutattalvar, *Irandam Tiruvantati* 1

NOTES

1. Ramanujan, A. K. Hymns for the Drowning (Princetown University Press, 1981), 132.

2. The word *talelo* ends all Tamil lullabies.

3. *Calal* is a word without meaning and seems to refer to a Tamil game where one girl comes up with a thesis and the second seemingly contradicts her with an antithesis.

4. Tamil: *purintu*, "desire"; also "shine."

5. The Tamil words are ambiguous. The line could read: "like red-hot iron sucking water, / I drank you, my life, to exhaustion."

8

Maharashtra: Games with God: *Sakhya-bhakti* in Marathi *Sant* Poetry

Vidyut Aklujkar

The major medieval Marathi-speaking *sants* of Maharashtra are
Dnyandev (1275–96), Namdev (1270–1350), Eknath (1533–99), and
Tukaram (1598–1649). All these worship God as Vithoba, or Vitthala,
whose dark, short *murti* (image) stands in a small temple at Pandhari,
or Pandharpur, with hands on waist, and both feet rested on a
brick. All of the *sants* identify Vithoba with Vishnu as Krishna.
Rakhuma (also called Rakhumabai, Rukmabai, or Rakhumadevi),
the consort of Vithoba, is thus equated with Rukmini, and Vithoba
is often addressed as "Father, the Groom of Goddess Rakhuma"
(*bapa rakhuma-devi-varu*).

The Marathi *sant* poets' Krishna is essentially the one portrayed in the *Bhagavata Purana*. However, they indulge in describing his childhood and young boyhood pranks in detail. They talk
fondly about his butter theft, his naughty pranks in the households of cowherds, his performing of miracles in order to save his
friends and his people from the evil emissaries of Kamsa, and his
going to Mathura to kill the evil king. The *sants* mainly focus on
Krishna of Gokula, or of Vrindavan, and add a lot of local color to the
games he plays. Krishna the king of Dvaraka is sometimes remembered, and we even find a wonderful song in the voice of a young
cowherd about the regal splendors of the old familiar cowherd Krishna
[see Namdev, *Sakala-santa-gatha*, ed, R. C. Dhere (1985/1908)]. But
what the *sants* revel in singing the most, especially as his eye-witnesses,
by claiming to be there with him as his buddies, are the exploits of
the young Krishna on the banks of the Yamuna. The most preferred
mode of *bhakti* in Maharashtra is *sakhya-bhakti*, "friendly worship."

I was on my way
fetching water
from Yamuna
when on the road
I met
the Dark One.
On his head was the
peacock-feathersh hat,
on his shouldersh
a quilt.
He made fun of me,
so I ran from the shpot
but I shlipped on the road,
and fell down;
broke the pitcher
on my head,
my kneesh
got shcraped
and I began to cry.

Kishna came
right there
and held me close
to Himshelf,
and cuddled me and calmed me.
Dnyandev got this bliss
by the grace of Nivritti.

In an intense love song full of traditional imagery, Dnyandev describes the state of mind of a milkmaid waiting anxiously for Krishna/Kanha.

D 632

The cloud is drumming,
the wind is blowing,
will I be meeting Kanha,
the savior of the world?
The moon, the moonbeams,
the frangipani, the sandalwood,
I like nothing at all,
without
the darling of Devaki.
The sandalwood paste
on my breast

burns my body
entirely.
Hurry!
Will I meet Kanho
who wears garlands of forest flowers?
This bed of buds
supposedly so soothing
sets me on fire.
Hurry! Put it out!
O you Kokila birds,
you sing sweet notes,
listen to me, answer me
or cut it out.
When I look in the mirror,
I cannot see my own face,
This is what he did to me,
the Father,
the Lord of Goddess Rakhuma,
Vitthala.

We find a statement of Dnyandev's *sakhya-bhakti* in an "eye-witness" style of *abhanga* that describes a familiar pastoral scene in the early life of Krishna, as the poet claims to be there.

D 584

The cows are going toward the woods,
Pendha, the cowherd is walking along.
"O cowherd Kanhoba,
take them to Yamuna for a drink."
Enchanted
by the call of the flute,
all the cows return.
They forget to graze
and stand still, mesmerized.
Dnyandev [is] there
as a buddy,
holding a stick,
a cowherd
herding the cows
on that riverbank.

Here is another eye-witness picture of pastoral joy with Krishna and his buddies.

D 600

Charmed by the flute
engrossed in Govinda,
how the cowherds dance
in bliss!
Hari herds the cows
on the bank of the Yamuna.
The cowherds
enjoy
and chant.
Here, there,
and everywhere
Pendha goes on frolicking.
Krishna is mimicking
and making faces at him.
The cows stand still,
forgetting their calves.
Krishna rushes them
along homeward.
In the heart of Dnyandev
Krishna goes on living . . .
the cowherd entertaining
His people with love.

Namdev, the Pampered Buddy

The most influential *sant* from Maharashtra, whose teachings found followers
at home and as far away as the Punjab, was Namdev. A younger contemporary
of Dnyandev, he was known as a devotee of Vithoba even in his childhood. Legend has it that he made the God in the temple eat from his plate. He
is described in his *abhangas* and those of the others as being "the best buddy"
to God. His worship sometimes takes the form of a child's mode of *bhakti*,
in which he experiences God as his mother. More often, he engages in *sakhya-
bhakti*, where he becomes the favorite buddy and talks of sharing God's
food, feeding God from his own lunch-sack, playing and frolicking with God,
quarreling with God, being annoyed with God, even cursing God and then
making up with him.

Here is a statement of Namdev's seeing all relations in God. The name
he uses to talk to God is a female form of the name Panduranga, "the fair
one."

N 270

You are my mother,
I'm your infant,
Nurse me with love
O Pandurangay!
You are my cow-mom,
I am your calf,
Don't hold the milk back
O Pandurangay!
You are my deer-mom,
I am your fawn,
Cut off my world-ties
O Pandurangay!
You are my bird-mom,
I am your egg-born,
Bring me my food
O Pandurangay!
Nama says,
You are our loving Lord,
You stand on all sides,
You care for us.

Namdev describes Krishna's childhood at length. The contrast of a tottering toddler who really is the omnipotent God is appealing to the *sant*. Here, Namdev describes the antics of the brothers, very young Krishna and Balarama, otherwise recognized as Vishnu and the great serpent Shesha, in graphic terms.

N1527

They pee
and use their palms
to smear the ground,
then wipe
their hands on their bellies.
When they grab a twig
and clean their teeth,
they make faces at Nanda.
In the middle of their meal
they run outside
and call for the dogs,
"You, yu, yu, yu, you."
They offer their bowls

to the dog
and hug him by his neck.
The neighbors see them
and laugh and laugh
and come and tell Yashoda
with fondness.
The two stand up
holding on to a wall . . .
the ones who support
the world.
When the two go
to play along,
Namdev's body
is blessed.

Namdev as an eye-witness recalls the butter-snatching tricks of Krishna, or, as they call him, Murari, Vanamali, Govinda.

N 1528

He rounds up his buddies
and says, "Come, I'll give you
cow-juice!"
"That milkmaid has gone
to fetch water,
Let's go to her place."
"We can't reach
that hanger,
the milk is high up there.
How shall we get it, Murari?"
Vanamali stacks the wooden seats
one upon the other
and brings down the hanger
with his stick.
Pendha hops around
beating his bottom:
"Oh what a trick,
Govinda, what a trick!"
"Hush! Buddy, don't make noise!
Here, hold on to this butterball!"
Some drink milk,
some eat the curds . . .
Oh oh!
The milkmaid rushes in.

"Everyday I wait to catch you,
you thief!
Now let me see how you can escape."
Nama says, He squirts milk from his mouth
straight in her eye,
and tells us "Run!"

Usually in Krishna literature, the corresponce between Krishna the cowherd of
Gokula and Krishna the king of Dvaraka is tenuously established. Usually the
gopis reminisce and pine for Krishna when they no longer see him in their
midst. But in the following poem by Namdev, where he narrates an incident
from his vantage point, the cowherd boys, as friends of young Krishna, are
discussing the change of his identity and planning to visit him.

N1713

"Hey, buddies,
did you hear?
He has become a king!
Our Krishna
now sits on a throne!
We used to play
on the banks of the Yamuna
with our sticks and quilts,
we used to dance bending our feet
to the tune
of his enchanting flute.
Krishna was our own
buddy.
When we played *hututoo*
and *humbri*
we slapped each other
on the bottom.
Now
he walks alongside an army,
Hari, the son of our Yashoda.
When we wrestled together,
and he had a runny nose,
we picked him up
and held him close.
Now
we are scared of him.
Let us go together
to herd the cows

and offer him
pats on his back . . .
but we are afraid to approach him."
Nama says,"Yes, let us go,
Let's stand in front
with folded palms,
let's fall at his feet and ask
that we may meditate on the same Krishna
whether in the forest
or in the middle of his folks."

Eknath, the Erudite Scholar

Eknath's poems describing the games with God are the most philosophically charged and socially potent of the Marathi *sant* poems. From his privileged position as a brahmin *sant*, Eknath used his traditional scholarship to enlighten people and teach them the intricacies of Vedanta philosophy. As a *sant* poet with a social conscience, he deliberately engaged in defying caste boundaries throughout his life. He was truly liberal in spirit, and so he regarded any expression of *bhakti* using any name for God, for example Krishna, Rama, Shiva, or Dattatreya of the Hindu pantheon or even Allah of the Muslims, as legitimate.

Eknath used the imagery of God's cowherds and their practices of playing together and eating a communal meal (*kala*) to endorse his ideas of equality and fraternity among all worshipers. The two *kala* poems here speak of their joy.

E 241

Hari from the heaven
dons the garment of a cowherd
and starts for the woods
with a lunch-sack in his hand.
His younger companions
follow him there,
and the wealth of the cows
goes after them
everywhere.
The lad dwelling in the *Brahman*
plays the maddening flute
as they go on playing
with each other.
Shrihari himself serves them

dishes of all sorts,
curds and rice,
the pickles,
and the morsels of *bhakri*.
Shrihari serves food,
and the cowherds enjoy,
and the leftovers are eaten up
by Eka of Janardan.

E 243

The friends all urge Krishna,
"Come on, you take the first bite."
Hari tells them instead,
"No, you go first."
The friends do not listen,
no way.
Hari says, "I won't go first."
He really gets annoyed,
and Krishna starts to leave.
"Krishna, don't go away,
here, we'll do as you say."
They all humor him
and bring Krishna back.
Eka in Janardan sees
the subtlety of Chakra-pani
who elevates his devotee
and makes him
praise the glory.

Eknath's signature in his *abhangas* is a combination of a form of his own name,
Eka, and Janardan, which was the name of his spiritual teacher, and also is
one of several names of God. Eknath often engages in exploiting all the possible meanings in the combinations of Eka and Janardan. In Eknath's *abhangas*,
we find expressions of several nuances of *bhakti* (some of them bold or even
outrageous) that are not found listed in any analysis. For example, at one place,
he says that God becomes great only because of his worshipers. Such a stance
can only be understood to be an expression of his *sakhya-bhakti*.

E 2943

First God, then the devotee;
that is the old tradition.
But to say this is wrong.

How can God be
before
the devotee?
The worshiper is
the crown jewel of
Love,
who truly charms
the God.
He reincarnates
for the worshiper.
That is for sure.
The worshiper
is the elder,
the God
is small,
Eka Janardan
says, "There is
no doubt
at all."

Every game played with God assumes metaphysical significance for Eknath. Sometimes God is a player, a teammate, or an opponent; at other times, he is just a witness. For example, here is Eknath's description of a game of swirling, with ribbons in hand, to make a braid. The presence of God in this game is understood as manifesting only in the attitude of the player.

E 180

I go swirling with Myself
and braid the strands
of three qualities.
I am not scared of anyone,
I swear
by the feet of my mentor
I go on swirling today,
I go on dancing all day.
Eka is His own
in Janardan
Let me fall at the feet
of the good ones.

Another is a game of *tipri,* in which the players have to hit the sticks in each other's hands without missing a beat. Haste or unmindfulness results in defeat, or death. Only focusing on God assures the players victory: victory in the game, victory over death, and the ultimate goal of realizing the divine in this existence.

E 190

You are playing
a game of *tipri*
in a hurry.
You should sing
the Name of Hari.
When you miss
the beat of a *tipri*,
you will fall in the trap
of Death,
my brother.
There are six
and four
and eighteen playmates
playing a game of *tipri*.
All are trapped
in a single game,
Death will wink
and trick for sure.
Why play a futile game,
dear child?
Be alert
and open your eyes.
When you take resort
in Eka Janardan,
that's when
you'll escape
Death.

Sometimes a poem about the games reveals the point of no return, that is, of salvation, thus displaying its metaphysical meaning, as here.

E 231

They play together
hamama and *humbri*,
the cowherds of all kinds
meet together.
One runs ahead,
the other runs behind,
one runs

killing his uncle (Kamsa) and aunt (a reference to Putana), and say that death and destruction follow in His company. In effect, they are describing God's capacity for granting salvation and actually praising him with their abuses.

E 237

Don't you play with us.
You've embarrassed us a lot.
How often can we say it?
You listen, but
You don't take it in, Kanhoba.
Go, sort your own cows out.
Don't bother us.
We won't keep track,
You can go, you can stay,
as you please, Kanhoba.
We know the worth
of your friendship.
You are the one
who killed your uncle,
sent your aunt
to see her maker.
We know very well
what you are.
There is death
and destruction
in your company
for sure.
We will never be
born again.
Eka of Janardan says
we will meditate on you
and relish the butter
with pleasure,
Kanhoba.

Here is another poem where Eknath is upset with God. The context is of being bereft of God's help in minding the cows (the senses), which are often unruly, and go after the sense-objects. The daily routine of cowherds can be as simple as a game, or it can turn into a nightmare, when God turns his face the other way. God is the trickster, the player who is silent, and aloof, gobbling up his friends' food, and allowing them to be harassed in gathering up the herd, instead of coming to their help in time. When God plays such games with his people, it is very hard for Eknath to be cross with him. Where will he go?

Who will he beseech with his complaints? Chiding God for not behaving himself is charming and is the ultimate expression of friendly worship. The poem ends with an expression of Eknath's utter helplessness, and total surrender in this game of cow-minding or, on the whole, just living.

E 236

Kanhoba, mind your own wealth of the cows.
If I don't speak up,
It's because I care for you.
You go and relax
under that Kadamba tree,
while we break our legs
going after these.
So unruly are your cows,
that they run and run
as soon as they see
anything anywhere green.
You sit there and eat our lunches
as you gather our sacks,
and you gobble
curds and rice
without so much
as a glance toward us.
You have pierced our being,
You have swindled us outright.
Eka in Janardan recounts,
full of highest bliss,
we are charmed by you,
O Govinda.

REFERENCES

Aklujkar, Vidyut. 1992. "Sharing the Divine Feast: Evolution of a Food Metaphor in Marathi Sant Poetry." In *The Eternal Food: Gastronomic Ideas and Experiences of Hindus and Buddhists,* edited by R. S. Khare for the SUNY Series in Hinduism (Wendy Doniger, editor), Albany: SUNY Press, 95–115.
Dhere, R. C., ed. [1908] 1985. *Sakala santa gatha (gatha pancaka).* Vols. 1–5. Pune. A compendium of major Marathi *sants'* works based on the Sakhare tradition of manuscripts.

9

Braj: Fishing in Sur's Ocean

John Stratton Hawley

From the sixteenth century until the early decades of the twentieth, the most influential literary medium within the span we now call "Hindi" was Braj Bhasha. As the name implies, this language had its natural home in the Braj area, which fans out from either side of the Yamuna (Jamuna, Jumna) River not far south of Delhi, but it was also a familiar medium of composition in much more distant parts. This was especially so wherever Krishna was worshiped, since Braj was held to be his native region and Braj Bhasha, therefore, his native tongue.

Already by the time Nabhadas composed his *Bhaktamal* in about 1600 C.E., one poet—Surdas, or Sur for short—was celebrated as setting the standard for what could be achieved in Braj Bhasha poetry. Nabhadas heralded him as the poet to whom other poets should turn to gain a true sense of their craft:

> What poet, hearing the poems Sur has made,
>   will not nod his head?
> The wording, pithy sayings, the alliteration,
>   the description—his standing is very great:
> He sustains the meanings of speech and loving sentiment,
>   conveying them in wondrous rhyme.
> In words he expresses Hari's playful acts,
>   reflected in his heart through divine vision:
> Birth, deeds, virtues, and beautiful form—
>   all are brought to light by his tongue.

Others' powers of insight are cleansed by those virtues
if they keep his virtues in their ears.
What poet, hearing the poems Sur has made,
will not nod his head?[1]

By the middle of the seventeenth century, the collection of poems attributed to Surdas had become sufficiently extensive that it began to be called "a
sea"—*Sursagar,* or *Sur's Ocean*—and the title has stuck up to the present day.
Like an ocean, it is composed of numerous drops that form themselves into
multiple, complexly related currents. No linear riverine narrative, the *Sursagar*
is an anthology of individual lyrics called *pads,* most of them containing six to
ten rhymed (or alternately rhymed) verses. It is likely that already in Sur's own
century, the sixteenth, other poet-performers besides the biological Surdas
contributed to the corpus bearing his name. Clearly this pattern continued in
the centuries that followed, right up to the present moment. Thus *Sur's Ocean*
continues to expand, and only a certain proportion of the Surdas compositions
that are held dearest by contemporary audiences can be traced back to Sur's
own time.[2]

Nonetheless, for present purposes, I have confined this selection to poems
that do appear in sixteenth-century manuscripts or can be shown, through a
comparison of seventeenth-century manuscripts, to have been in circulation in
the sixteenth century. While this leaves aside a much-cherished poem such as
Maiya mai nahin makhan khayau ("I didn't eat the butter, Ma"), it leaves us with
upward of four hundred poems whose general standard of excellence helps us
understand why Nabhadas thought as highly of Surdas as he did. These have
been drawn together in a forthcoming critical edition by Kenneth E. Bryant and
a team of scholars working with him. The verse translations offered here are
based on that edition.

As the title *Sursagar* suggests, these poems cover a substantial range of subject matter. They address themselves primarily to Krishna and the persons surrounding him, but one also finds a substantial collection of poems celebrating
Rama and Sita, the encounter of Vishnu with the demon-king Bali or the ele-
phant-king Gajendra, and the spiritual struggles of the poet himself. Other poems
address Hari apart from any clear narrative frame, or move out of the Vaishnava
realm altogether and evoke Shiva or the Ganges. Even within the spectrum that
concerns Krishna himself, we find a wide array of episodes—his birth at Mathura;
his childhood and adolescence in Braj; his heroic maturity at Girivraj, Kundan-
pur, and Dvaraka; his involvement in the conflicts reported in the *Mahabharata;*
even the last moments of his earthly life, refracted through his final separation
from his trusted friend and messenger, Uddhava (in Braj Bhasha, Udho).

Undoubtedly, however, the emphasis falls on Krishna's years in Braj; and in
several of the performance traditions based in Braj, it is forbidden to make ritual use of poems that "pollute" that Braj focus by taking up other aspects of

Krishna's career. Such traditions insist that the Braj years were the truly magical ones, and that the ultimate purpose of Vaishnava liturgy in general—and of singing Sur's songs in particular—is to draw the audience into an experience of that magic. That urge is honored in the selection offered here, which leaves aside any poems that cannot be understood to belong within the Braj domain.

The selection begins with the principal dramatis personae, featuring poems about Krishna and Radha that are so purely intended to conjure up a vision (*darshan*) of the figures in question that they cast aside any narrative anchor. For purposes of comparison—and perhaps a little comic relief—a portrait of Krishna's raucous, hard-drinking brother Balaram is also included. Next we meet a set of poems that focus on Krishna's childhood, beginning with the moment of his birth (celebrated every year on the festival of that name, *Krishnajanmashtami*) and taking us into the joys and conflicts caused by his famous appetite for butter.[3] Sur is widely regarded as the paradigmatic poet of this aspect of Krishna's personality, and I hope to convey some sense of his virtuosity by including poems that adopt several contrasting perspectives. In some, the cowherd girls and women taunt Yashoda by asking why she can't control her son—or conversely, by criticizing her for punishing him too sternly for his misbehavior. In others she criticizes them back, saying in effect that they protest too much and pointing to their overeager interest in this side of his personality, which so clearly presages his robustly erotic adolescence. Indeed, there is nothing accidental about Krishna's lust for butter. Butter, after all, is the concentrated form of milk; milk is the paradigmatic liquid of love; and many Surdas poems make us ask where the maternal realm leaves off and its amorous counterpart begins. Not a few celebrate the beauties of the breast.

Next we move into the erotic domain itself. Here there is such a weight of poetry in the *Sursagar*—and such a range of moods—that we have to make radical choices. Because of their relative continuity with the childhood poems, I present two groups. The first cluster depicts Krishna's relationship to his flute, Murali—who is personified as a woman—and reports what the sometimes envious *gopis* have to say about that tie. The second cluster is also relational. Here one of the *gopis* reacts to the sight of a morning-after Krishna who slinks in after spending the night with another woman.

Our selection concludes with a few poems that step back from such specific emplotments of the battle of love (*kama samgrama*) and take satisfaction in the overall love-play that emerges between Krishna and the *gopis*, especially Radha. These poems also celebrate the pleasure of being able to observe that play. Yet the ability to see is not always the ability to say. The last poem in our series bemoans the inadequacy of words when faced with a subject like Krishna. This is ironic, of course, because the visions recorded by Surdas are mediated to us in words alone. In fact, the poet is familiarly memorialized as being blind. When Nabhadas says that Surdas "expresses Hari's playful acts, reflected in his heart through divine vision," he may well have that in mind.

Loosely speaking, we present these poems attributed to Surdas in narrative order, but the reader is cautioned not to think they would be encountered as such in actual performance. While several poems addressing a single theme might be performed on a single occasion—poems appropriate for Krishna's birthday, say, or for the festival of Holi—these are quite individual compositions, each with a logic all its own. That logic unfolds in conversation with what the poet expects the audience will know. In many poems, part of the listeners' pleasure comes from locating the subject or moment of the poem as it proceeds—sometimes working against the poet's subterfuge—and they know the poem is about to conclude when they hear his oral signature.[4] Poems may be performed in various styles, but always the title line functions as a refrain—sometimes just once (as indicated by italics in the Nabhadas poem earlier), sometimes several times as the singer works his way through the verses; sometimes in its entirety and sometimes in part.

Many reductions are implied by presenting poems from the *Sursagar* as we do here. Readers of this book may not be as knowledgeable about Braj culture as the audiences that greet these poems in Braj Bhasha, and they may not have Krishna and Radha before them in image form, as so often happens when poems like these are performed in Braj. Most important, the original language and its musical setting are lost. One only hopes that something survives.[5]

Visions

> A necklace of pearls to captivate the mind
> Glistens on the beautiful chest of Shyam—
> > a Ganges descending from Himalayan heights to earth.
> Its banks are his biceps; its whirlpools, Bhrigu's scar;[6]
> > and its oh-so-lovely waves, his sandal-paste designs.
> Fish shimmer brightly in the sparkle of his jewels:
> > they've left their lakes to come and join
> > > his earring-crocodiles.
> Sur says, a lovely sacred thread flows down his chest
> > as if within the stream there were
> > > a yet more splendid stream,
> And the conch, disk, club, and lotus in his hands
> > are ganders come to rest on his lovely lotus pond.
> > > *SO 87; NPS 2376*
>
> Radha is lost to the onslaught of love.
> She weeps from tree to tree and finally succumbs,
> > searching through the forests and groves.
> Her braid—a peacock grasps it, thinking it a snake;
> > her lotus feet attract the bees;

Her voice with its honey makes the crow in the *kadamb* tree
   think her a cuckoo, and caw her away;
Her hands—the tender leaves of blossom-bringing spring:
   thinking so, parrots come to peck;
And thinking her face to be the moon on a full-moon night,
   the *chakor* bird drinks the water from her eyes.[7]
Desperate at thinking perhaps she'd been dismembered,
   the Joy of the Yadus appears in the nick of time:
Surdas's Lord takes that seedbud of new birth
   and cradles it, a newborn in his arms.

SO 60; NPS 1744

Wine shows her strength in the red of his eyes:
   he roams through the forest finding pleasure
With the splendor of an elephant king in rut
   trailing a harem of mates.
Beautiful the visage of his free-flying hair
   and his lovely garments of blue;
A full golden bowl he holds in his hand:
   he drinks from it; he makes his girlfriends taste.
He laughs, he sputters anger. He beckons, sends away.
   He pinches his eyebrows in a scolding scowl,
Then weeps, exults, rises, and staggers
   as his mind fills with thoughts of his little brother.
His color is the moon's. His strength supports the earth.
   The darling girls of Braj adore him,
And the thing that makes them flow with so much joy
   is his singing of the virtues of Sur's Shyam.

SO 332; NPS 4819

Birth and Childhood

"This night in the month of *Bhadon*, this dark night—[8]
Soldiers have closed the streets, dear, they've shut the doors,
   and the fear of Kamsa is heavy everywhere.
The clouds are rumbling. Now it's started to pour.
   The Yamuna's waves are high, its waters black,
And the only thought in every heart is this:
   how to keep the child's bright face obscured?
Husband, why did I heed your words that day?
   Better I'd been slaughtered there and then,

For look at this child, and tell me how a mother
  could live if torn from such a son."
Devaki's wail was heard by the One
  who pities the poor and removes his servants' pain:
The chains were loosed, says Sur, the gates undone.
  He gave her his wisdom and banished her distress.
            SO 1; NPS 629

"Braj has been blessed with a headman's son"—[9]
  and when the news traveled to everyone
How they were filled with joy!
  The worthy astrologers of Gokul,
Seeing that all the merits of the family's past
  had planted in the earth an unshakable pillar,
Searched pairings of planets, the powers of the stars,
  and chanted the sounds of the Veda.
When the Braj women heard, they all came running,
  dressed in their natural way,
Yet decking themselves with their newest clothes
  and applying mascara to their eyes.
Their forehead-marks all set in place,
  blouses on bosoms, necklaces on breasts,
With braceleted hands braced to hold
  auspicious golden offering-plates,
Group by group they left their houses
  in a lovely way, lovely to see,
Looking like a line of red *muni* birds
  that had broken free from their cages.
Friends gathered in clusters—five or ten—
  and sang their songs of blessing
Like early morning's lotus blossoms
  blooming at the sight of sun.
They didn't know—or care—that the breeze
  had blown their scarlet saris from their breasts.
On their faces and limbs was spread red powder,
  vermilion was daubed in the parts of their hair,
Earrings dangled in tandem from their ears,
  their hair was tied in loosely fastened braids,
And their exertion made sweat appear on their brows
  like droplets sprinkling from clouds.
The first to arrive at the darling baby's door
  was overcome with joy:

She called the others inside.
   They bowed, touching the feet of the child,
And when the veil was lifted from Hari's face
   they showered forth their blessings:
"Long live the one who fulfills
   every wish of Yashoda and Nanda!
Praise this day! Praise this night!
   Praise this watch, this hour!
Praise the womb of this mother,
   so full of wifely fortune
To have given birth to such a son—
   the ripened fruits of joy!
In him the whole clan has found a foundation.
   From every heart the spear of pain is gone."
Hearing the news, the cowherds urged their boys
   to herd home the cows.
They threaded garlands of *gunja* berries,
   found chalk in the forest to rub on their limbs,
And with pots of curd and butter on their heads
   they sang new songs as they went,
Making their way to Nanda's house
   with cymbals and drums.
One of them danced an uproarious dance,
   spattering the others with turmeric curd
As if rains in the month of *bhadon*
   had flooded the rivers with milk and ghee.
Wherever their minds might take them
   it seemed there was marvel there,
And they gave no thought to anyone else,
   so utterly absorbed were they in joy.
One of them rushed to Nanda,
   repeatedly touching his feet;
One of them laughed and laughed to himself,
   then fell into an embrace;
One of them stripped off his clothes
   and cheerfully gave them away;
Another took a blade of *dub* grass,
   daubing every head with cow-powder and curd.
Then Nanda bathed and reappeared
   with *kusha* grass in his hand,
To honor his ancestors with the *nandimukh* rite
   so that every inner worry would be gone.

He chose his priest for the ritual and gave out clothes
    to him and the other brahmins—whatever they might wish—
And in doing so, with hands together in honor,
    he touched their feet. He was moved with love.
Cows, there were countless cows—
    young cows, mother cows with fine big calves,
The kind of cows that give double the milk
    from grazing on the Yamuna's shores,
Gilt-horned cows with silver-shodden hooves
    and backs all covered with copper—
These cows he gave to numerous brahmins,
    who joyfully responded with words of blessing.
Others crowded into the house and its courtyard—
    minstrels, genealogists, and bards:
They sang out all the family's names,
    forgetting none whom they held dear.
King Nanda gave cheerfully to anyone who begged,
    gave to overflowing,
So from that moment all who'd ever begged
    now would beg no more.
Then laughing, he summoned those near to him—
    clan, friends, all his kin—
And marked their foreheads with a paste he prepared
    from musk and saffron and camphor.
With wildflower garlands he draped their breasts
    and gave them clothes of various colors,
Making it seem as if the rains of *ashadh*
    had brought to life the peacocks and frogs.
Then he had masses of saris brought,
    saris of beautiful colors,
And gave them out to the womenfolk.
    They took whatever caught their eye.
Happy, so happy, those cowherds, made rich,
    returned to the houses from which they had come,
Dispensing blessings as they went on their way,
    distributing however they pleased.
From house to house you could hear the drums—
    bheri, mridang, patah, nisan—
Garlands of special leaves were strung above doors,
    there were celebratory pots and flags,
And ever since that day those folk have lacked nothing,
    neither happiness nor wealth.

So says Sur: that will also be the fate
　　of all who fall in praise at Hari's feet.
　　　　　　SO 3; NPS 642

How radiant!—fresh butter in his hand,
Crawling on his knees, his body adorned with dust,
　　face all smeared with curd,
Cheeks so winsome, eyes so supple,
　　a cow-powder mark on his head,
Curls swinging to and fro like swarms of bees
　　besotted by drinking drafts of honey.
At his neck an infant's necklace, and on his lovely chest
　　the glint of a diamond and a tiger-nail amulet.
Blessed, says Sur, is one instant of this joy.
　　Why live a hundred eons more?
　　　　　　SO 7; NPS 717

"If you drink the milk of the black cow, Gopal,
　　you'll see your black braid grow.
Little son, listen, among all the little boys
　　you'll be the finest, most splendid one.
Look at the other lads in Braj and see:
　　it's milk that brought them their strength.
So drink: the fires daily burn in the bellies
　　of your foes—Kamsa and Keshi and the crane."[10]
He takes a little bit and tugs his hair a little bit
　　to see if his mother's telling lies.
Sur says, Yashoda looks at his face and laughs
　　when he tries to coax his curls beyond his ear.
　　　　　　SO 15; NPS 792

Today, my friend, at the first moments of dawn,
　　restless, I rose to start churning curd:
I filled up a vessel, put it down near a polished pillar,
　　and set the churning rope running through my hands.
Such a sweet sound—hearing it, Hari too
　　stirred awake and scampered to the scene.
His quick and flickering movements captured my mind—
　　my gaze froze, my mind glazed—
And I quite forgot my body as he studied his reflection;
　　my heart was cooled with utter joy.
I saw him take both hands and halve a lump of butter.
　　He offered it to the face he saw, and smiled.
Surdas says, the way that boy behaves
　　is more than my heart can contain:

These childish antics of the God of every mercy
    entrance me, and cause my eyes to dance.
                SO 17; NPS 796

Why don't you reprimand that boy?
What can I say? Every day it happens.
    I haven't the strength to endure:
He swallows the butter, spills milk on the floor,
    smears his body with curd,
Then chases after the children left at home,
    spraying them with butter-whey.
If ever I hide a thing, even in places
    far-off and secret, he knows where.
What to do? Defeated, undone,
    I'm driven to despair by your son.
His thefts are so clever—that wish-fulfilling jewel!—
    that their tale cannot be told,
And so, to get a hold on him, says Sur,
    all of Braj is flowing,
        dashing here and there.
                SO 23; NPS 909

Dark one, stop, don't go away.[11]
I'm doing it for you, my cowherd boy—
    listen to me, my lovely little lad—
        I'm filling the vessels full as they'll go
        with all six tastes of food.
Why go off where others live?
    Why make such elaborate plans
        to get the milk and curd and ghee
        and butter they too have to give?
They hardly seem to find it a crime
    to come and rehearse it a thousand times—
        that endlessly shameless company
        of newly married brides.
Big, uncouth Braj cowherd girls!
    Out in the streets they hawk their goods,
        shouting their taunts carelessly, always picking quarrels.
I've listened to them till I'm thin and ill.
    How much longer can I live with such bile?
        It's only guile, says Sur: they want
        to see that dear, dark face.
                SO 24; NPS 913

Take a hard look at Hari's face and body.
How could such a little bit of curd, Yashoda,
   provoke in you such wrath?
His eyes look with fear at the stick you're holding;
   they tremble and shimmer with tears
As if a bee had settled on a blue lotus petal
   and made the dewdrops shiver.
It seems indeed as if a lotus—sheath and stem—
   has been bent by a brisk morning breeze,
For his face and lips are similarly lowered,
   speaking through their shame some sullen pique.
How much cow's wealth could you possibly have lost
   to account for berating him so?
The tiny fear-erect hairs of Sur's Lord
   should suffice to make you sacrifice
     both body and breath.
        SO 28; NPS 968

Look toward the boy who is Nanda's joy:
His body is fevered with heat as he peers
   from the corners of his eyes toward your face.
Over and over he shudders with fear,
   some syllables escape his lips,
     and the color drains from its rightful place:
His face mirrors the harsh, round sun
   so that every passing minute squanders
     that much more of his charm.
His pupils, *chakor* birds that make the dark their home,
   are faced with a moon that has entered
     some new house.
They dart about like bumblebees buzzing inside a lotus
   filled at dawn with new nectar
And frighten at the sight of your stick, which so alarmed him
   that his eyes turned red, like blood.
Ah, Sur's Lord is such a treasury of beauty—
   though a butter thief he may be.
        SO 30; NPS 982

   Even then he wouldn't let go of the curd,
     Grasped it as if it held the four fruits of life
       until the Enemy of Night
         turned to a deer-faced new moon:

Relishing the pleasures of ambrosial words,
   he stuck to his stubborn, cajoling debate.
The lotuses of night began to bloom,
   and I wilted as the horses of the sun sank to earth;
I watched as he took on a lunar form,
   knowing it was night:
     adolescent, new-found youth.
The Lord of Surdas: why has he left me now—
   now that he's claimed my heart?
      SO 82; NPS 2289

Murali

These days Murali has become so proud
   she refuses to speak to a soul,
As if she'd found in the land of his lotus mouth
   a kingdom to supply her every joy.
Insolent girl—his hands are her throne,
   his lips her parasol,
His hair her whisk as she reigns, my friend,
   over a court of cows.
There she decrees that the waters of the Yamuna
   stop on their course to the sea,
And as for the gods in the city of the gods,
   she summons their chariots to earth.
Stable things move, and moving things are still—
   both are triumphs for her
As she cancels the way the Creator set things up
   to institute her own design.
That bamboo flute rules all, says Sur—
   god, sage, man, and snake:
Even Shri's Lord—he forgets his Shri,
   obsessed with his new-found love.
      SO 45; NPS 1271

Murali adorns Balaram's brother's lips.
Just one sound and all the women are transfixed;
   clothes slip unnoticed from their breasts.
Birds close their eyes, motionless as *yogis*
   intent on a night of meditation.
No vine rustles or sways on its tree,
   so weary and sluggish the breeze;

Cows and deer have abandoned their grass;
    calves disdain their milk.
Sur says, on hearing that beguiling sound,
    the waters of the Yamuna stand still.
        SO 47; NPS 1276

Murali has become Mohini:
You know what she did to the gods
    and antigods: she's done it again.
They churned the milk sea. We've churned a sea of vows
    and obtained a new immortal nectar:
An oceanic liquid, held in Hari's lunar face—
    that she stealthily snatches away
And quaffs down, making us drink octaves of sound
    that pour from her victory tour.
One single vessel—then it held elixir
    but now, says Sur, intoxicating liquor.[12]
        SO 70; NPS 1893

A beautiful flute glistens on his lotus mouth.
Mohan is playing and singing his ragas
    as he comes back from grazing the cows.
His curly, tousled hair is so lovely it looks
    like the maneuvers of a militia of bees
Who resent that Murali alone drinks his honey
    and want to capture some of their own.
His eyebrows arch as if Kama too had come,
    charming bow in hand, to give them aid,
For the nectar of the lips of the Lord of Surdas
    has bred in them a deep unease.
        SO 73; NPS 1995

Early Morning Lover

Away! Go back to where you spent the night!
Manmohan, what clues are you trying to erase?
    Signs of tight embraces are not so quickly hid.
A necklace, now stringless, is etched into your chest:
    what clever girl slept pressed against your heart?
Your garments, hair, and jewels are all askew:
    they were tangled in a bout with her lust-hardened breasts.
Teethmarks, nailmarks—oh what you've endured
    to have your fill of passion in that other woman's lair!

Surdas says, your honey lips have lost their sheen
   and your sleepless eyes bear the weight of lethargy.
SO 134; NPS 3122

Madhav, what a fine appearance!
Your eyes droop with sleep, your turban is askew,
   your hair flies beautifully wild,
And someone's nailmarks embellish your chest
   like newly risen slivers of moons.
Your lips have lost their color: the coral spark has paled.
   They seem pasted to your lotus-blue face.
Your clothes are all undone, and your feet—how they stumble
   and sway in a lionlike gait.
Lord of Surij,[13] you're in another's thrall,
   but still my heart responds to your appeal.
SO 135; NPS 3136

I became so aggrieved at Hari
When he came in lazy from another woman's love
   that I simply slammed the door to my room,
And with my own hands I took the huge chain
   and wound it, wound it, locked it tight,
But I looked: and there on the bed, his lovely image!
   My heart trembled with rage.
I bent, I recoiled, I raced to the courtyard,
   writhed, as with a seizure, on the floor,
And what can I say? There was nothing I could say,
   for now I saw another Govind.
I forgot all my anger, forgot all his faults,
   as the god of desire beguiled my mind again
And Surdas's Lord, so deft in every limb,
   slyly sipped the nectar of my lips.
SO 137; NPS 3150

Not to be hidden, such blood-red eyes
Resemble great wide *bandhuk* blossoms,
   and the pupils beautiful dark bees.
Those curls in your hair make treacherous snares
   when you try so hard to focus on me,
And your eyebrow bows are slack:
   they've lost the force of lust
     and their lotus-red arrows lie forgotten.

The eyelids droop beneath so matchless a power
   that even tugs and pulls can't pry them open.
Tell me, Lord of Surdas, this woman—
   who is she? Who's made you lose
     the battle of passion?
              SO 150; NPS 3301

A glance from the corners of those agile eyes,
And mind-churning Kama's sharp-pointed arrows
   have burst apart his heart from either side.
Utterly shaken, he slumps to the ground
   like a young *tamal* tree felled in a windstorm—[14]
Here lies his flute, his wondrous staff, his clothes;
   here, his peacock plumes crowned with all their moons.
His speech has no vigor; his sight remains sheathed
   like a lotus whose morning didn't dawn;
And the waters of love have so drenched your dear one's body
   that in trying to wring his garments dry
     he's shredded the edges.
One moment he sinks in the sea of separation,
   the next, he swells with the waves:
Sur says, sprinkle on him your lips' elixir
   and take away the swoon
     of Nanda's youthful son.
              SO 154; NPS 3357

Do with me now what you think I deserve.
Listen to me, Radha—so says Madhav—
   exact whatever punishment you will.
Crush my breast with yours.
   Bind me with your arms.
     Find some tender flesh to gore with your arrow-nails.
Lift your eyebrows—string those bows.
   Grind your angry teeth.
     Gorge yourself on the nectar of my lips.
Tangle me in your limbs.
   Squeeze with such anger
     that my body sweats passion,
Then take your many traits,
   braid them in a secret knot,
     and soak that knot in sweat till it won't slacken.
Lovely friend, I touch your feet,
   begging you to listen:
     from so much bitterness, great passion thins.

Sur says, the good life lasts but a few short days,
    so tame your enmity
        and let the world live.

SO 171; NPS 3441

Their Love-Play Observed

"On the banks of the River Yamuna,
In a secluded spot, alone,
    I was filling my pots with water
        when Kanh caught hold of my hair.[15]
I placed the pitchers on my head, but the path
    was winding, and he was garbed all in yellow,
And the more I looked, the lovelier he seemed;
    his little waist-bells so fine."
The milkmaid's touch of embarrassment
    told how that warrior had won the battle—
Surdas's cowherd: he'd taken her in his arms
    and given her golden pitchers their reward.

SO 64; absent in NPS

Black storm clouds have risen in the sky,
    pierced by herons in an eerie row.
Please, Kanh, look: a rainbow—such beauty!—
    bearer of all colors,
        bow for the arrows of the gods.
Lightning flashes forth and strikes here and there
    like an eager, restless woman
Whose lover is outside, while her husband is still at home:
    she moves away, returns, helpless,
        burned by the god of love.
Peacocks and crested cuckoos cry out in the woods,
    dispatched as messenger girls by the trees,
And just so the vines, love-deprived women,
    paragons of amorous anger and pride,
        break their vow of silence
            with another kind of poetry:
They mate with every tree they meet
    in a web of darkened groves.
Kama, the expert, awakens to the wish
    of Sur's dark Shyam: he lifts his own hand
        to decorate a bower as a home.

SO 65; NPS 1806

The Dark One and his dear one—what a lovely pair!
At the tying of their happy knot, Radha is pleased:
   she smiles a knowing smile, she turns her head away.
He is the bee; she, a *champa* bud.
   He is urbane; she, a simple girl.
Teach them, then, how to show each other love;
   steal them away from their fathers and mothers.
He is a sapphire daubed with sandal, and she—
   she is fair-skinned, like a golden vine.
Nanda's youthful lad is newly clever, and she—
   she's a clever girl newly blossomed into youth.
An emerald on a golden chain, lightning in dark clouds—
   similes like these cannot suffice.
Surdas says, for them, one has just *them*:
   to search for metaphors yields nothing at all.
           SO 105; NPS 2522

NOTES

1. Nabhadas, *Bhaktamal* (Lucknow: Tejkumar Press, 1969), p. 557.

2. In regard to the limitations of biographical information about Surdas and the cumulative nature of the *Sursagar*, see J. S. Hawley, *Sur Das: Poet, Singer, Saint* (Seattle: University of Washington Press, 1984), chaps. 1–2.

3. See J. S. Hawley, *Krishna, the Butter Thief* (Princeton: Princeton University Press, 1983).

4. A handsome analysis of these and related dynamics may be found in Kenneth E. Bryant, *Poems to the Child-God: Structures and Strategies in the Poetry of Surdas* (Berkeley: University of California Press, 1978), 1–141. See also J. S. Hawley and K. E. Bryant, *Sur's Ocean* (New York: Oxford University Press, forthcoming), especially Hawley's introduction, vol. 1, chap. 2.

5. The abbreviation SO introduces the number that has been assigned a given poem in Hawley and Bryant, *Sur's Ocean*. The abbreviation NPS refers to the version of the poem that appears in the currently standard edition produced by the Kasi Nagaripracarini Sabha: *Sur Sagar*, edited by Jagannathdas "Ratnakar," Nandadulari Vajpeyi et al., 2 vols. (Varanasi: Nagaripracarini Sabha, 1972–76). I acknowledge with gratitude the many contributions Mark Juergensmeyer has made toward producing the translations that follow. Numerous translations would have been more awkward without his intervention.

6. *Bhrigu's scar* is the dark tuft of hair, called *shrivatsa*, that grew up on the spot in the middle of Vishnu's (and by extension Krishna's) chest where the sage Bhrigu kicked him. Finding Vishnu recumbent, Bhrigu had misjudged him, thinking he was napping on the job and neglecting his duty to preserve the world. Actually, of course, he was supporting it in every way. This episode appears in one of many stories in which an effort is made to judge which of the *trimurti* deserves to be regarded as the supreme deity, superior to the other two. Here Vishnu wins out over Shiva and Brahma, who also

encounter the sage's peremptory behavior, because he is least ruffled by it. To the contrary, he actually begs the irascible sage's pardon, thus demonstrating his overarching grace and compassion and showing that he preserves even those who might turn against him.

7. The mythical *chakor* bird survives only on moonbeams. *Joy of the Yadus* (*jadunandan*) is a title that identifies Krishna by means of his position in the Yadu clan.

8. The poem is set in the lunar month of *bhadon* (Skt. *bhadrapada*, August/ September), which comes toward the end of the rainy season and is the month of Krishna's birth. The poem is addressed by Krishna's mother Devaki to her husband Vasudev, and her reference to *that day* denotes the day of her wedding. On that occasion her kinsman Kamsa had an ominous vision informing him that Devaki's eighth son would be his nemesis. He responded by wanting to kill her on the spot, but Vasudev argued against it by promising to deliver all of Devaki's offspring into Kamsa's hands. Now, seeing the splendor of the newborn Krishna, Devaki wishes she had surrendered her life instead of his when she had the chance.

9. This unusually long poem is traditionally performed in Braj on Nandotsav, "Nanda's festival"—the day after Krishna's birthday. It records and serves as charter for the actions that are expected on that day. One of the most formal of these is the *nandimukh* rite (v. 38), in which past generations are honored. Because he is now father to a son (or believes himself to be such—actually he is Krishna's foster father)— Nanda can be assured that he and his progenitors will be cared for by an ongoing male line. Only such sons can perform the rituals required to protect the dead, adjust their status as generations pass, and keep their memory alive. *Ashadh* (June/July, v. 52) is normally the month in which the monsoon arrives in north-central India.

10. *Keshi* is the horse-demon who attacked Krishna in his childhood, and the crane- or heron-demon (*bakasur*) is another of his childhood adversaries.

11. The long, rolling rhythm of this poem is unusual. It is measured out in lines whose standard length is 29 syllables, grouped 8/8/8/5. The final syllables in all six verses rhyme—the normal pattern—but in addition there is an internal rhyme at the conclusion of the first and second octads within each verse, which I sometimes retain in English (e.g., "crime . . . times," v. 4).

12. At the beginning of the present cycle of Creation, the gods and demons cooperated in churning the primordial Milk Ocean in search of the liquor of immortality (*amrt*, v. 6; *piyus*, v. 3). When it appeared, cooperation turned to dissension as the two groups struggled against one another for possession of the priceless liquid. The victory of the gods was secured only through a ruse of Vishnu, who manifested himself as Mohini (literally, "a bewitching woman") and distracted the demons from their purpose. In this and the following poems, we meet a number of alternative names for Krisha: Hari, Mohan, Manmohan, Madhov, Gopal, Govind, and Shyam. Each has an independent range of meanings, but for the present purposes they can simply be understood as proper nouns.

13. The name Sur designates the sun. Here we have the variant Surij (Skt. *surya*), which carries the same meaning.

14. The very dark bark of the *tamal* tree (v. 3) makes it a frequent term of comparison for Krishna.

15. *Kanh*, a vernacularization of *Krsna* (Krishna), has a somewhat more informal, familiar tone than its Sanskrit counterpart.

10

Rajasthan: Mirabai and Her Poetry

Nancy M. Martin

Mirabai (born c. 1500) is among the most well-known and loved of the Hindu women saints devoted to Krishna. Her devotion to her Lord is absolute, as her life and songs attest. Her story is a romantic tale of star-crossed lovers—one human, the other divine—marked by perseverance and triumph in the midst of great suffering. Songs sung in her name speak of the joys and trials of the devotional life and evoke the full range of romantic love, from the devastating longing that marks separated lovers and the blazing anger of a woman betrayed to the sweet and intoxicating pleasures of union. This woman of the sixteenth century has inspired and captured the imagination of fellow devotees across the centuries, so much so that her story has been told and retold in innumerable forms and more than a thousand songs have been sung in her name. Within the context of the wider Krishna tradition, this exemplary devotee provides an important bridge between the idyllic and eternal world of Braj, where the *gopis* and Radha sport with Krishna, and the world of *samsara,* wherein ordinary people must practice their devotion to the amorous Dark Lord.

The Life of Mirabai

So who was this extraordinary saint? We find her story first among those of other saints, preserved and recounted by devotees of God. But even here, there is no original or first telling that we can identify and of which all others would be variants. Instead, across the centuries a vast family of related but different stories are told about her, found not only in hagiographic literature but now also in religious, folk and dance dramas, epic songs, film, novels, comic books, and even a television serial that aired in 1997.

Though these stories differ considerably from one another, a general outline of her life story might go as follows. Mirabai was the daughter of the Rathor Rajput royal house of Merta within the feudal kingdom of Marwar (western Rajasthan). Even as a child, she already showed signs of great devotion to God. When she came of age, her marriage was arranged—against her will, by most accounts—into the Sisodiya Rajput royal family of the kingdom of Mewar (southern Rajasthan). As a young bride, she angered her marital family, in the fortress city of Chittor, by her refusal to fulfill her conjugal duties or to follow the rules of behavior for a woman of a royal household and of a Rajput or warrior caste. She should have remained secluded in the women's apartments of the palace, but she sang and danced in the public space of the temple and associated freely with holy men and with people of every caste and class, caring little for the material and social privileges that her royal status afforded her. Though she was praised by some, her behavior outraged others, particularly among her in-laws, who saw her actions as bringing dishonor to the family.

After efforts to dissuade her and then to confine and isolate her failed, attempts were made to kill her. The method and the murderer vary from story to story. Poison is the most commonly recounted method, with the poison said to be *charanamrit*, the holy water used to wash the deity's feet and thus imbued with grace—an ambrosia no devotee would refuse to drink. Other methods include a venomous cobra in a basket, scorpions with a deadly sting, a ravenous lion in a cage, and a bed of thorns, all said to be sent to her by the *rana*, the ruler of Mewar (sometimes identified as Mirabai's husband, sometimes as her father-in-law, and sometimes as her brother-in-law, acting after her husband's death). She is maliciously told that the snake is a diamond necklace or flower garland and the scorpions are jeweled toe rings to be opened only in the dark. But each becomes these harmless and beautiful gifts in Mira's hands. When she worships the lion as Vishnu's man-lion incarnation Narasimha, it lies down harmlessly before her, and thorns placed in her bed turn to flowers. Direct assaults are no more effective. In one telling, when the *rana* receives reports that she is speaking words of love to a man in her private chambers, he draws his sword to kill her. But when he enters the room, he suddenly sees four Miras, and bewildered, he backs away. In another account, when the *rana* orders her to drown herself, Krishna intervenes to stop her.

In the face of such persecution, Mira chooses to leave the great city of Chittor, or in other accounts is forced to do so. Some say she returns to her natal home for a time, but eventually she becomes a wandering holy woman, renouncing all that the world offers by way of pleasure and fulfillment, completely absorbed in the love of God. She composes innumerable songs of unmatched beauty, singing in the company of the devout and dancing in the temples before her Lord.

She is said to go to Vrindavan, the land of Krishna's youthful incarnation, where she meets Chaitanya's great disciple, Jiva Goswami. In some tellings, he refuses to see her because he has made a vow not to interact with women. She sends back a message, thanking him for enlightening her, for she had mistakenly thought that there was only one man in this holy city (all souls being feminine in their love for the amorous and very male Lord Krishna). Chagrined, Jiva Goswami immediately agrees to see her. Some also say that she took the untouchable leather-worker Raidas as her *guru* and that the Muslim emperor Akbar came to see this great devotee. In both cases, her family members are outraged, but Mira draws no distinctions between those who love God, regardless of caste or religion.

Finally she makes her way to the city of Dvaraka, where Krishna is said to have established his kingdom after leaving the cowherding community of his youth to fulfill his destiny. There she remains, until a delegation of brahmins arrives from the kingdom of Mewar. The *rana*'s motivation in sending the delegation is unclear. He may be genuinely repentant for his mistreatment of Mira, and he may have experienced a conversion to the devotional path. His decision may also be merely a matter of expedience—things are not going well in the kingdom, and many lay the blame at his feet for abusing the saint. Or he may want to regain some control over this woman whose actions continue to bring shame upon his family.

Whatever the reason, the priests arrive, insisting on Mira's return to Mewar. When she refuses, they vow to fast until death if she does not do as they say. In the face of such coercion (to cause the death of a brahmin priest is a great sin), she asks only to visit the temple one last time before departing, in order to take leave of Krishna. When others come looking for her within the temple, however, she is nowhere to be found, and only her clothing remains, draped across the image. Krishna has absorbed her into himself, the story goes, freeing her from the world's persecution and liberating her through a union with him. Thus ends this inspiring tale of unwavering devotion and love, in spite of horrific persecution, and of holding fast to the truth, regardless of the consequences.

Songs of Mirabai

Mirabai's unshakable love, her total dedication, and her suffering and triumph over adversity find expression in the songs sung in her name as well as in her story. We do not actually know which songs might have been composed by the

1

Mine is the mountain-lifting Gopal, there is no other.
There is no other, O *Sadhus*,
   though I have searched the three worlds.
Mine is the mountain-bearing Gopal, there is no other.

Brother, friend, relative, kin—all I left behind.
Sitting in the company of *sadhus*,
   I abandoned the world's expectations.
Mine is the mountain-bearing Cowherd, there is no other.

Watching devotees, I was delighted;
   Looking at the world, I wept.
The vine of love grew, watered by the river of my tears.
Mine is the mountain-bearing Gopal, there is no other.

Churning the milk, I extracted the ghee
   and discarded the buttermilk.
Drinking the poison the *rana* sent, I attained bliss.
Mine is the mountain-bearing Cowherd, there is no other.

Mira has bound herself to love;
   what was to be has come to pass.
Mine is the mountain-bearing Gopal, there is no other.[3]

2

Tying bells to her ankles, Mira danced away.

"I choose to serve Narayan," [she said.]
   "Freely I take the servant's role."
Tying bells to her ankles, Mira danced away.

"Mirabai's crazy!" they said,
   Mother-in-law said "family destroyer!"
Tying bells to her ankles, Mira danced away.

The *rana's* gift, a poison cup—
   Laughing, Mira drank it down.
Tying bells to her ankles, Mira danced away.

Mira's Lord, that gallant Mountain Bearer,
   so easily the Indestructible One was hers!
Tying bells to her ankles, Mira danced away.[4]

3

Rana, why should I marry a man
   who will die in birth after birth?

I will marry the Dark One, Shyam,
  and forever wear his wedding bangles.

What are you doing, Mother?
Marry Mira to the Dark Lover, Sanvara.
Bring joy, not sorrow, Mother—
Marry Mira to the Mountain Bearer, Girdhari.

A deadly snake the *rana* sent
  to be placed in Mira's hands;
Making it a garland, Mira was delighted.
Marry Mira to the Dark Lover, Sanvara.

A cup of poison the *rana* sent
  to be placed in Mira's hands;
Taking it as holy nectar, Mira drank it down.
Marry Mira to the Dark Lover, Sanvara.

Mirabai says, I sing the Mountain Bearer's praise.
Marry Mira to the Dark Lover, Sanvara.[5]

5

Make me your servant, dear Mountain Bearer,
  make me your servant.

Your servant, I'll plant a garden.
Arising each day, I'll come before you.
In the groves and lanes of Vrindavan,
  I'll sing of your love play, Govind.
Let me serve you, dear Mountain Bearer.

In serving you, our eyes will meet.
  Remembrance will be my wages.
The land-grant of loving devotion my payment—
  Desire of birth after birth.
Make me your servant, dear Mountain Bearer.

Peacock-feather crown,
  yellow silk at your waist,
    jeweled garland adorning your chest.
Enchanting flute player, Vrindavan's grazer of cows,
Let me serve you, dear Mountain Bearer.

Oh, Lord, I'll plant new groves
  with fragrant gardens beneath them.
Dressed in a red sari,
  I'll come to meet my Dark Love.

Mira obtained the Mountain Bearer—
    Her destiny of lives gone by.[13]

9

Friend, my eyes have been hit by the arrow of love.

His sweet form has taken over my thoughts
and pierced my heart to the depths.
Friend, my eyes are acting so strangely . . .

How long have I been standing here in this house,
gazing down the road?
Friend, my eyes have been hit by the arrow of love.

The dear Dark Lover is my breath,
The root, the source of my life.
Friend, my eyes are acting so strangely . . .

Mira is sold into the hands of the Mountain Bearer.
People say she has lost her mind . . .[14]

10

Hari, I am mad with love—
No one knows my pain.

Only the wounded know what the wounded endure—
the flames that engulf the heart.

Only the jeweler knows the value of the gem—
not the one who carelessly loses it.

Wandering from door to door in agony,
I find no doctor to heal my wound.

Lord of Mira, her pain will lessen
only when the Dark Lover comes to her aid.[15]

11

Having enticed me with affection,
Lord, where have you gone?

Having set the lamp of love ablaze,
You left your faithful companion behind.
Lord, where have you gone?

Having launched the boat of passion,
You abandoned it on the sea of separation.
 Lord, where have you gone?

Mira's Lord, when will we meet?
I cannot go on living without you.[16]

12

You've done it—you've utterly enchanted me.
Now when will you come to meet me again, O Renouncer?

Because of you I've taken up a renouncer's ways—
I wake the inhabitants of every house
In the name of the Unseen One.

Having utterly enchanted me,
When will you come to me again, you yogi?

In the day no hunger arises,
In the night no sleep comes.
Without you, nothing brings any pleasure.

Having utterly enchanted me,
When will you come to meet me again, O Renouncer?

Mira's Lord is the Indestructible Hari,
In meeting him, the flame is extinguished.[17]

13

Come to my home, Dwarka[18]-Dweller.
Taking your name, all my troubles go.
Taking your name, all obstacles dissolve.
Come into my home, Dwarka-Dweller.

The shoot bursts forth from the lotus of the navel,
The shoot grows from the center of my being.
It will reach the house of eternity.
Come into my home, Dwarka-Dweller.

Step by step I will dig this well,
For you, I'll be a servant to fetch water.
Come to my home, Dwarka-Dweller.

I'll make a sacred fire of cloves and fragrant nutshells,
Then the Wanderer will come to Mira's temple.
Taking your name, all obstacles dissolve.

In the sky, I'll lay out a beautiful bed.
Your pretty maid will cover it with flowers.
Come into my home, Dwarka-Dweller.

2. For further information about Mirabai's life, songs, and impact in India and beyond, see my book *Mirabai*, forthcoming from Oxford University Press.

3. This *bhajan*, or devotional song, appears in many printed *bhajan* books and is the first poem of the famous Dakor manuscript, supposedly dated 1585 C.E., published by Lalita Prasad Sukul as "Mira Padavali," in *Mira Smriti Granth*, edited by Sakal Narayan Sharma, Ram Prasad Tripani, Lalita Prasad Sukul, Vipin Bihari Trivedi, Kamali Devi Garg, and Sarak Nath Agrawal (Calcutta: Bangiya Hindi Parishad, 1949), pt. 2, p. 1. This *bhajan* appears in various forms in numerous other collections of Mira's songs as well. *Sadhus* are people who have renounced the world and dedicated their life to religious pursuits. Women renunciants exist, but this term generally refers to men. Gopal is a name for Krishna meaning "protector of cows."

4. This is a popular *bhajan*-book version of this song attributed to Mirabai.

5. Text of a song performed by the Meghwal singer Padmaram in western Rajasthan, recorded in 1993 and available on the compact disc "Meera: Voices from the Deserts of India" (Patrika TV/Ninaad Music, 2000).

6. Dakor MS, *pad* 35 ("Mira Padavali" in *Mira Smriti Granth*). Additional variants are presented by Bhagwandas Tiwari, *Mira ki Pramanik Padavali* (Ilahabad: Sahitya Bhavan, 1974), 183–186.

7. Dakor MS, *pad* 13; Parashuram Chaturvedi, *Mirabai ki Padavali* (Prayag: Hindi Sahitya Sammelan, 1973), *pad* 22; Narotamdas Swami, *Mira Mandakini* (Agra: Gaya Prasad, 1930), *pad* 18.

8. Dakor MS, *pad* 13.

9. Dakor MS, *pad* 46; Chaturvedi, *Mirabai ki Padavali*, *pad* 3; Swami, *Mira Mandakini*, *pad* 1. A *tilak* is a Hindu sectarian mark painted on the forehead.

10. In the translation of this line, I am indebted to A. J. Alston's translation. His choice to interpret the lightning that abandons shame as dancing and his selection of the word *exulting* to describe Indra here are wonderful. *The Devotional Poems of Mirabai* (Delhi: Motilal Banarsidass, 1980), 93.

11. Dakor MS, *pad* 45; Chaturvedi, *Mirabai ki Padavali*, *pad* 143, Swami, *Mira Mandakini*, *pad* 70. The *papiha* is a pied cuckoo.

12. The term translated as "auspicious bride" is *suhag*.

13. This song appears in many collections, including Chaturvedi, *Mirabai ki Padavali*, *pad* 27.

14. Dakor MS, *pad* 15; Chaturvedi, *Mirabai ki Padavali*, *pad* 14, Swami, *Mira Mandakini*, *pad* 26.

15. Dakor MS, *pad* 19; Chaturvedi, *Mirabai ki Padavali*, *pad* 70; Swami, *Mira Mandakini*, *pad* 57.

16. Dakor MS, *pad* 11; Chaturvedi, *Mirabai ki Padavali*, *pad* 64; Swami, *Mira Mandakini*, *pad* 27.

17. Swami, *Mira Mandakini*, *pad* 146.

18. After leaving Vrindavan to fulfill his destiny, Krishna settled in Dvaraka, far from his *gopi* lovers, who continued to long for him.

19. Text of song from the repertoire of Padmaram, recorded in 1993.

20. Text of song from the repertoire of Padmaram, recorded in 1993.

21. Text of song from the repertoire of Padmaram, recorded in 1993.

22. Text of song from the repertoire of Padmaram, recorded in 1993.

11

Gujarat: Govinda's Glory: Krishna-*Lila* in the Songs of Narasinha Mehta

Neelima Shukla-Bhatt

A frequently quoted verse from a Hindu sacred text, the *Padma Purana*, which traces the development of the tradition of *bhakti* (devotion) through various regions of India, is quite unflattering to Gujarat in western India. It speaks of *bhakti* as a beautiful woman who was born in Tamil South India, attained youth in Karnataka, grew old and feeble in Gujarat, but was rejuvenated back to a youthful state in Vrindavan in north India, the region traditionally associated with Krishna's early life.[1] In responding to this verse, many in *bhakti* communities of Gujarat refer to the songs belonging to the tradition of Narasinha Mehta (c. 1414–80 c.e.), an ardent Krishna devotee and a beloved saint of the region who is also honored as the first poet of the Gujarati language. "Just listen to Narasinha Mehta's songs; and you will know how wrong the writer of the *Padma Purana* was," they say. Their response indicates not only their confidence in the devotional fervor of Narasinha's songs but also their greater attachment to Gujarati *bhakti* lyrics over a Sanskrit Purana. While Sanskrit texts of Krishna devotion, especially the *Bhagavata Purana*, are read widely in Gujarat, they are read mostly in Gujarati translations. In gatherings of devotional communities too, the preferred medium for expression of devotion remains Gujarati songs, rather than Sanskrit hymns.

Some songs in Narashinha Mehta's tradition are among the most popular Krishna-*lila* songs in Gujarat.[2] Five centuries after their composition, these songs have such an appeal for the people of the region that an All-India Radio staff person once jokingly remarked, "If deceased poets had to be paid royalties, Narasinha Mehta would have to be paid the highest royalties by the radio stations of Gujarat."[3]

Even with his unique place in the history of Krishna *bhakti* in Gujarat, however, Narasinha was not the first to sing about Krishna-*lila* in the region. Krishna themes had been popular in Gujarat's cultural milieu long before him.

Krishna in the Culture of Gujarat

Gujarat claims a special bond with Krishna because one of its coastal cities, Dwaraka, is believed to have been established by Krishna as his princely capital after he migrated here with his people from Mathura in North India. According to tradition, Krishna spent the later part of his life in Dwaraka until his death near Prabhas, a pilgrimage place about 150 miles southeast of the city. While Krishna's life in Dwaraka is not celebrated much by most of his devotees, it is important for many people in Gujarat.[4] Several communities in Gujarat, especially in the peninsular region of Saurashtra where Dwaraka is located, claim descent from Krishna's companions. Their self-understanding is reflected in association of many components of the folk culture of Gujarat with Krishna.

A folk dance of the region, *ras*, in which men and women take alternate positions and dance with short sticks in their hands, is claimed to be the same dance that Krishna danced with the *gopis* in Vrindavan—his famous *ras-lila*. In various types of folksongs such as lullabies, wedding songs, and festival songs, too, themes of Krishna-*lila* are pervasive. Lullabies are often in the voice of Krishna's foster mother, Yashoda, and the child she rocks to sleep is Krishna. The young girl in folksongs often refers to her lover as Krishna; for the young man, his beloved is as beautiful as Radha. As Hasu Yagnik suggests, the charm of Krishna's character in a whole range of moods and situations has made him so easily accessible and so irresistibly attractive for everyone—the rich and the poor, the young and the old, men and women—it is no wonder that people seek to enhance the meanings of their ordinary existence by interweaving Krishna themes in the songs they use for their auspicious occasions.[5] As in many parts of India, in Gujarat, too, Krishna appears in the folklore not as the transcendent Lord but as an integral part of the very fabric of life. While it is difficult to trace the origin of the folksongs that are popular now, H. C. Bhayani indicates that he was able to compile a list of approximately two hundred popular Krishna songs of the early medieval period that he located in anthologies of Jain hymns of that time. In these anthologies, refrains of popular Krishna songs were written at the top of the hymn texts to indicate their tunes.[6]

In addition to folklore, Krishna themes are also found recurrently in literary works written in Gujarat since the late first millennium C.E. Significant among these are works of Jain monks in Sanskrit and Apabhramsha (the language of the region before the development of the Gujarati language), especially those dedicated to their twenty-second *tirthankara* ("ford-maker," a realized soul), Neminath, who is believed to be Krishna's cousin.[7] Examples of

Apabhramsha verses with Radha-Krishna themes are also given by the twelfth-century Jain grammarian Hemachandracharya in his work.[8] These early literary references clearly indicate the appeal Krishna-*lila* themes had for the people of the region from the end of the first millennium c.e. Their significance, however, is mainly historical; they are known only to a few specialists in today's Gujarat. It remained for Narasinha to compose songs of unprecedented devotional lyricism in the Gujarati language that have been transmitted through traditions of singing since the fifteenth century. One would find few Gujaratis, Hindu or non-Hindu, who do not know at least a few lines of his Krishna-*lila* songs by heart. While the issue of authenticity of some songs attributed to Narasinha continues to be a matter of scholarly debates in Gujarat, the songs translated below are selected from the critical edition compiled by Shivlal Jesalpura, ("*Narasinha Mehta ni Kavya Krutio*," 1981, *NKK* hereafter) which has been acclaimed and used widely by the scholarly community in Gujarat.[9] Jesalpura's compilation is based on a careful examination of more than three hundred manuscripts, which led him to exclude several hundred lyrics found in earlier editions. In the rest of this essay, "Narasinha" refers to the figure of the poet that emerges from Jesalpura's edition, with a keen awareness that the issue of authenticity of many songs attributed to him remains to be resolved. The singers of Narasinha's songs, of course, have little concern about the matter.

The immense popularity of Narasinha's songs is augmented by the high esteem in which he is held as a Krishna devotee all over India. Hagiographic narratives about Narasinha are found in several Indian languages in addition to Gujarati since the sixteenth century c.e.[10] In Gujarat, they are extremely popular and have been retold for generations through a variety of media—traditionally, through songs, tales, and folk drama, and now also through television, and films. They provide important pointers to the understanding of Krishna-*lila* in Narasinha's songs and form a significant regional source of Krishna *bhakti* in themselves. Along with Narasinha's songs, these stories exemplifying Krishna's ongoing *lila* in the human world are viewed by devotional communities of Gujarat as the distinctive contribution of their region to the larger pan-Indian current of Krishna *bhakti*.

Krishna Bhakti Themes in the Hagiography of Narasinha Mehta

According to hagiographic narratives, Narasinha was born in a small town, Talaja, in a family of Nagar brahmins who have traditionally been worshipers of Hindu deity Shiva. Narasinha lost his parents at a young age and lived with his elder brother and sister-in-law. He was married to Manekbai and had two children. Spending a great deal of time wandering around in the company of holy men, however, he did not make a proper living. One day, as he was entering his home, his sister-in-law called him foolish and a burden on the family. Deeply hurt, Narasinha turned around and wandered aimlessly until he reached a deserted Shiva temple. He decided to end his life there, meditating on Shiva. For seven days, he sat there meditating without food or water. Pleased with Narasinha's steadfast devotion, Shiva appeared before him and offered to grant any wish he expressed. Narasinha was overwhelmed and could not ask for anything specific. He simply said, "Kindly give me whatever is dear to you." In response, Shiva first revealed to Narasinha his own devotion to Krishnna. Then, placing his hand on Narasinha's head, he transported his new devotee to the heavenly abode of Krishna, where he dances in eternal *ras-lila* (circular dance) with the *gopis*, the cowherd women of Braj, who are upheld as Krishna's most exalted devotees. Here, a miracle occurred. As Narasinha stood entranced with the heavenly dance, he lost his male consciousness and acquired that of a *sakhi* (female friend) of the *gopis*.

Seeing Narasinha's total absorption in the *ras*, Krishna also asked him to select a reward. Narasinha urged that his wish to sing Krishna's praise all his life and in future rebirths be granted. Krishna not only granted him that wish, he also endowed Narasinha with a constant vision (*darshan*) of Krishna-*lila*. In addition, Krishna promised that he would be forever at Narasinha's beck and call. Narasinha was thus doubly blessed, by both Shiva and Krishna. He returned to the earth and began his vocation of singing the glory of Krishna-*lila* in the city of Junagadh. He danced ecstatically on the streets of the city with other Krishna devotees, including women and members of lower castes. Many stories are told about Narasinha's persecution by other brahmins and the king of Junagadh. In these narratives, Krishna appears on the scene at the critical moment every time and rescues Narasinha, declaring himself to be Narasinha's servant.

In stressing the power of *bhakti*, Narasinha's hagiography follows a recurrent pattern in hagiographic narratives of medieval North India. In addition, it interweaves some *bhakti* themes that are either particularly emphasized in Narasinha's songs or are associated with the *bhakti* milieu of Gujarat. The depiction of the transformation of Narasinha's consciousness, for example, explicitly stresses a theological concept that is implicit in much of Krishna *bhakti* poetry, where male poets take the persona of a *gopi*: To be a devotee of Krishna requires emulating the consciousness of the *gopis*, who loved him unconditionally and above everything. In many of Narasinha's songs this concept is reinforced through exaltation of not just the *gopis* but of all women as having a greater capacity for love. Similarly, stories about Narasinha's acceptance of women and people of lower castes as his *bhakti* companions are linked to repeated declarations in his songs that social rank has no relevance on the path of loving devotion to Krishna. The incident of receiving double blessing by Shiva and Krishna reflects the nonsectarian, eclectic *bhakti* that is followed by a large number of people in Gujarat. Such elements in Narasinha's hagiography greatly enhance the appeal of his songs; for they suggest that his songs are not lyrics of an ordinary poet, but are rooted in an exalted form of *bhakti* of a saint.

Narasinha's Songs in the History of Krishna-*Lila* Poetry

If hagiographic narratives highlight important themes in Narasinha's songs, his generally accepted dates (1414–80 C.E.) help us appreciate the place of his songs in the history of Krishna *bhakti* poetry in North India.[11] Like Vidyapati of Mithila and Chandidas of Bengal, Narasinha lived during the early phase of the flourishing of Krishna *bhakti* poetry in the regional languages of North India. His songs belong to the period between the composition of two pivotal Sanskrit sources of Krishna-*lila* themes—the *Bhagavata Purana* (ninth century C.E.) and the *Gitagovinda* of Jayadeva (twelfth century C.E.)—and the upsurge of Krishna-*lila* songs in the sixteenth century C.E. in North India with poets like Surdas and Mirabai. It is significant that while Vidyapati and Chandidas choose to focus on the Radha-Krishna love story, Narasinha portrays a range of aspects of Krishna's life in Braj. Reputed Gujarati scholar Umashankar Joshi suggests that in the early period of Krishna-*lila* poetry, Narasinha's voice is distinctive even in the larger context of North India.[12] While Krishna *bhakti* poetry in Hindi has been extensively studied in the English speaking world, examining poems of other regional poets such as Narasinha adds to our understanding of the history of Krishna *bhakti* in North India.

   In addition to well known Krishna *bhakti* poets, Narasinha also predates the establishment of the two widely successful sects of Krishna devotion in North India—the Gaudiya tradition, founded by Chaitanya of Bengal (c. 1486–1533), and the *Pushti-marg*, founded by Vallabha (c. 1479–1531). Narasinha did not belong to any Krishna *bhakti* sect. Furthermore, unlike most other well-known male saint-poets of medieval North India who were incorporated into various sectarian traditions during or after their lifetimes, he was not appropriated by any sect, even at a later date.[13] Often, as the religious sects that appropriated popular saint-poets spread, they took the songs of these saint-poets to even larger audiences preserved them in manuscripts, and bestowed on them an aura of authority by incorporating them into liturgy. Narasinha, along with Mirabai, the most famous woman Krishna *bhakti* poet of North India, did not receive this benefit. It is significant, then, that despite the absence of sectarian support, Narasinha's songs and hagiography have become a treasured part of the cultural heritage of Gujarat. His songs set the tone for all subsequent Krishna *bhakti* poetry in Gujarati and continue to inspire poets and singers even today.

Krishna and His *Lila* in Narasinha Mehta's Songs

As a Krishna-*lila* poet of a regional language, Narasinha had two types of resources from which to draw: (1) Sanskrit sources of Krishna *bhakti* with pan-Indian popularity, and (2) regional cultural resources. Narasinha repeatedly expresses his indebtedness to the two Sanskrit texts mentioned above: the *Bhagavata Purana* and the *Gitagovinda*.[14] Their influence on his songs is manifold. What he draws from them, however, is creatively interpreted and interwoven with regional cultural elements in his songs, giving them their distinctive quality. In this, his songs follow a pattern found in much of vernacular Krishna-*bhakti* songs by the saint-poets of medieval India, which links them to both transregional and region specific devotional currents. The elements that vernacular songs of a region share with Sanskrit sources link them to the larger pan-Indian network of Krishna *bhakti*. The regional elements ground them firmly in the land, making them popular among its people. In a country as linguistically diverse as India, the layered linking of vernacular Krishna *bhakti* songs provides an interesting cultural phenomenon of the pre-modern times.

Sanskrit Sources and Narasinha's Songs

Narasinha's reliance on the *Bhagavata Purana* is apparent in three major aspects of his songs. First, a number of popular Krishna-*lila* episodes from the *Bhagavata*—the theft of butter, the complaints of the *gopis*, the subjugation of the serpent Kaliya, the restlessness of the *gopis* on hearing Krishna's flute, their circle dance on an autumn night, the disappearance of Krishna from the circle and his reappearance, the pain of separation experienced by the *gopis* on Krishna's departure from Braj—have found a place in Narasinha's songs.[15] The *Bhagavata* influence is also evident in some lines from Narasinha's songs that closely parallel some verses from this Sanskrit *Purana*.[16] At the same time, since his audiences would already be familiar with the Puranic stories about Krishna, like all major poets of Krishna-*lila* in regional languages, Narasinha surprises his audiences with a fresh interpretation of the stories to which he refers in his songs. It is in the interpretation of a Puranic episode or situation in the pithy form of a lyric, that each Krishna-*lila* poet makes his or her mark.[17] Narasinha seems keenly aware of the poetic need of new interpretation. In the two songs about the *gopis'* complaints to Yashoda (selections 4 and 5 here), for example, there is a poetic suggestion that for the *gopis*, the complaint was only an excuse to get a glimpse of Krishna. In the original *Bhagavata* episode, the *gopis* look at Krishna's face as he pretends to be afraid, but there is no suggestion that the complaint is itself a pretense. Further, in the *Bhagavata* episode, Yashoda does not respond; she just laughs the whole thing away.[18] In Narasinha's very popular song (selection 5 here) Yashoda does respond; and her response ("My Kanji was at home, inside; when did you see him outside?") plays cleverly with the concept of Krishna being the inner-dweller (*antaryamin*) of all.

Second, as in the *Bhagavata Purana*, Narasinha's Krishna-*lila* songs stress the significance of the human body and emotions as means for relating to the divine.[19] In the *Bhagavata Purana*, this is conveyed through Krishna's relationships with the people of Braj, as child, friend, and lover that involve bodily activities such as eating and dancing. This theme is taken even further in Narasinha's songs wherein the simple folks of Braj, the low-caste cowherds, occupy as central a place as Krishna himself. As the following excerpt (from selection 2) shows, Narasinha conveys that the all-powerful Lord, is not just graciously accessible to his devotees; he is, in fact, dependent on their love and very eager to please them.

> Unasked, he runs errands,
> Supreme *Brahman* Indestructible.
> For a little butter,
>   he stands here before a cowherdess
>   with his mouth wide open.
>   (*NKK*, 12, p. 13a)

In another song Narasinha stresses even more explicitly that elevated social position (possessed by those of high caste) or cosmic status (represented by Brahma) have little significance in Krishna's eyes. The Lord who is inaccessible even to the gods dances happily among loving cowherds of low caste.

> Look, Narahari dances daily
>   in the courtyard of a cowherd.
> The one who is disinclined to enter Brahma's dream
>   is bound here to affection.
>
> How beautiful Hari looks
>   with his anklets ringing sweetly!
> Blessed are the cowherds;
>   what [is to be gained] from belonging to the highest caste?
>   (*NKK*, 3, p. 135)

By making a reference to Krishna's transcendence, brought into focus here through a reference to Brahma, songs of this type on one hand stress his abounding grace in mingling freely with people whom other humans consider low. On the other hand, they highlight the significance of the love of Krishna's devotees in making his earthly *lila* meaningful. In the song about the subjugation of the serpent Kaliya (selection 6 here), the female serpents play the central role. They are the ones who get "the serpent freed, from Narasainya's Lord." In the original *Bhagavata* narrative, too, the release of the serpent is a result of his wives' plea to Krishna. The agency of the female serpents, which highlights dependence of *lila* on *bhakti*, however, is not highlighted in the *Bhagavata* as it is in Narasinha's song.[20]

The third aspect of the *Bhagavata*'s influence on Narasinha seems rather paradoxical in conjunction with the foregoing at first glance. A metaphysical vision conveyed in some of Narasinha's songs parallels the one presented in some hymns in the *Bhagavata Purana*.[21] Friedhelm Hardy terms the

Bhagavata's metaphysical vision a "projection of *advaita-vedanta* on to the *gopi*-story."[22] Such a projection is achieved through a monistic interpretation of *lila*.

> In the final analysis, the whole *lila*, including its actors, are but Krishna, who very frequently in the BhP is thus defined as *atmarama* "who sports with himself" literally "whose pleasure-garden is the self," and that without any discernible motive, since "all his desires are fulfilled."[23]

In a large number of Narasinha's songs, such an understanding is implicit or is referenced in one line or phrase, as is commonly found in Krishna poetry in North India. In a group of songs often classified as *gyan-bhakti-vairagya na pad* (songs of knowledge-devotion-detachment), however, such a vision is explicitly expounded. Songs in this category are not based on specific episodes of Krishna's earthly *lila* during his *avatara* (divine descent). They are lyrics of contemplation on Krishna's sporting in the universe as the all-pervasive Ultimate Reality—*Brahman*. A major theme of these songs is the human struggle to relate to this form and to represent it in language. What Vijay Mishra says about Indian devotional poetry in general is particularly applicable to these poems; their vitality "arises precisely out of the tension between the sublime object and its representation in language."[24] The poetic tension often leads to use of paradox or expression of bafflement as found in the following lines (from selections 23 and 24 here):

> He is the Lord of a million universes.
>   He is the holder of the earth.
> A million universes are but a cell in his body.
>   (*NKK*, 54, p. 386)

> The expanse of Shyam's beauty,
>   is far beyond the mind's reach.
> The mind loses its way in this beauty's endless festival.
>   (*NKK*, 53, p. 385)

Composed in a vernacular that had hitherto not been considered a proper vehicle for metaphysical reflection, these songs are remarkable, in that the grand vision they convey does not detract from their accessibility. Sung in a morning melody called *prabhatiya*, many of them are among the most popular devotional songs in Gujarat.[25] In a glowing tribute to the poet, Umashankar Joshi suggests that people of Gujarat will forever remain indebted to Narasinha for the songs wherein he has given them Vedanta immersed in *bhakti*.[26] The cosmic scale sketched in this group of songs seems to contradict the songs about Krishna-*lila* in the idyllic landscape of Braj at first; but, in fact, it complements them. Narasinha repeatedly stresses that the Lord whose energy pulsates throughout the universe is the same Lord who danced with the *gopis* in Vrindavan. Krishna is still bound to the love of his devotees.[27]

The influence of the other Sanskrit text, the *Gitagovinda,* is most clearly evident in two aspects of Narasinha's songs: in his treatment of *shringar-bhakti* (devotion through the mood of erotic love), and in his use of popular folk tunes (*deshis*) (discussed further later).[28] In the best of Narasinha's *shringar* songs, Jayadeva's influence can easily be seen in the tender reciprocity of lovemaking. The following lines of Jayadeva's *Gitagovinda,* quoted directly here in Sanskrit by Narasinha in his Gujarati song, clearly demonstrate the extent of Jayadeva's influence on him.

> *Gitagovinda* 10.4.1–2
>
> *tvamasi mama jivana,*
> *tvamasi mama bhushana*
>
> You are my ornament, my life
> My jewel in the sea of existence.[29]
>
> Narasinha
>
> With arms around Krishna
> the pretty one says:
> "*Tvamasi mama jivana,*
> You are my life, Lord,
> *tvamasi shringar mama,*
> You are my ornament,
> the necklace on my heart"...
>
> "O pretty woman, you are
> the dear breath of my life" (Krishna says)
> (*NKK,* 375, p. 310)

There is also a cycle of songs attributed to Narasinha that closely follows the *Gitagovinda* theme of Krishna and Radha's separation and union. A fully developed Radha-Krishna story with all its complexity and movements of emotions as found in the *Gitagovinda,* however, is missing in Narasinha. As a result, Narasinha's Radha is not portrayed as a complex heroine, as "an intense, solitary, proud female" who is "Krishna's partner in a secret and exclusive love"[30] as in the *Gitagovinda.* Importantly, even though there are some songs with specific references to Radha, a large number of Narasinha's songs in a variety of moods are in the voice of Krishna's beloved who may or may not be identified as Radha. For any poet drawing from both the *Bhagavata* and the *Gitagovinda,* Radha's portrayal poses a theological challenge. In the *Bhagavata,* Radha is not identified by name. The exclusive nature of a favored unnamed *gopi*'s tryst with Krishna is presented there in negative terms.[31] In the *Gitagovinda,* Radha's emotional journey in her exclusive encounter with Krishna is celebrated. Should the poet drawing from both these texts present love for the divine as a shared experience, as presented in the *Bhagavata,* or should the poet present it as an individual's journey through intense emotions, as presented in the *Gitagovinda*? Narasinha attempts to strike a balance. He recognizes Radha as the supreme beloved of Krishna, but not by placing her apart from everyone else. He presents her as the finest representative of the simple rustic folks of Braj who loved Krishna unconditionally. Narasinha's Radha is like Surdas's Radha, whose supremacy, as Hawley points out, emerges out of the "representative role she plays in relation to the rest of *gopis*."[32] A fine example of the Braj residents' recognition of Radha as their representative is found in a popular Narasinha song about Radha's necklace (from selection 19 here):

> Today, our dear Kanuda has distanced himself from us,
>   stealing Radhika's necklace, he has given it to Rukmini.
>   (*NKK*, 282, p. 273)

This song is in the voice of the entire Braj Community; the complaint is against Krishna himself. In the end, the almighty gives in. He orders a necklace of unpierced (the purest, unpolluted) pearls for Radha. As is evident, what Narasinha draws from classical Sanskrit sources is reshaped in his songs through an interpretive imagination.

Regional Elements in Narasinha's Songs

If Narasinha's songs are bound to the transregional Sanskritic tradition of *bhakti* through their close links with the *Bhagavata* and the *Gitagovinda*, they are bound to the land of Gujarat through their creative use of colloquial Gujarati, their depiction of the Gujarati cultural milieu, and above all, through their musical structures, which are embedded in the region's folk tunes and rhythms. As the quote from Jayadeva indiacates, Narasinha seems to have been well versed in Sanskrit literature. He does not write, however, in heavily Sanskritized Gujarati. The diction in most of his Krishna songs remains close to the colloquial Gujarati of folk songs, which present Krishna-*lila* episodes mainly through dialogues, monologues, or simple narrative/descriptive lines, without much figurative embellishment. Their appeal is dramatic. In a large number of Narasinha's songs, too, the narrative unfolds in a dramatic manner, and the diction remains simple. His song about Kaliya's subjugation (selection 6 here) provides a good example of his ability to use dramatic irony and is acclaimed by some scholars as among the best on this theme in the corpus of Krishna *bhakti* poetry of North India.[33] Further, like Gujarati folk songs, Narasinha's songs take optimum advantage of the inherent rhythm and music of the language, often using alliteration. Their linguistic as well as stylistic affinity with folksongs significantly enhances their appeal across class/caste boundaries.

Another reason why Narasinha's Krishna-*lila* songs resonate so well with the people of Gujarat is that the landscape of the region—both physical and cultural—is ever-present in them. While some fundamental aspects of Krishna's portrayal, such as his yellow silk garment, his flute, and his love for butter, remain unchanged, in many other aspects, Krishna and the Braj residents get "Gujaratized" to a large degree in his songs. Mothers of cowherd boys offer them popular medieval Gujarati dishes like *karamalo*—a mix of rice and yogurt; *dahithara*—a dainty bun made with wheat flour, yogurt, and ghee; and *ghebar*—a sweet full of ghee. Krishna drinks *kadhial dudh*—fresh milk.[34] Radha and her friends put on Gujarati attire and jewelry such as *patoli* (famous silk sari of Gujarat), *vinchia* (toe rings), and *kambi* (a heavy silver foot ornament, especially popular among Gujarat's pastoral communities). During *ras-lila* in Vrindavan, they perform Gujarati folk dances such as *hamchi* and *garbi*. The arrival of spring is here marked by the blossoming of *kesu* flowers, found plentiful in the forests of Gujarat.[35] Krishna is often addressed using diminutives like Kanudo, Kahan, and Mavo, found extensively in Gujarati folk songs. As a result, in Narasinha's lyrics, Braj does not remain a distant, purely mythical landscape. While retaining its mythical appeal, it becomes a place with which Krishna devotees in Gujarat can identify. Here, they find it easier to relate to Krishna.

Along with the poetic diction and the descriptions of the landscape, the melodic structures of Narasinha's songs are also rooted in the folk culture of Gujarat. Narasinha is traditionally thought to be a *vaggeyakar*—a poet who is also a skilled musician, a poet who sings rather than recites or writes his poems. His command over melodies (*ragas*) of Indian classical music, such as the Kedar and Prabhat is stressed in his hagiography. A large number of his songs are, however, *deshis*, lyrics composed in popular folk tunes. This type of lyric, found pervasively in vernacular literatures of medieval India, uses quantitative meters that provide considerable flexibility and easily fit into folk rhythms, unlike the meters of classical Sanskrit poetry, which require a strict order of syllables. Narasinha's choice of *deshis* is a key to his popularity. Especially beloved are his morning hymns, *prabhatiya*, in a meter called *zulna*. Even today, one can hear them being sung early in the morning by women cleaning their yards or working at the grinding stone, by farmers walking to their farms, by people doing their *puja*, and even on All India Radio stations.[36]

Devotional lyricism of Narasinha's Krishna-*lila* songs has left an unmistakable imprint on Krishna-*bhakti* poetry of the region. One can hear the echoes of Narasinha's phrases, lines, tunes, and theological interpretations in the Krishna-*lila* lyrics of innumerable Gujarati poets since his time, including Dayaram (1777–1852 C.E.), his most famous successor, who, unlike him, was a follower of sectarian Krishna-*bhakti*, Pushtimarga.[37] In the larger context of North India, Narasinha's songs are often compared with the songs of the two most celebrated Krishna-*bhakti* poets of North India—Mirabai, the woman saint of Rajasthan, and Surdas, the poet of Braj.[38] Mirabai, with the unique intensity of longing in her songs, and Surdas, with the superb delineation of the emotional states of the participants in Krishna-*lila* in his songs, are popular throughout India. Compared to these two later poets belonging to the sixteenth century, Narasinha is recognized more as a regional poet of Gujarat (even though some of his songs are sung also in Rajashtan). Within the region, however, with his ability to lead audiences directly into the heart of *lila* through the use of dramatic irony and the lyricism of his songs, he remains the singer of the Krishna-*lila* par excellence. A large number of Gujaratis would agree with poet Harindra Dave's comment: "If there was a conference of the saint-poets of medieval India, Narasinha would be unanimously chosen by Gujaratis as their representative."[39] The following selection includes songs that are among the most widely sung Krishna *bhajans* in Gujarat.

Note on Lyrics and Translation

Narasinha refers to Krishna by a number of his popular names in Gujarat. Each name is indicated by an asterisk when it occurs for the first time. In the signature lines of the poems, "Narasainya," the diminutive by which Narasinha refers to himself to convey humility, is retained. Lyrics under each heading are associated with a theme. Lyrics 1 and 2 refer to Krishna's foster mother Yashoda who raised him in the village of Gokul. Lyric 2 also has references to the myth of churning of the milky ocean by gods and demons. Lyric 3 depicts Krishna's relationship with people of Braj. Lyrics 4 and 5 are based on the episode of the *gopis'* complaint to Yashoda about Krishna stealing butter from their homes. Lyric 6 refers to the popular narrative about subjugation of serpent Kaliya who lived in the river Jamuna and made it poisonous. Lyrics 7–19 depict various moods of love between Krishna and the *gopis*. Lyrics 21 and 22 equate the *gopis'* absorption in love for Krishna with meditative states of yogis. Lyrics 23 and 24 belong to the group that is often termed "songs of knowledge-devotion-detachment."

Yashoda's Bliss

1

Friends! Let's go!
Let's go, and see Nanda's son.*
Take platters full of pearls and sing joyous songs!

Blessed Yashoda has given birth to Jivan.*
   She has performed perfect *tapas* [asceticism].
   She has beheld Supreme *Brahman* so closely!
   She has attained all desired fruits.

Narayan [Vishnu] has descended to perfect the bliss of his devotees.
His grace to Narasainya
   that he [Narasainya] sang Govinda's* glory.
                    NKK, 5, p. 131

2

Yashoda-ji woke up early to churn the curds;
  the Holder of the *Sarang* bow*[41]
  [offered] to give her a helping hand.

"Ma, Yashoda, let me churn your curds, please.
I will not break your pot, don't worry, please."

Mount Meru shuddered, "I certainly will break,
  if he makes me the churning pole."
"What will happen to me?" Vasuki panicked,
  "It will take my life to be the churning cord."

"I have jewels no more," the ocean said,
  "I will be churned in vain this time."
"What will become of me?" Mahadev worried,
  "How will I drink the poison this time?"

Brahma, Indra, and other gods clasped his feet:
  "Lord of Gokul,* drop the cord, please!"
Yashoda said, "I have all nine treasures with me;
  I have Narsainya's Lord, the lover of devotees."[42]
              NKK, 12, p. 139

Krishna among Braj Residents

3

The tiny village of Gokul—
My beloved has turned it into Vaikuntha,[40]
  pampering devotees and giving joy to the *gopis*.

The one who is unfathomable through reflection,
  who refuses to appear in *yogis'* meditation;
that dear one churns curds at Nanda's
  and grazes cows in Vrindavan.

Unasked, he runs errands,
Supreme *Brahman* Indestructible.
For a little butter,
  he stands here before a cowherdess
  with his mouth wide open.

Whom Brahma cannot know,
  whom Shiva is happy to serve,
  he, Narasainya's Lord, is bound to his devotees,
  with *Mukti* [liberation] as his serving-maid.
              NKK, 13, p. 139

The *Gopis'* Complaints

4

"Look! Look at the footprints of your son!
Running away, the little one took such huge steps!"

"How did he bring my curds down from the hanging pot?
He gulped what he liked
and then spilled it away."

"He smashed all my pots.
To whom could we complain?"

"He woke my sleeping children up!
We know him only too well in our hearts."

Just then Shyam* arrived, throwing a mischievous glance!
Gopis lost their way back home.
Narasainya says: "Couldn't take a step,
hearts so taken by love!"

                              NKK, 14, p. 140

5

"Yashoda, yell at your Kanuda*and stop him.
He has entire Braj in commotion.
Is there no one to check him?

"He opened my doors, broke the butter-pot,
    and spilled the curds all over.
He ate some butter
    and then splattered the rest all around.
    He has truly wreaked havoc this time."

"He marches ransacking everything,
    and knows no fear.
He even smashed my churning pot.
What kind of pampering is this?"

"I have complained to you many times;
    now, I won't be courteous.
Living in the same town,
    how much could we bear day after day?"

"My Kanji* was at home, inside.
When did you see him outside?
We have pots full of milk and curds;
    but he doesn't even touch them.
You are all fine ladies,
Crowding in a group of ten-twelve and complaining!"

Narasainya's Lord is right.
Women of Braj are lying.
                    NKK, 17, p. 141

The Subjugation of the Serpent Kaliya

6

"Drop the water-lilies and take off, child!
Our lord will wake up.
He will wake up and kill you,
and I will bear the sin of child-killing.

"Tell me child, are you lost?
Or has your enemy misled you?
Certainly your days are over;
    why else would you venture here?"

"No, Serpentess, I am not lost;
    nor has my enemy misled me.

"Gambling in the city of Mathura,
I have lost a wager for your serpent's head."

"With lovely complexion and perfect form,
    you look so handsome and so full of dreams.
How many children does your mother have?
Among them, are you the unloved one?"

"My mother has only two sons;
    of them, I am the younger.
Now, go! Wake up your serpent!
My name is Krishna—little Kahan.*"

"I will give you my necklace worth a million;
    I will also give you my chain.
I will give you both,
    hiding them from my serpent."

"What would I do with your necklace, Serpentess?
What would I do with your chain?
And why should you, O Serpentess,
    steal from your own home?"

Pressing his feet and twisting his whiskers,
the serpentess woke the serpent up:
    "Wake up, O Mighty One!
    There is some child at our door."

Both the mighty ones entered a combat.
Krishna yoked Kaliya soon.

With a thousand hoods he hissed,
   like the thundering clouds of monsoon.

The serpentesses sighed:
"He will surely torment the serpent.
   He will take him to the city of Mathura,
   and sever his head."

Folding both hands, they began to pray:
   "Lord, please let go of our husband.
   We are the guilty ones;
      we failed to see.
   We couldn't recognize the Lord!"

They duly honored Shri Krishna,
   showering platefuls of pearls.
The serpentesses got the serpent freed
   from Narasainya's Lord.
                NKK, 21, p. 143

Moods of Love–Krishna and the *Gopis*

7

Melodious and beautiful,
   it is your flute, Kahan!*
I hear it in my house, friend.
Tell me, my friend, how could I stay home,
   with my heart so utterly restless?

I rushed out to see [him];
   the excuse—fetching water!
I hung the pot-holder on the mango tree.
I left the pot at the lake's side.
Loving Kahan came soon and grasped my *sari*'s edge.

"Let me go, let me go, handsome Kahan!" I said,
   "I have already lost my senses."
My friend, there I met Narasainya's Lord.
   He made the night six months long,
and fulfilled the desire of my heart."
                NKK, 114, p. 198

8

Fair woman's anklet tinkled sweetly
   in the middle of a dark night:
"My friend dear, come, listen to my tale:

[The other day, I sat thinking:]
"For one, here is my foe—this terribly dark night.
   Second, at home is my surly mother-in-law.
Then, there is the cuckoo-bird, singing away in woods,
   and there is the *bapaiya* bird,
   sweetly chirping along.
The moon also has risen to its height.
   So much love, and such a short night!

"If I see Shamaliya* this time,
   I will tell him things hidden in my heart.
Someone unite me with Mavji,*
      I will hold him in my arms."
[But then]
"Narasainya's lord met me with love,
      darling came and held my hand."
                    NKK, 138, p. 208

9

Let's play, friend, drop churning curds!
The spring is here:
   creepers have blossomed;
   mango groves have burgeoned;
   the cuckoo sings on the Kadamb tree;
   from flower to flower fly black-bees!

Woman with graceful gait,
   adorn yourself, put on a necklace,
   get up and go!
I have been urging for so long.

Let's kiss our beloved's mouth;
   let's embrace him; let's sway with joy.
Today, let coyness have no power!

Entice Hari* with love,
   revel clasping him close to heart!
Taking your hand, Krishnaji will bow lovingly.
Narasainya will be enraptured by the euphoric mood.
That will be the atonement for the lost day!
                    NKK, 81, p. 182

10

It is a beautiful season my darling;
   beautiful is springtime.

Beautiful *kesu* flowers have blossomed in the forest.
Beautiful is Radha's Lord.*

Beautifully blooms Vrindavan;
    beautiful is Yamuna's bank;
immensely beautiful, the cowherds' band;
    so beautiful is he, Balaram's kin.*

Beautifully rings the lute;
    young girls clap along.
A gifted woman plays *chang* drum,
    and the flute is played by Madangopal.*

Beautiful are colors—vermilion, saffron;
    beautiful are betel leaves in mouths.
Strikingly beautiful is Narasainya's lord,
    radiant with bliss each day.
        NKK, 77, p. 181

11

Oh, what elixir is flooding Yamuna's banks!
Instruments are playing and the Lord is dancing.

With their arms entwined,
    the *gopis* are singing together,
    happily, harmoniously.

No one sees anyone else;
    each has Krishna, pressed close to her heart.
Each is drinking nectar of his lips,
    facing an enraptured Shyam*
    who holds her gently, close to his heart.

Hari has adoring women wrapped in love.
Loving mood has gently settled on the forest.
    Watching, Narasainya is immersed in it,
    singing the glory of Krishna's play!
        NKK, 41, p. 166

12

Oh, flute resounds in Vrindavan;
    gopis and Govinda dance in *ras*.
Keshav* dark and *gopis* fair
    together weave a fine design.
The luminous night passes by gently.
The lord has mustered a unique play.

Women fling colors—white and red.
   Sandalwood slush is all around.
Their saris' laces flutter;
   their glances fly over their shoulders.
They laugh and joke and clap their hands.
   They dance and invite others to dance.

Their faces glisten with sweat;
   their bodies are exhausted in ecstatic dance.
Each *gopi* offers Yamuna water to others,
   as Narasainya gives their feet massage.
         NKK, 66, p. 174

13

Krishna, drenched in saffron-yellow,
   and the maiden, soaked in *kasumbal* red,[43]
are standing at the portal of the grove
   Their eyes are moist with tenderness.

Whom would you call more beautiful?
The maiden or the Lord of Braj*?
I look and keep looking at Purushottam*
   with his ruby-adorned hands.

He hastened to the grove;
   with his touch, it bloomed to perfection.
Blessed is meeting Narasainya's Lord,
   Each moment overflowing with joy.
         NKK, 430, p. 332

14

An unusual mood and a novel play
   Nanda's prince* has gaily invented!
He has dressed himself in an elegant way
   in order to please the proud woman!

He swings high on a bejeweled swing.
Lucky women get glimpses of his face,
   veiled behind the sari's edge.

He has smeared saffron-paste all over.
What a matchless spectacle!
In his nose-ring hangs a huge pearl,
   and his lips are ruby red.

Joyfully as he puts his *pitambar* (yellow garb) on,
   a dark *sari* he wears today.

His anklets tinkle sweetly;
   his bodice is fairly tight.
He has painted his feet red,
   and has worn a gem-studded armlet.
His golden bangles make a sweet sound.

He gracefully sways his long braid.
His hair is adorned with flowers,
   and his eyes are dark with *kohl*.
Auspicious is meeting Narasainya's Lord.
   Oh, what beauty my friend!
            NKK, 252, p. 258

15

Mother, the black cobra, Kahan, has bit me in my mind!
With every breath, life departs.
   Someone please halt it!

Don't give me herbs; don't take me to a healer!
In Gokul is the snake-charmer Govinda.*
   Place me at his feet.

The healer saw and thought:
   "The wound really is deep!"
Auspicious was meeting Narasainya Lord;
   all poison was withdrawn from the maiden!
            NKK, 307, p. 284

16

"In what auspicious moment
   did you get stuck to my *bindi*, Shyam?[44]
You don't part with me even for a moment;
   my breath, my life, my handsome friend!

"I turn to the door,
   you stand there touching me.
I look at the window,
   and you are sitting there.
On the street, I see you approaching,
   so much sweeter than nectar!

"I sit down to dine, and you are sitting along.
   I lie down, and see you in my bed.

On my way to Vrindavan,
>   you meet me and walk holding my hand!

"Mother and sister-in-law keep taunting me:
>   'You are dear to Nanda's prince!*
On your way to Yamuna to fetch water,
>   he comes and grabs your sari's edge.'"

He does not leave alone whom he loves;
>   such is the dear one, the delightful one;
Auspicious is meeting Narasainya's lord
>   who resides in the lotus of heart.

>   *NKK*, 141, p. 209

17

Mohan* passed through our front yard, playing flute.
How do I live now, mother?
Wicked Kahan has pierced my heart;
>   it hurts deeply inside.

I was just standing inside my house
when I saw Kahan passing by.
That's when our eyes met
and my darling threw such a glance!

Jivanji* left;
I still did not die; lived on,
>   only to dissolve limb by limb.
Someone please tell me of his whereabouts.
Now, I have put all shame aside.

All of my friends together searched through Vrindavan.
>   We looked even in Yamuna's waters.
Tears trickled ceaselessly,
>   as we kept recalling his love.

Friend, unite me with my heart's desire,
the sustenance of the women of Braj.
If ever I see Narasainya's Lord,
>   I will make him the adornment of my heart.

>   *NKK*, 104, p. 193

18

Look at me just once, my beloved,
>   and cool the fire in my heart!
From your eyes flows elixir
>   that rejuvenates my limbs!

How can there be joy without your grace,
  no matter how one tries?
The pain won't go without serving you,
  no matter how many gods one serves.

Precious is [the] human body
  and taking birth on earth.
Be it your grace to Narasainya
  that he keeps singing your praise!
                    NKK, 192, p. 230

19

"Today, dear Kanuda* has distanced himself from us!
Stealing Radhika's necklace,
  he has given it to Rukmini."[45]

"Street to street I paced, crying aloud.
  I went searching house to house.
There! I spotted my pearls on queen Rukmini's neck.

"Had I been awake,
  I wouldn't have let them be snatched.
My *karma*, I fell asleep.
Deceitful sleep seized me,
  but soon I woke up, saying 'Hari, Hari.'

"I will pump the blacksmith's bellows,
    and heat up an iron ball.
I will have him swear by life [holding it].
For the sake of my necklace,
  today I will even summon Narad [to intervene]."

Radhaji fumed with rage,
  with tears overflowing her eyes.
"Hari! Give me my necklace back,
 or here ends my life!"

He ordered a heap of pearls and
  got them strung unpierced.
Auspicious was meeting Narasainya's Lord
  who appeased enraged Radhika.
                    NKK, 282, p. 273

20

Odhav! Tell Kubja[46]:
  "You've got a diamond in Hari!

My advice to you is
    to take good care of him!"

Early in the morning, ask him what he wants
    and give that to him instantly.
He likes nothing else;
    he is only used to butter and curds!

Bedeck his bed with flowers.
    Present a new mood every day.
And listen, don't keep him awake too long,
    lest his tender body wither.

Shuka, Sanak, and great sages,
    no one knows him fully;
Don't part with him even for a moment, O naïve one!
Don't let arrogance enter your heart!

Kubja, Kamsa's maid,
    She has the dark one as her husband!
    She has Narasainya's Lord in her power,
    Her merit is limitless!
                    NKK, 181, p. 225

Absorption in Love as Meditation

21

Naïve cowherdess set out to sell Hari,
    filling her pot with the darling
    of sixteen thousand *gopis*.

The cowherd woman went around,
    selling the Lord of the destitute,
    crying aloud on streets, "Get Murari* for yourself!"

When she put the pot down,
    the flute resounded within it.
One look at his face
    and she lost consciousness.

Brahma, Indra, and the celestials witnessed this miracle.
They saw the Lord of all worlds
    in an earthen pot.

Due to *gopi*'s good fortune,
    the inner-dweller appeared.
Narasainya's Lord so pampers his devotees!
                    NKK, 33, p. 375

22

Tonight the flute played in Vrindavan.
I heard and lost my heart, dear friend!
I woke up from deep sleep.

Sleep, wakefulness, dream,
    and the fourth state,
I sported in a realm beyond them,
        in the realm of the ultimate bliss.
My mind got cleansed of the three qualities.
    All illusions were dispelled.

Everywhere I look, my friend,
    shine countless pearls of liberation.
Walking around, I see with joy
    the enchanting play of Narasainya's Lord.
                        NKK, 61, p. 389

From Songs of "knowledge–devotion–detachment"

23

The beginning, the middle, and the end—
    it is all you, Shri Hari!*
The one, the only, the only Self!
Even Brahma cannot grasp
    the *Brahman* permeating everything.
Foolish people look for him elsewhere!

Millions of suns and moons shine in his face.
His face is beyond probing sight,
    like the darkness that cannot be seen in the sunlight!
About him, the *Vedas* say "Not this, not this."

He is the Lord of a million universes.
        He is the holder of the earth.
A million universes are but a cell in his body.

The illusion will not shatter without grasping the essence.
The one without attributes [*nirguna*]
    has a form that has attributes [*saguna*].

He lives not in solitude;
    nor is he apart from the world.
His energy pulsates in everything.
Perfect, Beginningless, Bliss Incarnate—Krishnaji.
    Beautiful Radhika is his *bhakti*!

No one grasps the mystery of the *Vedas*.
  Only a rare one knows its essence.
Shuka, Sanaka, and the divine sage Narada—
  they meditate on Supreme *Brahman*!
That Supreme *Brahman* sports with loving women.
An adoring woman takes him on her lap.

The elixir that is enjoyed by women of Braj forever
  Narasainya drank it, taking the form of a female friend!
  NKK, 54, p. 386

24

Look who is strolling across the expanses of space,
  saying "I am that, I am that!"
I long for death at Shyam's* feet.
  No one here compares to Krishna!

The expanse of Shyam's beauty
  is far beyond the mind's reach.
The mind loses its way in this beauty's endless festival.
Know the nonliving and the living with *rasa*,
  holding the rejuvenating herb of love.

[His beauty is]
Comparable to the golden rim
  of the flame radiating from a million suns.
There, the Supreme sports in bliss,
  rocking in a cradle of gold.

Without lamp, without oil, without a cotton wick,
  an unfluttering flame shines for eternity.
See it without eyes, know it without form,
  Drink the ambrosia without tongue.

Indestructible, incomprehensible,
  he remains beyond intellect.
Sporting everywhere between high and low,
  Narasainya's Lord permeates the entirety.
A saint binds him with the fiber of love.
  NKK, 53, p. 385

NOTES

1. *Padma Purana, Uttarkhand, Shrimad Bhagavata Mahatmya* 1.48–49. In *Shrimad Bhagavatam*, edited by Krishnashankar Shastri (Sola, Gujarat: Shri Bhagavata Vidyapith, 1998), 2.

2. The term *lila* denotes "divine sporting" in the Hindu tradition. The range of its connotations include: the activity of a divine descent during his or her time on the earth, the working of the universe as divine play, and also the divine will as it works in an individual's life. The concept behind the term is that whatever is and happens is a part of the divine sporting, and has as its end bliss, *ananda*. In relation to Vishnu's *avatara* Krishna, the term *lila* becomes all the more meaningful because of his joyous life as a naughty child and as an amorous adolescent among the cowherds of Braj. Krishna's *lila* has, therefore, inspired the richest traditions of songs, paintings, and dances in India.

3. Conversation with Kiran Patel, announcer, All India Radio, Vadodara, Gujarat, June 14, 2001.

4. Kenneth Bryant stresses the point that Krishna-*bhakti* poets have treated Krishna's dealings with Kamsa and his life in Dwaraka only as a frame, almost as an excuse for his life in Braj. See Kenneth Bryant, *Poems to the Child God, Structures and Strategies in the Poems of Surdas* (Berkeley: University of California Press, 1978), 11.

5. Hasu Yagnik, *Gujarati Lokasahitya* (Gujarati: "Gujarati folk literature") (Gandhinagar: Gujarat Sahitya Akadami, 1995), 14.

6. See H. C. Bhayani, inntroduction to Yagnik, *Gujarati Loksahitya*, 15. Also see H. C. Bhayani and Hasu Yagnik, "Krishna in Gujarati Folk-Song Tradition," in *Devotion Divine: Bhakti Traditions from the Regions of India, Studies in Honor of Charlotte Vaudeville*, edited by Diana Eck and Françoise Mallison (Groningen, Netherlands: Egber Forsten, 1991), 43.

7. As early as the eighth century, Jinsensuri's *Harivamshapurana* (Sanskrit) incorporates a life of Krishna. For reference, see Ambalal Shah, *"Bhasha ane Sahitya"* ("Language and Literature") in *Gujarat no Rajakiya ane Sanskrutik Itihas* (Gujarati: Cultural and political history of Gujarat), Vol. 3, edited by Rasiklal C. Parikh and Hariprasad C. Shastri (Ahmedabad: B. J. Institute, 1974), 230.

8. See Barbara Stoler Miller Introduction, *Love Song of the Dark Lord: Jayadeva's Gitagovinda,* (New York: Columbia University Press, 1997), 35, for the example in translation, and p. 65 for notes.

9. The issue of authenticity of some popular songs attributed to Narasinha is not completely resolved in the scholarly debates in Gujarat, as is commonly the case with saint-poets of medieval India. Leading Gujarati scholars have elaborately discussed the problems that arise from this issue in preparing editions of Narasinha's lyrics. See, for example, H. C. Bhayani's essay *"Narasinha na sampadan ni samasyao"* (The problems of editing Narasinha's poetry), in *Krishna Kavya* (Gujarati: Krishna Poetry) (Ahmedabad: Rangdwar Prakashan, 1986), 79–83. For this selection, I follow Shivalal Jesalpura's critical edition: *Narasinha Mehta ni Kavyakrutio* (Poetic works of Narasinha Mehta) (Ahmedabad: Sahitya Sanshodhan Prakashan, 1981). While there is general consensus among scholars about the songs included in this edition, some scholars have expressed doubts about songs that convey a grand metaphysical vision. Jayant Kothari wrote about this issue in a three part essay *"Narasinha Mehta na Pado – Kartutva no Koyado"* ("Narasinha Mehta's lyrica: The problem of Authorship), *Uddesh* Vol. 9, May 1999, 380–387; and July 1999, 445–454; Vol. 10, September 1999, 49–58.

10. For hagiographic accounts about Narasinha, a good source in English is Justin Abbot's translation, *Bhaktavijaya: Stories of Indian Saints, English Translation of Mahipati's Marathi Bhaktavijaya*, vol. 2 (London: Arthur Probsthain, 1933), 415–466.

11. While these are generally accepted as Narasinha's dates now, there was a long and complicated debate about them among Gujarati scholars lasting several decades in the twentieth century. For an overview of this debate see K. K. Shastri, *Narasinha Maheto, Ek Adhyayan* (Gujarati: "Narasinha Mehta: A study") (Ahmedabad: B. J. Institute, 1971), 44–136.

12. Umashankar Joshi, "Narasinha Mehta," in *Gujarati Sahityano Itihas* (Gujarati: The history of Gujarati literature), vol. 2, edited by Umashankar Joshi, Anantarai Raval, and Yashavant Shukla (Ahmedabad: Gujarati Sahitya Parishad, 1976), 82.

13. Surdas, for example, is a part of Vallabhacharya's Pushtimarga; religious sects have developed around even a completely nonconventional figure like Kabir.

14. There are a number of songs (no. 493, p. 356; no. 6, p. 362, no. 62, p. 390 in *Narasinha Mehta ni Kavyakrutio*) in which there are references to Shukadev and Jayadeva as the ones who knew experientially and conveyed to others the joy of Krishna-*lila*.

15. A notable exception is the episode of the lifting of Mount Govardhan.

16. For a detailed discussion of these parallels see Shastri, *Narasinha Maheto, Ek Adhyayan*, 184–190.

17. John Hawley remarks on Surdas's ability to surprise "his listeners with a point of view that would enable them to see it all afresh." John Stratton Hawley, *Sur Das, Poet, Singer, Saint* (Seattle: University of Washington Press, 1984), 73.

18. *Bhagavata Purana*, 10.8.30–31, *Srimad Bhagavata*, vol. 3, Skandha 10, trans. Swami Tapasyananda (Madras: Ramakrishna Matha, 1981), 68.

19. For a discussion of the emotional nature of *bhakti* in the *Bhagavata Purana*, see Friedhelm Hardy, *Viraha-Bhakti: The Early History of Krishna Devotion in South India* (Oxford: Oxford University Press, 1983), 496–497, 542–544, 555.

20. See the same episode in the *Bhagavata Purana* 10.16 (*Srimad Bhagavata*, trans. Swami Tapasyananda, 106–117), where the female serpents appear only at the end.

21. Two hymns of this type are the *Bhagavata Purana* 10.14, "The Hymn of Brahma"; and 10.87, "The Hymn of the *Vedas*," *Srimad Bhagavata*, trans. Swami Tapasyananda, 95–104, 421–431. These hymns present theism and monism, meditative practices and loving devotion, as complementary approaches to the same ultimate reality.

22. Hardy, *Viraha-Bhakti*, 538.

23. Hardy, *Viraha-Bhakti*, 541.

24. Vijay Mishra, *Devotional Poetics and the Indian Sublime* (Albany: State University of New York Press, 1998), 126.

25. For a detailed discussion of Narasinha's morning melodies see Françoise Mallison, *Au Point de jour: Les Prabhatiyande Narasimha Maheta, Poet et saint Vishnouite de Gujarat* (Paris: École Française d'Extrême-Orient, 1986).

26. Joshi, "Narasinha Mehta," 2:100.

27. See for example the last stanzas of selections 23 and 24 here.

28. Shastri has discussed the two *deshis* that are found in both Jayadeva and Narasinha. See Shastri, *Narasinha Maheto, Ek Adhyayan*, 178–180.

29. *Love Song of the Dark Lord*, 112.

30. *Love Song of the Dark Lord*, 26.

31. *Bhagavata Purana*, 10.13.13, *Srimad Bhagavata*, 164.

32. Hawley, *Sur Das*, 89.

33. Jayendra Trivedi has made a comparative analysis of this song with Surdas's cycle of sixty-seven songs dealing with the episode. He argues that even though Surdas's creative genius is evident in his delineation of emotions of all characters involved, the dramatic economy with which Narasinha deals with the episode is more successful in capturing the essence of the episode. See his article in *Narasinha Mehta, Aswad ane Swadhyaya* (Gujarati: Narasinha Mehta, Appreciation of poems and studies), edited by Raghuvir Chaudhari (Bombay: M. P. Shah Women's College, 1983), 67–73.

34. See, for example, song nos. 23.4 (p. 144) and 7.3 (p. 362), in *Narasinha Mehta ni Kavyakrutio*.

35. For these, see songs under the headings "*Ras na pad*" (pp. 144–180), "*Vasant na pad*" (pp. 181–190), and "*Zanzar na pad*" (pp. 202–209), in *Narasinha Mehta ni Kavyakrutio*. Also see M. R. Majmudar, "The Aesthetic Factor: Arts of Pleasure," in *Cultural History of Gujarat* (Bombay: Popular Prakashan, 1965), chap. 8, 257–202. Here, Majmudar quotes from a number of Narasinha's songs discussing attire, food, and folk dances of Gujarat.

36. For the metrical and musical aspects of Narasinha's songs see Shastri, *Narasinha Maheto, Ek Adhyayan*, 174–183; Amubhai Doshi "*Narasinha na Pado ma Geyata ane Sangit-tattva*" ("Singability and musical element in Narasinha's lyrics") in *Narasinha Mehta Adhyayan Granth* (Gujarati: A collection of critical essays on Narasinha Mehta), edited by Rasik L. Mehta and Anant V. Dave (Junagadh: Bahauddin College, 1983), 158–169; and Harikrishna Pathak, "*Narasinha ni Kavita ma Laya ane Geyata*," (Rhythm and singability in Narasinha's lyrics") in Chaudhari, *Narasinha Mehta*, 79–87.

37. For more on Dayaram, see Rachel Dwyer, *The Poetics of Devotion: The Gujrati Lyrics of Dayaram* (London: SOAS, 2001).

38. For comparison with Mirabai, see, for example, the essay by Ushanas, "*Narasinha and Mira*," ("Narasinha and Mira") in Mehta and Dave, *Narasinha Mehta Adhyayan Granth*, 1–4; for comparison with Surdas, see Bhramarlal Joshi, *Surdas aur Nartasinha Mehta: Ek Tulanatmak Adhyayan* (Hindi: Surdas and Narasinha Mehta: A comparative study) (Ahmedabad: Gurjar Bharati, 1968).

39. Harindra Dave, commentary to performances of Narasinha's songs during the fifth centenary celebrations in 1981, as recorded in the memorial audio cassette *Narasainyo Bhakta Hari no* (Narasinha, the Devotee of Hari), distributed by Bahauddin College, Junaghadh.

40. Vaikuntha: Vishnu's abode.

41. *Sarang*: Krishna's bow, known for its strength. This poem uses as frame the myth of the churning of the milky ocean by gods and demons for obtaining nectar of immortality. The churners used Mount Meru as the churning pole and serpent Vasuki as the churning chord. When potent poison came out of the ocean before the nectar, Mahadeva, Shiva, drank it. In this poem, the actors in the cosmic play are afraid of child Krishna taking up churning to help his mother, Yashoda.

42. Nine treasures belong to the god of wealth Kubera.

43. *Kasumbal* red: color extracted from a wildflower of springtime, often mixed with water for using in the Holi festival when people throw colors at one another.

44. *Bindi*: Vermilion dot made on foreheads by married Hindu women whose husbands are alive, as a sign of good fortune.

45. Rukmini: Krishna's chief queen.

46. Kubja: a hunch-backed woman at the court of Krishna is foe Kamsa's court in Mathura. Krishna left Braj to defeat Kamsa and then stayed in Mathura. Kubja served him dearly. In this poem, the gopis are sending a message to Kubja somewhat enviously.

REFERENCES

English

Bryant, Kenneth. 1978. *Poems to the Child God: Structures and Strategies in the Poems of Surdas*. Berkeley: University of California Press.

Dwyer, Rachel. 2001. *The Poetics of Devotion: The Gujrati Lyrics of Dayaram*. London: SOAS.

Eck, Diana, and Françoise Mallison, eds. 1991. *Devotion Divine: Bhakti Traditions from the Regions of India, Studies in Honor of Charlotte Vaudeville*. Groningen: Egber Forsten.

Hardy, Friedhelm. 1983. *Viraha-Bhakti: The Early History of Krsna Devotion in South India*. Oxford: Oxford University Press.

Hawley, John Stratton. 1984. *Sur Das, Poet, Singer, Saint*. Seattle: University of Washington Press.

Jayadeva. 1997. *Love Song of the Dark Lord: Jayadeva's Gitagovinda*. Translated by Barbara Stoler Miller. New York: Columbia University Press.

Mahipati. 1933. *Stories of Indian Saints: English Translation of Mahipati's Marathi Bhaktavijaya*. Translated by Justin E. Abbot. London: Arthur Probsthain.

Majmudar, M. R. 1965. *Cultural History of Gujarat*. Bombay: Popular Prakashan.

Mishra, Vijay. 1998. *Devotional Poetics and the Indian Sublime*. Albany: SUNY Press.

Srimad Bhagavata Vol. 3, Canto 10. 1981. Translated by Swami Tapasyananda. Madras: Ramakrishna Matha.

French

Mallison, Françoise. 1986. *Au point du jour: les Prabhatiyam de Narasimha Maheta, poète et saint vishnouite du Gujarat*. Paris: Ecole française d'Extrême-Orient.

Gujarati

Primary Sources

Bhaktamal. 1998. With commentary by Priyadas in Gujarati translation. Translated by Dasanudas. Rajkot: Pravin Pustak Bhandar.

Mehta, Narasinha. 1981. *Narasinha Mehta ni Kavyakrutio* (Poetic works of Narasinha Mehta). Edited by Shivalal Jesalpura. Ahemedabad: Sahitya Sanshodhan Prakashan.

something else happened, something more than ritual graces, or the inevitable results of polished, disciplined meditation and practice of *Pancharatra rites.*

He was touched. Inhabited.

Late one night, long after evening worship, while he stood before the
Devanayaka image in Tiruvahindrapuram temple, he was beheld by the god,
and so transported—to another world, to the Krishna-world within that image
of Vishnu. Held in thrall by that gaze, he saw, and he sang what he saw in
verses of exquisite Sanskrit.

Though all forms of Lord Vishnu are here in this temple image and unfold
in serried theological array before his willing singers, the Boar and the Warrior
Brahmin, Tortoise, Man-Lion, and Dwarf, Buddha and Rama—that evening
the poet Venkatesha was struck by the luminous beauty of the Lord's most
sweet form as Krishna, the cowherd and king, handsome Kannan, lover of
gopis and child-prince of thieves from the forests of Vrindavan.

It is said that then he composed this poem, the *Gopalavimshati*, at Tiruvahindrapuram. After praising the manifold forms and powers and exploits
of Vishnu as Devanayaka in Sanskrit, Tamil, and Maharashtri poems of great
power and theological sophistication, he also sung this praise of Vishnu as
Krishna come down from the north. This Krishna who had, from an early time,
already entered Tamil consciousness as the god of the jasmine landscape.

It is to this poem we will turn, after some words of introduction. We need
to explore who this Venkatesha is, and the significance of his praises of Krishna
in the thirteenth–fourteenth centuries in Tamil Nadu.

Vedantadeshika: A "Lion among Poets and Philosophers"

The medieval South Indian saint-poet, theologian, and philosopher Venkata-
natha, or Venkatesha (c. 1268–1369) is most commonly known by his epithet
Vedantadeshika ("preceptor of the Vedanta"), or Deshika. Vedantadeshika is one
of the most important brahmin *acharyas* (sectarian preceptors) of the Sri-
vaishnava community of South India, a particular Vaishnava community that
worships a personal god in the form of Lord Vishnu, one of the high gods of
Hindu tradition, along with his consort-goddess Sri, or Lakshmi.[1] This community, which first developed around the tenth–eleventh centuries, claims the
Tamil poems of the *alvars*, especially those of the saint-poet Nammalvar, as
equal in status to the Sanskrit Veda (see chapter 7 here). Long after Deshika's
death, he was claimed as the founding *acharya* of the Vatakalai, or "northern"
school of Srivaishnavism, centered in the ancient holy city of Kanchipuram in
northern Tamil Nadu. Deshika's early association with the northern city of
Kanchi would be a significant source of his broad learning, his polylinguism,

and what might be termed his "cosmopolitanism." For Kanchipuram, even before the time of Deshika, had long been associated with multiple religious communities—Buddhist, Jain, Hindu—and a decidedly cosmopolitan atmosphere. The city had deep roots in transregional brahminical Sanskrit learning, though it also fostered the development of regional cosmopolitan literatures, most notably in Pali and Tamil.

Along with working in three major languages of his southern tradition, Deshika was a master of many genres of philosophical prose and poetry. He wrote long ornate religious poems (kavyas) in Sanskrit; a Sanskrit allegorical drama (natyam); long religious lyric hymns (stotras and prabandhams) in Sanskrit, Maharashtri Prakrit, and Tamil; and commentaries and original works of philosophy, theology, and logic in Sanskrit and in a hybrid combination of the Sanskrit and Tamil languages called Manipravala ("jewels" and "coral"). Tradition ascribes to him the resounding epithets kavitarkikasimha, "a lion among poets and philosophers" (or "logicians"), and sarvatantrasvatantra, "master of all the arts and sciences." Such epithets embody a certain spirit of creative cultural and linguistic synthesis. Deshika was master of all tantras (this term embraces multiple genres of texts); he was also both a kavi (master poet) and a tarkika (logician/debater/philosopher). Tensions and complementarities between poet and philosopher, the devotional lyric and theological prose, are enacted within the same person.

Deshika's devotional poetry combines in a dynamic way the local/regional literary prestige of Tamil with the pan-regional aesthetic prestige and power of Sanskrit (with Maharashtri as Middle Indo-Aryan literary spice). Deshika's writings expand the linguistic field of South Indian devotion beyond the normative claims either of Sanskrit or Tamil devotional texts. His language choices embrace both the singularity of Sanskrit as divine "primordial tongue" and the subordinate but equally divine claims of his mother tongue, Tamil.

Krishna in a World of Vishnu

In the Tamil religious literature of South India, Krishna rarely stands alone as an object of devotion. In the poetry of saint-poets, from the earliest Tamil alvars around the eighth–tenth centuries to the Sanskrit stotras of acharyas from the twelfth to the fourteenth centuries, Krishna comes, as it were, layered with other forms (avataras, or incarnations) of Vishnu. As Vidya Dehejia noted long ago, even in the tirumolis of the woman alvar Antal, one of the most passionate poets of Krishna the Cowherd Lover, Krishna and Vishnu are "not sharply differentiated."[2] Krishna in Antal is a composite god who mirrors various forms of Vishnu, whether it be the cosmic form of Ranganatha, asleep on the ocean of milk between creations, Vamana, the Dwarf who spanned and (literary ornamentations/figures of speech).[8] A luminous work on the model of Kalidasa's *Raghuvamsha* on the life of Rama and the *Krishnakarnamritam*, a South Indian Krishna *kavya* that became so influential in later Bengali Vaishnavism,[9] Deshika's *kavya* on Krishna is an encyclopedic treatment of the Krishna-*katha* (narrative) and *lila* (divine "play"). The poem mingles religious and "secular" forms of love and separation, the erotic (*shringara*), the heroic (*vira*), and awesome (*adbhuta*) forms of aesthetic experience (*rasa*), the royal and pastoral forms of narrative, and charm and gravity in ways distinctly suited to this polymorphous child-cowherd-lover-god-king.

After a first *sarga* of praise-verses (*stotras*), Deshika depicts, in the meticulous word-pictures of *kavya* style, the remarkable progress of Devaki's pregnancy, with descriptions of twilight (*samdhya*), the moon, and the cries of *chakravaka* birds. The third and forth *sargas* speak, respectively, of Krishna's coming to Gokula, his substitution for the girl-child Maya, and the destruction of various demons and pests sent to kill him, such as Putana, the "false mother" demoness (*rakshasi*) and the great *naga* Kaliya. *Sarga* 5 is an exquisite description of the seasons (*ritumala*), replete with descriptions of the paddy harvest, red *indragopa* bugs, dark monsoon clouds, dark hills, rain and rushing rivers in autumn, and intoxicated peahens. *Sarga* 6 is a *chitra-kavya*, filled with word-pictures, puns, and all manner of verbal conceits, including the visualization of *yantras*, or ritual devices for meditation. The seventh *sarga* describes Krishna lifting up Govardhan Hill—with expansive natural description—and the eighth contains the famous *ras-lila*, Krishna's circle-dance with the *gopis*, and their subsequent "watersports" (*jalakrida*). The latter *sarga* contains many technical references to dance and to music, consonant with the encyclopedic spirit of the *mahakavya*. Later *sargas* deal with various seminal events, such as Krishna's return to Mathura after the message of Akrura; his conquering of Kamsa; his kingship in Dvaraka and his marriage to Rukmini; the killing of Narakasura and his marriage to the sixteen thousand women; the theft of the *parijata* from Indra's realm and his return by "aerial car" over a dizzying landscape; a series of vivid "waking verses" in the erotic mode (*tiruppalliyelucci* in Tamil), and a remarkable *digvijaya*, or royal progress through his lands that includes a virtual social and political map of the North. Next comes a summary of the Mahabharata war, and finally, in *sarga* 24, a auspicious description of Krishna with his innumerable wives at home in Dvaraka, stopping short before his legendary ignominious death at the hands of a hunter in the epic *Mahabharata* account.

The Yadava *kavya* ends, unlike the *Mahabharata*, with auspicious images of Krishna as loving householder and husband; it also qualifies his worldly pleasures with the chastening warning that, while Krishna seems to be one whose mind is bent on sense-pleasures (*sambhoge ca pravanamanasah*), he is (at the same time) "perpetually" celibate (*brahmacharyam*). This is no worldly story of love, loss, and recovery: Dvaraka is not only some North Indian kingdom but is the "entire universe" (sarvalokam). One who knows this will ford the unfordable river of Maya, the splendid "illusion" of samsara.[10]

This tension between ascetic and erotic modes of discourse is one that runs through all of the Krishna literature. Yet in Deshika's kavya itself, as in the Bhagavata Purana and in various other Sanskrit or vernacular devotional texts, it is finally the sensuous vigor of the verses that belies any easy reduction of the Krishna-lila to some intellectualized and normative ascetic form of bhakti, or some kind of purely spiritual detachment, untethered from eros: in Krishna, as with the god Shiva, the erotic and ascetic dimensions are of course distinct, but inseparable; they interanimate, informing and, in many ways, defining each other.

The following verse from the last sarga of the Yadavabhyudaya is similar in vocabulary and syntactic structure to one of the most famous descriptions of loving embrace in Sanskrit literature, the great eighth-century playwright and poet Bhavabhuti's verse on Rama and Sita's loving "close embrace" that takes place as the night watches pass by "unnoticed," a verse that knits together the religious and the human language of love. Here we are with Krishna in his "inner apartments."[11]

> The fierce chill of winter air
> unchecked
> even by little clay pots
> with their red eyes
> of coal
> that burned between their heavy breasts
>
> was suddenly
> cut off
>
> by the heat of the Lord's
> passionate
> close
> embrace.

A Praise-Poem for Krishna as "Lord of Gods"

The Yadavabhyudayam itself, of course, is far too long to translate for a volume such as this. Even selections from this sprawling work would give little sense of its cumulative power and richly configured world, something only experienced in a full reading, and best left for a separate study, which would include detailed treatment of the influential commentary of the Shaiva philosopher-poet Appaya Dikshita.[12] What follows is a complete translation, with detailed thematic, grammatical, and philological notes, of Deshika's other Sanskrit poem for Krishna, the Gopalavimshati.

The *Gopalavimshati* is a praise-poem (*stotra*) and not a *kavya*. It is said to have been composed by Deshika for Vishnu as Devanayaka, or "Lord of Gods," at Tiruvahindrapuram, the "town of the Serpent King," near the coastal town of Cuddalore in Tamil Nadu. This *stotra* has a rich liturgical history at Deva-nayaka Swami Temple, which includes its use as a marriage hymn and as a blessing over food offered to the temple image (the *tadiyaradhanams*). On Krishna Jayanti, the image (*murti*; *archa*) of Devanayaka is taken in procession to the chanting of this hymn. Deshika composed for Devanayaka other very important Sanskrit *stotras*, Tamil *prabandhams*, and one long Maharashtri Pra-krit *stotra*, poems I have analyzed in some detail elsewhere.[13] They are dis-tinctive in their passionate devotion to this particular form of Vishnu and for their use of the first person and various erotic motifs from Sanskrit literature and *akam* conventions of classical love poetry in ancient Tamil. It thus comes as no surprise that Deshika identified this particularly beloved form of Vishnu as Gopala, the sensually evocative and emotionally accessible cowherd youth and god of the Vrindavan pastorale.

This comparatively short *stotra* gives the reader a very vivid sense of Krishna in the Tamil Land through one of South India's most gifted medieval saint-poets. It includes set descriptions and "enjoyments" of the body of Krishna that are meant to inspire devotional feeling (*bhava*) in the hearer: we move from the cosmological, in the evocation of the birth date, to ritual forms of meditation, the shining *yantra* of many colors: soon we are at the heart of the emotional *imaginaire* of Vrindavan pastorale, where the transcendent *Brahman*, incon-ceivable, unknowable, formless Being, has become a tiny, cranky baby, a tod-dler butter thief and trickster, a dancer in the courtyard, a flute-playing cow-herd, a merciless killer of demons, a handsome lover who plays at concealing and revealing his divine power. Like so many poets in South Indian *bhakti* tradition from the earliest period, Deshika delights in juxtaposing the Lord's awesome extremes: the big and the little, child and primal being, unknown god and intimate friend and lover, extremes that meet in this god of love, and *in* love (*kami*).

I hope, in the translation that follows, to bring into contemporary Ameri-can English verse something of the energies, the audacity, and literary elegance of the original Sanskrit.[14] (The text is taken from the 1966 *Sri Tecikastotramala*, Sanskrit text with Tamil commentary, by Sri Ramatecikacaryar.)[15]

I

His shining body lights up the woods
of Vrindavan;

cherished lover of the simple
cowherd girls,[16]

he was born on Jayanti
when Rohini touches,
on the eighth day,
the waning moon
in *Avani*:[17]

this luminous power[18]

that wears *Vaijayanti*,

the long garland of victory,

I praise Him![19]

2

We see him
as he fills with delight,
on his very own lap,
Sarasvati
goddess of speech;[20]

as he raises to his lotus lips
the royal conch shell,
Panchajanya.

Seated firm
in a lotus flower

set in the center
of a shining *yantra* of many colors,[21]

praise him,

great monarch of cowherds![22]

3

His lower lip trembles
as he begins
to cry—
the air fills
with the fragrance
of Veda;

at one moment
he is all sweet smiles,

then
suddenly

blooms
into a smile:

I recall in silence[33]
that young prince

who drags the big mortar
through the garden
and tearing the trees from their roots
frees
the two spirits.

8

I see him here always
before my eyes.[34]

This lovely boy
whom even the highest wisdom
of the Veda
seeks to have
by its side:

the two Arjuna trees
were witness
to his childish pranks
and the Yamuna
the long days
of his youth.[35]

9

You are the shortest path
to liberation,
a dark monsoon cloud
that hangs over the forest
raining
joy and wealth.[36]

A bamboo flute thrills at the touch
of your ruddy
lower lip:[37]

I love you
and worship you,[38]
root cause of creation,
pure compassion
in the body
of a man.[39]

10

We must honor him
with unblinking eyes:

eternally youthful,[40]
his curly locks of black hair
vie in battle

with the black eyes
of peacock feathers:

may this luminous beauty
whose intensity
maddens my senses[41]

be always
present
in my mind!

11

The sweet reed flute calls them,
sending every cowherd girl
it touches
with its music
into ecstasies;[42]

the flood of his glancing
eyes,

red lilies
in the river of his mercy,
cooled by his flawless
smile:[43]

may He protect me.

12

The lovely reed flute
that presses
against his lower lip;

the garland of peacock feathers
that adorn his crown;

a darkness luminous
as shards of cool
blue
sapphire:[44]

praise him,
adorned

in so many ways,

some strange kind of Trickster[57]
who steals

the youth
of the cowherd
girls. [58]

18

He holds the playful shepherd's crook
in the tender sprout
of his right hand;

his other hand
fondles
the slender
shoulders
of the lady
who trills at his touch—

the hairs on her body

shining

stand erect.[59]

Lovely, dark as the monsoon cloud,
his flute
tucked into the folds
of his yellow
waist-cloth,
and his hair shimmering
with garlands
of *gunja*-
beads,
praise Him,
tender lover of the *gopis*.[60]

19

He gazes at his lover,
her eyes
half-

closed
in ecstasy,

whom he embraced
from behind—

his hands tightly
circling
the curve of her waist—

as she struck a pose
to shoot
the sweet water.[61]

In one hand
he grasps his own
long syringe,[62]

and with the other
he cinches
tight
his dress

for water-sports:[63]

cherished lover of simple cowherd girls,[64]
good life-giving
medicine
for the devotees,[65]

may he protect us!

20

After stealing the cowherd girls' dresses
as they lay
strewn along the banks
of the Yamuna,
bright river-daughter of the Sun,[66]
smiling playfully,[67]

he sat in the branches
of a lovely Kunda tree.

And when,
burning with shame,
they pleaded
for their clothes,
he commanded they come
one by one

out of the water,
their lotus hands raised high
over their
heads
in prayer:

Praise this fabulous lover,
this god
in love![68]

21

Those who study with one-pointed mind
this praise-poem
composed by
Venkatesha

will see
before their very eyes
this inconceivable
unknowable god[69]

who is so dear to young girls,

deft connoisseur
of the holy
reed
flute![70]

NOTES

1. See my full-length study of Vedantadeshika, *Singing the Body of God: The Hymns of Vedantadesika in Their South Indian Tradition* (New York: Oxford University Press, 2002), and my anthology of translations, *An Ornament for Jewels: Poems for the Lord of Gods by Vedantadesika* (New York: Oxford University Press, forthcoming).

2. See Vidya Dehejia, *Antal and Her Path of Love: Poems of a Woman Saint from South India* (New York: State University of New York Press, 1990), 14–15.

3. For an elaborate argument for a specifically southern Tamil "Krishnaism" and its subsequent influence in the *Bhagavata Purana* and northern Krishna devotion, see Friedhelm Hardy, *Viraha-Bhakti: The Early History of Krsna Devotion in South India* (Delhi: Oxford University Press, 1983), especially pt. 4, "Mayon Mysticism: The Alvars."

4. See Vasudha Narayanan, *The Way and the Goal: Expressions of Devotion in Early Sri Vaisnava Tradition* (Washington, D.C.: Institute for Vaishnava Studies, 1987), 25–26. Narayanan goes on to argue the importance of the figure of Rama in Alvar devotion.

5. See Narayanan, *The Way and the Goal*, 106–112. See also, for this kind of layering, where images of Rama, Krishna, and other *avataras* intermingle, the great

Tamil praise-poem of Tiruppanalvar, the *Amalanatipiran*, translated in my study of Deshika, *Singing the Body of God*, 141–144.

6. See full translation of poem and discussion in my *Singing the Body of God*, 93–94. His other Tamil *prabandhams*, such as *Mummanikkovai* and *Navamanimalai*, are strewn with references to Krishna, mingled with other *avataras*, all present in his experience of the specific temple image being praised. See "The Fruits of Mukunda's Mercy," chap. 4 in *Singing the Body of God*.

7. From *Devanayakapanchashat* 27, cited in *Singing the Body of God*, 208–209.

8. See discussion in A. K. Warder, *Indian Kavya Literature* (1972; reprint, Delhi: Motilal Banarsidass, 1989), 1:1–53.

9. See Francis Wilson, *The Love of Krishna: The Krsnakarnamrta of Lilasuka Bilvamangala* (Philadelphia: University of Pennsylvania Press, 1975), for a translation and critical study of this remarkable devotional text, so close in spirit and style to Deshika.

10. *Yadavabhyudayam* 24:93. For verses of the *Yadavabhyudayam* see *Shrimatvedantadeshikagranthamala*, edited by K. P. B. Annankaracariyar and Shri Sampatkumaracaryasvamin, 3 vols. (Kanchi: 1940–58), the collected Sanskrit works of Deshika without commentary. See also text of *sargas* 9–12, with the Sanskrit commentary of Appaya Dikshita: *Yadavabhyudaya by Sriman Vedanta Desika* (Sri Rangam: Sri Vani Vilas Press, 1924), and cantos 13–18: *Yadavabhyudayam*, with Apayya Dikshita's commentary, edited by Vidvan T. T. Srinivasa Gopalachar (Mysore: Government Oriental Library, 1944). See also *Yadavabhyudayam: A Kavya on the Life of Lord Krishna*, edited with Sanskrit text and translation of first seven cantos by K. S. Krishna Thathachariar (Madras: Vedanta Desika Research Society, 1976), which includes eight essays by various scholars. For a brief discussion of the poem in relation to Deshika's life narrative, see my *Singing the Body of God*, 66–67.

11. *Yadavabhyudayam* 24:38. The phrase "passionate close embrace" (*aviralaparirambhalambhaniyaih*) is close to a phrase in Bhavabhuti's verse that describes Rama and Sita's arms as "busy in close embrace" (*ashithilaparirambha*). For a discussion on the Shrivaishnava use of Bhavabhuti's love lyric in commentaries on Deshika's *stotras*, see my *Singing the Body of God*, 162–163.

12. I plan some day to tackle just such a study.

13. See the introduction to my *Singing the Body of God*, and especially chaps. 4 and 7, 115–134 and 199–231. See also my *An Ornament for Jewels* (Oxford, forthcoming), which will include full translations of the Devanayaka *stotras* and *prabhandams*, along with the *Gopalavimshati*.

14. For a detailed account of my method of translation, including my use of visual spacing of phrases and individual words on the page, see the discussion in my *Singing the Body of God*, 15–21.

15. (1966; reprint, Cennai: Lifco, 1982), 637–657.

16. "Cherished lover of simple cowherd girls" *Vallavijanavallabham*, a phrase with a certain alliterative charm. This phrase is also said to point to Krishna's *saushilya*, or "gracious condescension."

17. *Jayantisambhavam*: I have expanded this phrase for clarity and detail, following the commentators. "*Jayanti*" is an astrological conjunction that can be described with some poetic grace. Ramatecikacaryar's Tamil gloss describes *Jayanti* as

the time when "the constellation *Rohini* is united with the eighth day of the dark of the moon in the month of *Simha Shravana*, or *Avani:" jayanti enpatu simha cravana (avani) mattatil kirushnapakshattu ashtamiyutan cerukinra rohini nakshtra matum*. This descriptive epithet is said to refer to Krishna's *saulabhyam*, or "easy accessibility."

18. "Luminous power" and "shining body" both translate the rich word *dhama*, meaning "majesty," "glory," "luminary," "effulgence," "power." I follow commentators in identifying this luminous power with the beautiful body of the Lord Krishna that "moves about" or "wanders" in Vrindavan, implied in the phrase *vrindavanacharam* in the first *pada* of the verse. This can also imply the "feet" of the Lord. In Ramatecikacharyar's Tamil gloss, *dhama* is a kind of *jyoti*, or radiant light, identified with Lord Krishna's "lovely body" (*vativu*): *Kannapiranenapatum oru coti vativai tolukinren* ("I adore/worship the lovely form/body, a radiant light that is called Lord Krishna"). The mention of Vrindavan here is said to index Krishna's *vatsalyam*, "tender loving affection [of a cow for her calf]."

19. The image of Krishna as wearing the "victory" garland indexes his *svamitvam*, his "independent mastery" or "supreme lordship." The entire verse, in its simple compass, is said to embrace various attributes of Krishna, from the tender love of a mother or a lover, and easy accessibility, to supreme lordship of the universe. The verse is also analyzed by commentators to include three major *rasas* (aesthetic "flavors" or experience) that are important to Krishna's "play" in the world: *shringara*, the "erotic" (in the allusion to *gopis*); *vira*, the "heroic," indicated by the *vaijayanti* garland; and *adbhuta*, or "wonder," indexed by his "moving about" in the forests, where, as we will see in the body of the *stotra*, he performs a variety of awesome feats of divine power. See Appayya Dikshita's commentary on this verse where it also appears as the first verse of Deshika's *Yadavabhyudayam*.

20. The identification of Deshika himself with *vach*, speech (glossed here and in the commentaries as Sarasvati), who "delights" (Tamil gloss *mukil*) or "relishes" being on the very lap of the Lord, is a common one in praise-verses of the poet, and points to his eloquence and mastery of language.

21. *Varnatrikonaruchire varapundarike*.

22. This verse has the flavor of a visualization used in ritual meditation of the Lord and his powers.

23. This descending, broken episodic phrase translates the first four *padas* of the verse, two long, elegant, and alliterative compounds in Sanskrit:

> *Amnayagandhiruditaspuritagharoshtham asravilekshanam anukshanamandahasyam.*

24. *Gopaladimbhavapusham*.

25. *Pranastanandhayam*.

26. *Param pumamsam*, glossed as the more common epithet *parama purusha*, or "Supreme Person," a phrase that hearkens back to the Upanishads and the *Bhagavad Gita*. This of course stresses the wonder of Krishna's play, which brings together opposing forms of the big and the little, the earthly and the cosmic, the awesome and powerful and the tiny and vulnerable: Krishna is no less than the Supreme Person in the tiny body of an infant who cries and fusses and suckles, but when he breathes,

one smells the fragrance of *Vedas*, and when the breasts he happens to suckle are those of the demon Putana, he kills without mercy.

27. *Anibhritabharanam*: "ornaments/jewels that tremble/move/stir." Tamil gloss: *anikal achaiyapperratay*. Because the dancing feet are being described, I take this reference to mean the anklets on the feet: see subsequent verses describing the rattling of jewels in anklets.

28. *Dadhna nimithamukharena nibadhatalam*: a vivid, vigorous phrase, literally: "unrestrained/vigorous rhythms with noisy/talkative ['mouthy'] churning of curds." I try in my translation to capture the clever use in this phrase of *mukharena* (noisy/talkative, "mouthy") with an aural/audial and rather fanciful phrase "thwacking ruckus."

29. In the loping *mandakranta* meter: *hartum kumbhe vinihitakarah svadu haiyangavinam*.

30. *Ishat pracalitapado napagacchan na tishthan*: "neither fleeing nor standing still, trembling just a little." The sense of the verse is that this god-child pretends to be frightened, or perhaps more accurately, "plays" (*lila*) at being frightened.

31. *Mithyagopah*. Verses 3, 4 and 5 are all in the long-lined, loping, rhythmic *mandakranta* meter, suitable to its subject: the dancing and pranks of the child Krishna. I have tried, in my translation, mostly visually on the page, to reproduce this loping, shifting rhythm, in the spacing of broken words and phrases. See also verses 17–20.

32. *Tat kimapi brahma*: literally, "that I-don't-know-what-kind-of *Brahman*," a deceptively short phrase that appears in other *stotras* of Deshika, where it is used to evoke the unknowable, inconceivable, and "transcendent" ultimate reality of the Upanishads. The power of this verse, of course, lies in Deshika's juxtaposition of this phrase with the erotic and maternal affective dimensions of this "lovable" *Brahman*.

33. *Smarami*, "I remember, visualize"; "I meditate on"—a verb commonly used in texts describing devotional meditations/visualizations of the qualities of a god (or of the Buddha in the Buddhist context). To "remember" here is to evoke the meditative *presence*, the presentational reality, of the god or Buddha.

34. *Nishamayami nityam*.

35. *Yamalarjunadrishtabalakelim yamunasakshikayauvanam yuvanam*.

36. "Joy and wealth," *sampadam*.

37. The original phrase contains, like so much of Deshika's Sanskrit, some lovely music: *arunadharasabhilashavamsham*.

38. *Bhajami*.

39. *Karunam karanamanushim*.

40. *Ajahadyauvanam*.

41. *Karanonmadakavibhramam maho*.

42. "Sweet reed flute," *manojnavamshanalah*. Tamil gloss: *iniya kulalin*. "Ecstasies," *vimoha* (Tamil *mayakkam*).

43. "Flood," *rasa*, water.

44. *Harinilashilavibhanganilah*.

45. "Glorious visions": *pratibhah*, "images," "appearances."

46. *Akhilan ... kalan*: "at every moment/time/waking hour."

13

Krishna in Advaita Vedanta: The Supreme *Brahman* in Human Form

Lance E. Nelson

I worship that great Light, the son of Nanda, the supreme Brahman in human form, who removes the bondage of the world.
—Madhusudana Sarasvati

Advaita, Shankara, and Madhusudana

Among the various schools of Hindu theology, Advaita (nondualist) Vedanta has historically, and perhaps even more in recent times, had an influence out of proportion to its actual number of adherents. In addition to being the oldest of the surviving schools of Vedanta, it has long been associated with the high-caste Brahmin community known as the Smartas, whose members are known for orthodoxy and ritual purity.[1] In the late nineteenth and early twentieth century, through the efforts of such figures as Swami Vivekananda and Sarvepalli Radhakrishnan, Advaita was transformed into the theological basis of the neo-Hindu revival whose apologists presented Hinduism as a universalist, inclusive faith, as compared with the narrow exclusivism of Western religion.[2] In this form, widely propagated in English, Advaita has become the faith and life-philosophy of many modern, Western-educated, urbanized Hindus, as well as the image of the Hindu tradition that appears most widely in textbooks and other popular presentations in the West.

The common understanding of Hinduism as a religion that, though polytheistic in popular practice, subsumes the many deities in one transcendent, impersonal Absolute, ultimately relegating both deities and world to the status of illusion, is more accurately understood as a presentation—however simplistic—of the views of Advaita Vedanta. Other chapters in this volume show very clearly that Hinduism offers a good number of compelling, alternate visions, each embodied in its own tradition of theology and ritual practice. Here I simply note that such theologies exist and must be taken seriously. The task of this chapter will be to indicate the basic theological position of Advaita and the place of Krishna therein.

It is indeed true that Advaita regards *Brahman* in its highest aspect as being impersonal—or, better, *trans*personal. For this reason, the nature and relative merits of particular deities have not been of special theological interest, or the subject of extensive theological disquisition, in Advaita. This is not to say, however, that the concept of God as such is unimportant for Advaitins, or exponents of Advaita. Nor is it to deny that for individual Advaitins, particular embodiments of Deity—including, but not of course limited to, Krishna—have loomed large in religious awareness. I shall then, after presenting a short overview of Advaita theology, consider first the place of Deity in the tradition and then look at what the tradition has had to say about Krishna in particular. Needless to say, an examination of the entire history of Advaita is impossible in the space allowed here. I shall therefore focus on two of the most relevant sources: the commentaries[3] of Shankara (c. 650–750 CE), the first systematizer of Advaita, regarded with reverence by the tradition as its founding preceptor (*acharya*), and the works of Madhusudana Sarasvati (sixteenth–seventeenth century), the last of the great classical exponents of Advaita.

The Concept of Deity in Shankara's Advaita

A well-known epitome of Shankara's theological vision is contained in the half-verse "*Brahman* is real; the world is a false projection; the individual self is exactly *Brahman*, nothing less."[5] Shankara defines the real as that which never changes and never proves false. For him, only *Brahman* has these qualities. The changing world of multiplicity (*jagat*) and the innumerable individual beings (*jiva*) that inhabit it are all "adjuncts" (*upadhi*), erroneously projected on *Brahman*, in a phenomenon termed superimposition (*adhyasa*). This occurs through the force of *maya*, a mysterious power that both projects the world appearance and conceals its real nature. While it is thus ultimately less than real, the universe—seen from within the realm of *maya*—has been here since beginningless time and will never come to an end. Like the universe, each *jiva* has been present for an infinite duration, migrating through countless rebirths. But, unlike the universe, the individual soul can bring its own existence—as individual—to an end, attaining liberation (*moksha, mukti*) from the world of reincarnation (*samsara*). This can be achieved, says Shankara, by those following the intellectual/ascetic discipline of the advaitic world-renouncers, through direct knowledge of the oneness of the inner Self (*atman*) and *Brahman*. When (and, as we shall see, only when) this oneness is directly realized, the false superimpositions of individuality and world are seen for what they are, and any claim to reality they had is effectively canceled (*badhita*). Upon gaining such knowledge, the *jiva* is liberated from the painful bondage of *samsara*, irrespective of the persistence or otherwise of physical embodiment.[6]

Fundamental to Shankara's thought is the distinction between the *para* (higher) and the *apara* (lower) *Brahman*. The higher *Brahman* is the Absolute as it exists in itself, free from all the limitations conjured by *maya*. The lower is *Brahman* in association with *maya*, seemingly limited by superimposed adjuncts of "name and form," i.e., the world of multiplicity. Of these two forms of *Brahman*, it is the lower that is described at BS 1.1.2 as the source, the support, and the end of the world; it is the lower that is, in a word, the supreme Deity. *Ishvara* (the "Lord"), as this conception of God is termed, is the transcendent, supreme *Brahman* appearing as if conditioned and personalized by virtue of its relation to *maya*, the principle of phenomenality.

Using the scheme of the twofold *Brahman*, Shankara seeks to arrive at a consistent interpretation of the Upanishads, which speak of the ultimate sometimes as an active, cosmically involved, conditioned, quasi-theistic or personal being and sometimes as inactive, acosmic, unconditioned, transpersonal Absolute. The descriptions of *Brahman* in the former mode, termed "qualified," or *saguna*, Shankara assigns to its lower aspect, and the descriptions of it in the latter mode, termed "unqualified," or *nirguna*, he attributes to its higher aspect. The scriptural revelation (*shruti*) is thus interpreted as a unified whole. The *para/apara*, higher/lower, distinction is thus the same as the well-known advaitic distinction between the *nirguna* (unqualified, attributeless) and the *saguna* (qualified, possessed of attributes) *Brahman*.

Shankara does not, as is commonly supposed, teach that everything other than the highest, unqualified Absolute is a bare illusion. He speaks, instead, of three levels of being or reality (*satta*). Within the realm of becoming and appearance, he makes a clear distinction between the ontological status of illusory objects (*pratibhashika-satta*), such as those produced by hallucinations and mirages, and that of the everyday empirical world (*vyavaharika-satta*). Shankara goes on to make a similar distinction between the truth of the empirical or phenomenal level of experience and that of the transcendental or noumenal level, the level of ultimate Reality (*paramarthika-satta*), identified with the *para Brahman*.[7] Illusions can be easily overcome by empirical knowledge of various sorts, but the empirical level of experience itself is much more difficult to transcend. Nothing but direct realization of the Absolute can take us beyond it. While the individual soul, the world, and even the personal God are ultimately seen to be false appearances, reminiscent of a great cosmic dream, they are not exactly illusory, for they are constantly present to the experience of all *jivas*.

This ontologically indeterminate mode of being, which belongs to all phenomenal existence, is characterized as *sad-asad-anirvachaniya*, "inexpressible as either real or unreal."

As long as one has not realized the ultimate truth, the world has empirical reality (*vyavaharika-satta*). Within this empirical reality, external objects are quite as real as the cognitions we have of them; they exist in their own right, independent of the individual mind. The same is true of the world as a whole and of *Ishvara*. When one *jiva* realizes its identity with *Brahman*, the activity of the manifest universe is not thereby terminated. It continues on its ordinary course, being experienced by other souls, directed as always by the personal God.[8] *Ishvara*, as creator and sustainer of the world, has at least as real an independent existence as anything else. From the point of view of embodied beings, *Ishvara* is in fact the most real of all conditioned entities, since he is the source of all levels of empirical existence other than his own. Moreover, *Ishvara* is eternal (*nitya*), having no beginning and no end, like the universe *Ishvara* rules (*BhG* 3.19).

Ishvara and Advaita Theism

Shankara's distinction between levels of reality and his acceptance of the complete—and, we might emphasize, eternal—functionality of *Ishvara* allows him to retain a theism that, far from making light of the notion of Deity, involves serious religious intent. While it is doubtful whether his analysis is adequate in the end from the devotional theists' point of view, it was not without reason that even a Christian theologian such as Rudolph Otto was able to recognize Shankara's relationship to the theistic worldview of the *Bhagavad Gita*, the epics, and the Puranas as an "inner one."[9] Indeed, as Hacker has shown, there is good evidence that Shankara and his early followers came from strong Vaishnava backgrounds.[10]

Ishvara is *Brahman* associated–not with a limited mind and body like the *jiva*—but with *maya*, the universal creative matrix, the divine energy (*shakti*) that projects the entire cosmos. Unlike the *jiva*, again, the Lord is not taken in by the delusive, concealing power (*avarana-shakti*) of *maya*. On the contrary, the true nature of reality, including especially *Ishvara*'s identity as the highest *Brahman*, is eternally transparent to *Ishvara*.[11] While the *jiva* is controlled by *maya*, *Ishvara* is the *mayavin*, the omnipotent, omniscient controller of *maya* (*BS* 1.1.3). The Lord has the power of manifesting, sustaining, and destroying the world. The ruler of the universe and all in it, *Ishvara* is "all knowing, all perceiving," the "absolute ruler of past and present" (*BS* 1.2.21, 1.3.24). Shankara makes it clear that the *jiva* is totally dependent on the Lord's grace for both the experience of *samsara* and the knowledge that effects *moksha* (*BS* 2.3.41). Shankara advances several proofs for the existence of God, of the sort that would be entirely acceptable in theistic circles, and he deals extensively with the problem of theodicity.[12] He also explicitly accepts that element so central to Hindu devotional religion, the doctrine of periodic divine incarnation (*avatara*) on earth (*BSSh* 1.1.20; *BhGSh*, introduction).

While Shankara may have come from a Vaishnava background, and while he opens his commentary on the *Bhagavad Gita* with an invocation of Narayana, there is nothing in his system of thought that would exalt any form of Deity over the other. He has been identified in the tradition as a devotee of Krishna on the basis of a devotional hymn, the *Bhaja Govindam*, and a few other texts that have been (dubiously) ascribed to him.[13] But he has also been identified as a Shakta tantric, and indeed as being himself an incarnation of Shiva. Tradition regards him as the *shan-mata-sthapaka*, "founder of the six doctrines," recommending for his lay followers worship of the five deities (*panchayatana*) Surya, Devi, Vishnu, Ganesh, and Shiva—plus Kumara. Since all are manifestations of the same Ultimate, the thinking goes, devotees are free to focus on the *ishta-devata*, chosen Deity, that is most meaningful to them.[14] In his commentaries, Shankara shows no special preference for Krishna, nor does he invest him with any special status vis-à-vis other forms of the supreme Deity. He describes Krishna as an *avatara* of Vishnu/Narayana, indeed as a partial (*amsha*) incarnation.[15] However, he also indicates that, in some unspecified sense, Krishna can be identified with the supreme *Brahman*, as is apparent in the readings that follow.

Scholars have long noted Shankara's tendency to employ such designations of the transpersonal Absolute as *para-brahman* (supreme *Brahman*), *atman* (Self), and *paramatman* (supreme Self) interchangeably with *ishvara*, *parameshvara* (supreme Lord), and *bhagavan* (Blessed Lord), which are titles of the personal God, and even with Narayana and Vishnu, which are personal names derived from mythology.[16] This habit of thought will be apparent in the readings that follow. Once having established the distinction between *para* and *apara*, *nirguna* and *saguna*, *Brahman* and *Ishvara*, Shankara does not remain fixated upon it. The Lord, we have seen, is nothing less than the supreme Reality itself in its aspect of relatedness to the phenomenal world; as such— religiously speaking—*Ishvara* truly *is Brahman*. Any attempt to maintain a constant and rigorous distinction between the *paramarthika* and *vyavaharika* standpoints in this respect would make the discussion unbearably cumbersome. Furthermore, by virtue of overemphasis, it would imply a devaluation of Deity that is not intended.[17]

Shankara's Final Transtheism

Still, there comes a time, at least for the Advaita *samnyasin* (renunciant) seeking final release, when ordinary piety is set aside in the quest for what is perceived as a higher level of truth. *Ishvara* may be God in all his glory from the point of view of the world, but from the point of view of liberation he is, as *Ishvara* (though not as *Brahman*), dependent on the world, just as the space limited by pots and jars is, for its existence as such, dependent on those vessels. When the pot is broken, so does the particular configuration of space it contained; when the world disappears for the one who has realized identity with *Brahman*, so does God (*BSSh* 2.1.14). This kind of thinking does not quite place *Ishvara* within the realm of *maya*,[18] but it does seem to remove Deity from the sphere of final truth in a way that a true theist could not tolerate. Advaitic theism emerges as, so to say, a kind of transtheism.

Advaita's view of the nature and status of God is of course very closely related to its understanding of the liberating power of knowledge (*jnana*), as compared with loving devotion (*bhakti*) to a Deity. The classical Advaita tradition is emphatic that the only means to *moksha* is *jnana*. While Shankara condones image worship and related expressions of *bhakti* spirituality as preparatory for advaitic knowledge, because they are a means to purification of the mind (*citta-shuddhi*),[19] in the end, for his *samnyasin* followers, he seeks to undercut anything, including *bhakti*, that smacks of dualism. Speaking for the benefit of ascetics on the brink of liberation, Shankara teaches (*BhG* 12.13) that any attitude that posits difference between the Self and God (*atmeshvara-bheda*) is a serious hindrance on the steep ascent to advaitic realization. Devotion may be useful for those who—whether because of caste, gender, family obligations, or aptitude—do not possess the qualification (*adhikara*) for advaitic discipline.[20] Still, Shankara suggests, the very idea is repugnant to the elite Advaitin world-renouncers who have "become the very Self of God" (*ishvarasya atma-bhutah*).[21]

It must be remembered that Shankara was writing at a time when the great *bhakti* revolution that originated in the South and swept eventually through North India was just in its beginning stages. Far more important to him as interlocutor and opponent was the then well-established orthodoxy of Vedic ritualism, promoted by the teachers of the Purva Mimamsa.[22] The vast bulk of Shankara's polemical efforts were devoted to a refutation of their denial of the validity of the advaitic path of knowledge and renunciation. *Bhakti* theism was by comparison a much less significant player in Shankara's religious environment.

Madhusudana Sarasvati's Advaitic Valorization of Krishna

By the time of Madhusudana Sarasvati (sixteenth–seventeeth century) nearly a millennium later, the religious landscape was quite different. Staunchly theistic *bhakti* movements, having triumphed in the South, had spread, flowered, and likewise triumphed in the West and North. Bengal, where Madhusudana (by most accounts) was born, was by this time a center of a great flourishing of Krishnaite *bhakti* inspired by Chaitanya (1486–1533). Indeed, Madhusudana was a younger contemporary of the great Bengal Vaishnava theologian Rupa Gosvami (1480–1564) and, according to tradition, also of the equally important Vaishnava *acharya* Vallabha (1481–1533), whom Madhusudana is said to have met. Madhusudana, unlike Shankara, has a good deal to say about Krishna.

Considered one of the great expositors of classical Advaita and a major figure in the tradition, Madhusudana is revered as a champion of nondualism and a brilliant polemicist against Vaishnava Vedanta, particularly Madhva's theistic dualism. His major works—including the *Vedantakalpalatika*, the *Siddhantabindu*, and his masterwork, the *Advaitasiddhi*—are still regarded as essential texts of Advaita scholarship.

It is intriguing, therefore, that Madhusudana is also known as a fervent devotee of Krishna. This devotion he expresses in a number of well-known devotional verses scattered through his works, particularly in passages of his famous *Bhagavad Gita Gudarthadipika* (Light on the Hidden Meaning of the *Bhagavad Gita*), his famous commentary on that text. A number of these verses are included in the readings here. Madhusudana is, moreover, the author of the only independent treatise on *bhakti* written by a major exponent of the classical Advaita tradition. Titled the *Bhaktirasayana* (Elixir of Devotion), this work expounds an advaitic theory of devotion and devotional sentiment (*bhaktirasa*) on the basis of the *Bhagavata Purana*, with the aid of abundant citations therefrom.[23]

Theistically inclined readers of Madhusudana, however, will find little to celebrate in this theologian's descriptions of Krishna. True, Madhusudana, like the Bengal Vaishnavas and the followers of Vallabha (and most likely under their influence), identifies the supreme Deity exclusively as Krishna, whom he speaks of almost invariably as Bhagavan (the Blessed Lord), instead of using the less devotionally charged term *ishvara*. Moreover, at least in the *Bhaktirasayana*, he breaks with Advaita tradition to the extent of placing *bhakti* on a par with *jnana* as a valid spiritual path.[24] But he also revives Shankara's habit of blurring the distinction between the *para-brahman* and the *saguna* Deity. As in Shankara, Krishna in Madhusudana's commentary on the *Gita* becomes primarily the *avatara* of the *nirguna Brahman*, of which he becomes— perhaps paradoxically—the earthly voice. Often, in this author's paraphrasing of the text, Krishna explicitly identifies himself as the *nirguna*. As we shall see, Madhusudana in his *Bhaktirasayana* defines Bhagavan as "the nondual Self, a mass of perfect Being, Consciousness, and Bliss, the pure Existence which is the substratum of all."[25] Therefore, despite his striking declaration "Beyond Krishna, I do not know of any higher Reality,"[26] it is clear that his conception of the Deity remains transtheistic.

Krishna in Advaita Texts

From Shankara's *Brahmasutrabhashya* (Commentary on the *Brahmasutras*)

Brahman is known as having two forms (*dvirupa*), [one] qualified by adjuncts (*upadhi*), which are the differences caused by the transformations of name and form, and [the other being] the opposite of that, free of all adjuncts. A multitude of scriptural texts show the twofold nature of *Brahman*, according as it is the object of knowledge or ignorance. For example: "For, where there is duality, as it were, one sees the other, but where all has become one's own Self, then who and with what shall one see?" [*BU* 4.5.15]; "Where one sees no other, hears no other, knows no other, that is the Infinite, but where one sees another, hears another, knows another, that is the finite. The Infinite is the immortal; the finite, the mortal" [*ChU* 7.24.1]. . . . This being the case, all discussions of *Brahman* as characterized by distinctions such as worshiper and object of worship are from within the state of ignorance (*avidya*). (*BSSh* 1.1.11, pp. 49–50)

There [in *ChU* 3.14.3] it is taught that the Lord—having qualities such as minuteness—is perceptible, that is, visible, in the lotus of the heart, just as Hari [is perceptible] in the *shalagrama* stone. In this case, the means of perception is an [interior] awareness of the intellect (*buddhi-vijnana*). Even though omnipresent, the Lord is pleased when meditated upon there [in the heart]. And this is to be understood by the analogy of space. Just as space, though being omnipresent, is spoken of as small or minute in reference to [its association with] such things as the eye of a needle, so it is with *Brahman* also. So the smallness or minuteness of *Brahman* is [mentioned] in reference to its being an object of meditation, not in terms of the highest Reality (*paramarthika*). (*BSSh* 1.2.7; pp. 102–103)[27]

Prior to the knowledge of the identity of the Self and *Brahman*, it is proper to regard the entirety of ordinary existence as true, as the events in a dream [are experienced as genuine] prior to awakening. As long as the true oneness of the Self is not apprehended, no one has the idea of unreality in reference to [empirical] transformations, which take the form of the means of knowledge, their objects, and their consequences. . . . Therefore, prior to knowledge of the Self's identity with *Brahman*, all activities, secular and religious, are appropriate. . . .

The omniscience (*sarvajnatva*) [of God] depends upon the manifestation of the seeds of name and form, the nature of which is
ignorance (*avidya*). According to scriptures such as "From that very
Self arose the ether" [*TU* 2.1], the origin, sustenance, and dissolution
of the world are from the Lord, who is by nature eternally pure,
awakened, and liberated (*nitya-shuddha-buddha-mukta*),[28] omniscient
and omnipotent (*sarva-shakti*). . . . This idea is also taught [by *BS*
1.1.4]: "From which is the origin, and so on, [of the world]." . . .

Name and form, fabricated by ignorance, which are the seed
of the manifest universe known as *samsara*, are indeterminable as
being either real or otherwise.[29] They are spoken of in scripture
(*shruti*) and traditional texts (*smriti*) as the *maya*-power (*maya-shakti*)
or the primordial matter (*prakriti*) of the omniscient Lord, seeming to
be identical (*atma-bhuta iva*) with the omniscient Lord. But the omniscient Lord is different from them.[30] . . .

Thus the Lord conforms to the adjuncts (*upadhi*) of name and
form, created by ignorance, as space conforms to the adjuncts such as
pots and jars. And, within the realm of empirical existence, He
rules over [the entities] called souls (*jiva*), identified with the mind,
who—like the space in pots—conform to a collection of [bodily] instruments that are effects created by name and form as conjured
forth by ignorance, the souls being [in reality] identical with His own
Self (*svatma-bhuta*). And thus the lordship, the omniscience, and
the omnipotence of the Lord are dependent on the distinctions of the
adjuncts whose nature is ignorance. But in reality (*paramarthatah*)
such [terms] as "ruler," "ruled," and "omniscience" do not apply to
the Self that has been cleared of all adjuncts by knowledge. (*BSSh*
2.1.14; pp. 311, 314–316)

In the world, kings or royal ministers, [persons] who have had all
their desires fulfilled, might engage in activities that are mere
play (*lila*), such as sports and games, not envisioning any particular goal. Likewise, breathing out and breathing in and similar activities occur simply because of [one's] inherent nature (*svabhava*), not
intending any external purpose. So it is that for the Lord [all] activities are mere play, arising out of [his own] inherent nature, not
considering any other aim. It is not possible to determine [that the
Lord has] any other purpose, either using reason or on the basis
of scripture. Neither can [the fact that playful creativity is the Lord's]
inherent nature be questioned. Although to us the creation of this
world looks like an enormous undertaking, for the Supreme Lord
(*parameshvara*) it is mere play, owing to his unlimited power (*shakti*).
And if nevertheless in ordinary life we might discern some subtle

purpose even in acts of play, still it is not at all possible to ascertain any motive in this case, because scripture affirms that [the Lord] is one for whom all desires are already fulfilled. (*BSSh* 2.1.33; pp. 340–341)

On this point the Bhagavatas[31] believe that the one Blessed Lord (*Bhagavan*)[32] Vasudeva, whose nature is pure knowledge, is the highest Reality. Having divided himself, He abides in the form of the four emanations (*vyuha*) Vasudeva, Sankarshana, Pradyumna, and Aniruddha. The supreme Self is called Vasudeva, the individual soul (*jiva*) is called Sankarshana, the mind is called Pradyumna, and the ego-sense is called Aniruddha. Among these, [the emanation] Vasudeva is the highest material cause (*prakriti*), [of which] the others—Sankarshana and the rest—are effects. Having—for a hundred years—worshiped the supreme Lord, the Blessed Lord, whose nature is such, by means of approaching [Him in temples], preparation [of materials for worship], the giving of offerings, recitation [of prayers, etc.], and meditation (*yoga*), one becomes free of afflictions and attains the Blessed Lord.

In reference to this, the following can be said. The idea that Narayana–who is well known as being beyond the unmanifest (*avyakta*),[33] the supreme Self, the Self of all–establishes Himself by Himself in multiple emanations (*vyuha*) is not at all disputed. From scriptures such as "He becomes one, then becomes threefold" [*ChU* 7.24.2], it is understood that the supreme Self becomes manifold. If in addition the constant worship of the Blessed Lord with completely concentrated mind through approaching [Him in temples], and so on, is being promoted, that also should not be discouraged, for meditation on the Lord is recommended everywhere in *shruti* and *smriti*. However, in reference to the idea that Sankarshana arises from Vasudeva, Pradyumna from Sankarshana, and Aniruddha from Pradyumna, we must object. The production (*utpatti*) of the individual soul, called Sankarshana, from the supreme Self, called Vasudeva, is not possible, because this would entail such defects as [the soul's] impermanence. If it is allowed that the individual soul has an origin, then defects such as impermanence invariably follow. On this account [for example], liberation (*moksha*), which consists in attaining the Blessed Lord, would not be possible, because an effect inevitably becomes completely destroyed when it returns to its cause.[34] (*BSSh* 2.2.42; pp. 415–416)

From Shankara's *Bhagavadgitabhashya* (Commentary on the *Bhagavad Gita*)

Om! Narayana is beyond the unmanifest (*avyakta*).[35] The Cosmic Egg (*anda*) comes forth from the unmanifest. These worlds,

together with the earth and its seven islands, are contained
within the Cosmic Egg.

Having projected this world, and desiring to maintain its stability, the
Blessed Lord projected the ancient progenitors and caused them to
follow the path (*dharma*) of ritual action, as declared in the *Vedas*.
Then, having manifested others—Sanaka, Sanandana, and the other
[eternal renouncers]—He caused them to follow the path of cessation from action, characterized by knowledge and renunciation. For
the *dharma* declared in the Veda is of two types, one defined by
action and the other by cessation from action. This *dharma*, which is
the cause of the preservation of the world and directly leads to [both]
worldly prosperity and final beatitude for living beings, has been
followed by Brahmins and others belonging to the [system of] caste
and stage of life who desire the best.

   After a long passage of time, *dharma* was being overpowered by
non-*dharma*, owing to the rise of desire in [the minds of] its practitioners, who had abandoned knowledge and discrimination, and
non-*dharma* was thriving. Then Vishnu, the primal creator, known as
Narayana, desiring to protect the stability of the world, and for the
sake of protecting Brahmins, who are *Brahman* manifest on earth,
took birth with a portion (*amshena*) [of Himself] as Krishna, [son] of
Devaki and Vasudeva....

   The Blessed Lord, always endowed with knowledge, dominion,
power, strength, valor, and glory,[36] manipulated His own *maya*,
belonging to Him as Vishnu, the primordial matter consisting of the
three *gunas*. Although the unborn, immutable Lord of [all] beings,
eternally pure, enlightened, and liberated,[37] He appeared (*lakshyate*),
by the [power of] His *maya*, as if (*iva*) born, as if possessed of a body,
bestowing His grace on the world. (*BhGSh*, introduction, pp. 1–5)

7.16. Persons of good deeds who worship Me, O Arjuna, are of four
types: the afflicted, the seeker of knowledge, the seeker of material
well-being, and the knower.[38]
7.17. Among these, the knower, ever disciplined, who has single-
minded devotion, excels. For I am exceedingly dear to the knower,
and he is dear to me.

Among them, between those four, the knower, who possesses knowledge of Reality, and who, on account of having knowledge of Reality,
is ever disciplined and, on account of not seeing any other object
of worship, has single-minded devotion—that person excels, that is,
is endowed with excellent qualities in abundance. He[39] goes beyond [all others]. This is the idea. Since I am the Self of the knower,

therefore I am exceedingly dear to him. It is well known in the world that the Self is dear. Therefore, Vasudeva, on account of being the Self, is dear to the knower. This is the idea. And the knower, being the very Self of Me who am Vasudeva,[40] is exceedingly dear to Me.

7.18. All these are noble, but the knower I deem to be My very Self, for he—with disciplined mind—is fixed on Me alone, the unexcelled goal.

... But the knower is the very Self, not different from Me, this is my settled conclusion. The knower is disciplined in mind, that is, mentally concentrated, having the idea "I myself am the Blessed Lord Vasudeva, nothing less." Being such, he rises to attain Me, the supreme *Brahman*, the ultimate goal.

7.19. At the end of many births, one possessed of knowledge attains Me, thinking, "Vasudeva is all!" Such a great soul is exceedingly difficult to find.

The knower is again praised. At the end or conclusion of many births, which are the foundation for [accumulating] the mental impressions necessary for knowledge, the one possessed of knowledge, that is, whose knowledge has attained maturation, attains—through direct perception (*pratyakshatah*)—Me, Vasudeva, the innermost Self. How [can this realization be expressed]? [The verse answers:] "Vasudeva is all!" Whoever thus attains me, the Self of all, that great soul has no one equal to him and none greater. Therefore, among thousands of human beings [such a one] is exceedingly difficult to find. This is the idea. (*BhG* 7.16–19, with *BhGSh*, pp. 362–365)

From Madhusudana Sarasvati's *Advaitasiddhi* (The Vindication of Nondualism)

> His hand is adorned by the flute, His complexion is like a fresh dark cloud laden with water. He wears beautiful yellow silk, and His reddish lips are like the *bimba* fruit. His face is as beautiful as the full moon, with eyes like lotuses. Beyond Krishna, I do not know of any higher reality. (*AS* 2.7, p. 750; also *GAD*, concluding invocation, p. 775)

From Madhusudana Sarasvati's *Samkshepashariraka Sarasamgraha* (The Compendium of the Essential Meaning of the *Samkshepasariraka*)

> I worship that *Brahman* truth, knowledge, infinite, nondual Bliss—which is directly realized for the sake of *moksha* by most excellent sages who have approached a *guru*, engaged in

reflection, and attained *samadhi*, Who was born in Vrindavana for the joy of all as a result of the austerity of Nanda, playing on the flute, with face as beautiful as the moon, having eyes like lotuses. (*SShSS*, opening invocation, p. 3)

265. This entire world arose, without thought, from the Lord, [Krishna,] the son of Anakadundubhi,[41] the pure Consciousness that neither arises nor disappears, transcending mind and the Vedic word.

The author says "from the Lord [Krishna], the son of Anaka-dundubhi" in order to proclaim [His] being the *avatara* of That [pure Consciousness]. (*SShSS*, p. 303)

From Madhusudana Sarasvati's *Bhagavad Gita Gudharthadipika* (Light on the Hidden Meaning of the *Bhagavad Gita*)

if the *yogins*, with their minds controlled by the practice of meditation, see that indescribable Light—attributeless, action-less, and supreme—let them see it! But as for me, may that wondrous blue Effulgence which runs about and plays on the banks of the Yamuna long be the joy of my eyes. (*GAD* 13, opening invocation, p. 521)[42]

4.6. Even though I am birthless, undying by nature, the Lord of [all] beings, commanding My primordial matter, I take birth by [the power of] My own *maya*.

... In the first half of the verse it is accepted that God cannot have a physical body. He excludes [first, the idea of His] taking on a new body [by saying] "even though I am birthless," [second, the idea of His] separation from an old body, by saying "undying by nature," and [third, the idea of His] being subject to merit and demerit [by saying] that He is "the Lord of [all] beings" from Brahma down to a blade of grass.

What then is the nature of this embodiment? [He answers this question] in the second half of this verse. There he says "Com-manding My own primordial matter, I take birth." Primordial matter, [also] called *maya*, possessed of many and variegated powers, clever in accomplishing that which is impossible, is "My own," it belongs to Me as an adjunct. Commanding this (*maya*), controlling it with the light of Consciousness, I take birth. By a particular transformation of that (*maya*), I am born, as it were, possessed of a body, as it were.[43] ...

How then is there the perception of a body in reference to the pure Being-Consciousness-Bliss that is devoid of any embodiment? To answer this, He says: It is nothing but *maya* when [embodied]

end of many births, one possessed of knowledge attains Me, thinking, 'Vasudeva is all!' Such a great soul is exceedingly difficult to find"
(*BhG* 7.19). The meaning is: Everything other than Vasudeva, since it
is a product of *maya*, is not real. Vasudeva alone is real, is the dearest,
because He is the Self. (*BhR* 1.32, pp. 76–88)

ABBREVIATIONS

AS   *Advaitasiddhi of Madhusudanasarasvati*. Edited by N. S. Ananta Krishna
        Sastri. Delhi: Parimal, 1982.

BhG   *Bhagavad Gita*.

BhGSh   *Srimadbhagavadgita with the Commentaries Srimat-Sankarabhashya with
        Anandagiri, Nilakanthi, Bhasyotkarsadipika of Dhanapati, Sridhari, Gitartha-
        samgraha of Abhinavaguptacarya, and*
        Gudharthadipika of Madhusudana. Edited by Wasudev Laxman
        Sastri Pansikar. 2nd ed. Delhi: Munshiram Manoharlal, 1978.

BhP   *Bhagavata Purana*.

BhR   *Sribhagavadbhaktirasayana* [*Bhaktirasayana*]. Edited with the author's *Tika*
        and the editor's Hindi *Anuvada* by Janardana Sastri Pandeya. Banaras:
        Motilal Banarsidass, c. 1961.

BSSh   *Brahmasutrabhasya* [*Brahmasutra with Shankara's Commentary*]. *Complete
        Works of Sri Sankaracharya in the Original Sanskrit*, vol. 7. Rev. ed. Madras:
        Samata Books, 1983.

BU   *Brihadaranyaka Upanishad*.

ChU   *Chandogya Upanishad*.

GAD   [*Bhagavad Gita*] *Gudharthadipika of Madhusudana* [*Sarasvati*]. In *BhGSh*.

SShSS   *Samksepasariraka of Sarvajnatman, with a Gloss called Sarasamgraha by Ma-
        dhusudana Sarasvati* [*Samkshepashariraka Sarasamgraha*]. Edited by Bhau
        Sastri Vajhe. Kashi Sanskrit Series 18. Banaras: Chowkhamba Sanskrit
        Series Office, 1924–25.

NOTES

1. See Yoshitsugu Sawai, *The Faith of Ascetics and Lay Smartas: A Study of the
Sankaran Tradition of Sringeri* (Vienna: Sammlung De Nobili, 1992).

2. See Wilhelm Halbfass, *India and Europe: An Essay in Understanding* (Albany:
State University of New York Press, 1988), 217–262.

3. For purposes of limiting this discussion, I define Shankara as the author of the
major commentaries on the *Brahmasutras*, the *Upanishads*, and the *Bhagavad Gita*,
and the independent treatise the *Upadeshasahasri*. Proponents of the idea that
Shankara was a practitioner of *bhakti* as well as a nondualist commonly seek support
in the so-called minor works (*prakaranas*) and the many devotional hymns (*stotras*)
attributed to him. See, e.g., S. Radhakrishnan, *The Brahma Sutra: The Philosophy of
the Spiritual Life* (London: Allen and Unwin, 1960), 37–38. Unfortunately, critical
scholarship suggests that these works were almost certainly not written by the great
Advaitin himself. Even as orthodox a Hindu scholar as the highly respected Maha-

mahopadhyaya Gopi Nath Kaviraj writes regarding the hymns: "No doubt, most of these *stotras* must have been written by the later Sankaracaryas but all of them have been attributed to the first Sankaracarya." In reference to the treatises, he says: "It is difficult to decide about the authorship and genuineness of these works"; quoted and translated from the Hindi by A. P. Mishra, *The Development and Place of Bhakti in Sankara Vedanta* (Allahabad: University of Allahabad, 1967), 128. Of the *prakaranas*, Hacker, Ingalls, and Mayeda recognize only the *Upadeshasahasri* as genuine; Karl H. Potter, *Advaita Vedanta up to Sankara and His Pupils, Encyclopedia of Indian Philosophies*, vol. 3, edited by Karl H. Potter (Delhi: Motilal Banarsidass, 1981), 116, 32. For the attitude of Shankara the commentator toward *bhakti*, see his comments on *BhG* 13, briefly considered later.

For abbreviations used here for the titles of texts, see the list at the end of the chapter.

4. The epigraph at the head of this chapter is the concluding benediction of *GAD* 14, p. 608.

5. *Brahma satyam jagan mithya jivo brahmaiva na parah* (traditional verse).

6. On the concept of liberation in Advaita, see Lance E. Nelson, "Living Liberation in Sankara and Classical Advaita: Sharing the Holy Waiting of God," in *Living Liberation in Indian Thought*, edited by Andrew O. Fort and Patricia Y. Mumme (Albany: State University of New York Press, 1996), 17–62. For a more complete discussion of Advaita theology and its implications, see Lance E. Nelson, "The Dualism of Nondualism: Advaita Vedanta and the Irrelevance of Nature," in *Purifying the Earthly Body of God: Religion and Ecology in Hindu India*, edited by Lance E. Nelson (Albany: State University of New York Press, 1998), 61–88.

7. See his commentary on *Brhadaranyaka Upanisad* 3.5.1. See also Eliot Deutsch, *Advaita Vedanta: A Philosophical Reconstruction* (Honolulu: East-West Center Press, 1969), chap. 3.

8. Shankara is not a subjective idealist. For him, God and the world are much more than mere creations of the mind. He takes pains to refute the views of the Vijnanavada Buddhist idealists, who deny the existence of external objects independent of perception. Shankara does not see such subjectivism as a necessary consequence of the doctrine of *maya* (*BSSh* 2.2.28–32). In post-Shankara Advaita, a kind of subjective idealism called *drishti-srishti-vada* (the doctrine of creation through perception) was put forward by Prakashananda (twelfth century), but there is no doubt that this view would have been rejected by Shankara.

9. Rudolph Otto, *Mysticism East and West* (New York: Macmillan, 1970), 123. Later on the same page, Otto speaks of the *"aparavidya* Shankara" as a "passionate theist." Considering what will be said about Shankara's views below, I think this latter statement is something of an exaggeration. I do, however, agree with Otto's observation that the great Advaitin stands sympathetically on the inside of the theistic tradition. He transcends it by moving "deeper," so to say, "from within." See note 10.

10. Hacker's study of Shankara's authentic works demonstrates that the latter's thinking on conventional religious matters, as well as that of his disciples, is consistently Vaishnava in tone and language; Paul Hacker, "Relations of Early Advaitins to Vaisnavism," in *Philology and Confrontation: Paul Hacker on Traditional and Modern Vedanta*, edited by Wilhelm Halbfass (Albany: State University of New York Press,

34. Hacker comments on this passage, "Relations of Early Advaitins," 37.

35. Compare Shankara's prominently placed declaration, here in the *mangala* (benedictory) verse with which he opens his commentary—that Narayana is "beyond the unmanifest," i.e., beyond *maya*, with his comments on *BhG* 15.16–17, where, following the text, he distinguishes the imperishable (*akshara*), identified with *maya*, from the *Purushottama*, identified as Narayana.

36. *jnanaishvarya-shakti-bala-tejobhih sada sampannah, BhGSh*, p. 4.

37. Again, *nitya-shuddha-buddha-mukta*.

38. The *jnanin*, the one "possessed of knowledge," i.e. (for Shankara), the one who has directly realized the identity of *Atman* and *Brahman*.

39. The male pronoun (*sah*) is used in the text. In Shankara's thought, only male Brahmin renunciants were qualified for the path of knowledge (see note 20). To attempt gender inclusive language here would therefore be misleading.

40. *Mama vasudevasyatmaiveti.*

41. *Anakadundubhi* is a name of Vasudeva, Krishna's father.

42. For further examples of devotional verses attributed to Madhusudana, see *Siddhanta Bindu; Being Madhusudana's Commentary on the Dasasloki of Sri Sankaracharya*, translated by P. M. Modi (Allahabad: Vohra, 1985), app. 4.

43. Compare with Shankara's introduction to the BhGSh, translated earlier.

44. The editor places in brackets the following additional epithets: "shining with a pair of lotus feet whose beauty exceeds that of a fresh lotus, incessantly playing the flute, whose mind is attached to delightful sports in Vrindavana, by whom the mountain called Govardhana was held high in play, Gopala, by whom droves of wicked ones such as Shishupala, Kamsa were slain." However, he notes: "This ornamented portion is not included in some manuscripts" (*GAD*, p. 361).

45. Bhagavan is clearly identified, elsewhere in this text, as Mukunda, Govinda, etc. Madhusudana also quotes literally hundreds of verses from the *Bhagavata Purana* in support of his ideas. In short, it is clear that here Bhagavan is Krishna and not, for example, Vishnu or Narayana.

46. A reference to *Yoga-sutra* 1.15.

14

Ramanuja and the Meaning of Krishna's Descent and Embodiment on This Earth

Francis X. Clooney

Ramanuja (1017–1137) is considered one of the greatest Shrivaishnava theologians in the South Indian Tamil area, and the most prominent expositor of what came to be known as the qualified nondualist (Vishishtadvaita) school of Vedanta theology. Ramanuja defended the notion that *Brahman* is the highest and uncompromised unitary reality, perfect in every way; material and conscious beings exist in *Brahman*, who, though unitary and undivided, includes all conscious and nonconscious beings as parts of himself. In Ramanuja's view, this *Brahman* is in fact Lord Narayana, to whom all beings must surrender in devotion if they are to reach liberation. He also asserts, accordingly, that this ultimate reality, *Brahman* who is Narayana, also becomes embodied as Rama, as Krishna, and in other forms, so that conscious beings may reach him and worship him lovingly in a way that is possible for humans.

The excerpts that follow are from two of his works: his *Gita Bhashya* commentary on the *Bhagavad Gita*, in which he explains and defends the notion of divine embodiment, and his *Shri Bhashya* treatment of embodiment (in one of the topical discussions, *adhikarana*, that make up the *Uttara Mimamsa Sutras* systematization of Upanishadic wisdom).

There are of course commentaries on all of Ramanuja's works, and they, too, are rich in faith, ideas, and arguments. On the *Gita Bhashya* passages, I have included comments from the *Tatparya Chandrika* of Vedantadeshika (1270–1369), who succinctly and astutely brings out the fuller meaning of Ramanuja's key theological and devotional insights into the *Gita*. On the *Shri Bhashya* passages I include comments from the *Shrutaprakashika* of Sudarshana Suri (twelfth century), who likewise elaborates Ramanuja's text, drawing out and elucidating his insights. Finally, I include two verses from Vedantadeshika's *Adhikarana Saravali*, a work in which he synthesizes the meaning of each of the topical discussions in the *Shri Bhashya*, and in which he further develops the implications of Ramanuja's ideas. In the two verses included here, Deshika summarizes and explains points made more expansively in the *Shri Bhashya* treatment of embodiment. Finally, I have added several insightful comments from two commentaries on Deshika's *Saravali*, the *Adhikarana Chintamani* of Vaishvamitra Shrivaradaguru and the *Sarartha Ratnaprabha* of Vatsya Viraraghavacarya.

On the whole, I have given preference to passages mentioning Krishna, and also passages examining the idea of divine descents of Narayana in the world. Nonetheless, it is striking how little is said explicitly about Krishna in what follows; most might apply just as well to Rama and even, though less importantly, to other divine descents. Nevertheless, we find numerous clues indicating that Krishna is very much in the mind of Ramanuja and his commentators. His overall goal is to defend the notion that Narayana could plausibly appear as Krishna in this world, and accordingly he confronts the philosophical and theological problems related to divine embodiment: if embodiment is real, does it not diminish the divine perfection? If embodiment is not real, does it not diminish the graced opportunity supposedly made available to devotees in the divine descents?

There are two major strategies by which Ramanuja, Vedantadeshika, and Sudarshana Suri address these questions and defend the notion that the perfect Lord can become embodied. First, and without embarrassment at the paradox, they insist that it is simply a fact that the divine births are real just as human births are real; and it is another fact that these births are entirely free from the defects and compulsions entailed by human births, their rootedness in *karma*, and so on. There is scriptural warrant for the reality of the births and for the undefiled divine perfection, so both positions must be true, and neither is to be surrendered for the sake of the other.

Second, Ramanuja, Vedantadeshika, and Sudarshana Suri little by little work out the distinction between bodies made of material nature (*prakriti*) and made up of the three constituents (*sattva, rajas, tamas*), and the divine bodies of Rama, Krishna, and so on, which are either entirely pure being, free of the disruptions and faults accruing to *rajas* and *tamas*, or instead stipulated to be "not made of material nature" (*aprakrita*).

Both strategies exemplify the virtues and weaknesses of theological reasoning: scripture establishes normatively the range of truths that must be held even when it is not clear how they fit together. New concepts—such as "body not made of material nature"—are devised as needed, in order to complete arguments for which some required components are lacking. Since there is a need for a body that is both really material and yet unlike matter as it is commonly known, then it must be the case that such a body does exist and is made up of some special kind of matter. Ramanuja and his heirs vigorously defend the reasonability of the positions they put forth, even if they do not claim that one could arrive by reasoning alone at the positions they argue.

The conclusion, they insist, is spectacular and efficacious: there is a divine body that is accessible to the senses, real, and nearby—and yet at the same time luminous and perfect, the flawlessly beautiful and immensely attractive presence of God among humans. This of course is where Krishna comes in. He most perfectly exemplifies the divine nearness, rare embodiment, extraordinary loveliness, and most astonishing acts of divine tenderness.

Ramanuja's chosen task is to defend and elaborate the intellectual implications of the doctrines and piety of the tradition. Ramanuja's writing is for the most part exegetical, logical, and apologetic, and rarely does he wax eloquent in words of praise. Complexities aside, it should be evident how Shrivaishnava intellectual piety infuses even the most abstract discussions, as he, Vedantadeshika, and Sudarshana Suri emphasize that the highest value of divine descents lies simply in divine nearness. They defend, on solid intellectual grounds, benefits and pleasures already known with certainty by devotees. Reason illumines what one believes; beliefs energize and give purpose to one's reasoning.

Ramanuja's insights are expressed in the logic and by the stylistic technicalities of expert exegesis, and it is important to notice how he writes. By correlating his words to those of the texts he comments on, and then to those of his commentators, I have attempted to render the commentarial project evident yet intelligible in translation. Like the other translators contributing to this volume, I have striven for accuracy and clarity in an unencumbered style that allows the translation to speak for itself.

As noted in the references, I have also gratefully consulted some of the available translations, although what follows is my own translation.

Selections from Ramanuja's Commentary on the Bhagavad Gita with Further Comments from Vedantadeshika's Tatparya Candrika

Text 1: Ramanuja's Commentary on the Introduction to the Bhagavad Gita

Ramanuja.[1] The highest *Brahman*, the highest person, Narayana, emitted the entire universe beginning with Brahma all the way down to immovable objects, [a]*while yet remaining in His own form.* He was [b]*inaccessible in meditation, worship, and so on,* [c]*to Brahma and the other gods and humans.*

Vedantadeshika.[2] In the passage beginning with [a]*while yet remaining in His own form* and ending with [b]*inaccessible in meditation, worship, and so on, to Brahma and the other gods and humans,* Ramanuja indicates that the divine descent is due to Krishna's own will. He explains its purpose and how that purpose is not complete until Krishna is in the state of divine descent. Krishna's state is [b]*inaccessible* because it is unmanifest. As has been said, "By those qualities with which Hari is equipped even in bearing an unmanifest form, by those qualities you two [Nara and Narayana] are equipped even when bearing a manifest form."[3] [c]*Brahma and the other gods and humans* indicates that the competence even of Brahma, Rudra, Indra, and other gods for meditation on the highest self is made possible only in accord with their desire and their capability, as is said, "Badarayana says that [conscious beings are capable of meditation] because it is possible [in terms of capacity and motivation]."[4]

Ramanuja. Yet, since He was also [d]*a vast ocean of boundless mercy, affability, affection and generosity,* [e]*He emitted His own form in a configuration appropriate to each kind of being, yet without giving up His own proper nature.* Thus He descended again and again into each world, was worshiped in each world, and bestowed the results known as righteousness, wealth, enjoyment, and liberation,[5] according to the desires of each person.

Vedantadeshika. But if He lacks any personal motive how it is that He still acts this way? This is explained by [d]*a vast ocean of boundless mercy, affability, affection and generosity.* He is not concerned about His own interests; He is unable to endure the suffering of others; nothing contradicts His own greatness; He desires unbroken union with even the slow-witted; His specific relationship [to people] is natural to Him and covers over the faults of others; He is greatly generous and has the disposition to ask "Can't still more be given, after one has already surrendered oneself to demons, cowherds, and cowherd women, and so on?" Because of all this, He is prompted to descend [into this world].

After Ramanuja has reflected on the Lord's form [mentioned in the section on weapons and ornaments], he then shows that unique part of the forms of divine descents that has as its basis the highest heaven and no natural matter. This is in accord with the statement "O king, where all these powers are established, that is the form of the universal form, the other form of Hari, the great. There, O ruler of the people, by his own play he makes forms of all the powers, the deeds of gods, animals, and humans, to help the worlds; they do not originate due to *karma*."[6] All this is explained when Ramanuja says, [e]*He emitted His own form in a configuration appropriate to each kind of being, yet without giving up His own proper nature,* and so on.

Ramanuja.[7] [a]*Under the pretext of removing the burden of the earth,* but really for the purpose of becoming the place of refuge even for [b]*people like us,* He descended to the earth and made Himself visible to the eyes of [c]*all* those born human. He performed [d]*divine deeds* of a sort that ravished the minds and eyes of [e]*everyone,* both [f]*the high and the low.*

Vedantadeshika.[8] The general nature of divine descent and its purpose have already been shown. Now he makes some specifications related to the topic, by [a]*under the pretext of removing the burden of the earth* and what follows. Descending to support the earth is merely a pretext; becoming refuge for all is the evident intent. Destroying evildoers is part of a greater purpose, the protection of the good. All this is explained here by [a]*under the pretext of removing the burden of the earth.*

[b]*People like us,* that is, people who are not *yogins.* By saying [c]*all,* Ramanuja explains how He is the refuge of [c]*all.* He is hard to grasp even by the purified minds of great *yogins;* as it says, "That which neither the gods nor silent sages nor I nor Shankara know, that is the highest place of the highest Lord, Vishnu."[9] Due to bountiful accessibility toward humans [on this earth] as cowherd, however, He became visible even to the eyes of those humans who ignore the differences between what is contradicted and what is not.[10]

The goal of His coming down and becoming the object of human eyes is not merely that He be worshiped but also that He be experienced. Ramanuja explains this by mentioning [f]*the high and the low.* The *high* are those capable of meditation, for example, Brahma, Rudra, Bhishma, Akrura, and so on. The *low* are the Abhiras and others. [e]*Everyone* indicates that there is no distinction between males and females here; as it says, "He captivated men's minds and vision."[11] [d]*Divine deeds* indicate [eating the] butter, dancing, and so on. Thus Ramanuja intends two specifications when he specifies how the good are protected.[12]

Ramanuja. He killed [g]*Putana,* Shakata, the twin Arjuna trees, Arishta, Pralambha, Dhenuka, Kaliya, Keshin, Kuvalayapida, Chanura, Mushtika, Tosala, Kamsa, and others. He refreshed everything with the nectar of His looks and with His words pregnant with [h]*boundless compassion, friendliness, and love.* He made Akrura, Malakara, and others into the greatest of devotees by manifesting His surpassing beauty, affability, and a host of other such qualities.

Vedantadeshika. [Ramanuja] also explains that destruction of evil that is connected with the protection of the good, by mentioning [g]*Putana*, and so on. Because [His brother] Lord Balabhadra is a portion of Him, the killing of Pralambha, Mushtika, and so on are mentioned as if He were the agent. Ramanuja shows the enjoyment that comes with protecting the good by mentioning [h]*boundless compassion, friendliness, and love.* Seeing His most desirable and lovely form is [His devotees'] support. Seeing His deeds is their nourishment. Speaking with Him is their mode of pleasure. Such is the point of listing separately seeing Him with the eyes, and observing His deeds, and so on.

Ramanuja.[13] [i]*Under the* [j]*pretext of encouraging the son of Pandu to fight,* He promulgated that *yoga* of devotion that accords with knowledge and works, that has Himself for its object, and that in the Vedanta is declared to be the means to the attainment of liberation, the highest of human ends.

Vedantadeshika.[14] Now Ramanuja connects the Lord's deeds with the teaching of the *Bhagavad Gita.* The connection with the plot of the *Mahabharata* is indicated by [i]*under the pretext of encouraging the son of Pandu to fight.* How it is a [j]*pretext* is explained in the text that says "The exposition of this teaching [the *Bhagavad Gita*] was made for the sake of the instruction of Arjuna who had sought refuge when, due to his ungrounded love and pity, he was troubled by thinking that what is not righteous is righteous."[15]

Ramanuja.[16] [k]*At that point, when that war between the sons of Pandu and the descendants of Kuru began,* [l]*He, the* [m]*master, the* [n]*highest person, the* [o]*Lord of all lords,* [p]*who became mortal to help the world, who is overpowered by His affection for those who seek refuge with Him*—He made Arjuna the rider in the chariot and Himself the charioteer, as was witnessed by the whole world.

Vedantadeshika.[17] After summarizing the [*Gita's*] teaching, Ramanuja now summarizes what is connected with it by mentioning previous events, [k]*at that point, when that war between the sons of Pandu and the descendants of Kuru began.* . . .

He fends off the objection that in acting as a teacher the Lord is only pretending to be a charioteer, by saying [k]*at that point,* and so on. He means at the point when the Lord is to expound the *yoga* of devotion; or, when the battle is about to begin.

[Krishna] is called [m]*master* in order to emphasize His form as *guru,* and so on, even in the performance of the lowly work of charioteer. This form [as guru] is rooted in His tenderness and is characterized by His fullness and freedom even in the context of a divine descent. [1]*He, *[m]*the master, *[n]*the highest person, *[o]*Lord of all lords*: these four words summarize His transcendence by expounding His proper nature, exceptional qualities, pervasiveness, and so on.

[o]*Lord of all lords* is to be understood according to the text where it says "Krishna [is proclaimed as] the Lord of all lords [by all the learned; but however great their praise may be, it captures only a particle of His reality]."[18] This expresses His freedom and yet also that He has the world as His household. [p]*Who became mortal to help the world, who is overpowered by His affection for those who seek refuge with Him* summarizes His accessibility; that He is not deceptive is also suggested. One remembers here the text, "Who is able to conquer the unborn, unmade Lord, the eternal one, who [by His own will] became mortal to aid the world . . . ,"[19] and as it says elsewhere, "[He comes] for the sake of helping the world."[20]

Text 2: Ramanuja's Comment after Bhagavad Gita 4.4

Ramanuja.[21] This [truth about Krishna] was also often heard [by Arjuna] from Bhishma and others during the *rajasuya* sacrifice of Yudhishthira and on similar occasions mentioned in sentences such as the following: "Krishna alone is the origin and dissolution of all the worlds. For this universe, containing things both animate and inanimate, was brought into existence and exists for the sake of Krishna."[22] "For the sake of Krishna" means that the entire universe is subservient to Krishna.

The following may also be added. The [a]*son of Prithu* [Arjuna] [b]*certainly knows the* [c]*son of Vasudeva* as Lord, but although he knows Him, he asks questions [d]*as if he did not know* Him: is this the birth of [e]*the Lord of all,* [f]*who is the opposite of all that is evil and who is* [g]*the sole seat of auspicious qualities* [h]*who is omniscient,* [i]*whose will is unfailingly true and* [j]*all of whose desires are fulfilled?* And [k]*is His birth the same as that of gods, humans, and others who are subject to the influence of deeds?* Is it unreal like [l]*Indra's net,* [m]*and so on,* or is it real? [n]*If it is real,* [o]*how does His birth take place,* [p]*what is* [q]*this* [r]*body made of,* [s]*what is the reason for His birth,* [t]*when does His birth take place, and* [u]*for what purpose?* The point of the questions is known by way of the refutations [they anticipate].

Vedantadeshika.[23] [a]*The son of Prithu* [Arjuna] certainly knows the son of Vasudeva as the Lord. "Lord" indicates both His name and His qualities. The words [c]*son of Vasudeva* and [a]*son of Prithu* indicate that there is a relation to what is natural, as is indicated by being the son of a maternal uncle or of a paternal aunt. As with other people, this relation conceals His state as Lord. Nevertheless, Arjuna knows Krishna due to the good things He has done and the power of His teaching. The suspicion [that he does not seem to know Krishna] is ruled out by asserting that he [b]*certainly knows*. Arjuna does not ask about what is entirely unknown; rather, what is known is being investigated in order to learn another specific part of it. By [d]*as if he did not know* Ramanuja suggests that the question is prompted by modesty.

By mentioning [e]*the Lord of all,* [f]*who is the opposite of all that is evil,* [g]*who is the sole seat of auspicious qualities,* [h]*who is omniscient,* [i]*whose will is unfailingly true and* [j]*all of whose desires are fulfilled,* Ramanuja ascertains what is already known regarding the Lord by someone who wants to understand what is not known. That is, Arjuna recognizes that there are questions regarding the falsity of the birth, and so on of the Lord. The words [f]*who is the opposite of all that is evil* highlight the question, "If He ends the undesirable features of birth, age, and so on, when these pertain to others, how can He Himself assume these features?" By saying [g]*the sole seat of auspicious qualities* Ramanuja asks, "What does one who delights in the bliss of His own proper form have to do with birth at all?" Calling Him [e]*Lord of all* recognizes that if there were someone else who were independent and in charge of Him, then birth, and so on, might ensue [for Him]; but for Him there can be no such person. [h]*Who is omniscient* indicates that if He did not know what is beneficial or not for Him, He might on that account have taken on birth, and so on, like children touching fire, and so on. [i]*Whose will is unfailingly true* recognizes that even if someone knows what is good and not good for himself, and even if he thinks, "I will walk on the dry ground," nonetheless he might still step right into the mud. The point is that it is not this way with Him.

But the best answer is that He descends solely for the sake of protecting the world. By saying, [j]*all of whose desires are fulfilled,* Ramanuja's point is that if something needed to be accomplished, some goal, then birth, and so on, might be taken on for that purpose. But that too is not the case here . . .

The manner of birth as generally understood occasions suspicions about the falsity [of His birth], since [undergoing birth] seems contrary to His previously stated [perfect] form. This is indicated in the question, [k]*is His birth the same as that of gods, men, and others who are subject to the influence of deeds?*

. . . or, "birth" may mean an [extrinsic] form that is undergoing birth. If so, then the point would be that because the Lord assumes it, it is like [l]*Indra's net,* which by its own will creates diverse confusions for others. Such would be a distinctive characteristic indicative of His appearing. [m]*And so on* indicates taking on an actor's role, and so on.

If one holds the position that His body is false, the manner [of embodiment] need not be established. Therefore, by saying [n]*if it is real* Ramanuja suggests that there is a [real] body and then raises a doubt about it. By [o]*how* Ramanuja asks whether He is born by abandoning His proper nature as highest Lord or in some other way. [p]*What is this body made of?* asks whether this body is made of the three constituents[24] or [instead, of something that is] not natural. [q]*This* indicates that it is [at least] perceived as a configuration, an aggregate of elements. [r]*Body* indicates that it is perceived in the form of a mass. [s]*What is the reason for His birth?* asks whether the reason [for this body] is simply an act of [divine] intention or rather merit and demerit accepted by the Lord by His own will. The word [t]*when* asks whether it occurs in the time of the ripening of [His own] merit and demerit, or only in times when *dharma* is in decline, and so on. By asking [u]*for what purpose,* he is asking whether the goal is to experience [*karmic*] pain and pleasure or rather to save good people ...

Text 3: Ramanuja's Comment on Bhagavad Gita 4.6

Bhagavad Gita 4.6. Though I am [a]*unborn* and [b]*an imperishable self,* [c]*though I am the Lord of all beings,* [d]*having established My own nature* nonetheless [e]*I make myself become,* [f]*by the* [g]*maya of My own self.*

Ramanuja.[25] Here [the Lord] explains [h]*the manner of divine descent,* the nature of His body, and the cause for His birth.

Without giving up My manner of being the highest Lord— having qualities such as being [a]*unborn* and [b]*imperishable,* being of the Lord of all, and [d]"*having established My own nature*"—[e]I make Myself become, [f]"*by the maya of My own self.*" [d]"*Having established My own nature*" means "having established my proper way of being." [e]"*I make Myself become*" strictly according to My own form, that is, by My own will ...

Vedantadeshika.[26] Now the next verse answers three questions regarding the [g]*manner of divine descent,* and so on. By the words [a]*unborn* and [b]*imperishable* is explained that there are no changes here in His proper form or in His characteristics as would be the case with material nature or [individual] persons. Or, the words [a]*unborn* and [b]*imperishable* indicate the absence of birth and death such as are caused by deeds. [c]"*Though I am Lord of all beings*" indicates that He is unfailing in having as His figure all auspicious qualities. Or, by the word [a]*unborn* is excluded the unconsciousness and condition of being a limited knower that accompany birth . . .

Ramanuja. [f]*By the maya of My own self,* that is, by My own *maya.* In this verse *maya* is synonymous with knowledge, as has been stated,[27] "*Maya* is wisdom, knowledge." Accordingly too there is the text, "By His *maya* He continually knows the good and evil of beings." [j]*By My own knowledge* [*maya*] means [k]*by My own will.*[28]

Without giving up My own nature, as Lord of all, [l]*possessed of all auspicious qualities,* without sin, and so on, I make for Myself forms like the forms of gods, humans, and so on, due solely to My own will. The sacred text, [m]*He who is unborn* [n]*is born many times,*[29] teaches the same thing. That is, without making His birth the same as that of other persons, He is born in the form of gods, and so on, in the manner described here, by His own free choice. For there is no contradiction between prior and later claims such as the following: [o]"*Many are* My [p]*past* births and yours, Arjuna; [q]*I know* them all," (4.5), "Then [r]*I emit* My self" (4.7), and "Who thus knows truly My [s]*birth* and action as [t]*divine* . . ." (4.9)

Vedantadeshika. [f]*By the maya of My own self* cannot properly mean, "[His birth] is not like ordinary [births] with respect to the highest reality," since as such it would not be different from the births of others, which too are false according to [the Advaitin's] reasoning.[30] Rather, [j]*by My own knowledge [maya]* speaks fruitfully to the proper point. How can knowledge alone be the cause of divine descents? To avoid the conclusion that the divine descents would then occur at all times he says [j]*by My own knowledge* [*maya*]" *means* [k]*by My own will* . . .[31] [l]*Possessed of all auspicious qualities* recalls the text, "He possesses all auspicious qualities, and all beings have but a small portion of His own power. His are bodily forms He chooses to assume by His own will, His is the benefit of the entire world He has made."[32]

[m]*He who is unborn* excludes in general [the notion that the Lord is merely like other beings who undergo birth]. The ensuing positive statement, [n]*is born many times,* serves to restrict the scope of the prior exclusion [by allowing an exception]. Since the danger of contradiction is thus alleviated, no other intent for the statement need be construed. Nor is this a general statement about His becoming multiple as the world form, as when it says, "May I become many."[33] For it is proper to say that only the knowledge of the mystery of divine descent is very helpful to those seeking liberation, as in subsequent statements such as "The wise know His womb."[34] The statement under discussion ["He who is never born is born many times"]

shares a single purpose with that latter statement ["The wise know His womb."]

In order to dispel the doubt that he is avoiding contradiction [merely] by distinguishing true [birth] and false [birth], Ramanuja gives another reason, [o]"*Many are My* [p]*past* births and yours, Arjuna; [q]*I know* them all," (*Bhagavad Gita* 4.5); The Lord says [d]*having established My own nature,* and with respect to His own form he refers to His [g]*maya* [*Bhagavad Gita* 4.6]) with respect to knowledge.[35]

The words [q]*I know,* [r]*I emit,* and [t]*divine* are to be construed as indicating respectively that His [s]*birth* is preceded by understanding, that it is done solely by His will, and that it is [t]*divine.* Words such as "*maya,*" and so on, indicate ignorance, and so on and all else that should be ruled out.

Here [s]*birth* does not indicate a false appearance of birth, nor does the word [p]*past,* synonymous with "destroyed," imply a contradiction. Nor can [q]*I know them all* belong to a person held by that *maya*; so too, [r]*I emit* cannot refer to what is false, nor can [t]*divine* apply to what is merely an offshoot of the three constituents.

Text 4: Ramanuja's Comment on Bhagavad Gita *4.8*

Bhagavad Gita 4.8. For the protection of the good, for the destruction of evildoers, for the establishment of righteousness I come into being age after age.

4.8 Ramanuja.[36] [a]*The good* are [b]*those who are disposed toward dharma,* as explained above.[37] They are the [c]*foremost Vaishnavas* and are [d]*bent on taking refuge with Me.* [e]*Although My names,* works, and forms are beyond the range of speech and mind, [f]*[these devotees] do not gain support, sustenance, and so on, for their selves without seeing Me.*[38] They [g]*consider even a moment of time* [spent away from Me] *as a thousand aeons.* [h]*They will become weak and unnerved in every limb* [on account of separation from Me], so *I am born from age to age in the forms of gods, men, and so on,* [i]*for the sake of protecting them by* [j]*giving them opportunities of talking, looking at My proper nature and My activities,* for the destruction of those who are the opposite of these, and "for the firm establishment of Vedic righteousness when it is has declined"—*a righteousness that is of the nature of worship of Me* — [k]*by showing My proper form that is the worthy object of adoration.*

Vedantadeshika.[39] [a]*The good* here does not name merely those who are incapable [of protecting themselves], since it is meant as the opposite to the word "doers of evil"; here it must mean those who actually do good. Ramanuja explains this by saying [b]*those who are*

disposed toward dharma as explained above, that is, as was explained
earlier at *"dharma* explained in the Veda,"[40] and so on. There are
those who worship other deities according to *dharma* as previously
explained; there are also some Vaishnavas who worship the Lord
in the form of specific deities, according to the rule enunciated in the
Pratardana Meditation.[41] Neither group has a very urgent disposition to see the divine descents. [Yet] because by the circumscribed
force of those other deities they can plausibly be said to gain everything they want, they are nonetheless still called ᶜ*foremost Vaishnavas*
. . . For these ᶜ*foremost Vaishnavas,* what is undesirable is not gaining the Lord. Gaining Him, after taking refuge with Him, terminates
whatever is undesirable. Such is the point of the words from ᵈ*bent
on taking refuge with Me* up to ʲ*giving them opportunities of talking,
looking.* Such people do not have rice, drink, betel nut, and so on, as
their sustenance and nourishment. The idea is, "I, Krishna, am all
this," and this is the point of his saying that ᶠ*[these devotees] do not gain
support, sustenance, and so on, for their selves without seeing Me.* This
"not seeing" is due to incomplete *yoga.* Were such persons able
to close their eyes and endure even for a short time without My
manifestation, then I too could endure this condition of theirs. But
since they cannot endure [even briefly without Me] neither can I
[without them]. This is why Ramanuja adds that they ᵍ*consider even
a moment of time* [spent away from Me] *as a thousand aeons . . .*

He describes the final condition of those who suffer from not
seeing the Lord by adding, ʰthey *will become weak and unnerved in
every limb.* The forms experienced by such devotees are intended to
keep alive people who are distressed by separation from Him, so
Ramanuja adds, ⁱ*for the sake of protecting them by* ʲ*giving them opportunities of talking, looking at My proper nature and My activities.* Unlike
the joys of liberation,[42] He cannot by His mere wish, apart from
a divine descent, give them such opportunities.

Text 5: Ramanuja's Comment on Bhagavad Gita 4.9

Bhagavad Gita 4.9. ᵃ*Whoever thus truly knows My* ᵇ*divine birth and
action, leaving his body behind,* ᶜ*is never born again;* ᵈ*he comes to Me.*

Ramanuja.[43] ᵃ*Whoever thus truly knows* My unique birth and action,
which are ᵇ*divine* and not comprised of material nature, which are
intended solely for the protection of the good and enabling them
to take refuge with Me, which belong to Me who am free from birth
such as is caused by actions and takes the form of contact with
material nature comprised of the three constituents, and which are

endowed with all auspicious qualities such as lordship over all, omniscience, a will that is unfailingly true—whoever knows in this way, when he has given up the present body, ^c*is never born again*, but ^d*he comes to Me* alone.

Through discerning knowledge of the truth about My divine birth and work, all the sins that stand in the way of his resorting to Me are destroyed, and in this very birth he takes refuge with Me in the manner already stated. Being pleased with Me alone and having a mind for Me alone, he obtains Me alone.

Text 6: Ramanuja's Comment on Bhagavad Gita 4.11

Bhagavad Gita 4.11. ^a*However people take refuge with Me,* ^b*in that way do I favor them,* O Arjuna; humans travel ^c*My path* ^d*in every way.*

Ramanuja.[44] ^e*Not only* do I descend in the forms of gods, humans, and so on, and so bestow protection on those who desire refuge with Me, but also, ^a*however people* desire to *take refuge with Me,* that is, in whatever manner they imagine Me and ^f*in accord with their desire*—^b*in that way,* that is, *in that human form,* ^g*I show myself* to them.

What is more, ^h*all* ⁱ*men* who are focused solely on following Me on ^c*My path* shall ^j*keep on experiencing* ^k*My proper nature,* even if it is ^l*beyond the range of the speech and thought even of* ^m*those practiced in yoga.* They ^j*keep on experiencing Me* ^d*in every way desired by them* with their own eyes and other organs of sense.[45]

Vedantadeshika.[46] The Lord's own accessibility, which is connected with meditation,[47] has been explained. This has been done primarily by way of describing His divine descents in the same form as gods, humans, and so on, as due to His own choice, for the sake of protecting the good, and so on. Now Ramanuja shows the condition that is achieved as the highest reach of that state: ^a*However people* desire to *take refuge with Me,* ^b*in that way do I favor them.* Here, along with the event of divine descent as Krishna, and so on, also included is the event of temple forms.[48]

The words ^a*however people* desire to *take refuge in Me* are intended to set aside the previously mentioned restrictions[49] regarding who is a competent person, and regarding approved actions, modes of action, and so on. Therefore he says ^e*not only.* ^f*In accord with their desire* refers to the modes of His being lord, son, charioteer, boar, man-lion, and so on...

[Ramanuja] says ^g*I show myself* in order to indicate that He who is served offers access to vision and devout participation to those who serve Him. [i]*Men* is coupled here with [h]*all* to indicate that women too are included.

[c]*My path* ought not be taken as indicating a literal road, lest the statement thereby seem out of context. Nor does it merely signify behavior, since that too would make the statement appear out of context. Similarly excluded is the idea of following along the path mentioned in 3.16, "Thus the wheel was set in motion," and mentioned where it says, "By Him alone is established the boundaries of *Brahman* that make the world come into being."[50] Rather, in this context where accessibility is being taught, [Ramanuja] glosses [c]*My path* as [k]*My proper nature* in order to indicate that he means the aggregate [of qualities] in [the Lord's] proper nature, His extraordinary form and deeds, His good disposition, and so on. . . .

What Ramanuja means by [i]*men* is glossed as [m]*those practiced in yoga*. He means that [devout] *men* with their external senses and physical eyes can experience what is beyond words and even beyond minds purified by *yoga*. When Ramanuja says [d]*in every way* he indicates the forms of father, son, friend, brother, servant, charioteer, and so on, and the divine descents in temple forms, since all of these are indicated by [d]*in every way desired by them*. They [j]*keep on experiencing* [k]*My proper nature*, that is, experiencing Me, they progress.

Or, in this context [d]*in every way* may indicate decorations, processions, festivals, acts of service, and so on. In keeping with the reference to what is [l]*beyond the range of the speech and thought even of those practiced in yoga*, one can reflect on the transcendent form even in its temple form.

One might object, "If protecting the good, and so on, might be achieved simply by His wish, what then is the point of divine descent?" This has already been countered by Ramanuja in his commentary on 4.8,[51] beginning with *although My names*[52] and up to *for the sake of protecting them by giving them opportunities*.[53] In commenting on "for the firm establishment of Vedic righteousness when it has declined,"[54] Ramanuja added *by showing My proper form that is the worthy object of adoration*.[55] When the Lord says, [a]*however people take refuge with Me . . .*, He shows that His accessibility is different from the ordinary accessibility common to all.

Text 7: Ramanuja's Comment on Bhagavad Gita 9.14

*Bhagavad Gita 9.14.*Those [who wish to be] in constant union [with Me] worship Me out of devotion, [a]*always* [b]*singing My praises,* [c]*putting forth endeavors* [to serve Me] with firm resolution, and [d]*bowing to Me in reverence.*

Ramanuja.[56] On account of My being *exceedingly dear* to them they are unable to find sustenance for their selves even for the slightest fraction of a moment without *singing My praises,* *putting forth endeavors [to serve Me] and* *bowing in reverence.* *Their voices made low and indistinct with joy* and *every part of their bodies thrilled remembering My* *names that* *are expressive of particular qualities of mine,* they *always* offer praise using names such as Narayana, Krishna, Vasudeva.

With firm purpose they resolve to act on My behalf by acts of worship, and so on, and other acts auxiliary to those acts, such as making dwellings and gardens, and so on With the eight organs—the mind, the understanding, the ego, the two feet, the two hands and the head—made to bend low by *the weight of loving devotion,* they prostrate themselves on the earth itself like sticks [that fall down], not caring about dust, wet mud, small stones, and other such things. Thus they are unfailingly united with Me, that is, they desire permanent union and they worship Me, dedicating the full extent of their selves to My service.

Vedantadeshika.[57] At "they participate" (9.13),[58] meditation was the topic. Now, with *always,* [participation] is further specified by the condition of extreme delight that is due to *singing my praises,* *putting forth endeavors,* and *bowing in reverence.* The triad of praise, and so on, takes form respectively in acts of word, mind, and body, the modes of which are known in other contexts. *Always* is specified in acts of meditation that are permanently linked to acts of praise, endeavors, and bowing in reverence, as is shown by *exceedingly dear,* which is indicative of devotion.

To show the extreme sweetness of His *names,* Ramanuja adds that they *are expressive of particular qualities of mine.* Praising His names also presumes praising His deeds, and so on. The point is that even if one does not meditate on the qualities, the *names* generate pleasure even of themselves. With *every part of their bodies thrilled* because, as it says, "The eminent person has his hairs standing on end due to remembering [the Lord's] names."[59] *Their voices made low and indistinct with joy* recalls texts that similarly define devotion, mentioning "changes in voice, eyes, and limbs."[60]

"Krishna" indicates primarily the cause of the human goal, since "krish" indicates "the earth," and "na" indicates "completion."[61] "Krishna" is mentioned between two limiting terms [Narayana and Vasudeva] in order to indicate how [the Lord as named "Krishna"] is common to all states, the transcendent, the evolved, and so on. But Krishna is also mentioned among the divine descents, "You are uplifted by the boar, by Krishna with a hundred arms."[62] One might also say that "Narayana" indicates transcendence while "Krishna" and "Vasudeva" indicate accessibility with reference to specific divine descents. The power of praise is everywhere well known, as these texts show: "King Bharata spoke only the names of Hari, 'Reverence to you, Lord of the sacrifice, Govinda, Madhava, Ananta, Keshava, Krishna, Vishnu, Hrishikesha, Vasudeva,' "[63] "There is so much power in the name 'Hari' that it removes sins,"[64] "Lotus-eyed Vasudeva, Vishnu, sustainer of the earth, the unfallen one, whose hands hold the conch and wheel,"[65] "It is sufficient to remove the impurity of men,"[66] "Giving praise solely with the word 'Narayana,' "[67] and other such texts.

[k]*The weight of loving devotion*, and so on, explains how offering reverence is accomplished due to desire. The act of reverence done with the eight limbs is explained where it says, "By mind, understanding and self, he surrenders himself on the ground like a tortoise, with his four limbs and his head as a fifth."[68]

Text 8: Ramanuja's Comment on *Bhagavad Gita* 9.15

Bhagavad Gita 9.15. [a]*Others*, offering in addition [b]*the sacrifice of knowledge,* [c]*worship* [d]*Me* [e]*who am* [f]*one though I face in all directions,* [g]*in many ways, distinctly.*

Ramanuja.[69] [a]*Others*, that is, great selves, [c]*worship* [d]*Me* by previously mentioned acts of praise, and so on, and by offering [b]*the sacrifice* known as "knowledge." How? They worship [d]*"Me"* as [f]*one*, [g]*in many ways, distinctly,* in the form of the world, [d]*Me* [e]*who am* [f]*one though I face in all directions,* that is, [h]*who has all things as modes of myself.*

[i]*The following is what is being said.* The [j]*Lord* [k]*Vasudeva* Himself is possessed of a body consisting of intelligent and inanimate things in an extremely subtle state that cannot be differentiated into names and forms. He has a will that is unfailingly true. He resolves, "May I become one who has a body of intelligent and inanimate things in a gross state, differentiated variously into names and forms." He then abides as one alone who [nevertheless] has as His body the varied world consisting of gods, animals, humans, and inanimate things. By meditating on Me in this manner, so they worship Me.

Vedantadeshika.[70] [Ramanuja] explains [e]*who am* [f]*one though I face in all directions* in keeping with its well-known meaning, [h]*who has all things as modes.* But how does Ramanuja explain the connection between [f]*one* and [g]*in many ways, distinctly?* That is, how can a being who is one only be established as many? Moreover, this [seeming many-ness] suggests the flaws of being subject to modification, being caught in this world, and so on. So too, a person who meditates on a being established to be multiple as if it were one would be suffering from defective vision.

Ramanuja responds beginning with ⁱ*the following is what is being said*. He is speaking against the explanation, given by others, that the threefold difference[71] exists in meditation only, and so too against the theory of some others about difference and nondifference.[72]

ʲ*Lord* indicates the expansion of constituent elements[73] that is the means of creation, and so on. The first part of the word ᵏ*Vasudeva* specifics the pervasiveness accomplished by His having all as His body. This can be expressed in the claim that everything has the same referent.[74] The second part of the word ᵏ*Vasu-deva* expresses His play, and so on, activities that have as their purpose creation. Together, the two words ["Lord" and "Vasu-deva"] express the special *mantra*[75] used by people who are focused solely on Him and no one else.

The simple multiplicity of the world, and so on, is known from perception and other sources. But the fact that this world is a multiplicity of what is really one is known only from scripture. So the point of the statement is that all this is one, and so too that all this has evolved as the body of the one.

From Ramanuja's *Shri Bhashya* Commentary on the *Uttara Mimamsa Sutras* with Additional Comments from Sudarshana Suri's *Shrutaprakasika*

Text 9: Shri Bhashya *Commentary on the* Uttara Mimamsa Sutras *1.1.21*

> *Ramanuja.*[76] There is no truth in the contention that because he ["the person within the sun"] is connected with a body He cannot be different from individual selves [who are subject to *karma*]. For it is not true that the mere fact of embodiment proves subjection to *karma*. A being whose will is unfailingly true can assume a body by its mere wish.
>
> But it may be said that by "body" we understand a certain combination of elements that evolves from material nature made of the three constituents. Connection with such a body cannot possibly be brought about by the wish of a person who is free from all evil and whose will is unfailingly true. For such a connection would not be to the person's own benefit. In the case of a self that is subject to *karma* and that does not know its own proper nature, connection with a body cannot be avoided and takes place quite apart from

the self's desire, in order that the self may experience the fruits of its actions.

This would be so, we reply, if the body of the highest *Brahman* were made of material nature as comprised of its three constituents. But since this is rather a body suitable to the nature and intentions of that self, [this kind of embodiment] is plausible.

[a]*The point is the following:* [b]*only the highest Brahman* has a nature that is fundamentally antagonistic to all evil and that in its proper form is composed of infinite knowledge and bliss, and thus different from all other selves. It has a host of innumerable auspicious qualities that are natural to it, flawless, and in abundance.

Sudarshana Suri.[77]Because the Lord's omniscience is founded in Himself, His omnipotence does not depend on organs for action or knowledge, so He has no need of a body. If His body were to have [ordinary] forms, and so on, it would merely be a body made of material nature. Or, were it [exclusively] eternal, there would be no possibility of multiple, impermanent divine descents. Were He to take on the forms of animals, and so on, He would have a connection with *karma* such as underlies [such forms], as is described in texts such as "A man becomes . . . a bird or wild animal as a result of faults that are the effects of things he said . . ."[78]

To avoid such suspicions Ramanuja responds, [a]*the point is the following.* Just as it is on the basis of authoritative knowledge that one accepts both the proper nature of the highest *Brahman* as a subject and also its innate qualities, [on the same basis] it must be understood that He possesses an extraordinary body. To indicate all this Ramanuja mentions [b]*only the highest Brahman.*

Ramanuja.[79] Similarly, [a]*in a single form* conformed to His intentions, He is possessed of endless [b]*unthinkable,* [c]*divine,* [d]*astounding,* [e]*permanent* and [f]*flawless* qualities, a treasure of [g]*unsurpassable* splendor, beauty, fragrance, tenderness, loveliness, youthfulness, [h]*and so on.* Such is the [i]*divine form that is natural to Him.* He is a boundless ocean of compassion, favorable disposition, tenderness, generosity, and lordly power. In it the scent of all that is undesirable is [j]*annihilated.* It is not afflicted by sin. He is the highest Self, the highest *Brahman,* the supreme person, [k]*Narayana.* It is [l]*that form alone* that [m]*He individualizes* out of favor to the person meditating on Him, [n]*so as to render it suitable to their apprehension.*

Sudarshana Suri.[80] The point of [a]*in a single form* ff., is as follows. Although His act of knowing does not depend on sense organs, the material form of the highest one still exists for the sake of pleasure.

That is, although His bliss is unsurpassable, He has regard for specific pleasures; it is evident that those who have had experiences of bliss still have interest in other experiences of bliss. [a]*in a single form* indicates a unity of form such as is averse to all that is to be avoided. It is therefore also auspicious, and so on. By [b]*unthinkable* he means that it is not within the scope of acts of reasoning such as "Because He has a body, that body must endure suffering just like our bodies." By mentioning [c]*divine* [in "unthinkable, divine, astounding"] he gives a reason for [b]*unthinkable* and indicates a unique substance. This is to exclude the idea that merely because it is natural it would have to have form, and so on, such as would contradict the character of the referent.[81]

The second mention of [i]*divine* [in *divine form that is natural to Him*] indicates His uniqueness. As it says, "That is the form of the universal form, the other form of Hari, the great."[82] [d]*Astounding* indicates He is "new every moment." [e]*Permanent* rules out the [flawed] inference, "It is impermanent because it has parts," an inference that would contradict the character of the referent. [f]*Flawless* is meant to exclude the doubt that although His form is auspicious, it might still include some admixture with [flaws] to be avoided. [g]*Unsurpassable* indicates that He has all good qualities, as is explained later. By [h]*and so on* His power and other good qualities are meant.

But if He is permanent, how are multiple impermanent divine descents possible? How can He become of the same kind as inferior gods, and so on.? [Ramanuja] answers with the words [m]*He individualizes* that same form [n]*so as to render it suitable to their apprehension.* [l]*that form alone* indicates His unfallen condition. Although He has no weakness in form, [individualization] brings about multiple bodies for gods, and so on. This is seen with respect to the body of the four-faced god and is appropriate too regarding the highest form . . .[83]

[*That the scent of all that is undesirable is*] [j]*annihilated* indicates the Lord's transcendence. That is, His transcendence and accessibility both support the fact that He is an object of meditation. But in order to indicate that when He shares a common nature with humans, and so on, He is not touched by the grief, confusion, and so on, they experience, he adds the word [j]*annihilated.* Even when He enters into individual selves, their grief, and so on, pertain only to the portion that is the individual self.[84] In full divine descents, however, grief, and so on, are simply dramatic gestures.[85]

[k]*Narayana* is the inclusive term. Just as "highest self" and "highest *Brahman*" are two generic words with the same referent, and just as "highest person" and "Narayana" are two specific words

with the same referent, so too both the general and specific words have the same referent [Narayana].

Here too is refuted a doubt regarding whether His proper form is deficient in its capacity for enjoyment. His ability to experience enjoyment in relation to other things does not contradict the fact that His enjoyment is of Himself. Rather, that the host of things related to Himself is an object of enjoyment points to the unsurpassable quality of His self-enjoyment. It is not a deficiency in the fragrance of musk that the musk-like fragrance also attaches to everything that comes in contact with it; indeed, such is its excellence. So too, that He experiences enjoyment in His material forms because they are related to Him attests to the unsurpassability of enjoyment in Himself.

Ramanuja.[86] There is a scriptural text, [a]*Though unborn, He is* [b]*born many times.*[87] There is also the traditional text, "Though I am the Lord of all beings, having established My own nature nonetheless I make myself become, by the *maya* of My own self . . . For the protection of the good, for the destruction of evildoers, for the establishment of righteousness I come into being age after age." (*Bhagavad Gita* 4.6, 8) . . . Lord Parashara has said, "O king, where all these powers are established, that is the form of the universal form, the other form of Hari, the great. There, O ruler of the people, by his own play he makes forms of all the powers, the deeds of gods, animals, and humans, to help the worlds; they do not originate due to *karma.*"[88] In the *Mahabharata* too, is mentioned the form of his divine descents, such as is not made of material nature: "The body of the highest self is not an arrangement founded on an aggregate of elements."[89] [c]*Such is his unique character*, since he is possessed of a form of that sort.

Sudarshana Suri.[90] Surely it seems that [a]*unborn* prohibits any real births, while [b]*born many times* offers a rule for interpreting "births" that are not real.

No, there would be no point in arguing that births are entirely false. Merely by stating the falsity of the world one could prove the falsity of the Lord's forms too. What then would be the point of further, specific designations [of births as false]? [Such designations] would also be improper, since what is asserted [[b]*born many times*] cannot at the same time be ruled out [by [a]*unborn*]. After asserting births such as are not known by other means of knowledge, how could they then be denied?

Suppose that He is not born in His proper nature, but that He only assumes multiple "becomings" by means of bodies? No. That there can be births by means of bodies even though the proper nature is unchanging is just the same with [ordinary] individual selves too. It would be inappropriate to claim, [in *Taittiriya Aranyaka* 3.13.3], that "The wise know His womb," since this claim has a point only if His manner of birth is different from that known in the world as common to all. It need not be said that Devadatta's birth can be known only by the wise, since his is not different from Yajnadatta's.

Suppose then that although He is unborn in His proper nature, He undergoes multiple births by taking on the entirety of the forms found in the world? This certainly is something individual selves cannot do.

No. [In *Taittiriya* 3.12] it said, "Spreading out all forms, the wise one makes names for them, speaks them." Then, in the next section [*Taittiriya* 3.13.1], His multiple births are mentioned: "As Tvashtri, He radiates forth His form." It would therefore be super-fluous suddenly to refer to something other than divine descents [by adding "The wise know His womb" [in 3.13.3]. So we must inter-pret [*Taittiriya* 3.13.3, ᵃ*though unborn,* ᵇ*He is born many times*] as likewise referring to divine descents. If so, one can say that there is a coherent and continuous meaning to the statement, ᵃ*though un-born,* ᵇ*He is born many times.* ᶜ*Such is his unique character* settles the fact that his form, as described, is different from that of the indi-vidual self.

The *Adhikarana Saravali* of Vedantadeshika with additional comments from the *Adhikarana Cintamani* of Vaishvamitra Shrivaradaguru and the *Sarartha Ratnaprabha* of Vatsya Viraraghavacarya

Text 10: Adhikarana Saravali, *Verse 64*

Vedantadeshika.[91] ᵃ*His body has been described as* ᵇ*untainted being, flawless,* ᶜ*a substance of some sort, and* ᵈ*different than what is unmanifest;* ᵉ*this form is a lordly form, it shines even in heaven, and so too in Shesha, Vishvaksena,*[92] *and so on.;* ᶠ*this God never loses His proper nature;* *His form is eternal, honored by heavenly beings, ever higher; but to extinguish the worldly existence of humans He undergoes modification, in divisions beginning with the emanations.*[93]

Vaishvamitra Shrivaradaguru.[94] [Objection:] You claim that the highest *Brahman* has a body. But is this body comprised of mate-rial nature, or is it not made of material nature? If it is not made of material nature, is it simply the Lord's proper form, or is it some other reality? The first view [that it is comprised of material nature] is the position we have proposed, and it concedes that He is within worldly existence. [Though you claim to differ], you would merely be coming to the same conclusion by a round-about means. The second view [that the body is the Lord's proper form] would mean that His proper form evolves [and this is not possible]. Nor can the third view [that His body is some other reality] be true, since there is no other reality apart from material nature, individual persons, the Lord, and time.

He responds by saying, ᵃHis body has been described in texts such as: "All beings are one foot, while of three feet is comprised the immortal in heaven";⁹⁵ "in Vaikuntha, the highest place [is the Lord of the world, with Shri as half of Himself]";⁹⁶ "the highest establisher of tamas [bearer of the conch, discus and club...";⁹⁷ "pure being, shining as His being."⁹⁸ It is comprised of ᵇuntainted being, without rajas and tamas; it is ᶜa substance of some sort. It is ᵇuntainted because it lacks the instruments by which it would proceed [to be entangled] in worldly existence. Yet it is also ᵈdifferent than what is unmanifest. Only its manifest part is meant in the verse, "Of three feet is comprised the immortal in heaven." Therefore Deshika says ᵉthis form. For the Lord's form is made of ordinary material nature, while His proper form is not thus made.⁹⁹ It is rather some other, non-natural thing. Thus Lord Parashara said, "That is the form of the universal form, the other form of Hari, the great."¹⁰⁰

[... Objection:] Let us grant that everything born of qualities of the Lord who dwells in Vaikuntha [is thus free from flaws]. But Rama, Krishna, and so on, have a material nature, and they participate in the joys and sorrows born of karma. How are we to gain liberation by worshipping them?

[Deshika] answers this by saying, ᶠThis God never loses His proper nature. In keeping with Parashara and according to Parashara's tradition, [the bodies of Rama, Krishna, and so on, too] are possessed of qualities not comprised of material nature. As Parashara says, "Having all powers...,"¹⁰¹ and similarly in keeping with what Parashara says, "The body of the highest self is not an arrangement founded on an aggregate of elements."¹⁰² As Valmiki says, "He is manifest, the great yogi, the eternal highest self."¹⁰³ We conclude that the Lord's actions [during divine descents] are actions modeled on grief, confusion, and so on, just as performances on a stage occur for the sake of amusement.

Text 11: Adhikarana Saravali, Verse 65

Vedantadeshika.¹⁰⁴ Objection: because [the Lord's body] is a body and because it has parts, it must also have the seven physical components and the three impurities. It must be flawed and painful, it must cause suffering, and it must be destined for destruction.

Not so, we reply. Such a view is contradicted by authoritative knowledge about the possessor of that body. There can be no contradiction regarding the one who is known only from scripture. Otherwise, there would be the grave danger [of uncertainty about scripture and its truth].

Rather, ªwhatever His dramatic gestures during His divine descents, all of them are freely intended by His own will for ᵇthe overthrow of demons.

Vaishvamitra Shrivaradaguru.[105] That the Lord has a body is proven from scripture. References to His [body] being mixed with sorrow, and so on, contribute to ᵇ*the overthrow of demons.* These demons are Kamsa, and so on. They think that when Krishna and the other divine descents act as children, and so on, such is their complete reality. So again and again they move against them. But when they act thus they themselves perish. Thus the Lord's behaving like a child, and so on, has as its fruit the destruction of evildoers. As it says, "for the destruction of evildoers . . . [I come into being age after age]."[106]

Viraraghavacarya.[107] Learned Vedic scholars who are deluded by logic accept the Lord but hate the idea that He takes on material forms. To refute their logic he shows in this verse how their views are inconsistent with the meaning of the Veda . . .

[Objection:] It must be admitted on the basis of scripture that the Lord does experience some powerlessness and some suffering.

[Deshika] responds by saying ª*whatever His dramatic gestures.* It is known authoritatively that He suffers due to the suffering of others, as is shown in the text, "He was sorely grieved . . ."[108] With respect to His own self, it is shown in the text, "Exiled from His kingdom, living in the forest, [Sita lost, a brahmin killed: such is My misfortune that it could burn even fire]."[109] The Lord acts out this suffering by dramatic gesture, and only during His divine descents. Were divine descents dependent on deeds, then deeds would be the cause of His suffering. But His divine descents are due to His own will. He would not will His own birth were it the cause of His own suffering. So it is certain that this suffering is simply dramatic gesture.

What is its use then? He responds that it is for ᵇ*the overthrow of demons.* Its use is that demons see His suffering, impotence, and so on, and think Him inferior. They become particularly hostile toward Him, do not take refuge with Him, but instead sink down to the lowest place.[110]

Moreover, devotees see Him suffering in ways that are without limit and without precedent, and so on. They cry out, "How could
this little one suffer in this way?" Seeing His dramatic gestures of
suffering and exhaustion, and not realizing that it is just performance, even His friends are distressed. But this confusion is due to
their affection, and it is for their protection. By contrast, the confusion of others is due to their hatred and is for their confusion
and overthrow.

We can reflect on texts such as these: "The wise know His
womb";[111] "I make Myself become, by the *maya* of My own self";[112]
"He cannot have a natural form, flesh, marrow, bone";[113] "the body
of the highest self is not a collection of elements";[114] "ruler, great
yogin, Lord of all the world, He begins to do deeds, weak like a
low person, and in this way, by the *yoga* of His *maya*, Keshava de-
ceives the worlds."[115]

Scripture thus informs us that the Lord really has a body, is born,
and so on, but also that He lacks the affliction, weakness, and so on.
that belong to a body made of flesh and blood and ordinary material nature. Thus it is certain that only certain aspects [of embodi-
ment] are ruled out, but not form, and so on, as such. Thus, His form
is truly opposite to anything that should be avoided.[116]

NOTES

1. P. 10. All page references are to Sanskrit editions.

2. P. 10.

3. *Mahabharata* (Shanti Parvan) 12.331.37. In the *Narayaniya* discourse in the
epic, Nara and Narayana, sons of Dharma, embody in visible form the qualities
of the unseen transcendent Krishna.

4. *Uttara Mimamsa Sutras* 1.3.25.

5. The traditional four goals of life, respectively, *dharma, artha, kama,* and
moksha.

6. *Vishnu Purana* 6.7.69B–71B.

7. Pp. 11–12.

8. Pp. 11–12.

9. *Vishnu Purana* 1.9.55.

10. That is, people who are intellectually inattentive and ill prepared, in contrast
with the great *yogins.*

11. *Ramayana, Ayodhya Kanda* 3.29; in the citation, "men's" is *pumsam,* which
indicates males.

12. Krishna protects the virtuous from their enemies, and he gives them great
pleasure by the proximity of his lovable form.

13. Pp. 12–13.

14. P. 12.

15. From the *Gitartha Samgraha* of Yamuna, v. 5.

16. P. 13.

17. Pp. 13–14.

18. *Vishnu Dharmottara Purana* 75.44.

19. *Vishnu Purana* 5.30.80.

20. *Vishnu Purana* 6.7.72.

21. Introducing *Gita* 4.5–11; pp. 143–145.

22. *Mahabharata* (*Sabha Parvan*) 2.35.22.

23. Pp. 144–145.

24. The three constituent elements (*gunas*) are *sattva* (pure being), *rajas* (passion, energy), and *tamas* (dark inertia).

25. Pp. 146–149.

26. Pp. 146–149.

27. The *Nirukta* of Yaska, 3.9.

28. Ramanuja thus equates *maya* with knowledge, and knowledge with knowing (free) choice.

29. *Taittiriya Aranyaka* 3.13.3, which reads in full: "The lord of creatures moves about inside the inner place, unborn he is born many times; the wise know his womb, makers desire the place of the Marichas."

30. Earlier, Deshika has indicated that Shankara is the opponent here; he is portrayed as holding that all births are illusory.

31. Thus, *maya*, knowledge, and will are correlated and declared to pertain to real knowledge, in a real world.

32. *Vishnu Purana* 6.5.84.

33. *Chandogya Upanishad* 6.2.

34. *Taittiriya Aranyaka* 3.13.3.

35. That is, his astounding power, *maya*, is not illusion or lack of knowledge but a higher realization that confounds ordinary thinking.

36. P. 150.

37. Unidentified.

38. The editor of Ramanuja's *Gita Bhashya* cites here a relevant verse from the Tamil *Tiruvaymoli* that may be in Ramanuja's mind here: "My rice for eating, my water for drinking, my betel for chewing, my Lord Krishna!" her eyes flowing tears, she keeps crying" (6.7.1).

39. P. 150.

40. At the beginning of *Gita* 4.7.

41. *Kaushitaki Upanishad* 3.2.

42. Which can be given by the Lord from His transcendental realm, without appearing in the world.

43. Pp. 151–152.

44. Pp. 153–154.

45. At *Gita* 4.9, p. 108.

46. Pp. 153–154.

47. That is, one comes to realize his proximity through meditation.

48. *Archa-avatara*, in the consecrated image in the temple; there are five modes of Vishnu's presence: the transcendent, the cosmic evolutions, the descents, the inner controller, and the temple presence.

49. See Deshika's comments in the introduction to the *Gita* on competence for meditation.

50. Unidentified.

51. P. 150.

52. "e" at *Gita* 4.8.

53. "i" at *Gita* 4.8.

54. *Gita* 4.8.

55. "k" at *Gita* 4.8.

56. Pp. 302–303.

57. Pp. 302–303.

58. "They participate in Me, without minds for anyone else, knowing the beginning of what has come to be, the imperishable" (*Gita* 9.13.b).

59. *Vishnu Dharma* 74.48.

60. The editor identifies the text as *Mahabharata, Ashvamedhika Parvan* 115, but I have been unable to locate the citation there.

61. *Mahabharata* (Udyoga Parvan) 5.68.5.

62. The editor identifies the source as the *Narayaniya* section of the *Mahabharata*, but I have not found the cited text there.

63. *Vishnu Purana* 2.13.9.

64. *Visishtadvaita Kosha*, vol. 4 (p. 235) attributes the definition to Vyasa.

65. *Vishnu Purana* 3.7.33.

66. *Bhagavata Purana* 6.3.24.

67. Unidentified.

68. *Satvata Samhita* 6.187.

69. P. 303.

70. Pp. 303–304.

71. According to the editor (p. 303), the three views are: pure unity of *Brahman*; divisions such as the sun, moon, etc.; the all-inclusive universal form of the Lord.

72. Intended here is the refutation of those (unidentified) thinkers who posit that differences in *Brahman* are differences operative only in meditation, and those who adopt the "difference and nondifference" theory by which *Brahman* is "partly" nondifferent and "partly" differentiated.

73. On the constituent elements of reality (*gunas*), see note 24 here.

74. That is, all realities and words refer ultimately to a single referent, the Lord.

75. According to the editor, it is the twelve-syllable *mantra*, probably "*Om namo bhagavate vasudevaya,*" "Om, reverence to Lord Vasudeva."

76. P. 244. In this section of the *Uttara Mimamsa Sutras*, the debate pertains to a person described in *Chandogya Upanishad* 1.6, particularly in 1.6.6b: "Now, the person made of gold seen within the sun—he has a golden beard and golden hair; he is completely golden, down to the very tips of his nails." One of the objections, dealt with in the *Bhashya* passage translated here, argues that since this golden person is embodied, he cannot be *Brahman*, the Lord. Ramanuja argues that embodiment is not necessarily an obstacle.

77. P. 244.

78. *The Laws of Manu* 12.9, Doniger translation.

79. Pp. 244–245.

80. Pp. 244–245.

81. I.e., *Brahman*, the Lord.

82. *Vishnu Purana* 6.7.69b.

83. P. 245.

84. That is, insofar as he is human, he suffers, but he does not suffer in his true self.

85. *Abhinaya* is a "dramatic gesture" that is cultivated and practiced, yet it also becomes heartfelt and expressive of the actor's identity.

86. P. 246.

87. *Taittiriya Aranyaka* 3.13.3.

88. *Vishnu Purana* 6.7.69B-71B.

89. *Mahabharata* (Shanti Parvan) 12.206.60.

90. Pp. 246–247.

91. P. 123.

92. Not only does the Lord's material form shine splendidly for all eternity but so, too, do the forms of his eternal servants such as Shesha, the serpent on whom he rests, and Vishvaksena.

93. See earlier.

94. Pp. 123–125.

95. *Rig Veda* 10.90.3.

96. *Vayu Purana.*

97. *Ramayana, Yuddha Kanda,* 114.15.

98. Unidentified.

99. Form (*rupa*) and proper form (*svarupa*) are distinguished here.

100. *Vishnu Purana* 6.7.70a.

101. *Vishnu Purana* 6.7.69b.

102. See *Mahabharata* (Shanti Parvan) 12.206.60. See also *Shribhashya* 1.1.21 and *Tanishloka* at *Yuddha Kanda* 114.14; p. 484.

103. *Ramayana, Yuddha Kanda* 114.14.

104. P. 125.

105. P. 126.

106. *Bhagavad Gita* 4.7.

107. Pp. 125, 126–127.

108. Unidentified.

109. *Ramayana, Aranya Kanda* 67.24.

110. P. 126.

111. *Taittiriya Aranyaka* 3.13.3.

112. *Gita* 4.6.

113. Unidentified.

114. Unidentified.

115. Unidentified.

REFERENCES

Sanskrit

The Adhikarana Saravali of Shrimad Vedanta Deshika with the Adhikarana Chintamani of Vaishvamitrashrivaradaguru and the Sarartha Ratnaprabha of Vatsya Viraragha-vacarya. 1974. Chennai: Ubhaya Vedanta Granthamala.

The Bhagavad Gita with Shri Bhagavad Ramanuja's Bhashya and Shrimad Vedanta Deshika's Commentary named Tatparya Candrika. 1972. Edited by Sri Abhinava Desika (Uttamur) T. Viraraghavacharya. Chennai: Ubhaya Vedanta Granthamala.

The Brahmasutra Shribhashya of Ramanuja with the Shrutaprakashika of Sudarshana Suri. 1989. Edited by Sri Uttamur T. Viraraghavacharya. 2 vols. Chennai: Visishtadvaita Pracharini Sabha.

Translations Consulted

The Laws of Manu. 1991. Translated by Wendy Doniger with Brian Smith. London: Penguin Books.

Ramanuja. 1985. *The Gitabhashya of Ramanuja*. Translated by M. R. Sampatkumaran. Mumbai: Ananthacharya Indological Research Institute.

The Vedanta Sutras with the Commentary of Ramanuja. 1976. Translated by George Thibaut. Delhi: Motilal Banarsidass.

The Vishnu Purana. 1980. Sanskrit text, with English translation by H. H. Wilson. 2 vols. Delhi: Nag.

15

Madhva Vedanta and Krishna

Deepak Sarma

The Madhva School of Vedanta is a Vaishnava tradition developed
by Madhvacharya (1238–1317 C.E.) in the thirteenth century on
the west coast of South India near Udupi. Though known among
adherents to be next to Pajakakshetra, the birthplace of Madhvacharya,
Udupi is better known throughout India as a pilgrimage site for
Krishna *bhaktas* (devotees). The goal of their journey is the Udupi Shri
Krishna temple whose *murti* (image) was discovered in a lump of
gopichandan (clay) by Madhvacharya himself. Although Krishna is the
center of lay Madhva activities and worship, he assumes much less
importance in the doctrines of the tradition in comparison to
Vishnu, of whom he is an *avatara* (incarnation). Foremost, Madhva
Vedanta is a Vaishnava tradition and only secondarily is it a tradition
of Krishna worship.

Still, Krishna is mentioned far less frequently in the Madhva
corpus than one would think, given his predominance in the activities of the worship practices of lay Madhvas. Out of a total of thirty-
seven texts, only five are focused on Krishna. Krishna is an essential character in the *Bhagavata Purana*, the *Mahabharata*, and the
Bhagavad Gita, but Madhvacharya's commentaries on these texts
treat him as no more than one *avatara* of Vishnu among many.
Madhvacharya also has written several zealous *strotras* on Krishna,
including his [*Krishna*] *Jayanti Nirnaya* (The Discussion of Krishna's
Birthday), and his laconic *Krishnastuti* (Hymn to Krishna). Madhvacharya supposedly composed the latter as a boy. Its inclusion in the
corpus of Madhva texts is not without controversy, although B. N. K.
Sharma believes that it is authentic.[1]

For these reasons, it would be misleading to focus on Krishna exclusively in Madhva Vedanta, especially since all inquiries about him lead ultimately to Vishnu. A proper understanding of Krishna's place in Madhva Vedanta thus necessitates an understanding of the centrality of Vishnu Himself.

How does Vishnu fit into the Madhva system? What is Krishna's relationship to Him? What are some of the popular legends about Krishna told by Madhva devotees?

Basic Madhva Ontology

The following passage, taken from Madhvacharya's *Vishnutattva(vi)nirnaya*, summarizes the chief elements in Madhva Vedanta.[2] "As stated in the *Parama Shruti*: '. . . the wise [recognize] that [the universe] is known and protected by Vishnu. Therefore it, [the universe,] is proclaimed to be real. But Hari [that is, Vishnu] alone is supreme.'"[3] For Madhvacharya, the universe is unquestionably real, as are its components. Vishnu, who is the pinnacle of the Madhva system, governs all things. Furthermore, correct knowledge of Vishnu and the nature and function of the universe is the prerequisite for *moksha* (liberation).

Vishnu is the facilitator of all entities and all possible events. The entire universe is manifested as a result of His activity and is utterly dependent upon Him. To reflect this dualism in his ontology, Madhvacharya separates all of reality into *svatantra* (independent) and *asvatantra* (dependent) entities. The only *svatantra* entity is Vishnu, while all other entities are *asvatantra*.[4] All things, moreover, are in a hierarchical relationship with one another and with Vishnu, where Vishnu is at the zenith. This chain of command is known as Madhvacharya's doctrine of *taratamya* (gradation). The hierarchy pervades every aspect of the Madhva system and can be found even in *moksha*. There is *taratamya* in *moksha* because of the gradation in the devotion toward Vishnu.[5] This is known as Madhvacharya's *ananda-taratamya-vada* (theory of a gradation in bliss).[6]

Madhvacharya's characterization of Vishnu is very similar to those offered by other Vaishnava traditions that existed in medieval Karnataka. Such descriptions rely primarily on accounts found in the *Puranas*, the *Mahabharata*, and the *Ramayana*, which are portrayals of Vishnu's *avataras*, and Vishnu is depicted as a personal God in them. These accounts are intended to inspire proper *bhakti* in the devotee. Vishnu possesses attributes such as beauty, *ananda* (bliss), and intelligence.[7] He is held to be all-pervading and to be one who devours everything. He possesses all characteristics, such as being immanent in the universe and in the individual selves and the like.[8] Lists of these and other attributes can be found in Madhvacharya's *Dvadasha Stotra*, a text dedicated almost exclusively to propitiating Vishnu.[9]

Knowledge of Vishnu alone is insufficient for attaining *moksha*. Devotees must also obtain the grace of Vishnu in order to obtain *moksha*. Madhvacharya writes: "Direct realization of the highest Lord [comes] only from grace and not [from] the efforts of the *jiva*."[10] The *jiva* (individual self) is utterly dependent on Lord Vishnu, as is exemplified in the need for Vishnu-*prasada* (grace). The reward of Vishnu-*prasada* is a natural outcome of *bhakti-yoga* (the path to *moksha* via devotion). When *bhaktas* show their awareness of the hierarchy of the universe, namely the supremacy of Lord Vishnu, and act accordingly, then they are rewarded for their submission. Madhvacharya explains: "Hari [that is, Vishnu] is the master of all for [all] eternity. [All] are under the control [of the] Highest [One]. This *taratamya* and the supremacy of Hari are to be known."[11]

Vishnu's *Vyuhas* and *Avataras*

Madhvacharya separates Vishnu's manifestations into two groups: Vishnu's *vyuhas* (emanations) and His *avataras* (incarnations). The *vyuhas* have their basis in the *Pancharatragamas,* a sectarian text that was accepted as authoritative by both the Vishishtadvaita and Madhva schools of Vedanta.[12] They are mechanisms by which the universe is ordered, was created, and evolves. According to Madhvacharya, Vishnu has either four or five *vyuhas*, named Vasudeva, Sankarshana, Pradyumna, Aniruddha, and Narayana, which evolve one after the other in the development of the universe.[13] The status of the fifth *vyuha*, Narayana, is not clear, and in some passages he is not even mentioned.[14] The names of the first four *vyuhas* are connected with the stories of Krishna taken from the *Mahabharata*. Vasudeva is another name for Krishna, and Pradyumna is Krishna's son. Aniruddha is Pradyumna's son, and Sankarshana is another name of Balarama, Krishna's older brother. The *vyuhas* function in the evolution of *prakriti* (material stuff) and are each attached to its development. Vasudeva is associated with *mahat* (the great principle) and with granting *moksha*. Sankarshana is affiliated with *ahamkara* ("I"-ness) and is believed by Madhvacharya to be the destroyer. Pradyumna helps to convey the *jivas* during their rebirth. Aniruddha is associated with *manas* (mind) and functions to maintain the status quo.[15] Though the mythology of Krishna clearly plays a role in the names of each of these emanations, Madhvacharya did not derive them independently, for they originated in the *Pancharatra* texts and the *Mahabharata*.[16] Pratap Kumar and Jan Gonda argue that the *vyuha* doctrine permits the highest being to maintain unity while still having multiple manifestations. God can simultaneously have multiple functions in the evolution of the universe and can remain changeless.[17] This ability of Vishnu to be multiple yet ultimately unified is taken further in connection with His *avataras*.

In contrast to *vyuhas*, *avataras* are manifestations of Vishnu that appear and act in the world of humans. Vishnu appears on the earth in order to defend both *dharma* (law, duty, order) and his devotees, and this is established

5. Those who are liberated are only fivefold: the gods, the seers, the ancestors, the protectors [of the world], and the [highest among] men. Only these [sentient beings] are fit [to obtain] liberation. And those not fit for liberation are twofold: those fit for the darkness and those who are eternally in *samsara* [literally, those who remain in the journey].

6. Those fit for darkness are proclaimed to be fourfold: the *daityas* [demons], the *rakshasas* [orcs], the *pishachas* [ghastly lurkers], and the *martyadhamas* [the vilest of the mortals].

7. These [vilest who are fit for darkness] are twofold: those who suffer in complete darkness and those whose way [to darkness is through] *samsara*. Nonsentient things are known to be threefold: eternal, noneternal, and transitory.

8. The *Vedas* are eternal. The *Puranas* and the other [texts], time, and *prakriti* [material cause] are proclaimed to be both eternal and non-eternal. Noneternal things are known to be twofold: combined and not combined.

9. Not combined [i.e. atomic] things are: the *mahat* [the great principle], the *aham[kara]* ["I"-ness], the *buddhi* [intellect], the *manas* [mind], the ten openings [*indriyas*], the *pancha-tanmatras* [five subtle elements], and the *pancha-bhutas* [the five elements].

10–11. Combined things are proclaimed to be the [primordial] Egg [of *Brahman*] and other [things found] in it. Creation, preservation, destruction, and governance [of the world], knowledge and ignorance, fettering, freedom, pleasure, pain, the repetition [of birth and rebirth], and light exist because of Vishnu. He is the cause of all of the combination and separation.

Madhvacharya's *Tattvaviveka* (The Delineation of Reality)

1. Knowable things are regarded as twofold: independent and dependent things. Lord Vishnu, who is filled with all excellent attributes [and is] without defects, is independent.

2. Dependent things are said to be twofold: existent and nonexistent. Nonexistent things are threefold: prior, subsequent, and always [nonexistent] things.

3. Mutual nonexistence [which occurs when two things have nothing in common] does not exist separately [from *bhava* (existents) and *abhava* (nonexistents)] because it consists of existent and nonexistent

things. Existent things are traditionally held to be twofold: sentient and nonsentient.

4–5. Dependent sentients are only twofold: those who are eternally released and those who are joined to transmigration. Shri is eternally released. Those who are joined to transmigration are known to be twofold: released and not-released.

6. Those who are released are said to have hundreds of types of qualities [that increase] higher and higher, culminating with [the god] Brahma. Ramaa [that is, Shri] exceeds them many times over with all her qualities. Beyond that, Hari [that is Vishnu] has endless qualities. Those who are not released are thus threefold: the highest, middling, and the lowest.

7. Those who are able to attain liberation are the highest, those who are eternally existing [in *samsara*] are the middling, and those who are eternally fit for darkness are the lowest. Nonsentient things are re-garded as twofold by their division into eternal and noneternal things.

8. Eternal things are space, time, *shruti*, the [five] elements [namely *prithvi* (earth), *ap* (water), *tejas* (light), *vayu* (wind), and *akasha*, (ether)], the [eleven] senses [namely *ghrana* (smell), *rasana* (taste), *chakshus* (sight), *shrotra* (hearing), *tvak* (touch), *vach* (speaking), *pani* (grasping), *pada* (going), *payu* (excreting), and *upastha* (procrea-tion)], the breath, the [three] qualities [namely *sattva, rajas, tamas*], and the subtle elements [namely the five *tanmatras* [*shabda* (sound), *sparsha* (touch), *rupa* (color), *rasa* (taste), and *gandha* (smell), *buddhi, mahat, ahamkara*, etc.].

9. A modification of these would be a noneternal thing. Sentients are only eternal [and cannot be modified]. All attributes of a thing be-ginning with universals, actions, and qualities, are [identical with] its [very] form.

10. That [attribute] is twofold: those [that coexist with the substance and remain] as long as the substance [exists] and those [that change and] are perishable [even when the substance remains]. In the [at-tribute that is] perishable, there is [both a] difference and an identity [with the substance]. The [attribute that exists] as long as the sub-stance [exists] is without difference [from the substance].

11–12. The modification of the modified thing is precisely its perish-able form. Likewise [there is difference and unity in the case of] the cause and effect, the particular and the universal, the qualified and pure, and also the part and whole.

13. [The existence of] all dependent things is the will of Hari.

Madhvacharya's *Anubhashya* (Brief Commentary [on the *Brahma Sutras*])

1.1. Bowing to Narayana, who excels with all qualities, who is without defects, who is the object of knowledge, who is the intended [goal] for the teachers, the meaning of the [*Brahma*] *Sutras* [of Badarayana] is being presented.

1.2. Vishnu, the creator of all, is the origin of the sacred texts. He alone is to be known. He is the object of [the Divine] vision in accordance [with the gradation of *jivas*]. He is filled with bliss. He is inside [all and is like the] ether.

1.3. Vishnu, who is the creator, who is entirely virtuous, is alone designated by all [words such as] "light" and so on [which have] other meanings in mundane [usage].

1.4. He is all-pervading. He devours [everything] and is eternally free from being able to be perceived and other [defects]. Indeed He possesses all characteristics [such as] being immanent in the universe and in the individual selves and the like.

1.5. He is the refuge for all [beings]. He is filled with [all] virtues. He is indestructible. He exists [in] the heart-lotus [of all]. He is the illuminator of the sun and the like. He is the progenitor for creation. He is [to be known] even by the gods.

1.6. *Shudras* and others cannot know him by means of the *Vedas*. And he causes [all beings] to tremble. And he is other than the *jivas* [individual selves]. He possesses attributes, [one of which is] being the ruler. And He [is even] designated [by words that have] other [meanings in mundane usage].

1.7. Janardan alone is preeminently signified by all words. He is not manifested and is even signified by words that express actions. He, [though] one, possesses unlimited forms.

1.8. The terms "antecedent cause" and "subordinate cause," and the terms "nature" and even "void," among others, signify [Him] preeminently. Therefore, He [is understood to] have infinite virtues [when] words are etymologically derived.

2.1. The *smriti* [traditional texts] are unable to reject the qualities of Hari [simply] from their being contradictory [with other] *smriti* texts [that agree with] *shruti* [orally revealed texts], that is, the *Vedas*]. The *Vedas* are the most authoritative form of knowledge because of their eternality.

2.2. The passages such as "[the earth spoke and] the waters spoke" [from *Shatapathabrahmana* 6.1.3] and the like are not wrong because they refer to gods. Nowhere is it seen [that] nonexistent [things can be] the cause.

2.3. The terms "nonbeing," "self," originator," and so on signify *Brahman* alone [as] the cause and nowhere anything else. Hari is filled with virtuous qualities.

2.4. *Shruti* do not state anything wrong because [Hari] is independent and the cause of all. There is an incoherence in all other doctrinal systems because they are founded on false premises.

2.5. Vedic statements would not become doubtful [just] because of [any] opposition to them. All things, like *akasha* [ether] and the rest, are born from Him and dissolve because of Him.

2.6. He is without origination and dissolution. He is the maker [of all]. The *jivas* are eternally under [His] control and are [His] reflection. Hari is eternally the same in all [His] forms.

2.7. The *Mukhyaprana* [Primary Breath], the senses, and also the body arise from Him. All [else that is] under the control of the *Mukhya-prana* is eternally under the control of Vishnu.

2.8. The Lord is the Supreme Being, and therefore is free from all flaws. His attributes, declared by the *Vedas*, are entirely without contradiction.

3.1. By good deeds, [one goes] to heaven and by bad deeds, to [a place of] suffering. And by false knowledge [one is led to] darkness. Only by knowledge [does one attain] the highest goal [i.e. *moksha*].

3.2. From this, it follows that one should renounce and resort only to knowledge [of Him]. He [Vishnu] actuates all states and is without difference in all [His forms].

3.3. He is in all places and at all times. He alone is the highest Lord. There is gradation in *moksha* because of the gradation in the devotion toward Him.

3.4. [He is to be meditated on] by men as "the *atman* [the Self] [of] being, consciousness, and bliss," by the lord of the gods with many attributes in due order, and by Brahma as [possessing] all of the attributes.

3.5. [He is] honored by all the *Vedas*. And Vishnu is to be known by all [beings] to the best of their abilities. But there will be difference in knowledge [of Him] in accordance with the gradation [of *jivas*].

3.6. All the objects of aspiration will be [realized] because of the knowledge [of Him]. There is no doubt [of this]. He who knows [Him] is not at all polluted by any afflictions.

3.7. Even the happiness in liberation increases and decreases because of [the performance of] good and bad deeds. The happiness of humans and gods in *moksha* is determined by the gradation [of their natures].

4.1. Vishnu must be eternally worshiped as "*Brahman*" even in times of crisis. *Brahman* is immediately perceived through this [worship].

4.2. The experience of all the disagreeable *karmas*, other than those currently manifesting, ends as a result of knowledge [of Him]. [There is a destruction] of the other [i.e. those currently manifesting by means of their being] experienced.

4.3. Hierarchically arranged, those who are liberated enjoy the internal and external happiness until they reach Vayu.

4.4. And Vayu also enters into Vishnu [in *moksha*]. The pleasures [of *moksha*] are [linked to the] gradation [of the individual *jiva*]. Having died, humans reach *moksha*. Gods [reach *moksha*] by leaving their bodies.

4.5. The highest [*jivas*], who are comprised of the highest humans and others, having reached Vayu through the path, beginning with the Light [and then] from the world of Brahma along with Amuna [four-faced Brahma], go to Janardan.

4.6–7. Those whose bodies are [of the nature of] consciousness and bliss enjoy [liberation according to their] desire. And they are without the great power in emitting, and creating, and so on, the universe. And they are powerful according to their desire due to their excellent inherent natures. They are under no one's control and are free from increase and decrease [of the body]. They are free from suffering and other [imperfections and] delight [in] pleasure eternally [and] continually.

4.8. This collection of the meanings of the entire *Shastra* [is composed] by the sage Purnapragya [i.e. Madhvacharya]. May the great spirit, the Lord of Ramaa [Lakshmi], be pleased with this [collection].

4.9. Salutations again and again to you who is without imperfections, who is full of [auspicious] attributes, who is venerated by the praised [gods] such as Brahma and Shiva and others, and who chooses Shri [as His consort].

Madhvacharya's *Upadhikhandanam* (The Refutation of
the [Concept of] the Limiting Adjunct)

1. May [Lord] Narayana [Vishnu], whose form alone is permanent
[and filled with] countless qualities, who is free from all faults, [and]
who is the abode of Kamala [i.e. Lakshmi], be pleased. [Attributing]
ignorance to the One Who Knows All is absolutely not proper.

2. If [you] hold that [this ignorance is] possible because of the difference [caused by] the limiting adjunct, then either it is [part] of the
self-nature [of *Brahman*] or it is [caused by] ignorance. If it is intrinsic [to *Brahman*], then dualism is [established as] true.

3. When the cause [of the limiting adjunct] is [held to be] ignorance,
then [there is the fallacy of] infinite regress or reciprocal dependence.
Or [there is the] calamity of circularity. And, [moreover,] how can
difference [be caused by] the limiting adjunct?

4. In all cases previously seen, [the limiting adjunct] is the indicator of a difference [that already] exists. [It does not] create new
[differences]. When it, [the limiting adjunct, differentiates] portions from other portions, it indicates a difference [that already] exists. [The limiting adjunct] is for the consideration of those who are
stupid!

5. If not, then is there a relation of the limiting adjunct with one part
[of the space] or with the whole? [If it were the first], with one
part, then there would be an infinite regress. [If it were the second],
with the whole, then there is no difference [that is created].

6. And if one [self] is identical [with another, then] there would be
no difference [between their individual] experience of pleasure and
pain. Despite the difference [caused by] the limiting adjunct such as
the hands, feet, and so on [they are not experienced as different
from the one who experiences them].

7. There is also the case of the *yogi* who investigates the experiences of
different bodies. If [the bodies were] not [different from one another],
then how can the *yogi*'s desire to investigate the experiences [of different bodies be understood]?

8. [It may be argued that] possessing various bodies [is possible]
without the plan [to investigate]. [If so, then] how is the *yogi* [able to
choose] particular [bodies]?

9. If it were argued that [the difference in limiting adjuncts] is due to
the difference in *karma*, then there would also be a difference in the

Kanakadasa's *Krishna Ni Bhegane Bharo* (O Krishna, Please
Come Here Quickly!)

O Krishna, please come here quickly.
Please come quickly and show your face.
Beautiful tinkling bells upon your ankles,
    blue jewels [on your arms].
O blue-colored one, please come here dancing,
    with bells on your waist,
    rings on your fingers,
    and the garland of flowers called Vaijayanti around your neck,
dressed in yellow-Kashi-silk, flute in your hands,
    your beautiful body anointed with sandalwood paste,
the one who showed his mother the three worlds in his mouth,
that one who uplifts the world is [our] Udupi Shri Krishna!

NOTES

1. Sharma, *History of the Dvaita School of Vedanta and Its Literature*, 190–191.
My thanks to Professor Edwin Gerow for confirming much of what I suspected regarding the status of Krishna in Madhva Vedanta.

2. See Sarma, *An Introduction to Madhva Vedanta*, for more on the fundamentals
of the Madhva system.

3. *Matam hi jnaninametasmitam tratam cha vishnuna / tasmat satyam iti prok-
tam paramo harir eva tu iti paramashrutih / Vishnutattva(vi)nirnaya*. This passage is
found on p. 35 of Govindacharya's edition of the text and p. 122 of Prabhanjancharya's.

4. *Svatantram asvatantram cha dvividham tattvam ishyate / svatantro bhagavan
vishnur / Tattvasamkhyana* 1.

5. *Taratamyam vimuktigam / Anubhashya* 3.3.

6. *Yatha yatha 'dhikaro vishishyate evam muktavanando vishishyate / Brahma Sutra
Bhashya* 3.3.33.

7. *Namo 'mandanijanandasandrasundaramurtaye / indirapataye
nityanandabhojanadayine / Upadhikhandanam* 20.

8. *Sarvago 'tta niyanta cha drishyatvadyujjhitah sada / vishvajivantaratvadyair
lingaih sarvair yutah sa hi / Anubhashya* 1.4.

9. See Puthiadam, *Vishnu*, for more on Vishnu's attributes.

10. *Paramatmaparokshyam cha tatprasadad eva na jivashaktyeti . . . / Brahma Sutra
Bhashya* 3.2.22.

11. *Sarvesham cha harirnityam niyanta tadvashah pare / taratmyam tato gyeyam
sarvoccatvam harestatha / Mahabharatatatparyanirnaya* (hereafter MBhTN) 1.79.

12. See Sarma, *An Introduction to Madhva Vedanta*, for more on these texts.

13. In his *Anuvyakhyana*, Madhvacharya mentions the five: *eko narayano
devo . . . vasudevadirupena chaturmurtish cha sarvasha atahava panchamurtih sa prokto
'dhikaranam / Anuvyakhyana* 1.1.252. I owe this citation to Glasenapp. See Glasenapp,
Madhva's Philosophie des Vishnu-Glauben, 35 n. 3. See Pratap Kumar, *The Goddess
Lakshmi*, 24–30, for more on the vyuhas.

14. For example: *vasudevah sankarshanah pradyumno 'niruddho 'ham / Brahma Sutra Bhashya* 2.3.48.

15. *Ittham vichintya pramassa tu vasudevanama babhuva nijamuktipadapradata /* MBhTN 1.6. *Sankarshanash cha sa babhuva punassunityah sanharakaranavapustadanugyayaiva /* MBhTN 1.7 *sthitva svamurtibhiramubhirachintyashakti pradyumnarupaka imamsh charamatmane 'dat /* MBhTN 1.8. *sthityai punah sa bhagavananiruddhanama /* MBhTN 1.8.

16. See Schrader, *Introduction to the Pancaratra and the Ahirbudhnya Samhita,* 40–49.

17. Kumar, *The Goddess Lakshmi,* 30. Kumar cites Gonda here as well.

18. *Yada yada hi dharmasya glanirbhvati bharata / abhyutthanam adharmasya tada 'tmanmµ; srijamy aham / paritranaya sadhunam vinashaya cha dushkritam / dharmasamsthapanarthaya sambhavami yuge yuge / Bhagavad-gita Bhashya* 4.7–8. I am indebted to Puthiadam for these citations, Puthiadam, *Vishnu,* 141–142. This passage is directly from the *Gita.*

19. *Aham matsyah kurmo varaho narasimho vamano ramo ramah krishno buddhah kalkir aham shatadha 'ham sahasradha 'ham amito 'ham ananto 'ham... / Brahma Sutra Bhashya* 2.3.48.

20. *Evamabedhenaiva / chashabdadanantarupatvam chaike shakhinah pathanti / amatro 'nantamatrash cha dvaitasyopashamah shiva / Brahma Sutra Bhashya* 3.2.13.

21. *Svamshashchatho vibhinnamsha iti dvedham 'sha ishyate / amshino yullu samarthyam yathasthitih / Brahma Sutra Bhashya* 2.3.47.

22. Thanks to Professor Srinivasa Varakhedi.

23. My translation of the *Tattvaviveka* along with a commentary was first published in the premier issue of *Namarupa.* I am grateful to Robert Moses and Eddie Stern, its editors, for kindly granting me the permission to reproduce it here.

24. My translation of the *Upadhikhandanam* was first published in my book *An Introduction to Madhva Vedanta.* I am grateful to Ashgate Publications for kindly granting me permission to reproduce it here.

25. For more on Kanakadasa, see Jackson, *Songs of Three Great South Indian Saints.*

26. Olivelle, *Upanishads.*

27. Translation of the *Rig Veda* is from R. T. H. Griffith, *The Hymns of the Rgveda.*

REFERENCES

Primary Sources

Chalari Sheshacarya. 1985. *Tattvaprakashikavyakhyana.* In *Anubhashya of Sri Madhvacarya with the commentary Tattvaprakashikavyakhyana, of Sri Chalari Seshacarya.* Edited by R. G. Malagi. Mysore: Oriental Research Institute.

Griffith, R.T. H. 1963. *The Hymns of the Rgveda.* Varanasi: Chowkhamba Sanskrit Series Office.

Jayatirtha. 1994. *Tattvaprakashika.* Edited by Panchamukhi. Delhi: Indological Research Centre.

Madhvacharya. 1969–74. *Sarvamulagrantha.* Edited by Govindacharya Gov Bangalore: Akhila Bharata Madhwa Mahamandala.

————. 1985. *Anubhashya.* In *Anubhashya of Sri Madhvacarya with the commentary Tattvaprakashikavyakhyana, of Sri Chalari Seshacarya.* Edited by Malledevaru Mysore: Oriental Research Institute.

————. 1999. *Sarvamulagranthah.* Edited by Prabhanjanacharya. Bangalore: Sri Vyasa Madhwa Seva Pratishthana.

Narayana Panditacarya. 1996. *Sumadhvavijayah.* Edited by Prabhanjanacharya. Bangalore: Varna Graphics.

Olivelle, Patrick. 1996. *Upanishads.* Oxford: Oxford University Press.

Panditacharya, Narayana. 1989. *Sumadhvavijayah, Bhavaprakashikasametah.* Edited by Prabhanjanacarya. Bangalore: Sri Man Madhwa Siddantonnahini Sabha.

Secondary Sources

Glasenapp, Helmuth von. 1923. *Madhva's Philosophie des Vishnu-Glauben.* Bonn: Kurt Schroeder.

Govindacarya, Bannanje. 1995. *Udupi: Past and Present.* Udupi: Puthige Mutt.

Jackson, William J. 1998. *Songs of Three Great South Indian Saints.* Delhi: Oxford University Press.

Kumar, Pratap. 1997. *The Goddess Lakshmi: The Divine Consort in South Indian Vaishnava Tradition.* Atlanta: Scholars Press.

Puthiadam, I. 1985. *Vishnu: The Ever Free.* Dialogue Series no. 5. Varanasi: Arul Anandar College.

Sarma, Deepak. 2003. *An Introduction to Madhva Vedanta.* London: Ashgate.

————. 2003. "Madhvacarya's *Tattvaviveka*: A Translation and Annotated Commentary." *Namarupa* 1, 84–89.

Schrader, F. Otto. 1916. *Introduction to the Pañcaratra and the Ahirbudhnya Samhita.* Madras: Adyar Library.

Sharma, B. N. K. 1981. *History of the Dvaita School of Vedanta and Its Literature.* Delhi: Motilal Banarsidass.

16

The Six *Sandarbhas* of Jiva Gosvami

Satyanarayana Dasa

Background of the Chaitanya Tradition

Among the various schools of Vedanta, the school of Gaudiya Vaishnavism is the most recently established. It was founded by Chaitanya Mahaprabhu, who was born in Navadvipa, Bengal, in 1486 c.e. In his short span of life, lasting about forty-eight years, he initiated one of India's most vigorous *bhakti* movements. Thus he was a major contributor to the flood of *bhakti* that swept across the plains of northern India, in the period that has sometimes been compared to the Renaissance period in Europe. Although *bhakti* was preached by many medieval saints, such as Guru Nanak, Kabir, Surdas, and Mirabai, the followers of Chaitanya were especially noteworthy in producing extensive literature delineating the theology of *bhakti*.

With some exceptions, the *bhakti* that flourished in this period was emotional in nature and was typically manifested in devotional chanting of the names of God, spiritual egalitarianism, social renunciation, and a rejection of brahminical Sanskritic hegemony. Certain of Chaitanya's disciples, however, had been thoroughly schooled in the various branches of Indian philosophy and Sanskrit letters, and thus brought significant erudition to articulating a theology of *bhakti*. Therefore, Chaitanya's school evolved as a distinct and well-knit philosophical system with a unique contribution to the fields of epistemology, metaphysics, religion, and aesthetics. The original writings were in Sanskrit and Bengali. Later, much poetry was also composed in Hindi. This strong undercurrent of philosophy and theological writing was the unique feature of the stream of *bhakti* unleashed by Chaitanya.

Although social reform was not Chaitanya's primary interest, he fought against and resolved many of the social ills of his time. His life and teachings had a great impact in the north of the subcontinent. He popularized congregational chanting and met and interacted with many great teachers of his time, including Vallabhacharya, the founder of the Pushtimarga school.

During the period of Chaitanya's birth, Navadvipa was a major center of learning in India. Navadvipa produced some of the greatest logicians of the time, such as Raghunatha Shiromani, Mathura Natha, Jagadish, and Gadadhar Bhattacharya, who in turn produced voluminous literature in *navya-nyaya*, the "new logic," including *Didhiti* and *Rahasya*.[1] Chaitanya himself was a great scholar of *navya-nyaya* and was popularly known as *pandit*, or "learned." Even as a boy of sixteen, he was running a school teaching hundreds of students. According to his biographers, some of them contemporaries, he demonstrated his acumen in scholarship while debating with some of the greatest scholars of India, such as Keshava Kashmiri.

After his father's demise, Chaitanya's life took a turn. He gave up his pursuit of scholarship and became absorbed in devotion to Krishna, starting the *sankirtana* movement, whose followers practiced congregational singing of the names of Krishna. During these *kirtanas* he would go into rapturous states, losing all external consciousness. Such devotional exhibitions were not in vogue in the contemporary Hindu society, and the orthodox brahmins opposed Chaitanya's new mode of religion. As a consequence, Chaitanya took to ascetic life as people had respect for ascetics and not oppose their actions. For a few years he traveled in the southern states of India, and he finally settled down in Puri in Orissa. He had many followers, and his *sankirtana* movement influenced the lives of millions of people in India.

Although a scholar himself, Chaitanya left behind no writings on philosophical or theological aspects of his school except eight verses known as the *Shikshashtaka*. He entrusted the formulation of his doctrine to two scholarly brothers named Rupa and Sanatana, later famous as two of the Six Gosvamis of Vrindavan. Chaitanya personally instructed them on the subtle principles of philosophy and religion related to his new school, and he asked them to compose literature and teach. At the behest of Chaitanya, Rupa and Sanatana made their base at Vrindavan, the playground of Krishna.

These two brothers wrote many books expounding the principles of love for Krishna, as imbibed from Chaitanya. They also excavated many of the lost places of pilgrimage associated with Krishna's pastimes and established several temples that formed the nucleus for the development of Vrindavan, which has since become one of the most vibrant holy places in North India.

Later they were joined by some other followers of Chaitanya, including Jiva Gosvami, their nephew. Together they created the core literature of the school of Chaitanya.

Jiva Gosvami, the Author of the *Six Sandarbhas*

Jiva Gosvami was the youngest of the Gosvamis and the most prolific writer. Out of the numerous books he compiled, the six *Sandarbhas* occupy a special position and deserve the credit of giving final shape to the philosophy of the school of Chaitanya. These *Sandarbhas* are accepted by the school as the authoritative and definitive canon of Chaitanya's theology and philosophy. These six books are called *Tattva, Bhagavat, Paramatma, Krishna, Bhakti,* and *Priti.* According to the author himself, the *Sandarbhas* are an analysis of the *Bhagavata Purana,*[2] delineating the true message of the book. Chaitanya considered the *Bhagavata Purana* (also known simply as the *Bhagavata*) to be the natural commentary on the *Vedanta Sutras* by the author of the *Sutras.* He therefore held the *Bhagavata* to be the cream of Vedic literature and made it the source for his philosophy and theology.

In conformity with this understanding, Jiva compiled the *Sandarbhas* elucidating the entire philosophy and theology in a systematic form. According to Jiva, the *Bhagavata Purana,* which gives the essence of the *Vedas,* deals with three subjects: *sambandha, abhidheya,* and *prayojana. Sambandha,* "relation," means the relation of the Absolute Reality with its *shaktis,* "energies," in the form of *jivas,* "living beings" (the word *jiva* here should not to be confused with Jiva Gosvami, the author, whose name is shown with an upper-case *J*), and *prakriti,* "matter" (the relationship between these ontological categories is the primary subject matter of all Vedantic hermeneutics). *Abhidheya,* "to be executed," refers to the prescribed process by which this relation can be actualized. And *prayojana,* "purpose," is the ultimate goal, which is to be acquired by the *jiva* when his relation matures through execution of the prescribed process. The first four *Sandarbhas* are an exposition of the principles of *sambandha,* the fifth of *abhidheya,* and the last of *prayojana.*

Jiva Gosvami informs his readers that in composing the *Sandarbhas* he has taken help from the treatises of previous Vaishnavas, such as Madhvacharya and Ramanujacharya. He had the advantage of the whole heritage of Vaishnava philosophical thought as expressed in these earlier schools. He also accepts the explanations of Shridhara Svami, the renowned *Bhagavata* commentator, when they are not contrary to Vaishnava philosophy, and cites the *Upanishads,* the *Puranas,* and the *Samhitas.* He draws freely from all these sources in his writings, and does not put forth any important proposition without supporting it with such scriptural reference. However, his thought is not just a repetition of established principles but a further development of them.

The Content of the *Six Sandarbhas*

The Tattva Sandarbha

Tattva means the essence, or the reality. The *Tattva Sandarbha* defines the Absolute Reality. The first part of the book deals with epistemology and the second with ontology. Ontology is further elucidated in the next three books.

In the part dealing with epistemology, Jiva says that the ordinary person is naturally liable to four kinds of defects: delusion, error, the tendency to deceive, and imperfection of the senses. Therefore, direct perception, inference, and similar knowledge-acquiring methods are inadequate for leading one to perfect knowledge. These methodologies are particularly ineffective in comprehending metaphysical reality. In line with most traditional commentators, he concludes that *shabda*, or revealed scriptural knowledge, is the definitive *pramana*, or means of valid knowledge. He does not reject other means but places them as subsidiary to *shabda*, considering them inadequate as independent means of acquiring true knowledge of the Absolute.

Jiva supports his conclusion on the authority of *Vedanta Sutra*. *Shabda* primarily refers to the *Vedas*, but in the present age, the *Vedas* are difficult to understand. The complete body of the *Vedas* is unavailable, and their commentators are not in agreement as to their meaning. Jiva Gosvami argues that the *Itihasas* and *Puranas* are regarded as the fifth *Veda*, and as such, can rightly determine the sense of the *Vedas*. Among them, the *Bhagavata Purana* is accepted as supreme by the Chaitanya school on the grounds that it is Vyasa's own commentary on the brief and cryptic *Vedanta Sutras*, which in turn claims to be an elucidation of the Upanishadic tradition of the *Vedas*. The *Bhagavata Purana* (literally: "history of Bhagavan, or Krishna") has been accepted as authority by previous *acharyas* (teachers), such as Madhvacharya, Shridhara Svami, Vallabha, Chitsukha, and so on. Jiva gives a list of about nine commentaries and three essays on the *Bhagavata* that were available to him, to show its popularity. The categorical acceptance of the *Bhagavata* is one of the fundamental postulates of the Chaitanya school.

Having established epistemology by demonstrating the superiority of the *Bhagavata Purana* as the topmost and flawless *pramana*, Jiva proceeds to elucidate Gaudiya ontology by an analysis of the book.[3] He explains that *sambandha* relates to Krishna, *abhidheya* is devotion to Krishna, and *prayojana* is *priti*, or love for Krishna. To highlight this, he analyzes the statements from the *Bhagavata Purana* that relate the trance of Vyasa, which formed the core of the *Bhagavata Purana*. Devotion necessitates the existence of a worshipable deity, which is Krishna, the worshiper, and the process of worship. The attainment of divine love is the highest bliss, higher even than the bliss of attaining *Brahman*. For this reason, the *Bhagavata* itself describes how Shuka, an adept in the monistic realization of *Brahman* and eventual speaker of the *Bhagavata*, gave up his attraction for the formless conception of *Brahman* and studied the *Bhagavata* from his father, Vyasa. He thus became devoted to the personal form of Krishna, who is considered by the Chaitanya school to be *para-Brahman*, or the highest manifestation of *Brahman*.

Jiva then argues that the essential truths that Vyasa realized in his trance unite the various schools of Indian philosophy. He points to the *Bhagavata* 1.2.11, which forms the central theme of the book: "The knowers of the Absolute Reality call that Reality *advaya-jnana*, 'nondual consciousness,' which is designated as *Brahman*, Paramatma or Bhagavan." That one Absolute Reality is perceived by the *advaitins* as all-pervasive *Brahman*, by the yogis as Paramatma, the Supreme Soul situated within the heart of all living beings, and by the Vaishnavas as Bhagavan, the Supreme Lord, endowed with transcendent form, features, and qualities. Thus for Jiva there is no contradiction among the varying schools. It is only a matter of the degree of completeness of perception of the one Absolute Truth.

This verse succinctly states what the reality or *tattva* propounded by the *Bhagavata* is. The rest of the *Tattva Sandarbha* is an elaboration of the nondual consciousness stated in the foregoing verse. Jiva Gosvami argues that the nondual consciousness is not limited to the qualityless, formless reality of the monists. Rather, it refers to that Absolute Reality that can accommodate all three aspects of *Brahman*, Paramatma, and Bhagavan. The thrust of Jiva's argument is to establish Bhagavan as the most complete aspect of the Absolute upon which the other two aspects are based. This, he demonstrates, is the ultimate principle described in the *Bhagavata*. Next Jiva analyzes the ten topics discussed in the *Bhagavata* and shows that Krishna is the chief subject of the text. The following three *Sandarbhas* are devoted to a more detailed exposition of *Brahman*, Paramatma, and Bhagavan.

The Bhagavat Sandarbha

This *Sandarbha* describes the concept of Bhagavan alluded to in *Bhagavata* 1.2.11. Jiva explains that although the Absolute Reality is one and indivisible (nondual), it has three aspects according to the capacity or qualification of the individual person aspiring for realization of the Absolute, as noted earlier. The one Absolute Reality, therefore, is perceived as *Brahman*, Paramatma, and Bhagavan by three different classes of spiritual aspirants.

Bhagavan refers to the feature of the Absolute as the most perfect person who possesses multifarious potencies and qualities. These qualities and potencies remain *avivikta*, or indistinct, in *Brahman*. *Brahman* is a substantive object in which the distinctions between the object itself (*visheshya*), its qualifying attributes (*visheshana*), and the same object when qualified (*vishishta*) by those attributes remain undifferentiated, whereas Bhagavan is a differentiated object qualified by unlimited manifest potencies and attributes (*vishishta shakti-shaktimat*).[4] Therefore, Jiva describes *Brahman* as *asamyag avirbhava*, an incomplete manifestation of the Absolute. *Brahman* is included in Bhagavan. In the *Bhagavad Gita* (14.27), Krishna states that He is the *pratishtha* or "substratum" of *Brahman*. *Brahman* is the object of realization of the *jnana-yogis* and Bhagavan of the *bhakti-yogis*.

Bhagavan's attributes and potencies eternally reside in him in the relation known as *samavaya-sambandha* (perpetual coinherence). This refers to the inseparable relation that exists between a substance and its qualities. These attributes and potencies form the intrinsic nature of Bhagavan. According to the *Vishnu Purana*, Bhagavan refers to a person who possesses six virtues to the highest possible limit: controlling power (*aishvarya*), potency (*virya*), fame (*yasha*), prosperity (*shri*), knowledge (*jnana*), and renunciation (*vairagya*). The attributes of the Supreme Lord are not material but transcendental.

Bhagavan has divine potency that is inconceivable to the human mind and that enables him to accomplish acts that are impossible for any other being. This potency is natural to the Lord and constitutes His very essence. The relation between Bhagavan and His potency is one of inconceivable difference in non-difference, known as *achintya-bhedabheda*.[5] It is in recognition of the nature of this relation that Chaitanya's philosophy is called *Achintya bhedaabheda-vada*.

The potency of Bhagavan has many divisions, among which three are primary: *antaranga-shakti* (internal), also known as *svarupa-shakti*, or the potency that constitutes the Lord's form, abode, associates, and the activities of the spiritual realm; *tatastha* (marginal), referring to the living beings who belong neither to the spiritual nor to the material energies but can be influenced by either; and *bahiranga* (external), or the potency that functions in the material world. *Bhagavat Sandarbha* deals primarily with the internal potency of Bhagavan, and *Paramatma Sandarbha* deals with the other two potencies.

The external potency is sheltered in Bhagavan, but it does not influence him. It is also called *maya*, but it is not the same as the *maya* of Shankara's *advaita-vada*. The marginal potency refers to the living beings who remain either under the influence of the internal or the external potency. The potency of *maya* is directly controlled by an expansion of Bhagavan called Paramatma, or the Supreme Soul. The living entity can transcend the influence of the external potency by taking shelter of Bhagavan.

Next, Jiva Gosvami explains an aspect of the *antaranga-shakti*—namely, the intrinsic nature of the body of Bhagavan. His body is beyond the qualities of matter; it is eternal and is nondifferent from His own self. It does not undergo any transformations like material objects. Although situated in one place, it is all-pervading. He says that such a thing is possible by the inconceivable potency of Bhagavan. As mentioned earlier, His inconceivable potency can make possible even the impossible. Among various attributes of Bhagavan, one unique feature is the ability to possess contradictory qualities. Therefore His body can be all-pervasive and yet situated in one place. This was depicted in the pastime of Krishna when His mother, Yashoda, tried to bind him with numerous ropes. No matter how many ropes she strung together, they always ended up two fingers short of the circumference of His belly.

Jiva then describes another aspect of the *antaranga-shakti*, the abode of Bhagavan, known as Vaikuntha. He says it is beyond the phenomenal world, just like Bhagavan himself. The material qualities cannot touch it, and the residents of Vaikuntha never fall down to the temporal realm. The bliss experienced in Vaikuntha is superior even to the experience of the formless monistic *Brahman*. Vaikuntha is eternal, beyond time or material actions, and can be attained only through devotion to Bhagavan. This means that one cannot reach it by any material means. But it can manifest in this world, just as the *avataras* (literally descents), or "incarnations," of Bhagavan do. Whenever Bhagavan descends to the temporal world, His abode also becomes manifest here.

After establishing the spiritual nature of Vaikuntha, Jiva describes its denizens. They are on a par with Bhagavan, being manifestations of His internal energy, and their attributes are similar to His. The bliss enjoyed by the Lord's associates through worshiping him is supreme, and thus superior even to the bliss of merging in monistic *Brahman*. Therefore, the residents of Vaikuntha desire only loving service to Bhagavan.

The rest of the discussion is devoted to showing the distinction between *Brahman* and Bhagavan. The Ultimate Reality is one, but by Bhagavan's internal power of differentiation, known as *vishesha*, there is distinction between *Brahman* and Bhagavan. Bhagavan is the complete manifestation of the Absolute. The complete vision of the Absolute can be acquired only through *bhakti*. Jiva analyzes the four seed-verses of the *Bhagavata* and shows that their purport is *prema-bhakti*, or devotion in divine love. Thus, for Jiva, the *Bhagavata Purana* is the synthesis of all Vedic literature and therefore the cream of all scriptures.

The Paramatma Sandarbha

The *Paramatma Sandarbha* deals with Paramatma, a partial manifestation of Bhagavan related chiefly to the *bahiranga* (external) and *tatastha* (intermediate) potencies. Paramatma is immanent in the *jiva* (the living being) as well as in *prakriti*, or matter. He exists in a four-handed form as the witness to all activities of living beings. His size varies according to the size of the body. He exists within the smallest manifestations of matter. The living being is part of the *jiva-shakti* of Paramatma. This potency is called *tatastha*, or "situated on the margin," because it belongs neither to *svarupa-shakti* nor to *maya-shakti* (just as the shoreline, *tata*, is neither sea nor land).

with reference to numerous texts, as well as by pointing to the beatific visions of many great sages and devotees. This form existed even before Krishna's manifest pastimes on earth at the end of Dvapara Yuga. Krishna carries a flute in his hand and is ever youthful. He is most charming and beautiful and is therefore called Krishna, or all-attractive.

Jiva then deals with the abode of Krishna, called Vrindavan or Goloka, which he holds to be the highest of all spiritual planets. Krishna always resides there along with His associates. Goloka is manifest in three abodes, called Dvaraka, Mathura, and Gokula, according to the difference in his *lilas* (pastimes) and *parikaras* (associates).

Next Jiva describes the associates of Krishna in these three abodes. He shows that Krishna's activities are eternal and beyond time, although they appear to be transient. Krishna's pastimes are eternally going on in these three places. When they are visible to the eyes of mortals, they are called *prakata*, or manifest pastimes. According to Jiva, the pastimes can be seen even today by some devotees who are spiritually qualified.

Jiva throws light on the relation between Krishna and the *gopis*, the cowherd girls of Vrindavan. He says that the spiritual import of their seemingly erotic relation is pure devotion. Their pastimes in the *Bhagavata* have been depicted according to the principles of *rasa-shastra*.[9] The *gopis* are Krishna's eternal beloveds and are manifestations of His *svarupa-shakti*, or internal spiritual potency. They are superior to His queens in Dvaraka. Among the *gopis*, Radha is chief. She is the personification of *hladini-shakti*, or the bliss potency of Krishna, which is an aspect of *svarupa-shakti*. She alone manifests the stage of *mahabhava*, or supreme love for Krishna. Jiva concludes *Krishna Sandarbha* by interpreting the first verse of the *Bhagavata* to show how it can be applied to Radha.

The Bhakti Sandarbha

The *Bhakti Sandarbha* delineates the *abhidheya-tattva*, or the prescribed process for attaining the ultimate goal of life. It shows how *bhakti*, devotion, is the fundamental process given in the *Bhagavata* for attaining Krishna-*prema*, or love for Krishna. There are two types of living beings: those who are naturally devoted to Bhagavan and those who are averse to him. *Bhakti* is the *abhidheya* for the second class of living beings to remove their aversion. The influence of *maya*, or the deluding potency, can be counteracted only by *bhakti*, because it is the Lord's *svarupa-shakti*. True knowledge of Bhagavan is bestowed through *bhakti*. *Bhakti* is not just a means but also the end, because the bliss of service to Bhagavan is so fulfilling that a devotee continues to serve the Lord even after attaining liberation from this world. Therefore, according to the *Bhagavata*, *bhakti* is the *para-dharma*, or highest duty.

According to Jiva, *bhakti* is superior to the paths of *yoga*, *karma*, and *jnana*, which lead to *Brahman* or Paramatma realization. It is the summum bonum and surpasses all *dharma*, or duty. It is causeless and cannot be obstructed. *Jnana* and *vairagya* (detachment) follow automatically for a devotee. Without *bhakti*, the paths of *jnana*, *karma*, and *yoga* cannot yield their respective results. Jiva does not reject any of these paths, but he proceeds to show their incompleteness and thus their inferiority to *bhakti*. *Bhakti* is capable of bestowing the results derived from all other paths, if a devotee so desires.

Jiva does not accept the dedication of the fruits of *karma* as *bhakti* (as outlined in the *Gita*). He says that *bhakti* is of two types: mixed and pure. The first one refers to *bhakti* mixed with *karma*, *jnana*, or *yoga*. A mixture means desiring something other than the pleasure of the Lord. Pure *bhakti* purges the mind of all motives, removes the bondage of *maya*, and grants direct vision of Bhagavan. In the eleventh canto of the *Bhagavata* (11.14.9), Krishna tells Uddhava that people whose discrimination is covered by *maya* speak of many different paths, such as *karma* and *jnana*, as the most effective means to attain their goals, according to their previous *karma* and personal inclinations. Therefore, worship of Bhagavan is supreme. However, other deities, such as Brahma and Shiva, should not be disrespected. If one is to worship them, one should regard them as Vaishnavas or as dwelling places of Bhagavan.

Jiva then demonstrates that *bhakti* is the central theme of the *Bhagavata*. It can be executed at all times, in all places, by all species of life, and under all conditions. It is applicable to those who desire liberation as well as those who have achieved liberation. The prescriptions to follow other processes are ultimately to make one inclined toward *bhakti*. *Bhakti* alone dispels the aversion to Bhagavan.

The characteristics of *bhakti* are outlined as follows: (1) it cleanses sins, (2) it removes desires for sinful acts, (3) it dispels nescience, (4) it awards *jnana* and *vairagya*, (5) it is beyond the *gunas*, or constituent qualities of *prakriti*, material nature, (6) it is supreme bliss, (7) it belongs to the internal potency, (8) it bestows attachment to Bhagavan, and (9) it attracts Bhagavan himself. *Bhakti* descends by the grace of a devotee. Bhagavan's grace cannot descend directly to a living being because the Lord, being completely beyond the contact of material influences, cannot empathize with the sorrow of the living being. The first cause of *bhakti* is the grace of the Lord because He invests the power of compassion in His devotees. But direct association with devotees is the most important medium through which this divine grace is communicated.

According to the *Garuda Purana* (*Purva-khanda* 231.3), the derivative meaning of the word *bhakti* is "complete servitude." This is the essential characteristic of *bhakti*. This includes complete submission of the body, mind, and words. Jiva describes various divisions of *bhakti*. Then he proceeds to say that *bhakti* is either *vaidhi* or *raganuga*. *Vaidhi* is inspired by the injunctions of scripture, whereas *raganuga* is prompted by natural inclination, regardless of any injunction. *Raganuga* is spontaneous and follows the natural course of emotions. Jiva then describes eleven steps in *vaidhi-bhakti*.

The Special Contribution of the *Sandarbhas* to Vaishnava Thought

Although *bhakti* has been treated by all Vaishnava teachers as the only means of emancipation, their views differ as to the true nature of devotion. Ramanujacharya defines devotion as continuous recollection of God.[10] For him, love is a kind of knowledge,[11] and *bhakti* is of two types, called *sadhana* (practice) and *phala* (the fruit), attainable through the performance of religious duties and the grace of God, respectively.[12] Madhvacharya considers devotion to be a strong emotion of love accompanied by knowledge of the majesty of God.[13] Nimbarkacharya defines devotion as a special kind of love having the stages of *sadhana* and *phala*.[14] Vallabhacharya also makes two divisions of *bhakti*, called *maryada* and *pushti*, which are predominated by the knowledge of the Lord's majestic feature and love, respectively.[15]

Shri Jiva Gosvami, basing his exposition on the *Bhagavata Purana*, presents a new concept of devotion. According to him, pure devotion is not a mere emotion of love but is the very essence of God's internal potency of bliss, which is supreme among the potencies of God. By His own grace, God grants this energy to a particular living being. It manifests in the form of loving service toward God with complete submission of the body, mind, and speech.[16] It is not mixed with the sense of awe that is evoked by awareness of the Lord's majesty. It is causeless and is absolutely devoid of any personal motive. There is nothing that can impede this spiritual potency of love, since there is no pleasure more consuming than loving service and no misery more acute than abandonment of such service.

Without devotion, the paths of *jnana* and *karma* are completely futile. But devotion can yield the desired results of all other paths. Devotion is supremely independent and cannot be subjugated by *maya*, the external potency of God. While other Vaishnava teachers have stated that liberation is attained through devotion, Shri Jiva stresses that a devotee is not interested in the five types of liberation. He is concerned only with loving service. Jiva has analyzed *bhakti* in a very detailed manner. His explanation of the abode of Krishna, *bhakti* as *rasa*, *priti* as the ultimate end of human life, elaborate taxonomies of *bhakti*, *bhakti* as the internal potency of God, Krishna as the original form of the Absolute, the *Bhagavata* as the supreme authority, the *gopis* as the topmost devotees, and Radha as chief among the *gopis* are new additions to Vaishnava philosophy and theology.

Therefore, the Chaitanya school is a significant addition to mainstream Indian philosophy. Its contribution in the field of epistemology, metaphysics, religion, and ethics is unique, and it offers a vast literature for study.

It is well known that what has been termed the Hindu Renaissance flourished across the north of the subcontinent in the sixteenth century. While the movement was basically emotional in nature, the erudite scholasticism of Chaitanya's followers, and Jiva in particular, are noteworthy in having produced analytical literature to articulate the theology of *bhakti* and situate it within the established traditions of Indian philosophy.

Although in the past the Chaitanya school has not received the attention it deserves in terms of its unique contribution to Indian philosophy and theology, scholars have now begun to realize its importance. The *Sandarbhas* of Jiva Gosvami are considered by the school to be the most important exposition of its theology.

Selections from the *Tattva, Bhagavat,* and *Bhakti Sandarbhas*

The *Tattva-sandarbha*

8. The aspect of Shri Krishna as pure consciousness, without any manifest characteristics, is called *Brahman* in some portions of the *Vedas*. In another aspect he exists as the Purusha, who controls the external potency, *maya*, by his many plenary portions. In yet another of his forms, he is present as Narayana in the transcendent realm [Vaikuntha]. May that Shri Krishna, the original source of all manifestations of Godhead, bestow love for himself on those who worship his lotus feet in this world.

9. Four topics were implied in the previous verse: Shri Krishna as the subject to be ascertained [*vishaya*]; the connection [*sambandha*] between him, as that which is signified [*vachya*]; in the text, and the signifier, or the actual words of the text that describe him; service to him as the recommended process of attainment [*abhidheya* or *vidheya*]; and pure love for him as the ultimate goal [*prayojana*]. Now to understand these we should first determine a valid means of evidence.

Human beings are bound to have four defects: they are subject to delusion, they make mistakes, they tend to cheat, and they have imperfect senses. Furthermore, empirical methods of acquiring knowledge are unable to approach the inconceivable spiritual reality. Thus direct perception, inference, and other such methods of ascertainment are deficient.

10. Consequently, these empirical methods are not valid means of evidence. For we who desire to know that which is beyond everything, which is the support of all, which is fully inconceivable and wondrous in nature, the *Vedas* are the only suitable means of knowledge. This is because the *Vedas* exist without beginning, they have been passed down in disciplic succession, they are the source of

all material and spiritual knowledge, and they are full of transcendental words.

11. The following scriptural statements confirm this conclusion:

"Logic cannot provide conclusive proof." (*Brahma-sutra* 2.1.11)

"One should not use logic to ascertain that which is inconceivable." (*Mahabharata, Bhishma-parva* 5.22)

"Scriptures are the source of knowledge of the Absolute Truth." (*Brahma-sutra1.1.3*)

"But this has to be accepted on the authority of the *Vedas*, because they are the source of knowledge of the Absolute Truth." (*Brahma-sutra* 2.1.27)

"O Lord, your Veda is the supreme guide for the forefathers, the *devas*, and human beings. By it they can understand the truth that lies beyond the scope of the mind and senses, as well as the ultimate goal of life and the means to attain it." (*Bhagavata* 11.20.4)

12.1. Because at present it is difficult to study the *Vedas* in their entirety, because it is difficult to understand their meaning, and because the great thinkers who have commented on the *Vedas* interpret them in contradictory ways, we should therefore study only the *Itihasas* and *Puranas*, since they are Vedic in nature and are conclusive in determining the meaning of the *Vedas*. Moreover, with the help of the *Itihasas* and *Puranas* we can infer the meaning of the unavailable portions of the *Vedas*. Thus, at present only the *Itihasas* and *Puranas* are appropriate sources of valid knowledge.

12.2. This is why the *Mahabharata* (*Adi-parva* 1.269) and *Manu-samhita* state: "One should complement one's understanding of the *Vedas* with the help of the *Itihasas* and *Puranas*." And elsewhere it is stated: "The *Puranas* are called by that name because they complete." It is not possible to "complete" or explain the meaning of the *Vedas* with something that is not Vedic in nature, just as it is improper to finish an incomplete gold bracelet with lead.

12.3. But, one might object, if the literature we know as *Itihasas* and *Puranas* are actually part of the *Vedas*, there must exist other literatures that go by the same name but are not part of the *Vedas*; otherwise the literature we call *Itihasas* and *Puranas* cannot be accepted as nondifferent from the *Vedas*.

To this we reply that the *Itihasas* and *Puranas* are nondifferent from the *Vedas*, inasmuch as both kinds of literature have no human author and present the same object of knowledge. Nonetheless, there is some difference between them with regard to intonation and word order.

12.4. The *Madhyandina-shruti* (*Brihad-aranyaka Upanishad* 2.4.10) implies the oneness of the *Itihasas* and *Puranas* with the *Rig* and other *Vedas* in terms of the *apaurusheya* nature all these works share: "My dear Maitreyi, the *Rig, Yajur, Sama,* and *Atharva Vedas,* as well as the *Itihasas* and *Puranas,* all appear from the breathing of the Supreme Being."

13.1. Therefore, the *Prabhasa-khanda* of the *Skanda Purana* (2.3.5) states: "Long ago, Brahma, the grandfather of the demigods, performed severe penances, and as a result the *Vedas* appeared along with their six supplements and their *pada* and *krama* texts. Then the entire *Purana* emanated from his mouth. Composed of eternal sound and consisting of one billion verses, it is the unchanging, sacred embodiment of all scriptures. Please hear the various divisions of this *Purana,* of which *Brahma Purana* is the first."

13.2. The figure one billion cited above refers to the number of verses existing in Brahma's domain. *Shrimad-Bhagavata's* third canto gives a similar description in the passage starting with the words *rig-yajuh-samatharvakhyan vedan purvadibhir mukhaih*: "From his four mouths, beginning from the one facing east, Brahma, manifested the four *Vedas*—*Rig, Yajur, Sama,* and *Atharva*—respectively" (*Shrimad-Bhagavata* 3.12.37). In this passage we find the statement "Then the all-seeing Lord Brahma created the fifth *Veda*—the *Puranas* and the *Itihasas*—from all his mouths" (*Shrimad-Bhagavata* 3.12.39). Here the word *Veda* is used specifically in reference to the *Itihasas* and *Puranas.*

13.3. And elsewhere it is said: "The *Puranas* are the fifth *Veda*"; "The *Itihasas* and *Puranas* are called the fifth *Veda*" (*Shrimad-Bhagavata* 1.4.20); and "He taught the *Vedas* along with the fifth of their number, the *Mahabharata*" (*Mahabharata, Adi-parva* 63.89).

If the *Itihasas* and *Puranas* were not Vedic, it would have been inappropriate for the preceding verses to include them as the fifth *Veda,* since normally one counts together only objects of the same category.

13.4. Also, the *Bhavishya Purana* states: "The fifth *Veda,* written by Shri Krishna Dvaipayana Vyasa, is called the *Mahabharata.*"

Another reference is found in the *Chandogya Upanishad* of the Kauthumiya school of the *Sama Veda*: "Venerable Sir, I have studied the *Rig, Yajur, Sama,* and *Atharva Vedas,* and also the *Itihasas* and *Puranas,* which are the fifth *Veda*" (*Kauthumiya, Chandogya Upanishad* 7.1.2).

13.5. This refutes the frequently raised objection that the *Itihasas* and *Puranas,* said in the *Brihad-aranyaka Upanishad* to emanate from the breathing of the Supreme Being, are included in the four *Vedas* and therefore have no separate existence. The same is stated in the words "*Brahma Purana* is the first of the *Puranas* that appeared from the mouth of Brahma [after the emanation of the four *Vedas*]" (cited above in 13.1 from the *Skanda Purana*].

14.1. In the *Vayu Purana* (60.16–18, 21–22) Suta Gosvami explains why the *Itihasas* and *Puranas* are considered the fifth *Veda*: "Shrila Vyasadeva, the almighty Supreme Lord, accepted me [Suta Gosvami] as the authorized speaker of the *Itihasas* and *Puranas*. In the beginning there was only one *Veda*, the *Yajur Veda*, which Shrila Vyasa divided into four parts. These gave rise to the four activities called *chatur-hotra*, by means of which Shrila Vyasa arranged for the performance of sacrifice.

"The *adhvaryu* priests carry out their responsibilities with *Yajur-mantras*, the *hota* priests with *Rig-mantras*, the *udgata* priests with *Sama-mantras*, and the *brahma* priests with *Atharva-mantras*."

Suta Gosvami further states: "O best of the twice-born, thereafter Shrila Vyasa, who best knows the meaning of the *Puranas*, compiled them and the *Itihasas* by combining various *Akhyanas* [stories], *upakhyanas* [subordinate tales], and *gathas* [songs]. Whatever remained after Vyasa divided the *Vedas* into four parts was also the *Yajur Veda*. This is the conclusion of the scriptures."

14.2. The *Puranas* are also used in the formal study of the *Vedas* called *brahma-yagya*: *yad brahmananitihasa-puranani*, "The *Itihasas* and *Puranas* are *Vedas*" (*Taittiriya Aranyaka* 2.9). Consequently, the *Itihasas* and *Puranas* cannot be non-Vedic, otherwise they would not be used in this way in the *brahma-yagya*.

Therefore, in the *Matsya Purana* (53.8–9) the Supreme Lord says: "O best of the twice-born, foreseeing that the *Purana* will gradually be neglected, in every age I assume the form of Vyasa and abridge it." In other words, Shrila Vyasa condenses the already existing *Purana* so that people can easily comprehend it.

14.3. The *Matsya Purana* (53.9–11) also states: "The *Purana* consisting of four hundred thousand verses is divided into eighteen parts, then it is passed on by oral recitation in every dvapara-yuga here on earth. Even today the original *Purana* of one billion verses exists in the planets of the demigods. The essential meaning of that *Purana* is contained in the abridged version of four hundred thousand verses."

14.4. Suta's statement that "whatever remained after Vyasa had divided the *Vedas* into four parts was also the *Yajur Veda*" (cited in 14.1) indicates that the essence of the original *Purana*, which was the remaining portion of the *Yajur Veda*, formed the abridged version of four hundred thousand verses in the world of mortals. It is not a different composition.

15.1. Similarly, the *Vayaviya-samhita* of the *Shiva Purana* indicates the Vedic nature of the *Puranas* by discussing their appearance along with the *Vedas*:

"The Lord abridged the four *Vedas* and then divided them [*vyasta*] into four. Therefore he became known as Veda-Vyasa. He also summarized into four hundred thousand verses the *Purana*, which still comprises one billion verses in the higher planets" (*Shiva Purana* 7.1.1.37–38).

Here the word *sankshiptam* [condensed] implies "condensed by him."

15.2. The name of a *Purana*—*Skanda, Agni,* and so on—refers to its original speaker, as with the *Katha Upanishad*, which was promulgated by the sage Katha. Otherwise the name refers to the person who arranged the *Purana*'s contents. The reason the *Puranas* are occasionally described as impermanent is that they are sometimes manifest and sometimes not.

In this way by the arguments and evidence provided in *anucchedas* 13, 14, and 15.1–2, the Vedic nature of the *Itihasas* and *Puranas* is established.

15.3. Yet Suta Gosvami [Suta, here, does not refer to the *suta* caste, but refers to a particular person, the first speaker of the Puranas] and others (who are not twice-born) are qualified to recite the *Puranas* in the same way that every person is qualified to chant the holy name of Shri Krishna, the transcendental fruit of the creeper of all the *Vedas*. As stated in the *Prabhasa-khanda* of the *Skanda Purana*:

"O best of the Bhrigu dynasty, the holy name of Krishna is the sweetest of the sweet and the most auspicious of the auspicious. It is the transcendental fruit of the creeper of the entire *Vedas* and is the embodiment of pure spiritual consciousness. If anyone chants the name of Krishna even once, whether with faith or with contempt, the holy name delivers him."

15.4. The *Vishnu Dharma Purana* states:

"A person who chants the two syllables *ha-ri* has already completed the study of the *Rig, Yajur, Sama,* and *Atharva Vedas*."

And the *Vishnu Purana* affirms that the *Puranas* and *Itihasas* establish the meaning of the *Vedas*:

"On the pretext of writing the *Mahabharata*, Shrila Vyasa explained the meaning of the *Vedas*. Without doubt, all the ideas of the *Vedas* are firmly rooted in the *Puranas*."

15.5. Moreover, even if we count the *Itihasas* and *Puranas* among the books illuminating the meaning of the *Vedas*, still they are unique because of the eminence of their compiler. The *Padma Purana* says: "Brahma and others do not know what Dyaipayana Vyasa knows. Indeed, he knows everything known to others, and he knows what is beyond everyone else's grasp."

16.1. The *Skanda Purana* states: "Many people have taken fragments of knowledge from the sky of Vyasa's heart for their own use, just as others acquire items from a householder's home and use them."

16.2. We also find this statement by Parashara Rishi in the *Vishnu Purana* (3.4.2–5): "Thereafter, during the twenty-eighth *manvantara*, the Lord in the form of my son Vyasa took the one *Veda*, consisting of four sections, and divided it into four separate parts. Just as this intelligent Vyasa divided the *Veda*, previously all other Vyasas, including myself, also divided it. O best of the twice-born, understand that in every cycle of four *yugas* a Vyasa comes and arranges the *Veda* into various branches. But know, O Maitreya, that Shri Krishna-dvaipayana Vyasa is Lord Narayana himself. Who else in this world could have written the great epic *Mahabharata*?"

16.3. The *Skanda Purana* further states: "In *satya-yuga* the knowledge that emanated from Lord Narayana remained pure. It became somewhat distorted in *treta-yuga* and completely so in *dvapara-yuga*. When ignorance had covered that knowledge because of Gautama Rishi's curse, the demigods became perplexed. Led by Brahma and Rudra, they approached Lord Narayana, the Supreme Person and faultless refuge, and told him why they had come. On the request of the demigods, Lord Hari then descended as the great *yogi* Vyasa, son of Satyavati and Parashara, and reestablished the forgotten *Vedas*."

16.4. Here the word *Veda* also indicates the *Itihasas* and *Puranas*. Thus it is established that studying the *Itihasas* and *Puranas* is supremely beneficial. And of these two, the *Puranas* are more excellent. Lord Shiva confirms this in the *Naradiya Purana*: "O lovely one, I consider the meaning of the *Puranas* to be more important than that of the *Vedas*, because the *Puranas* firmly establish all the Vedic meanings. There is no doubt of this. One who considers the *Puranas* to be apart from the *Vedas* will take birth as an animal; even if he can expertly control his senses and mind, he can attain no good destination."

17.1. Furthermore, the *Prabhasa-khanda* of the *Skanda Purana* (5.3.121–24) states: "O best of the twice-born, I consider the meaning of the *Puranas* to be as immutable as that of the *Vedas*. Without doubt, the *Puranas* firmly establish the meaning of all the *Vedas*. The *Veda* once became afraid of those who would insufficiently hear from her, and she thought, 'This sort of person will distort my meaning.' For this reason, the *Itihasas* and *Puranas* firmly established the meaning of the *Veda* in ancient times. What cannot be found in the *Vedas* is found in the *smriti*, and what cannot be found in either is clearly explained in the *Puranas*. O learned Brahmins, even if a person has studied the four *Vedas* along with the *Vedangas* and *Upanishads*, he is not considered learned unless he knows the *Puranas*."

17.2. Next, we must consider the following doubt concerning the status of the *Puranas*: although their authority has been established [in the previous *anucchedas*], still it is difficult for the less intelligent men of the modern age to comprehend their ultimate meaning. The reasons for this difficulty are that the *Puranas*, like the *Vedas*, are only partially available and that the *Puranas* generally try to establish the supremacy of various deities.

17.3. As stated in the *Matsya Purana* (53.65, 68–69): "A history is called a *Purana* if it has the five defining characteristics; otherwise it is called an *akhyana*. The *sattvic Puranas* primarily glorify Lord Hari; the *rajasic Puranas*, Lord Brahma; and the *tamasic Puranas*, Lord Shiva and Agni. The *Puranas* in mixed modes glorify Sarasvati and the *Pitas*."

17.4. In this statement, the glories of Agni (fire] refer to the Vedic sacrifices performed by making offerings into various sacred fires. The word *cha* in the phrase *Shivasya cha* implies the glories of the wife of Lord Shiva. Sankirneshu [in those that are mixed] means "in the various *Puranas* that represent mixtures of the modes of *sattva, rajas,* and *tamas.*" Sarasvatyah [the glories of Sarasvati] means "of the presiding deity of speech" and, by implication, "of the various deities referred to in the numerous scriptural texts she embodies." According to *shruti, karmana pitri-lokah*: "By ritualistic ceremonies one can attain the abode of the forefathers." The word *pitrinam* [the glories of the forefathers] refers to the rituals meant for attaining the planet of the forefathers.

18.1. This being the case [that the *Puranas* are in various modes of nature], the *Matsya Purana* classifies the *Puranas* into three divisions based on the descriptions found in them. But how can we determine the relative importance of the *Puranas* so that we can then learn about the other subjects under discussion [namely, *sambandha*, *abhidheya*, and *prayojana*]? If we use the three modes of nature as the basis for categorizing the *Puranas*, then on the strength of statements such as "The mode of goodness produces knowledge" [*Bhagavata*. 14.17] and "the mode of goodness leads to realization of the Absolute Truth" [*Bhagavata*. 1.2.24], we will conclude that the *Puranas* and other literature in the mode of goodness are superior means for gaining knowledge of the Absolute Truth.

18.2. But even then, how can we reconcile the different inconclusive views put forward regarding the Absolute Truth? Someone may propose study of the *Brahma-sutra* as the solution, claiming that Bhagavan Vyasa compiled the *Brahma-sutra* to present the decisive conclusion of both the *Vedas* and the *Puranas* concerning the Absolute Truth. But then the followers of sages who wrote other *sutras* may be dissatisfied. Moreover, since the aphorisms of the *Brahma-sutra* are terse and extremely esoteric, and since they are also subject to varying interpretations, someone will always express a contrary idea. What, then, can resolve disputes concerning the meaning of the *Brahma-sutras*?

18.3. This problem could be solved if there were one scripture that had the characteristics of a *Purana*, that had no human origin, that presented the essence of all the *Vedas*, *Itihasas*, and *Puranas*, that was based on the *Brahma-sutra*, and that was available throughout the land in its complete form.

Well said, Sir, because you have reminded us about our revered *Shrimad-Bhagavata*, the emperor of all *pramanas*.

19.1. Indeed, Lord Vyasa was not satisfied even after compiling all the *Puranas* and the *Brahma-sutra*. He therefore wrote *Shrimad-Bhagavata*, which was revealed to him in trance, as the natural commentary on his own *sutras*. In *Shrimad-Bhagavata* alone we find the consistent reconciliation of all scriptures, shown by its opening with the *Gayatri mantra*, which is characterized as the essence of all the *Vedas*.

19.2. The characteristics of *Shrimad-Bhagavata* are further described in the *Matsya Purana* (53.20–22): "That *Purana* is known as the *Bhagavata* that explains at length the principles of religion with reference to the *Gayatri mantra*, and that tells of the killing of the demon Vritra. This *Purana* has eighteen thousand verses. Whoever writes out a copy of the *Bhagavata*, places it on a golden throne, and presents it to a qualified person on the full-moon day of the month of Bhadra [August–September] will attain the supreme goal."

19.3. The word *Gayatri* in the preceding verse refers to the word *dhimahi* [let us meditate on the Supreme Truth], which is always found in *Gayatri* and thus serves as an indicator of *Gayatri*. The meaning of *Gayatri* is specifically implied by the word *dhimahi*, since it would be improper to directly utter Gayatri itself, the origin of all Vedic *mantras*. The first verse of *Shrimad-Bhagavata* (1.1.1) alludes to the meaning of *Gayatri* by the phrases: *janmady asya yatah* [by him this universe is created, maintained, and destroyed] and *tene brahma hrida* [He revealed Vedic knowledge in Brahma's heart]. These phrases express the same meaning as *Gayatri*, by describing the Lord as the basis of all the universes and as he who inspires everyone's intellect.

The word *dharma* in the compound *dharma-vistara* [also from the preceding verse] refers to the supreme religion, as expressed in the *Bhagavata* by the words *dharmah projjhita-kaitavo 'tra paramah* (*Bhagavata*. 1.1.2): "In this book is found the supreme religion, devoid of all cheating propensities." And, as will become clear in upcoming *anucchedas*, this *dharma* is indeed characterized by meditation on the Supreme Lord.

26.1. Shri Vyasa and Narada were present in that assembly. Although these two sages were Shri Shuka's guru and grand-guru, respectively, when they heard *Shrimad-Bhagavata* issuing from his lips, they felt as if they had never heard it before. For this reason it is said here that Shuka taught this most significant wisdom even to them. As mentioned earlier, *shuka-mukhad amrita-drava-samyutam*: "The *Bhagavata* is enriched with immortal nectar flowing from the mouth of Shuka" (*Bhagavata*. 1.1.3). Thus in this sense also *Shrimad-Bhagavata* is more glorious than any other scripture. Statements about the superiority of other *Puranas*, such as the *Matsya Purana*, are only relatively true. What more need be said! Indeed, *Shrimad-Bhagavata* is the very representation of Shri Krishna.

26.2. As the first canto states: "Now that Krishna has returned to his own abode, along with religion, knowledge, and so on, this *Purana* has risen like the sun for those bereft of sight in the Kali-yuga" (*Bhagavata*. 1.3.43).

In this way we can see that only *Shrimad-Bhagavata* is endowed with all virtues, as stated in the second verse of the first canto: "In this book the supreme *dharma* is explained and all cheating propensities are rejected."

The supremacy of the *Bhagavata* is also confirmed by the words of both the author of *Mukta-phala* [Vopadeva] and Hemadri [its commentator]: "The *Vedas* instruct one like a master, the *Puranas* like a friend, and *Kavya* (poetry] like a beloved. But *Shrimad-Bhagavata* instructs in all three manners."

26.3. Consequently, while some may think that other *Puranas* are dependent on the *Vedas*, *Shrimad-Bhagavata* explicitly refutes the possibility that it may be dependent in this way; we thus receive the *Bhagavata* on its own authority. For this reason it is in fact the highest manifestation of *shruti* [the original *Vedas*]. As it is said, "O beloved teacher, how did the dialogue between King Parikshit and the sage Shuka come about, as a result of which this *satvati shruti* became manifest?" (*Bhagavata*. 1.4.7)

That Vyasa composed *Shrimad-Bhagavata* only after completing all of the other *Puranas*, as mentioned earlier, can be verified from the dialogue between Shri Vyasa and Narada in the first canto.

27.1. Therefore, we will examine the *Bhagavata* alone, observing the consistency between preceding and succeeding statements, in order to determine the ultimate good. In these six *Sandarbhas*, the statements with which we introduce our explanation of the *Bhagavata* verses will serve as the *sutras*, the *Bhagavata* verses themselves will serve as the scriptural text to be analyzed, and the commentary on the *sutras* will be the explanations of the *Bhagavata* verses given by the great Vaishnava Shridhara Svami. His views will be quoted verbatim only when they conform to strict Vaishnava principles, since his writings are interspersed with the doctrines of *advaita*. This he did to awaken an appreciation for the Lord's greatness in the *advaitins*, who are now quite prevalent, especially in central India.

27.2. Sometimes we shall follow the views Shridhara Svami has expressed in writings other than his *Bhagavata* commentary. In other cases, we shall follow the original meaning of the text by basing our explanations on the authoritative opinions of the venerable Ramanujacharya, expressed in such works as *Shri-bhashya*. He is the renowned leader of the Vaishnavas of the Shri Sampradaya, which originated directly from the Goddess Shri [Lakshmi]. These great devotees are famous throughout India's southern region [*Dravida-desh*] and elsewhere. *Shrimad-Bhagavata* itself states that they are well known as devotees of Vishnu in the South:

"O King, a few Vaishnavas can be seen here and there in this age, but they can be found in abundance in the *Dravida*" (*Bhagavata*. 11.5.39).

Since the principles of *advaita-vada* are already well known, we shall not discuss them at length.

28.1. Here in the *Shat-Sandarbha* I will quote the authoritative words of the *shrutis*, the *Puranas*, and other such scriptures, just as I have seen them. I will quote these passages to verify my own interpretations, not the statements of *Shrimad-Bhagavata*. Some of the verses quoted here I have not seen in their original texts but have gleaned from citations in the *Bhagavata-tatparya*, *Bharata-tatparya*, *Brahma-sutra bhashya*, and other works by the venerable Madhva-charya, the ancient preceptor of the doctrine of *Tattvavada*. Shri Madhva brought forth numerous distinctive Vaishnava doctrines, he was an eminent scholar of the *Vedas* and their interpretation, he was greatly renowned in the South and elsewhere, and his disciples and grand-disciples include Vijayadhvaja Tirtha and Vyasa Tirtha.

28.2. In *Bharata-tatparya*, Sri Madhvacharya states: "Having understood other scriptures with the help of the *Vedanta-sutra*, and having looked at various kinds of scripture in different parts of the country, I shall give my explanation in strict accordance with what Shri Vyasadeva, who is none other than the Supreme Lord Narayana, has spoken in *Mahabharata* and other works" (*Bharata-tatparya* 2.7.8).

The texts we will cite from the works of Shri Madhvacharya will include portions from Vedic *shrutis*, such as the *Chatur-veda-shikha*, Puranic texts from unavailable parts of the *Garuda Purana* and other works, *samhita* texts from the *Maha-samhita* and similar works, and *tantra* texts from the *Tantra-Bhagavata*, *Brahma-tarka*, and so on.

29.1. Such being the status of *Shrimad-Bhagavata*, Suta Gosvami concisely defines its basic message by turning our attention to the disposition of the heart of its speaker while offering him obeisances:

"I offer obeisance unto Vyasa's son, who destroys all sins, whose consciousness was absorbed in the bliss of Self, and who was thus free from any other worldly thought. Yet his heart became attracted by the beautiful pastimes of Lord Ajita, Krishna. Out of compassion he narrated this *Purana*, which illumines reality" (*Bhagavata.* 12.12.69).

29.2. Shridhara Swami explains in his commentary. "Suta Gosvami offers obeisances to his guru [Shri Shuka], whose consciousness was filled with the bliss of Self, and who had thus put aside all other thoughts. But even at that elevated stage, his inner essence consisting of his fixity in the bliss of Self was drawn to the enchanting pastimes of Lord Ajita. I offer my obeisances unto him, the speaker of *Shrimad-Bhagavata*, which illumines the supreme goal of life."

29.3. Similarly worth examining are the three verses Shri Shuka spoke in the second canto that begin with *prayena munayo rajan* (*Bhagavata.* 2.1.7–9). In the verse under discussion (*Bhagavata.* 12.12.69) we should understand that the words *akhila-vrijinam* [all inauspicious things] indicate everything averse or indifferent to such a feeling [of attraction to Krishna's pastimes]. Therefore the subject of this book [sambandhi-tattva] is *Shriman* Ajita, who is distinguished by his enchanting pleasure pastimes and who thus transcends the bliss of realization of the nondual Absolute [Brahmanda]. Later, in the context of our discussion of Shrila Vyasa's trance, it will be made clear that in his fullest manifestation, Lord Ajita is primarily named Shri Krishna.

Similarly, the final goal [prayojana-tattva] is the happiness of love for Krishna, which leads to the sort of attachment to him that Shri Shuka experienced. And thus our means [abhidheya] is service to him, characterized by such devotional processes as hearing his divine pastimes; this activity generates love for him, as it did in the case of Shri Shuka. The identity of each of these three principles [sambandha, abhidheya, and prayojana] follows as a natural logical sequence.

The phrase *vyasa-sunum* [son of Shri Vyasa] in *Shrimad-Bhagavata* 12.12.69 alludes to an incident described in the *Brahma-Vaivarta Purana*—namely, that Shuka, because of Shri Krishna's benediction, remained untouched by *maya* from his very birth.

The verse under discussion was spoken by Shri Suta to Shri Shaunaka.

30.1. Shri Suta Suta Gosvami elucidated the same basic message of the *Bhagavata* while describing the meditative trance of its author, Shrila Vyasadeva. What Vyasadeva experienced indicated the principles he would later establish in his book, *Shrimad-Bhagavata*. Shri Suta described this trance in brief:

"His heart being purified and perfectly concentrated through *bhakti-yoga*, he saw the Absolute Lord along with his external energy [maya], which was subordinate to him. The living entity, deluded by *maya*, considers himself a product of the three *gunas*, though really beyond them, and consequently comes to grief. Vyasadeva composed this *Satvata-samhita* [Shrimad-Bhagavata] for those people ignorant of the fact that *bhakti-yoga* directed toward Adhokshaja [Krishna] directly puts an end to misfortune. Simply by hearing this *Satvata-samhita*, devotion for the Supreme Lord, Krishna, will grow in him, putting an end to lamentation, delusion, and fear. After composing and arranging this *Bhagavati-samhita*, Vyasa taught it to his son, Shuka, who was situated on the path of renunciation" (*Bhagavata*. 1.7.4–8).

30.2. Shaunaka Rishi then inquired: "But why did the sage (Shuka], who was situated in renunciation, indifferent toward everything, and rejoicing in the Self alone, take the trouble to study such a vast literature?" (*Bhagavata*. 1.7.9)

In reply to Shri Saunaka's query, Suta said: "Although such sages rejoice in the Self alone, and are free from all bounds, they cherish unmotivated devotion unto Urukrama [Krishna]; such are the virtues of Hari. The venerable son of Vyasa became captivated at heart by the qualities of Hari and studied this great narrative daily. From that point on the devotees of Vishnu became dear to his heart" (*Bhagavata.* 1.7.10–11).

The phrase *bhakti-yogena* [through devotional service] [in *Bhagavata* 1.7.4] means "through love of God," since the same meaning is conveyed in the following statement: "My dear King, the Supreme Lord, Mukunda, grants liberation to those who offer him [mere] worship, but he never bestows *bhakti-yoga*, pure love for him" (*Bhagavata.* 5.6.18).

30.3. The word *pranihite* [fixed] means "concentrated in meditation," since Vyasa had been instructed earlier by Narada to recall the events of Krishna's *lila* by means of *samadhi* [trance] (*Bhag.* 1.5.13).

The word *purna* [complete—qualifying *purusha*] should be understood here in its unrestricted sense, as corroborated by the *Padma Purana* (*Uttara-khanda* 226.68): "The words *bhagavan* and *purusha*, when free from limiting modifiers, refer to Lord Vasudeva [Krishna], the Supreme Soul of all." This is further verified in Shridhara Svami's commentary on the following two verses: "One who desires worldly enjoyment should worship Soma [the predominating deity of the moon], but one who has no material desires should worship the Supreme Lord. A high-minded person, whether free from desires, full of desires, or desiring liberation, should worship the Supreme Lord through ardent devotion [*bhakti-yoga*]" (*Bhagavata.* 2.3.9–10).

Shrila Shridhara Svami states that the word *purusha* in the first of these two verses indicates the Supreme Soul [Paramatma], whose sole *upadhi* [apparently limiting qualification] is material nature, while the same word in the second verse indicates the complete Personality of Godhead [*purna-purusha*], who is free from all *upadhis*. Thus the phrase *purna-purusha* [in *Bhagavata* 1.7.4, quoted in Anuccheda 30.1] refers to the original Personality of Godhead (svayam Bhagavan).

31.1. Even if we consider the alternative reading of *purvam* instead of *purnam* (in *Bhagavata* 1.7.4 quoted above), still the reference here will be to the Supreme Lord. This is shown by the statements of Vedic *shruti*: "[The Lord said] I existed here prior [*purvam*] to everything else" and "That [existing prior to everything else] is the essential characteristic of the Lord."

When it is said that Shri Veda-Vyasa saw the Lord, it is self-evident that he saw the Lord endowed with his internal potency [*svarupa-shakti*], just as when it is said that a person sees the full moon, the implication is that he also sees its effulgence.

31.2. Thus it is said: "You are the original Supreme Lord, the controller of all creations and transcendental to the material energy. You have cast aside the effects of the material energy by your spiritual potency [*chit-shakti*]. You are always situated in eternal bliss in your own Self" (*Bhagavata.* 1.7.23).

Therefore we understand the phrase *mayan cha tad-apashrayam* [in *Bhagavata* 1.7.4] to mean that *maya* takes shelter of him in an inferior position, being concealed from his sight; thus she does not constitute his *svarupa*, or essential nature. As said later on, "*Maya*, feeling ashamed, flees from the Lord's direct presence" (*Bhagavata.* 2.7.47).

31.3. We will now explain the Lord's *svarupa-shakti* with reference to the two verses, beginning *anarthopashaman sakshad bhakti-yogam adhokshaje* and *atmaramash cha* [*Bhagavata.* 1.7.6 and 10, respectively]. From the statement in the first of these two verses that *bhakti* can subdue the material energy, *maya*, we can infer that the power of *bhakti* is a function of the Lord's internal energy. The second verse implies that the qualities of Lord Hari constitute the *svarupa-shakti*'s highest function, superior even to the bliss of *Brahman*.

It should be understood that no separate mention is made of the *Purusha* who presides over *maya* [Paramatma], or of *Brahman*, since both are considered to fall within the domain of the *Purna Purusha*, the former as a partial aspect of him, and the latter as his nondifferentiated manifestation. This fact we will thoroughly demonstrate later, in the second and third *Sandarbhas*. Thus here, as before, the *sambandhi-tattva*, or the essential topic of discussion in *Shrimad-Bhagavata*, has been defined.

32.1. Then, Vyasa perceived the essential distinction between the Lord and the living entity, which forms the basis for the process [*abhidheya*] and the goal [*prayojana*] of this work, as we have defined them earlier. This is indicated in the verse beginning with *yaya* [*Bhagavata*. 1.7.5]. Although the living entity is by nature pure spirit, transcendental to the three inert material modes, when deluded by *maya* he considers himself a product of those modes, and thus misidentifies himself with the inert material body. This delusion causes the living entity to suffer unwanted consequences, namely the miseries of repeated birth and death.

32.2. Furthermore, not only does the living being consist of pure spiritual consciousness, but, just as light, which consists of nothing but illumination, also has the capacity to illumine itself and other things, the living being possesses consciousness as a component of his essential nature. This is implied [in *Bhagavata*. 1.7.5] by the words *yaya sammohitah*, "deluded by *maya*" [the implication being that if consciousness were not an attribute of the living being, there would be nothing that becomes bewildered], and *manute*, "he considers" [the act of reflection itself being a symptom of consciousness]. This is further confirmed by the following words from *Bhagavad-gita* (5.15): "Living beings are bewildered because their consciousness is covered by ignorance." Thus the contrary opinion that the *jiva* exists only as an *upadhi*, or a limited adjunct of *Brahman*, and that liberation is only the elimination of this *upadhi* is refuted.

Here [in *Bhagavata*. 1.7.5] the phrase *yaya sammohitah* shows that *maya* alone is responsible for deluding the living being; the Lord remains uninvolved.

32.3. Later *Shrimad-Bhagavata* [2.5.13] states: "The external energy of the Lord cannot stand in front of him, being ashamed of her deeds. Less intelligent people, being bewildered by her, boast of "I" and "mine."

Here we can infer from the phrase "being ashamed" [*vilajjamanaya*] that although *maya* knows that her work of bewildering the living beings does not please the Supreme Lord, still she cannot tolerate their turning their backs on him because of ignorance that is beginningless. *Shrimad-Bhagavata* (11.2.37) describes the result of the *jivas'* turning from the Lord: "When the living beings are indifferent to the Lord, they become fearful because of absorption in that which is secondary." Therefore *maya* covers their real nature and entices them to identify with matter.

The *Bhagavat-sandarbha*

Anuccheda

In the previous [*Tattva*] *Sandarbha* I have described in a general way the nature of the nondual Absolute Truth and the eternal distinction between that Absolute and the individual living entities, who are naturally the servants and worshipers of the Absolute. Now I shall describe some of the variegated features of the Absolute. The Absolute is known in three features, called *Brahman*, Paramatma, and Bhagavan. This is described in the following statement of *Shrimad Bhagavata* (1.2.11): "Learned transcendentalists who know the Absolute Truth call this nondual substance *Brahman*, Paramatma, or Bhagavan."

The *Bhakti-sandarbha*

text 1

The topic of *sambandha*—the relation between the Supreme Being, His potencies, and the living beings—was explained in the previous four *sandarbhas*. In those four books, the complete, eternal, and supremely blissful Absolute Reality, which is also known as *sambandhi*, the subject of our inquiry, was described. That Absolute Reality was referred to by its threefold manifestations as *Brahman*, nondual being, Paramatma, the Supreme Soul, and Bhagavan, the Supreme Lord. Among these three, the preeminence of the manifestation as Bhagavan was also established. Other *avataras*, or incarnations of the Lord, such as Vishnu and Chatuhsana, the four Kumara brothers, were described in the course of such discussions. It was concluded that Bhagavan is Shri Krishna himself.

While enumerating the magnificence of Paramatma, the material misery of the living entities, who are marginal potencies of Paramatma, was expounded. Although purely conscious by nature, their knowledge about their own intrinsic nature is covered by His external potency, *maya*, because she finds in them the defect of aversion to him, which is in the form of beginningless ignorance about the Absolute Reality.[17] She herself furnished them with the consciousness of identifying with the primordial state of nature known as *pradhana*, the undifferentiated state of the three fundamental qualities of nature, *sattva*, luminosity, *rajas*, dynamism, and *tamas*, inertia.

As the Lord says in the eleventh canto of *Shrimad-Bhagavata*: "The controversy as to whether the Lord exists or not is rooted in the propensity for argumentation and betrays a basic ignorance of the Supreme Self. Although such controversy is meaningless, those whose intelligence is averted from Me, the ultimate shelter, cannot give it up" (*Shrimad-Bhagavata* 11.22.34).

In light of this reality, scripture, possessing the characteristic of supreme munificence, offers instruction for the enlightenment of such souls who are in a state of forgetfulness of the Lord. Out of them, some living beings have had some experience of the Absolute Reality in past lives, which has left impressions on them lying in a latent form. There are others who attain a vision of the Absolute by the liberal grace of a devotee. In the case of both of these types of individuals, as soon as they begin to hear instructions about the perfect, ever-existing entity, characterized as the Absolute Reality, they immediately and simultaneously become devoted to the Absolute and are endowed with realization of the same. This is indicated in *Shrimad-Bhagavata*: "As soon as pious people become eager to hear *Shrimad-Bhagavata*, the Supreme Lord is immediately captured within their hearts. Therefore, what need is there of any other literature?" (*Bhagavata.* 1.1.2)

Therefore, such people do not need any other instruction. Incidental hearing of other instructions acts only to incite their specific permanent disposition of love for the Lord, in the same manner that hearing the Lord's pastimes does so. Such an effect was seen in the case of devotees like Prahlada and others.

Even for others who have no such latent impressions of experiences of the Absolute from past lives or who have not received the special mercy of perfected souls, the seed of realization of the Absolute can come into being merely by hearing instructions about the Lord, although it remains suppressed by defects such as material desires. The following statement of the illustrious devotee Prahlada, who considered himself wretched, is applicable in earnest to others: "O Lord of Vaikuntha, my mind does not take pleasure in hearing Your pastimes because it is polluted by sinful desires, utterly impious, agitated by lust, and distressed by material happiness, lamentation, fear, and worldly hankerings. With a mind such as this, how can I, a pitiable person, meditate on You?" (*Bhagavata.* 7.9.39)

A similar statement is made in the *Brahma-vaivarta Purana*: "As long as the heart is polluted by sins, one will not develop faith in scripture and in a bona fide spiritual teacher. The manifestation of love occurs only by hearing scripture in the association of saints as the exceptional fruit of accumulated piety earned over many lifetimes."

Even though the prime import of scripture culminates in identifying the Absolute Reality, instructions on the Absolute in scripture give rise to two more essential questions: what is to be done to approach the Absolute, and what is the goal to be attained in respect of that Reality? Consequently, there is need for instruction in two further topics as the secondary import of scripture. These are known as *abhidheya*, the methodology by which one realizes the Absolute, and *prayojana*, the goal to be attained in relation to the Supreme. Out of these two, the methodology, *abhidheya*, involves turning one's awareness toward the Absolute, which is just the opposite of the former attitude of apathy towards the Ultimate Reality. This attitude is characterized by worship of the Supreme, the very means by which knowledge of the Absolute manifests. The purpose, *prayojana*, refers to experience of the Absolute, which means direct witnessing of the Truth both internally and externally. It is by such direct experience that all miseries are dispelled of their own accord.

These two topics were implied in the earlier descriptions of the Absolute known as *siddhopadesh*,[18] instructions that do not require injunctions. Just as a poor man after hearing "there is wealth hidden in your house" endeavors to find that wealth [without being ordered to do so] and then obtains it, a similar intention applies here. Yet [despite the scripture offering instructions about our real wealth] we may still not endeavor to uncover it. To dispel any laxity in this regard, the scripture again explains that it is our apathy toward the Absolute, rooted in our beginningless ignorance of the Lord, that is the cause of our misery. The scripture instructs us to focus our attention on the Absolute, which is like a treatment meant to nullify the cause of our disease.

This situation is summed up in *Shrimad-Bhagavata* in the statement of the sage Shri Kavi to the King of Videha: "A person who is not devoted to the Lord because of the influence of the Lord's deluding energy, *maya*, succumbs to forgetfulness, misapprehension, and fear arising out of absorption in that which is secondary to the Lord. Therefore, the intelligent should worship the Lord with exclusive devotion, considering their teacher as their worshipful deity and object of love" (*Bhagavata* 11.2.37).

Shridhara Svami, the famous *Bhagavatam* annotator, comments:

> Because fear is brought about by the Lord's deluding potency, an intelligent person should worship only him. A doubt may be raised in this regard. Since fear arises out of attachment to the body, which stems from misidentifying the body as the self, which itself originates in ignorance of one's own intrinsic nature, what role does *maya* play in the arousal of fear?
>
> The first part of this verse addresses this type of question. The words *ishad apetasya* refer to a person who is not devoted to the Lord. Such a person is under the influence of the Lord's deluding potency, which induces a state of *asmriti*, or forgetfulness, which here refers to ignorance of one's own intrinsic nature. This ignorance leads to the misconception of identifying the body as the self. It is this misidentification that leads to absorption in the nonessential from which fear arises. The principle of how fear can be aroused due to the misapprehension of reality brought about by delusion is well known even in the case of *laukiki-maya*, or ordinary magic.
>
> The Lord also said in *Bhagavad Gita*: 'This divine potency of Mine, consisting of the three *gunas*, or constituent qualities of

nature, is very difficult to cross over. Those who surrender unto Me alone can cross beyond this *maya.*' (*Bhagavad Gita* 7.14)

The verse [*Bhagavata* 11.2.37] further states that one should worship the Lord with unswerving devotion, *ekaya bhaktya.* Moreover, one should regard one's spiritual teacher as one's worshipful deity, or as the Lord, and also as the dearest person, *guru-devatatma.* It is with this vision that one should worship the Lord. This is the implication of the verse.

text 6

In this matter, there are some who think that the object of *dharma* is wealth, that wealth is meant to facilitate enjoyment, that enjoyment is meant for sensual pleasure, and that sensual pleasure again leads to the cycle of *dharma,* and so on. This is certainly a misconception. Suta Gosvami has addressed this idea in two verses: "Transcendent *dharma* is not meant for amassing wealth. Wealth that is meant only for *dharma* should not be used to facilitate enjoyment. The objects of enjoyment should not be used for sensual indulgence, but only for maintenance of life. The goal of life is to know the Absolute and not to acquire wealth in this world by carrying out one's prescribed duty" (*Bhagavata* 1.2.9–10).

According to the following prose from the fifth canto of *Shrimad-Bhagavata,* the word *apavarjnasya* [from *Bhagavata* 1.2.9] means *bhakti:* "By following one's prescribed duty according to the *varna* system, one also obtains *apavarga,* which is causeless *bhakti-yoga* for Lord Vasudeva, who is the Supreme Soul, the shelter of all, beyond mind and speech, free from attachment and the Soul of all. This happens only when one obtains the association of a devotee of the Lord, by which the knot of ignorance, the cause of being subjected to various destinations in the material world, is cut asunder" (*Bhagavata* 5.19.18–19).

The same point is made in the *Reva-khanda* of the *Skanda-Purana:* "O Lord Janardana, unflinching *bhakti* for you, is indeed *mukti,* or liberation. Therefore only liberated souls, O Lord Vishnu, O Hari, are Your devotees."

Thus, from the above statements the word *apavargyasya,* which qualifies the word *dharma* in *Shrimad-Bhagavata* 1.2.9, means "that which brings about *bhakti.*"

In his commentary on the two verses of *Shrimad-Bhagavata* (1.2.9–10) quoted above, Shridhara Svami says: "The words *artho nopakalpate arthaya* mean that it is not appropriate to consider wealth as the result [of *dharma*]. The knowers of the Absolute say that the result of *artha*, wealth, which is the unfailing companion of such *dharma*, is not for material enjoyment. The goal of consuming sense objects is not sensual delight, but life maintenance. This means that one should consume sense objects only sufficient for the preservation of life. The purpose of life is not to achieve the much-sought-after destination of heaven by the performance of *dharma*, but to know the Absolute."

In this way, only *bhakti*, the concomitant factor of which is said to be knowledge of the Absolute, is the supreme result.

What then is the Absolute? To answer this question, Suta Gosvami recited the following verse: "The knowers of the Absolute say that the Absolute is nondual consciousness. It is referred to as *Brahman*, Paramatma, and Bhagavan" (*Shrimad-Bhagavata* 1.2.11).

After specifying the indivisibility of the Absolute by using the word *advayam*, nondual, Suta Gosvami accepts all other phenomena as the energy of the Absolute, just to make it clear that there is nothing separate from it. When the nondual Absolute is manifest as pure consciousness devoid of any attributes in the form of various potencies, it is called *Brahman*. When the same Absolute is endowed with the feature of immanence, and manifests a prominence of the external potency along with parts of the *chit-shakti*, or conscious potency, it is called Paramatma. The same Absolute, possessing all potencies in fullness, is called Bhagavan. This has been described in the first three *Sandarbhas*.

NOTES

1. *Navya-nyaya*, or neo-logic, is an improvisation on the old school of *nyaya*. It began with the *Tattva-cintamani* of Gangesh Upadhyaya in the thirteenth century C.E.

2. The *Bhagavata Purana* is one of the eighteen principal *Puranas* attributed to Vedavyasa, and the most prominent of all of them. There have been far more traditional commentaries and writings on it than on any other *Purana*.

3. The word *Gaudiya* comes from the word *Gauda-bhumi*, or the land of Gauda. According to the *Shakti-sangama Tantra*, this corresponds to West Bengal and includes some parts of modern-day Bangladesh and Orissa (extending as far as Bhuvaneshvara). In ancient times the residents of this tract of land were known as Gaudiyas. After the appearance of Chaitanya in Bengal, the term *Gaudiya* became associated with the followers of Chaitanya because his influence was so widespread throughout the land of Gauda.

4. This concept may be understood from the example of "blue lotus." In this phrase, lotus by itself is the *visheshya*, or substantive, without any adjective; blue is the *visheshana*, or qualifying attribute, and "blue lotus" is the *vishishta*, or qualified object. *Brahman* is compared to the lotus devoid of all attributes; whereas Bhagavan is

compared to the same lotus when endowed with all attributes. As "blue lotus" includes and envelops lotus, Bhagavan includes and transcends *Brahman*.

5. The concept of difference in nondifference is like the relation between heat and its source, fire. Heat is separate from fire because it can be felt outside fire. Yet it is integrally connected with and wholly dependent on fire; it cannot exist without it. *Achintya*, or inconceivable, means that which can be known only from scripture.

6. *Prakriti*, or primal matter, has three aspects or constituents called *gunas*: *sattva* (illumination), *rajas* (vibrancy), and *tamas* (indolence). The *gunas* have distinctive characteristics and pervade all material objects. They are always intermixed with each other.

7. According to Jiva Gosvami, the relation between energy and energetic—the possessor of energy—is that of oneness and difference. There is oneness because energy is never separate from its source, yet being but a part of the whole that includes it, energy is different from its energetic agent. Similarly, because the living entities are fractions of the Lord's *tatastha-shakti*, their relation with him is that of oneness and difference. This relation is termed *achintya*, or inconceivable, because it can be comprehended only through revealed scripture, being beyond the scope of logic.

8. According to *Jaimini-Sutra* 3.3.14, *shruti*, *linga*, *vakya*, *prakarana*, *sthana*, and *samakhya* are criteria for determining the meaning of a text in decreasing order of importance. In this list *shruti* means an independent direct statement, which is considered most authoritative.

9. *Rasa-shastra* is a particular type of literature that sets standards regarding the depiction of sentiments between the hero and heroine in a poetic composition. It defines *rasa*, or "relish," its types, how it manifests, its ingredients, people eligible to taste it, and so on.

10. *Shri Bhashya* 1.1.1.

11. *Vedartha-sangraha*.

12. *Yatindramata-dipika*, seventh *avatara*.

13. *Mahabharata-tatparya-nirnaya*.

14. *Dasha-shloki*, 9.

15. *Anubhashya* 3.3; 4.4.

16. According to Jiva, *bhakti* is divided into *vaidhi*, which draws its inspiration from scriptural injunctions, and *raganuga*, which is prompted by natural liking, following the ideals of the eternal associates of Krishna in Braj. The latter is akin to the Pushtimarga of Vallabhacharya.

17. The exact word used here for ignorance is *sansarga-abhava*. This is a term used in the *vaisheshika* school of philosophy. *Sansarga-abhava* is of three types: *prag-abhava*, *pradhvamsa-abhava*, and *atyanta-abhava*. The type of ignorance referred to here is *prag-abhava*, or pre-nonexistence. This refers to the absence of an object before it is acquired or produced. This term implies that the absence is beginningless but comes to an end when the object is acquired or produced. In the present context, *prag-abhava* refers to an absence of knowledge of the Absolute Reality. This means that this ignorance, although beginningless, will come to an end when a particular living entity attains knowledge of the Absolute Reality.

18. According to the *purva-mimamsa* school of thought, the Vedic injunctions, which result in auspiciousness if executed by a person, are called *dharma*. These injunctions inspire or impel a person to act. As such, they are generally expressed in the imperative, optative, or subjunctive moods (referred to by Panini as *lot, lin,* and *let,* respectively) or by use of the potential passive participle (suffix *tavya*). All of these verbal forms imply advice, obligation, or command. Injunctions stated in any of these ways are called *vidhi*. Sometimes, however, a descriptive statement is given that is not a direct order but that naturally inspires one to act, as in the foregoing example. This type of description is known as *siddhopadesh*.

17

A Selection from the *Bhaktirasamritasindhu* of Rupa Gosvamin: *The Foundational Emotions (Sthayi-bhavas)*

David L. Haberman

The *Bhaktirasamritasindu* is a Sanskrit text that was written in the sixteenth century by Rupa Gosvamin, a famous Krishnaite theologian and theoretician of aesthetics.[1] This text presents religious experience in terms of the classical aesthetic (*rasa*) theory of India and systematizes a way of thinking about religion that has had a lasting influence. This text, whose title can be translated "The Ocean of the Essence of Devotional Rasa," is a vast compendium of devotional aesthetics. The selection translated here makes up just one of the twenty-three chapters of this large text; I have chosen it because it gives access to *bhava* theory, which is in many ways the very core of the religious experience expressed in this text.

Although Krishna devotionalism has had a long history in India, the kind of religion represented in the *Bhaktirasamritasindhu* has many new elements that arise at a unique historical moment. In many ways, the religion presented here is a full flowering of what Friedhelm Hardy calls "emotional Krishna *bhakti*."[2] This form of religion focuses exclusively on Krishna as the supreme reality, and therefore might be distinguished from "Vaishnavism," if the latter term is used to indicate that Krishna is an *avatara* of Vishnu. This new form of religion is very much associated with the *Bhagavata Purana*, which introduces passionate emotionalism into the world of intellectual Krishna *bhakti*, represented in such texts as the *Vishnu Purana*. The religion presented in the *Bhaktirasamritasindhu*, then, is one that represents Krishna as the supreme reality and as the focus for a passionate form of devotionalism.

At least since the time of Shridhara's commentary on the *Bhagavata Purana* in the thirteenth century, this text began to be understood as a presentation of the religious life as a relishing of an emotional relationship (*rasa*) with the Lord. What began in earlier ages in seminal form reached full culmination in the *Bhaktirasamritasindhu*. This text was composed at a time when emotional Krishna *bhakti* as expressed in the tenth canto of the *Bhagavata Purana* became the very center of far-reaching cultural activities in the north-central region of India known as Braj, or sometimes simply Vrindavan (or Mathura).

Little is known for certain about the early years of Rupa Gosvamin's life.[3] It seems almost certain, however, that he was born sometime between 1470 and 1490, the earlier date being more plausible.[4] Rupa belonged to a branch of a family of Karnataka brahmins who were forced to leave the South because of conflicts over land within the family and eventually ended up in the region that is now Bengal. Rupa was one of three sons; the eldest was Sanatana, acknowledged in many of Rupa's writings as his guru, and the youngest was Anupama, the father of Jiva Gosvami.[5] Sanatana, Rupa, and Jiva were to form the hub of what became a circle of prolific Gaudiya theologians located in Vrindavan.

As young men, Sanatana and Rupa took up residence at Ramakeli near the capital city of Gauda, the seat of Muslim power represented by the nawab Husain Shah. Since the two were widely known for their learned abilities, they were recommended to the nawab as promising assistants.[6] Despite the fact that the two brothers held high positions in the Muslim court, they were apparently unhappy with their situation. They invited Chaitanya, the great Bengali saint who was the inspirational source of the movement that came to be known as Gaudiya Vaishnavism, to Ramakeli in 1514, while he was attempting a journey to Vrindavan.[7] This meeting transformed their lives, for after it they were determined to leave the service of the nawab and dedicate their lives to Vaishnava scholarship. Rupa left Ramakeli secretly with his younger brother Anupama and joined Chaitanya in Allahabad during Chaitanya's return from Vrindavan; Sanatana managed to escape at a later date. Chaitanya instructed Rupa in Krishna devotionalism in Allahabad for a period of ten days.[8] Rupa wanted to accompany Chaitanya to Varanasi (Benares), but recognizing him to be a very talented and learned man, Chaitanya sent him instead to Vrindavan to restore its sacred sites and to write treatises to establish the theological foundation of Krishna devotionalism. Rupa visited Chaitanya later at his residence in Puri for a period of ten months and there received further instruction from him. Rupa returned to Vrindavan after this final meeting in 1516 to settle there permanently, establish the worship of Govindadeva, and carry out the work Chaitanya had assigned him. The exact date of Rupa's death is unknown, but it is likely that he died sometime in 1557.[9] After his death, the tradition of Gaudiya

Vaishnavism that he helped to found increasingly viewed Rupa as a saint and an exemplar of the type of devotional practice he established.[10]

Rupa completed the *Bhaktirasamritasindhu* in the vicinity of Vrindavan in the year 1541. Gaudiya sources record between thirteen and seventeen works authored by him, including dramas based on the activities of Krishna, dramaturgical treatises, and collections of devotional poetry. His most important works by far, however, are the *Bhaktirasamritasindhu* and its sequel, the *Ujjvalanilamani*. These two Sanskrit texts became very influential among learned groups of scholars in northern India, and much of their content found its way into Krishnadasa Kaviraja's immensely popular Bengali text the *Chaitanya Charitamrita*, thus ensuring a wide-ranging audience for the text among Gaudiya Vaishnavas living in Bengal. One of the major cultural products of the creative fermentation that was taking place in Braj in the sixteenth century, the *Bhaktirasamritasindhu* was the only text of its kind to systematize the new religion of emotional Krishna *bhakti* in terms of aesthetic theory. Although the influence of devotional aesthetics is apparent in the writings of other saint-scholars,[11] Rupa was the sole writer to create a systematic formulation of a uniquely Vaishnava aesthetic, one that is still vitally alive today.

Rupa's ideas about aesthetics, or *rasa,* to use the Sanskrit term, are better understood when viewed in the larger context of this concept. Reflections on the nature and experience of *rasa* have had a long and fascinating history in India. The term *rasa* originally meant "sap," "juice," or "essence," and by extension "flavor," "taste," and "enjoyment." *Rasa* was used in the early *Upanishads* to mean "essence" or "joy" (*ananda*) and was associated with the highest reality. The *Taittiriya Upanishad,* for example, claims: "Verily he [*atman*] is *rasa.* One becomes joyful only after obtaining *rasa.*"[12] Although later aestheticians easily read their meaning back into these early Upanishadic texts, the concept of *rasa* inherited by Rupa came out of the specific context of aesthetics, particularly out of reflections on the nature of dramatic experience expressed in the *Natya Shastra* of the legendary sage Bharata. Within this context, the term *rasa* is best translated as "dramatic sentiment" or "aesthetic enjoyment."

The West has generally followed Aristotle's notion that plot is the central organizing feature of drama. Bharata, however, articulated a theory wherein the evocation of *rasa* assumes that position. The central challenge for the dramatist, therefore, was to determine how this "aesthetic enjoyment" could be evoked in the audience of a drama. Bharata's resulting project involved a detailed analysis of emotional experience to determine how various types of emotions could be reproduced on stage and evoked in the audience of a drama. This endeavor led him to a very sophisticated analysis of human emotions. Bharata began with the observation that the human being experiences a wide range of psychological states or emotions (*bhavas*). He produced a list of forty-one possible emotions, but did not give all of them equal value.[13] Eight were marked as having a dominant or durable (*sthayin*) effect on the human personality. These he called the *sthayi-bhavas*, which I have translated "Foundational Emotions." Dominance or durability, in this case, seems to mean that these emotional states are so engrossing, and affect the person feeling them so greatly, that for the time being that person is aware of nothing else.[14] The remainder of the emotions presumably lack this characteristic. The eight Foundational Emotions listed by Bharata are love (*rati*), humor (*hasa*), sorrow (*shoka*), anger (*krodha*), effort (*utsaha*), fear (*bhaya*), disgust (*jugupsa*), and astonishment (*vismaya*). Although these Foundational Emotions may be experienced by anyone, Bharata's particular task was to determine how they could be raised to a "relishable" state and thereby experienced in the dramatic context.

His solution was seemingly simple. If an emotion arises in a certain environment and produces certain responses and gestures in a human being, cannot a representation of that environment and an imitation of those responses and gestures reproduce the emotion in the sensitive and cultured viewer? Acting on this assumption, Bharata analyzed the emotions of everyday life in great detail. This analysis revealed to him that emotions are manifested by three components: the environmental conditions or causes (*karana*), the external responses or effects (*karya*), and accompanying supportive emotions (*sahakarin*). Bharata then proceeded to define the specific characteristics of each of the components for each of the eight Foundational Emotions so that they could be imitated on stage and thus reproduce the desired emotion for the audience. When the environmental conditions, the external responses, and the accompanying emotional states are not part of ordinary life but are components of artistic expression, they are technically renamed the *vibhavas*, the *anubhavas*, and the *vyabhichari-bhavas*, respectively.[15] (Rupa refers to these in verses 85–86.) The proper combination of these components, Bharata maintained, would allow an emotion to be reproduced and "relished" as *rasa*. This leads to the famous *rasa-sutra* found in the sixth chapter of Bharata's text: "*Rasa* is produced (*nishpatti•*) from the combination of the *vibhava*, *anubhava*, and *vyabhichari-bhava*."[16]

The *vibhava* is generally explained as denoting that which makes the Foundational Emotion (*sthayi-bhava*) capable of being sensed. For this reason I have translated it here as the "Excitant." In this sense, it is said to be the primary "cause" (*karana, nimitta,* or *hetu*) of the aesthetic experience.[17] *Anubhavas* are said to be the vocal, physical, and mental gestures (*abhinaya*) by which the meaning is expressed and conveyed; they are the means by which the emotions are made to be felt.[18] For this reason, I have translated *anubhavas* "Indications." The *vyabhichari-bhavas* are temporary accompanying accessory emotions that foster, support, and give fresh impetus to the Foundational Emotion. I have translated *vyabhichari-bhavas* "Transitory Emotions." Being thirty-three in number, they also account for the variety within a single Foundational Emotion, since each combines with the Foundational Emotion in its own unique way. Bharata introduces yet another category of emotions, the *sattvika-bhavas*, which are involuntary and uncontrollable physical responses produced from certain mental states.[19] I have translated *sattvika-bhavas* "Responses." Since examples include perspiration, goose bumps, and trembling, many later writers have considered them a type of Indication.

When combined with the proper combination of Excitants, Indications, and Transitory Emotions in the controlled environment of the theatre, the eight Foundational Emotions are somehow raised in the sympathetic spectator to a relishable state of aesthetic enjoyment and become the eight *rasas*: amorous (*shringara*), humorous (*hasya*), compassionate (*karuna*), furious (*raudra*), heroic (*vira*), dreadful (*bhayanaka*), abhorrent (*bibhatsa*), and wonderful (*adbhuta*). This is Bharata's theory in a nutshell; although it was worked out in the context of drama, over time it was applied to a variety of arts, and later by theologians to religious experience itself. Rupa was one of the most prominent among the latter group, and the *Bhaktirasamritasindhu* gives expression to his efforts.

Rupa's understanding of *rasa* differs greatly from those of other theoreticians who preceded him. Whereas previous writers normally restricted the *rasa* experience to the limited space of the theatre, he extends it to all of life. *Rasa* is now not understood to be simply a temporary aesthetic experience but rather as the culminating core of a genuine human life. For Rupa there is only one true *rasa*, love of God, which constitutes the highest religious experience. This one true *rasa* is to be distinguished from the ordinary (*laukika*) *rasas* of classical theory, for it is understood to be extraordinary (*alaukika*), even an aspect of divinity (*shuddha sattva*).

The special nature of devotional *rasa* for Rupa, however, can best be seen by closely examining his understanding of its Foundational Emotion (*sthayi-bhava*); in fact, an understanding of the uniqueness of this foundational emotion is the key to understanding Rupa's entire system. Rupa states: "The Foundational Emotion here is declared to be that love [*rati*] which takes Shri Krishna as its object [*vishaya*]" (verse 2). As was already mentioned, the classical *rasa* theory passed down from Bharata recognized eight Foundational Emotions; a ninth was added later. Although Rupa will proceed to introduce variety into love, it is clear that *bhakti-rasa* has a single and very special Foundational Emotion. For him, then, all genuine *rasa* is based on some form of love, or more specifically, some form of love for Krishna.

So important is this special Foundational Emotion for Rupa that a major portion of his text is concerned with determining how to cultivate it. This leads him to a lengthy consideration of *sadhana*, or religious practice.[20] The aim of this religious practice is the production of the Foundational Emotion. Although Rupa will go on to discuss various types of *rasa*, it is important to understand that for him all *rasas* are rooted in the single Foundational Emotion of love for Krishna (*krishna-rati*). Rupa has a keen awareness of the great differences found among the various kinds of devotees. In fact, he claims that the type of love experienced is dependent upon the type of "vessel" (*patra* or *ashraya*) experiencing it; thus he is able to develop a system that simultaneously recognizes the oneness and multiplicity of love. He writes: "The particular form that love takes is determined by the specific nature of the individual experiencing it, just as a reflected image of the sun is determined by the nature of the jewel through which it is being reflected" (verse 7). Though love is one, it is experienced as many because of the different types of people experiencing it. Concomitantly, the form in which Krishna appears is determined by the perceptual disposition of the devotee; this means that divinity is also simultaneously one and multiple. This allows Rupa to develop what amounts to a typology of religious experience. Though he has declared devotional *rasa* to be one, a typology of religious experience (or *bhavas*, to use his Sanskrit term) enables him to correlate his theory to the previous theories that recognize a number of *rasas*, while at the same time maintaining that all *rasas* are rooted in the same Foundational Emotion of love for Krishna.

Rupa divides the *rasas* into Primary *Rasas* and Secondary *Rasas*. The Primary *Rasas* are five in number (verse 115) and are understood to be direct forms of *rati*, or "love" for Krishna. The Secondary *Rasas* are seven in number (verse 116) and correspond to the remaining *rasas* of the classical theory. The ninth *rasa* of classical theory, the Peaceful *Rasa* of *shanta*, is included as the first of the Primary *Rasas* by being defined as a particular type of love. What distinguishes a Primary *Rasa* from a Secondary *Rasa* is that the former are based on a Foundational Emotion that is "self-supporting," whereas the Secondary *Rasas* are based on Foundational Emotions that are supported by a Primary Foundational Emotion.[21] In all cases, the Primary Foundational Emotion is a form of love (*rati*), defined as "a special form of the pure and luminous quality" (verse 3), an aspect of divinity. On their own, the Secondary Foundational Emotions lack this essential quality, but they come to share in it through association with a Primary form of love. Once again, we observe the centrality of love, or *rati*, in Rupa's system. In effect, then, the five Primary *Rasas* are simply variant forms of what is called the *shringara rasa* in the classical theory, since this is the *rasa* based on the Foundational Emotion of *rati*. Rupa employs the terminology of all the aesthetic components to lay out his twelvefold schema of *rasa*. He first does this in a generic way, devoting five respective chapters to a general discussion of the Excitants, Indications, Responses, Transitory Emotions, and Foundational Emotions; he proceeds to a detailed analysis of the five forms of Primary *Rasa* in the second half of his text.

The five forms of Primary *Rasa*—Peaceful, Respectful, Companionable, Parentally Affectionate, and Amorous—are presented in a hierarchical manner by Rupa, with the last clearly being the highest (verse 115). The criterion of hierarchical judgment employed is the intensity of emotional connectedness (*sambandha*), expressed in terms of several related concepts. One of these has to do with a particular understanding of the sense of "myness" (*mamata*), which signals personal attachment. Although this term is frequently assumed to have negative connotations in philosophical literature concerned with achieving absolute unity with *Brahman*, Rupa uses it in a very positive fashion to indicate an important ingredient of a strong relationship with Krishna. Gaudiya Vaishnava philosophy rejects the realization of absolute unity with *Brahman* in favor of an intimate relationship with *Brahman* as the infinitely qualified Bhagavan Krishna. This requires personal attachment, which depends on a sense of ownership and individuality. This is what is being expressed by the positive use of the term "myness." Rupa employs this term to define the Foundational Emotion of the Peaceful *Rasa*: "Generally, Peaceful Love arises in tranquil people who comprehend Krishna as the highest Self [*paramatman*] but are without even a trace of the sense of 'myness'" (verse 18). Accordingly, he places the Peaceful *Rasa* (*shanta*) on the bottom of his hierarchical list of the Primary *Rasas*, for the others involve increasing amounts of this sense of myness (verse 22), and the Amorous *Rasa* identifies most intensely with this sentiment.

The particular typology of religious experience Rupa presents in the *Bhaktirasamritasindhu* utilizes all the aesthetic components of the classical tradition. In the selection translated here, the Foundational Emotions of this typology are discussed. The chief elements of Rupa's typology are the varying object (*vishaya*), shifting vessels (*ashraya*), and the resulting different religious experiences (*bhavas*). Rupa begins his presentation and analysis of the Primary *Rasas* with the Peaceful *Rasa* (*shanta-bhakti-rasa*), whose Foundational Emotion is Nondistinct Love (verses 8–26). The particular form in which Krishna is encountered in Nondistinct Love is one appropriate to *yogic* meditation, the four-armed Vishnu, which is described as being appropriate for *yogic* meditation in texts such as the *Bhagavata Purana*.[22] The vessels of this *rasa* are the peaceful (*shanta*) devotees, defined as those who have achieved tranquillity and then go on to experience a love for Krishna. Rupa represents the resulting emotional experience (*bhava*) as being somewhat similar to the joy of the *yogis*, except that the object of the *yogis*' quest is said to be the Self (*atman*), whereas the object (*vishaya*) of this *rasa* is the Lord (*isha*). This is what makes the Peaceful *Rasa* a devotional *rasa* for Rupa; it is still a form of love (*rati*) directed toward Krishna. The classical understanding of the Peaceful *Rasa* is that it is the absence of all emotions; it is the still ocean in which all waves of passion have been eliminated. This, however, would not be a true *rasa*, according to Rupa, who defines the experience of *rasa* as involving some type of love. The Peaceful *Rasa* is also placed lowest on the hierarchical scale because it involves only an encounter with the essential form (*svarupa*) of the Lord, and is not connected in any way with his charming *lila*s or divine play.

Moving up the hierarchical ladder, the next type of religious experience, or devotional *rasa*, is the Respectful *Rasa* (*prita-bhakti-rasa*),[23] whose Foundational Emotion is Respect (verses 27–29). Here Krishna appears as a superior master or protective elder, and the devotees take on the forms of his servants or younger relatives. The resulting religio-emotional experience is connected with a relationship in which Krishna as the supreme Lord is encountered as the worshiper's own caretaker. Since the intensity of this type of relationship is compromised by a differential in power, it is surpassed by the following types.

The third type of devotional *rasa* is that of Companionship (*preyo-bhakti-rasa*, also known as *sakhya* or *maitri-maya rasa*), whose Foundational Emotion is Friendship (verses 30–32). Here Krishna appears as the devotee's friend, and the devotee assumes the position of Krishna's equal friend. The devotees who experience this *rasa* are completely unrestrained and enjoy confident familiarity with Krishna. We begin to see the positive effects of the increasing presence of "myness" (*mamata*) and approachability, and the concomitant fading of the majestic perspective that was dominant in the previous *rasa*. The unique feature of this *rasa* is its Foundational Emotion of Friendship (*sakhya*), which exists between two persons of approximately equal status; it consists of confident familiarity and lacks any sense of awesome respect. Because of the more equal power relationship, intimate friendship is possible, making this *rasa* much more intense than the previous two.

The second most intense *rasa*, according to Rupa, is the *rasa* of Parental Affection (*vatsala-bhakti-rasa*). Here Krishna (as the *vishaya*) appears as a child in need of nurturing protection, and the devotee (as the *ashraya*) assumes the position of an elder who cares for young Krishna. These are opposite to the conditions of the Respectful *Rasa*. Since Krishna is here the recipient of kindness and protection, his majestic power is not manifest. Krishna's foster parents Yashoda and Nanda are ranked the highest among this type of devotee. The Foundational Emotion of this *rasa* is defined as Parental Affection (verses 33–35), which consists of a kind and caring love that is devoid of deferential respect. This *rasa*, too, has a unique feature: it will not diminish when not reciprocated. When mutual friendship is not returned, it disappears, whereas there is no expectation of mutual friendship from a tiny baby. Rupa, therefore, recognizes a unique strength in this kind of love.

The most supreme devotional *rasa* and the highest type of religious experience possible is the Amorous *Rasa* (*madhura-bhakti-rasa*), whose Foundational Emotion is Amorous Love (verses 36–37). Rupa has written another book devoted entirely to this single *rasa*, the *Ujjvalanilamani*. This is clearly the highest *rasa* for him, and he presents it in the familiar terms of the classical *rasa* theory. The erotically charming Krishna is the object (*vishaya*) of this *rasa*, and the *gopis* of Braj are its vessels (*ashrayas*). The most exalted of all the women—of all vessels or devotees, for that matter—is Radha, daughter of Vrishabhanu. The Foundational Emotion of Amorous Love (*madhura-rati*) is explored elsewhere in the text in terms of the various states of union and separation. The distinctive feature of this *rasa* is that it is not diminished by any circumstances. It is clear from Rupa's statements that this *rasa* encompasses the strengths of all the other forms of love, making it the *rasa* par excellence.

In summary, Rupa has created a typology of religious experience that ranks the various types of possible ultimate relationships in terms of intimacy with the divine and intensity of emotion. Within this typology Rupa is able to place both the Peaceful (*shanta*) experience of the ascetic *yoga* traditions, which often define the ultimate state as the absence of all emotions, and the Amorous (*shringara*) experience of passionate devotion, which seeks to utilize the power of all emotions to establish a solid connection with the divine as beloved. These two impulses represent polar tensions that have defined and enlivened much creative debate within Hindu philosophy, and Rupa's presentation provides yet another important way of viewing their relationship.[24]

Rupa's view of the Foundational Emotion appears fairly unique and radical when compared with the classical *rasa* theory of Bharata, for whom the Excitant causes the emotion. In this section, Rupa asserts: "This charming love makes Krishna and related factors into an Excitant and other related aesthetic components, and then expands itself by means of these very components" (verse 94). What he is saying here is that the Foundational Emotion of love makes objects into Excitants, or opportunities to experience love in intense ways. "Ordinary" objects then become occasions for the expression or experience of love. An ordinary cloud, for example, may evoke the experience of love, but it is the *bhava* or Foundational Emotion that makes the cloud into an object of love that determines the experience. This may be illustrated with an everyday example. Say one person is madly in love with another, but for some reason is separated from the beloved. If the beloved happened to leave a jacket behind, the sight of that jacket will be an occasion to experience the pangs of love. The jacket itself is not the foundational cause of the love, however, but is rather an object that evokes a preexisting love. Another person may very well walk past the jacket and experience nothing whatsoever, viewing it simply as an old piece of clothing. Again, the *bhava* is the determining factor, and this is what makes Rupa's system quite different from Bharata's, wherein the dramatic objects function as Excitants to create a particular feeling. For Rupa, love is and remains Foundational, or, to repeat (and reverse) the common adage: "Love is God." Once it has sprouted in the heart, it expands and expresses itself by means of various aesthetic components. In this regard, Rupa writes: "This process is just like the ocean that, having filled clouds with its own water, increases itself by means of this very rain water" (verse 95). Besides suggesting the identity of love and Krishna, this verse indicates more about the expanding nature of love; once established, it goes on increasing its own delight through its joyful play with various components, now seen as part of itself. This is the eternal play of love as understood by Rupa and other Gaudiya theologians.

The ultimate experience, according to Rupa in the *Bhaktirasamritasindhu*, then, is one continual and expansive religio-aesthetic experience of love. This involves playful interaction between the dynamically interconnected lover, the beloved, and love itself. Once love has been established in the purified heart, the entire world becomes a divine stage and an occasion for experiencing blissful love for Krishna, who in fact (according to Gaudiya theology) is not different from the world—not, at least, from the world seen with a clear mind and a soft heart characterized by the state of pure luminosity (shuddha-sattva).

Bhaktirasamritasindhu, Southern Quadrant, Fifth Wave: The Foundational Emotions

Now the Foundational Emotions [sthayi-bhavas]:
1. That emotion that dominates all compatible and incompatible emotions and shines forth like the best of kings is called a Foundational Emotion.[25]

2. The Foundational Emotion here is declared to be that love [rati] which takes Shri Krishna as its object [vishaya]. The knowers of rasa say it is of two types: Primary [mukhya] and Secondary [gauni].

Primary Love:
3. Love, which is a special form of the pure and luminous quality,[26] is called Primary. Primary love itself is further divided into two types: "self-supporting" [svartha] and "supportive of another" [parartha].

Self-supporting:
4. Love that clearly nourishes its own self with compatible emotions, and is not diminished by incompatible emotions is called "Self-supporting" love.

Supportive of another:
5. Love that contracts itself and supports both compatible and incompatible emotions is called "supportive of another."[27]

6. The Primary Foundational Emotions, which consist of Love that is both Self-Supporting and Supportive of Another, are of five types: Nondistinction [shuddha], Respect [priti], Friendship [sakhya], Parental Affection [vatsalya], and Amorousness [priyata].[28]

7. The particular form that love takes is determined by the specific nature of the individual experiencing it, just as a reflected image of the sun is determined by the nature of the jewel through which it is being reflected.[29]

Nondistinct Love:
8. Nondistinct Love, which is indicated by shaking limbs and blinking eyes,[30] is of three kinds: common [samanya], clear [svaccha], and peaceful [shanti].

Common:
9. The love for Krishna that has no special characteristics and is seen in the common people and the small girls of Braj is considered to be "common."

An illustration:
[Upon seeing Krishna, who had just arrived in Mathura, a resident of Mathura says:]
10. When that sweet sun rose before me on this street in Mathura, my heart melted like wax. Tell me, O Friend, what has happened?[31]

Another illustration:
11. Old Woman, take a close look at this three-year-old girl! Upon seeing Krishna, she let out a shout and is rushing toward him.

Clear:
12. Love that takes a variety of forms in the practitioners due to different types of spiritual practices and association with different types of devotees is considered to be "clear."

13. It assumes the form [or color] of the particular type of love possessed by the devotee to whom one is attracted, just like a transparent crystal.[32] For this reason it is called "clear."

An illustration:
14. There was a noble brahmin who experienced a variety of emotional states through a variety of services. Sometimes he would consider the Lord as an all-powerful master and praise him, sometimes he would consider the Lord as a friend and laugh with him, sometimes he would consider the Lord as his son and care for him, sometimes he would consider the Lord as his beloved and make love to him, and sometimes he would consider the Lord as the highest Self and meditate upon him in his mind.

15. As a general rule, Clear Love is for those noble persons whose minds are extremely pure, but who have not yet sipped from the ocean of happiness that yields the variety of particular emotions.[33]

Peaceful
16. The cessation of any fluctuations of the mind[34] is called "tranquillity" [*shama*].

It has been said:
17. That natural state of the Self, after one has abandoned engagement in sense-objects and is situated in the joy of the Self, is here called tranquillity.[35]

18. Generally, Peaceful Love arises in tranquil people who comprehend Krishna as the highest Self [*paramatman*] but are without even a trace of the sense of "myness" [*mamata*].[36]

An illustration:
19. When the divine sage Narada began to sing with his lute in the great celebration of Hari's *lila*, the body of Sanaka[37] trembled, even though he had realized the highest reality of *Brahman*.

Another illustration:
20. Having completely disregarded the experience of liberation [*moksha*] under the influence of service to Hari's dear devotees, my mind longs to see that form of the greatly desired and highest *Brahman* who is as beautiful as a dark cloud.

21. Since this form of love has no connection with the particular tastes and experiences associated with the other forms of love that are about to be explained, it is called "nondistinct."[38]

22. Now, the three types of love that are soothing to the heart—called Respect [*priti*], Friendship [*sakhya*], and Parental Affection [*vatsalya*]—are born from a deep sense of kindness [*anukulata*] and are always associated with the sense of "myness" [*mamata*].[39]

23. These three types of love, Respect, Friendship, and Parental Affection, are found in three types of Krishna's devotees, respectively, those he favors, his friends, and his elders.

24. This threefold love, which causes such Indications as wide-open eyes, yawning, and trembling, can take two forms: single [*kevala*] and mixed [*sankula*].

Single:
25. A single love is without even a trace of another type of love, and is exemplified, respectively, in the servants of Braj such as Rasala, the friends such as Shridama, and the elders such as Nanda, the king of Braj.

Mixed:
26. A mixed love is a combination of two or three types of love and is exemplified respectively in such characters as Uddhava, Bhima, and Mukhara. The particular name is determined according to which love is dominant.[40]

Respect:
27. Those who think of themselves as inferior to Hari are considered to be His favored subordinates. The love found in them, which consists of honor, is called "Respect."[41]

28. This kind of love produces attachment to Hari and destroys affection for everything else.

An illustration is in the *Mukundamala*:
29. I don't care if my residence is to be in heaven, on earth, or in hell, O Destroyer of Hell. My prayer is simply that at the moment of death I will think of your feet, which are far more beautiful than autumn lotuses.[42]

Friendship:
30. The wise have determined that those who consider themselves to be equal to Mukunda are his friends. Their love, which takes the form of the intimacy that comes from a sense of equality, is called "Friendship." It is free from restraint and produces such actions as joking and laughing.[43]

An illustration:
31. I had gone off desirous of seeing the flowering forest. When I returned, those boys—whose hearts are broken from just a moment of separation from me—saw me from a distance, and with their hair standing on end, played a game to see who could run and touch me first.

Another illustration:
32. Even though you arm-wrestle playfully with Shridama and thereby destroy your heap of pride by losing, O Damodara, still every day you continue to boast and thereby wash your hands of all shame.

Parental Affection:
33. Hari's supervisors are considered to be his respected elders.[44] Their love, which consists of kindness, is called "Parental Affection." It produces such actions as caressing him, giving auspicious blessings, and tickling his chin.[45]

An illustration:
[Yashoda says:]
34. That boy Krishna is always going into the dense forest to watch over the cows, which are continually threatened by the huge, mountainous servants of Kamsa, who is extremely hostile for no reason whatsoever. Ah, what am I to do?

Another illustration:
35. The breasts of Yashoda, wife of the king of Braj, flowed with milk and her heart was filled with tenderness as she placed her fingers on the tip of the chin of her son, who was standing in front of the house, and gently began to caress him.

Amorous Love:

36. That love, which is the primary cause of the mutual sensual pleasure of Hari and the doe-eyed women, is called "Amorous Love" [*priyata*]; it is also known as "Sweet Love" [*madhura*]. It produces such acts as sidelong glances, raising the eyebrows, love-talk, and smiles.[46]

An illustration is in the *Govindavilasa*:

37. May that extraordinary sprout of anticipation, born from the desire to see each other in a secret place, grow victoriously for Radha and Krishna, whose hearts have been longing for each other for a long time.

38. Even though Primary Love always consists of the joy of a particular taste, it is differentiated in a hierarchical manner as the five forms of love. The particular form that love takes for a given individual is determined by unconscious impressions from previous experiences [*vasanas*].[47]

Secondary Love:

39. A particular emotion that is born from the excellence of the Excitants and is nourished by a Primary Love that has contracted[48] itself is called a Secondary Love [*gauni-rati*].

40. There are seven types of such particular emotions: Humor [*hasa*], Amazement [*vismaya*], Effort [*utsaha*], Sorrow [*shoka*], Anger [*krodha*], Fear [*bhaya*], and Disgust [*jugupsa*].

41. Although the Excitant for the first six is Krishna, the Excitant for the seventh is the body. This is because under the influence of love, there can never be any disgust for Krishna.[49]

42. Here Humor and the other forms of Secondary Love are different from the forms of Primary Love in that they are not a special form of the pure and luminous quality;[50] however, because of their association with a Primary Love that is "supportive of another,"[51] the word "love" remains applicable.

43. Love that is predominantly humorous is called "Humorous Love" [*hasa-rati*]. In a like manner, the other six forms of Secondary Love are to be understood.

44. In some situations for certain devotees, Humor and the other types of Secondary Love achieve the state of a Foundational Emotion when they become enhanced by a Primary Love, as determined by specific forms of Krishna's divine play [*lila*].

45. Therefore, these seven forms of Secondary Love are only temporary and have no steady foundation. Though they occur naturally in some devotees, they disappear when overwhelmed by more powerful emotions.

46. A Primary Love never deviates from its own foundation or from its own nature, and is established as the perfect Foundational Emotion in all devotees. Without Primary Love, all other emotions are worthless.[52]

47. Although emotions such as anger always achieve the state of a Foundational Emotion in Krishna's enemies, they are not suitable for *Bhakti-Rasa*, since they are devoid of love.[53]

48. Even when they are reinforced by compatible emotions, all Transitory Emotions eventually fade away. Therefore, they are not worthy of being considered Foundational Emotions.

49. For this reason, Transitory Emotions such as understanding and arrogance are never Foundational Emotions, though they are declared to be so by some people.[54] Our authorities on this matter are such knowledgeable people as Bharata.[55]

50. But when the seven forms of Secondary Love attain the state of a Foundational Emotion in the devotees and are well nourished by the various Transitory Emotions, their enjoyment is expanded.

Thus it is said:
51. It has been determined that the eight forms of love [one Primary Love and seven Secondary Loves] are rooted in deep and lasting impressions, whereas other types of emotions [such as the Transitory Emotions] are not; therefore the latter are not proper Foundational Emotions.[56]

Humorous Love:
52. Humor is a cheerful expansion of the heart in response to some unusual change in speech, dress, or behavior. It causes the eyes to widen, and the nose, lips, and cheeks to quiver.

53. When humor is caused by some behavior of Krishna and is nourished by a Primary Love that contracts itself, it becomes "Humorous Love" [*hasa-rati*].[57]

An illustration:
[Radha was going with her girlfriends to worship the sun and were carrying pots of yogurt for the occasion. They stopped to gather flowers and Radha met Krishna alone in the forest. They embraced

and began to enjoy each other when a messenger of Radha's came upon them and caught Radha kissing Krishna. The following is Krishna's response.]

54. "Hey Beautiful-Faced Lady, I swear to you that I did not even look at your pots of yogurt, but your shameless friend suspects me anyway and is smelling my mouth to see if I have eaten any. Set her straight about my innocence!" Upon hearing Achyuta speak these words, the messenger was unable to stop her laughter.

Amazed Love:
55. "Amazement" is a loss of mind due to some extraordinary surprise. It produces behavior such as wide-opened eyes, glorifying speech, and goose bumps. When the amazement is caused by Krishna and is associated with a contracting Primary Love, it becomes "Amazed Love" [vismaya-rati].

An illustration:
[Brahma steals the cows and cowherd boys of Braj and hides them in a cave to trick Krishna, who responds by replacing them with duplicates produced out of himself. Upon seeing the reduplicated forms Brahma says:]

56. All the young cows and cowherds are dressed in yellow, they bear the shining shrivatsa mark, their beauty is enhanced with four huge arms, they sing the praises of infinite universes, and they possess the excellent qualities of the Highest Reality. What's going on? Ah, what's going on?

Energetic Love:
57. "Effort" is a concentration of the mind that is quick and firm in mighty acts, such as war, and whose results are praised by the sages.

58. Effort involves perseverance, a disregard for time, and the abandonment of patience; when it is caused by Krishna and is associated with a contracting Primary Love, it is perfected and becomes "Energetic Love" [utsaha-rati].

An illustration:
59. When the sky was filled with the sounds of a horn, a flute, and weapons on the bank of the Yamuna, Shridama resolutely girded his loins, eager to fight with Krishna, the Destroyer of Demonic Agha, who was shouting out a challenge.[58]

Sorrowful Love:
60. Sorrow is defined as that burden of pain in the heart that is due to separation from the beloved. It produces weeping, falling to the

ground, sighing, dryness of the mouth, and confusion. When it is caused by Krishna and is associated with a contracting Primary Love, it is perfected and becomes "Sorrowful Love" [*shoka-rati*].

An illustration is in the tenth canto (*Bh.P.* 10.7.25):
61. When the force of the dust storm caused by the tornado abated, the *gopis* heard Yashoda's wailing. Not seeing Nanda's son anywhere, they became greatly agitated and began to cry, soaking their faces with tears.

Another illustration:
[Upon seeing Krishna captured by the snake demon Kaliya, Nanda laments:]
62. Seeing my son, who is dearer to me than a thousand lives, wrapped in the coils of the king of snakes, my heart still does not break in two. Shame on the hardness of this mortal body!

Angry Love:
63. Anger is defined as a burning in the heart when faced with conflict. It produces such things as harsh speech, frowning with knitted eyebrows, and a reddening of the eyes.

64. When it is caused by Krishna and is associated with a contracting Primary Love, it is perfected and becomes "Angry Love" [*krodha-rati*]. Angry Love is of two kinds: that which takes Krishna as the Excitant, and that which takes an enemy of Krishna as the Excitant.[59]

An illustration in which Krishna is the Excitant:
65. Seeing Radha's shining necklace of pearls around the neck of Hari, Radha's mother-in-law, Jatila, stared at him for a long time with a frightening look and a dreadful frown.[60]

An illustration in which Krishna's enemy is the Excitant:
66. When Kamsa's brother became a violent weapon in the form of a fierce forest fire and surrounded Hari, Balarama, the Enemy of Pralamba, immediately knitted his eyebrows in anger, thereby releasing what appeared to be a string of dark clouds onto the sky of his forehead.[61]

Fearful Love:
67. Fear is an extreme unsteadiness of the mind that is brought on by such things as one's own transgressions or some terrifying sight. It produces such reactions as hiding, dulling of the mind, flight, and aimless wandering.

68. When it is caused by Krishna and is associated with a contracting Primary Love, it becomes "Fearful Love" [*bhaya-rati*]. The wise

have said that like Angry Love, it, too, is of two types [i.e., that which takes Krishna as the Excitant, and that which takes an enemy of Krishna as the Excitant].

An illustration in which Krishna is the Excitant:
69. In the assembly, Krishna angrily asked Akrura, the son of Gandhini, for the Syamantaka jewel, which he had hidden in his clothing; Akrura was rendered senseless with fright, and his mouth became dry.[62]

An illustration in which Krishna's enemy is the Excitant:
70. Ah! When the bull demon roared violently like a thundering cloud at the entrance of the cowherd village, Yashoda, queen of Braj, trembled with fear and became single-mindedly intent upon protecting her son.

Disgusted Love:
71. Disgust is a withdrawal of the mind from an unpleasant experience. It produces such behavior as spitting, contorting the face, and words of contempt. When it is born from a supportive form of Primary Love, it is judged to be "Disgusted Love" [jugupsa-rati].[63]

An illustration:
72. Ever since my mind has begun to delight in the lotus-feet of Krishna, which are the abode of new and ever-fresh rasas, I spit and my face becomes contorted when remembering my sexual escapades with women.

73. Until Primary Love and the seven forms of Secondary Love reach the position of a rasa, they remain the eight Foundational Emotions.

74. The Transitory Emotions counted independently are thirty-three; when combined with the eight Foundational Emotions and the Eight Responses, there are forty-nine emotions in all.

75. Since all these emotions are associated with Krishna, they completely transcend the three ordinary qualities of existence [gunas] and consist of abundant joy [ananda]. Nevertheless, they look as though they consist of the happiness and sorrow that is produced from the three ordinary qualities of existence.[64]

76. Therefore, such emotions as shyness, awakening, and effort appear to be related to the pure quality [sattvika-guna]; such emotions as arrogance, happiness, dreaming, and humor appear to be related to the energetic quality [rajasa-guna]; and such emotions as

grief, depression, confusion, and sorrow appear to be related to the heavy quality [*tamasa-guna*].

77. Happy emotions are generally cool, and the sad emotions are generally hot. What is amazing here is that even though love is a concentration of the highest joy [*paramananda*], it can appear to be hot.[65]

78. When nourished by powerful cool emotions, love becomes cooling, but when nourished by hot emotions, it appears very hot, as if it were heating. Therefore, in separation it is called the semblance of the burden of sorrow.

79. Both types of love [Primary and Secondary] are transformed into *rasa* in the devotees when they hear, see, or remember Krishna and related factors that function as the Excitants and the other related aesthetic components.[66]

80. Just as a substance consisting of yogurt and other ingredients is mixed in a special way with sugar and spices [and] becomes the drink called *Rasala*,

81. So here, too, in the same way, the devotees relish the inexpressible wonder of abundant joy [i.e., *rasa*] from a direct experience of Krishna and the other aesthetic components.[67]

82. Even though the *rasa* has become one with love and the other aesthetic components, such as the Excitant, the special qualities of the various components of the *rasa* can be perceived distinctly.[68]

For as it is said:
83. The Excitants and other aesthetic components are first recognized as separate units, but upon becoming *rasa*, they are mixed and achieve a seamless unity.

84. Sometimes the individual ingredients can be tasted in sherbet, even though there is a oneness of the sugar and spices. In a like manner, the individual Excitants and other aesthetic components can sometimes be experienced distinctly in *rasa*, even though they have achieved a oneness.

85. Krishna and Krishna's dear devotees are the "cause" [*karana*] of love [*rati*]; emotions such as stupefaction are the "results" [*karya*] of love, and such emotions as indifference are its "companions" [*sahayaka*].

86. In the context of *rasa*, the ordinary meaning of the terms "cause," "results," and "companions" is left behind, and they assume the

names "Excitant" [*vibhava*], "Indications" [*anubhava*],[69] and "Transitory Emotions" [*vyabhichari-bhava*].

87. The Excitants are so called by the wise because they make possible the various kinds of special experiences of love.

88. Such actions as sidelong glances, along with the Responses, are called Indications because they allow the love to be perceived and cause a deep experience of the love to permeate the heart.

89. Emotions such as indifference are judged to be Transitory Emotions because they cause love to wander and in this way lead to variety in the love.

90. Some scholars partial to poetry and drama are of the opinion that the involvement in poetry and drama about the Lord is the primary cause of the aforementioned aesthetic components.[70]

91. However, the ultimate cause of the aesthetic components is the power of love itself, which is the wonderful perfection of a sweetness [*madhurya*] that is beyond reason.[71]

92. That emotion called love [*rati*] shares in the inconceivable divine nature [*achintyasvarupa*], and its essence is the playful emanation of the great power [*mahashakti*].[72] As such, it cannot be invalidated by reason. Indeed, the ancient ones have illustrated this with a passage from the *Mahabharata*.

It is said in the *Udyama Parva*:
93. Those emotions that are inconceivable are unable to unite with reason. "Inconceivable" is defined as something that is beyond all ordinary nature.

94. This charming love makes Krishna and related factors into an Excitant and other related aesthetic components, and then expands itself by means of these very components.[73]

95. This process is just like the ocean, which, having filled clouds with its own water, increases itself by means of this very rain water.[74]

96. In the case of an inexperienced devotee who has just experienced a young sprout of love, a poem or drama about Hari may be somewhat effective in providing the Excitants and other aesthetic components.[75]

97. But saints with a mature love experience *rasa* upon hearing about Hari in the slightest degree; and in this case, the cause of the aesthetic components is clearly the powerful influence of their love.[76]

98. Love makes Krishna and related factors vessels of sweetness, and then when Krishna and the related factors are experienced as such, they expand the love.

99. Therefore, here a perpetual and mutual support can clearly be seen between this love [the Foundational Emotion] and the four aesthetic components of the Excitants, the Indications, the Responses, and the Transitory Emotions.

100. But when there is a deformity in the Excitant or other aesthetic components, then even the power of love contracts itself. A deformity is defined as an impropriety [*anaucityam*] in the aesthetic components.[77]
101. Because of its extraordinary [*alaukika*] nature, the state of *Rasa*, wherein all the aesthetic components clearly appear as "generalized" [*sadharanata*], is extremely difficult to understand.[78]

102. Ancient sages have defined the "generalization" [*sadharanya*] of the aesthetic components as the disregard of the sense of "my" and "another."[79]

Shri Bharata has said:
103. In generalized actions there is a special power of the Excitants and other aesthetic components by which the experiencer apprehends them as his own.[80]

104. In aesthetic experience, even if one sometimes experiences a sorrow that appears to relate to one's self, the wonder of concentrated joy is still experienced.[81]

105. Also, the abundance of supreme joy increases when happy emotions appear in the heart, although sometimes they seem to belong to another.[82]

106. If a true emotion [*sad-bhava*] is born from only slight exposure to one of the aesthetic components, then it will proceed to the full state of *Rasa* from the immediate supplementation of the other four aesthetic components.[83]

107. The knowers of drama are of the opinion that love [the Foundational Emotion] situated in the original characters by ordinary causes cannot become *Rasa*.[84] What they say is correct.

108. However, the extraordinary love for Krishna [*Krishna-rati*], which is the wonder of all wonders, does proceed to a special *Rasa* in the beloved ones of Hari in union with Him.[85]

109. In separation, however, even though this powerful love is really a mature and wonderful joy, it assumes the semblance of excessive pain.

110. Therefore, that love that takes the son of the chief of the cow-herds as its Substantial Excitant reaches the highest limit of the wonder of the most concentrated joy.[86]

111. Just as the sage Agastya instantly drinks up the entire ocean by his own power, so too does this special love [which has Krishna of Braj as its object] drink up the sweet ocean of joy resulting from the direct perception of other forms of divinity, such as the Lord of Rukmini.[87]

112. In fact, since the Foundational Emotion of love and all the other aesthetic components are identical with the highest joy [para-mananda],[88] the self-manifesting and indivisible nature of Rasa is established.

113. Love was previously declared to be divided into two types: Primary and Secondary. Accordingly, Bhakti-Rasa is also of two types: Primary and Secondary.

114. Although love has a fivefold nature, because of its unity the Primary Rasas are here counted as one; when combined with the seven Secondary Rasas, the Bhakti-Rasas number eight.

Primary Bhakti-Rasas:
115. The fivefold Primary Bhakti-Rasas are Peacefulness [shanta], Respectfulness [prita], Companionship [preyas], Parental Affection [vatsala], and Amorousness [madhura]. These are to be regarded in a hierarchical manner in which the first is considered the lowest.

Secondary Bhakti-Rasas:
116. The seven Secondary Bhakti-Rasas are: Humorousness [hasya], Wonder [adbhuta], Heroism [vira], Compassion [karuna], Fury [raudra], Dreadfulness [bhayanaka], Abhorrence [bibhatsa].

117. Thus, from this twofold division, Bhakti-Rasa is said to be of twelve kinds. But, in fact, in the Puranas only five kinds are to be seen.[89]

118. The colors of the twelve Bhakti-Rasas are, respectively: white, variegated, pink, crimson, dark blue, pale yellow, bright yellow, golden, purple, red, black, and blue.

119. The gods of the twelve Bhakti-Rasas are, respectively: Kapila, Madhava, Upendra, Nrisimha, Nandanandana, Balarama, Kurma, Kalki, Raghava [Rama], Bhargava [Parashurama], Kiri [Varaha], and Mina.[90]

120. The aesthetic experience of all *Bhakti-Rasas* is said to be of five kinds: (1) completion [*purtti*], (2) openness [*vikasha*], (3) expansion [*vistara*], (4) bewilderment [*vikshepa*], and (5) agitation [*kshobha*].

121. The wise have declared that in the Peaceful *Rasa* there is "completion"; in Respectfulness, Companionship, Parental Affection, Amorousness, and Humorousness there is "openness"; in Wonder and Heroism there is "expansion"; in Compassion and Fury there is "bewilderment"; and in Dreadfulness and Abhorrence there is "agitation."

122. Even though all the *rasas* are of a nature that is entirely pleasurable, from time to time there is an inexplicable kind of special experience in the *rasas*.

123. Even though such *rasas* as Compassion immediately strike both the ignorant and the uncouth rustics as sorrowful, the cultured know them truly to consist of abundant joy [*ananda*].[91]

124. It is well established that happiness can clearly result from such *rasas* [as Compassion] when by the play of love and the instruction of the wise the extraordinary [i.e., Krishna] becomes their Excitant.

As it says in the dramatic literature:
125. That even a *rasa* like Compassion can produce supreme happiness needs no other proof than the fact that the intelligent experience it as such.[92]

126. If this were not so, then works such as the *Ramayana* would cause sorrow, since the *rasa* called Compassion appears throughout it.

127. But if this were the case, then how could Hanuman, who is an ocean filled with waves of supreme love for the lotus-feet of Rama, listen continually to the *Ramayana* with pleasure?

Moreover,
128. If the love for a friend [with similar devotional feelings] is the same as or less than the love for Krishna, then it is a Transitory Emotion; but if this love grows to the point where it exceeds the love for Krishna, then it is called "Emotional Rapture" [*bhavollasa*].[93]

129. Those who are burned out by worthless asceticism, those who possess dry knowledge,[94] the logicians, and especially the Mimamsakas [specialists of rituals designed to control karma] are all incapable of experiencing devotion.

130. Because of this, the connoisseurs of devotion should always protect the *Rasa* of devotion to Krishna from the dried-up old Mimamsakas, just as one would protect a valuable treasure from a thief.

131. The *Rasa* associated with the Lord is incomprehensible in every respect for those without devotion; it can be relished only by those devotees who have made the lotus-feet of Krishna their all in all.

132. *Rasa* is judged to be that which passes beyond the course of contemplation [*bhavana*] and becomes an experience of abundant amazement that is relished intensely in a heart illuminated by purity.[95]

133. Emotion [*bhava*], however, is said to be that state of contemplation [*bhavana*] which is experienced by means of the deep unconscious impressions [*samskaras*][96] in the heart of a wise person with focused intelligence.

134. May the Eternal Lord, who expands the *Bhava* of Raghunath [i.e., Rama] by assuming the beautiful form of Gopala, be pleased with this Southern Quadrant of the *Ocean of the Essence of Devotional Rasa.*

[This verse can also be translated as:]
134. May Sanatana Gosvamin, who enhances the *Bhava* of Raghunath Dasa Gosvamin while enlightening Gopala Bhatta Gosvamin and Rupa Gosvamin, be pleased with this Southern Quadrant of this *Ocean of the Essence of Devotional Rasa.*

NOTES

1. I have translated this entire text. See *The Bhaktirasamritasindhu of Rupa Gosvamin*, translated introduction and notes by David L. Haberman (New Delhi: Indira Gandhi National Centre for the Arts, 2002).

2. Friedhelm Hardy, *Viraha-Bhakti: The Early History of Krsna Devotion in South India* (Delhi: Oxford University Press, 1983), 6–10.

3. Gaudiya sources for the life story of Rupa Gosvamin include the *Chaitanya Charitamrita* of Krishnadasa Kaviraja, the *Laghuvaishnava Toshani* of Jiva Gosvamin, and the *Bhaktiratnakara* of Narahari Chakravartin. A good Bengali account of Rupa's life can be found in Nareshchandra Jana, *Vrindavaner Chaya Gosvami* (Calcutta: Kalikata Vishvavidyalaya, 1970), 83–147. A fairly solid account in English is available in S. K. De, *Early History of the Vaisnava Faith and Movement in Bengal* (Calcutta: Firma KLM, 1962). A good account in Hindi is available in Prabhudayal Mital, *Braj ke Dharma-Sampradayo ka Itihas* (Delhi: National Publishing House, 1968), 311–314.

4. Jana, *Vrindavaner Chaya Gosvami*, 19–21. See also the fine discussion of the dating of Rupa's life by Neal Delmonico, "Sacred Rapture: A Study of the Religious Aesthetic of Rupa Gosvamin" (Ph.D. diss., University of Chicago, 1990), 279–280.

5. These are the names given to the three brothers later by Chaitanya. Anupama's original name is recorded as Vallabha, but information is uncertain about the original names of Sanatana and Rupa. Mital and others have stated that their names were Amara and Santosh, respectively. See Mital, *Braj ke Dharma-Sampradayo ka Itihas*, 311.

6. Some Gaudiya sources claim that Sanatana and Rupa were forced into the service of the nawab. See Mital, *Braj ke Dharma-Sampradayo ka Itihas*, 28.

7. A sense of his discontent may be gleaned from this verse Rupa is reported to have sent his brother Sanatana after leaving his post in the Muslim court:

Where, alas, is Ayodhya, the kingdom of Rama now? Its glories have disappeared. And where is the famous Mathura of Krishna? It also is devoid of its former splendor. Think of the fleeting nature of things and settle your course. (Quoted in Dinesh Chandra Sen, *Chaitanya and His Age* [Calcutta: University of Calcutta, 1924], 220)

8. This is recorded in Krishnadasa Kaviraja's *Chaitanya Charitamrita* 2.19, especially 104 and the following pages.

9. A document recently translated by Irfan Habib, however, suggests that Rupa may have been alive still in 1566. See Irfan Habib, "A Documentary History of the Gosains (Gosvamis) of the Caitanya Sect at Vrindavana," in *Govindadeva: A Dialogue in Stone*, edited by Margaret H. Case (New Delhi: Indira Gandhi National Centre for the Arts, 1996), 156.

10. In fact, Rupa came to be identified by later practitioners of his *Raganuga Bhakti Sadhana* as an eternal character in Krishna's *lila*, most specifically as Rupa Manjari, the chief assistant of the important *sakhi*, Lalita. See my *Acting as a Way of Salvation: A Study of Raganuga Bhakti Sadhana* (1988; reprint, Delhi: Motilal Banarsidass, 2001), 90–91, 107, and 113–114.

11. For example, Vallabha's *Subhodini* is filled with uses of and references to the *rasa* theory and its vital components, such as the *vibhava*, *anubhava*, and *vyabhichari-bhava*.

12. *Raso vai sah. rasam hyevayam labdhvanandi bhavati*. Verse 2.7.

13. This list includes eight *sthayi-bhavas* and thirty-three *vyabhichari-bhavas*. See *Natya Shastra* 7.6. The text I translate from is *Natya Shastram of Bharatamuni*, with the commentary of Abhinavagupta, edited with Sanskrit and Hindi commentaries by Madhusudan Shastri, 2 vols. (Varanasi: Banaras Hindu University, 1971). If the eight *sattvika-bhavas* are added, the list becomes forty-nine, but many later writers consider the *sattvika-bhavas* to be types of *anubhavas*.

14. The *Natya Shastra* says that the *sthayi-bhava* is greatest among the *bhavas*, just as a king is greatest among people and the *guru* is greatest among the disciples (7.8).

15. A good discussion of these components of dramatic experience is found in S. K. De, *History of Sanskrit Poetics* (Calcutta: K. L. Mukhopadhyay, 1960), vol. 2. I have translated these terms, respectively, as the Excitants, Indications, and Transitory Emotions.

16. NÍ 6.32. Although Bharata does not mention the *sthayi-bhavas* in this *sutra*, in a statement that follows soon after the *sutra* he states that the *sthayi-bhavas* attain the state of Rasa (*rasatva*) in combination with the various *bhavas* (*tatha nanabhavopagata api sthayino bhava rasatvam apnuvanti*).

17. NÍ 7.4.

18. NÍ 7.5.

19. NÍ 7.93.

44. Although, in reality, Krishna is superior to all, for the sake of relishing *Rasa*, he appears as a small and helpless child. This apparent transformation is an important ingredient of the love-play of Braj.

45. Jiva glosses Parental Affection as "love consisting of an identity of elderness" (*gurutva-abhimana-maya-rati*).

46. Jiva makes it clear that for this type of love, Krishna is the "object" (*vishaya*) for the devotees, and the devotees themselves are the "objects" for Krishna. In this sense, Amorous Love is declared to be "mutual." Jiva goes on to mark the latter kind of love (wherein the devotees are the objects) as an Enhancing Excitant (*uddipana-vibhava*) of the former (wherein Krishna is the object for the devotees).

47. The specific order of hierarchy is as follows. Amorous Love is greater than Parental Affection, which is greater than Friendship, which is greater than Respect, which is greater than Nondistinct Love. The ranking depends on the power of attraction (*utkarsha*) inherent in each emotion. The *vasana*s are karmic residues from previous lives or experiences that determine one's present disposition. Vishvanath makes it clear that the hierarchy implies that a lower form of love is present in the higher, but not the other way around. There is no Amorousness in Parental Affection, for example, but there might be Parental Affection in Amorousness.

48. Contraction here means that the Primary Love pulls in and conceals its dominant nature so that the nature of the Secondary Love can shine forth. Though concealed, however, the Primary Love remains the animating force. Jiva has an interesting explanation of this. He says people sitting on a platform make a lot of noise, not the platform itself; however, in a figurative sense it is said that the platform is noisy. In a similar manner, he explains, the Secondary Love (the platform) is called love by its association with the Primary Love (the noisy people on the platform).

49. The major difference between ordinary fear or sorrow and the Fear or Sorrow referred to here is that here fear and sorrow are under the influence of a Primary Love (which has contracted itself but remains the animating force). Being animated by Primary Love, these secondary emotions, too, are forms of love. But in any case, Krishna cannot be the object of disgust.

50. As defined in 1.3.1, the pure and luminous quality (*shuddha-sattva*) is the essential characteristic of the *bhava* of love.

51. That is, the Secondary Loves are animated by a contracted Primary Love, which does possess the special and pure and luminous quality of *shuddha-sattva*. See verse 5. The seven types of Secondary Love possess no love themselves, but being animated by a Primary Love become a form of love (*rati*).

52. The point here is that a Primary Love is always present, even when a Secondary Love is manifest.

53. The great exemplars of such emotions are Kamsa and Shishupal.

54. Bhoja does not seem to make a sharp distinction between the Foundational Emotions and the Transitory Emotions. Perhaps his position is what Rupa has in mind here.

55. I follow Jiva's gloss of knowledgeable people as "Bharata and others."

56. Vishvanath explains that even when a Secondary Love is unmanifest, it still exists in latent form (via its *samskaras*), but when a Transitory Emotion is no longer manifest, it completely vanishes. However, the Transitory Emotions—though they

cannot become Foundational Emotions—can serve to promote the Secondary loves so that their enjoyment is enhanced. The secondary emotions become Secondary Loves when associated with a Primary Love. Again, love (*rati*) is the only Foundational Emotion, or *sthayi-bhava*, of *Bhakti-Rasa*.

57. That is, the humor must be directed toward Krishna (the *vishaya*) and in association with a Primary Love (*mukhya-rati*) in order to be considered a Foundational Emotion of Krishna *bhakti*. Specifically, this involves only a Primary Love that contracts itself and supports another (*parartha-mukhya-rati*), since a self-supporting Primary Love (*svartha mukhya-rati*) would overwhelm it.

58. Here the eagerness to fight with Krishna is still a sign of Shridama's great love for him.

59. Specifically the "object" of the Substantial Excitant (*vishaya-alambana-vibhava*).

60. Jiva comments that the assumption here is that Jatila loves Krishna; otherwise this would not be Angry Love.

61. Here the anger is motivated by a love for Krishna. In this case, the objects of the love and fear are different.

62. Here too, Akrura loves Krishna, although in this case that love is covered by fear.

63. It was established in verse 41 that Krishna is never the object of this kind of love. This is made clear in the following verse.

64. The point being made here is that since Krishna himself consists of joy and transcends the three ordinary qualities of existence (as stated in *Bhagavata Purana* 11.25.24), so do all emotions associated with him. How then can sorrowful emotions, such as grief, be associated with Krishna? Jiva answers this by explaining that joy underlies all the devotional emotions, but to enhance the joy of reunion, the devotees must experience the grief or sorrow of separation from him. So whereas these emotions appear sorrowful, as ingredients of the dynamic play of love, they are really forms of joy.

65. Again, the point is that whereas the love for Krishna is always delightful (cool), it can appear to be distressful (hot). In this case, the heat is understood to come from the hot emotions themselves, such as grief, not from the love, which is ever joyful. The sorrow involved in the love of Krishna, then, must be a "semblance" of sorrow, as is stated in the following verse. In sum, even the distress of sorrow is a joyful experience when it is associated with Krishna.

66. This is another clear indication of Rupa's view on the relationship between the Foundational Emotion (*sthayi-bhava*) and Rasa. Whereas theorists such as Abhinavagupta contend that there is no ultimate relationship between the Foundational Emotion and Rasa, Rupa, in agreement with theorists such as Bhoja, holds that the Foundational Emotion is merely an underdeveloped form of *Rasa* that moves to the position of *Rasa* in the presence of the Excitants and other aesthetic components. For more on this, see the introduction to the chapter.

67. Love (*rati*), which exists in the heart of the devotee, manifests as *Rasa* when mixed with the Excitants (*vibhavas*) and other aesthetic components. In this metaphor, the yogurt substance is the Foundational Emotion of love, and the sugar and spices the Excitant and other aesthetic components that produce the special taste.

68. Rupa clearly indicates that whereas *Rasa* is one, its tastes are many. This is so because all *Rasa* is based on the same Foundational Emotion of love (Krishna-*rati*); however, that love itself takes many forms, depending on the particular aesthetic components with which it is mixed. But even in the unified mixture of *Rasa*, the distinctive tastes of each ingredient is subtly present. This is illustrated in the next two verses.

69. Rupa here includes the Responses (*sattvikas*) as types of Indications.

70. Rupa's point is that while in ordinary *rasa* theory the components of the drama are considered to be the cause of the manifestation of an emotion, here in the *Rasa* theory of Krishna, *bhakti* love is considered to be self-manifesting, as is evident in the following verse.

71. The point Rupa is making here is that love, because of its special nature identified in the following verse, itself turns things into aesthetic components, which then go on to enable the love to further manifest itself. He states this directly in verses 94 and 95. This is one of the unique features of Rupa's Rasa theory. Jiva comments that the love referred to here relates specifically to Shri Bhagavan.

72. Jiva glosses *mahashakti* as *Hladini Shakti*, the blissful energy of Krishna. As R. K. Sen says: "It should be distinctly understood that *Rasa* enjoyment always presupposes the philosophy of *shakti*. No enjoyment is possible without *shakti*." See his *Aesthetic Enjoyment* (Calcutta: University of Calcutta, 1966), 17.

73. This statement indicates a remarkable development within Indian aesthetic theory. What Rupa in effect is saying is that the Foundational Emotion is the cause of the Excitants and other aesthetic components; this is the opposite of what many other theoreticians have said. Whereas in the standard theory the aesthetic components are determinative of the aesthetic experience, here everything depends upon the essential Foundational Emotion of Krishna-*rati*. For further discussion of this point, see the introduction to this chapter. (This is quite different from Bharata, and his followers, such as Abhinavagupta, who stated that *Rasa* arises from the combination of the *vibhava*, *anubhava*, and *vyabhichari-bhava*.)

74. Again, love makes surrounding things into aesthetic components that then go on to enhance that very love. Or, put slightly differently, love makes all things into an opportunity for the experience of love. For the advanced devotee, the entire world becomes a theatre in which to experience *Rasa*.

75. Here is an admission that the ordinary way of understanding the relationship between the Foundational Emotions and other aesthetic components may have a limited value.

76. Although the poem or drama may appear to be the cause of the aesthetic components, Rupa insists that the Foundational Emotion of love for Krishna is the major determinative factor. That is, the poem or drama is just an opportunity for love, as is anything for the mature devotee. This point is reinforced in the next verse.

77. Jiva states the obvious: that the deformity is with the Excitant and other aesthetic components, and not with Krishna and his devotees (who function as Excitants). Vishvanath comments that this specifically has to do with the way Radha and Krishna are portrayed by actors on stage. For example, if Krishna appears to be older than Radha, the devotees watching the play would experience a contraction of love.

78. Jiva comments that generalization is what allows contemporary devotees to experience the emotions (*bhavas*) of ancient devotees.

79. "Generalization" involves that obliteration of egoistic consciousness that accompanies the connoisseur's identification with the aesthetic situation, and involves the union of a spectator's and actor's emotions, or an actor's and original character's emotions. In this sense, it is what makes identification with the depicted emotions possible. This facet of the aesthetic experience has been explored by the tenth-century writer Bhatta Nayaka. For further discussion of this issue, see my *Acting as a Way of Salvation*, 16–17. Vishvanath gives two interesting examples of generalization. The first concerns a sensitive devotee who was listening to the story of the *Ramayana* being recited by some sages. When they came to the part where Hanuman leaps over the ocean to reach the island of Lanka, the sensitive devotee so identified with Hanuman that he himself got up and started leaping around. The second example concerns a sensitive actor playing the part of Dasharath, Rama's father, in a dramatic performance of the *Ramayana*. When the actor playing Dasharath heard that Rama had left for the forest, he so identified with his part that he actually died of grief.

80. Vishvanath remarks that generalized emotional experience both does and does not belong to the other, and both does and does not belong to one's self (*parasya na parasyeti mameti na mameti cha*). I have not been able to locate this quotation in the *Natya Shastra*.

81. That is, *Rasa* occurs since the emotion is generalized, though it may appear to be a personal emotion. In this way, the sorrow is "aestheticized" and thus still gives pleasure. Or, more to the point, the sorrow of the *gopis* leads to increased joy.

82. The point Rupa seems to be making here is that although the emotion is located in the original character, a sensitive spectator can experience it due to its "generalized" nature.

83. Jiva makes it clear that here Rupa is identifying yet another of the special powers of love for Krishna.

84. Since the emotions situated in the original characters in ordinary drama are by definition the personal emotions of those characters, the standard theory has it that these emotions can never become *rasa*. This seems to be the position of Abhinavagupta. Rupa agrees with this, but goes on in the next verse to distinguish the extraordinary nature of *Krishna-rati* from ordinary emotions. Jiva comments that this is also the case for ordinary actors, since the actors are too involved in the business of performance to experience *rasa*. There is much debate among theorists of *rasa* regarding who can experience *rasa*. There are three possibilities: the original character (*anukarya*), the actor (*anukarta*), and the spectator (*samajika*). Abhinavagupta, for example, restricted the experience of *rasa* to the latter category. Rupa agrees in the case of ordinary drama, but in the case of love for Krishna, all changes. What he says in the next verse is that anyone who experiences Krishna-*rati* can experience *Rasa*, no matter which of the three positions that person occupies. Again, love for Krishna is the central and essential defining feature of the ultimate *Rasa* experience.

85. The point that Rupa wants to make here is that the original characters in the Krishna *lila*, such as the *gopis*, do indeed experience Rasa. For Rupa, the devotee in any position can experience *Rasa*. The deciding factor is the Foundational Emotion of love for Krishna, not one's position.

86. That is, Rupa is claiming that the highest experience of *Rasa* is that which takes Krishna Gopala as its object. Jiva relates this to *Bhagavata Purana* 2.1.121, in which it is stated that Krishna is the complete form of God (*Harih purnatama*).

87. The point here is that the love for Krishna is all-encompassing and is therefore the highest type of love possible. Jiva identifies the other form of divinity referred to here is the Lord of Shri Rukmini, stressing the superiority of the Braja-*lila* over the Dvaraka-*lila*, and the love of Krishna and the *gopis* over the love of Krishna and his wives.

88. Jiva identifies this term with the *Hladini Shakti*, Krishna's energy of bliss. He goes on to say that since Krishna himself is the Excitant of this love, there is a oneness between the aesthetic components and the highest joy, just as there is a oneness between *shakti* and *shaktiman*.

89. This means that the seven Secondary *Rasas* are not accepted as true *Bhakti-Rasas* in the Puranas. Jiva says that this is because there they are really considered Transitory Emotions.

90. Some manuscripts substitute Buddha for Mina; others substitute Buddha for Madhava.

91. Jiva adds that there are five types of people: (1) worshipful devotees (*bhavya-bhakta*), who participate in Krishna's *lila*; (2) appreciative devotees (*bhavaka-bhakta*), who view Krishna's *lilas*; (3) the insightful (*pragya*), who know the true meaning of treatises on *Rasa*; (4) the ignorant (*agya*), who may know other scriptures, but not the treatises on *Rasa*; and (5) the uncouth rustics (*gramya*), who know nothing whatsoever about devotion. Jiva explains that the first three types are able to experience such *rasas* as Compassion as joyful, whereas the last two types cannot.

92. This is a quotation from the *Sahitya Darpana* (3.4), a treatise on drama written in the fourteenth century by Vishvanath Kaviraja.

93. A friend here means one who has similar devotional feelings. *Bhavollasa*, which also could be translated as "the brilliance of another's emotion," is a technical term of great importance for the later tradition, for it opens the way for the love of Radha, which is the foundation of the important meditative path of *Manjari Sadhana*. Whereas in much of Rupa's theory Radha is an *ashraya*, or "vessel" of devotion, in *Manjari Sadhana*, Radha becomes the *vishaya*, or "object" of devotion. Therefore, the love of Radha experienced by her close girlfriends, in effect, amounts to another type of Foundational Emotion for devotion. See my *Acting as a Way of Salvation*, 108–114.

94. Jiva glosses this as knowledge that is indifferent to devotion (*bhakti-udasinadi-gyanam*).

95. The point is that *Rasa* has passed beyond the state of a Bhava to the condition of full manifestation. Here the agency of manifestation is purity (*sattva*), not the unconscious impressions (*samskaras*) of the next verse.

96. These seem to refer to the types of unconscious impressions (*vasanas*) mentioned in 2.1.6 and 2.5.39; they are the agency of contemplation. Love remains a *bhava* until fully manifest as a *Rasa*. In these two verses, Rupa has given a concise definition of *bhava* (or Foundational Emotion, *sthayi-bhava*) and *Rasa*, and indicated the relationship between them. Jiva explains that *bhava* and *Rasa* are related like cause (*karana*) and effect (*karya*). He also compares the two to *yogic* meditation (*dhyana*) and final trance (*samadhi*).

18

The Divine Feminine
in the Theology of Krishna

Graham M. Schweig

Nowhere in the panorama of world religious traditions, from ancient
times to the present, do we find such a strong presence of the feminine voice within the divinity as we do in the Hindu complex of
religion.[1] In light of the widespread interest in the role of the feminine throughout religion during the past three decades, the prominence of the divine feminine in the Krishna *bhakti* traditions of
Vaishnavism is certainly worthy of our attention.

While the theologies among later traditions of Krishna *bhakti*
in northern India are diverse and complex, there are prominent
themes concerning the feminine within and in relation to the divinity. In this essay, I will briefly discuss five forms of the divine
feminine and present demonstrative examples from scriptural
and poetic sources. Expression of the feminine takes many shapes,
beginning, perhaps surprisingly, with Krishna himself.

The Divine Androgyny of Krishna

Krishna's attributes clearly reveal his androgynous nature. Certain
schools of Krishna theology project a supreme *anima* and *animus* of
the godhead. Though Krishna is commonly known as a "male" deity,
his bodily features are predominantly feminine; his innermost nature is also described by theologians as both masculine and feminine.
Furthermore, Krishna's divine consort, the supreme goddess Radha,
who amorously attends him, is originally nondifferent from his supreme self. As a famous Chaitanyaite theologian stated, "Radha

and Krishna are one Soul, yet they possess two bodily forms."[2] Although she is part *of* him, she becomes eternally separate *from* him in order to enter into supreme loving relation (*rasa*) *with* him.

The special attributes of the feminine are appreciated as early as the *Bhagavad Gita*, the original theological discourse on Krishna *bhakti*. Krishna boldly identifies with these feminine excellences, thus declaring their superlative state:

> Of feminine attributes
> [and their presiding goddesses],
> I am fame, beauty, speech,
> Remembrance, intelligence,
> Constancy, and forbearance.[3]

Krishna's recognition of feminine traits as his own indicates his divinely androgynous nature.

Krishna is usually depicted as an eternally youthful male adolescent, yet his masculine body appears to possess many feminine attributes. The significance of such feminine aspects of the visage and bodily appearance of Krishna have yet to be fully appreciated by Western scholars. It is no accident that most Westerners, unfamiliar with the deity of Krishna, take artistic renderings of Krishna's form to be that of a woman! This is conceivable when one considers that Krishna's loveliness and beauty, along with his sweetness and grace, are often portrayed or praised in Vaishnava literature: "Whose loveliness is distinguished from and more charming than countless love-gods" and "whose limbs are beautiful";[4] the "original form of the treasure of beauty and grace";[5] "the oversoul, which has embodied/itself in the beautiful blue body of infinite/ sweetness";[6] and "I sing praise of the boy cowherd who is the dark/color of a blue water-lily petal."[7]

Other feminine features of Krishna include his curling locks of hair and various hair and bodily ornamentations: "who has a cap of clustering curls";[8] "whose head is bedecked with ornaments";[9] and "with a bright peacock plume hair ornament."[10] Flowers are also used to decorate Krishna, and are often compared to the beauty of his form: "clusters of *kadamba* flowers hanging from each ear";[11] "whose eyes blossom like lotus flowers";[12] and "whose smile, as it were, is made of jasmine and *mandara* flowers."[13] The divine cowherd's body is repeatedly presented as being soft as a lotus and pleasingly curved, bending in three places, and his hair as long and curly. Very few masculine qualities are associated with Krishna's form in the traditional literature; rather, predominantly feminine characteristics are used to identify and extol the beauty of the deity.

These depictions are found throughout the sacred text of the *Bhagavata Purana*, the literary masterpiece that has been recognized as the ultimate scriptural, most authoritative text by later major Vaishnava sects. I will present foundational materials for the Vaishnava theology of the divine feminine from this text, and also draw from northern Indian *bhakti* traditions appearing in the later medieval period, written or dramatic traditions that further illuminate the vision of the Goddess. In addition, a dialogue within a modern dramatic performance will be presented. These selections will illustrate perhaps the five most significant manifestations of the feminine within Vaishnavism: (1) the queens of Dvaraka, wives of Krishna; (2) the wives of the brahmins of Braj; (3) the cowherd girls of Braj, the *gopis*; (4) the supreme goddess Radha, the favorite *gopi* of Krishna; and (5) the independently powerful goddess Yogamaya.

In the West, we typically think of God as a supreme "masculine" being or person, whereas in India, as we shall see, the divinity manifests in both genders. The two major traditions within the Hindu complex of religion focus upon the worship of supreme masculine and feminine divinities. There are those sects centered on the worship of the masculine deities of Vishnu (Krishna), and of Shiva (Rudra). In these traditions, the Goddess acts dependently, either as the consort of Vishnu, named Lakshmi, or as the consort of Shiva, named Parvati. Here God and Goddess within the godhead are complementary and inseparable, manifest as "spirit," *purusha* (masculine), and "matter," *prakriti* (feminine), for the living beings of this world. Ultimately, the Vaishnava traditions conceive of a bimonotheism, the concept of a type of androgynous deity—a divinity made up of two persons who pose as the supreme divine couple, namely the Goddess Radha and the God Krishna.

The vision of the Goddess and the role of the divine feminine in Vaishnava traditions is complex, and many aspects may challenge our Western theological assumptions. Specifically, the concept of "the one and the many" poses certain problems. In the West, we readily relate to either "monotheism" or "polytheism," and no other arrangement is conceivable. The exception to this might be the Christian trinity, in which the one supreme deity assumes three forms. For the ancient Indian mind, however, the supreme is described as having unlimited forms, *ananta-rupa,* since it is believed that God has no limitations.

As the Christian mind never considers the three members of the trinity to be polytheistic, so the Indian mind never considers the unlimited forms of the supreme to be disunited. A common theological structure could easily be characterized as a "polymorphic theism," or the concept of the many forms of the one deity. This is clearly demonstrated when we consider the one supreme Goddess, Krishna's beloved Radha, along with her many forms or manifestations, known as the *gopis*, or cowherd girls.

Also problematic or confusing for the Western mind would perhaps be the independence of the feminine deity. The Goddess, or Devi, for example, when separated from the masculine divinity, appears in her own tradition, named Shaktism (the tradition worshiping the "divine feminine power"), in which she reigns supreme and autonomous, apart from being paired with any masculine divinities. Thus, in the theology of Krishna, the Goddess functions both in her constituent dependent role, reviewed briefly earlier, as well as in her disassociated, segregated role. Her independent identity within the Shakta traditions takes many forms, such as the more benign deity Durga, and at the other end of the spectrum the fierce and terrific deity Kali Ma. Some sects of Vaishnavism also preserve a unique place for the powerful and independent goddess who assumes the name of Yogamaya, presented in the final section of this chapter.

Krishna's 16,108 Wives—The Queens of Dvaraka

Within the *Bhagavata Purana*, which considers the ultimate form of the deity to be Krishna, the role of the feminine is paramount. Many great female devotees of Krishna are highlighted, especially in the famed tenth book, in which the intimate divine acts, or *lilas*, of the deity are displayed. Here it is said that Krishna married 16,108 princesses, all of whom are understood to be manifestations of the goddess Lakshmi. Every one of these princess wives had fervently desired to have Krishna as her husband. Each princess successfully attained him as her beloved spouse, yet due to Krishna's special power of duplication and his ability to act lovingly with each wife, each one considered Krishna to be her husband alone: "Seeing that Achyuta stayed at home and never left the house, each princess regarded her beloved as exclusively her own. These women were not aware of his real nature."[14] The intense devotion of the princesses is displayed in their prayers that appear in the final chapter of the tenth book, thus expressing the preeminence of the divine feminine voice in the *Bhagavata*. These prayerful words are translated by Edwin F. Bryant in the summarizing chapter in *Krishna: The Beautiful Legend of God*, "Description of Krishna's Activities," as follows:[15]

> 15. The queens said: "O *kurari* bird, the Lord is sleeping in the world at night, his consciousness overtaken [by sleep], but you do not rest. You have been deprived of sleep and are lamenting. Has your mind been deeply wounded like ours, O friend, by the noble playful glances and smiles of the lotus-eyed Lord?

> 16. Alas, O *cakravaki* bird, your friend is not to be found at night, and so you close your eyes and wail piteously. Have you become a servant [of the Lord] like us? Or is it that you wish to wear the garland that has touched Acyuta's feet on your braid of hair?

> 17. *Bho! Bho!* You thunder continuously, O ocean. You are not able to sleep, and have fallen into a state of insomnia. Or have your personal possessions been taken away by Mukunda? You have entered the state in which we find ourselves—it is impossible to overcome.

18. O moon! You have been seized by powerful consumption, and do not dispel the darkness with your rays! Have you forgotten the words of Mukunda like we have? *Bho!* You appear to us to be dumbstruck!

19. What have we done that is displeasing to you, O Malayan breeze? You are arousing lust in our hearts, which have been pierced by Govinda's glances.

20. O beautiful cloud! You must certainly be dear to the Lord of the Yadavas. Bound by love, you meditate on Krishna, who bears the *shrivatsa* on his body, just as we do. Remembering him again and again with an anguished heart, like us you pine intensely and release endless torrents of tears. Attachment to Krishna brings unhappiness.

21. O cuckoo! You utter such melodious sounds about my beloved with words that can animate the dead. Tell me, what nice thing can I do for you today? You utter such pleasing sounds.

22. O noble-minded mountain, supporter of the earth, you do not move, you do not speak! Are you thinking about some grave matter or, alas, do you yearn to place the lotus feet of the son of Nanda on your breast, as we do?

23. O rivers, wives of the ocean! Alas, your lakes are dry and you are much reduced. Desiring your Lord, your beauty in the form of lotuses has vanished now. You are just like us: our hearts have been stolen, and we are quite withered from being deprived of the loving glance of Krishna, the Lord of Madhu.

24. Welcome, O swan, and be seated! Drink milk and tell us stories about Shauri [Krishna]. We know that you are the messenger of Krishna. Is the invincible one well? Does our fickle friend remember the words he spoke to us before? Why should we worship him, O [messenger of] a cruel person? He fulfils desires, but speak to him when Sri, the goddess of fortune, is not present—she among women is exclusively devoted to him, without a doubt."

The Wives of the Brahmins of Braj

The women of Braj that we hear the least about from the tenth book are the "Wives of the Brahmanas."[16] In this narration, in which pride is considered the enemy of humility and devotion, the husbands recognize the superior, unconditional love of their wives, who surpass their prideful husbands in worship due to their selfless devotion to God. This story illustrates how the feminine has been honored in the eyes of the *Bhagavata's* author, and reflects much about how various Vaishnava sects exalt the feminine to the highest devotional status. (The following verses are drawn from Edwin F. Bryant's translation of the story of the brahmanas' wives in *Krishna: The Beautiful Legend of God.*)[17]

1. The *gopas* said: "Balarama, mighty-armed Balarama! Krishna, the annihilator of the wicked! Our hunger is really troubling us; please satisfy it."

2. *Sri* Suka said: *Bhagavan*, the son of Devaki, was feeling pleased with his devotees, the wives of the *Brahmanas*. When he was appealed to in this way, he spoke as follows:

3. "Go to the sacrificial arena. Desiring to attain *svarga* [the celestial abode of the gods], the *Brahmana* reciters of the *Vedas* are taking part in a sacrifice called *angirasa*.

4. Go there and request some cooked rice, mentioning the names of the worthy *Bhagavan* Balarama, and of me myself; say that you have been dispatched by us."

5. Directed thus by *Bhagavan*, the boys went and asked as suggested. They fell on the ground before the *Brahmanas* like sticks, their hands cupped in supplication:

6. "You are gods on earth, please listen. May good fortune be with you. Please know that we *gopas* have been dispatched by Balarama and come to you to execute Krishna's instructions.

7. Balarama and Acyuta have become hungry while grazing the cows not far from here, and desire cooked rice from you. You are distinguished in the knowledge of *dharma*, and if you have any respect for them, give them cooked rice. They entreat you, O *brahmanas*.

9. Although they heard *Bhagavan's* request, the *Brahmanas* did not listen to it. They had petty aspirations. They thought themselves distinguished, but despite the fact that they performed numerous rituals, they were ignorant nevertheless.

12. When they did not respond either with a "yes" or a "no," the *gopas* returned dejected and reported what had happened to Krishna and Balarama, O scorcher of the enemies.

13. After listening to this, *Bhagavan*, the Lord of the universe, laughed, pointing out the materialistic ways of the world. He then spoke again to the *gopas*:

14. "Inform the wives that I have arrived, along with Sankarshana [Balarama]. They will give you as much food as you wish. They are affectionate, and their minds dwell in me."

15. So, the *gopas* went to the *patnishala* [women's quarters], where they saw them sitting down, prettily bedecked. They humbly paid homage to the wives of the *Brahmanas* and spoke as follows:

16. "Greetings to you, O wives of *Brahmanas*; please listen to what we have to say. We have been sent by Krishna who is passing by not far from here.

17. He has come from afar, and has been grazing the cows with Balarama and the *gopas*. Please give food to him. He and his companions desire to eat."

18. The women had always been eager for a glimpse of Acyuta, because they had been captivated by accounts of him. When they heard that he had arrived nearby, they became flustered.

19. Taking along a great variety of the four types of food in pots, they surged forth to meet their beloved, like rivers to an ocean.

20. [Although] they were obstructed by their husbands, brothers, relatives and sons, their hopes [of meeting Krishna] had long been sustained by hearing about him. He is *Bhagavan*, who is praised in the best of hymns.

21. The women saw Krishna surrounded by the *gopas* and wandering about with his elder brother in the grove on the Yamuna, which was a picturesque sight with fresh buds of *ashoka* trees.

22. He was dark blue in colour, and wearing a golden garment. He was dressed like an actor with fresh shoots, minerals, a peacock feather and a forest garland. One hand was placed on the shoulder of a companion, the other was twirling a lotus flower. His smiling lotus face had curls on the cheeks and lotuses behind the ears.

23. The women had heard so much about their beloved, and his celebrity had so filled their ears that their minds had become absorbed in him. Now, they drew him into [their hearts] through the openings of their eyes. They embraced him for a long time and cast off their distress, just like false notions of the self are cast off after wisdom is embraced....

35. So *Bhagavan*, Govinda, the Lord, fed the *gopas* with the four kinds of foodstuffs, and then he himself ate.

36. Imitating the world of men in a human body for the purpose of *lila*, he brought pleasure to the cows, *gopas* and *gopis* through his deeds, words and beauty.

37. Later, those *Brahmanas* repented in retrospect: "We have committed an offence because we ignored the request of the two lords of the universe. They are playing the role of mortals."

38. Seeing the supreme devotion of the women to *Bhagavan* Krishna, they lamented their own lack of it, and rebuked themselves:

39. "Curses on that birth which is threefold, curses on vows, curses on extensive learning, curses on our family lineage, curses on skill in rituals: we still remain averse to Adhokshaja [Krishna]. . . .

41. "*Aho!* See the unlimited devotion of these very women to Krishna, the *guru* of the world. It has pierced the fetters of death under the guise of household life.

42. "Neither the *samskara* purificatory rites of the twice-born, nor residence in the house of the *guru*, nor austerity, nor inquiry into the self, nor rites of cleanliness, nor auspicious rituals were [practiced] by these women.

43. "Nonetheless, they were constant in devotion to Krishna, the Lord of the lords of *yoga*, whose glories are renowned. This was not the case with us, even though we have undergone the *samskara* and other such rites. . . .

48. "He, indeed, is *Bhagavan* himself, Vishnu, the Lord of the lords of *yoga*, born amongst the Yadus. Although we had heard this, being fools, we did not understand.

49. "*Aho!* How fortunate we are to have wives such as these! Their devoutness has given rise to unwavering devotion to Hari in us."

The *Gopis*: Cowherd Maidens of Braj

The Sanskrit word *gopi* refers to "a female cowherder," or "cowherd maiden." The word in its plural form, "the *gopis*," names the group of married or unmarried cowherd women and girls who are passionately devoted to the deity of Krishna.[18] The word in its singular form, as "the Gopi," can refer to the favored *gopi* of Krishna, named Radha. The *gopis* appear in the ancient literature of India known as the *Puranas*. It is in the tenth book of the popular *Bhagavata Purana* (here abbreviated as BhP), famed for the stories of Krishna as an infant, child, and youth in the region of Braj, in northern India, that the *gopis* receive the greatest attention as intimate lovers of the flute-playing Lord.

The young cowherd maidens are honored by certain traditions within Vaishnavism as the ultimate example of devotion. The most revered and most often contemplated presentation of the *gopis* for these traditions is found within a dramatic story in the *Bhagavata*, the *Rasa Lila Panchadhyaya* ("the five chapters on the story of the Rasa dance," BhP 10.29–33). Throughout the drama, various types of behavior and emotions of the *gopis* are displayed, which the Chaitanya school of Vaishnavism accepts as the highest level of worship in *bhakti* ("devotional love") for the deity Krishna. Thus, among all the stories involving Krishna and the cowherd maidens in the *Bhagavata* text, it is this portrayal of the *gopis* that Vaishnava devotees, especially in the Chaitanya school, worship as the model of loving service and ideal devotion.

The *Rasa Lila* story commences on an enchanting autumn evening as the full moon is rising. Krishna himself is so inspired by the beauteous landscape that he is moved toward amorous love, and produces irresistible flute music, alluring the *gopis*. They suddenly abandon everything—their household duties, their families, their homes, even their physical bodies—to run off to the forest to be with him. Several chapters earlier (BhP 10.22), the *gopis* had performed a particular form of worship in order to gain the favor of the supreme Goddess, with the intention of attaining Krishna as their husband. It is in the *Ras Lila* that the *gopis* are said to have this desire fulfilled. The climactic scene occurs when the *gopis* form a great circle around Krishna, who miraculously duplicates himself so that he can dance with each and every *gopi* simultaneously, though each feels that Krishna is with her alone.

Description of the Gopis' Abandonment

The verses that follow describe the different domestic activities in which the *gopis* are engaged at the time of hearing Krishna's intoxicating flute music. The abrupt abandonment of their various duties is described as virtually a physical and social death for the *gopis*, as they desert their physical bodies and adopt new spiritual forms, while giving up all consideration for proper social and ethical behavior. This lack of concern for such conventions symbolizes their natural renunciation born of love, as well as their unconditional, passionate devotion to Krishna. (The following selection of verses is my own translation, taken from *Dance of Divine Love: The Rasa Lila of Krishna and the Cowherd Maidens of Braj from the Bhagavata Purana*.)[19]

> Seeing lotus flowers bloom
> and the perfect circle of the moon
> Beaming like the face of Rama,
> reddish as fresh *kunkuma;*

O unattainable one,
   do not reject us—
   accept us as your devotees
Just as you, the Lord,
   the original Person,
   accept those who desire liberation.

O dear one, as you
   who knows *dharma*
   have stated,
The proper duty for women
   is to be loyal to husbands,
   children and close friends.
Let this *dharma* of ours be for you,
   O Lord, since you are
   the true object of such teachings.
Truly you are the dearest
   beloved of all living beings,
   the most intimate relation,
   for you are the supreme Soul.

O Soul, the spiritually advanced
   certainly feel attraction to you
   as their eternal beloved.
With these husbands, children, and
   others causing much trouble,
   what is to be done?
O supreme Lord,
   please be merciful unto us.
O one with eyes like lotus flowers,
   do not destroy our hopes
   that we have held for so long.

While in our homes, our minds
   were easily stolen by you;
So also were our hands
   engaged in housework.
Our feet will not move even one step
   from the soles of your feet.
How shall we return to Braj
   what would we do there?

Krishna's Words to the Gopis

The following words of Krishna, from the fourth chapter of the *Rasa Lila*, are in response to the *gopis'* question on the nature of love. Krishna speaks of the *gopis'* love as being so pure that even he is unable to fully reciprocate. (The verses that follow are excerpted from my translation, *Dance of Divine Love*.)[21]

> Dear ladies,
>   indeed, for my sake alone
> You have abandoned the world,
>   the *Vedas*, and
> even your relatives,
>   out of love for me.
> It was out of love for you
>   that I became invisible,
>   though you were never
>   removed from my sight.
> Therefore, you should not be
>   discontented with me—
>   O dearest ones,
> I am your beloved!
>
> I am unable to reciprocate,
>   your faultless love for me
>   your own purity,
> And all that you have
>   sacrificed for me,
>   even over the long lifetime
>   of a great divinity.
> Severing strong ties
>   to your homes so difficult
>   to overcome, you have
>   lovingly worshiped me.
> May your reward be
>   your own purity.

Portrayal of the Gopis' Dancing

The lively dance movements and singing of the *gopis* are described in the climactic verse of the *Rasa Lila* story (taken from my translation, *Dance of Divine Love*).[22]

> With their feet
>   stepping to the dance;
>   with gestures of their hands,
>   loving smiles and sporting eyebrows;
> With waists bending
>   and the rhythmic movements

of garments covering their breasts;
with earrings swinging
on their cheeks;
The spiritual wives of Krishna,
with moistened faces
and braids and belts
tied tightly,
sang his praises—
They appeared
like lustrous flashes
of radiant lightning
engulfed by a ring of dark clouds.

Poetic Descriptions of the Gopis

Poetic descriptions of the *gopis* are colorfully presented in the *Krishna Karnamritam of Bilvamangala Thakur*, translated by Frances Wilson. The absorption of the *gopis* in thoughts of Krishna while they are performing their household duties is revealed here in the second of these two verses from the *Krishna Karnamritam.*[23]

Hail to the beneficent lord of
the three worlds
who has a forehead mark of musk
and whose amorous advances are
encouraged by the love play
of the Braj women.

May he ever protect us—the yellow clad one
to whom the milkmaids in Gokula at the end of night
joyfully sing praises so that by the abundance of
luster from their own teeth they repel the rays
of the moon
while they quickly churn the curd so that the jingling
of the bangles on their wrists keeps time to their
singing, and the ends of their upper garments dance.

The Gopis' Words on the Flute

The *gopis* are well known for their "songs" of love and separation. In the *Venu Gita*, "Song of the Flute" (BhP 10.21), they long to be with Krishna after becoming mesmerized by his flute music that captivates all living beings. The *gopis* are depicted as being in a perpetual state of remembrance of Krishna, as presented as follows, in my translation of the twenty-first chapter of the *Bhagavata Purana*.[24]

> Those young women of Braj
>   were aroused by Passion
>   after hearing
>   the song of his flute.
> Some of them, in his absence,
>   were moved to describe
>   the qualities of Krishna
>   to their intimate friends.
>
> As they began to describe him,
>   they remembered
>   the playful activities of Krishna.
> Their minds again became
>   disturbed by the force of Passion
>   and they could no longer speak, O king.
>
> Thus hearing, O king,
>   the sound of the flute
>   that captivates
>   the hearts of all beings,
> The young women of Braj
>   began describing
>   that alluring sound yet again,
> embracing him within their minds.

The *gopis* also recognize the effect of Krishna's flute music on other women, as well as on the flute itself, rivers, and bamboo trees! Their words are expressed, along with appreciation of Krishna's loveliness, in the following verses of the *Venu Gita* (my translation).[25]

> The beautiful *gopis* spoke:
> O friends,
>   for those who have eyes,
>   we know of no greater
>   reward than this—
> Entering the forest
>   with their companions and
>   herding the cows before them,
> The two sons of the ruler of Braj,
>   whose faces are adorned
>   by the flutes they play,
> Cast loving glances
>   all around them—

it is this vision that
is constantly imbibed.

O *gopis*, what auspicious acts
    must have been performed
    by this flute,
For it enjoys the nectar flowing
    from the lips of Damodara,
    leaving only a taste for us cowherd girls
    to whom this nectar truly belongs.
The rivers, themselves
    mothers of the bamboo
    from which the flute is made,
    feel jubilant with blooming lotuses;
And the forefathers of the flute,
    the bamboo trees, shed tears
    of joy with their flowing sap.

Gazing at Krishna, whose
    pleasing form and behavior
    are utterly elating for all women,
And hearing
    the enchanting music
    emanating from his flute,
The hearts of the gods' wives
    are agitated by Passion while
    they move in heavenly chariots;
They become bewildered
    and their belts loosen,
    as flowers fall from their hair.

When rivers hear
    the music of Mukunda,
    their flowing currents are broken
And their waters swirl
    out of intense love for him.
The two feet of Murari
    are made stationary,
    seized by the embrace of
Arm-like waves that present
    offerings of lotus flowers.

The native women of Pulinda
    are fully satisfied by contact with
The *kumkuma* powder that decorates

the breasts of his beloveds,
    released from the beautiful
    reddish lotus feet
    of the greatly praised Lord.
Even though they feel
    tormented by the sight
    of reddened blades of grass,
They also experience relief from
    the pangs of that vision of Passion
    when they spread the powder upon
    their own faces and breasts.

The Gopis' Words in Songs of Separation

The middle chapter of the *Rasa Lila* (BhP 10.31) presents the famed *Gopi Gita,*
"Song of the *Gopis,*" in which the *gopis* yearn intensely for Krishna's return after his disappearance. In their loving madness of separation, they even claim
that Krishna's beauty is "killing" them, and ask "Is this not murder?" (The following verses are excerpts from my translation of the *Dance of Divine Love.*)[26]

With your eyes,
    you steal the beauty
    of the center
Of an exquisite fully bloomed
    lotus flower, rising out
    of a serene autumn pond,
O Lord of love,
    and it is killing us,
    your voluntary maidservants—
O bestower of benedictions,
    in this world,
    is this not murder?

The nectar that
    strengthens our love
    and vanquishes our grief;
The nectar that
    is abundantly kissed
    by the flute you play,
Making everyone forget
    all other attachments;
O hero, please bestow
    upon us this nectar
    of your lips!

Who would not be available to him,
 with his playful arching eyebrows
 and deceptive, charming smiles?
After all, what are we to him,
 the dust of whose feet is worshiped
 by the goddess Lakshmi herself?
Nevertheless, those who are destitute
 are favored by the words of
 the most excellent and famous one.

Please keep your head
 away from my foot!
 I understand you very well—
You know how to offer flattering words
 while acting as his messenger,
 because you have been trained by Mukunda.
Now he has abandoned us,
 who have given up our children, husbands,
 and all others in the world for his sake—
Therefore, why, since he is ungrateful,
 should we make up with him?

Behaving like
 a cruel-hearted hunter,
 he shot arrows
 at the king of monkeys;
While dominated by one woman,
 he disfigured another
 who approached him
 with passionate desires;
Even after accepting the worship of Bali,
 he tied him up with ropes like a crow
 who, after devouring its prey,
 hovers over it.
So enough of this friendship
 with that dark-complexioned one,
 even if the treasure of such stories
 about him is impossible to give up!
For one who constantly seeks
 to hear of his divine acts,
 the ears are filled with nectar,
A drop of which, if relished even once,
 destroys all attachment to worldly duties
 filled with conflict and duality.

Such irresponsible persons promptly
   give up their families and homes,
   leaving them in a wretched condition.
Here, many of them wander about
   acting as mendicants,
   begging for their livelihood
   like so many birds.

We had faith
   that his deceptive speech was true,
Just as the foolish female companion
   of the black deer is deceived
   by mimicking sounds of a hunter.
We, the maidservants of Krishna,
   have experienced repeatedly
   the pain of his amorous love
Created by the ardent touch of his nails—
   O messenger, please speak of other things!

O friend of my dear one,
   have you been sent here
   once again by my beloved?
You ought to be honored
   by me, my friend—
   so what do you wish from me?
How will you lead us who
   remain here to his side,
   he with whom togetherness
   is too difficult to give up?
After all, O gentle one,
   the Goddess Shri, his consort,
   is forever present with him,
   resting upon his chest.

Oh, indeed! Is it not regrettable
   that the son of a highly esteemed man
   now resides in the city of Mathura?
O gentle one, does he remember
   his father's house, his family relations
   and his cowherd friends?
Does he ever relate to you
   any words about us,
   his maidservants?
When might he place his hand,
   with the fragrant scent of

> soothing aloe-wood balm,
> on our heads?

WORDS DESCRIBING RADHA. Along with the spirited portrayal of the *gopis* presented earlier, the amorous relationship between Radha and Krishna is vividly described in the *Krishna Karnamritam of Bilvamangala* (translated by Frances Wilson).[28]

> May Radha purify the world who, all her thoughts
>   given up to the Eternal Lord, Krishna, kept
>   churning in a vessel empty of curds.
> May the Lord purify the world who, intending to
>   milk a cow, ropes a bull while he looks with
>   impatient ardor at Radha's breasts fluttering
>   like a bouquet.
>
> Although but a boy, you hold a mountain aloft
>   with a finger tip.
> Although dark, you are a light in the deep darkness.
> Although immovable, you are drawn by the eyes of Radha.
> Although an adulterer, you destroy the inevitability of
>   rebirth. How are you all this?
>
> I take refuge in Glory incarnate as the enchantingly
>   sweet boy crowned king of flute players,
> who elicits the feeling of wonder by the
>   amours enjoyed by Radha, who is a treasury of
>   graces,
> whose lotus face with natural smiles is beyond
>   the ordinary,
> who shatters the proud importance of the emerald.

RADHA'S WORDS OF REMEMBRANCE. A sampling of Radha's reminiscent words, spoken to a friend, appears in the *Gitagovinda* of Jayadeva. Radha acknowledges the "sweet notes from his alluring flute," and observes Krishna's intimate interactions with the other *gopis*. She remembers her personal encounter with him "under a flowering tree," and recalls the *Rasa* dance repeatedly in the refrain, "My heart recalls Hari here in his love dance." (The verses that follow are taken from Barbara Stoler Miller's translation, *Love Song of the Dark Lord: Jayadeva's Gitagovinda.*)[29]

> Sweet notes from his alluring flute echo nectar from his lips.
> His restless eyes glance, his head sways, earrings
>   play at his cheeks.

My heart recalls Hari here in his love dance,
Playing seductively, laughing, mocking me.

A circle of peacock plumes caressed by moonlight crowns his hair.
A rainbow colors the fine cloth on his cloud-dark body.
My heart recalls Hari here in his love dance,
Playing seductively, laughing, mocking me.

Kissing mouths of round-hipped cowherd girls whets his lust.
Brilliant smiles flash from the ruby-red buds of his sweet lips.
My heart recalls Hari here in his love dance,
Playing seductively, laughing, mocking me.

Vines of his great throbbing arms circle a thousand cowherdesses.
Jewel rays from his hands and feet and chest break the dark night.
My heart recalls Hari here in his love dance,
Playing seductively, laughing, mocking me.

Jeweled earrings in sea-serpent form adorn his sublime cheeks.
His trailing yellow cloth is a retinue of sages, gods, and spirits.
My heart recalls Hari here in his love dance,
Playing seductively, laughing, mocking me.

Meeting me under a flowering tree, he calms my fear of dark time,
Delighting me deeply by quickly glancing looks at my heart.
My heart recalls Hari here in his love dance,
Playing seductively, laughing, mocking me.

RADHA'S WORDS OF TORMENT. In a later chapter of Jayadeva's *Gitagovinda*, Radha expresses the torment and intensity of her love for Krishna, wherein she announces her desire to give up her life, in the agony of separation (translation of Barbara Stoler Miller).[30]

Sandalwood mountain wind,
As you blow southern breezes
To spread the bliss of love,
Soothe me! End the paradox!
Lifebreath of the world,
If you bring me Madhava
For a moment,
You may take my life!

Friends are hostile,
Cool wind is like fire,
Moon nectar is poison,
Krishna torments me in my heart.

But even when he is cruel
I am forced to take him back.
Women with night-lily eyes feel love
In a paradox of passion-bound infinity.

Command my torment, sandal mountain wind!
Take my lifebreath with arrows, Love!
I will not go home for refuge again!
Jumna river, sister of Death,
Why should you be kind?
Drown my limbs with waves!
Let my body's burning be quenched!

POETS HEAR WORDS OF RADHA. The next three selections are by two medieval Vaishnava poets, Vidyapati and Chandidasa, who witness Radha's actions and words. In the first poem, Vidyapati hears Radha's words of separation, then offers a reflective question to Radha herself in the *bhanita*, or signature line of the poem. (These selections are taken from *In Praise of Krishna: Songs from the Bengali*, translated by Edward C. Dimock, Jr., and Denise Levertov.)[31]

O my friend, my sorrow is unending.
It is the rainy season, my house is empty,
the sky is filled with seething clouds,
the earth sodden with rain,
and my love far away.

Cruel Kama pierces me with his arrows:
the lightning flashes, the peacocks dance,
frogs and waterbirds, drunk with delight,
call incessantly—and my heart is heavy.
Darkness on earth,
the sky intermittently lit with a sullen glare...

Vidyapati says,
How will you pass this night without your lord?

In the next of Vidyapati's poems, Radha's thoughts on her own identity in relation to her beloved are expressed. The *bhanita* in this instance is addressed to the reader (Dimock and Levertov translation).

As the mirror to my hand,
the flowers to my hair,
kohl to my eyes,
tambul to my mouth,
musk to my breast,
necklace to my throat,

ecstasy to my flesh,
heart to my home—

as wing to bird,
water to fish,
life to the living—
so you to me.
But tell me,
Madhava, beloved,
who are you?
Who are you really?

Vidyapati says, they are one another.

The following poem by Chandidasa expresses Radha's fear that Krishna's love for her could come to an end. In the *bhanita*, Chandidasa enters into the world of the poem and offers Radha consoling words (Dimock and Levertov translation).

Suddenly I am afraid.
At any moment, Kanu's love for me may cease.
A building can collapse because of a single flaw—
who knows in what ways I, who desire to be
a palace for his pleasure, may be faulty?
And few are those who can restore
what once is broken ...
Distracted, I wander
from place to place, everywhere finding
only anxiety. Oh, to see
his smile!
       My love,
whoever brings down the house of our love
will have murdered a woman!

Chandidasa says, O Radha, you reflect too much;
without your love he could not live a moment.

The saintly poet Surdas presents exotic imagery of Radha, who attracts even the birds and bees of the forest. (The following poem is taken from *Songs of the Saints of India*, translated by John Stratton Hawley and Mark Juergensmeyer.)[32]

Radha is lost to the onslaught of love.
She weeps from tree to tree and finally succumbs,
searching through the forests and groves.
Her braid—a peacock grasps it, thinking it a snake;
her lotus feet attract the bees;
The honey of her voice makes the crow in the *kadamb* tree

caw, caw to mimic its cuckoo;
Her hands—the tender leaves of blossom-bringing Spring:
the parrot, when he sees, comes near to taste;
And the full moon in her face inspires the *cakor* bird
to drink the water washing from her eyes.
Her despair, her desperation—the Joy of the Yadus sees it
and appears at her side just in time;
Surdas's Lord takes that seedbud of new birth
and cradles it, a newborn in his arms.

RADHA AND THE *RAS-LILA*. The stanzas that follow are representative of the esoteric vision of the poet Havivamsh, who speaks of a *ras-lila* that takes place in spring rather than autumn. Shri Hit Harivamsh opens the following stanza by pleading with Radha to respond to Krishna's call, then concludes by informing the reader of their achieved divine union. (These selections are from *The Caurasi Pad of Sri Hit Harivams*, translated by Charles S. J. White.)[33]

O Radha, look at the Rasa Lila in the forest.

In the season of vasant
There are numberless half-opened kusum blossoms
And fruits and leaves.

The note of Nandlal's flute
Has called. Listen!
Why do you drowse away?

Why do you delay?
O Lady, the time
Goes vainly by!

Your Darling is handsome—
Like a sapphire. You are the one
With a golden body.

Sri Hit Harivamsh says,
The Couple, united,
Overwhelm each other with a host of virtues.

The poet again attempts to convince Radha to join her beloved in the forest in the next stanza. Here, however, the *bhanita* is addressed to Radha on Krishna's behalf.

For your welfare I have come to fetch you—
Shyam has sent for you from the forest.
Dispel, O Passionate Lady, the severe distress of his desire.

Why make obstacles? Listen, O wise Radha!
At your meeting, O Sakhi,
Wipe out the manifest tenth stage of *viraha*.

Look . . . Oh, the night is beautiful!
The Beloved's preparations are charming. There are lotuses
At the riverside. The Lover of Rohini is arisen in the sky.

O Sakhi, You are very artful. You didn't assent
To a single one of my proposals. In speaking to you,
O Young Lady, I failed in cleverness!

Mohan Lal is handsome.
Entranced with his own feelings:
The sweet sound of his flute enchants the birds and animals.

Shri Hit Harivamsh says,
O Lady, if you love Hari,
Then he will accept his body, life, and youth as yours!

Radha and Krishna are joyfully united in the following stanza. Harivamsh relieves the reader in his final reassuring words.

Together with Shyam in the Rasa circle Radhika looks beautiful.

Nandalal is in the midst of the Braj maidens, the color
Of *champak* flowers, as though a cloud were surrounded
By lightning or an emerald set in gold.

The one who gives joy does the steps,
Pauses and *tatta thei* hand motions,
According to the seven tones, *sa ri ga ma pa dha ni.*

In the emotion of the dance she is a picture
In the blue costume she wears: Her face shines
Like moonlight in the cloudy skies in the sign of *makar.*

The ragas and raginis and various rhythms
Adhere to musical science. The full moon rests
In the heaven in a night in Sharad.

The one who moves like an intoxicated female elephant
Has dispelled the madness of Kamadeva from the Lord,
The Swan who has the waist of a Lion, says Shri Hit Harivansh.

Yogamaya: The Illusive Power for Loving Union

Yogamaya, also known as Mahamaya and often referred to as simply Maya, is both a goddess and a power.[34] She originates in God, belongs to God, and cannot exist without God or act without his sanction. Yogamaya, who acts both as a restrictive force for unqualified souls entrapped in the physical world and as a uniting force for lovers of God, has a wide range of functions.

Even so, she is unique in her complete separateness from the manifestations of God:

> [Varuna speaks:]
> I offer my respects unto you, the supreme Lord [bhagavan],
>   who is the supreme spirit [Brahman]
>   and the supreme soul [paramatman],
> within whom, it is heard, Maya does not exist,
>   yet she arranges the creation
>   of all the worlds.[35]

Here, it is said that Maya possesses the power of "creation of all the worlds," which includes Krishna's eternal abode of intimate play. Maya is therefore an independent force. If this were not so, the supreme Lord would be unable to submit himself to her, which clearly he does in the first verse of the *Rasa Lila*.

> Even the Beloved Lord,
>   seeing those nights
>   in autumn filled with
>   blooming jasmine flowers,
> Turned his mind toward
>   love's delights,
>   fully taking refuge in
>   Yogamaya's illusive powers.[36]

Yogamaya, then, is a separate divine agency intended for Krishna's direct use in his *lila* of loving intimacy.

What is perhaps most intriguing is that Maya is independent to the point that she has her own persona (indeed, even personae) apart from her originator. Maya manifests multipersonifications identified by various names, as Krishna explains to Yogamaya herself in the *Bhagavata* text.

> People from all over the earth
>   will give you various names
> Such as Durga, Bhadrakali,
>   Vijaya, and Vaishnavi.
>
> Kumuda, Candika, Krishnaa,
>   Madhavi, and Kanyaka;
> Maya, Narayani, Ishani,
>   Sharada, and Ambika.[37]

The author of the *Bhagavata* acknowledges the femininity of Maya through such nomenclature, clearly identifying this phenomenon as a *shakti* ("power" or "energy") of God, within the Goddess or Devi tradition. Furthermore, the empowered Goddess is described as one who is appointed by God to assist him in his divine work:

The Maya of Vishnu,
>by which this whole world is captivated,
>is known as Bhagavati.

She, who has been directed by her master [God],
>will become manifested with her various parts
>for the purpose of fulfilling his work.[38]

The role of Maya functions both in concealing and revealing ways. She conceals the true nature of the Self in relation to the Divine through delusion: "This whole world is bewildered by such a power in which persons are constantly forgetful of their [true] selves."[39] Through the agency of Maya, the Lord disguises himself from one who is bound to this world, as smoke covers the light of fire.[40] And she conceals the truth of the divinity from lovers of God through a certain kind of divine deception. Concealing the greatness, aishvarya, of God in order for the sweetness, madhurya, of the divinity to be revealed is a primary function of Maya.

The liberated associates of God are "covered by a curtain of divine illusion," so that any awareness of God's majesty is eclipsed, allowing for more intimacy with the deity. A classic example occurs in a story in which the divine mother of the Lord, Yashoda, inspects her child's opened mouth for dirt particles.[41] While doing so, an overwhelming vision of the universe is revealed to her. The potency of Maya thereafter conceals this aishvarya manifestation of God, deceiving Yashoda so that she will not be distracted from her maternal affection for Krishna:

[Shuka narrates]
When she understood reality in this way,
>the supreme Lord of the gopi, Yashoda,
Manifested the power [Maya] known as Vaishnavi,
>that she [Yashoda] may [again] possess intimate affection
>for the omnipotent Lord as her son.[42]

Throughout the tenth book one finds the phrase maya-mohita, "bewildered by Maya," in relation to Krishna's closest associates:

Thus both of them [Krishna's mother and father]
>who were bewildered [mohita]
>by the words of the [supreme] Soul of all, who is Hari,
Whose appearance in the human form
>was made possible by Maya,
>joyfully placed him on their laps and embraced him.[43]

It can be understood that the force of Maya acts as a veritable catalyst for intimacy, as she camouflages manifestations of God's almighty aspect by providing him with a form that his devotees can relate to personally and affectionately. It is said that God appears, by the arrangement of Maya, to be just like an ordinary human, causing Yashoda to think as follows.

> I am this, this is my husband,
>   this is my son,
> I am the wife of the Lord of Braj (Nanda)
>   and I am the owner of all his wealth.
> And all of the cowherdsmen are mine,
>   along with their wealth of cows—
> thus it is he who is my shelter whose power (Maya)
>   is causing me to think wrongly in these ways.[44]

Interestingly, God's manifestation in such a human-like form appears ordinary to those attached to this temporary world, and at the same time appears intimately to those bound to him through loving devotion.[45]

The complex phenomenon of Yogamaya, an essential element of intimate divine love, is recognized even by common practitioners of Vaishnavism. It should therefore be no surprise that a lucid portrayal of Yogamaya is given dramatic expression within the tradition. Yogamaya's identity and various functions are recorded in a script of charming dialogue between Krishna and Yogamaya personified, appearing in the popular *"ras lila"* dramatic productions regularly performed in Vrindaban. The passage demonstrates the significant effect of Yogamaya on the popular folk culture of the Braj region. This is hardly an unsophisticated understanding of Yogamaya, despite the spontaneous and casual, nonscriptural presentation. (The following excerpt is from *At Play with Krishna: Pilgrimage Dramas from Brindavan*, by John Stratton Hawley in association with Shrivatsa Goswami.)[46]

KRISHNA   Yogamaya, come over here quickly...

YOGAMAYA   Greetings, world-encompassing, lotus-blue Govind, fount of joy....

KRISHNA   I thought of you, Yogamaya, because today I am going to play the great *ras* with thousands of young women here. It's a task that's impossible from start to finish, and I need you to make it possible. The burden is on you, you see, because I'll be out in the forest tasting the liquid of love. If any problems occur in arranging the whole thing, you will have to solve them—I'll be too involved. But keep this in mind. You mustn't do anything that would obstruct my tasting the mood of the occasion or debase the girls' experience by interjecting an element of worldly love.

YOGAMAYA   ...First of all, when you set your lips to the flute I'll arrange it so that the only ones who hear are those girls whose hearts are filled with amorous emotion for you. The other women of Braj and the men will be completely unaware of what's going on....

KRISHNA   And after that, what, Yogamaya?

YOGAMAYA   My second task, Lord, will be to make sure that when the girls hear the sound of the flute and rise to answer its call, their relatives and family won't stop them. What I'll do is to produce a living copy of every girl who departs. . . .

KRISHNA   Good. Without that my great ras could not come to be. And what else?

YOGAMAYA   My third service will be to take the little circle on the banks of the Jumna where you dance and make it so enormous that thousands upon thousands of Braj milk-maids can dance and sport there with complete abandon. . . . I'll make it so that you have all the room you want to dance with all those countless women, but to the uninitiated eye it will still look like the same little clearing in the forest.

KRISHNA   And for your fourth act?

YOGAMAYA   I'll multiply you when you dance with the girls.

KRISHNA   You'll what?

YOGAMAYA   Multiply you! Just as one flame gives birth to many, I'll make your dark brilliance shine many times.

> Just as the fire from a single flame
>   can repeat, in igniting other lights,
> So will I kindle and multiply you,
>   a Madhav for every cowherd maid.
> One image will seem a multitude,
>   as root expands to the many branches,
> With not a mar, or a shade of difference
>   between them all, original and copies.
> As hundreds of thousands of girls gather,
>   hundreds and thousands of Krishnas will rise
> And live in a tiny place, in a corner of town,
>   and find room to move and room to dance.
> Never has such a thing been thought.
>   It requires some magic, a miraculous act
> For me to create; and the gods will meet,
>   says Bihari, and cheer the great ras.

KRISHNA   Wonderful, Yogamaya! And what's the next impossible feat you'll accomplish?

YOGAMAYA   My fifth impossible possibility will be to make your great dance last not one night but one night of Brahma, that is 4,032,000,000 human nights.

KRISHNA   But why make it so long? One night for the gods only amounts to six months in human time.

YOGAMAYA   True enough, Lord. But you're not just a god; you're the god of gods, and supremely supernatural. And these Braj girls are supernatural too, and so is their love, and so is the desire that animates their love. The time of the dance will have to be as extraordinary as all of its elements: I have no choice. . . .

KRISHNA   Good. What else will you do?

YOGAMAYA   There's a sixth measure I'll take. As the girls trip out into the forest they're sure to jingle their anklets and let happy little cries escape their throats. But never mind, I'll cast such a magic mantle over the earth that those sounds will go straight to heaven, and the only ones to hear them aside from the girls themselves will be the heavenly musicians and the gods who have gathered in their flying chariots to witness the event.

KRISHNA   Perfect. Now there's nothing to worry about at all, and I can just lose myself in the tasting of emotions. But you be careful to stay alert. You've got a lot to do.

YOGAMAYA   Lord, I always stand ready to perform your every wish. But really, it isn't right for me to get the credit when they say you go to the forest "with the support of Yogamaya." Actually it is all your doing. But never mind, off I go.

NOTES

1. Scholars have observed this prominence of the divine feminine in India as compared with other world religions. See David Kinsley, *Hindu Goddesses: Visions of the Divine Feminine in the Hindu Religious Tradition* (Berkeley: University of California Press, 1986), especially his introduction, 1–5; and John Stratton Hawley, prologue to *Devi: Goddesses of India,* edited by John Stratton Hawley and Donna Marie Wulff (Berkeley: University of California Press, 1996), 1–3.

2. *Chaitanya Charitamrita* 1.4.56. Translation mine. (All translations are mine unless otherwise indicated.)

3. *Bhagavad Gita* 10.34 (second half of verse).

4. *Brahma Samhita* 5.30.

5. *Krishna Karnamritam* 3.43.

6. *Krishna Karnamritam* 3.49.

7. *Krishna Karnamritam* 2.88.

8. *Krishna Karnamritam* 2.88.

9. *Brahma Samhita* 5.30.

10. *Krishna Karnamritam* 1.4.

11. *Krishna Karnamritam* 2.31.

12. *Brahma Samhita* 5.30.

13. *Krishna Karnamritam* 2.48.

14. BhP 10.61.2, from *Krishna: The Beautiful Legend of God,* translated with an introduction and notes by Edwin F. Bryant (New York: Penguin Books, 2004).

15. BhP 10.90.15–24, from *Krishna: The Beautiful Legend of God.* For an explanation of the *shrivatsa* in verse 20, see chapter 9 here, note 6.

16. BhP 10.23.

17. BhP 10.23.1–7, 9, 12–23, 35–39, 41–43, 48–49 from *Krishna: The Beautiful Legend of God.*

18. "The *gopis*" refers to the particular cowherd women of Braj; it is the common epithetical name utilized in the *Bhagavata* text.

19. *Dance of Divine Love: The Rasa Lila of Krishna and the Cowherd Maidens of Vraja from the Bhagavata Purana* (Princeton: Princeton University Press, 2005) (hereafter abbreviated RL), 1.3–11 (BhP 10.29.3–11).

20. *Dance of Divine Love,* RL 1.31–34 (BhP 10.29.31–34).

21. *Dance of Divine Love,* RL 4.21–22 (BhP 10.32.21–22).

22. *Dance of Divine Love,* RL 5.8 (BhP 10.33.8).

23. Francis Wilson, *The Love of Krishna: The Krsnakarnamrta of Lilasuka Bilvamangala* (Philadelphia: University of Pennsylvania Press, 1975), *Krishna Karnamritam,* 1.103 and 2.101.

24. *Venu Gita* (BhP 10.21.3, 4, and 6) from *Dance of Divine Love.*

25. *Venu Gita* (BhP 10.21.7, 9, 12, 15, and 17) from *Dance of Divine Love.*

26. *Dance of Divine Love,* RL 3 (BhP 10.31) 2, 14, 15, and 16.

27. "The Song of the Black Bee," BhP 10.47.11–21, from *Dance of Divine Love.*

28. *Krishna Karnamritam* 2.25, 2.73, and 3.2.

29. Jayadeva, *Love Song of the Dark Lord: Jayadeva's Gitagovinda,* translated by Barbara Stoler Miller (New York: Columbia University Press, 1977), 2.2–7.

30. *Love Song of the Dark Lord,* 7.39–41.

31. *In Praise of Krishna: Songs from the Bengali,* translated by Edward C. Dimock, Jr. and Denise Levertov (Chicago: University of Chicago Press, 1965), 61, 15, and 49.

32. *Songs of the Saints of India,* translated by John Stratton Hawley and Mark Juergensmeyer (New York: Oxford University Press, 1988), 107.

33. *The Caurasi Pad of Sri Hit Harivams,* translated by Charles S. J. White (Honolulu: University of Hawaii Press, 1977), stanzas 28, 58, and 71.

34. For the Chaitanya school, Yogamaya is the term generally reserved for Maya when she acts in positive ways within the divine world. Mahamaya, on the other hand, is the term reserved for Maya when she acts in negative ways within the world of the endless cycle of birth and death, *samsara.* However, the *Bhagavata* text itself utilizes these terms more loosely and interchangeably.

35. BhP 10.28.6.

36. *Dance of Divine Love,* RL 1.1 (BhP 10.29.1).

37. BhP 10.2.11–12.

38. BhP 10.1.25.

39. BhP 10.14.44cd.

40. BhP 10.70.37.

41. See BhP 10.8 for the story of Krishna and his mother Yashoda.

42. BhP 10.8.43.

43. BhP 10.45.10.

44. BhP 10.8.42.

45. This type of human-like appearance by God is expressed in phrases such as *maya-manushya*, "the appearance as a human"; *maya-martya*, "appearance of an ordinary mortal"; and *maya-manujam*, "appearance like a human being."

46. John Stratton Hawley in association with Shrivatsa Goswami, *At Play with Krishna: Pilgrimage Dramas from Brindavan* (Princeton: Princeton University Press, 1981), 191–193.

PART IV

Hagiography and Praxis

19

Kumbhandas: The Devotee as Salt of the Earth

Richard Barz

Vallabha

Vallabha (1478–1530), to whose name is often suffixed the title *acharya*, "teacher," is one of the major formulators of *bhakti* thought.[1] With one of contemporary Hinduism's leading religious organizations, the Vallabha sect, being directly descended from the movement which he established and another, the Brahma Kumaris World Spiritual University, influenced indirectly by his teachings, his thought continues to be a living presence in contemporary Hinduism.[2]

Vallabha's Sect

According to the theology of the Vallabha sect, Vallabha was not an ordinary person but was the incarnation of the mouth of Bhagavan Krishna, the Supreme Being. As the incarnation of the divine mouth, Vallabha could, through his *bhakti* philosophy, convey transcendent knowledge to his followers. Since Krishna's mouth is the receptacle of the Vedic fire, which purifies earthly offerings and then transmits them to the gods, Vallabha could also cleanse his followers of their spiritual defects and guide them to well-being in communion with Krishna. For the *bhagavadiya,* "devotee of Bhagavan Krishna," who adheres to Vallabha's teachings, Vallabha was Shri Acharyaji Mahaprabhu—"the auspicious great master teacher" who was the intermediary between flawed humanity and divine perfection.

Vallabha established his sect in order to promulgate his philosophy and practice of *bhakti*. After Vallabha's death, the survival of his form of *bhakti* was ensured by the sectarian doctrine that his status as intermediary between human and divine passes down from generation to generation through his direct descendants in the male line. Only these descendants have the right to administer the *brahmasambandha,* the "union with *Brahman*"[3] rite of initiation by which new members surrender themselves to Krishna and are inducted into the sect. Each descendant has in his care the temple of an image of Krishna. The foremost of these images is Shri Govardhannathji, "the auspicious lord of Govardhan," usually called Shri Nathji, "the auspicious lord," disclosed by Vallabha himself to be the epiphany of Bhagavan Krishna.[4] Shri Nathji's temple is the primary center of the sect. Originally Shri Nathji's temple was located on Govardhan Hill, west of Mathura in the Braj region of Uttar Pradesh. Since the late seventeenth century, it has been at Nathdwara in Rajasthan.

Sectarian worship is known as *seva,* "service," and is communal. The order of *seva* at the temple of Shri Nathji is the prototype for *seva* at all sectarian temples. At eight periods through the day, the temple sanctuary is opened, and worshipers are admitted to have *darshan,* "viewing," of the image of Krishna. Each of the *darshan* periods focuses on a particular phase of Krishna's daily life during his incarnation as a member of a *gopa* or "cowherd" community in Braj. At dawn, in the first *darshan* period, the divine image is awakened and given a light breakfast of fruit. In the second period, it is dressed for the day. Since the image is considered sentient, the clothing and jewelry chosen for it change in harmony with the weather in each season of the year. In the third period, the image is shown taking cows out to graze. At the fourth *darshan* period, in midmorning, it is offered an elaborate array of delicious foods as the main meal of the day. The fifth, sixth, and seventh periods are occasions, respectively, for the image to be awakened from a nap, offered a light lunch, and given the evening meal. At the eighth and last *darshan* period of the day, the image is put to bed and left with a bedside snack in case of hunger during the night. At each of the *darshan* periods there is hung behind the image a large cloth *pichhvai,* "backdrop," on which is illustrated the activity in which Krishna's image is participating at that period. The food that has been set before the image is available to the worshipers as Krishna's *prasad,* "favor." At each *darshan* period, singers accompanied by musicians sing *kirtan,* "songs of devotion," reinforcing the emotions aroused by that period. The intention is to concentrate the worshipers' senses of sight, taste, and hearing on Krishna so that they will be transported out of their ordinary, self-centered lives into an all-encompassing mood of *bhakti*.

Vallabha's Shuddhadvaita Philosophy

Vallabha held that the universe arises out of only one entity: Bhagavan Krishna. In his conception of ultimate reality as a single entity he was in agreement with such metaphysicians of *advaita*, "monism," as Shankara (788–820 C.E.). Vallabha also was in accord with the assertion of Shankara's school that it is *maya*, "illusion," that causes the one existent entity to appear as the manifold universe. He was, on the other hand, vehemently opposed to Shankara's view that *maya* is unreal and, therefore, not a part of that single existent entity. In Vallabha's view, an *advaita* that posited any presence, even a presence considered false, that is distinct from Bhagavan Krishna is an impure *advaita*. Vallabha's strict interpretation of *advaita* philosophy, which he called *shuddhadvaita*, "pure monism," required that *maya* be part of Krishna as his power of manifestation.

According to Vallabha, the universe is Krishna's unity dispersed along the spectrum of his self-revelation through the operation of his *maya*. The innumerable calibrations of this spectrum can be grouped into three major sections, each section being equivalent to one of the three components that Vallabha held to be the constituents of infinite, eternal, omniscient Bhagavan Krishna. The first of these components is *sat*, "existence." *Sat* is the limited end of the spectrum. It is Krishna's revelation of himself as the matter of the universe. The next component, moving further up the spectrum, is *chit*, "consciousness." The *jivas*, "souls," that dwell within human beings partake of Krishna's *chit*. The third section is *ananda*, "joy," the total revelation of Krishna. On this spectrum, the entire universe of living and nonliving things is a manifestation of Krishna. For Vallabha, both matter and *jivas* are, consequently, real.

In verses 5–9 of his brief treatise the *Siddhantamuktavali*,[5] within his *Shodashagrantha*, Vallabha illustrates this spectrum with the analogy of the Ganga River. At the *sat* end of the spectrum, the Ganga is visible as a stream of water. In the middle of the spectrum, where revelation is more comprehensive, the Ganga appears as an agent of spiritual cleansing. At the *ananda* end of the spectrum, where the divine revelation is complete, the Ganga is a goddess to be worshiped. Not just the Ganga but any feature of the world can be observed through this spectrum. For instance, it can be applied to the Braj region. With limited revelation, Braj is a portion of the landmass of India. Further up the spectrum, it is a pilgrimage place full of spiritual benefit. At the apex of the spectrum of revelation, Braj is the earthly manifestation of Goloka, Bhagavan Krishna's paradise beyond time and space.

Human beings, as presented in Vallabha's *shuddhadvaita*, lie along the same spectrum. At the *sat* end of the scale a human being appears as a body, in the *chit* portion he or she is a *jiva*, and in the complete *ananda* revelation each human being is Bhagavan Krishna. Through his own will, Krishna casts his *maya* as an amnesia over countless *jivas*, each a fragment of himself, so that each *jiva* forgets that it is a part of him. Under this forgetfulness, each *jiva* imagines itself to be a unique human ego. Though the *jivas* are real, their imagined egos are a product of misconception and are unreal. Similarly, the universe in which the *jivas* move is authentic, but the *samsara*, "cycle of births and deaths," that endlessly plays itself out in that universe is false. It has reality only in the deluded minds of the *jivas* who pass through it. Under the spell of *maya*, each *jiva* is oblivious of its source in Krishna and concentrates its attention on its ego as its identity, so tainting itself with the flaw of self-centeredness. Vallabha portrays this flaw of self-centeredness as the root of all wrongdoing and sin. It is the defect that stands as a barrier between the *jiva* in every man and woman and Bhagavan Krishna.

In Vallabha's reasoning, then, Bhagavan Krishna emits the *maya* that gives rise to the flaw that excludes the *jivas* from himself and leaves them helplessly enmeshed in the misery of an unending series of births and deaths. Why does he do this? The answer is the logical result of Vallabha's uncompromising *advaita*, according to which Krishna is all *chit*. Since *chit* includes all consciousness, it must comprise self-consciousness. Self-consciousness is possible, however, only if there is a nonself in distinction to which the self can conceive of itself. Since the *shuddhadvaita* philosophical view leaves no possibility of anything other than Krishna, only Krishna himself can be any entity or entities appearing to be outside of himself. Krishna accomplishes the paradoxical feat of becoming other than himself without violating his essential unity by exercising his *maya* to bring on the amnesia that leaves his *jivas* with the mistaken notion that they are other than himself.

Through the limited, self-centered consciousness of each one of the multitude of *jivas*, Bhagavan Krishna can be conscious of himself in his universe. Krishna's experience of himself through his *jivas* in his universe is his *lila*, "play." While experiencing his *lila*, Krishna also participates in it by entering into the flow of time in his universe in a series of partial revelations of himself. Once, just before the great war described in the *Mahabharata* epic, Krishna revealed himself in Braj in his complete form as the foster son of Nanda, a *gopa* headman, and his wife Yashoda. Togther with his self-revelation, Krishna also allowed his divine Goloka to become coincident with Braj. The scripture in which this revelation is described, the *Bhagavata Purana*, was for Vallabha the paradigm for the conduct of a *bhakti*-centered life. Through the *Bhagavata Purana*, he held that human beings can witness the revelation that is the culmination of divine *lila* and the nexus between Goloka and the ordinary world.

By means of his *lila* Bhagavan Krishna is aware of himself in his universe but not of himself as Supreme Being. Krishna's awareness of himself as Supreme Being comes when one of his *jivas* awakens from the delusion of *samsara* to remember its original oneness with Krishna in Goloka. Krishna desires the awakening of each *jiva* so that he can know himself through the *jiva*'s rediscovery of its identity with him. As it was through Krishna's *maya* that each *jiva* fell into *samsara*, so it is through his *anugraha*, "grace," that Krishna continually offers each *jiva* freedom from *samsara* in remembrance of its primeval consubstantiality with himself.

Vallabha's Pushtimarga Guide to the Practice of *Bhakti*

For Vallabha the purpose of *bhakti* is the reorientation of the *bhagavadiya* away from the ego and toward Krishna. As this reorientation proceeds, the *bhagavadiya*'s *jiva*, realizing that its self-centeredness is a deception, becomes able to receive Krishna's *anugraha*. Because Vallabha considered the well-being of the *jiva* to result from the reception of *anugraha*, he called his guide to the practice of *bhakti* the Pushtimarga, "way of well-being."

After undergoing the *brahmasambandha* initiation and internalizing the *shuddhadvaita* philosophy, the *bhagavadiya* is ready to embark on the Pushtimarga in earnest. The first step on the Pushtimarga is the acceptance of the key presupposition of Vallabha's concept of *bhakti*: there can be no spiritual advancement without Bhagavan Krishna's *anugraha*. The corollary to this is that the *bhagavadiya* who does not put all trust in *anugraha* but who relies on self-effort for progress in *bhakti* is doomed to failure. This is because any initial success achieved through self-effort makes a *bhagavadiya* proud and arrogant, convinced that he or she has spiritual prowess. Such pride bolsters self-centeredness and strengthens the barrier between the *jiva* and *anugraha*.

Since self-effort is counterproductive, it is futile for the *bhagavadiya* following the Pushtimarga to try to distort his or her personality to fit an ideal of holiness. Instead, according to Vallabha, the *bhagavadiya* should learn to express love for Krishna in a way that is in harmony with his or her own personal inclination.

Like many other *bhakti* theoreticians, Vallabha recognized five main varieties of human love through which a *bhagavadiya*, according to personal temperament, might channel the expression of *bhakti*. These five channels are: servile love, in which the *bhagavadiya* approaches the divine being as a servant; parental love, in which the aspirant feels the affection Nanda and Yashoda had for their child Krishna; comradely love, in which the devotee is a *sakha*, "friend," of Krishna as cowherd boy; erotic love, in which the *bhagavadiya*, whether male or female, is a *gopi*, "cowherd woman," in love with Krishna; serene love, in which the divine is contemplated as the Supreme Being beyond name and form. Of these channels, practitioners of the Pushtimarga have tended to be little attracted to servile love and have usually found serene love to be too emotionally cold. All three of the other varieties are popular in the sect. Sectarian traditions maintain that Vallabha himself preferred to express his *bhakti* through parental love while his younger son and successor Vitthalnath (1516–86) chose erotic love as the channel for his devotion.

Vitthalnath

After a period of uncertain direction following Vallabha's death, Vitthalnath succeeded to the leadership of the Vallabha sect in 1543. Vitthalnath, called Shri Gusainji, "the auspicious master," in the sectarian literature, was an energetic and skillful administrator. Under his supervision the Vallabha sect enjoyed good relations with the Mughal government and entered into a period of temporal expansion. Vitthalnath also used his talent as a philosopher to reinforce the sect's theological underpinnings and increase its prestige in the Vaishnava[6] community. With his interest in the esthetics of religion, he was able to draw new members to the sect by extensively elaborating its temple *seva*.

As in most theistic varieties of Hinduism, in the Vallabha sect, both a masculine and a feminine aspect is attributed to the Supreme Being. Followers of Vallabha use the title Svaminiji, "mistress",[7] for the feminine counterpart of Bhagavan Krishna. Though sectarian literature indicates that some of the *bhagavadiyas* who followed Vallabha had great respect for Svaminiji, her role in the *bhakti* of the Pushtimarga seems to have become much more important in the time of Vitthalnath. Parallel with Svaminiji's increased influence in the sect is the enhanced position of those *gopis* who were her *sakhis*, "women friends," in Braj. For *bhagavadiyas* living by the Pushtimarga, Svaminiji's *sakhis* set the standard for devotional love. When they left their husbands and families to join Krishna in amorous intimacy, they exemplified the disdain that every *bhagavadiya* should cultivate for egotistic concern with worldly reputation. Later, when Krishna forsook them, through their suffering in *viraha*, "separation," they forgot their egos and centered themselves on him. In the imagery of Vallabha sectarian literature, they burnt away their egos in the fire of *viraha*. In so doing, they demonstrated the obliteration of self-centeredness that is the goal of the Pushtimarga.

The *Chaurasi Vaishnavan ki Varta*

During his career as a *bhakti* philosopher and religious leader, Vallabha attracted a sizeable number of Vaishnavas to take up his Pushtimarga. Of these Vaishnavas, eighty-four were so accomplished in their practice of the Pushtimarga that their lives became examples to be emulated by the members of the Vallabha sect. To aid in this emulation, noteworthy episodes in the life of each Vaishnava were handed down within the sect as oral *vartas*, "accounts," in the Brajbhasha language.[8] It is the opinion of scholars of the Vallabha sect that these *vartas* were gathered together by Vitthalnath's fourth son, Gokulnath (1552–1641), and were included in his sermons on the Pushtimarga. One of the *bhagavadiyas* listening to these sermons is said to have taken the *vartas* down in writing. Later, the *vartas* were organized into the *Chaurasi Vaishnavan ki Varta*, "accounts of the eighty-four Vaishnavas," the oldest manuscript of which dates from 1640.[9]

The *Chaurasi Vaishnavan ki Varta* has been the preeminent vernacular text for the edification of members of the Vallabha sect from the time of its composition to the present day. The text exists within the sect in two main recensions, called here recension A and recension B. Both are in Brajbhasha prose with occasional quotations in verse. Although no thoroughgoing analysis of the two recensions has been made, the text of recension B seems to be an elaboration of recension A and, therefore, recension A is probably the older of the two. No commentary is associated with recension A[10] while recension B is usually combined with the *Bhavprakash*, "light on emotion," commentary of Hariraya (died 1716).[11] Neither recension A nor recension B has been translated into English, though an English paraphrase of recension A is available.[12]

Since Vallabha, and Vitthalnath after him, believed that a *bhagavadiya*'s *bhakti* should be empathetic with his or her personality, the Vaishnavas whose hagiographies make up the *Chaurasi Vaishnavan ki Varta* comprise men and women of many different character traits. While most of these Vaishnavas are portrayed as fundamentally pious and righteous, a few appear capricious, cantankerous or even dissolute. Two of the most colorful are Krishnadas, the manager of Shri Nathji's temple on Govardhan Hill, and Kumbhandas Gorva,[13] whose *varta* is the subject of this study. Aspects of Krishnadas's behavior are so reprehensible that sectarian apologists have had to strain hard to explain them away.[14] While Kumbhandas was unassailable in his personal morality, he is shown in his *varta* to be capable of a bluntness embarrassing to the sensitive. This bluntness is apparent from the very first episode of Kumbhandas's *varta* when he composes a verse with an insult in the closing line that has a coarseness that is perhaps unparalleled in *bhakti* poetry. In any case, the fact that not every one of the *bhagavadiyas* in the *Chaurasi Vaishnavan ki Varta* is blandly decorous is confirmation of the universality of the premise of Vallabha's Pushtimarga that, since Bhagavan Krishna's *anugraha* is available to everyone, *bhagavadiyas* of every personality type should have a precursor to follow in their cultivation of *bhakti*.

Kumbhandas

In the *Chaurasi Vaishnavan ki Varta* and other hagiographies of the Vallabha sect,[15] Kumbhandas Gorva (1468–c. 1582) is depicted as both a straightforward, plain-speaking farmer and a paragon of devotional virtue. The down-to-earth, no-nonsense side of his disposition has made him accessible to those members of the Vallabha sect who might find the exaggerated saintliness of others among the eighty-four Vaishnavas unattainable and discouraging. At the same time, the fearless and unyielding loyalty to Krishna that Kumbhandas displays gives him an archetypal quality as a *bhagavadiya* that has made him an attractive model for many following the Pushtimarga.[16] Because of this combination of unpretentious honesty with perfection in *bhakti*, Kumbhandas could best be described in English as "the salt of the earth."

As is true of most of the eighty-four Vaishnavas, there is no historical evidence of Kumbhandas other than in the traditions of the Vallabha sect. Nonetheless, the events of his life as related in the *Chaurasi Vaishnavan ki Varta* are, apart from the unlikely lifespan of more than one hundred years needed to encompass those events, mostly free of the miraculous and incredible. Moreover, a body of *kirtan* poetry is preserved under his name in sectarian libraries.[17] Finally, he is associated in a plausible way with such historical figures as, in episode 2, the Mughal emperor Akbar (reigned 1556–1605) and, in episode 3, Akbar's officer and courtier Raja Man Singh Kachhwaha of Amber (1550–1614). It is quite probable that there was a Kumbhandas appointed by Vallabha to sing *kirtan* before Shri Nathji who lived a life more or less as recounted in the *Chaurasi Vaishnavan ki Varta*.

The translation given here of the *varta* of Kumbhandas from the *Chaurasi Vaishnavan ki Varta* has been made from the Kanhaiyalal edition of recension A. This version of the *varta* has been chosen because it has an unadorned narrative flow and naïveté of style that both brings out in bold relief the exemplary *bhakti* of Kumbhandas and vividly evokes the oral roots of the *Chaurasi Vaishnavan ki Varta* in Gokulnath's sermons. The greater stylistic polish of the recension B version of the *varta* increases its literary appeal but makes it more remote from the discursive nature of the original account. This translation is the first rendering of the recension A version of Kumbhandas's *varta* into English. Two English translations of the recension B version have been published.[18]

The *Varta* of Vallabha's Follower Kumbhandas Gorva

Episode 1

The first part of this episode describes Vallabha's foundation of the temple of Shri Nathji at Govardhan Hill. The second part is a good illustration of the approach to *bhakti* through comradely love. Moved by this sort of *bhakti*, Kumbhandas feels himself to be such a close *sakha* of Shri Nathji that he can chide him in a satirical verse.

Kumbhandas's village was Jamnauta near Govardhan Hill. The village had received its name because in ancient times a channel of the

Jamna River[19] flowed nearby. The land that Kumbhandas used to farm was located not far away at Parasoli on Chandra Lake.[20] Later, the *bhagavadiya* Kumbhandas was so favored by Shri Nathji that he became famous as one of his foremost *sakhas*.

As soon as Shri Nathji had manifested himself, he wished to summon Vallabha and appeared to him when he had reached Jharkhand[21] in the course of his pilgrimage around India. There Shri Nathji gave him this command: "I am the three conquerors in Govardhan Hill: Nagdaman 'the conqueror of the serpent,' Devdaman 'the conqueror of the gods,' and Indradaman, 'the conqueror of Indra.' The middle one is Devdaman, and that is what people there call me. You must come and install me and establish the rite of my *seva*."

Vallabha suspended his tour right there and set out immediately for Govardhan Hill. With him went his five disciples Damodardas Harsani, Krishnadas Meghan, Govind Dube, Jagannath Josi, and Ramdas. When they got to Govardhan Hill, Vallabha and his men went to Saddu Pande's house and seated themselves on his veranda. Vallabha allowed Saddu Pande, his wife, Bhavani, and their daughter Naro, all of whom had become his followers, to carry on the *seva* of Shri Nathji for the time being. Among the many Brajvasis[22] who took spiritual refuge in those days with Vallabha was Kumbhandas.

On Govardhan Hill Vallabha had a small temple constructed, installed Shri Nathji in it, and directed Ramdas Chauhan to perform *seva* there. Brajvasis brought milk, yogurt, and butter for Shri Nathji to eat. Whatever food divine providence might ordain Ramdas first offered to Shri Nathji and then received for himself as *prasad*. Vallabha instructed those Brajvasis who had become his followers: "You are to try to keep matters in good order and to be assiduous in engaging in *seva*. This is of utmost importance to me." And he commanded Kumbhandas and his other disciples: "Don't take *prasad* without first having *darshan* of Devdaman."[23] After giving these instructions, Vallabha returned to Jharkhand and resumed his pilgrimage tour of India.

Vallabha had divulged the *mantra* of the divine name to Kumbhandas and had administered the *brahmasambandha* initiation to him. By Vallabha's favor, Kumbhandas regularly had *darshan* of Shri Nathji, composed beautiful *kirtan* verses, and sang them before him. In turn, Shri Nathji showed much favor to Kumbhandas, visiting him at his house and talking and playing games with him there. Meanwhile, Shri Nathji's *seva* continued to be conducted by Ramdas.

One time there came to Braj a *mlechchh*, "barbarian,"[24] who was the enemy of the Hindu religion. As the *mlechchh* was creating havoc in the area, Manikchand Pande, Saddu Pande, Ramdas Chauhan, and Kumbhandas all got together to consider what to do. In their uncertainty they decided to consult Shri Nathji. They asked, "Maharaj, what shall we do?" Shri Nathji commanded, "Pick me up and take me away from here." The devotees responded, "Maharaj, where shall we take you?" From his holy mouth Shri Nathji replied, "We will go into the Tond Thicket." So the Vaishnavas obtained a buffalo bull, seated Shri Nathji on it, and with Ramdas holding him on one side and Kumbhandas on the other, they all set off. The thicket was a mass of thorns and brambles, and in no time the four devotees were in considerable pain, with their bodies covered with cuts and lacerations and their clothes ripped to shreds.

In the very center of the thicket there was a pond in a clearing surrounded by trees. After the Vaishnavas had seated Shri Nathji under a large tree, Ramdas set out the materials necessary for making a food offering, first filling a pitcher with water and placing it in front of Shri Nathji. When all four devotees had sat down, Shri Nathji said to Kumbhandas, "Sing something, Kumbhandas."

Although he didn't feel much like singing, Kumbhandas composed this poem in *Raga Sarang*[25] and sang it for Shri Nathji:

> You might really like this Thicket of Tond,
> But as we ran through it our bodies were cut by burrs and
> brambles.
> What kind of mockery is this? Since when is a lion afraid of
> a fox?
> Kumbhandas says: you are the Lord of Govardhan Hill,
> Who is he but the son of a low-down slut.[26]

Listening to Kumbhandas's verse, Shri Nathji smiled but didn't say anything. After a while, news came from Govardhan that the *mlechchh* army had withdrawn, and Shri Nathji returned to his temple on Govardhan Hill.

Episode 2

This episode has two themes: first, the *bhagavadiya* who loves Krishna cannot bear to be apart from him, and second, one who follows the Pushtimarga should have no interest in currying favor with the rich and powerful. The last three poems in this episode are typical of Kumbhandas's compositions inspired by the erotic mode of *bhakti*. In them he assumes the identity of a *gopi*

confiding to her *sakhis* her love for Krishna. In the two final poems, he voices
the Pushtimarga doctrine that *bhakti* expunges regard for egotistic morality and
shame. Although Kumbhandas at times expressed his *bhakti* through comradely
affection, the greater part of his poetry was composed under the influence of the
bhakti of erotic love, and that mode of *bhakti* was evidently most compatible with
his personality.

The Brajvasis were delighted to have Shri Nathji, whom they
called Devdaman, back in his temple on Govardhan Hill and gave
thanks to him. They said it was his grandeur that had averted the
disaster that the *mlechchh* had threatened. Kumbhandas also was very
happy, and in the presence of Shri Nathji he sang two verses, one
opening with the words "Victory to Hari, the savior of all his servants" and the other beginning "Krishna on the banks of the
Yamuna, Daughter of the Sun."[27]

Kumbhandas sang so many fine verses like these before Devdaman that his poems achieved renown throughout the land. His
verses were on everyone's lips. For instance, a minstrel learned some
of his poetry and sang it before the emperor[28] at Fatehpur Sikri.
The emperor was so deeply moved by Kumbhandas's verses that he
buried his head in his hands and said that the man who had composed such poetry was inspired and had had *darshan* of the Supreme
Being. When the minstrel heard this, he said, "Sahib, the poet is
Kumbhandas and he is still alive."

This news greatly pleased the emperor, and he asked the minstrel where Kumbhandas could be found. When the minstrel told
him that the poet lived near Govardhan Hill in a village called
Jamnauta, the emperor decided that he must meet Kumbhandas
and sent men with a horse cart to bring him to Fatehpur Sikri. When
the emperor's men did not find Kumbhandas in his house, they
went on to Parasoli in search of him and located him there. But
when they told him that he had found favor with the emperor,
he said, "Brothers, I am not one of the emperor's servants, so what
do I have to do with him?"

In reply the emperor's men said, "Baba, we don't know anything about that. All we know is that the emperor has ordered us to
bring you back with us. We have this horse cart or we can get you a
palanquin. Kindly take whichever you want and come with us. We are
here to escort you to Fatehpur Sikri and that is what we will do."

Kumbhandas realized that he had no choice but to go with them
and so, without further ado, he put on a pair of shoes and got ready to
depart. At this, the men who had come for Kumbhandas brought up

One summer, when he had returned home after campaigning victoriously against many countries, Raja Man Singh[34] decided that he should go on pilgrimage to Mathura and Brindaban, as it had been a long time since he had last visited those places. After leaving Agra, he went first to Mathura,[35] stopping at Vishram Ghat and having *darshan* at the temple of Keshavray, and then proceeded to Brindaban.

Because they had been informed that Raja Man Singh would come on that day for *darshan*, the chief priests in all the temples in Brindaban had arranged to have their images of the Lord dressed in the very finest garments of gold brocade and lavishly adorned with jewelry. They had also placed canopies of heavy gold cloth over the images and attached the *pichhvais* behind them with pins of gold and silver.

The weather that summer was so hot that the *raja* could hardly stand up when he went into temples for *darshan* of the Lord. So, after he had had *darshan* in four or five great temples, he decided to go back to his camp. In camp, it occurred to him that he ought to go to Govardhan, and so that same afternoon he mounted his horse and set out with his entourage for that town. In Govardhan, after he had arranged for his camp to be set up, he had *darshan* of Haridevji. Just as had happened in Brindaban, in Govardhan worship was performed with great opulence. After Raja Man Singh had had *darshan*, someone said to him, "Maharaj, Shri Nathji is a very attractive form of the Lord and you should have *darshan* of him." In response, the *raja* said, "That form of the Lord is the king of all Braj. I must go to have *darshan* of him."

As soon as he got to Gopalpur[36] village, Raja Man Singh asked when the next *darshan* period would be. He was told that the fifth *darshan* period, when the deity had been awakened from his afternoon nap, had just finished but that he could have *darshan* in the temple at the sixth period, at which time the deity would be given a light lunch. The *raja* felt quite weary and uncomfortable after walking up Govardhan Hill in the extreme heat to have *darshan* of Shri Nathji.

As the sixth *darshan* period was beginning, Raja Man Singh was conducted into the shrine. There, magnificent *seva* of Shri Nathji was in progress. Shri Nathji had been sprinkled with rose water, and water was flowing all through his shrine from sanctuary to entryway. When he had had *darshan*, Raja Man Singh threw himself down in homage before Shri Nathji. He had arrived miserable with the heat, but now he felt cool and refreshed. Having beheld the holy face of Shri Nathji, he was filled with joy and exclaimed, "I have seen

in person the consummate *Brahman* Krishna who is the Moon
of Brindaban and the Lord of Govardhan. Today I have actually seen what before I had only heard of in the *Bhagavata Purana*.
This is a day of great blessing." And he whispered to himself, "At this
sixth *darshan* period the Lord sits majestically in state."

And then, to the beat of *mridang* drums, Kumbhandas, moved by
darshan, began to sing *kirtan* there in the shrine. The verses of
Kumbhandas's *kirtan* went straight to the heart of Raja Man Singh,
and the divine form appeared before him with all the splendor of millions of gods of love. In his *kirtan* that day Kumbhandas sang these two
verses, the first in *Raga Nat* and the second in *Raga Dhanashri*:

> Not for an instant do my eyes blink when I look at his form,
> Watching the Holder of Govardhan, my eyes and heart are trans-
> fixed,
> When he asks for yogurt,[37] he steals away my mind and I stand
> stunned, unable to talk.
> Kumbhandas says: I tell my *sakhis* about my delightful time
> with the Lord.

> Mohan has come and taken away my heart,
> I was sitting blithely at home when he came into view and all
> my concern about modesty vanished,
> Nanda's son is the treasury of beauty who knows all about love,
> and my eyes can't stay still when I see him.
> Kumbhandas says: the Lord is the Holder of Govardhan, and
> the nectar of love fills his body.

When *darshan* had finished, the *raja* prostrated himself and returned to his camp. At the end of the seventh *darshan*, Kumbhandas's
period of *seva* was over and he left for home.

Meanwhile, while discussing the adornment of Shri Nathji with
the men in his camp, Raja Man Singh asked if anyone knew who
it was who had been singing the indescribably beautiful Vaishnava
verses in front of Shri Nathji. One of them replied, "Maharaj, you've
heard about the Brajvasi Kumbhandas who went to meet the emperor? Well that was him." Then Raja Man Singh said, "I also would
like to meet him."

Next morning, as soon as he got up, the *raja* went around Govardhan Hill to Parasoli. Just as Kumbhandas was sitting down to
relax after his bath, Shri Nathji appeared and said that he wanted to
tell him something. At that precise moment, Raja Man Singh turned
up, greeted Kumbhandas, and sat down. This startled Shri Nathji,
and he ran a little distance away and stayed there, looking back at

Kumbhandas. Kumbhandas kept his gaze fixed on Shri Nathji. In the meantime, Kumbhandas's niece had also arrived. She said to him, "Baba, the *raja* is sitting here."

Kumbhandas answered, "What should I do? The one who[38] is over there was going to tell me something, but then he ran away. Now he may never tell me!"

From where he was waiting, Shri Nathji called out, "Kumbhandas, I will tell you." This made Kumbhandas happy, and he said to his niece, "Bring my mirror so that I can apply my *tilak*."[39]

But Kumbhandas's niece replied, "Baba, the female buffalo calf has gotten loose and drunk up the mirror." Then she filled a wooden bowl with water and set it in front of Kumbhandas. Kumbhandas looked at his reflection in the water and began to apply his *tilak*.

At this, the *raja* set his golden mirror in front of Kumbhandas and said, "Baba, take this and look in it when you put on your *tilak*." Kumbhandas replied, "Look, Brother, what good would this be to me? I live in a thatched house. Anyone can easily break into it and murder me for this mirror. I don't want it."

Then Raja Man Singh placed a purse full of gold before Kumbhandas. Kumbhandas said, "Brother, I don't need riches. I till the soil here and earn enough to support myself that way."

When the *raja* said, "All right, but let me sign over your village to you,"[40] Kumbhandas responded, "I'm no brahmin that I should accept your charity."

Finally, Raja Man Singh said, "Baba, give me a command."

At this Kumbhandas asked, "Will you do whatever I say?"

The *raja* joined his hands respectfully and said, "Maharaj, whatever you say I will do."

Then Kumbhandas said, "Don't ever come near me again."

Raja Man Singh said, "Maharaj, you have favored me. I have traveled over this broad earth and seen many devotees of *maya*, but you are the only true devotee of Bhagavan that I have ever seen." With these words, Raja Man Singh first prostrated himself before Kumbhandas and then arose and departed.

After the *raja* had gone, Shri Nathji came back to Kumbhandas and told him what it was that he had been going to say. This made Kumbhandas very happy, and he went back up Govardhan Hill to perform the *seva* of Shri Nathji.

Episode 4

In this episode Kumabhandas composes a hymn in praise of Svaminiji at the request of Hit Harivansh (1502–52), the founder of the Radhavallabha sect.

This gives credence to the opinion of some scholars that reverence for Sva-miniji in the Vallabha sect was stimulated by influence from other Vaishnava groups.

One day the religious leader Harivansh came from Brindaban with some of his followers to meet Kumbhandas. Harivansh knew that Kumbhandas was such an inspired man that the Lord used to come to chat with him. He also had heard the beautiful *kirtan* songs that Kumbhandas composed and knew that such verses could not have been produced without direct experience of the Lord. With all this in mind, Harivansh went to meet Kumbhandas in person, and when he had met him, he felt great joy. In the course of conversation, Harivansh said, "Kumbhandas, you have written many Vaishnava verses, and I have come here to hear them, but I have not yet heard any verse of yours that is about Svaminiji." On hearing this, Kumbhandas composed this verse about Svaminiji and sang it in *Raga Ramkali* and *Tal Charchari*:[41]

> Radha, full of youth and boundless good fortune, for your face I
>   would sacrifice hundreds of millions of moons,
> In my heart I know that hundreds of millions of deer or *khanjan*
>   birds[42] are no match for your eyes,
> I would offer up hundreds of millions of banana trees for your
>   thighs and hundreds of millions of lions for your waist,
> Hundreds of millions of rutting elephants can't rival your gait,
>   and hundreds of millions of ewers are not worth your breasts,
> Hundreds of millions of parrots are not the equal of your
>   nose, and hundreds of millions of jasmine blossoms can't
>   compare with your teeth,
> I would give up hundreds of millions of fragrant oleander
>   blossoms for the beauty of your lips,
> Hundreds of millions of cobras are nothing to your braid, and I
>   would dismiss hundreds of millions of doves for your neck,
> I can find nothing, not hundreds of millions of lotuses, to
>   compare with your hands,
> Kumbhandas cannot begin to describe Svaminiji, wondrously
>   lovely from head to foot, and Krishna, the young man who
>   holds the mountain, says that he will gaze on her every
>   moment as long as he lives.

When Harivansh had heard Kumbhandas sing this verse, he was filled with joy and complimented Kumbhandas in these words: "Kumbhandas, you have made many more comparisons with Sva-miniji than I ever could in my verses about her. You are a very inspired man. How can I praise you enough?" Greatly pleased, Harivansh and his followers took leave of Kumbhandas and returned to Brindaban.

Episode 5

Episode 5 describes Vitthalnath's unsuccessful attempt to take Kumbhandas with him on a fund-raising tour of Gujarat. Even though Kumbhandas is impoverished and desperately needs the money that he will obtain as his share of the contributions received on the trip, he is so deeply attached to Shri Nathji that he cannot go more than a mile from Shri Nathji's temple without suffering *viraha*. The episode also illustrates Vallabha's postulation that since Bhagavan Krishna knows himself through his *bhagavadiyas*, he needs them as much as they need him.

Vitthalnath had decided that he should visit Dvaraka.[43] After asking his divine image Navnitapriyaji[44] for permission to make the journey, he went to the temple of Shri Nathji and performed *seva* from the second to the fourth *darshan* periods. Then, when he had had something to eat, he seated himself in his audience chamber so that his followers could have *darshan* and speak with him.

The Vaishnavas were talking about Kumbhandas when one of them said, "Maharaj, Kumbhandas has great financial difficulty. He has seven sons, but he has only what he can produce with a single yoke of oxen. He has to support his family on what he earns from that."

Vitthalnath thought this over, and when Kumbhandas arrived for the fifth *darshan* period, he said, "Kumbhandas, I am going to Dvaraka to have *darshan* of Ranchorji. I also intend to tour the countryside around Dvaraka because many Vaishnavas there have written inviting me to come. I would like you to accompany me, for it would be disturbing to travel without a *bhagavadiya* in that distant land. With a *bhagavadiya* like you with me, the time will pass propitiously. Besides, I have heard that you have some financial problems. On our tour donations will be received, and your money problems will be solved. You really must come with me."[45] Kumbhandas replied, "As you command."

Because it was time for the fifth *darshan* period, Vitthalnath bathed and entered the temple of Shri Nathji. After he had seen to the remaining *darshan* periods and Shri Nathji had been put to bed, Vitthalnath withdrew to his audience chamber and told Kumbhandas, "Kumbhandas, tomorrow come quickly as soon as the fourth *darshan* period is over, because that's when I will depart for

Apsarakund."[46] Kumbhandas prostrated himself before Vitthalnath and went to his house.

The next day Kumbhandas, after attending Shri Nathji's first four *darshan* periods, went with all haste to Apsarakund. Meanwhile, Vitthalnath had taken leave of Shri Nathji, gone down the hill to take his meal, and had *prasad* from the temple distributed among his followers. As he had determined that hour to be the auspicious time to begin his journey, Vitthalnath then left Govardhan Hill for Apsarakund. There his people were awaiting him. Earlier they had come with his baggage and had already set up camp. As soon as he arrived in Apsarakund, Vitthalnath retired to sleep. At the same time, Kumbhandas was sitting there in Apsarakund with his mind on Shri Nathji, saying to him, "Tell me what I should do, Lord of my Life. No one knows what pain I am suffering in separation from you." When it came to be the fifth *darshan* period when Shri Nathji is awakened from his midday nap, Vitthalnath woke up in his camp. Pining for *darshan*, Kumbhandas went to a secluded spot near the village of Punchhari. There he sat down and sang *kirtan*, with a stream of tears flowing from his eyes. Kumbhandas sang this verse in *Ragu Sarang*:

> So many days have gone by since I saw my suave young lover,
> Nanda's son,
> With the hint of a moustache over his mouth,
> Ten million moons can't equal the radiance of his handsome face,
> His glances, his smile, the elegant clothes on his graceful body
> hold my heart enraptured,
> My heart yearns to meet and play with that charming dark man.
> Kumbhandas says: without the young man who holds up the
> mountain my life is pointless.

In his camp Vitthalnath heard Kumbhandas singing this verse and could not bear Kumbhandas's anxiety. So Vitthalnath came out of his camp and said, "Kumbhandas, now you go home quickly. Your foreign tour is over. And your condition is also Shri Nathji's condition. How do I know that Shri Nathji was also suffering? I know because of the case of Gajjan.[47] Mother[48] had sent Gajjan to get some *pan*. But Gajjan was so attached to Bhagavan Krishna that he could not remain a moment without seeing him. He was not able to get the *pan* because he had gone only a short distance from the house when he was stricken with a fever and fell down unconscious. And at that time Mother was offering food to Navnitapriyaji. But Navnitapriyaji did not hear Gajjan's voice and so said, "Where is my Gajjan?" And Mother replied that he had gone to get *pan*, and so Navnitapriyaji said that he would not take any food until his

Gajjan had returned. And there he sat refusing further communication. Gajjan was quickly summoned. When he arrived and asked Navnitapriyaji to eat, then Navnitapriyaji accepted the offered food. It is one of Vallabha's doctrines that however much love the devotee has for the Lord, so much love does the Lord have for his devotee. And in the *Bhagavad Gita* Bhagavan Krishna has said: 'In whatsoever way [devoted] men approach Me, in that same way do I return their love.' "[49] And when he had quoted this passage, he went on to say, "Kumbhandas, your condition is the same as Shri Nathji's condition. When you suffer in the absence of Shri Nathji, Shri Nathji is also suffering in your absence."

That is the instruction that Vitthalnath gave to Kumbhandas, and Kumbhandas went to have *darshan* of Shri Nathji and sang this verse before him in *Raga Sarang*:

> Listen to me, my friend, I can't stay here doing nothing,
> So I'll try in a hundred thousand ways to meet him,
> With the pain of *viraha* pervading my heart, how should I care
>   about my shame before my family and the rules of the world.
> Kumbhandas says: I am attracted to his body and don't care
>   for anything else, when I can't see the young mountain holder
>   every moment is an eternity.

Kumbhandas sang this verse in the presence of Shri Nathji, and Shri Nathji was delighted when he heard it. Kumbhandas was very happy to see Shri Nathji again.

Episode 6

This episode deals with *seva* and *viraha*. In addition to temple worship, the term *seva* designates any service done by a devotee for Shri Nathji. In the preliminary part of this episode, Kumbhandas uses his sons to illustrate different degrees in the performance of *seva*. He does not consider five of his seven sons to be his true sons because they do not do *seva* at all.[50] Of his true sons, one, Krishnadas, does *seva* for Shri Nathji by herding his cattle. In Kumbhandas's opinion, Krishnadas's performance of *seva* is not complete because it does not include a spirit of *viraha*. Krishnadas, therefore, can be no more than half his son. Because the other true son Chaturbhujdas[51] suffers *viraha* when he cannot be with Shri Nathji in the forest,[52] he fully performs *seva*. In consequence, Kumbhandas regards Chaturbhujdas as entirely his son. The second section of the episode, made up of the *varta* of Kumbhandas's son Krishnadas, further emphasizes the importance of *viraha* in the Pushtimarga. In this section, Kumbhandas suffers grief not from the death of his son but from *viraha*, being barred from *darshan* at Shri Nathji's temple by the ritual pollution arising from that death.

And one time Kumbhandas was sitting near Vitthalnath and said to him, "Maharaj, I have one and a half sons." But Vitthalnath replied, "You have seven sons, so how can you say you have one and a half sons?" Kumbhandas explained, "Maharaj, Chaturbhujdas is a whole son and Krishnadas, who serves Shri Nathji by tending his cows, is half a son."

The reason that Kumbhandas called Krishnadas half a son has to do with the Pushtimarga that Vallabha revealed. Vallabha revealed the Pushtimarga for the sake of those Brajvasis who adhere to *bhakti*. That's why *bhagavadiyas* sing: "He showed Brajvasi adherents of *bhakti* how to perform *seva* through love for the benefit of human beings in the world." And how do they do it? They do *seva* both by staying with the Lord when he herds cattle and also by honoring him with cries of "Farewell!" when he leaves for the forest. But some do only the one and not the other and so are only half devoted. For example, Chaturbhujdas does both kinds of *seva*, and so he is wholly devoted; but Krishnadas does only the first kind of *seva*, and so he is half devoted.[53]

Then Vitthalnath remarked, "The only son worth having is one who belongs to Bhagavan."

The Varta of Krishnadas

Krishnadas[54] was a herdsman, and Vitthalnath had assigned him the *seva* of tending Shri Nathji's cows. Every day Krishnadas used to go out in the morning to graze the cows. One day he had gone with them over toward Punchhari. All of the cows had gone into the corral, except for one large cow with a very heavy udder and a very slow gait. Then, as that cow passed by a dark place at the base of Govardhan Hill, out of the shadows sprang a tiger. The tiger was about to pounce upon the cow when Krishnadas screamed out, "Hey, scoundrel, that cow belongs to Shri Nathji! If you're hungry then eat me!" This gave the cow time to run into the corral, but the tiger killed Krishnadas.

So, when Kumbhandas arrived at the corral, all the cows were safely inside. There, Kumbhandas received this *darshan* of Shri Nathji: in a little while, Shri Nathji himself came with the cowherds to milk the cows. Shri Nathji sat down to milk the big cow, and Krishnadas held the cow's calf while the cow licked it.[55] After milking the cow, Shri Nathji returned to the temple on Govardhan Hill.

At the same time that Vitthalnath was offering food at the sixth *darshan* period in Shri Nathji's temple, Kumbhandas was coming from the corral. He had reached Dandauti Sila[56] when he received the news that a tiger had killed his son Krishnadas. As soon as he had heard this news, Kumbhandas fainted away and fell into a coma. His companions tried to revive him, but he showed no sign of consciousness. One of the Vaishnavas took the news to Vitthalnath, saying "Maharaj, Krishnadas has been killed while saving a cow from a tiger. He is lying dead over by Punchhari."

Then Vitthalnath said, "A cow would never desert anyone. When, as he is dying, a person promises to donate a cow, then the cow takes that person to the highest world.[57] Since Krishnadas saved Shri Nathji's cow, how could the cow ever abandon Krishnadas? And where is Kumbhandas now?"

The Vaishnava replied, "Maharaj, grief has deeply distressed Kumbhandas. Kumbhandas was on his way here when he learned of the death of Krishnadas. As soon as he heard the news he fell into a swoon and, try as they may, no one has been able to restore him to consciousness.

Then Vitthalnath said, "Go again and examine Kumbhandas's body and bring me news of him." The Vaishnavas again tried to resuscitate Kumbhandas but were unsuccessful. They returned to Vitthalnath, reporting that they still could not get Kumbhandas to respond.

After Vitthalnath had put Shri Nathji to bed at the last *darshan* period of the day, he went down the hill and saw that Kumbhandas was lying by the side of the road surrounded by a crowd. The people were saying, "Kumbhandas is a great *bhagavadiya*, but even he has been devastated by the loss of a son. No one can escape this pain. A son is as dear as one's self."

When Vitthalnath heard the people talking this way, he thought to himself, "Something else is wrong with Kumbhandas." And so, in order that they might know the nature of a *bhagavadiya* like Kumbhandas, Vitthalnath showed the people what really had happened by calling out to Kumbhandas, "Kumbhandas, come quickly in the morning and you will be allowed to have *darshan* of Shri Nathji. Have no sorrow about this in your heart."

As soon as Vitthalnath had said this, Kumbhandas, full of joy, got to his feet. After he had prostrated himself before Vitthalnath, he arranged for the funeral rites for Krishnadas. The next morning he arrived for *darshan* of Shri Nathji. Vitthalnath was preparing Shri Nathji for the first *darshan* of the day. He gave instructions that Kumbhandas should be allowed to have *darshan* alone before anyone else. So it was that Kumbhandas set the precedent for any Vaishnava who had been defiled by the death of a family member to be able to enter the temple. By the favor of Kumbhandas, everyone may have *darshan*.

So Kumbhandas was able to have *darshan* once a day and then go to Parasoli and stay there, singing verses of *viraha* like these three, the first two in *Raga Dhanashri* and the third in *Raga Kedara*:

> Because the beautiful women of Braj can't meet with you they
> are sad, Gopal,[58]
> O Beloved, they are restless and miserable in the pain of their
> *viraha*,
> The cool moon for them is hot, and its rays burn, while lotuses
> seem like water snakes,
> Sandalwood and flowers have lost their beauty, and fever rages
> in their bodies.
> Kumbhandas says: without you, dark youth, these women are
> withered like *kanak* vines[59] in the hot season.

> Ever since Hari went to Mathura,
> Time hasn't moved, and the nights and days are as still as
> mountains,
> As if the Creator had made a new law that each hour should
> last an eon.
> What kind of lover is he to keep us lying awake
> Like fish out of water gasping for breath? All the Brajvasis are
> floundering, restless, anxious, and dejected at heart.
> Kumbhandas says: their eyes are brimful of water, but still they
> burn in separation from Nanda's son who holds up the
> mountain.

> Other women stay close to him, but for me there's only
> separation,
> Everyone else can sleep soundly, *sakhi*, while the four winds
> are heavy with my pining.
> Who can know the Creator's mind? Was he angry when he wrote
> my fate?
> Kumbhandas says: my lord is the Mountain Holder, and day
> and night I call for him like a *chatak*[60] thirsting for rain.

While he was defiled by his son's death, Kumbhandas sang verses like these. As soon as the period of his pollution was over, Kumbhandas resumed the *seva* of Bhagavan. He had *darshan* and worshiped by presenting lamps before the Lord. Kumbhandas had received such favor from Vallabha that he had become a perfect *bhagavadiya*. His *varta* can never be experienced completely, nor can it be written down in full.

At this point, the *varta* of Kumbhandas in recension A of the *Chaurasi Vaishnavan ki Varta* comes to a close.[61] The life of Kumbhandas, as presented in the *Chaurasi Vaishnavan ki Varta*, illustrates the practice of these primary doctrines of the Pushtimarga: love of Bhagavan Krishna through one of the modes of *bhakti*; replacement of concern for ego-centered morality with devotion to Krishna; emphasis on *seva* of Shri Nathji as the revelation of the Supreme Being; the mutual love of Bhagavan Krishna and his *bhagavadiyas*; the central role of *viraha* as the fire that burns away self-centeredness. For sectarian devotees, the *varta* of Kumbhandas in the *Chaurasi Vaishnavan ki Varta* is a classic guide to the practical application of the principles of *bhakti*.

NOTES

1. Only a brief outline of Vallabha's thought can be given here. A more detailed discussion will be found in Richard Barz, *The Bhakti Sect of Vallabhacarya* (New Delhi: Munshiram Manoharlal, 1992), 16–93. In the writing of this chapter I have benefited from suggestions offered by Yogendra Yadav.

2. R. K. Barz, "A Reinterpretation of Bhakti Theology: from the *Pustimarg* to the Brahma Kumaris," in *Devotional Literature in South Asia*, edited by R. S. McGregor (Cambridge: University of Cambridge Press, 1992), 298–313.

3. According to Vallabha, *Brahman* is an alternate name for Bhagavan Krishna.

4. The manifestation of Shri Nathji on Govardhan Hill has been discussed within the larger Hindu context by Charlotte Vaudeville, "Multiple Approaches to a living Hindu Myth: The Lord of the Govardhan Hill," in *Hinduism Reconsidered*, edited by G. D. Sontheimer and H. Kulke (New Delhi: Manohar, 1989), 105–125.

5. English translations of the *Siddhantamuktavali* are given in Manilal C. Parekh, *Sri Vallabhacharya: Life, Teachings and Movement* (Rajkot: Sri Bhagavata Dharma Mission, 1943), 459–462 and in James D. Redington, *The Grace of Lord Krishna: The Sixteen Verse-Treatises (Sodasagranthah) of Vallabhacharya* (Delhi: Sri Satguru, 2000), 26–42.

6. Vaishnava, used as a noun or adjective, is a more general term than *bhagavadiya* and refers to a devotee of Vishnu or any of the other deities, including Krishna and Rama, related to Vishnu.

7. Svaminiji's personal name is Radha.

8. Brajbhasha is closely related to standard Hindi.

9. I discuss the textual history of the *Chaurasi Vaishnavan ki Varta* in "*Chaurasi Vaishnavan ki Varta* and the Hagiography of the Pustimarg," in *According to Tradition: Hagiographical Writing in India*, edited by W. M. Callewaert and R. Snell (Wiesbaden: Harrassowitz, 1994), 43–64.

10. *Caurasi Barta*, edited by Kanhaiyalal (Mathura: Navalkishor Press, 1883), is the standard edition of recension A. In the contemporary Vallabha sect recension A is transmitted mainly in Gujarati translation, e.g., *Sri Acaryaji (Shrimad Vallabhacharyaji) na 84 Vaishnavni Varta*, edited by Lallubhai Ch. Desai (Ahmadabad: Shri Lakshmi Pustak Bhandar, 1971).

11. The standard edition of recension B, *Chaurasi Vaishnavan ki Varta: Tin Janm ki Lila Bhavna Vali*, edited by Dvarkadas Parikh (Mathura: Shri Bajrang

Pustakalay, 1971) (referred to hereafter as recension B), includes Hariraya's commentary.

12. *Eighty-four Vaishnavas,* translated by Shyam Das (Baroda: Shri Vallabha, 1985).

13. The surname Gorva identifies Kumbhandas as belonging to the Gorva, or Gaurva, caste within the *kshatriya varna.*

14. For Krishnadas's career see R. K. Barz, "Krsnadas Adhikari: An Irascible Devotee's Approach to the Divine," in *Bhakti Studies,* edited by G. Bailey and I. Kesarcodi-Watson (New Delhi: Sterling, 1992), 236–250.

15. The *Chaurasi Vaishnavan ki Varta* is concerned only with Kumbhandas's life after he was initiated by Vallabha. Details of Kumbhandas's life before his initiation are related in the *Shri Nathji ki Prakatya Varta,* translated into English by Charlotte Vaudeville in "The Govardhan Myth in Northern India," in *Indo-Iranian Journal* 22 (1980), 18–45 (passages related to Kumbhandas are on pp. 21–22 with a note on pp. 30–31).

16. Kumbhandas's reputation within the Vallabha Sect can be gauged from Shrikrishnagopal Mathur, "Bhakt Kumbhandasji" *Shrivallabh-Vigyan* 8, no. 3 (1968), 12–15.

17. One of the published collections of Kumbhandas's poetry is *Kumbhandas ke Pad,* edited by Rajesh Dikshit (Mathura: Shri Ji Prakashan Mandir, 1966).

18. Richard Barz, *The Bhakti Sect,* 165–206, and *Ashta Chhap: Lord Krishna's Eight Poet Friends,* translated by Shyam Das (Baroda: Shri Vallabha, 1985), 127–178.

19. Jamna is the Brajbhasha name for the Yamuna River.

20. Further information on Chandra Lake (Chandrasarovar) and the other places in Braj mentioned in the episodes of Kumbhandas's *varta* will be found in A. W. Entwistle, *Braj: Centre of Krishna Pilgrimage* (Groningen: Egbert Forsten, 1987).

21. In Vallabha's time the Jharkhand region included the modern state of the same name along with part of neighboring Orissa.

22. A Brajvasi is a native of Braj.

23. Vallabha's use of Shri Nathji's previous name Devdaman when addressing the Brajvasis indicates that at this stage the local population had not yet fully accepted his identification of Shri Nathji with their deity Devdaman.

24. The *mlechchh* was one of several Muslim freebooters and warlords who disturbed the Mathura region before Humayun began the re-establishment of Mughal control in 1555.

25. Kumbhandas composed each of his verses to be sung in a particular *raga,* "musical arrangement." *Raga Sarang* and the other *ragas* in Kumbhandas's *varta* are described in Alain Daniélou, *The Ragas of Northern Indian Music* (London: Barrie and Rockliff, 1968)

26. In this poem, "you" refers to Shri Nathji and "he" to the *mlechchh* raider.

27. The poems are quoted in full in recension B, pp. 485–486.

28. The emperor, who is unnamed in recension A of the *Chaurasi Vaishnavan ki Varta,* is identified as the Mughal emperor Akbar in recension B, p. 489.

29. It can be inferred from this mention of the emperor's camp that this episode took place in the early 1570s, before the construction of the imperial palace in Fatehpur Sikri.

30. *Hees* is a tall grass that grows luxuriantly along the banks of the Yamuna.

31. The Holder of Govardhan is an epithet of Krishna that refers to the event in his *lila* when he lifted up Govardhan Hill to shelter the *gopas* and *gopis* from torrential rain sent by Indra.

32. Krishna is called Mohan, "the beguiler," because of his *maya* power.

33. Hari is one of Krishna's names. Mountain Holder is a variant of Krishna's epithet Holder of Govardhan.

34. Raja Man Singh Kachhwaha of Amber (Jaipur).

35. A description of the atmosphere of Krishna *bhakti* that is as typical of Mathura today as it was in Man Singh's time can be found in my "Mathura Janmashtmi, 1967," in *Unfinished Journeys: India File from Canberra*, edited by D. Ganguly and K. Nandan (Adelaide: Centre for Research in the New Literatures in English, 1998), 219–230.

36. Gopalpur, also called Jatipura, is the village built around Shri Nathji's temple on Govardhan Hill.

37. The child Krishna is especially fond of yogurt and butter.

38. Kumbhandas refers to Shri Nathji with a circumlocution because Indian rules of courtesy discourage the use of personal names.

39. A *tilak* is a Hindu sectarian mark painted on the forehead.

40. Raja Man Singh was offering to give Kumbhandas the right to receive the revenue assessed from his village.

41. *Tal*, "rhythm," is discussed in Daniélou, *Ragas*, 66–74.

42. The *khanjan*, "wagtail" (*motacilla alba*), is a symbol in Brajbhasha poetry for the restless eyes of a woman in love.

43. Dvaraka, on the Arabian Sea coast of Gujarat, is an important Vaishnava center and the seat of the form of Krishna called Ranchorji, "the one who abandons conflict."

44. The image of Krishna known as Navnitapriyaji, "fond of butter," was originally installed in Vallabha's household. Later it was moved by Vitthalnath to Gokul, southeast of Mathura, and now it is in Nathdwara.

45. According to Vallabha scholars, Vitthalnath made this trip to Gujarat in 1574.

46. Apsarakund, "nymph pool," located near the village of Punchhari, is only about a mile from Shri Nathji's temple on Govardhan Hill.

47. Gajjan was one of the eighty-four Vaishnava followers of Vallabha. Gajjan's *varta* is the thirteenth *varta* in the *Chaurasi Vaishnavan ki Varta*.

48. Vitthalnath is referring to his own mother and to an event that happened in his childhood.

49. *Bhagavad Gita*. 4.11; the English translation is from *The Bhagavad Gita*, translated by R. C. Zaehner (Oxford University Press: 1973), 185.

50. Kumbhandas's opinion of his five sons is left implied in recension A but is plainly stated in recension B (Barz, *Bhakti Sect*, 187).

51. Events in the life of Chaturbhujdas are recorded in the third *varta* of the *Dosau Bavan Vaishnavan ki Varta*, a collection of episodes in the lives of the 252 followers of Vitthalnath.

52. According to the doctrines of the Pushtimarga, no man, including Krishna's *sakhas*, is permitted to be present when Krishna plays with the *gopis* in the forest.

53. This paragraph is one of the few recension A passages that seem to be part of a lost commentary.

54. Kumbhandas's son Krishnadas should not be confused with the Krishnadas referred to earlier as the manager of Shri Nathji's temple.

55. Here Kumbhandas is witnessing an apparition of his dead son with Shri Nathji in Goloka.

56. According to Entwistle, *Braj*, 355–356, Dandauti Shila, "Prostration Stone," is located in the path below Shri Nathji's temple.

57. That is, if a dying person mentally makes a religious vow to donate a cow to a religious individual or institution, then the cow will conduct that person to heaven.

58. Gopal, "protector of cows," is one of the epithets of Krishna.

59. The *kanak* is a type of *datura*.

60. It is a convention of Indian poetry that the *chatak*, "pied cuckoo," lives only on rain drops.

61. Recension B of Kumbhandas's *varta* continues on for eight more episodes.

REFERENCES

Ashta Chhap: Lord Krishna's Eight Poet Friends. 1985. Translated by Shyam Das. Baroda: Shri Vallabha.

Barz, Richard. 1992. *The Bhakti Sect of Vallabhacarya.* New Delhi: Munshiram Manoharlal.

———. 1992. "Krsnadas Adhikari: An Irascible Devotee's Approach to the Divine." In *Bhakti Studies*, edited by G. Bailey and I. Kesarcodi-Watson. New Delhi: Sterling, 236–250.

———. 1992. "A Reinterpretation of Bhakti Theology: From the *Pustimarg* to the Brahma Kumaris." In *Devotional Literature in South Asia: Current Research, 1985–1988*, edited by R. S. McGregor. Cambridge: University of Cambridge Press, 298–313.

———. 1994. "The *Caurasi Vaisnavan ki Varta* and the Hagiography of the Pustimarg." In *According to Tradition: Hagiographical Writing in India*, edited by W. M. Callewaert and R. Snell. Wiesbaden: Harrassowitz, 43–64.

———. 1998. "Mathura Janmashtmi, 1967." In *Unfinished Journeys: India File from Canberra*, edited by D. Ganguly and K. Nandan. Adelaide: Centre for Research in the New Literatures in English, 219–230.

The Bhagavad Gita. 1973. Translated by R. C. Zaehner. Oxford: Oxford University Press.

Caurasi Barta. 1883. Edited by Kanhaiyalal. Mathura: Navalkishor Press.

Caurasi Vaisnavan ki Varta: Tin Janm ki Lila Bhavna Vali. 1971. Edited by Dvarkadas Parikh. Mathura: Sri Bajrang Pustakalay.

Daniélou, Alain. 1968. *The Ragas of Northern Indian Music.* London: Barrie and Rockliff.

Eighty-Four Vaishnavas. 1985. Translated by Shyam Das. Baroda: Shri Vallabha.

Entwistle, A. W. 1987. *Braj: Centre of Krishna Pilgrimage.* Groningen: Egbert Forsten.

Kumbhandas ke Pad. 1966. Edited by Rajesh Diksit. Mathura: Sri Ji Prakashan Mandir.

Mathur, Srikrsnagopal. 1968. "Bhakt Kumbhandasji." *Sri Vallabh-Vigyan* 8, no. 3, 12–15.

Parekh, Manilal C. 1943. *Sri Vallabhacharya: Life, Teachings and Movement.* Rajkot: Sri Bhagavata Dharma Mission.

Redington, James D. 2000. *The Grace of Lord Krishna: The Sixteen Verse-Treatises (Sodasagranthah) of Vallabhacharya.* Delhi: Sri Satguru.

Sri Acaryaji (Srimad Vallabhacaryaji) na 84 Vaisnavni Varta. 1971. Translated by Lallubhai Ch. Desai. Ahmadabad: Sri Laksmi Pustak Bhandar.

Vaudeville, Charlotte. 1980. "The Govardhan Myth in Northern India." *Indo-Iranian Journal* 22, 1–45.

———. 1989. "Multiple Approaches to a Living Hindu Myth: the Lord of the Govardhan Hill." In *Hinduism Reconsidered,* edited by G. D. Sontheimer and H. Kulke. New Delhi: Manohar, 105–125.

20

The *Bade Shikshapatra*: A Vallabhite Guide to the Worship of Krishna's Divine Images

Paul Arney

The introduction to a translation of a primary religious text appearing within a volume such as *Krishna: A Sourcebook* should situate that text by demarcating in the most concise and rigorous terms possible the boundaries between it and the other translated texts.[1] We must now, however, briefly blur the categories of outside and inside, the divisions between *theoria* and *praxis*. This becomes necessary because, for the devotees of Krishna—that most colorful of all Hindu deities—"ultimate truth" is not a remote, nebulous abstraction consigned solely to the realm of philosophical speculation. Nor is it something bound up with theological dogma and imposed from above. Rather, it is constantly affirmed as an immediate reality to be validated by ordinary devotees themselves through direct perception. In other words, for the devotees of Krishna there are no rigid distinctions between theology and mysticism, or between religious faith and personal experience of the divine. No matter what their sectarian affiliation, Vaishnava devotees maintain that the ideologies to which they subscribe serve an eminently practical purpose: to shape all the circumstances of life, the "raw material of living," into a reflection of what is ultimately real so that they may not only act according to what they know intellectually but also *be* it. For genuine devotees, the point is not how to assimilate a particular body of religious doctrine to one's own mode of rational understanding but how to effect an inner transformation that will enable one to know ultimate truth in an essentially mystical manner.

And this is where a text like the *Bade Shikshapatra* ("The Great Epistles") is relevant. The *Bade Shikshapatra* is a manual of precept and practice that teaches the followers of the Pushtimarga the fundamentals of image-worship, or devotional service (*seva*).[2] Essentially a composite document in Sanskrit and Braj Bhasha authored by two of Vallabha's direct descendants, Hariray (traditional dates 1591–1716) and his brother Gopeshvar (b. 1593), the *Bade Shikshapatra* illuminates what devotees should see, think, feel, and do in the presence of a temple or household image of Krishna. Just as crucially, the text also explicitly details what devotees should see, think, feel, and do at all other times when absent from the image.

In all Vaishnava traditions, devotional service is considered to be a primary means of gaining access to the divine, and nowhere more so than in the Pushtimarga, wherein images of Krishna are called *svarups*, a term denoting that they are simultaneously Krishna's "own [outer] forms" and his "essential [inner] reality."[3] The most preeminent *svarup* in the Pushtimarga is Shri Govardhannathji ("Lord of Mt. Govardhan"), known more familiarly as simply Shri Nathji.

Shri Nathji and eight other "self-revealing" *svarups* are credited with having appeared in miraculous circumstances. Subsequently, these *svarups* came to be worshiped personally by Vallabha and his son and successor Vitthalnath (1531–86). Toward the end of his life, Vitthalnath made a decision to distribute them among his own seven sons. In this way, the custom was begun of handing down these especially prestigious *svarups*—along with the hereditary office of *guru* (or *maharaja*)—from generation to generation by patrilineal descent. Other "manufactured" or man-made images may also be consecrated as *svarups*, however, by a *guru* of Vallabha's lineage bathing them in *panchamrita* (lit., "the nectar of five substances") and offering them *prasad* (sanctified food) that has been presented to an established image.[4] A large number of such *svarups* reside in Pushtimarga temples (*havelis*) located in Rajasthan, Gujarat, southwestern Uttar Pradesh, and Mumbai.[5] In addition, the lay follower is given a *svarup* at the time of initiation for personal worship in his or her own household shrine.

The performance of devotional service, or *seva*, is characterized by an ardent striving to apprehend Krishna in concrete, palpable form. Followers of the Pushtimarga want not just to honor Krishna through his *svarups*, but also to be able to touch, bathe, decorate, and even "feed" him. No *svarup* is ever merely venerated as a physical likeness of the deity carved out of stone or wood or as a symbol to be used as a focus for meditation. All *svarups* are loved, worshiped, and served as conscious, living forms of Krishna who require constant care and attention. The function of fully revealing the otherworldly beauty of Krishna within tangible form belongs to the *svarup*, and the *svarup* possesses all of the sanctity of the figure whose likeness it bears. The *svarup* literally and intrinsically "is" the deity.

What fundamentally defines the practice of *seva*, then, is not the material out of which the *svarup* is crafted, or its style, appearance, or posture, but what devotees *believe* it to be. Since the *svarup*'s supramundane reality is imperceptible to gross consciousness, in the beginning stages of spiritual life it may appear as little more than a lifeless statue. As faith and focus increase, however, the image begins to take on the significance, reality, and personality of a sentient being with whom one may establish an almost "co-dependent," profoundly empathetic, personal relationship. The meditative practices and procedures of *seva* are said to promote an increasingly fervent, ceaseless recollection (*smaran*) of the Lord's name, form, and *lilas*. This purifies the heart's eye, enabling a person to not just intuitively feel but actually "see" that the *svarup* is an incarnation of Krishna. With the grace of God and *guru*, a favored devotee may then observe Krishna coming to life: living, breathing, eating, playing, and conversing with him or her through the *svarup*.

There is no "image" in the ordinary sense for a person who has developed this faculty of subtle sight. Rather, the *svarup* functions as a portal into another dimension. For when advanced practitioners of *seva* are able to offer themselves without hesitation or reservation to the *svarup* with an absolute faith that the form they are seeing before them is, in reality, Krishna himself, they are carried away in ecstasy, transported into that transcendental realm of divine play, or *lila*. Such accomplished devotees are provided with a subtle body (*alaukika deha*)[6] that allows them to enter the eternal dimension of *lila* and enjoy the unmediated vision of the deity with the same intense emotion originally experienced by Krishna's parents, lovers, friends, and servants when they beheld him face to face, incarnate in Braj, as the all-perfect *avatara*.

As with many of the temples affiliated with other Vaishnava communities, the *havelis* of the Pushtimarga are kept closed throughout the day, except for eight viewing periods (*darshans*) lasting only about fifteen to thirty minutes each, when worshipers are permitted to have an audience with the deity. Although the essential elements of devotional service are common to all Vaishnava traditions, the practice of *seva* has been developed within the Pushtimarga to an extent unsurpassed elsewhere in its sophistication and lavishness. Specific ritual acts, items of food, clothing, ornaments, flowers, perfumes, lights, toys, temple decorations, hymns, and *ragas* are selected, arranged, and blended for each *darshan* according to the principles of Indian aesthetics. These are designed to please Krishna and stimulate the devotion of his worshipers by being in perfect mystical accord with each other, the time of the day, the season of the year, and the "mood" of an associated *lila* episode.[7]

From the first *darshan* early in the morning when the image-incarnation is awoken until the last *darshan* at night when it is put back to sleep, the *svarup* is displayed and cared for in different devotional contexts signifying that it is engaged in various *lilas*. Behind the scenes, priests and temple functionaries are constantly occupied in a variety of *seva*-related tasks: Certain *darshans*

require that the *svarup* be bathed; that the *svarup* be dressed in colorful costumes and expensive jewelry; that a sumptuous array of food be presented
to the *svarup*; that painted backdrops illustrating incidents from Krishna's life
be placed along the walls of the inner sanctum; that toys and objects dear to
Krishna be positioned close by the *svarup*; that hymns of praise (*kirtan*) be sung
to the *svarup*; and then, most dramatically, that the doors or curtains parti-
tioning the sanctum from the audience hall of the temple be thrown open to
reveal the deity enthroned in all of its splendor before an adoring congregation
of believers.[8]

The priests and temple elders help recreate the events that occurred in
Krishna's daily routine as an infant and youth in Braj. This is not meant to be
done as a meticulously executed, rigid observance of ritual but rather as an
earnest, unfeigned expression of devotion intended to please the real Krishna
himself. Just as the *svarup* is not a "symbol" of the deity meant solely for
feebleminded individuals incapable of higher meditative efforts but Krishna's
"own form," *darshans* are not dramatic presentations addressed to the outer
faculties in order to remind otherwise unqualified temple-goers of unseen
spiritual verities. The episodes from Krishna's life acted out within the sacred
space of the temple are understood to be actualizations of *lila* taking place
within the home of Krishna's foster parents Nanda and Yashoda.

Temple *svarups* may only be directly ministered to by temple functionaries.
Nonetheless, lay worshipers perform all facets of *svarup seva* within their own
domestic shrines. Furthermore, when lay worshipers come to the temple for
darshan, they are more than just passive observers: they touch, savor, and drink
in the *svarup* with their gaze.[9] While either having *darshan* of a temple *svarup* or
directly attending to the needs of a personal *svarup* at home, worshipers strive
with all their heart, and with all their soul, and with all their mind, and with all
their strength (*sarvatmabhava*) to actualize the rapturous experience of being in
immediate contact with the highest metaphysical reality. They endeavor to visualize the *lila* that Krishna is supposed to be performing at that particular
time of the day and season of the year, while internalizing the devotional attitude (*bhava*) of one or another of the characters described in Vaishnava devotional literature as having had a role to play in that *lila*—Krishna's parents,
lovers, friends, and servants.

By modeling themselves on these paradigmatic figures of Braj, devotees
are trained for a role within Krishna's divine play until they understand that
they are, in fact, inhabiting the religious reality of the exemplary individuals
being emulated. In this way, even while still here on earth, the human soul
becomes gradually attuned to living in eternity with Krishna.

Non-Vaishnava sectarian opponents claim that it is not only logically inconceivable but simply childish to believe that the omnipotent creator, sustainer, and destroyer of the universe could entrust himself to human nurturing and safekeeping by appearing in the form of a material image subject to

hunger and thirst. According to the Vallabhites, however, people who hold such views are ignorant of the fact that Krishna's true greatness—and, indeed, grace—consists of him being a *viruddhadharmashraya*, a treasure-store of mutually contradictory properties and antagonistic principles that defy rational comprehension.[10] Krishna, the Supreme Lord, is perfectly free and willing to become dependent on his devotees, to morph into whatever form is most appropriate for them to love, serve, and relate to, according to their own individual character, disposition, and capacity.[11]

However, with regard to this last point and its implications for *seva*, the *Bade Shikshapatra* regularly sounds a note of caution. Until devotees have acquired purity of heart and can "see" Krishna manifesting within the *svarup* for themselves, they are exhorted to never forget that they are dependent on him. Until this happens, devotees must be careful to always wait upon the deity with humility, wonder, and awe; in imitation of an insignificant servant assiduously attending to a capricious emperor of inestimable power and infinite glory (i.e., with *dasya bhava*).[12]

Considerable importance is undoubtedly attached to such admonitions. Nonetheless, the Pushtimarga has long been the most renowned of all devotional communities in India for the way its adherents shower parental affection on their *svarups*. This is done with the same devotional attitude Krishna's mother Yashoda once displayed when caring for Krishna as an infant (i.e., with *vatsalya bhava*).[13] Since Krishna is understood to be particularly accessible and responsive to the attentions of devotees who adopt this poignant and tender mode of worship,[14] it is preeminent in all of the Pushtimarga's temples and shrines.

This emphasis on *Vatsalya Bhava* is curious for still another reason, however. The prominence that is given to parental affection in the performance of *svarup seva* belies the fact that in the Pushtimarga the most intense, intimate, and sublime form of devotion to God is conceived in terms of the sexually charged relationships that the *gopis* (cowherd women, milkmaids) established with Krishna when he was their adolescent lover (i.e., in terms of *shringara bhava*).[15] Why is this not reflected in Pushtimarga worship practices?

An examination of the *Bade Shikshapatra* helps make sense of this incongruity. Followers of the Pushtimarga do not cultivate—or outwardly manifest—the devotional sentiments associated with the adolescent Krishna's milkmaid lovers so much when they are performing *seva* in the presence of the *svarup* as in its absence[16] (i.e., during *anosar*).[17]

Except in unavoidable circumstances, the physical component of *seva* is never to be abandoned, even by the most advanced devotees, because to do so would cause Krishna distress.[18] However, the highest form of worshipful service is a mental discipline[19]—and it does not cease just because a devotee leaves the presence of the *svarup*. The Pushtimarga community is overwhelmingly made up of householders actively engaged in the world, and to afford Krishna privacy, even the most dedicated practitioners of *seva* are required to spend a considerable amount of each day away from the *svarup*. But if practitioners of *seva* feel elated in the presence of the *svarup* because they literally identify it with Krishna, then the obvious corollary is that they will also feel dejected in the absence of the *svarup*, because they are then separated from Krishna.

Paradoxically, though, the *Bade Shikshapatra* insists that to be overcome by suffering in the absence of the *svarup* is not a misfortune but the highest spiritual fulfillment. Followers of the Pushtimarga do not seek spiritual union with Krishna, "the pleasure, raised to the 'n-th' degree of human sexual union with him," but the very longing for union, the intense desire itself.[20] As in the various Bengali and other Vaishnava traditions, the ultimate goal is to suffer the intense agony of separation that the *gopis* experienced when their minds became entirely riveted on their lover Krishna in his absence. In short, the followers of the Pushtimarga want to burn:

> As the mind acquires increasing focus during the performance of *seva* the devotee begins to feel that he or she is being consumed from within by a burning desire to see Krishna. This experience reaches such an intensity that all defects vanish and the virtue of humility is perfected. The heart is then gripped by intense suffering in separation, and the love of the devout people of Braj [i.e., the *gopis*] becomes internalized. This is referred to as *manasi*, or "mental," *seva*, and it is the ultimate [fruit]. When the devout people of Braj were separated from Krishna they were set on fire. When a follower of the Pushtimarga comes to experience this same phenomenon he or she then knows that Vallabha has entered their heart. Vallabha's form is, verily, the "fire of love."[21]

Alternately experiencing the bliss of union (*samyoga rasa*) with Krishna in the presence of his *svarup*, and the pain of separation (*viprayoga rasa*, *viraha*, or *viyoga*) from Krishna in the absence of his *svarup*, the most accomplished devotees grow insane with desire. By constantly visualizing Krishna's form, remembering his *lilas*, and invoking his holy name with the utmost fervor (*sarvatmabhava*) during periods between *darshans*, pure love (*prema*) for the deity is transformed. First it evolves into an intense emotional "attachment" (*asakti*) and then into an acute "addiction" (*vyasana*). Devotees become consumed by an insatiable craving for Krishna that causes them to forget all else and not be able to tolerate anything but him. They start hallucinating their beloved Krishna everywhere and in everything. The restrictions of time and space dissolve, and the sacred and the profane merge into one another.[22] In this state, worshipers are so overcome by longing that when they return into the presence of the divine image again, they feel utterly bereft of Krishna even during those brief instants when their eyelids blink and they are deprived of the sight of the *svarup* for what seems to them like an eternity![23] The authors of the *Bade Shikshapatra* proclaim that the spiritual practices of *seva* reach their full fruition when one constantly suffers in separation. And, remarkably, this experience is also the sweetest bliss (*mukhya rasa*). For it involves Krishna himself, he who is made of love, becoming the center of one's being, one's own, innermost reality.[24]

The Pushtimarga practice of devotional service is not meant to be just one activity or pastime among many that are to be pursued. It is the foremost *dharma* of a devotee, that one duty which the *Bade Shikshapatra* tells us is to be given priority above all personal concerns, household obligations, and even a narrow adherence to Vedic injunctions. Although the Pushtimarga does not encourage a world-renouncing form of spirituality, it is nevertheless held to be crucial that devotees mentally turn from the empty glamour of passing things so as to be able to worship Krishna out of an utterly pure and selfless love (*premalakshana bhakti*). The *svarup* is not to be plied with offerings to propitiate the deity and gain some reward independent of *seva*. *Seva* is to be performed without any thought of recompense, favors, or consolations by those who would seek for themselves nothing but the happiness of Krishna. The profound sense of satisfaction that comes from actually seeing and knowing that Krishna is being pleased by one's worshipful service is, in itself, the devotee's true reward. If it asserted that this sense of satisfaction surpasses even the bliss of liberation.[25]

Let us now look more closely at the *Bade Shikshapatra* itself and the circumstances of its composition. The text seems to have come into existence sometime during the mid- to late seventeenth century, when Hariray sent forty-one didactic letters in Sanskrit verse to his younger brother Gopeshvar. Gopeshvar apparently then immediately composed or, more accurately, dictated a prose commentary on Hariray's letters in Braj Bhasha.

The siblings were fourth-generation descendants of Vallabha and hence venerated as *gurus* within the Pushtimarga. Not a great deal is known about Gopeshvar and, in terms of literary activity, he was not exceptionally prolific.[26] By contrast, Hariray was a figure of considerable prominence within the Pushtimarga. As the eldest son, he had automatically acquired the sect's second *gaddi* (seat of power, dynastic house), inheriting all of the honors and responsibilities associated with performing the *seva* of the prestigious Shri Vitthalnathji *svarup*. Moreover, Hariray was also a markedly charismatic figure in his own right. There is a belief in some quarters of the Pushtimarga that Hariray was an incarnation of Vallabha,[27] while others hold that Hariray was an *avatara* of the founder's son and successor Vitthalnath.[28] A massive amount of literature has been attributed to Hariray in Sanskrit, Braj Bhasha, Gujarati, Marwari, and Punjabi that in sheer volume surpasses the literary output of any other member of the *sampradaya*.[29] Furthermore, Hariray is given credit for having extended the mode of *seva* that was originally instigated by Vallabha and, at a later date, elaborated and systematized by Vitthalnath.[30]

Such being the case, it is not particularly surprising that a number of Sanskrit *shlokas* (paired verses) composed by Hariray for the *Bade Shikshapatra*—a text whose main subject is *seva*—should be incorporated into the daily religious observances of Pushtimarga temples, nor that children who attend sect-affiliated schools should be made to memorize them.[31] Yet nowadays at least the *Bade Shikshapatra* is invariably published with Gopeshvar's commentary, either in its original Braj Bhasha or else in Hindi or Gujarati translation or paraphrase. In fact, regardless of differences in language, style, and genre, Gopeshvar's vernacular prose elucidates and ideologically blends with Hariray's Sanskrit verses sufficiently well that a great many followers of the Pushtimarga regard the commentary as part of one coherent whole synonymous with the *Bade Shikshapatra*. Indeed, almost canonical status is bestowed on Gopeshvar's commentary by an origin myth that describes both the production and consumption of the text as being part of an overlapping process in which the roles of author, commentator, and "target audience" are deliberately blurred.

The story is told that Hariray possessed paranormal powers. He was once travelling in a distant region when he had a prophetic intuition that Gopeshvar's wife would die two months later. This woman was a great devotee, and Hariray knew how attached Gopeshvar was to her for this reason. Thus, he began sending Gopeshvar one letter each day to fortify him against the impending tragedy and assuage his grief. Gopeshvar was too preoccupied with devotional tasks to read even a single letter, however, and before long his wife died, just as Hariray had foreseen. Gopeshvar was devastated. He not only completely abandoned his priestly duties but alarmed relatives and personal followers alike when he began to talk of going away to live in the forest as a hermit.[32] A *sevak* (servant-devotee) then managed to cajole Gopeshvar into agreeing to at least glance at one of the hitherto-unread letters Hariray had been sending him. Scarcely had the first of Hariray's letters (the one partially translated here) been placed into his hands than the pall of grief that had been hanging over him evaporated. Empowered by a renewed sense of Krishna's compassion and grace, Gopeshvar embraced the *sevak* who had handed him the letter, bathed and ate for the first time in what was by then a number of days, and then immediately set to work dictating his contribution to what would become renowned as "The Great Epistles."[33]

In his commentary on the final *shloka* of Hariray's last letter, Gopeshvar makes use of a traditional Hindu conceit. He compares the *Bade Shikshapatra* to a priceless jewel whose very existence is to be kept hidden from all but those who are suitably qualified: the *pushti* (favored, chosen, elect) souls who belong to the Vallabha *sampradaya*.[34] The *Bade Shikshapatra* is, unequivocally, a sectarian manual intended primarily for a limited coterie of initiates; it may be regarded as a partisan, even an "esoteric," document.[35] Yet it is also an accessible guide to Vaishnava worship practices that has had an enduring and more general relevance. The *Bade Shikshapatra* is to this day highly valued for its insistence that selfless love is the characteristic emotion and most efficacious form of religion.

The *Bade Shikshapatra* of Hariray with
the Commentary of Gopeshvar[36]

Verses 1–2

Equanimous toward the outcome
Of personal affairs and Vedic rituals,
Yet constantly pining
For the sight of Krishna;
Restrained in speech,
Only talking when strictly necessary;
Keep the mind always absorbed
In the passing parade
Of Krishna's divine deeds.

Commentary on Verse 1. Do not be grieved by the vicissitudes of
the world or the burdens of Vedic religious obligations. If you feel
distressed by these matters in the presence of the divine image, then
Krishna will see your unhappy face and suffer too, even though he is
made entirely of bliss. Do not be dejected if your secular affairs or
Vedic rituals are not going well, or even if they turn out to be a
complete debacle. Understand that there is nothing of value in the
temporal world or Vedic ritualism. Followers of the Pushtimarga
should feel a sense of satisfaction whenever any action associated
with *seva* has a successful outcome; they should only ever feel troubled when unable to serve the Lord.

In the Pushtimarga, *seva* is to be performed in emulation of the
devout people of Braj. Whenever Krishna went out to graze his
cows in the woods, the cowherd women who were left behind in his
village would pine away singing songs of sorrow and separation
(*venugita, yugalagita*).[37] Later, however, Krishna would come back to
console them. In his presence once again they would experience
rapturous emotion. So this is precisely how *seva* is to be performed
in the Pushtimarga. During *anosar*, when you are away from Krishna's image, keep his lotuslike face constantly in mind as you experience the sorrow of separation. When you are once again in the
presence of the image, however, gaze with ardor at the sight of your
spiritual reward, the Supreme Being, Lord Krishna. Only after first
performing *seva* should you engage in any secular or formal religious activity. It is incumbent upon householders that they carry out
these secondary tasks so as to avoid any possible worldly disrepute
and to conform to the Vedic injunctions. But never allow yourself to
become entrapped in temporal affairs or ritual matters. Accustom

your mind to always being occupied with Krishna. Then during *darshan* you will remain free of all worries and be able to simply revel in the Lord's holy presence.

It is a rule that a person should never enter the temple in a state of *sutak*[38] because to do so would pollute it. In such circumstances *seva* is to be performed with devotion in the imagination.

Commentary on Verse 2. A devotee's speech should always be restrained. Do not talk excessively, only as much as is needed to conduct your daily business. The general ideal is that a devotee should only speak about topics relating to the divine. It is not practical, however, for householders to carry out the tasks of everyday life without some conversation relating to worldly topics. But do not talk any more than is strictly necessary; otherwise you will commit one of the sins of speech. Do not waste time in idle prattle. Divine sentiments are never able to establish themselves within the heart of a garrulous person. They dissipate outward through the voice. To be of measured speech is so vital because this path of devotional love is so delicate.[39]

It is the nature of the mind to always want to be jumping from one object to another. Therefore, keep it occupied with Krishna's infinite and multifarious *lilas*, recollecting them one after another in chronological succession. The mind is even more fickle than the wind. Although a person may attempt to check it by countless different means, it never stays focused on a single object for any length of time. So always keep it engaged in contemplating the Lord's various divine deeds. Whenever you become aware that your mind has wandered from Krishna, redirect your attention to the different *lilas* associated with the annual festivals: *Janmashtami* [Krishna's birthday], *Annakut* [the "mountain of food" feast day in celebration of Krishna raising up Govardhan Hill to protect the cowherds from the storms sent by the Vedic demi-god Indra], *Holi* [the famous spring festival when people throw colored powder over each other], and *Hindola* [the festival day when images of Krishna are carried about in ornamental cradles].

In this way devoutly meditate on and imaginatively enter into Krishna's various *lilas* according to the spiritual practices of the Pushtimarga. As well as the events associated with the festival days, you should visualize those activities that Krishna used to perform in Braj which form the basis of the daily *darshans*. Begin in the morning by contemplating the Lord waking up in his foster father Nanda's house, in a forest grove with Shri Svaminiji (Radha), or after having a tryst with one of his other *khandita* lovers.[40] Next recall the activities associated with the *mangal* viewing period [when Krishna is served a light breakfast and worshiped with burning lamps], *shringar* [the bathing and dressing of Krishna], *gval* [when Krishna and his companions take the cows out to graze], *palna* [when Krishna is envisaged as a tiny infant being rocked in his cradle; note that this is not classified as a discrete *darshan*], *rajbhog* [when Krishna is given a midday meal], *utthapan* [when Krishna is awoken from his afternoon nap], *bhog* [when Krishna is served a light snack], *sandhyarti* [when Krishna is imagined returning home with the cows, worshiped with burning lamps, and served a meal], and *shayan* [when Krishna is put to bed]. After the Lord has retired for the night, you may then meditate with a pure heart on the *ras lila*, the *man lila*, the *jalsthalvihar lila*, and such like.[41]

In addition, always be mindful of the gracious nature of Shri Acharyaji (Vallabha), Shri Gusaimji (Vitthalnath), and the lineage of *gurus*. Reflect repeatedly on the reason for Krishna's manifestation on earth. Meditate on the inner meaning of Krishna's assorted garments and his various ornaments. Continually contemplate the significance of each and every object that has a role to play in Krishna's love games so as to inspire a fervent devotion. Recall Krishna's *lilas* one after another so as to become completely filled with him. Keep your mind absorbed in the Lord's *lilas* twenty-four hours a day.

At this point we may note that there are two ways of performing *seva*. One of them is considered excellent, whereas the other has to be reckoned at best mediocre. To perform the best form of worshipful service, you should first purify yourself with a bath and then approach your *guru* with reverence. Take care of any personal needs your *guru* may have; then proceed to the temple in his company. After arriving at the temple, participate in temple service with humility according to your *guru's* instructions. If you physically visit the temple, then Krishna, the sum of all bliss, will not be troubled. He will quickly bless you. This is the highest form of devotional service. By contrast, the mediocre way of doing *seva* involves installing Krishna directly within the heart. The Lord is gracious. However, if you adopt this approach it causes him unnecessary trouble. For this reason it is not the sanctioned practice of the Pushtimarga.[42]

Verses 3–4

To protect all implements and materials,
Maintain the strictest discipline
While performing
Even the most menial
Devotional tasks.

Commentary on Verse 5. If your wife is averse to *seva* and puts obstacles in the way of its performance, all association with her ought to be given up. Why? Because it is only proper to abandon that which has no affinity with the Lord. If your wife is not spiritually minded, attempt to arouse her interest in Krishna. If she has received the *namanivedana* initiation[45] from a guru of Vallabha's lineage and follows the rules and regulations laid down by the tradition, she may be allowed to touch the *svarup*. If she is an initiated devotee but does not scrupulously follow the injunctions, have her do other sorts of devotional service. If, however, the woman actively obstructs the performance of *seva*, renounce her forthwith.

Avoid all attachments to money. It is said that to live in a dispassionate manner without concern for money is the most exalted way of life. To be realistic, however, we are living in the *Kali-yuga*, the last age of iniquity, in which people's ability to withstand hardship is greatly diminished. If you were to suddenly adopt a carefree attitude toward your finances, any wealth you had managed to accumulate would soon disappear. In such a situation, most people would quickly come to the end of their tether and start to regret having let all their money slip through their fingers. For this reason such a stance is not advisable.

Nonetheless, you should not be concerned about money for the sake of your own, personal happiness. Knowing that everything belongs to the Lord, take good care of your wealth so that it can be put to proper use in devotional service. If you are truly possessed by a spirit of renunciation, you need not even concern yourself with money. If you are not absolutely resolute in your renunciation, however, look after your money in a sensible manner, always remaining conscious of the fact that its sole purpose is to allow you to serve the Lord.

A fiendish mentality takes hold of a person who becomes totally absorbed in the pursuit of wealth and spends it all on worldly goods instead of utilizing it in Krishna's *seva*. Therefore, spend your money on such things as religious festivals, temples maintained by *gurus* of Vallabha's lineage, or needy devotees. Empty your mind of all attachments, take good care of your finances, and put to proper use whatever you can afford in the service of God and *guru*. If you behave wisely in this regard, love for the Lord will blossom within your soul.

Verse 6

When arranging a marriage,
Assess a prospective bride's

Aptitude for devotional service.
Associate with lovers of Krishna
To learn about him who is
Dearer than life itself.

Commentary on Verse 6. It was suggested above that money not be spent in the worldly sphere. But if this advice is followed, how is it possible to perform such necessary activities as marriages? Concerns of this sort may be addressed in the following manner: The marriage of a devotee, or the son of a devotee, ought to be arranged with a view to *seva.* If an additional person is found to assist in the Lord's *seva,* it can be performed all the better. However much money is required on marriages and the like. Obtain the blessing of the Lord, then carry out your worldly obligations with the attitude of a servant.

Do not seek the company of accomplished devotees out of any self-interest—a desire for the transient things of this world or the next—but only so as to be inspired by what they have to say about Krishna, he who is "dearer than life itself." It is important to associate with spiritual people, but do not harbor thoughts of gaining anything in return. Do not indulge in displays of piety in order to win praise from others. Behave in a religious manner, but do so in all humility, simply because it is your duty.

Verse 7

In the absence of the image,
Feel bereft.
In the presence of the image,
Strive to behold the Lord's divinity:
He will manifest within it.

Commentary on Verse 7. Whenever it is not the time to be ministering to the divine image, strive to experience the pain of separation felt by the cowherd women of Braj who sang songs of longing and loss in Krishna's absence. If you believe with all your soul that the *svarup* is in reality Krishna, the all-perfect Supreme Being will manifest within it. Until you have actually experienced this phenomenon, however, show the *svarup* the same respect you would if you were in the presence of the Lord himself. As you perform *seva* before the *svarup*—dressing, adorning, and presenting offerings to the divine image with a mind to how each item would suit Krishna himself—savor the sublime sweetness of those *lilas* that Krishna performed in the company of his devotees. During *anosar,* on the other hand, experience the agony of Krishna's absence. Having left the temple, cultivate the same tormented state of mind described in the songs of unrequited love that were sung by the cowherd women of Braj. As the lovelorn *gopis* ran throughout the woods frantically searching for Krishna, they would think to themselves, "In which forest grove would the Lord be now?" "Where could he be performing his love games with his devotees at this moment?" Make these *lilas* of separation vividly present to your mind, all the time becoming more and more distraught with the thought of how vile you must be not to be able to see the Lord. In this context, the following Sanskrit verse composed by Vitthalnath is exemplary: "My mind is corrupt, my speech is corrupt, my body is corrupt, my deeds are corrupt, my knowledge is corrupt, my devotion is corrupt: How can I even contemplate my myriad crimes?" In like manner, feel humble and contrite as you are overcome with misery for Krishna's loss.

As the time for *seva* approaches you should bathe, put on clean clothes, and proceed directly to the temple in a state of ritual purity (*apras*) according to the ordinances of the Pushtimarga. Once inside the temple, gaze ardently upon the blissful Lord's ambrosial face and divine limbs, ridding yourself of all the pain of separation. Aspire with all your heart to experience the same rapture as the residents of Braj when they came to see Krishna in Nanda's home. They will then favor you with a love for the Lord equal in intensity to their own.

Verse 8

Touch the image with love.
Perform each devotional act with love.
For it is only through love
That he who is made of love
Can be truly known.

Commentary on Verse 8. We have already intimated how after performing all necessary preliminaries such as bathing, and so on, the eyes of the worshiper are captivated when they behold the divine image of the Lord. It is important to realize, however, that all the senses are able to revel in the deity during the course of temple worship. When it is time for the *mangal darshan,* you should glorify Krishna, bathe him, put on his garments, and adorn him with jewelry that is appropriate for the season. As you are doing this, touch the Lord's form with love. If your heart is pure, you may adopt the persona of one of the devout people of Braj who would visit Krishna

early in the morning at Nanda's house. These devotees would present
Krishna with garments, ornaments, and toys before bathing and
dressing him. However, until you have acquired purity of heart, you
should always handle the Lord's form with some trepidation, as if
you were attending to a mighty emperor. Think to yourself: "If an
offense is committed, the God of all gods will punish me." Thus, if it
is a cold winter's day, be sure to first warm your hands before
touching the *svarup*. By touching the *svarup* with a consummate
awareness of the tenderness of the Lord's divine limbs, an intense
love for him will well up within you.

In this manner, throughout the day, from the first *mangal* period
in the morning until the last *shayan* period at night, perform each
act of worship with love. Offer homage to Krishna's image with the
utmost love, always conscious of the fact that every single item used
in *seva* is divine in nature (*svarupatmaka*). Do nothing without love.
When you are able to perform *seva* with an absolute dedication of
your entire being *(sarvatmabhava)*, you will experience the bliss of
which the divine image is constituted.

Verses 9–10

Hari[46] is unable to enter a defiled heart.
Yet in proportion to the spiritual assets
Of his devotees
He reveals himself in his immaculate image.
When the heart has been purified
He manifests within.

Commentary on Verse 9. While serving Krishna's divine image,
keep all of your heart, mind, and senses totally free of anything
profane. Do not be distracted by either worldly joys or sorrows, since
these both relate solely to the physical body: the pleasures and
pains that derive from the performance of secular works and religious
rituals enjoined by the *Vedas* are limited in their effect to the present
body. By contrast, the divine delights and poignant agonies of *seva*
affect the very soul, lifetime after lifetime.

The Lord's *svarup* is immaculate. Never for an instant imagine
that it is constituted of any material quality (*maya*). Krishna's feet,
hands, face, belly, and every other part of his body are made of bliss
itself. And a pure mind is capable of experiencing that bliss. The
Lord is without need, greed, pride, or selfishness. He is the remover
of all sorrow and the granter of transcendental bliss. After with-
drawing your attention from mundane matters, contemplate Krishna
as being endowed with all divine virtues. Strive constantly to keep

your mind enamored of Krishna's lotus feet to the exclusion of everything else. If you perform *seva* with ardent love, the Lord will bestow on you the experience of his reality.

Commentary on Verse 10. In the philosophical system of Vallabhacharya, the whole creation is broadly classified into things that are by nature *daivi* (divine) or *asuri* (demonic, evil). By further dividing the divine into that which is either *maryada* (discipline-bound, conforming to formal religious rites and rituals) or *pushti* (partaking of grace, favored, chosen, elect), three separate divisions are established. If you are able to inwardly discriminate between each of these divisions you will not fall victim to either delusory pain or pleasure.

Let us now look at a few examples to help us understand what those *pushti* things are that constitute a devotee's spiritual assets. First, if your body stays effortlessly engaged in *seva*, know that it is *pushti*. If, however, you buckle easily under feelings of lethargy while performing *seva*—that is, if you constantly make excuses of being unwell, only performing *seva* intermittently, say, if you happen to come into contact with some Vaishnava—know that you have an *asuri* type of body. Similarly, know that your mind is *pushti* if you experience the reality of the Lord's *svarup* during the performance of *seva*. If your mind is *asuri*, however, you will repeatedly become sidetracked by worldly preoccupations during the performance of *seva*. Hence, you will be unable to experience the bliss of the *svarup*. If your wife, children, or other relatives assist in *seva*, they should be considered *pushti*. If they obstruct the performance of *seva*, they should be considered *asuri*. On the other hand, people who habitually occupy themselves with the *karma marga*[47] should be considered *maryada*. The same applies to finances. Money that is put to use in *seva* should be considered *pushti*, whereas money outlaid on the *karma marga*— on such things as gifts [to brahmins or mendicants], fire sacrifices, or offerings to the ancestors—should be considered *maryada*. However, if money is spent on luxury items, it is stolen, or it goes in a tax or a fine, it should be deemed *asuri*.

The main principle is that all items employed in *seva* should be considered pure. On the other hand, anything that is not used in *seva* should be considered impure. Only pure things that have been dedicated to the Lord are beneficial to a devotee. Fully realize the implications of this. If you do, you will be purified. The Lord himself will then enter your heart so that you may delight in that bliss which is his reality. Renounce whatever is unrelated to *seva*. Perform *seva* with a thorough appreciation of the divine status of each and every one of the garments, implements, and other items utilized in the Lord's *seva*.

Verse 11

Won over by humility,
Krishna provides an immortal, subtle body.
Then, he who is made of love
Enters it,
Revealing his reality.

Commentary on Verse 11. Unless you perform *seva* with sincere humility, the Lord will neither be satisfied nor pleased. Krishna is the God of all gods who is endowed with all six divine perfections: *jnana* [omniscient knowledge], *vairagya* [serene dispassion], *aishvarya* [transcendent majesty], *virya* [creative power], *yasha* [universal honor], and *shri* [radiant beauty]. It is simply inconceivable that the Lord could ever lack anything. It is only through love and humility that he is won over. In the words of one eminent saint:

> *Seek the Beloved through love.*
> What matter whether you are shapely,
> Talented, virtuous, or charming;
> Whether you are high-born, meritorious, or fortunate;
> Whether you recite the Veda or Purana?
> Without love, Govinda[48] says,
> You might as well be wagging your tongue
> Like some witless parrot.

Krishna accepts any paltry object a humble person offers him out of love, just as he affectionately accepted the chick peas that were given to him by his poverty-stricken childhood friend Padmanabh Das. It is only when one becomes totally self-effacing that Krishna is truly satisfied. When that happens, Krishna will shower his grace upon you. He will perfect your subtle body so that you will be able to adore him in *lila* for all eternity. He who is made entirely of love will take up his abode within your heart and allow you to experience the reality of his own nature. You will then realize that this whole universe is nothing but Krishna's eternal play. Never more will you experience enmity toward any creature. You will obtain the goal of this path of grace, the Pushtimarga.

Verse 12

Deliberating constantly
On this eternal reward,
Be utterly dedicated
To praising Krishna.

Commentary on Verse 12. Attachments to things in the material sphere will not arise if you meditate unceasingly on your spiritual reward, the Supreme Being. If, however, remembrance of the Lord is not practiced at all times, you will begin to rely on external things. This will cause demonic states of consciousness to arise that are inimical to spirituality. Therefore, practice the sort of mindfulness that is described here—full of humility, fervor, and anguish. The deity should be attended to with profound reverence—not for show, for the sake of gaining a reputation as a holy person, nor any other such worldly motive. The principal duty of a Vaishnava who belongs to the Pushtimarga is to perform *seva* with the humble attitude of a servant who knows that selfless service is itself the supreme reward. Worship the Lord incessantly with heartfelt devotion. Do not think to yourself, "It will not matter if I do not perform *seva* today, I'll do it tomorrow." For goodness sake, you could give up the ghost at any moment! Put aside all sensual pleasures and bodily comforts in order to serve the Lord unceasingly. This is the highest doctrine.

Verse 13

This worship is performed
In the presence of the image,
And in its absence.
Hence it is unique and distinct.
Its devotional mood
Is considered intermingled,
Like that of the "singing" milkmaids.[49]

Commentary on Verse 13. We are told how the milkmaids initially experienced the bliss of Krishna's form. Later, however, Krishna suddenly disappeared from their midst. When that happened, the *gopis* gathered together to praise the Lord in song. In their distress, they then started rushing about like lunatics, searching high and low for him from forest grove to forest grove. Having lost Krishna, the distraught women became so obsessed with the thought of him that in their own minds they actually became him. They all began imitating Krishna performing his *lilas*, with each of them individually identifying herself with the Lord. It is this devotional state of consciousness (described in *Bhagavata Purana* 10.30) that consists of Krishna's presence being experienced in his absence that is to be cultivated through the practice of *seva*.

First worship in the presence of the image and savor the sweetness of union. Then, in the absence of the image, repeatedly recall to mind the forest-grove *lilas* and suffer the sorrow of separation. It is related in the *Rasapanchadhyayi*[50] how, without a second thought, the *gopis* deserted their households so as to experience the bliss of Krishna's company. It was not long though before Krishna had again vanished from their midst so as to reveal to them what it was like to be totally overcome by misery in his absence. Even in the worldly sphere we can observe that if a person amasses a huge fortune then suddenly loses it he or she undergoes immense suffering. But how would a person ever know such pain if they did not have a penny to their name to begin with?[51] Similarly, if the Lord had not first given the *gopis* a brief taste of union, they would never have been able to experience such intense agony in his absence. Krishna later reappeared before the women, and then the *jalsthal krida* took place, when they frolicked together on the banks of the Yamuna in mutual delight.

This, then, is the manner in which *seva* is to be performed in the Pushtimarga. Inside the temple, exult in face-to-face contact with Krishna while joyfully participating in the communal singing of *kirtan* (hymns) that describe the ecstasy of union. Outside the temple, consider yourself utterly bereft of the Lord while singing with great ardor devotional songs that have as their theme the loss, anguish, and yearning caused by separation from the beloved (*venugita, yugalagita,* and *gopikagita*).[52] The practice of the latter form of *seva*-in-separation accomplishes everything. If remembrance of Krishna is practiced constantly—alternately in the presence of the *svarup* and in its absence—a person becomes inflamed with devotion. The nature of that devotion is explained in the following verse.

Verse 14

Afterward,
There is only
Love in separation:
The ultimate attainment!

Commentary on Verse 14. If you sing Krishna's praises and worship him according to the directions given above, a state of consciousness arises in which you begin to experience the presence and the absence of the Lord simultaneously. The gift granted by Krishna subsequently, however, consists of pure, unalloyed yearning. This is the ultimate fruit of the Pushtimarga, beyond which there is nothing else. Everything is attained when Vallabhacharya favors you with an all-consuming fixation on Krishna's absence. What happens is this. When you suffer in separation while away from the *svarup*, you begin to see the Lord everywhere and in everything. The next time you come before the *svarup* and attend to the needs of the Lord again, however, you start to experience Krishna's absence at that time, too. Because it can seem as if the Lord vanishes even when your eyelids blink! You become agitated. You drown in waves of love, thinking, "Why has Krishna deserted me?" "Where could he have gone?" A profound anguish is now felt even in the presence of the *svarup* reminding you again of Krishna's forest-grove *lilas.* Your mind starts working frantically: "How could the Lord be going out and about at this time of the day in the heat to graze the cows with his bare feet so tender?" "Krishna would not have gone off to Dvaraka, would he?" "How will I be able to make it through the day without him?" Wave after wave of suffering in separation washes over you even in the presence of the image. Then, finally, as all hankerings and hopes for everything temporal fade, you realize you have won the ultimate prize, that devotion to Krishna which consists of nothing but utter love (*premalakshana bhakti*). This is the sweetest bliss (*mukhya rasa*).

Verse 15

If the heart hankers
For a spiritual reward,
Let it be Krishna's face.
The ever-blissful Krishna
Is the reward,
For he is the essence
Of your love.

Commentary on Verse 15. It was stated in the previous verse that if devotees give themselves over to serving the Lord and praising his infinite virtues with a pure heart, then the only thing they ever gain is an incessant longing, and that this is the ultimate goal. However, if an insatiable yearning for the Lord is all that one ever achieves, is this an attainment worth aspiring to? The Pushtimarga replies emphatically in the affirmative. This marvel of unquenchable desire is itself the ultimate reward. A hundred thousand other spiritual experiences combined could not even come close to the rapture of suffering in separation from the Lord. In truth, only Krishna's intimates in Braj are capable of knowing this state of mind. It is beyond the ken even of gods like Brahma and Shiva.

Now note this carefully: If you serve Krishna and sing his praises out of a desire for some worldly or heavenly reward—be it even liberation—you will never realize the ultimate goal of the Pushtimarga. If you must wish for anything, wish with all your might for the vision of Krishna's lotuslike face; wish with all your might for the vision of Vallabha, he who is the very incarnation of the Lord's mouth. Realize in the depths of your soul that the ultimate goal of all religion is to be able to perform *seva* in the presence of the divine form; to gaze again and again directly at the Lord's lotuslike face. Whenever the temple is closed, contemplate the moonlike radiance of the Lord's face while feeling more and more overcome with misery for his loss. This practice will culminate in the attainment of a pure and ardent love for Krishna in his absence. It will cause you to start seeing Krishna's moonlike face everywhere. Love in separation is your ultimate reward, because Krishna himself—he who is made entirely of love—becomes your innermost reality. May you consider the matter thus, practice the remembrance of the Lord, and serve his divine form.

Verse 16

This attainment is not gained
Through knowledge;
It is heedless of the Purushottama's[53] repute
As Being, Consciousness, and Bliss.

Commentary on Verse 16. According to the Pushtimarga, only devotees who have given themselves over wholly to the worship of the Lord are capable of realizing that his essence is the sweetness of love. However, a philosophical opponent may object to this doctrine on the grounds that the *Puranas* and various other sacred texts extol the path of knowledge (*jnana marga*) as not only the best but the only means of realizing God: the scriptures contradict the sect's claim that God can only be realized through unswerving devotion (*bhakti*). To this challenge the Pushtimarga declares that under no circumstances do the proponents of the path of knowledge—who meditate on the Absolute in the form of light—ever have any experiential relationship with, or indeed, are they qualified to even speculate about, Krishna's bliss-permeated form. The only connection such people ever establish with the Lord is with the imperishable aspect of the Absolute (*akshara*). Their individuality gets extinguished in the infinite spirit that pervades all things in an unmanifest form like the element of fire. Such people are simply incapable of experiencing the rapture of devotional love. It is for this reason that followers of the Pushtimarga are strictly enjoined never to discuss the nature of their attachment to the Lord's *svarup* with those who follow the path of knowledge.

Krishna's essence is love (*rasatmaka*). His essential form is being, consciousness, and bliss (*sachchidanandasvarupa*). The *jiva*, or individual soul, possesses being (*sat*) and consciousness (*chit*). However, the bliss (*ananda*) component in the *jiva* is ontologically

sampradaya to designate the building complexes that house the *svarups* and the *gurus* of the sect responsible for serving them. Nonetheless, *mandir*, the most common-place word for temple in northern India, is used throughout the *Bade Shikshapatra*.

6. For an analysis of the concept of the *alaukika* ("realm of the sacred") in the Pushtimarga, see Barz (1976, 9–15). An *alaukika deha* is also referred to in the Pushtimarga as a *sevopayogi deha* ("body useful for service"). In other Vaishnava traditions there is the analogous notion of a *siddha deha* or *siddha rupa* ("perfected body"), which is capable of entering Krishna's divine *lilas* (see Haberman, 1988; Das, 1998).

7. Bennett (1990, 194).

8. For a brief outline of the *darshans* and their associated *lilas*, see Gopeshvar, in Hariray and Gopeshvar 1.1 (1972), translated in this chapter. For more detailed de-scriptions of the *darshans*, see Bennett (1983, 194–211); Bennett (1990, 191–200); Gaston (1994, 247–256); and Barz (1976, 48–49).

9. On synaesthesia in Pushtimarga worship, see Entwhistle (1993, 84–103).

10. A lengthy discussion of Krishna's *viruddhadharmashrayatva* may be found in Hariray and Gopeshvar 4.1–16 (1972). This Pushtimarga concept is also somewhat analogous to the Christian notion of *coincidentia oppositorum* (coincidence of oppo-sites). The latter term was coined by Nicholas of Cusa as the least imperfect definition of God (Eliade, 1965, 81. See also Cousins, 1978; Awn, 1983, 190; McDermott, 1996, 284).

11. See, for example, Hariray and Gopeshvar 2.1–19 and, especially, 4.2–6 (1972). A key statement regarding Krishna's dependence on his devotees is to be found in *Bhagavata Purana* 9.4.63.

12. See Gopeshvar, in Hariray and Gopeshvar 1.7 and 1.8 (1972), translated in this chapter. *Dasya bhava* means, literally, the "attitude of a servant." Bennett com-ments with considerable pertinence that "the cultivation of this servile feeling-state is primarily conceived in subjective, moral, and affective terms, that is, as a means of removing selfishness, overcoming pride, and demonstrating one's dependence on Krishna, rather than affirming the latter's hierarchical superiority" (1990, 197).

13. Literally, "parental affection."

14. Hariray and Gopeshvar 2.5 (1972).

15. *Shringara bhava* is also known as *madhurya bhava* or *gopi bhava*. Little mention is made in the *Bade Shikshapatra* of the fourth Vaishnava devotional attitude, *sakhya bhava* (in which Krishna is loved out of affectionate playfulness as a friend of equal age and status). This would appear to be related to the fact that, in contrast to the *gopis*, who are celebrated as the *"gurus* of the Pushtimarga," the *gopas* (their male counterparts) are considered to have been *maryada* ("convention-bound" or "law-abiding") devotees of Krishna (see Gopeshvar, in Hariray and Gopeshvar 2.16 [1972]). *Maryada* devotees (also sometimes referred to as *vaidhi* devotees in other Vaish-nava traditions) are those so preoccupied with scriptural injunctions, ritual minu-tiae, or heavenly rewards that they are unable to serve Krishna with a spontaneous, selfless love.

16. This is perhaps stated most clearly by Gopeshvar at 5.1: "[Inside the temple] you should perform *seva* with the attitude that Krishna is engaged in the *lilas* of his infancy, whereas [outside the temple] you should practice remembrance (*smaran*)

of Krishna engaged in the *lilas* of his youth. The validity of this procedure is affirmed by Vitthalnath's statement that 'The Lord should always be wholeheartedly served as Gokuleshvar ["Lord of Gokul," i.e., as the child he was in Gokul], while [at all other times] he is to be meditatively imagined in amorous play with groups of *gopis* in Vrindavan.' " Different devotional sentiments are not mutually exclusive, however, and, as Gopeshvar goes on to note, the manner in which *seva* is to be performed is also affected by the particular *svarup* that is being worshiped (and, we may add, the time of day and season). Thus, Krishna's childhood *lilas* are preeminently associated with the Shri Navnitpriyaji ("He Who Is Fond of Butter") *svarup*, whereas Krishna's adolescent *ras lilas* are associated far more with the Shri Govardhannathji *svarup*. Gopeshvar, in Hariray and Gopeshvar 5.1 (1972).

17. From the Sanskrit: *an-avasara*, or "nonoccasion" for image-worship.

18. See Gopeshvar, in Hariray and Gopeshvar 1.3 (1972), translated in this chapter.

19. *Chetastatpravanam* (the mind being devoted to, intent upon, and absorbed in That [i.e., Krishna]) is the essential definition of *seva* given by Vallabhacharya in his *Siddhantamuktavali* 2. It is quoted by Hariray, in Hariray and Gopeshvar 9.30 (1972). For a translation of the *Siddhantamuktavali*, see Redington (2000).

20. Dimock (1966), p. 14.

21. Gopeshvar, in Hariray and Gopeshvar 20.12 (1972). Followers of the Pushtimarga maintain that Vallabhacharya declared himself to be an *avatara* of the fire god Agni in his *Tattvarthadipanibandha* 1.10 and in his *Anubhasha* commentary on the *Brahma Sutras* 2.2.26.

22. Experiencing *asakti* destroys a devotee's ability to operate competently in the everyday world. Experiencing *vyasana* annihilates even the perception of the existence of the everyday world. See Hariray and Gopeshvar 9.20 and 9.21 (1972).

23. Gopeshvar, in Hariray and Gopeshvar 1.14 (1972), translated in this chapter.

24. See Hariray and Gopeshvar 1.14 and 1.15 (1972), translated in this chapter. On the greatness of *viraha* as a spiritual attainment, see also *Bhagavata Purana* 10.47.27 and 10.47.34–37.

25. Gopeshvar, in Hariray and Gopeshvar 1.15 (1972), translated in this chapter. Several times throughout the *Bade Shikshapatra* Gopeshvar quotes a key verse from the *Bhagavata Purana* (9.4.67) in which Krishna states: "By performing my *seva*, devotees become so fulfilled (*purnah*) that no trace of desire remains for *salokya* or any of the four types of liberation, let alone the transient things of this world." See, for example, Gopeshvar, in Hariray and Gopeshvar 18.12 and 22.1 (1972).

26. In addition to his Braj Bhasha commentary on the *Bade Shikshapatra*, Gopeshvar is known to have composed Sanskrit commentaries on at least two of Vallabhacharya's brief treatises (the *Samnyasaniranaya* and the *Bhaktivardhini*), as well as a work in Braj Bhasha prose about shrines erected to the memory of Hariray (the *Shri Hariray ki Baithak ko Charitra*). Dasgupta (1949, 375 and 380) ascribes to Gopeshvar both the *Rashmi* commentary on the *Prakash* (of Purushottama on Vallabha's *Anu Bhasha* commentary on the *Brahma Sutras*) and the *Subodhinibubhutrabodhini*. However, these works were composed by Gopeshvar Yogi (1780–1830).

27. Anonymous (1970, 2).

28. Caturvedi (1976, 53); Mital (1962, 20).

29. Several hundred works in Sanskrit and Braj Bhasha prose (original compositions, as well as translations and commentaries on the treatises of Vallabhacharya and Vitthalnath) have been attributed to Hariray, in addition to over a thousand Braj Bhasha poems penned under the names Rasnidhi, Rasik, Rasikpritam, Rasikray, Haridas, Haridhan, Harijan, and Madhukarni (Caturvedi, 1976, 78–79; Mital, 1962, 1, 3, 11; Sharma, 1981, 219; Sukhabala, 1980, 32). Hariray is best known, however, for composing, collating, and/or editing the following Braj Bhasha prose works: the *Chaurasi Vaishnavan ki Varta* and the *Dau Sau Bhavan ki Varta* (both compilations of sectarian hagiography), the *Mahaprabhuji ki Prakatya Varta* (a hagiography of Vallabha), and the *Shri Nathji Prakatya ki Varta* (an account of the discovery of the Sri Nathji *svarup* and its subsequent history). The *vartas* are among the first examples of prose in the North Indian vernaculars. They provided a blueprint for pioneering Hindi prose writers such as Lallulal and Harishchandra who were active during the nineteenth century (Barz, 1994, 45–46; Vaudeville, 1980, 15).

30. Sukhabala (1980, 193).

31. Introduction to Hariray and Gopeshvar (1972).

32. The Vallabha *sampradaya* affirms family life as being the most conducive to performing a wide range of devotional services. An external renunciation of the world is not ordinarily countenanced, unless one is overcome by an overwhelming, incapacitating sense of *viraha* (see note 22 here; Smith, 1993, 135–156; Redington, 1993, 157–179). Thus, if Gopeshvar, a direct descendant of Vallabha, had renounced his priestly duties in the circumstances described here, it would not just have been a rash personal decision, it would have undermined the very foundations of the sect established by his illustrious forefather.

33. Introduction to Hariray and Gopeshvar (1972). This inspiring story of the *Bade Shikshapatra*'s origin is undoubtedly responsible for a great deal of the popularity the text enjoys. It accords Hariray the status of a great saint endowed with mystical powers, while casting Gopeshvar in the mold of an Arjuna-like "Everybody" figure representative of all devotees. Some westerners may find it difficult, however, to reconcile the origin myth with what the text itself says about Gopeshvar's personal circumstances (see Hariray and Gopeshvar 6.1 and 20.1 [1972]).

34. Gopeshvar, in Hariray and Gopeshvar 41.11 (1972).

35. Hariray and Gopeshvar repeatedly use the word *gudha* (esoteric, secret) in the *Bade Shikshapatra* when describing the erotic *bhavas* of the *gopis*. The authors declare that these *bhavas* are always to be kept hidden from *maryada* devotees. See, for example, Hariray and Gopeshvar 2.14–18 (1972).

36. The following is a translation from the Sanskrit of the first seventeen of the twenty-four *shlokas* that comprise Hariray's first letter, with a translation from the Braj Bhasha of Gopeshvar's accompanying prose commentary. It is based on Hariray and Gopeshvar (1972).

37. Literally, "song of the flute" and "song in couplets." The terms *venugita* and *yugalgita* denote the *Bhagavata Purana* chapters 10.21 and 10.35, respectively.

38. *Sutak* is a state of ritual impurity caused by a birth or death in the family.

39. Compare with the fourteenth-century English mystic Richard Rolle (1972, 49): "Love for God and love for the world cannot coexist in the same soul: the stronger drives out the weaker. . . . The elect of God, indeed, eat and drink 'in God,' and all their

thinking is directed Godwards; they attend to mundane matters only as need—not lust—may require. They have to talk of earthly things, of course, but they do so with reluctance, and they never dwell thereon. Mentally they turn back to God with all speed, and spend the rest of the time with divine duties."

40. The *khanditas* are, literally, "shattered" lovers; women who have waited up all night for their unfaithful lover, been temporarily deserted, or wronged by him in some other way.

41. The *ras lila* took place in the forest on the night of the full autumn moon when Krishna multiplied himself to appear in as many forms as there were *gopis* and danced with each of them individually. The *gopis* formed a circle, with Krishna appearing between two *gopis*, and each *gopi* between two Krishnas. At the same time, Krishna also stood in the center of the circle seductively playing his flute. Each of the *gopis* believed that Krishna was dancing with her alone. See *Bhagavata Purana* 10.29.33. After Krishna had performed the *ras lila*, each of the *gopis* began considering herself "superior to all other women on earth." To cure them of this hubris (*man*), Krishna temporarily vanished. This incident is referred to as the *man lila*. See *Bhagavata Purana* 10.29–30; and Hariray and Gopeshvar 1.13 (1972), translated here. The *jalsthalvihar lila* occurred when Krishna made love to the *gopis* on the banks of the Yamuna River. See *Bhagavata Purana* 10.32–33.

42. For a parable related by the nineteenth-century mystic Sri Ramakrishna about a devotee who did not wish to "trouble" God unnecessarily, see M. (1974, 165–166).

43. According to the teachings of the Pushtimarga, the greatest obstacle to spirituality is *anyashraya* (lit., "refuge in others"), the placing of one's hopes for personal happiness and security in the people, things, or situations of the everyday world. If a particular worldly attachment causes a sincere follower of the Pushtimarga to neglect *seva*, it is said that Krishna, out of his mercy, will snatch it away, so that the devotee is impelled to seek refuge with redoubled zeal exclusively in the divine. Whenever such a loss occurs, devotees are counseled to find solace in the knowledge that it is due to Krishna's grace. An extended discussion of how worldly suffering relates to God's grace may be found in Hariray and Gopeshvar 6.8–15 (1972).

44. Before approaching the *svarup*, a practitioner of *seva* must get into a state of ritual purity, or *apras* (from the Sanskrit: *asparsha*, noncontact, or *asprishya*, not to be touched). This involves bathing, putting on clean clothes, and avoiding being touched by anyone. If the temple offerings are touched, seen, or smelled by anyone not in a state of *apras*, they become polluted and rendered unfit for Krishna. It would be well to note here that nonvegetarian and other types of "impure" foods (including *rajasik*, "passion-inducing," onions and garlic) are also considered unworthy of being presented to Krishna. Likewise, anything that is acquired by immoral means or donated by an immoral person, a non-Vaishnava, or a person of low caste is considered unfit for use in *seva*.

45. During the *namanivedana* ("name-dedication") initiation, a person is given the *mantra shri krishnah sharanam mama* ("The Lord Krishna is my refuge."). A person is then considered to be a Pushtimarga Vaishnava but does not become a full member of the sect until he or she receives the *atmanivedana* ("self-dedication") initiation, during which the *brahmasambandha mantra* is given (see note 54 here). At the present time, most people are born into the Pushtimarga rather than converted to it. Children of both sexes are usually given the *namanivedana* initiation before the

age of five. However, whereas boys receive the *atmanivedana* initiation at about the age of twelve, girls receive it prior to marriage (Barz, 1976, 20).

46. A name of Krishna meaning "The Remover."

47. The text is not referring to the *karma marga* (*yoga*) of the *Bhagavad Gita* but rather to the performance of ceremonial and ritual observances enjoined by the *Vedas* for achieving transient material or heavenly gains.

48. Composed by Govindasvami, one of the *Ashtachap* (Eight Seals), poet-disciples of Vallabha and Vitthalnath. The *Ashtachap* are regarded as incarnations of the eight female companions who participated with Krishna in his secret, night-time *lilas* (Barz, 1976, 12–13). However, each of their names is also associated with one of the eight daily *darshans*. The most renowned of the *Ashtachap* was Sur Das. For an appraisal of the evidence linking Sur Das to Vallabhacharya and the Pushtimarga, see Hawley (1984, 3–33).

49. An alternative reading of this verse is possible: "This devotional service is performed in the presence of the image, and in its absence. Hence, it is distinct from the former [type of *seva* that is performed only in the presence of the image, as described earlier]. Its mood is considered intermingled, like that of the 'singing' milkmaids." The verse is quoting *Bhagavata Purana* 10.30.4: "Singing at the top of their voices the praises of [Krishna], [the *gopis*] gathered in a group. As if insane, they went from forest grove to forest grove, asking the trees whether they had seen that person who pervades all beings, within and without, like the element space."

50. The *Rasapanchadhyayi* is the name given to chap. 29–33 of the tenth canto of the *Bhagavata Purana*. This is the most celebrated section of the text describing Krishna's erotic dalliances with the *gopis*. The *Rasapanchadhyayi* with Vallabhacharya's *Subodhini* commentary has been translated by Redington (1983).

51. For Vallabhacharya's reflections on this metaphor, consult his *Subodhini* commentary on *Bhagavata Purana* 10.32.20; translated by Redington (1983, 253–255).

52. The *gopikagita* (lit., "song of the *gopis*") refers to *Bhagavata Purana* 10.31.

53. Purushottama is a name of Krishna meaning the Supreme Being.

54. The *brahmasambandha* ("bond to the Absolute") is a long, pledgelike Sanskrit *mantra* that echos *Bhagavata Purana* 9.4.65. It is received during the final *atmanivedana* initiation: "Om. The Lord Krishna is my refuge. For thousands of years and countless eons I have been lost in pain, grief, and sorrow caused by separation from Krishna. Together with my wife, home, children, elders, and all assets in this world and the next, I dedicate the functions of my body, senses, life, and soul to the Almighty, Lord Krishna. O Krishna, I am your servant! (Om Shri Krishnah Sharanam Mama Sahasraparivatsaramitakalasanjat Krishnaviyogajanitatapakleshananda Tirobhavoham Bhagavate Krishnaya Dehendriyapranantahkaranataddharmamshcha Daragaraputraptavittehpranyatmna Saha Samarpayami Dasoham Krishnatavasmi)."

REFERENCES

Anonymous. 1970, March. "Shiksha Patra Sar." *Shri Vallabha Vijnan* 9, 2.

Awn, P. J. 1983. *Satan's Tragedy and Redemption*. Leiden: Brill.

Barz, Richard. 1976. *The Bhakti Sect of Vallabhacarya*. Faridabad: Thomson Press. Reprint, New Delhi: Munshiram Manoharlal, 1992.

―――. 1994. "The *Chaurasi Vaishnavan ki Varta* and the Hagiography of the Pushtimarga." In *According to Tradition: Hagiographical Writing in India*, edited by Winand M. Callewaert and Rupert Snell. Wiesbaden: Harrassowitz, 43–64.

Bennett, Peter. 1983. "Temple Organisation and Worship among the Pushtimargiya-Vaishnavas of Ujjain." Ph.D. diss., School of Oriental and African Studies, University of London.

―――. 1990. "In Nanda Baba's House: The Devotional Experience in Pushti Marg Temples." In *Divine Passions: The Social Construction of Emotion in India*, edited by Owen L. Lynch. Berkeley: University of California Press, 182–211.

―――. 1993. "Krishna's Own Form: Image Worship and Pushti Marga." *Journal of Vaishnava Studies* 1, no. 4 (summer), 109–134.

Caturvedi, Visnu. 1976. *Gosvami Hariray aur unka Braj Bhasa Sahitya*. Mathura: Javahar Pustakalya.

Cousins, Ewert H. 1978. *Bonaventure and the Coincidence of Opposites*. Chicago: Franciscan Herald Press.

Das, Shukavak. 1998. "ISKON's Link to Sadhana-Bhakti within the Caitanya Vaishnava Tradition." *Journal of Vaishnava Studies* 6, no. 2 (spring), 189–212.

Dasgupta, Surendranath. 1922. *A History of Indian Philosophy*. Vol. 4. Cambridge: Cambridge University Press.

Dimock, Edward C. Jr. 1966. *The Place of the Hidden Moon: Erotic Mysticism in the Vaisnava-Sahajiya Cult of Bengal*. Chicago: University of Chicago Press.

Eliade, Mircea. 1965. *The Two and the One*. Translated by J. M. Cohen. London: Harvill.

Entwistle, Alan. W. 1993. "Synaesthesia in the Poetry and Ritual of the Pustimarga." *Journal of Vaishnava Studies* 1, no. 3 (spring), 84–103.

Gaston, Anne-Marie. 1994. "Continuity of Tradition in the Music of Nathdvara: A Participant-Observer's View." In *The Idea of Rajasthan: Explorations in Regional Identity*, vol. 1, edited by Karine Schomer, Joan L. Erdman, Deryck O. Lodrick, and Lloyd I. Rudolph. New Delhi: Manohar, 238–277.

Haberman, David L. 1988. *Acting as a Way of Salvation: A Study of Raganuga Bhakti Sadhana*. New York: Oxford University Press.

Hariray and Gopeshvar. 1972. *Shriharirayjikrt Bade Siksapatra: Shrigopeshvarjikrt Vrajbhasatikasahit*. Revised and edited by Shri Subodhini Sabha. Lucknow: Jankiprasad Agraval.

Hawley, John Stratton. 1984. *Sur Das: Poet, Singer, Saint*. Seattle: University of Washington Press.

M. [Mahendranath Gupta]. 1974. *The Gospel of Sri Ramakrishna*. Translated by Swami Nikhilananda. Madras: Sri Ramakrishna Math. Originally published 1942.

McDermott, Rachel Fell. 1996. "The Western Kali." In *Devi: Goddesses of India*, edited by John S. Hawley and Donna M. Wulff. Berkeley: University of California Press, 281–313.

Mital, Prabhudayal. 1962. *Gosvami Harirayji ka Pad Sahitya*. Mathura: Sahitya Sansthan.

Redington, James D. 1983. *Vallabhacarya on the Love Games of Krsna*. Delhi: Motilal Banarsidass.

————. 1993. "The Last Days of Vallabhacarya." Journal of Vaishnava Studies 1, no. 4 (summer), 157–179.

————. 2000. The Grace of Lord Krishna: The Sixteen Verse-Treatises (Sodasagranthah) of Vallabhacharya. Delhi: Sri Satguru.

Rolle, Richard. 1972. The Fire of Love. Translated by Clifton Walters. London: Penguin Books.

Sharma, Gajanan. 1981. Shrimad Vallabhacarya: Vyaktitva, Siddhant aur Sandesh. Indore: Pustimargiya Vaishnava Parishad.

Smith, Frederick M. 1993. "The Samnyasanirnaya: A Shuddhadvaita Text on Renunciation by Vallabhacharya." Journal of Vaishnava Studies 1, no. 4 (summer), 135–156.

Sukhabala, Radharani. 1980. Vallabha Sampradaya aur uske Siddhant. Beawar: Pandit Rampratap Shastri Charitable Trust.

Vaudeville, Charlotte. 1980 "The Govardhan Myth in Northern India." Indo-Iranian Journal 22, 1–45.

21

Vaishnava Pilgrimage: Select Puranic Texts

Paul H. Sherbow

Pilgrimage, by its very nature of movement from one place to another, reveals two of its own fundamental elements: first, as the object of pilgrimage is not where the pilgrim lives—it is somewhere else—the specialness of place, that some places are more special than others, is self-evident; and second, as travel separates the pilgrim from his or her home context and thus domestic routines are broken, the devotee is freed from entanglements of home and family.

Places are made special in a religious sense by the presence of spiritual or divine energies. The Vaishnava traditions of India distinguish categories of nature spirit, celestial deities, and Vishnu-*tattva*, each residing in different dimensions—subtle, celestial, and spiritual (*chit*). The descent (*avatarana*) of Vishnu, in various forms, from the spiritual world to a lower dimension, is known as an *avatara*. Wherever *avataras* of Vishnu descended in the physical dimension, displaying their pastimes (*lila*), was regarded as sacred (*punya*), worshipable (*pujya*), and worthy of a visit and service (*seva*). In a special category are the localities, such as Ayodhya, Dvaraka, Mathura, and Vrindavan, where Rama or Krishna resided and pursued many of their most famous pastimes, most of which have been commemorated with temples or shrines. These places are also magnets for devotees of Vishnu in both forms, as progress in one's spiritual practice (*sadhana*) may be exponentially increased by residence there.

Tirthas (sacred places) are located the length and breadth of India, from the peaks of the Himalayas, where Nara and Narayana *rishis* performed penance and there is still to be seen the cave of

Vyasa, the Vishnu *avatara* who arranged the *Vedas* and composed the *Mahabharata* and most *Puranas*, to Setubandha on the shore of southern India, where Rama with his army of monkeys crossed the ocean to Lanka over a bridge of stones. Sacred waters are associated in some sense with almost all *tirthas*, in the form of rivers, holy wells, or the ocean, and one of the principal activities involved in Vaishnava pilgrimage is ritual bathing (*snana*), both for purification from past misdeeds and the accumulation of blessings. India's two most famous sacred rivers—the Ganges and the Yamuna—possess the spiritual potency to purify all with which they come into contact by their direct association with the feet of Vishnu and Krishna, respectively.[1]

Reasons for making pilgrimage to such holy places run the spectrum of human desire (*purushartha*). In a sense, as repositories of potent spiritual energies, places of pilgrimage can be all things to all people: those desiring material benefits are assured of better opportunities in the future; those beset by life's problems are assured of purification and hence a decrease in their sufferings; and those seeking spiritual blessings, or the grace of God, are assured that such holy places are the optimum spots for their devotional practices (*sadhana-bhakti*). According to the *Bhagavata Purana*, the service of a sacred place or person (*punya-tirtha-nishevana*) is one of the elements of the path in developing taste for hearing about Krishna,[2] a sign of evolving love of God. Thus, according to Jiva Gosvami, one of the original theologians of the Gaudiya Vaishnava tradition, the beneficial effects of bathing in sacred rivers such as the Ganges serve as instrumental causes of *bhakti*, or devotion to God.[3] Long-term residence in a *tirtha*, or staying there until death, comes under a different category, indicating complete surrender (*saranapatti*) to God, rather than as an instrumental cause of devotion. Jiva's uncle, Rupa Gosvami, in his *Bhakti-rasamrita-sindhu*, lists "residence in an abode of the Lord" (*tad-vasati-sthale vasah*) as one of the five most important items of devotional service.

According to the standards of pure devotion (*shuddha-bhakti*) enunciated by the sixteenth-century Gaudiya Vaishnava authority Narottama Das, pilgrimage to *tirthas* for reasons other than cultivating surrender to Krishna is simply a form of mental illusion. The perfection (*siddhi*) of all benefits derived from visiting *tirthas* for other reasons is to be found in surrender at the feet of Govinda (*govinda-charana*).[4]

At particular times during the year, visits to *tirthas* are especially recommended. Pilgrims flock to Mathura-Vrindaban on the eighth day of the waning moon (*kishnashtami*) in the lunar month of *Bhadra* to celebrate *Janmashtami*, the appearance-day of Krishna, with fasting (*upavasa*), a night vigil (*jagarana*), and a festival (*mahotsava*) on the following day. On *Rama-navami*, the ninth day of the waxing moon (*shukla-navami*) in the lunar month of *Chaitra*, Vaishnavas congregate at Ayodhya to observe the appearance of Ramachandra, the incarnation of Vishnu. For Gaudiya Vaisnavas, the full-moon day in the month of *Phalguna* is the most popular day to visit Navadvipa (West Bengal), the appearance-place of Chaitanya, who is said to be Krishna himself in the mood of Radha.

These and most Vaishnava holy days are calculated on the basis of a lunar calendar, but others are determined by solar calendar. For example, there is *Makara-sankranti*, when the entrance of the sun into the constellation of Capricorn (*Makara*) draws millions for ritual bathing at sacred rivers and especially at *Ganga-sagara*, where the Ganges enters the Bay of Bengal—this is calculated by solar reckoning. Huge numbers of pilgrims gather at *tirthas* on the occurrence of solar and lunar eclipses when bathing is enjoined—very traditionally at Kurukshetra, where a massive tank has been constructed to accommodate the crowds. Certain large gatherings are held at wider stretches of time. Kumbha-mela, the world's largest religious gathering, rotating every twelve years between four ancient *tirthas*—Prayaga (the modern Allahabad), Haridwar, Ujjain, and Nashik—attracts Hindus of all sects; Vaishnava ascetic orders march in procession with their Shaiva counterparts to bathe at the most auspicious times.

Death also brings devotees to *tirthas*, many wishing to spend their retirement years or at least their final days within the sacred precincts of a *tirtha*. There always seems to be a large number of retired gentlemen or widows, some living independently, others cloistered in ashrams or hostels specifically created to accommodate them in tirthas. After death as well, the requisite memorial services (*shraddha*), necessarily performed by descendants, are traditionally offered at Gaya or other holy places.

Even when unable to personally visit a *tirtha*, Vaishnava devotees connect themselves with holy places through several items of daily ritual. For example, when ritually sipping water (*achamana*) for purification, a devotee remembers the seven sacred rivers—Ganga, Yamuna, Godavari, Sarasvati, Narmada, Sindhu, and Kaveri—as their presence is invoked in water by reciting a mantra.[5] A consecrated image (*archa-murti*) of Vishnu, in any of his various forms, whether Krishna, Rama, Nrisimha, Vamana, Varaha or any other, is also considered to include its personal abode (*dhama*) and associates. Hence the temple or home where such worship is practiced itself becomes a *tirtha* by virtue of the deity's presence.

Finally, the saint (*sadhu*) is also considered a *tirtha*. Indeed, *tirthas* in the solid or liquid forms of mountains or rivers are apt to become polluted (*malina*) by the accumulated sins (*papa*) of their pilgrim visitors, but the *sadhu* is held to be of such a supreme level of purity that he has the capacity to purify the *tirthas* themselves, as mentioned in the *Bhagavata Purana*: "Devotees of Bhagavan such as yourself are themselves places of pilgrimage (*tirtha-bhuta*), making *tirthas* pure [*tirtha*] by the presence of You who reside within them."[6]

The *Bhagavata* also warns against the mistaken perception that the potency of *tirthas* is present in the water of sacred rivers more than in the person of pure Vaishnavas. This would be as ignorant an idea as to consider the physical body composed of three material elements (*tridhatu*) to be the spirit (*atma*).[7] Elsewhere in the *Bhagavata* during his instruction to Uddhava, Krishna includes pilgrimage to *tirthas* in a list of fourteen practices that are unable to please him as much as association with *sadhus* (*sat-sanga*).[8]

The following three selections, from the *Bhagavata*, *Padma*, and other *Puranas*, illustrate, respectively, a traditional geography of well-known *tirthas*; a glorification (*mahatmya*) of Mathura, highly revered as the birthplace (*janma-sthana*) of Krishna; and the results obtainable by performing devotional practices in Mathura during the sacred lunar month of *Kartika*, its most popular pilgrimage season. The *Bhagavata Purana*, one of the most popular Vaishnava devotional texts, is assessed by modern European-model academics as a product of ninth-century South India, although orthodox Vaisnava scholars consider it to have been composed by the sage Vyasadeva nearly five thousand years ago. Included in the *Bhagavata* are summaries of the pastimes (*lila*) of the major *avataras* of Vishnu in twelve books (*skandhas*). The *Bhagavata's* tenth book, the longest by far (ninety *adhyayas*, or chapters), relates the history of Krishna. In its seventy-eighth chapter, Krishna's brother Balarama sets out on pilgrimage around India to avoid taking sides in the internecine battle brewing between his two sets of relatives, the Kauravas and their cousins, the Pandavas. His journey circulates through many of India's most famous *tirthas*.

The second selection consists of verses from various *Puranas* as cited in the eighteenth-century *Bhakti-ratnakara*, a Sanskrit and Bengali work written by Narahari Chakravarti, a famous Gaudiya writer of that period. Among its diverse contents are personal histories of noted Gaudiya Vaishnava saints, descriptions of the sacred geography of Vrindavan and Navadvipa, and technical expositions on music. The fifth section (*panchama-taranga*) excerpts verses from the *Padma*, *Vayu*, and other *Puranas* in praise of Mathura, which as the site of Krishna's appearance (*avirbhava*) on earth is a prime pilgrimage destination for Hindus in general, and for Vaishnavas in particular.

The third selection is a passage from the *Padma Purana* on the special benefits of observing the month of *Kartika* in Mathura as cited in the *Hari-bhakti-vilasa*, a sixteenth-century compendium of Vaishnava practice by Sanatana Gosvami (Rupa's elder brother), on the basis of materials compiled by his younger contemporary, Gopala Bhatta Gosvami. The book, divided into twenty *vilasas*, or sections, provides rules for every aspect of Vaishnava behavior, from initiation to personal hygiene, from designing and constructing a temple to the observation of fast days and repetition of *mantras*. The sixteenth *vilasa* details practices to be observed during the holy month of *Kartika*, including pilgrimage.

Text 1: *Bhagavata Purana* 10.78.17–20 and 10.79.9–21

Having heard of the Kurus' preparation for war with the Pandavas, Balarama, desiring to remain neutral, left on the pretext of going to bathe in sacred places of pilgrimage [*tirthabhiseka*]. (78.17)

After bathing and offering *tarpana* to the gods [*devas*], sages [*rsis*], and forefathers [*pitas*] in Prabhasa,[9] Balarama proceeded upstream along the bank of the Sarasvati River,[10] accompanied by brahmins. (78.18)

After visiting Prithudaka,[11] Bindusara,[12] Tritakupa,[13] Sudarshana,[14] Visala,[15] Brahmatirtha,[16] Chakratirtha,[17] the eastern Sarasvati River,[18] and all the *tirthas* along the banks of the Yamuna[19] and Ganga rivers,[20] Balarama went to the forest of Naimisha,[21] where the sages were engaged in performance of a sacrifice. (78.19–20)

Having obtained permission from those sages, Balarama went with the brahmins to the Kausiki[22] River and, having bathed there, proceeded to the lake from which the Sarayu[23] River originates. (79.9)

Reaching Prayag[24] by following the current of the Sarayu, and having bathed there and made offerings to the gods and others, he went to the ashram of the sage Pulaha.[25] (79.10)

Then having bathed in the Gomati,[26] Gandaki,[27] Vipasa[28] and Sone[29] rivers, he went to Gaya[30] and worshiped the forefathers [*pitas*] at Ganga-sagara.[31] (79.11)

Then he saw and praised Parashurama[32] at Mahendra Hill.[33] Having bathed in the sevenfold Godavari,[34] the Vena[35] and Bhimarathi[36] rivers, and the Pampa Lake,[37] Balarama visited Skanda,[38] and then went to Shrisaila,[39] the residence of Girisa (Shiva). From there, the Lord visited Venkatadri,[40] very sacred among the lands of South India. (79.12–13)

After seeing Kamakosni,[41] Kanchipuri,[42] the Kaveri,[43] considered the best among rivers, the very sacred place named Shriranga,[44] where Hari is present, and Rishabhadri,[45] the place of Hari, as well as southern Mathura,[46] he went to Setubandha,[47] which destroys great sins. (79.14–15)

There, Rama, bearing his plough, gave in charity ten thousand cows to the brahmins. After bathing in the Kritamala[48] and Tamraparni rivers,[49] he visited the Malaya mountains.[50] (16)

After bowing and praising the sage Agastya, who was seated there, and having been blessed by him and received his permission, Balarama went to the southern ocean and there visited the goddess Durga named Kanya.[51] (79.17)

Balarama then went to Phalguna Tirtha[52] and the Panchapsarasa Lake,[53] where Vishnu resides. After bathing there, he gave ten thousand cows in charity. (79.18)

Then Balarama visited the lands of Kerala[54] and Trigarta[55] and from there went to Gokarna,[56] the place of Shiva, where Shiva is present. (79.19)

From there, Baladeva visited the goddess Arya (Parvati)[57] on an island, and from there went to Surparaka.[58] After having bathed in the Tapti,[59] Payosni,[60] and Nirvindhya[61] rivers, he entered the Dandaka Forest. (79.20)

He then went to the Reva[62] (Narmada) River where the city Mahismati[63] is situated and after bathing in Manutirtha,[64] returned again to Prabhasa.[65] (79.21)

Text 2: Selected Verses from the *Adi-varaha, Padma,* and *Vayu Puranas*

These three *Puranas,* as cited in the eighteenth-century Vaishnava work *Bhakti-ratnakara*[66] by Narahari Chakravarti,[67] describe the results of pilgrimage to Mathura.

In the *Adi-varaha Purana* it is said—
My circle [*mandala*] of Mathura is twenty *yojanas,* where a man having bathed is freed from all sins [*papa*]. (5.41)

In the *Adi-varaha Purana* it is said—
As darkness is destroyed at sunrise, as mountains by fear of the thunderbolt [*vajra*], as snakes after seeing Tarksya,[68] as clouds buffeted by the wind, as misery from knowledge of the truth [*tattva-gyana*], as deer after seeing a lion—so sins are destroyed immediately on seeing Mathura. (5.46–47)

In the *Padma Purana, Patala-khanda* it is said—
As flames burn heaps of grass, so the city of Mathura burns great sins. (5.48)

My circle of Mathura is twenty *yojanas* in size. Here a pious result equal to an *ashvamedha*[69] can be obtained at each step—in this matter consideration [*vicharana*] is of no use. (5.50)

In the *Adi-varaha Purana* it is said—
Sin committed elsewhere—consciously or unconsciously—is destroyed in Mathura. (5.52)

In the *Padma Purana, Patala-khanda* it is said—
Those sins accumulated in many past births are destroyed in Mathura. Sin that has been committed in Mathura itself is destroyed in a moment. (5.54)

In the *Vayu Purana* it is said—
Sin committed in Mathura is destroyed in Mathura. Residing there, a man may obtain *dharma, artha, kama,* and *moksha.* (5.56)

In the *Padma Purana, Patala-khanda* it is said—
Ripened [*prarabdha*] sin [*kilbisa*][70] that is elsewhere experienced for ten years, O Mahadevi! is finished in ten days in Mathura. (5.58)

Text 3: *Padma Purana, Kartika-vrata-mahatmya*

This is a passage from the *Padma Purana,* as cited in the sixteenth-century *Hari-bhakti-vilasa*[71] (16.150–66), a Gaudiya Vaishnava compendium of rules for correct Vaishnava conduct (*sad-achara*) and ritual composed by Sanatana Gosvami on the basis of material compiled by Gopala Bhatta Gosvami. The passage tells about the performance of *Kartika-vrata*[72] in Mathura.

In the month of *Kartika,* bathing [*snana*], charity [*dana*], and especially ritual worship [*puja*], wheresoever one may perform them, are equal to an *agnihotra.*[73] (150)

Performed in Kurukshetra,[74] it is ten million times [*kotiguna*], on the Ganges equal to that, and the result is even more when performed in Pushkara.[75] O Bhargava! *Kartika* observed in Dvaraka[76] by ritual worship and bathing bestows residence in the same world [*salokya*][77] as Krishna. (151)

O sages! Other cities give a result equal to that mentioned above, except for Mathura; because in that place was manifested Hari's form of Damodara.[78] And therefore, if the month of *Kartika* is observed in Mathura, one's love for Hari increases. (152)

24. Prayag—sacred site at the confluence of the Ganges, Yamuna, and Sarasvati rivers, presently located in the city of Allahabad, and most famously the site, every twelve years, of the Kumbha Mela, the world's largest religious gathering.

25. Pulahashrama—hermitage of Pulaha, a mental son of Brahma and husband of Gati, daughter of Kardama and Devahuti (*Bhag.* 3.12.12).

26. Gomati—a well-known sacred river.

27. Gandaki—a sacred river originating in the Himalayan region and flowing into the Ganges at Sonepur in Bihar.

28. Vipasa—a sacred river in Punjab presently known as the Beas River.

29. Sone River—a sacred river.

30. Gaya—sacred place of pilgrimage at the present city of Gaya.

31. Ganga-sagara—sacred place at the mouth of the Ganges in the Bay of Bengal.

32. Mahendra Hill.

33. Godavari—one of the seven sacred rivers of India, the most famous of those in the South.

34. Vena—a sacred river.

35. Bhimarathi—a sacred river of South India, originating in the Sabya mountains and flowing into the Krishna River north of Raichur.

36. Pampa—a sacred river flowing through Kerala in South India.

37. Kartikeya—son of Shiva and Parvati.

38. Shrisaila—famous site of the Mallikarjunasvami temple in the present Andhra Pradesh.

39. Venkatadri—mountain in Andhra Pradesh, site of the famous temple of Venkateshvara, a form of Vishnu.

40. Kamakosni or Kamakosthi—the city of Kumbhakonam, former capital of the Chola kingdom.

41. Kanchi—two sacred places: Shiva-kanchi, sacred town of temples to Shiva; and Vishnu-kanchi, nearby town of temples to Vishnu, both in Tamil Nadu.

42. Kaveri—again, one of the seven sacred rivers, in South India.

43. Shrirangam—site of perhaps India's largest temple, Ranganatha Swami, located on an island in the Kaveri River, about five kilometers north of Tiruchirapally in Tamil Nadu. It draws multitudes of pilgrims on *Vaikuntha Ekadashi* in late autumn.

44. Rishabha Hill—located in Madura District of southern Karnataka, the present Palni Hill.

45. Southern Mathura—the present city of Madurai on the Bighai, site of the famous Minakshi temple.

46. Rameshvaram—site of Ramachandra's worship of Shiva, close to the mainland end of the stone bridge over which Rama and his monkey army marched to the island of Lanka; today the site of a massive Shiva temple.

47. Kritamala—sacred river of South India; mentioned in *Bhagavata Purana* 11.5.39.

48. Tamraparni—sacred river of South India, mentioned in *Bhagavata Purana* 11.5.39.

49. Malaya mountain.

50. Kanyakumari—*tirtha* at the southernmost tip of the Indian subcontinent.

51. Phalguna Tirtha—Anantapura (according to the commentator Shridhara Svami).

52. Panchapsarasa—sacred place in *Phalguna.*

53. Kerala—the country from Malabar to Kanyakumarika.

54. Trigarta—Jalandhar District in Panjab. The land between the Ravi, Vipasa, and Satadru rivers.

55. Gokarna—a special place located twenty miles southeast of Karoyara in North Karnataka, famous for the Mahabaleshvara Shivalinga. It was visited by Nityananda, one of Chaitanya's close companions.

56. Arya—visited by Chaitanya and Nityananda (*Chaitanya-bhag.* 1.9.150).

57. Surparaka—see *Bhag.* 10.79.20. Same as Sopara in Tana Distrist of Bombay Presidency. Or in Kerala, where Parashurama journeyed (*Brahmanda Purana*).

58. Tapti—a river flowing to the Arabian Sea.

59. Payosni—a river flowing to the south of Vindhyachala (see *Bhag.* 5.19.17).

60. Nirvindhya—a sacred river of South India.

61. Dandaka—a very ancient forest where many sages have performed penance on the banks of the Godavari River (see *Bhag.* 9.11.19).

62. Reva or Narmada—one of the famous seven sacred rivers, located in South India, much mentioned in the *Mahabharata* (*Sabha* and *Vana Parvas*).

63. Mahismati—an ancient city on the bank of the Narmada River, capital of Kartaviryarjuna.

64. Manutirtha—a sacred place on the bank of the Sarasvati River (*Bhag.* 3.1.22).

65. Prabhasa—a sacred place on the coast of Saurastra, also known as Soma-tirtha, where Arjuna performed penance.

66. The text of *Bhakti-ratnakara* is taken from a modern Bengali script edition: Narahari Chakravarti, *Sri Sri Bhakti-ratnakara,* edited by Sri Nandalal Vidyasagara (Calcutta: Gaudiya Mission, 1960).

67. Narahari Chakravarti was the son of Jagannath Chakravarti, a disciple of Vishvanath Chakravarti, the well-known seventeenth-century Gaudiya Vaishnava commentator on the *Bhagavata Purana, Bhagavad Gita,* and other works. After taking the renounced order of life, Narahari Chakravarti was known by the name Ghanashyama-dasa.

68. Tarksya—another name of Garuda, the eagle-mount of Vishnu and lethal enemy of the serpent species.

69. *Ashvamedha*—the Vedic horse sacrifice, performed by monarchs for the increase of their kingdoms.

70. Ripened (*prarabdha*) sin (*kilbisa*)—according to Rupa Gosvami's *Bhakti-rasamrita-sindhu* (1.1.19), sin (*papa*) is twofold: that which has ripened (*prarabdha*) and that which has not yet ripened (*aprarabdha*). Ripened sin is already manifested in the form of one's body and worldly circumstances. This verse points out that ripened *karma* that would normally have to be suffered for a lengthy period of time is drastically shortened by residence in Mathura.

71. The text of *Hari-bhakti-vilasa*, available in numerous editions in Bengali script, is based on the following edition: Sanatana Gosvami, *Shri Hari-bhakti-vilasa,* with the author's *Dig-darshini-tika.* Shridham Mayapur: Shri Chaitanya Math, 485 Gaurabda.

72. *Kartika-vrata*—observances enjoined for Vaishnavas during the month of Kartika (usually falling during October and November); mentioned in *Hari-bhakti-vilasa* (16.92) as five: night vigil on *Ekadashi* (*hari-jagarana*), early morning bath

(*pratah-snana*), service of Tulasi (*tulasi-sevana*), prayer (*udyapana*), and offering of lighted lamps (*dipa-dana*).

73. *Agnihotra*—ritual Vedic fire sacrifice.

74. Kurukshetra—field (*kshetra*) consecrated by King Kuru and located outside the present city of Kurukshetra; the site of Parashurama's exploits and the great battle between the Kauravas and Pandavas narrated in the *Mahabharata*. It is also the annual resort of huge numbers of pilgrims during solar eclipses.

75. Pushkara—a holy lake in Rajasthan.

76. Dvaraka—a city on the western coast of India reputed to be the site of Krishna's fantastic kingdom, much mentioned in the tenth *skandha* of the *Bhagavata Purana*.

77. One of five kinds of liberation listed in the *Bhagavata Purana* (3.29.13), *salokya* is defined by Shridhara Svami in his *Bhavartha-dipika* as "residence in one world with me [Krishna]" (*salokyam maya saha ekasmin loke vasam*). The other forms of liberation are: same power as the Lord (*sarshti*), same vicinity (*samipya*), same form (*sarupya*), and oneness (*ekatva*).

78. Damodara—name of Krishna derived from his being bound by a cord (*dama*) around the belly (*udara*) to a wooden mortar by his mother Yashoda when an infant. In the famous pastime described in *Bhag.* 10.10, Damodara drags the mortar (*ulukhala*) between two Arjuna trees, uprooting them and releasing Nalakubara and Manigriva, two *gandharvas* imprisoned there by the curse of Narada.

79. *Magha*—lunar month, occurring in January–February of the western Calendar, in which one is recommended to take daily early morning baths (*pratah-snana*). In his gloss on *Bhagavad Gita* 2.14, where Arjuna is instructed to tolerate sense impressions producing alternately heat and cold, happiness and distress, the eighteenth-century Gaudiya Vaishnava commentator Baladeva Vidyabhushana gives the sensation of water as an example: a refreshing summer bath produces happiness, but bathing in the month of *Magha* (*Magha-snana*) produces the opposite (*Vidyabhushana-bhashya* on Bg. 2.14).

80. Jahnavi—another name for the Ganges River.

81. *Vaishakha*—lunar month occurring in the late spring.

82. These two verses also appear in Rupa Gosvami's *Bhakti-rasamrita-sindhu* (1.2.220–21), where Jiva Gosvami comments on the phrase "because it puts Hari under their control" (*yato vasyakari hareh*) (*Durgama-sangamani-tika* 1.2.220–21).

83. Dhruva—son of Suniti and King Uttanapada, the story of his penance and attainment of Hari is told in *Bhag.* 4.8–9. He was instructed by Narada (*Bhag.* 4.8.42) to go to the sacred Madhuvana on the bank of the Yamuna River, where Hari is eternally present (*yatra samnidhyam nityada hareh*); Madhuvana is identified by commentators as the present-day Mathura.

84. Commenting on this verse, Sanatana Gosvami points out that this description refers to the history of a certain Prince Dhumrakesh, who, having been exiled by his royal father, becomes a thief and goes to live in Vrindavan, where he lives with a prostitute. Seeing the brahmin Satyavrata engaged in the service of the Lord, Dhumrakesh laughs at him. When, shortly thereafter, he is captured by the king's men and executed, he is greatly honored by Yamaraja, the god of death, and after instructing him, goes to Vaikuntha. This story, narrated in the *Kartika-mahatmya* section of the *Padma Purana*, shows the power of Mathura to liberate even those who laugh at devotional practices (*Dig-darshini-tika* on *Hari-bhakti-vilasa* 16.161).

22

Chaitanya Vaishnavism and the Holy Names

Neal Delmonico

Theology of the Holy Names

The form of Vaishnavism inspired by the sixteenth-century saint-reformer Shri Krishna Chaitanya (1486–1533 C.E.) rested heavily upon a belief in the purifying and salvific powers of the names of God, whose fullest self-revelation Chaitanya believed to be Krishna. While other medieval Vaishnava traditions certainly also shared this belief to some extent, none of those traditions placed as much stress on the Holy Names as the Chaitanya Vaishnava tradition. The Chaitanya tradition took quite seriously the idea, drawn from various passages of the *Puranas*, that *kirtana* or, more specifically, *sankirtana* is the proper form of religious practice for the current age, which the Hindu texts identify as the Age of *Kali*, the Age of Quarrel. *Kirtana* means "praising" or "glorifying," and *sankirtana* means loudly praising or glorifying. *Sankirtana* often takes the form of congregational singing of Krishna's names with the accompaniment of various kinds of musical instruments (drums, cymbals, harmoniums, and so forth). As the singing becomes emotionally charged, various kinds of dancing often break out as well. *Sankirtana* is generally a public performance, in that it is often carried out in public areas such as the streets and the squares of villages, towns, and cities.

The *Bhagavata Purana* provides the most famous stanza identifying *sankirtana* as the appropriate religious rite right for this age:

> The wise worship by sacrifices, primarily in the form of
> *sankirtana*, one whose letters are "krish-na" and whose

complexion is dark along with all his parts, subparts, weapons, and companions.[1]

There are many ways of praising Krishna. One may praise him by recounting his activities or "sports" (*lila*), as they are called, or by praising his good qualities (*guna*), or by describing the beauties of his forms (*rupa*), or by repeating his various names. For the followers of Chaitanya, the best way to praise Krishna is by means of his various names. An early follower of Chaitanya and one of the movement's first theologians, Sanatana Gosvamin (1465?–1554 C.E.), wrote that "among the various kinds of glorification [*kirtana*] of Krishna, loud glorification [*sankirtana*] by means of his names is the foremost. Since it is able to produce quickly the treasure of love for Krishna, it is considered the best of all."[2] He explains why in his commentary on that verse: "because it is able to cause love for Krishna to appear without dependence on anything else."[3] What is meant here is that the various names of Krishna encompass all the other forms of glorification mentioned above and thus are not dependent on any of them. Take, for instance, the name Shyamasundara, "beautiful dark one." Here one has a description of Krishna's beautiful dark form. Or, in the name Navanita-taskara, "butter thief," one has a name that refers to one of Krishna's childhood activities or sports, stealing butter. In the name Dina-dayalu, "compassionate to the poor," is indicated Krishna's quality of compassion for the downtrodden. Thus, all the other forms of praise can be encompassed within praise through Krishna's names. In other words, they can be accomplished through the vehicle of calling out to Krishna. The Chaitanya tradition, therefore, has concluded that praise of Krishna through his names is the best of all forms of praise.

Theology of the Holy Names

Because of its focus on the names of Krishna as a means for cultivating love for Krishna,[4] the Chaitanya Vaishnava tradition has developed over the centuries what might be called a theology of the names of Krishna, or a theology of the Holy Names. While there are many dimensions to that theology, especially as it has been developed by more recent authors, its fundamental insight is that Krishna and his names are, in all respects except one, nondifferent. Drawing on an important verse from the *Padma Purana* for support, the Chaitanya tradition asserts that by vocalizing or even just remembering his names, one is brought into the presence of Krishna himself. That verse is:

> Because the Holy Name and the Holy Named are nondifferent, the Name is a thought-jewel, the very embodiment of consciousness and joy (*rasa*), full, pure, eternally liberated, and Krishna himself.[5]

In this verse the Holy Name is called a "thought-jewel," which, like the mythic philosopher's stone, fulfills all of one's desires. One thinks it and one has it. The Holy Name, like the thought-jewel, is capable of granting all one's wishes; it is an embodiment of consciousness and joy; it is full and eternal, and it is eternally liberated because it is nondifferent from Krishna himself in all ways but one. The Holy Name, according to the Chaitanya tradition, is greater in compassion than even Krishna himself, because though the Name is beyond the grasp of material senses, as Krishna is, it appears in them anyway.[6] By that purifying contact with the nonmaterial Name, the material senses are cleansed of their materiality—so argue the theologians of the Holy Names—and become capable at last of perceiving the nonmaterial realm of Krishna. The Holy Names are thus like a perpetual descent (avatara) or an enduring appendage of Krishna in the world.

Although there are countless names of Krishna, the Chaitanya tradition, following the lead of Chaitanya himself, has given a place of special honor to a form of those names called the mahamantra, or great chant. The mahamantra is the well-known formula:

Hare Krishna Hare Krishna Krishna Krishna Hare Hare
Hare Rama Hare Rama Rama Rama Hare Hare[7]

This formula contains three names, Hari, Krishna, and Rama, all in the vocative case of the Sanskrit language. It thus essentially constitutes a series of calls to Vishnu, Krishna, and Rama. Hari is a common name of Vishnu; Krishna is his eighth descent, recognized as deity in the Mahabharata; and Rama is Vishnu's seventh descent, divine hero of the epic Ramayana. Sometimes in the Chaitanya tradition it is said that the Rama meant in the chant is not Sita's Rama of the Ramayana but Balarama, Krishna's older brother. Though exact meanings of the names are obscure, the tradition supplied meanings, based on imaginative etymologies, that could be pressed into theological service. Hari, for instance, is said to mean "he who takes away one's sufferings." Krishna means "the all-attractive one," and Rama "the pleasing one." All the names are then regarded as referring to aspects of Krishna himself in the Chaitanya tradition, since in that tradition Krishna has thoroughly superseded the ancient Vedic Vishnu in religious evaluation. Krishna is regarded as the source of Vishnu rather than Vishnu the source of Krishna.[8]

Not satisfied with the aforementioned understanding of the Great Chant, therefore, some members of the Chaitanya tradition have given other interpretations. Hari is replaced with the feminine name Hara, for instance, which in the vocative is also Hare. Hara is then made to refer to Radha, Krishna's primary lover and his pleasure-giving power (hladini-shakti), because she alone is able to steal away Krishna's mind and heart. Rama is also reinterpreted to mean Krishna as "the pleasing one" who makes passionate love (ramana) to Radha. Thus, the mantra is transformed into an expression of the love relationship between Radha and Krishna. In this way, the first line of the *mantra* indicates Radha and Krishna's mutual attraction to each other and the second their union with each other in conjugal love. The *mantra* has even been interpreted more elaborately by placing it within the frame of a story about Radha chanting it as she desires reuniting with Krishna.[9]

In one of the passages translated here, Shri Krishna Chaitanya is described as advising his followers to do *japa* of this *mahamantra*, to chant it day and night, and to know that there are no rules or regulations governing its chanting. *Japa* is the repetitive pronunciation of a *mantra*, either silently in one's mind or out loud in one's speech. In some texts it is said that there are three kinds of *japa*: mental, whispered, and vocal. All three types are accepted by the Chaitanya tradition, but the type of *japa* that is done loudly or vocally has generally been favored. The reasons for that can be found in another of the passages translated here. Basically, chanting to oneself, in one's mind or in a whisper, is beneficial for oneself, but chanting loudly is beneficial for oneself and for all those who hear. Loud chanting is thus said to be a hundred times more beneficial than silent chanting. The loud or vocal repetition (*japa*) of the names of Krishna is considered in fact to be a form of *kirtana*.[10]

There is another aspect of glorification through Krishna's names that should be mentioned before concluding this brief introduction. Those who chant or repeat Krishna's names sometimes experience intense joy and occasionally go into ecstatic trances. This was certainly typical of Shri Chaitanya's experience of glorification of the Names, as several of the translations below demonstrate. Chaitanya's frequent ecstasies during *kirtanas* have prompted some scholars to suggest that he was given to epileptic fits.[11] Be that is it may, the history of Chaitanya Vaishnavism is filled with saints who have experienced ecstatic trances in the context of *kirtana*. While this may be true of those who are regarded as elevated in the tradition, it is certainly not the case for those who are just beginning the practice of repeating the names of Krishna. Rupa Gosvamin (1470?–1555), one of the tradition's finest poets and theologians, has made an interesting comment on this in his *Upadeshamrita* ("Nectar of Instruction"):

> It may be that the sugar of the names and activities of Krishna is not pleasing to a tongue overheated by the bile of ignorance. Still, if one tastes them with respect every day, gradually they become delicious, destroying the source of that disease.[12]

In the beginning of the cultivation of *preman*, love, one may not feel much attraction to the Holy Names, but after one has practiced reciting them regularly for some time, one begins to taste their innate sweetness. Through the regular rubbing of the Holy Name against the mind, the same mind is gradually wiped free of its pollution of ignorance as a mirror is wiped free of dust and smudges. Ignorance takes the form of misconceptions about the nature of the self, misidentification with the body and things related to the body, and a truculent and intractable egotism. A sign that those effects of ignorance are becoming loosened is found in the development of a deep sense of humility. Then the Name is said to rise like the sun in the mind of the practitioner, and the practitioner's heart, softened by the warmth of that sun, becomes ripe for the experience of sacred rapture [bhakti-rasa]. This tasting of sacred rapture is what is manifested in the extraordinary joys and ecstatic trances that sometimes overcome those engaged in kirtana. The symptoms of ecstasy signal the appearance of the final goal as envisioned by the Chaitanya tradition, the development of bhakti as goal, bhakti as love (preman) for Krishna. This then is a very brief summary of the tradition's theology of the Holy Names.

Texts Presented Here

Most of the passages translated here come from Bengali texts dating from the early sixteenth century up to the twentieth century. However, since the Chaitanya tradition depends so heavily on the Puranas for support of its theology of the Holy Names, the textual translations begin with a small sampling of the numerous Sanskrit verses glorifying the recitation or chanting of the names of Krishna. Those verses are selected from the huge number of verses from the Puranas, Itihasas (Epics), and other texts that were collected together in the eleventh chapter (11.272 to 11.529) of the Hari-bhakti-vilsa ("Manifestations of Bhakti for Hari") compiled and arranged by Gopala Bhatta Gosvamin (1500–87). Next come some Sanskrit verses on the Holy Name by immediate followers of Chaitanya, along with a couple of verses on the same subject from the Shikshashtaka ("Eight Verses of Instruction"), which is attributed to Chaitanya himself. Following that is a Sanskrit hymn written by Rupa Gosvamin, called the Shri Krishna-namashtaka ("Eight Verses on the Names of Krishna"). This short hymn has been the springboard for much of the theology of the Holy Names that has developed in the Chaitanya tradition in the nineteenth and twentieth centuries.

The next section contains a few of the thousands of Bengali songs written by followers of Chaitanya, some of whom were his companions, portraying Chaitanya's own involvement in kirtana and the ecstatic moods and trances he experienced in that context. We turn next to one of the early hagiographies of Chaitanya, the Chaitanya-bhagavata by Vrindavan Dasa (flourished 1540). In it we find the story of Haridasa, a Muslim convert to Krishna bhakti, who is regarded by the tradition as the model teacher (acharya) of the chanting of the Holy Names. We also find there Chaitanya's own instructions to his followers on the chanting of the Holy Names. Next, we skip to the middle of the nineteenth century and witness an important event in the life of the Vaishnava saint Shri Radharamana Carana Dasa Baba, or Bodo Baba ("Big Baba") (b. 1853). During the *kirtana* described in that passage, Bodo Baba falls into a trance and reveals the chant (*Bhaja Nitai Gaura Radhe Shyam; japa Hare Krishna Hare Ram*) that became the primary form of *kirtana* for his community of followers, which is even today one of the most lively communities of modern Chaitanya Vaishnavism.

There are several outstanding figures in the more recent history of the Chaitanya Vaishnava tradition who have written on the theology of the Holy Names. I refer to them as the theologians of the Holy Names because of their efforts to try to flesh out that special domain of Chaitanya Vaishnava theology. Perhaps the earliest of them was Vipinvihari Gosvamin, whose work entitled the *Hari-namamrita-sindhu* ("Ocean of the Nectar of the Names of Hari") was completed in 1878.[13] He draws together hundreds of Sanskrit verses from a variety of sources, organizes them into twelve general headings, and provides his own translation-commentary on them in versified Bengali. One of Vipinvihari Gosvamin's major disciples was Thakura Bhaktivinoda (1838–1914), who wrote, among numerous other works on Chaitanya Vaishnavism, a classic work on the Holy Names called the *Shri Hari-nama-chintamani* ("Thought-Jewel of the Names of Hari"). A brief excerpt from his discussion of the phenomenon of "reflected light" of the Holy Name (*namabhasa*) is given here.

In the twentieth century, there were a number of writers on the Holy Names. Perhaps the greatest of them was Kanupriya Goswami. His work, which eventually extended to three volumes, is entitled the *Shri Shri Nama-chintamani* ("Thought-Jewel of the Holy Names"). Because of his work on the Holy Names, Kanupriya Goswami was recognized in the Vaishnava community as the "Teacher of the Science of the Holy Names" (*Nama-vijnanacharya*). Inspired by Kanupriya's work, another great scholar of the Vaishnava tradition, Sundarananda Vidyavinoda, wrote a work in Bengali on the theology of the Holy Names called *Shri Shri Nama-chintamani-kirana-kanika* ("A Small Ray of Light from the Thought-Jewel of the Holy Names"), spanning nearly six hundred pages. Perhaps the best short introduction to modern Vaishnava thinking and teaching about the Holy Names, however, comes from Manindranath Guha, one of the disciples of Kanupriya Goswami. His book *Shriman-namamrita-sindhu-bindu* ("A Drop from the Ocean of the Nectar of the Holy Name") presents a dialogue between a disciple and his *guru* on the subject of the Holy Name. A short passage on the nondifference between the Holy Name and the Holy Named from Manindranath's book is the final selection presented here.

Sanskrit Sources

Glorification of the Holy Names

From the Epics and *Puranas*

All of his names, king, bring about the achievement of all goals. Therefore, in all endeavors you may chant with devotion whichever of Krishna's names you wish.[14]

You are indeed pure, since, like the sun, attachment to glorifying Hari [Krishna] does not arise without destroying all the darkness in human beings.[15]

Let humans not fear the lighted flames of sin. Those are destroyed by the drops of water from the dense rain clouds of Govinda's names.[16]

"Govinda" spoken with devotion or even without burns away all sins like the conflagration at the end of the ages.[17]

The auspicious powers capable of destroying all sins, [powers] that are inherent in the giving of charity, the keeping of vows, austerities, the visiting of holy bathing sites and places of pilgrimage, and so forth, and that are in the *Rajasuya*, *Ashvamedha*, and the other sacrifices, and in knowledge of the higher self, all of those powers Hari has drawn together and placed in his own names.[18]

There is one great boon among the many faults characteristic of the Age of *Kali*, king, and that is that by glorification of Krishna one is freed from bondage and goes to the supreme.[19]

If one desires the highest knowledge and from that knowledge the highest abode, then with great respect, king of kings, glorify Govinda.[20]

Krishna [here referring to Princess Draupadi], this debt of mine is increased so much that I never leave the heart of someone who cries out "Govinda" to me though I live far away.[21]

If someone should sing my names and dance near me, this I say to you truthfully: I am purchased by that person, Arjuna.[22]

Sweetest of the sweet, most auspicious of the auspicious, true fruit of the vine of all revealed texts, consciousness by nature, the name of Krishna sung even once either with respect or by accident, best of Bhrigus, saves any human being.[23]

The name of Hari, the name of Hari, the name of Hari is my life. In the Age of *Kali* there is no other, is no other, is no other way.[24]

Because the Holy Name and the Holy Named are nondifferent, the Name is a thought-jewel, the very embodiment of consciousness and joy [*rasa*], full, pure, eternally liberated, and Krishna himself.[25]

From the Saints

May glorification of Krishna be most victorious! It cleanses the mirror of the mind, puts out the great fire of worldly existence, spreads moonlight to the lily of good fortune, is the life of the wife of wisdom, increases the ocean of bliss at each step, and causes the tasting of the fullest nectar.[26]

In your names are invested many of your own powers. The time for remembering them is not restricted. Such is your mercy, Lord, but such is my misfortune that no passion for them has been born [in me].[27]

Victory, victory to the blissful name of Murari [Krishna], which ends the drudgery of following one's own *dharma*, of meditation, of performing rites of worship and so forth; that name, if somehow uttered even once, gives liberation to living beings and is the greatest nectar. It is my whole life, my only ornament.[28]

Krishna! Getting free from the cords of hearing, you are caught by the ropes of meditation. Escaping from those, too, you are captured by the chains of glorification [*sankirtana*] of your Names. Now I, who am unsettled by *bhakti* for you, will never let you go. You are surrounded and firmly held, O Wearer of cloth of yellow silk![29]

Among the various kinds of glorification of Krishna, glorification through his names is the foremost. Since it is able to produce quickly the treasure of love for Krishna, it is the best.[30]

The name of the Lord is even more dear than his form. It benefits the whole world, is easily worshiped, and is enjoyable. [Therefore,] it has no equal.[31]

May they rule supreme, those syllables "Hare Krishna," springing from the mouth of Shri Chaitanya, his own names, inundating the whole world with love.[32]

I don't know how much nectar the two syllables "*krish-na*" are made with, but when they dance on my tongue, they create a desire for a whole string of tongues. When they blossom in the hollows of my ears, they create a desire for millions of ears. When they enter the courtyard of my mind, they overcome the operations of all my senses.[33]

Rupa's Eight Verses on the Names of Krishna

Holy Name! The luster of the crown jewels of all the *Vedas* illumine your lotus-like feet. I seek complete shelter in every way in you who are worshiped even by liberated souls. (1)

Victory to you, Holy Name, praised by the sages. You have a form of the highest syllables for the pleasure of the people. Even though pronounced without respect or only partly, you nevertheless destroy all fearsome sufferings. (2)

What talented person is able to describe your sublime greatness in the world, sun-like Name of the Lord? By even the first reflections of your arising, the darkness of the existence of those gripped by ignorance is destroyed, and you give the power of sight that guides to *bhakti* even those blind to the truth. (3)

The *Veda* roars out that what is not achieved by the direct experience of *Brahman*, namely the destruction of the effects of past actions that are already fructifying, is accomplished by the appearance of the Holy Name. (4)

Holy Name, let my love for you grow immensely, you who have many forms, like Aghadamana [Punisher of Agha], Yashodanandana [Son of Yashoda], Nandasunu [Son of Nanda], Kamalanayana [Lotus-Eyes], Gopichandra [Moon of the Gopis], Vrindavanendra [King of Vrindavana], Pranatakaruna [Merciful to the Surrendered], and Krishna. (5)

Holy Name, you have two natures: the conveyed and the conveyor. I understand the latter to be more merciful than the former, since even a living being who has committed some grievous offense to the former may honor the latter with his mouth and be ever submerged in an ocean of joy. (6)

Holy Name, obeisance to you, destroyer of the pains of those sheltered by you, lovely consciousness and joy in nature, great festival of Gokula, Krishna's full body. (7)

Name of Krishna, one who enlivens the *vina* of Narada, soaked in the sweetness of syrupy waves of nectar, please, if you wish, appear on my tongue joyfully [*rasena*] forever. (8)

Early Bengali Sources

SONGS

I

Long-armed Chaitanya Raya[34] used to dance.
Who knows how many
were his hundreds and hundreds of moods?
O Golden-hued was Gaura[35] Raya.
In love [*prema*] he fainted time and again,
his pure body decked with goose bumps.

What more can I say: his manifestations were endless
to draw to himself the greed in the minds of the world.
Hearing loud singing of his own qualities and names,
he was undone, his dancing broken.
The people of Nadiya forgot their pains and pleasures
and floated away on waves of love.
Passing out jewels and raining down love's nectar,
the whole world was drenched.
Chaitanya Dasa sings: "A matchless gift of love
and me, I've missed out!"[36]

2

Lord Gauranga[37] dances in Nadiya town.
Hearing this, the three types of people do not stay home.
Jewelry of gold and gems adorn his body,
his limbs smeared with sandal, a drop of musk within.
Is this the sandaled Moon or well-dressed Meru?
A garland of jasmine decorates his neck.
In front dances Advaita for whom he has descended.
Outside Gauranga dances, the joy of all.
Dancing, dancing whichever way Gaura goes,
thousands light lamps, some sing "Hari."
The wives of houses give up all and sing "Hari."
A river of love flows from the tears of everyone's eyes.
His curling hair is surrounded by many flowers,
a branch of oleander, some jasmine with leaves.
Is this a stylish dancer or my Lord dancing?
What need have I for austerity, recitation, or Vedic rules?
By the names of Hari he [Chaitanya] has saved even the outcastes.
Wives and the rest have left their household chores.
Ascetics quit their penances, renunciants their renunciation.
When he dances, sings, and chants the names of Hari,
Balarama Dasa is robbed of that nectar.[38]

3

His companions form a circle;
in its center is Gaura, the dancer.
Vishvambhara [Chaitanya] dances with Gadadhara;
Nityananda Raya dances too.
In his [Chaitanya's] former sports he tastes the joy of love,
realizing it in his own nature.

To one house after another
he gives love for Shyamasundara [Krishna].
He offers praise [*sankirtana*] and gives away love,
with all of his companions.
The male dances in the mood of the female;
The female in the mood of the male.
Whatsoever their nature, realizing their true nature,
how many hundreds of classes dance!
Says Nayanananda: "The joy of Nadiya
fills the world with bliss. Sad is my life. Therefore,
I beg shelter at the feet of Madhava [Krishna].[39]

4

Gaura dances filled with love; again and again he shouts "Hari,"
One moment recalling Vrindavana, the next the queen of his life.[40]
The color of *lac* [red] is the cloth round his hips; shining brightly
   Gaura sings.
Sometimes he shouts "Yamuna" and runs to the Ganges' bank.
"Thaw-thaw, thie-thie" sound the drums; " jhan-jhan" ring the bells.
From his lotus eyes a Ganges flows; on his neck a garland swings.
The source of all joy is Gaurachandra;[41] merciful to those who
   have nothing at all.
Govinda Dasa nourishes hope for the shade of those lotus feet.[42]

5

In the skies of Nadiya a "cloud of praise" forms.
Drums, cymbals, and from mouths, deep roars;
the thunder of tumult rises again and again.
The two lords [Chaitanya and Nityananda] rain dense showers
   of Names.
Their companions sing and dance in fits.
Lightning bolts of feelings flash brightly.
The downpour of love makes the river flood Shantipura.
[Sadly] Ananta Raya's heart is not charmed by that joy [*rasa*].[43]

6

His body fills up with goose bumps when he hears his own qualities.
Overwhelmed by love, he rolls about on the ground.
One moment he leans on Narahari's body.

Gazing at Gadadhara's face, he falls unconscious.
One moment he brags, the next he says "Hari."
Saying "Radha, Radha," he loudly weeps.
Saying "Lalita, Vishakha," he heaves deep sighs.
Govinda Dasa cannot maintain his composure.[44]

7

My Gaura is the limit of mercy, a treasury of qualities.
On the bank of the Suradhuni, in Nadiya,
Gauranga sports without limit.
Placing his two arms on the shoulders of his *bhaktas*,
he is not able to move. Shouting "Haribol,"[45] he weeps.
In love his two eyes are full of tears; how many rivers from
    them flow?
His whole body is covered with goose flesh; the earth cannot
    hold them.
With his companions he wanders around, constantly saying
    "Haribol."
Placing his two arms on the shoulders of friends, leaning and
    swaying he moves.
Filling the world with love, he fulfills his name, "Savior of the
    Fallen."
Hearing of it, no other hope enters Paramananda's mind.[46]

Hagiographies

Chaitanya-bhagavata

Victory, victory to Gaurasundara,[47] friend of the downtrodden.
Victory, victory to the Husband of Lakshmi [goddess of fortune],
    Lord of all.
Victory, victory to his descent for the protection of the devotees.
Victory to the sport of glorification [*kirtana*], true for all times.
Victory, victory to Gauranga[48] along with his devotees.
If one hears the story of Chaitanya, *bhakti* comes within reach.
The story of the first division[49] is a river of nectar
in which one hears of Gauranga's sports, enchanting to all.
In this way the Lord of Vaikuntha was in Navadvipa
living as a householder and teaching as a *Brahmana*.
His descent was to reveal the devotion of love.
He was not doing that at all, and that was the way he wanted
    it then.
Everyone's domestic life was completely void of the highest aims.

The insignificant joys of sense enjoyment had everyone's respect.
Those who taught the *Gita* or the *Bhagavata*
would not perform or encourage others to perform glorification.
Or, all of the devotees, clapping their hands
would get together with one another and sing in praise.
Even then they would ridicule it in their hearts.
"Why are these people shouting so loudly?
I am *Brahman*; in me sits the immaculate.
Why distinguish between master and servant? "
The materialists all would say: "They are just begging for food.
They call out 'Hari' to let everyone know.
Let's break down the doors of this bunch's houses."
All of Nadiya gathered together and argued like that.
Hearing this, all the devotees were saddened.
They did not find a person worthy of conversation.
The devotees saw the material life as empty.
Calling out "Alas, Krishna! " they felt boundless sadness.
At just that time, Haridasa arrived there,
a physical manifestation of pure devotion to Vishnu.
Now listen to Haridsa's story,
hearing which one reaches Krishna in his glory.
To Bhudan village descended Haridasa.[50]
By his good graces glorification appeared in all those places.
Staying for a while, he came to the Ganga's banks.
Arriving there, he settled at Phuliya and Shantipur.
There he met Acharya Gosai,[51]
who shouted loudly, no limit to his joy.
Haridasa felt the same in Advaitadeva's company.
On waves they floated in Govinda's [Krishna's] ocean of joy.
Continuously Haridasa on the Ganga's banks
wandered about merrily, saying "Krishna" quite loudly.
Foremost was he of those detached from sensuality;
His fortunate mouth filled with Krishna's names incessantly.
Not even for a moment did Govinda's names cease.
In tasting *bhakti*, many feelings rose from moment to moment.
Sometimes he danced all by himself.
Sometimes he roared like a lion vexed.
Sometimes he loudly wept.
Sometimes he laughed outlandishly.
Sometimes he shouted out ferocious growls.
Sometimes he fainted, falling hard to the ground.
One moment he yelled out an unworldly sound.
The next he gave it commentary most profound.

Squirting tears, horripilation, laughter, fainting, sweat—
all of Krishna-*bhakti*'s somatic perturbations—
as soon as Prabhu Haridasa began to dance,
they all arrived and swarmed through his body.
In this way his tears of joy dampened all his limbs.
Even the most wicked seeing him were greatly charmed.
So amazing were the goose bumps in his body
that Brahma and Shiva seeing them were delighted.
All of the *Brahmanas* of Phuliya
seeing him were filled with joy.
Everyone developed for him great respect.
In the village of Phuliya lived Prabhu Haridasa.
Bathing in the Ganga, incessantly Hari's names
he chanted loudly and wandered about to all places....[52]
In this way Haridasa in the company of the *Brahmanas*
fearlessly performed singing in praise with great delight.
All of the Yavanas[53] who had given him pain
perished with their families in a short while.
Then Haridasa in a cave on the bank of the Ganga
settled down, remembering Krishna day and night in solitude.
Three hundred thousand names he chanted every day.
That cave of his became a mansion of Vaikuntha....[54]
Seeing the people's lack of respect for *bhakti*,
Haridasa felt great sadness inside.
Still Haridasa in a loud voice
performed full-throated praising of the Lord.
Even then extremely wicked sinners
were not able to tolerate loud praise of Hari.
In the village of Harinadi lived a rascal *Brahmana*.
Seeing Haridasa, he said this to him angrily:
"Hey Haridasa! What are you doing
calling out the Name? What is the reason?
You should chant in your mind. That is the right way.
What scripture says to shout out the Holy Name?
Whose teaching is it to shout the name of Hari?
Tell it to this assembly of scholars."
Haridasa replied: "All the principles of this
you all know, you know the greatness of Hari's name.
After hearing of it from all of you, I am repeating it.
I shall describe whatever little I know.
If one chants it loudly, there is a hundred times more merit.
Scripture does not call it a fault; rather, it is a good trait.
'Loudly it becomes a hundred times more fruitful.' "[55]

The *Brahmana* asked: "If one chants the Name loudly,
the chanter gets a hundred times more merit? What is the reason?"
Haridasa replied: "Hear, great sir,
the teaching on this in the *Veda* and *Bhagavata*."
All the scriptures appeared in Haridasa's mouth.
He began to explain, feeling the bliss of Krishna.
"Listen, *Vipra* [scholar]! If they hear only once the name of
    Krishna,
animals, birds, even insects go the abode of Vaikuntha.
As it says in the tenth canto of the *Bhagavata*:

> Since chanting of your name immediately purifies all hearers
> as well as the one chanting, what more need be said of one who
> has been touched by your foot.[56]

Animals, birds, insects, and so forth are not able to speak,
but if they hear the Holy Name they all are saved.
A person who chants silently [*japa*] Krishna's name saves himself.
By chanting loudly a person helps others.
Therefore, if a person shouts praise out loudly,
the result is a hundred times greater, all the scriptures say.
As the *Naradiya Purana* says:

> Chanting loudly is a hundred times greater than the silent
> chanting of the names of Hari because by loud chanting one
> purifies oneself and the hearers.

Why is the loud chanter a hundred times greater
than the silent chanter according to the Puranas?
Listen, *Vipra*, carefully to the reason for this.
Chanting silently one only nourishes oneself.
If one loudly praises Govinda,
all living beings hearing it are liberated.
Even though they have tongues, all living beings, except
    for humans,
are not able to make such a sound as Krishna's name.
That from which these poor ones gain liberation—
what is wrong with doing that, please tell me.
Someone takes care of only himself.
Someone else takes care of a thousand persons.
Between these two who is greater, consider it for yourself.
For this reason there is goodness in loud praise."
That *Brahmana* hearing Haridasa's words
began to say terrible things in anger.
"Now Haridasa has become a philosopher.

We see over time how the Vedic path has been destroyed.
'At the end of the age, *shudras* will explain the *Vedas*.'
We see that now; why only at the end of the age?
In this way you have revealed yourself.
You wander from house to house eating good food.
The explanation you have given, if it is not correct,
may your nose burst into pieces in front of all."
Hearing the words of that lowest of *Brahmanas*,
Haridasa said "Hari" and smiled faintly.
Then, not giving him any reply,
he departed, singing praise loudly....[57]
"For so long have you studied and listened.
Now finish your education: glorify Krishna."
The disciples asked: "What sort of glorifying do you mean? "
The Son of Shachi, the Master himself [Shri Chaitanya], taught
    them.
Haraye namah Krishna Yadavaya namah
Gopala Govinda Rama Shri Madhusudana.[58]
Showing them the way, the Master raised his hands
and did *kirtana* himself with his disciples.
The Lord of Kirtana himself led *kirtana*;
And all the disciples sang, surrounding him on all sides....[59]
Bringing gifts, everyone came to visit the Master,
Seeing the Master all bowed down.
The Master said: "May everyone have *bhakti* for Krishna.
Speak of nothing else but Krishna's qualities and names."
Then the Master himself instructed them all:
"Listen to the details of Krishna's Name, the *maha-mantra*:
Hare Krishna Hare Krishna Krishna Krishna Hare Hare,
Hare Rama Hare Rama Rama Rama Hare Hare."
The Master said: "I have spoken this *maha-mantra*.
With it perform recitation [*japa*] with persistence [*nirbandha*].
From this, every perfection will arise for all.
Say it every second; there is no other rule.
Some of you should gather, sitting at the door, and all do
    kirtana clapping your hands:

Haraye namah Krishna Yadavaya namah
Gopala Govinda Rama Shri Madhusudana.
I have told you all of this *kirtana*.
Gathering together wives, sons, and fathers,
go to your homes and perform it."[60]

. . .

When invited for an alms-meal, the Master said, laughing:
"First you go and become lords of a hundred thousand.
I will eat where there is a lord of a hundred thousand."
Hearing this, all the *Brahmanas* became troubled.
The *Brahmanas* offered prayers and said: "Goswami,
What to speak of a hundred thousand, none of us has a
   thousand.
If you do not take alms-food from us, our households,
let them burn to ashes this instant!"
The Master said: "Do you know who is a lord of a hundred
   thousand?
He who chants a hundred thousand Holy Names every day.
I call that person a lord of a hundred thousand.
There do I take alms; I don't go to other homes."
Hearing the merciful words of the Master, the *Brahmanas*
gave up their worry and became joyful in heart.
"We will chant a hundred thousand Names, Master. Please take
   our alms.
What good fortune! In this way you teach us."
Every day all the *Brahmanas* chanted a hundred thousand Names
in order to have Chaitanyachandra take alms-food at their
   houses.[61]

Modern Bengali Reflections

Shri Radharamana Carana Dasa Baba's Revelation of the Nitai Gaura Mantra

Baba became overwhelmed with emotion and with a choked-up
voice began to sing:[62]

   Nitai[63] and Gaura dance like Radha and Krishna,
   Everyone sings "Hare Krishna, Hare Rama."
   If you really want this Gauranga,
   become a servant of Nityananda.
   Even one who says only with his mouth:
   "I am a servant of Nityananda"
   will perceive the true form of Gaura.
   The love of the *gopis* as in the *Bhagavata*
   one will get only from Nityananda in this world.
   Nityananda is the giver of love;
   Gauranga is his greatest treasure.
   In the pleasure of the Rasa dance,
   one will meet Shri Radharamana.

Climbing aboard the boat "Hare Krishna, Hare Rama,"
cross over the ocean of rebirth to Vrindavana.
My Nitai frolics, my Nitai plays,
All who are maddened with love he makes his own.
Here my Nitai dances, overwhelmed with emotion.
Whomever he finds, even a *Chandala*,[64] he pulls onto his lap.

While singing that song, Bodo Baba went into a deep trance. Tears began to flow from his eyes in streams, and his body was covered with goose bumps. A moment later his body shook violently like a tree in a powerful wind, and he fell to the ground unconscious. The devotees surrounded him and began to chant the Holy Names. Seeing in his body the rising and falling waves of powerful emotions, the devotees were astonished. When he became paralyzed with emotion, it seemed as if his body was devoid of life. Then a moment later he began to laugh, the next moment he cried, a moment later he shivered, and a moment after that he was covered with goose bumps. The devotees surrounded him, and after chanting the Holy Names for quite a while, he came halfway back to consciousness and stuttered the following words:

Bhaja Nitai Gaur pabe Radhe Shyam
japa Hare Krishna, Hare Ram
Worship Nitai and Gaura (Chaitanya)
and you will get Radha and Shyam.
Recite *Hare Krishna, Hare Rama*

All the devotees who surrounded him began to sing in unison these words, and that grew into a *kirtana* that lasted long into the night. By about 10:30 at night, no one even remembered their bodies. One group of them sang the first line, and another group responded with the second line: each group, seemingly trying to overpower the other, sang praise with all their might and danced, overwhelmed with emotion, their arms raised high. Some time later during the *kirtana*, Bodo Baba, leaning against a wall, his eyes half open, his body drenched in tears and covered with goose bumps, a smile on his face, raised the pointing finger of his right hand and swayed back and forth in intense emotion. At some point, too, a wonderful aroma, attracting hearts and minds, filled the place, and some of the devotees tried to find its source, but none of them were able to. The flood of Holy Names continued on in the same manner. Around about midnight, the *kirtana* began to wind down, but Bodo Baba continued to be overwhelmed with feeling, leaning up against one of the walls.[65]

Thakura Bhaktivinoda's Discussion of the Reflection of the Holy Name

> Glory to Gadai,[66] Gauranga, and the Life of Jahnava[67]
>   [Nityananda].
> To Sita and Advaita glory and to the devotees headed by
>   Shrivasa.
> Mahaprabhu, becoming compassionate toward Haridasa,
> arose and then, reaching out his lotus hands,
> said: "Listen, Haridasa, to my words.
> Tell us now clearly about the reflection of the Holy Name
>   [namabhasa].[68]
> If you inform us about the reflection of the Holy Name,
>   the Holy Name will become pure.
> The living beings will easily become freed by the qualities
>   of the Holy Name.
> The Name is like the sun; it destroys the darkness of maya.
> Fog and clouds cover the Name again and again.
> The ignorance of the living being and all its harmful habits
> are like powerful clouds and fog.
> The sun of the Name of Krishna has risen in the sky of
>   the mind.
> Fog and clouds again cover it over.
> One who does not know that the Name is consciousness
>   by nature
> brings on the darkness of the fog of ignorance.
> One who knows not that Krishna is lord of all
> worships many different gods and wanders the path of
>   works.
> One who knows not that the living being is by nature
>   consciousness
> is constantly in ignorance under the influence of maya's
>   matter."
> Then Haridasa said: "Today I am fortunate.
> Chaitanya will hear about the Holy Name from me.
> Krishna, the living being—lord, servant—and dull maya—
> one who does not know them has ignorance's shadow on
>   his head.
> Desire for the unreal, weakness of the heart, and the
>   offenses;
> All these harmful things are obstacles in the forms of
>   clouds.
> They cover the rays of the Name-sun, and reflection of the
>   Name occurs.

They perpetually cover the self-existent Name of Krishna.
As long as one does not have knowledge of relationship
    with God (sambandha),
the reflection of the Holy Name is the living being's shelter.
Even if a practitioner finds shelter with a real guru,
it is by expertise in worship that the clouds are driven away.
When the clouds and fog have dispersed, the Name-sun
appears and gives the devotee the gift of love.
The true guru gives knowledge of relationship
and encourages cultivation of the Name as the meaning.
The Name-sun in a short while becomes strong
and drives away the fog of harmful things.
Then it bestows the ultimate goal, the treasure of love.
The living being who has obtained that love sings the Names.
At the feet of a true guru, the living being with respect
first acquires knowledge of relationship with thoughtful
    discussion.
Krishna is the eternal master, the living being his eternal
    servant.
Love of Krishna is eternal, a manifestation of the living
    being's true nature.
The living being, the eternal servant of Krishna, has
    forgotten that
and wanders in the world of maya searching for happiness.
The world of maya is the living being's prison,
punishment for the living being's fault of aversion.
Then if the living being, by the grace of holy Vaishnavas,
through knowledge of relationship again finds the Name
    of Krishna,
it obtains the treasure of love, the essence of all religion,
before which [love] the five types of liberation are rejected.
As long as knowledge of relationship is not steady,
one remains, gripped by harmful habits, in the reflection
    of the Name.
Even in the stage of reflection of the Holy Name there are
    benefits.
The living being's merit becomes stronger.
By the reflection of the Name, sins are destroyed.
By the reflection of the Name, liberation comes and Kali is
    weakened.
By the reflection of the Name, a person purifies his
    community.
By the reflection of the Name, all diseases are impeded.

All doubts are chased away by reflection of the Name.
One in reflection of the Name finds peace from all
   misfortunes.
Yakshas, rakshas,[69] ghosts, ghouls, and all planetary
   influences
by reflection of the Name are driven far away.
A person fallen into hell easily gains liberation.
All emergent effects of past actions depart because of
   reflection of the Name.
It is greater than all the Vedas, better than all places of
   pilgrimage.
Reflection of the Name is the best of all auspicious rites.
It bestows the four goals: piety, wealth, sense-enjoyment,
   and liberation.
Reflection of the Name, the savior of the living being,
   possesses all powers.
It gives joy to the whole world and bestows the best abode.
It is the one goal of those without goals, the best abode of all.
By the reflection of the Name, one attains the worlds of
   Vaikuntha and the rest,
especially in the Age of Kali. So all the scriptures say.

From Manindranath Guha's *Shriman-namamrita-sindhu-bindu:* The
First Principles of the Holy Name

Just as iron in contact with fire gains the qualities of fire, by mere
contact with an immortal thing we, too, are able to become immortal.
That immortal thing is the Holy Name.[70]

> Because the Holy Name and the Holy Named are non-different,
> the Name is a thought-jewel, the very embodiment of con-
> sciousness and *rasa*, full [undivided] and pure [free of connec-
> tion with *maya*], eternally liberated [beyond *maya*], the very
> nature of Krishna.

Shri Jiva in a commentary on this verse has said:

> The Holy Name is a thought-jewel: it grants all one's desires
> [i.e., while in contact with the Holy Name, which has the na-
> ture of truth, whatever is thought of becomes true. Therefore it is
> a thought-jewel. See *Bhag.* 11.15.26: *yatha sankalpayet*...]. Since
> the Holy Name is Krishna, it has the nature of Krishna. Con-
> sciousness and so forth are adjectives of Krishna. The reason the
> Holy Name is Krishna is that the Holy Name and the Holy
> Named are not different. *One eternal, conscious, joyful, rapturous
> truth has appeared as two.*[71]

Joyful astonishment is called *rasa*. This *rasa* is consciousness *rasa*—it has no relationship with *maya*. It is as though a liquid substance, poured into two molds, one in the form of a human and the other in the form of syllables, settled in two forms. One is the human form—Shyamasundara, Vamsidhari, Tribhangi—and the other is the highest syllabic form "*krishna*." The two are embodied consciousness and *rasa*, the highest nectar,[72] a condensed ocean of the highest joy.[73] The Holy Name possesses a full form.[74]

Shri Sanatana Gosvamin, whose very life and decoration was the Holy Name, the highest of nectars, has revealed the truth of the Holy Name with his own lips in a rapturous outburst:

> Hey! The name of Krishna is an extremely elevated *rasa*-filled thing. Why *rasa*-filled? Because it is composed of soft, sweet syllables or, because it is made of the *rasa* of eternal being, consciousness, and joy, it is *rasa*-filled. Or, because it presents a particular kind of *rasa*, either the ninefold *rasa* headed by *shringara*, the *rasa* of *bhakti*, or the *rasa* of *preman*. Also, even in the states of separation and union the name appears—therefore it is *rasa*-filled. Or, *rasa* is meant in the sense of passion; this name is accompanied by passion. Or, it without failing brings about love of the Lord. Therefore this name is *rasa*-filled. Or, the name creates in the minds of its servants or of everyone love for itself—therefore it is *rasa*-filled. Or, *rasa* might be understood as a kind of potency this name possesses; it has the greatest of powers, therefore it is *rasa*-filled. Or, *rasa* can be a special kind of quality—this name delivers all distressed people—therefore it is *rasa*-filled.[75]

It is as if he drank so much *rasa* that his outburst will never end. Therefore again the outburst continues:

> If *rasa* is viewed as a kind of happiness, the name is made of intense happiness, and therefore it is filled with *rasa*. Or, the name is sweetness at its highest limit, or supremely sweet— therefore it is filled with *rasa*. This name is sweeter than sweet, extremely sweet, and therefore it is incomparable.[76]

The Named himself and the syllables of the Name, these are, without dependence on anything else, fully, that is, completely, nondifferent in power and in sweetness. They are just like the way a mango and an apple molded from solid sugar are independently the same in taste, in aroma, and in sweetness.

Therefore, even though Ajamila was completely devoid of any connection with the Named, Narayana, the Lord of Vaikuntha, at the time he called to his own son named Narayana, as a result of the contact of his tongue with those four syllables, he got sudden liberation.

Furthermore, in Rupa's play *Vidagdha-madhava* ("Clever Madhava"), Paurnamasi said: *no jane janita kiyadbhiramritaih krishnetivarnadvayi*, "I don't know how much nectar the two syllables *krish-na* are made of." This is the sweetness of the Holy Name. "One truth, in the form of eternal being, consciousness, joy, *rasa*, and so forth, has appeared as two."[77] This statement of Shri Jiva, in his discussion of the Holy Name, is the definitive statement. It has authority everywhere, or, in other words, it is the final conclusion.

The Holy Name is a Vaikuntha substance[78]—that is, a substance always without weakness; it does not become impure in any condition; it does not become corrupted by incursion of the faults of an offender, nor, in the reflection of the Name, is it changed.

NOTES

1. *Bhagavata Purana* (BP) 11.5.32. The connection of the practice of *sankirtana* with the Age of *Kali* is supplied by the context. The stanza just prior to this in the BP begins "Now hear about [*dharma*] in the Age of *Kali*" (*kalavapi tatha shrinu*). Parts and subparts refers to Krishna's various plenary expansions and subexpansions as represented by his elder brother Balarama and others in his own descent (*avatara*). By the clever application of the rules of *sandhi* in Sanskrit grammar and hermeneutics, the Chaitanya tradition has interpreted this verse as a reference to Shri Krishna Chaitanya himself. Thus, they see him as a descent of Krishna whose renunciation name, Krishna Chaitanya, contains the letters "k-r-s-n-a," who was by complexion "not dark" (*tvisha akrishnam* instead of *tvisha krishnam*), that is, light or golden. Shri Krishna Chaitanya's complexion is said to have been light or golden, and his enthusiasm for and participation in *sankirtana* is known from the many eyewitness accounts contained in his early biographies.

2. Sanatana Gosvamin, *Brihad-bhagavatamrita* (Bb), 2.3.158. Edited by Puri Dasa, with Sanatana's own *Dig-darshini* commentary, in Sanskrit (Bengali script). (Mayamanasimha: Sacinatha Raya Caturdhurina, Gaurabda 459 [1946])

3. Sanatana Gosvamin, *Dig-darshini* (Dd) on Bb, 2.3.158. See previous footnote for edition.

4. The Chaitanya tradition appears to be alone in its view that the highest goal of human life is not liberation (*moksha*) but love (*preman*) of Krishna. In the other Vaishnava traditions, *bhakti* (devotion) is regarded only as a means to liberation. In the Chaitanya tradition, *bhakti* has two aspects, as means and as goal. *Bhakti* as means is a set of practices, primarily hearing, glorifying, and remembering, aimed at cultivating *bhakti* as goal or *preman*. Once one has developed *bhakti* as goal, one does not discontinue the activities that formerly were viewed as means. Instead, one continues, only now the same activities become avenues of relishing and expressing one's love for Krishna. Thus, *bhakti* is both means and goal in this tradition and is promoted to a place above *mukti* as a goal of human life.

572 HAGIOGRAPHY AND PRAXIS

5. *Nama chintamanih krishnash chaitanya-rasa-vigrahah, purnah shuddho nitya-mukto 'bhinnatvan nama-naminoh; Padma Purana*, cited in the *Hari-bhakti-vilasa* (Hbv), 11.503. Gopala Bhatta Gosvamin, *Hari-bhakti-vilasa*, edited by Puri Dasa, with the *Dig-darshini* commentary of Sanatana Gosvamin, in Sanskrit (Bengali script). (Mayama-nasimha: Sacinatha Raya Caturdhurina, Gaurabda, 1946), 459.

6. See Rupa Gosvamin, *Bhakti-rasamrita-sindhu* (Brs), 1.2.234. Rupa Gosvamin, *Bhakti-rasamrita-sindhu*, edited by Haridasa Dasa with the commentaries of Jiva Gosvamin, Mukunda Dasa Gosvamin, and Vishvanatha Chakravartin and a Bengali translation. (Mathura and Navadvipa: Haribola Kutira, 3rd ed. Gaurabda, 1981), 495.

7. This form of the *mantra* is given in the *Brahmanda Purana, Uttara-khanda,* 6.55. In the *Kali-santaranopanishat* it is given with the *Hare Rama* half first.

8. This view is based on an important verse in the *BP* (1.3.28), *ete chamshakalah pumsah krishnastu bhagavan svayam*: "These [descents] are all portions and parts of the *Purusha*, but Krishna is the Lord himself."

9. As in Raghunatha Dasa Gosvamin's *Harinamartha-ratna-dipika*, for instance, in which Radha, feeling the pain of separation from Krishna, begins to chant the *mahamantra* and at each word imagines herself meeting with Krishna and fulfilling her desire to be with him. The *Harinamartha-ratna-dipika* is available in a collection of short works on the meaning of the *mahamantra* called *Mahamantra-vyakhya* with translation into English by Jan Brzezinski at the Gaudiya Grantha Mandira (www.granthamandira.org).

10. See Sanatana Gosvamin's commentary on Hbv, 11.472.

11. See Amulyachandra Sena, *Itihaser shri Caitanya*. (Kalikata: Shrikiranakumara Raya, 1965).

12. Rupa Gosvamin, *Upadeshamrita*, verse 7, in the *Shri Stava-kalpa-druma*, edited by Bhaktisaranga Gosvamin and Purushottama Dasa (pp. 787–8) (Vrindavana: Tridandibhikshu Bhaktisaurabhasara, 1959). The disease Rupa had in mind was something like jaundice, for which sugar is a cure (or at least an aid) but during which sugar is not pleasing to the taste.

13. It was apparently published in 1879. There is a copy of the 1879 edition in the British Library (shelf-mark VT1850). It has twelve chapters, called *tarangas* ("waves"). They are entitled: (1) The *dharma* of the age and the good quality of the Age of *Kali*, (2) The greatness of the names of Hari, (3) The method of glorifying Hari and the greatness of such glorification, (4) The method of hearing the names of Hari and the greatness of that hearing, (5) The method of remembering the names of Hari and the greatness of that remembering, (6) The method of thinking of Hari and the greatness of that thinking, (7) Description of the origination of the names of Hari, (8) Inquiry into Shri Radha, (9) Description of Hari and *Brahman* and the real difference between them, (10) The practice of cultivating the names of Hari, (11) Description of the way of attaining *bhakti* for Hari, and (12) Description of the different kinds of *bhakti* for Hari.

14. *Vishnu-dharmottara*, ited in Hbv, 11.314. This is the sage Markandeya addressing King Vajra, the grandson of Krishna.

15. *Hari-bhakti-sudhodaya*, cited in Hbv, 11.315. Spoken by the sage Narada.

16. *Garuda Purana*, cited in Hbv, 11.316.

17. *Skanda Purana*, cited in Hbv, 11.322.

18. *Skanda Purana*, cited in Hbv, 11.398–99.

19. *BP* 12.3.51.

20. *Garuda Purana*, cited in Hbv, 11.441. Spoken by Shuka to King Ambarisha.

21. Krishna speaking to Draupadi, also called Krishna (with a macron over the final *a*), in the *Mahabharata*, as cited in Hbv, 11.445.

22. Krishna speaking to Arjuna in the *Adi Purana*, cited in Hbv, 11.446

23. *Prabhasakhanda*, cited in Hbv, 11.451.

24. The words of Narada from the *Brihan-naradiya Purana*, cited in Hbv, 11.460.

25. *Padma Purana*, cited in Hbv, 11.503.

26. Shri Chaitanya, *Shikshashtaka*, 1, in *Shri Padyavali*, verse 22, collected by Rupa Gosvamin, edited by Vanamali Dasa Shastri with a Hindi translation (Vrindavana: Raghavachaitanya Dasa, 1949).

27. Shri Chaitanya, *Shikshashtaka*, 2. This is verse 31 in the *Padyavali* of Rupa Gosvamin. The author expresses his humility here when he says that he feels no passion for the names of Krishna. This kind of expression of humility, expressing a sense of one's own fallen-ness, is common among the writers and poets of the Chaitanya tradition.

28. Sanatana Gosvamin, Bb, 1.1.9.

29. Sanatana Gosvamin, Bb, 2.1.1. This verse is probably not Sanatana's. The text's editor, Puri Dasa, says that it is found in only one manuscript and in that manuscript it occurs immediately after the closing *pushpika* (a brief statement that signals the closing of sections of a work and also of a whole work) of the first section. He thinks it was added by a later copyist.

30. Sanatana Gosvamin, Bb, 2.3.158.

31. Sanatana Gosvamin, Bb, 2.3.184.

32. Rupa Gosvamin, *Laghu-bhagavatamrita*, 2nd ed., 1.4, edited by Bhaktivilasa Tirtha with a Bengali translation (Mayapura: Shri Chaitanya Matha, 1974), 488.

33. Rupa Gosvamin, *Vidagdha-madhava*, 2nd ed., 1.15, edited by Pandit Bhavadatta Shastri and Kashinath Pandurang Parab, with a commentary (Bombay: Pandurang Javaji, 1937).

34. Raya means "king," here used as an expression of respect.

35. Gaura means "golden" or "white." Chaitanya's skin color was white or golden.

36. Chaitanya Dasa in the *Shri Gaurapada-tarangini* (Gpt), 2nd ed., 4.2.1. (In Bengali) Edited by Mrinalakanti Ghosha Bhaktibhushana with a long introduction (Kalikata: Bangiya Sahitya Parishat Mandira, 1341 [1935]).

37. "Golden-limbed," an epithet of Chaitanya.

38. Balarma Dasa, Gpt, 4.2.3.

39. Nayanananda, Gpt, 4.2.8.

40. Radha.

41. "Golden-moon." Another name of Chaitanya.

42. Govinda Dasa, Gpt, 4.2.12.

43. Ananta Raya, Gpt, 4.2.79.

44. Govinda Dasa, Gpt, 4.3.5.

45. "Say Hari!"

574 HAGIOGRAPHY AND PRAXIS

46. Paramananda Sena, Gpt, 4.3.6.

47. Beautiful Golden One, Chaitanya.

48. Golden-Bodied One, Chaitanya.

49. The *Adi-lila*, or "First Division" of the Acts or Sport of Chaitanya. It is the first of the three parts of Vrindavana Dasa's *Chaitanya-bhagavata* covering the first twenty-four years of Chaitanya's life. Vrindavana Das, *Chaitanya-bhagavata* (Cb), edited by Radhagovinda Nath, with his commentary and translations into Bengali of the Sanskrit citations, in six volumes. (Kalikata: Sadhana Prakashani, 1966).

50. Haridasa Thakura was born into a Muslim family. He was drawn as a young man to the practice of reciting loudly the names of Krishna, and as a result he was persecuted by the leaders of his community.

51. Advaita Prabhu, an important senior companion of Chaitanya.

52. Vrindavana Dasa, *Cb*, 1.11.1–35.

53. I have skipped the account in this section of the story of the Muslims who arrested Haridasa and beat him.

54. *Cb*, 11.167–70. Vaikuntha is the transcendent realm of Vishnu beyond the material universe.

55. *Uccaih shatagunam bhavet*, source unidentified.

56. *BP*, 10.34.17.

57. *Cb*, 1.11.261–91.

58. Obeisance to Hari, O Krishna, obeisance to [you] descendant of Yadu, O Gopala [protector of cows], Govinda [pleaser of cows], Rama [pleasing one], Madhu-sudana [killer of the demon Madhu]!

59. *Cb*, 2.1.397–401.

60. *Cb*, 2.23.72–80.

61. *Cb*, 3.10.117–25.

62. The extraordinary chant described here, *bhaja Nitai Gaura Radhe Shyam, japa Hare Krishna, Hare Ram*, was revealed by Bodo Baba (Shri Radharamana Carana Dasa Baba) in the midst of an intense *kirtana* he led during a prolonged stay in the town of Krishnagar in Bengal. It has become one of the main songs used in the performance of *kirtana* by a sizable community of modern Chaitanya Vaishnavas. This selection is from Bodo Baba's biography, *Charita-sudha* (Cs), 2:33–34 4th ed. Compiled and edited by Ramadasa Babaji in six volumes (Bengali) (Navadvipa: Shriramadasa Babaji, Gaurabda 473–81 [1959–67])

63. An abbreviated form of Nityananda, one of Chaitanya's close companions.

64. A community beyond the pale of the caste hierarchy—an outcaste.

65. *Cs*, 2:33–34.

66. An abbreviated version of Gadadhara, one of Chaitanya's dear companions.

67. Jahnava or Jahnavi is the name of Nityananda's senior wife. After the death of Nityananda, she became an important leader in the Chaitanya movement.

68. This a translation of part of the third chapter of Bhaktivinoda's *Shri Hari-nama-cintamani* (Svarupaganja, Nadiya, West Bengal: Gaudiya Mission, 1963), 26–31. *Abhasa* is translated here as "reflection." The Holy Name is often compared with the sun. *Abhasa* is the indirect or diffused light of the sun just before it rises or when it is covered by clouds or fog. Like the sun, the Holy Name is sometimes thought to have a diffused or indirect influence. Though the sun is not directly

visible, its diffused or reflected light nevertheless destroys the darkness of night and brings warmth and the ability to see things. So does the reflected "light" of the Holy Name have beneficial effects on the practitioner.

69. *Yakshas* and *rakshas* are demonic beings of various sorts mentioned in the *Puranas.*

70. This translation is from Manindranath Guha, *Shriman-namamrita-sindhu-bindu*, 2nd ed. (Shri Vrindavana: Savitri Guha, n.d.), 10–14. The complete work is now available in English as *Nectar of the Holy Name*, translated with introduction and notes by Neal Delmonico (Kirksville, MO: Blazing Sapphire Press, 2005).

71. Jiva Gosvamin on *Brs*, 1.2.233.

72. Sanatana Gosvamin, *Bb*, 1.1.9.

73. Rupa Gosvamin, *Krishna-namashtaka*, 7, in *Shri Stava-kalpa-druma*, pp. 811–2.

74. Rupa Gosvamin, *Krishna-namashtaka*, 7.

75. Sanatana Gosvamin, Dd on Bb, 2.3.184.

76. Sanatana Gosvamin, Dd on Bb, 2.3.184.

77. From Jiva Gosvamin, commentary on Brs, 1.2.233.

78. *BP* 6.2.14.